Modern Capitalism

*A systematic historical depiction
of Pan-European economic life from
its origins to the present day*

Werner Sombart

Modern Capitalism

*A systematic historical depiction
of Pan-European economic life from
its origins to the present day*

Werner Sombart

II: The Historical Foundations of Modern Capitalism

K A Nitz

AUCKLAND, NEW ZEALAND

The 2nd edition of
Der moderne Kapitalismus
first published in German
1916

This translation into New Zealand English
Copyright © K A Nitz 2023
All rights reserved

ISBNs:
978-0-473-69132-5 (paperback)
978-0-473-69133-2 (hardback)

Table of Contents

Translator's Note

Sombart's work contains several untranslated quotations from sources in languages other than German. I have continued to follow the policy from the first volume of retaining each of these in its original language followed in square brackets by a rough (sometimes very rough) and fairly literal translation so as to retain more of the feel of what it would be like for someone with a basic familiarity with these other languages to read Sombart's original text. All such translations are my own unless explicitly noted otherwise.

I have endeavoured to clarify the citations used by Sombart (particularly expanding his abbreviations), and have provided the additional bibliographic details with these references where possible (and occasionally also provided a more recent work or English translation to aid those wishing to investigate the sources). I have also tried to add bibliographic details where possible for direct quotations (not always indicated as such by Sombart!) which did not have a source cited, and sometimes noted the absence of references. Where the original work was easily accessible to me, I have endeavoured to check passages cited and correct any inaccuracies (both in the text quoted and in the reference itself).

The formatting of glosses — used extensively throughout by Sombart to provide further detail and discuss the sources — has retained the smaller typeface as used in the German text, but with the addition of a vertical bar on the right-hand margin to help further distinguish them.

The extent of the footnotes in the original, and the addition of the translations of non-German passages, has regrettably necessitated the footnotes being moved to endnotes so as to aid the flow of the text on the page.

Measurements have been converted, where known, to the equivalent metric measures in most instances.

This volume incorporates the second book ("The Historical Foundations of Modern Capitalism"), which spanned both the half-volumes of the first volume of the original work. The previous volume of this work (published 2019) encompassed the introduction and first book ("The Pre-Capitalist Economy") from the first half-volume of the first volume of the original work. Note that the chapter numbering is a continuation from the previous volume.

As always, I accept all responsibility for any errors in this translation.

Source Abbreviations

MGH Monumenta Germaniae Historica

(http://www.dmgh.de)

LL   Leges

Const.   Constitutiones et acta publica imper-
                      atorum et regum

Acts of the Parliament of England, Great Britain, or the United Kingdom

The standard abbreviations have been used. For instance, the Exportation Act 1548 is cited as "2 & 3 Edw. 6 c.26", meaning the 26th act passed during the session that began in the 2nd year of Edward VI and ended in the 3rd year of his reign. Where the act has a defined name that has been given afterwards in brackets with the year, otherwise just the year.

Volume II

The Historical Foundations of Modern Capitalism

Section 1: The Nature and Inception of Capitalism

Chapter 19: The Capitalist Economic System

I will first, before I pursue the origin of the capitalist economy, portray the idea of this manner of economy, as it appears in the capitalist economic system, in conceptual purity.

I. Concept

We comprehend by capitalism a specific economic system[1] which can be described in the following way:

> It is an open economic organisation in which regularly two different populations, the owners of the means of production — who at the same time have command and are the economic subjects — and propertyless workers — who are exclusively workers (as economic objects) — are connected by the market, combine together, and are dominated by the principle of acquisition and economic rationalism.

The open economic organisation to which sole proprietors, private industry, professional differentiation between the specific industries, and market-like associations belong are things which capitalism has in common with craftwork[2]; morphologically it is distinguished from the latter by the social differentiation of the personal factors of production into the two components of workers who lead and workers who carry out the work, who face each other at the same time as possessors of the means of production and exclusively technical workers, and must be brought together by the market for the necessary merging into the production process.

The reigning *economic principles* are the principles of acquisition and economic rationalism which take the place of the principles of satisfaction of needs and traditionalism which, as we have seen*, infuse self-sufficiency and craftwork.

I have already explained the essence of these economic principles in the introduction† and add the following remarks only as an enlargement on that.

The *particular nature of the principle of acquisition* expresses itself in that under its dominion the immediate goal of economic activity is no longer the satisfaction of the needs of a living person, but instead exclusively the accumulation of a sum of money. This goal-setting is inherent to the idea of capitalist organisation; you can thus describe the obtaining of profit (that is, the enlargement of an initial sum through economic activity) as the objective goal of capitalist economy with which (especially with the completely capitalist economy) the subjective goal-setting of individual economic subjects need not necessarily coincide[3].

Economic rationalism, that is, the fundamental justification of all actions in the highest possible functionalism, expresses itself in three ways:

1) as systematic procedures in financial management;
2) as functionalism in the narrow sense; and
3) as a focus on calculation.

The systematic procedures brings into the capitalist economic system the management of money according to far-reaching plans; functionalism takes care of the right choice of means; a focus on calculation takes care of the exact numeric counting and registering of all economic events and their arithmetical summation into a meaningfully ordered numbering system.

II. The Capitalist Enterprise

The economic form of the capitalist economic system is the capitalist enterprise. It forms an abstract unity: the business. Its goal is the making of profit. The particular means for the fulfillment of this goal is the concluding of contracts over monetarily-valued payment and consideration. Any technical problem must in the framework of the capitalist enterprise be

---

*   [Tr.: see Volume I.]
†   [Tr.: the introduction forms the first part of Volume I.]

solved in the completion of a contract to whose advantageous arrangement all the thinking and striving of the capitalist entrepreneur is directed. It may be that personal effort is exchanged for tangible goods or tangible goods for tangible goods — it always amounts to whether in the end that surplus in exchange value (money) remains in the hands of the capitalist entrepreneur, the obtaining of which his entire activity is focused on. All economic processes as a result lose their qualitative aspect and become quantities expressible and expressed purely in money.

The capitalist enterprise exhibits *various forms* which we can distinguish as follows[4]:

1. according to the *content of the activity performed in an enterprise*:
   (a) enterprises for the production of goods;
   (b) enterprises for the distribution of tangible goods;
   (c) enterprises for the offering of services;
   (d) enterprises for the provision of highly enjoyable goods;
   (e) enterprises for the granting or arrangement of credit; and
   (f) enterprises with a content combined variously of a through e.

2. according to the *form of the enterprise's capital*:
   (a) sole proprietorships which rest on the assets of one person;
   (b) collective undertakings whose capital several people have accumulated.

3. according to the *position of the entrepreneur with respect to the workers*:
   As it is one of the most important tasks of the next volume to show how the capitalist enterprise was composed historically of loose opportunistic ties between investors and workers, I will, so as to avoid repetition, handle the various theoretical possibilities of the position of the entrepreneur with respect to the workers there when I portray the empirical evolution of the various work organisations.

4. according to the *position of the enterprise with respect to public authority*:

(a) free enterprises which are completely independent from public authority;

(b) bound enterprises which stand in some immediate dependency on public authority; a special case are the mixed public enterprises.

III. The Functions of the Capitalist Entrepreneur

These are:

1. organisational

Since the work which the entrepreneur accomplishes is constantly a work in which other people assist, and since other people thus make themselves subservient to his will so that they combine with it, the entrepreneur must above all be an *organiser*.

Organising means to combine many people into a happy, successful work, it means to plan for people and things so that the desired benefits come about without reservation. A whole variety of abilities and actions are again enclosed in that. First of all, anyone who wants to organise must possess the ability of assessing people with respect to their productivity, thus to pick out of a great heap those people suited to a specific goal. Then he must have the talent to have them work instead of himself, and indeed so that each stands in the right place from which they can accomplish the maximum performance, and to drive everyone along always so that they also really begin to display the highest sum of activity corresponding to their productivity. Finally, it lies with the entrepreneur to see to it that the people united to a common activity are also combined into a productive whole, that the juxtaposition and the positions above and below each other of individual participants in the work is well ordered, and that their activities interconnect properly in a sequential way — "collection of forces spatially" and "combination of forces in time", as Clausewitz desired of commanders.

2. commercially

The relations which the entrepreneur enters into with people are of yet another form when they are described with the word "organising". He has to first recruit his people himself; he then has to constantly make unfamiliar people serve his goals while he holds them to specific activities or restraints other than through compulsion — to this end he must "negotiate", hold a dialogue with someone else in order to move them, through providing reasons and rebuttals of the opposing grounds, to the acceptance of a specific suggestion, to the performance of or refraining from a specific activity. Negotiation is a wrestling match with intellectual weapons.

The entrepreneur must also thus be a *good negotiator, deal-maker, or dealer*, as we express the same process with a different nuance. The dealer in the narrow sense, that is the negotiator in financial affairs, is just one of many phenomena in which the negotiator appears.

It is always about convincing buyers (or sellers) on the advantageousness of concluding a contract. The ideal of the seller is then achieved when the entire population considers nothing to be more important than to buy the articles that have just been praised by him. Or when the human masses are seized by a panic that they will not be able punctually to acquire any more (as is the case in times of feverish excitement in the securities market).

To excite interest, to acquire trust, to awaken the desire to buy — the activity of the fortunate dealer presents itself in this climax. The means by which he achieves it remains the same. Enough that there are no external, but rather only internal means of coercion, that the counterpart enters into the pact not against his will, but rather from his own volition. Suggestion must be the effect of the dealer. But there are many internal means of coercion.

3. arithmetical-economical

If the previously named functions are common to all entrepreneurship, the capitalist entrepreneur has the specific function of carrying out the arithmetic (calculating). As his activity dissolves into concluding contracts over services and consideration valued monetarily, he must know how to represent the content of any contract immediately in a sum of money, which in constant taking in and giving out must in the end result in an active balance — we call this function, however, accounting. Where the accounting is an accounting with unknown magnitudes, we speak of speculation. He must,however, be a good budgeter since only by careful economy is the uppermost goal of the capitalist enterprise achieved.

IV. Capital and its Utilisation

The sum of exchangeable value serving as an actual base for a capitalist enterprise is *the capital*. This begins and ends in the form of money, whereas it appears in-between in alternating forms as the means of production or goods.

We call the production time that time which the capital spends in the sphere of production, and the circulation time that time which it spends in the sphere of circulation. Turnover time is the sum of production and circulation time[5].

We call real capital that which serves for the purchase of means of production, and personnel capital that which serves for the purchase of workers. This important distinction is complementary to the usual division into fixed or standing and circulating or revolving capital[6].

To "turn to account" the capital invested in an enterprise, that is, to reproduce with an increase (win, profit), is thus the goal of the capitalist economy. The possibilities for enlargement of the profit of capital from the given magnitude are the following.

I. When the profit ratio is given on the individual product, then *the quantity of production units produced in a given time* decides over the extent of the profit – this is enlarged by speeding up (intensifying) the production process or, expressed in a capitalist way, by speeding up the turnover of capital.

II. When the quantity of goods produced in a specified time is given, then *the profit ratio on the individual product* decides over the extent of the profit. This is formed by the difference between selling price and costs. The striving is thus directed at the enlargement of this difference. This enlargement can be achieved fundamentally in two ways:

1. By *increasing the selling price*. This finds its limit in the necessity of underbidding the competition in price. From that there arises for capital the paradox of selling at the same time at the dearest

possible price and at the cheapest possible. A solution to this paradox is strived for by the artificial exclusion of the competition, be it by statutory methods (monopoly, privileges, etc.) or by way of mutual understanding — tendencies to price arrangements, cartel forming, etc. Should the price not be raisable, then as a last means of raising the profit there remains:

2. the *reduction of costs*. This can be obtained by:

   a) by *cheapening production*, that is, producing more goods by increasing the productivity with the same expenditure. The increasing of productivity results from:

      A. improvement of the work process (organisation of the firm);

      B. improvement of technology;

   b) by *cheapening of the factors of production*, that is, producing the same quantity of product with lower expenditure, *without* a simultaneous increase in productivity, thus only by savings which are made in the outlay for procurement of the factors of production, and indeed:

      A. in the *objective factors of production*: by advantageous purchase, careful conservation, etc., utilisation of waste, etc.

      B. in the *personal factors of production*:

      - by cutting the rewards for the same work (wage pressure, employment of cheaper workers like children and women),
      - by increasing the work for the same reward, be it through extensification of the work (lengthening the time of work), or be it through intensification of the work (stricter oversight, piecework pay, etc.).

V. The Conditions of Capitalist Economy

Like any particular type of economy, capitalism is also tied to the fulfillment of specific conditions, be they situated in the economic persons or in the environment. To establish these conditions, two paths lie open to us. We can list conditions which any capitalism requires in order to exist. I took this path in this work when I depicted craftwork (see Chapter 13 in the previous volume), and with reference to capitalism in my treatment in the *Grundriss der Sozialökonomik* (Sombart 1925). Or, alternatively, we could establish those very events whose entry made possible an historical manifestation of capitalism, that of "modern" capitalism, possible and brought it to development. That is the path we have to tread here. For we want to recall the entire structure of this work, which set as its task the describing of the coming into existence and growth of the capitalist economic ways belonging to our time and our peoples. Thus it is our responsibility now to follow how modern capitalism has arisen in a slow reshaping from the familiar economic forms of the European Middle Ages. And precisely the proof of how the preconditions essential for its emergence were fulfilled has been made the main problem in this volume. The peculiar, historically narrowly defined formulation of the problem is thus this:

After the economy of the European peoples had assumed the particular form of the feudal-craftwork economy during the Middle Ages, which we thus take as a given, and after the new spirit has given birth to the wish for capitalism, what conditions coincided which made it possible that that wish arrived at its aim?

Several things are to be noted in connection with the above.

Chapter 20: The Inception of Capitalism

I. The Driving Forces

Capitalism grew from the depths of the European soul.

The same spirit from which the new state and the new religion, the new science and the new technology were born also created the new economic life. We know it is a spirit of earthliness and worldliness; a spirit with enormous power for the destruction of old natural forms, old connections, old limitations, but also strong for the rebuilding of new life forms, artistic and artificial constructions. It is that spirit which has since the outgoing Middle Ages torn people from the quiet, organically grown relationships of love and community and tossed them onto the path of restless selfishness and self-determination.

At first striking root in this or that strong man and chasing him out from the mass of his rest-loving, comfortable compatriots; then filling, enlivening and moving into ever wider circles.

It is the spirit of Faust – the spirit of unease, of unrest — which now animates people. "His spirit's ferment far aspireth."* If you wish to call what we see active here a striving for infinity, then you are right because the goal is pushed out into the boundless, because all natural measures of organic connections are felt by those pushing forward to be inadequate, constricting. If you want to call it striving for power, then you will also not be wrong, for this indescribable urge of strong individuals to assert themselves, to hold their ground

---

* [Tr.: Mephistopheles discussing Faust with the Lord, from the prelude to Faust (Goethe 1808, 26; 1890, 10), translation by Bayard Taylor. Cf. also Spengler (1920; 1922) and his concept of Faustian civilisation.]

against all forces, to subjugate others to their will and their actions, which we can describe as will to power, wells up from the deepest depths which our knowledge is incapable of looking down into. If you want to call it a spirit of enterprise, then you are also certainly always expressing there something correct where that will to power demands the collaboration with others for the completion of a common work. The "enterprising" are those who conquer the world; the creators, the animators; those who are not introspective, not savouring, not withdrawing from the world, not world-denying.

We know that in every region of human life this new "enterprising" spirit was taking command. Above all in states — there its goal was conquering, governing. But it was coming alive just as much in religion, in the churches — here it wanted to liberate, to unchain – in science – here it wanted to decipher — in technology — there it wanted to invent — on the surface of the earth – there it wanted to discover.

This same spirit now also began to govern economic life. It broke through the bounds of the static, feudal-craftwork economy of self-sufficiency, built on leisurely comfort and kept in balance by itself, and drove people into the whirl of the acquisition economy. Here, in the region of material striving, conquering meant acquiring — enlarging a sum of money. And nowhere did the striving for infinity, the striving for power find the field of activity so much in accordance with its innermost being as in the pursuit of money, this completely abstract symbol of value, relieved of all organic-natural limitations, whose possession then appeared more and more as a symbol of power.

I have given an in-depth account elsewhere of how this greed for gold and money at first and over a long period dug a bed next to economic life and led to a series of phenomena which have nothing to do with economic life, as at first people strove to obtain gold or money outside the circle of their normal economic activity. It is those mass phenomena characteristic of the last centuries of the Middle Ages and the first centuries of the new age:

    a) robber barons;
    b) treasure seeking;
    c) alchemy;

d) endless planning of fanciful projects;

e) loan usury.

But then this spirit of conquest also penetrated into economic life, and with that capitalism appeared on the scene — that economic system which in a wonderfully artificial way opens up an especially fruitful field of activity for the striving for infinity, the will to power, the spirit of enterprise as well, and precisely in the area of the everyday concern for ones livelihood. The capitalist economy possesses this suitability because under its dominance there stands in the centre of all goal-setting not a living person with their natural needs, but an abstraction — capital. In this abstractness of goals lies its unboundedness. In the overcoming of the concreteness of all goals lies the overcoming of their restrictiveness.

Striving for power and striving for acquisition now merged together — the capitalist entrepreneurs, for that is what we call the new economic subjects, strove for power in order to acquire, and wanted to acquire for the sake of power. Only someone who possesses power can acquire; and whoever acquires, increases their power. We will see that as a result the concept of power shifts in the course of the development. As consequently the types of entrepreneur also change; as gradually the means of power supplant trickery, and the persuasion of the means of power supplants violence; as more and more your commercial disposition decides over your fitness as an entrepreneur in economic life.

But capitalism was not only born from this infinite striving, from this desire for power, from this spirit of enterprise. With this another spirit paired itself, which brought to the economic life of the new age the secure order, the computational exactness, the cold finality of aims — that is the *bourgeois spirit* which can be very effective outside the sphere of the capitalist economy and was effective for centuries in the lower stratum of the civic economic subjects, the professional traders and craftsmen.

If the spirit of enterprise wants to conquer, to acquire, the bourgeois spirit wants to order, to preserve. It expresses itself in a series of virtues which everyone is in agreement with, that that behaviour is morally good which conceals a well-arranged capitalist housekeeping. Hence the virtues which adorn the bourgeois are above all industry, temperance, thrift, economy, honouring contracts. *We call the mental atmosphere which is interwoven from the spirit of enterprise and the bourgeois spirit into a unitary whole the capitalist spirit.* It created capitalism.

I have dealt with the problem of the "spirit of capitalism" in-depth and from all sides in my book over the bourgeois, which appeared in 1913 [Tr.: translated into English in 1915] and had the subtitle "A Study of the History and Psychology of the Modern Business Man" (Sombart 1913a; 1915). Hence here I have, *in that I refer to my book*, only sketched quite briefly the nature of the capitalist spirit and dispensed entirely in this place *with its derivation*, to which the greatest part of my book on the bourgeois was dedicated, so as to not have to repeat myself. Likewise I direct the reader who is interested in the problem, of whether the "spirit" "produces" the "economic life" or vice versa, to my explanations in the same place. I consider in addition that what I said there was a solution to this problem is surely very much in need of expansion and deepening, above all towards the metaphysical side, but I do not want to burden this work with the multi-layered discussion of just this theme, and leave it for myself to come back to it at another opportunity.

II. The Historical Building of Modern Capitalism

Writing history means furnishing the proof of by which paths the spirit of the peoples approached its goal, what assisted it in its striving, and what hindered it. Expressed in a different way, it means to show to what extent and by what means the idea at the basis of a people or a group of peoples was realised. Applied to economic history and our particular task, writing the history of modern capitalism means tracing how in the course of centuries the idea of the capitalist economic system was transformed into reality, how the economic life of the European peoples developed out of the new spirit in all it ramifications.

Spoken in metaphor (which also gave the title of this subsection its setting), we want to comprehend the "building" of modern capitalism. To this end, we assume the efficiency of some unknown master builder whose "building approach" is, however, quite well known to us because it is to us obvious in the mental disposition of striving men, and we now follow from what components he fits together his building. The building itself we will first see growing in the next volume of this work. Here it is worth at first getting to know the "foundations", and also the building materials and the building workers.

The reader may convince themselves by a look at the table of contents as to on which phenomena I place the decisive weight for the genetic examination of modern economic life. Whether I have made the correct choice can of course only be proved by the study of this work. Here I want to strive to make this easier for the reader by giving him an *overview of the multi-layered material*. I do this by showing him the connections which I observe between the operative forces and the various areas of historical effectiveness which the following seven sections embrace, between these in relation to each other, and between them and the capitalist economy.

I say in one place, "in the beginning was the army", and want to express thereby that I observe in the modern armies the first and most important tool for forming the new spirit so as to complete its work. With the help of the army, the *state* was created (Section 2), that first finished product of the new spirit in which and through which this above all produced its effects. To take control of the forces of nature, it then strove to reshape *technology* (Section 3), and its innate urge for money and power led it to the *stores of precious metals* (Section 4) which it exploited.

These three areas appear as independent fields of activity for the new spirit, and any *one* striving cannot be derived completely from the others. But we certainly note how all three stand in the closest interplay with one another. It is the interests of the state above all which, in order to raise the strike power of the army, was urged to incessant improvement of technology; it is that interest which considered the increase in stores of precious metals to be the most important goal of politics and hence pursued the increase in production of precious metals. But if technological progress and production of precious metals are processes caused by the state, then they are just as much conditions for the state's development — without the technology of blast furnaces, no cannons and hence no modern army; without compass and astrolabe, no discovery of America and no colonial empires. Without the opening up of rich silver mines and gold fields in America, no modern tax system, no government debt, no army, no professional bureaucracy, and thus no modern state. But technology and precious metals production also stand in a relationship of the closest interplay – without water pumping machinery, without amalgam processes, no silver production; without the progress in minting, no modern currency system. And in reverse, without the search for gold, not nearly so quick a progress in the area of technology.

State, technology, and the production of precious metals are likewise the basic conditions of capitalist development — always assuming the will for capitalism as a component of the new spirit. Each of these basic conditions is divided in its influence as follows.

The *state*, above all through its army, creates a large market for capitalism, and imbues economic life with the spirit of order and discipline. The state, by its policy towards religion, produces heretics and, in that it causes migrations for religious reasons, 'foreigners' – two elements that are indispensable for the building of capitalism. The state pushes into distant parts, it conquers the colonies and brings about with the help of slavery the first capitalist, large enterprises. The state looks after and advances by conscious intervention of its policies the capitalist interests.

Technology makes the production and transport of goods at a large scale possible (and necessary) for the first time; it creates through new processes the possibility of new industries which arise in the framework of capitalist organisation.

Precious metals influence economic life in myriad ways and independently bring about by their abundance miracles — they form the market in a direction beneficial to capitalist development; they intensify the capitalist spirit in that they strengthen the urge to acquire and perfect the arithmetic.

Thus state, technology, and precious metals had an immediate influence of capitalism. Their advancement of the capitalist development was, however, now in still greater measure an indirect one, in that they namely brought to fulfillment a series of other important conditions for this development.

It is they which made possible by their combination the *accruing of bourgeois wealth* (Section 5). But this was a necessary precondition of capitalism in so far as through it on the one hand the formation of capital was made easier, and on the other hand an expense fund was created which played an important role in the *reshaping of goods demand* (Section 6). By this the possibility of making a break like that which capitalism needed was given for the first time. This reshaping was, however, on the other hand the work of the three basic forces — state, technology, precious metals production — which in part exercised their influence directly (luxury demand at the court! army demand! ships demand! colonial demand!), and in part by the middle link of bourgeois wealth (luxury demand of the new rich!).

The *procurement of labour* (Section 7) took place under the influence of technology for the most part through the mediation of the state in a direct or indirect manner.

In *entrepreneurship*, whose origin is then revealed (Section 8), the forces come to life which were destined to meld together all the individually analysed elements into the cosmos of the capitalist economy. They had effects, and indeed variously in accordance with their origin; they were, however, just as much brought about and conditioned by all the circumstances which are enumerated in this book — the state influenced their composition in so far as it provided from its midst countless leaders of the new economic forms, in so far as it produced by its policies, as already stated, important types of new economic subjects; the accruing of bourgeois wealth brought it about that in non-bourgeois circles a spur for acquisitive entrepreneurship was offered, and in many cases the factual possibility of acting as an entrepreneur was first created, etc.

To prove all that in detail is indeed the task of this work.

I must yet send out a limiting remark in advance of the historical portrayal — in the following seven sections of this book are shown the preconditions of the capitalist economy which made possible its development from its beginnings *right up to the end of the age of early capitalism*. In order for capitalism to be able to enter into its high age, other conditions had to be fulfilled, as will be shown later. As long as they were not fulfilled, thus up to perhaps the second half of the 18th century, there were "inhibitions" on the capitalist development. What they were will also be stated at the given time.

Now we must first in a long, intimate reliving remind ourselves and keep sight of the enormous abundance of con-fusing and multifariously criss-crossing facts whose combina-tion first made capitalist economy in general possible. The constant orientation of all events and occurrences towards one point – *what did they signify for the development of capitalism?* – will enable us to master the enormous material which towers up before us.

Section 2: The State

Chapter 21: Nature and Origin of the Modern State

I. The Concept of the Modern State

The actual phenomenon of the princely state or the absolute state, as it had arisen since the end of the Middle Ages in Europe, rested on the fact that a large number of people — a large number means here more than the number that settle in a city borough or even a "region" – were made subject by the will of a sovereign (or a governor) to the interests of this ruler. That these people were not tied by any bond of community – not of blood, but also not that of neighbourhood or allegiance to one another – and that their "union" was more a "mechanical" (not "organic"), a made (not grown) one, that they came together under rational points of view, that is what essentially distinguishes this form from all previous political associations of people.

In the state that striving for infinity which fills the new age established itself for the first time and most successfully. We see at first powerful unique personalities setting themselves up as "tyrants", but who then as it were grew out of themselves in that they widen into the idea of the state. The *L'état, c'est moi* [the state, that's me] also has the meaning: *moi, c'est l'état* [me, that's the state]. And in this extension of princely interests into the interests of the state lay the distinctive feature of the development of the European state which divided it sharply from all oriental despotism. The welfare of the state coincided with the welfare of the prince from whose absolute power the idea of governmental authority developed.

But just as the idea of the state was decoupled from the person of the prince, who was only its visible leader, its "embodied manifestation", and became independent, so too did the thought of governmental authority set the state as something different from the people. And with that the idea of the state surely actually first won its expansive power, surely became for the first time qualified to serve as a regulative principle for the endless striving for power, and at the same time cleared the way for its activities.

Decoupled from the organic limits of the national community, the state developed according to mechanical principles into the *absolute state*. Externally, in that it strove for boundless expansion which it endeavoured to carry out through the mechanically linked and just as boundlessly expansible modern mass army, that is, in that it turned into a pure *power state*; internally, in that it subjugated all areas of life to a conscious regulation and had the tendency towards making its will the sole source of life, that is, in that it turned into a *police state*.

The correspondence of the developmental sequence of modern state life and modern economic life is odd. But it would be a futile endeavour to want to "derive" the one complex of phenomena from the other, the economy from the state, the state from the economy. Both arise from a common root, and then certainly also mutually require and determine each other.

How the state absolutely lives its own life, goes its own way independently from all economy, we will see as soon as we focus on its development.

II. The Origin of the Modern State

From where did the modern state take its origin, what model became decisive for it? – Attempts have often been made to answer these questions in quite various senses. If one, as often happens, describes the Holy Roman Emperor Frederick II as the first modern prince, then it suggests making the Constitutions of Melfi of 1231 responsible for the origin of the modern state, and tracing this back to Byzantine or Arab influence[7]. In fact the Constitutions of Melfi contained for the first time a series of entirely modern governing principles — above all the professional bureaucracy which reached back to Roger II of Sicily and experienced its systematic development in Frederick's Constitutions of Melfi. But then second thoughts arise. In the state of Frederick II components that were just as essential had remained feudal in a medieval way — the conduct of war was still founded on the idea of the fief and was something more like that. Then it is also doubtful whether the states of the Renaissance really trace back their lineage to Frederick's state. In Sicily itself, in particular on the Sicilian mainland, the definitions of Frederick's Constitutions of Melfi were soon overgrown by other laws. In Naples feudalism itself had not been overcome by Frederick II's law-making — under the Angevins feudalism again became the foundation of the constitution and economic life, and this was carried out so consistently that 200 years later it excited the astonishment of the Frenchman Comines — the relationships of possession to office, and of office to court service were strictly retained everywhere. Certainly we must also recall the fact that one of the first entirely modern princes is Alfonso V of Aragon, who was King of Naples 1416–1458, and whom we are accustomed to describe as the "model king of the Renaissance". Had he received his stimuli from his predecessors on the throne? Or had a Turkish influence come to life in him? For already when one begins to study and admire the Ottoman Empire which in the 16th century was at the centre of interest for all statesmen, and of which Luther writes, "they say that no finer worldly regiment exists anywhere but with the Turks."[8]

But perhaps we do not need to direct our eyes to the lands of the East at all when we want to explain the genesis of the modern state. Perhaps the elements of the European society of the Middle Ages completely suffice in order to derive from them the absolute princedom and with it the modern state. It seems to me though as if a large part of the principles and ideas of modern statecraft would consequently have developed from the medieval city right where it experienced its purest development — in Italy. Above all we find the two basic ideas of the absolute state — rationalism and much regulation — already completely developed in the Italian cities and city-states of the 14th century.

"The deliberate adaptation of means to ends, of which no prince out of Italy had at that time a conception, joined to almost absolute power within the limits of the state, produced among the despots both men and modes of life of a peculiar character."

(Burckhardt 1860, 6; 1878, 10)

"The prince [as we hear already at the time of the 14th century in Italy] is to be independent of his courtiers, but at the same time to govern with simplicity and modesty; he is to take everything into his charge, to maintain and restore churches and public buildings, to keep up the municipal police, to drain the marshes, to look after the supply of wine and corn; he is to exercise a strict justice, so to distribute taxes that the people can recognise their necessity and the regret of the ruler to be compelled to put his hands in the pockets of others; he is to support the sick and helpless, and to give his protection and society to distinguished scholars"[9].

On the other hand, the influence of the Italian developments on the other European states is not to be traced in detail without objections.

"It is unmistakeable, however, that the constitutions and statecraft of the Italian Renaissance did not occupy, attract and repel only the theorists, but also the world of political activity everywhere to the highest degree. The secularisation of the state became visible here more openly and lucidly than elsewhere. Here power became quite openly an end in itself, the *ratio status* [relative standing] rose to the highest law before whose omnipotence every moral and religious consideration [...] really took second place."[10]

The derivation of the idea of the modern state from the Italian city states will enlighten us still more when we recall that the word "state" was also first used in the modern sense in Italian. We first find the word *Stato* in connection with the name of a city (*stato di Firenze*, etc.), then used for any state. In the opinion of Jakob Burckhardt, "the rulers and their dependents were together called 'lo stato', and this name afterwards acquired the meaning of the collective existence of a territory" (1860, 2 n. 2; 1878, 5 n. 1). In this change of word-meaning the fundamental idea of modern princedom — that the welfare of the prince expands into the welfare of the state — comes to tangible expression. Cf. also Jellinek (1914, 131 f.).

When this idea then took hold in wider areas, when the petty tyrants of the Italian city states had become "kings" who now asserted a claim to the same absolute power for their great empires as that for their tiny principalities, then the idea soon had to emerge of intrinsically connecting these newly created power relationships with the old imperium. With the help of the Roman law, the 16th and 17th century teachers of constitutional law developed the modern concept of sovereignty — they thereby gave "to the enlightened despotism a good conscience and the power of conviction which it very much needed for its arbitrary behaviour."[11] Bodin (1530–1596), who began this work, defined sovereignty (*majestas*) as "summa in cives legibusque soluta potestas" [the highest power over citizens free of the laws] (1586, 78 Liber I Cap. VIII), thus giving theoretical blessing to the practical "l'état, c'est moi". What Bodin, Hobbes, etc. achieved for the formal theory of the state, Montchrétien undertook for the material theory of the state — the justification of the centralisation of the state. With that the modern *large* state was also completed as a systematic unity, after it had been practically brought to life by the "three magi", as the great kings are called who reigned at the end of the 15th century — Ferdinand the Catholic, Louis XI, and Henry Tudor.

The absolute state experienced a strengthening then through Protestantism, through which the concept of the Christian state and of a Christian authority which is immediately from God was established properly for the first time[12].

The ideas of the absolute state and its policies, particularly also its economic policies, then spread in the following centuries over all the lands. Whilst the enlightened principality perhaps also found its typical representative in the Sun King and in Prussia's kings, we find the fundamentals of its polices in use just as much in the Dutch free states as in the constitutional, in the republican, and in the absolute English state. We can even follow in detail how the policies of one land compelled the following of the same policies by another land, as for example Holland was drawn by the policies of England and then particularly France into the wake of the mercantilist

policies in which it then sailed in the 18th century when it concerned the protection of the industries called into life by the
French refugees[13].

III. The Significance of the State for Capitalism

The significant effects to which such an artificial bringing
together of many people under the will of one person leads
are above all the following.

Firstly, so that that goal of the prince's state is fulfilled —
that is, for the population of a wide stretch of land to serve
the goal of the state — a system of means is created which is
itself of the strongest influence in the fashioning of human
destiny — forces must be gathered, people must be taught
specific activities and omissions — an "organisation", an administrative machine arises. And this system of means of ruling then itself comes to life again and continues working as
subject and object in the course of history.

Secondly, the "subjects", that is thus the objects of the
goals of the state, are influenced in the fashioning of their
own lives — the institutions of the state grasp into every individual life, and bring together at the same time the masses
into a closer community of life, connecting those who were
previously unconnected.

In Europe, as we know, the long epoch from the Crusades
to the end of the 18th century, just that timespan which we describe as the epoch of early capitalism, was characterised by
the development of the absolute principality, in the bounds of
which modern capitalism thus developed purely on the face of
it.

But a great part of the signs of life of the modern state also
inwardly stand in some connection to the genesis of modern
capitalism, and also apply to it as precondition or impetus or
even as hindrance. That is, however, more than it seems at
first sight. For even if a consciously immediate impetus for
capitalist development became evident only in the economic
policies of "mercantilism", other branches of the state's life
though were unwanted and indirectly became of extremely
high significance for the impact of the capitalist nature, as
will be proven in detail in the course of these investigations.

Those areas of governmental authority which are thus of importance for our observations are the following:

1. the armed forces;
2. the business and trade policy;
3. transport policy;
4. currency policy;
5. colonial policy;
6. church policy;
7. labour policy;
8. public finances.

The first six areas are dealt with in this section, since they are exclusively expressions of the authority of the state and can be understood as such. The branch of policy named under 7 must on the contrary be treated in connection with other phenomena which first appear in a later stage of the development of the ideas, as they are not understandable without these. Hence it forms the object of a special section.

The public finances of the state will, pursuant to the plan of this work, be dealt with in the following connections:

1) in the chapter about finance;
2) as a "brake" on capitalist development (next volume);
3) as a stimulator for signs of life of the capitalist nature whose discussion and genetic portrayal is reserved for a later volume (the nature of the stock exchange and securities);
4) the public finances of modern states find extensive consideration as a source of enrichment in the section dedicated to the wealth of the bourgeois.

Specifying *literature* for these few general remarks over the nature and origin of the modern state, which has merely the goal of an introduction to the following, does not make much sense. There are to my knowledge no works which have fundamentally and in general retrospect made their special theme the problem discussed here. Books like that by J. Ferrari (1860) (which incidentally is valuable for its peculiar bibliography of Italian political literature of the 16th and 17th century), F. Oppenheimer (1907; 1926), and the like are though of too general a content to be of substantial assistance for the understanding being sought here. The work of S. M. Mélamed (1910) does not contain what you expect from the title *Der Staat im Wandel der Jahrhunderte* [*The State Through the Centuries*] — not the state, but rather the theories of the state are followed in their changes. A few of the *general works on the theory of the state* contain short historical overviews of the various forms of the state in the past. Thus in particular Jellinek (1914, 287 ff.).

But you must essentially rely here on the historical depictions which have this period as their subject. Eager students interested in the general patterns of the development will still find the most enlightenment in Jacob Burckhardt's unsurpassed *Civilisation of the Renaissance in Italy*, as well as in the works of Ranke which occupy themselves particularly in-depth with the 16th, 17th, and 18th centuries. Unfortunately Ranke fails of course in the parts on economic history almost completely. From the new literature, refer to the volume from the series *Kultur der Gegenwart* which considers *Staat und Gesellschaft der neueren Zeit* [*The State and Society of the Newer Period*] (Bezold, Gothein, and Koser 1908), and in which the work of Bezold over the time of the Reformation is especially valuable.

That, in the sphere of interests described here, that literature also towers which portrays the *theories of the state in their historical development* is understood by itself. An interesting attempt to describe the formation of modern states under an essentially geographical point of view is contained in the book of Auguste Himly (1876).

Chapter 22: The Armed Forces

Preliminary Remarks. Literature.

The modest prince's state is built from blood and iron. Inwardly as well as outwardly it becomes as strong and as large as the power of its sword reaches. Development of the modern state and development of the armed forces are thus homologous concepts. For this reason anyone who wants to say something about the modern state will have to give consideration to the particular nature of the military relationships.

But not only because of that do I speak here of the founding and expansion of the modern army, but also and above all for the reason that precisely from this side did capitalism experience an expansion that was fundamental and touched wide areas, thus that the development of militarism appears to be one of the preconditions for capitalism.

I have pursued these connections which prevail between militarism and capitalism in my study of *war and capitalism* (Sombart 1913b), to which I refer the reader when he wants to learn about the facts in more detail than I can portray here. The reader will find listed there in the appendix also a selection of the most important works of military science, which can serve him as a *literary guide* to further penetration into the area of problems in military history.

In accordance with the overall plan of this work, I treat in this capital firstly only the facts of the military organisation of modern armies and fleets, which appears as a work of public administration, as well as its manner of arising as far as it is necessary for comprehension. In each particular place the effects will then later be demonstrated which the new ordering of the armed forces had on the path of economic development.

I. The Origin of the Modern Armed Forces

1. The Development of New Forms of Organisation

a) The Army

The modern army is a *standing* army and a state's army. Both already existing tendencies — making the prince (as representative of the state) the sole commander, and placing the

45

troops permanently at his disposal — have an effect right down to the final details, until the principles achieve a general applicability. This victory of both principles finds it outward, it is tempting to say its symbolic expression, if this expression did not have such a very real significance for the basic ideas of the modern army, in the permanent state of readiness or provision of monetary means for the procurement and outfitting of standing, state troops — means of which the prince is free to dispose, thus that he can thereby make the temporal duration as well as the administration of the army dependent on his will — in this henceforth created material power of the prince the two essential characteristics of the modern army — that it is standing and that it belongs to the state — are united as if by themselves into an organic unity. The prince disposes now over "means and people", and with that the army is guaranteed in its new form, with that it became what it is destined to be — the sword in the hand of the prince, whom it in turn helps to realise his nature — since in the political world "a lord is of no consideration when he has himself no means or people", as the Great Elector* expressed it in his political testament of 1667.

If the inner relatedness of the three factors — creation of means, continuity, and state administration — and their fundamental significance for the development of the modern army is recognised, then one is inclined admittedly to attribute an epoch-making character to the reforms of Charles VII of France[14].

What was playing out already in France in the middle of the 15th century first repeated itself in other European states two centuries later. In England the consolidation of the army first took place in the time of the Commonwealth[15].

For Germany, that is for the German sovereign princes, it appears to me, Article 180 of the closing of the parliament from 17 May 1654 became of decisive importance[16].

At the beginning of the 18th century the modern army stood finished in its constitutional and administrative form.

---

*   [Tr.: Frederick William I (1620–1688), Elector of Brandenburg and Duke of Prussia.]

In Prussia, from now on the leading nation, the cabinet order of 15 May 1713 applied the seal to the new form[17].

But when we focus on "the modern army" in its entire nature, then other features than its constitutional and administrative character distinctly appear in the image – the modern army is also peculiarly defined by military technology. And indeed it portrays itself as what you could call a collective army or a *mass army* or even an army of troops in service, and is distinguished thereby just as sharply from all medieval armies.

The distinctive feature of such a mass army lies in that it has the effect, above all through its size, pulled together by it into a tactical unit, of a many-headed troop of soldiers animated by a common spirit. The community of spirit is produced by the command which emanates from the leaders. The functions of (intellectual) direction and (physical) action are thus separated and are exercised by different persons, whereas earlier they were amalgamated in one and the same person. That process of differentiation has taken place which is so extraordinarily characteristic for the entire modern cultural development.

The analogy of development imposes itself above all on the organisation of economic life — from craftwork to capitalism.

This *differentiation of the directing and the performative functions* then draws a whole crowd of phenomena after itself, phenomena which typify the modern armed forces — above all the exercising and the discipline by which they must produce in a mechanical way the connection between the directing and the performative organs. In the "lockstep" which the Greeks and Romans had practised, which the Swiss and Sweden again practised, which Leopold I, Prince of Anhalt-Dessau, made the rule in the Prussian army, the modern army likewise welcomes its symbol.

Certainly the modern principality would have produced this form of army creation out of itself, even without models, just as modern capitalism had to develop with urgent necessity the large scale enterprise as a form of work organisation from itself and its innermost being, because this external manifestation lay enclosed within itself.

The modern principality had to produce the differentiated mass army out of itself, because this alone would fulfill its innate *urge towards expansion*, towards expansion of power. Weapons technology may have had a say in it. But it was not a primary cause in the development of the modern organisation of the army (just as little — the comparison instinctively imposes itself again and again — as with the development of the forms of large scale enterprise in the framework of the capitalist economic system). The tactical unity of the square of men in which the modern mass army first appeared had its foundation in the weapons technology of the pike, and had to at first be heavily altered in order to enable shooting with firearms. Then later, of course, *firearms technology* established with its monotonously mechanical effects the organisation of the mass army, stamped on it as it were the automatic trait, and made a necessity out of the formation which had been formed previously purely out of free volition (like steam technology transferred manufacturing to the factory).

But originally the form of the mass army was openly created by the modern prince to give expression to his innermost being — only in him lay enclosed the possibility of a quick and constant expansion. In the differentiation between directing and performative work, in the thereby conditioned mechanical transfer of skills lay the guarantee of training in a short time any desired mass of unschooled men into efficient soldiers. In mass, of course, as tactical success was built more and more on the mass effect, which to an increasing extent was the case with the infiltration of firearms, the urge grew for an enlargement of the army, on whose extent (with otherwise equal extents of training, equipment, etc.) the size of the state's power was from now on dependent.

b) The Fleet

Certainly the organisation of sea warfare exhibits many common traits with that of land warfare. Above all we encounter with the marine frequently the same forms of raising forces as with the army — there are just as much contingents, as there are mercenaries and condottieri, on water as on land.

But what differentiates the nature of sea warfare from land warfare is perhaps still greater and more significant. Above all, there was never a knight at sea. Those individual soldiers grown from the topsoil of their own clods of earth, who formed the armed forces of the Middle Ages so characteristically, are missing in sea warfare for purely external reasons. The tactics here had to be based fundamentally from the beginning on mass effects. Even if single combat were pursued on the boarding of an enemy ship, martial success depended in essence on the good manoeuvres of the ship, which was always the work of many among whom one commanded, whilst the others carried out his orders. What a difference (precisely in the same centuries) between a battle of knights and the battle between say Venetian and Genoan galleys where hundreds of slaves sat on the oar benches!

The second peculiarity of sea warfare lies grounded in the fact that the conduct of war is always bound to an extraordinarily strong expenditure of a tangible nature which often significantly exceeds the capacity of the individual. For the complete equipping of the fighter there is still the ship to think of, which demands inordinately much greater means to produce and to move than the provision of weapons for the individual soldier and even than the obtaining of a warhorse.

And the strange thing is that these all-important accessories for the conduct of war were kept ready at any time by the common merchant in the form of his trading ships.

From this strange reality developed a system of organisation peculiar to sea forces — the utilisation of the trading fleet for war aims. We find this system in use by all the seafaring nations of Europe during the entire Middle Ages[18].

On the other hand, the overwhelming significance of tangible expenditure with sea warfare led earlier to such a thing as can be called a *standing fleet*. Once a prince has the means to build himself ships, they remain at his disposal for a longer time. They do not demand expenditure constantly like soldiers. Naturally it still needed now sailors and marines to conduct war. But in the ships the prince possesses a considerable part of the forces which are thus "standing", so long as the ships are usable. It seems almost as if kings and cities already early on had a stock of their own ships[19].

Even the *nationalisation of the navy* reaches much further back than the nationalisation of the army. It seems here that the judge-like power of the king formed the bridge between the independent ship's crews and the supreme power of the king[20].

2. The Expansion of the Armed Body

I said that the tendency for enlargement innate to the modern army depicts that peculiarity of it which is most important to us in this respect because, as will be shown later, it results in the most important economic effects.

So as to give a clearer idea of this phenomenon of expansion of the modern army, I want to share here the *numbers for the strengths of the armies* of the main states.

a) The Armies

One of the most important results to which Hans Delbrück arrives in the third volume of his history of the art of war[21] is the proof that the *Middle Ages had throughout smaller armies* than was previously assumed. In addition, the same is shown for the conduct of war as I have shown for trade, and what many others have already shown previously for the general population ratios, in particular the number of inhabitants of cities — the outward smallness of the medieval world (which makes its inward greatness all the more imposing). In the battle of Hastings previously hundred of thousands, even millions (one estimate comes to 1,200,000) were supposed to have fought one another — most probably the Norman army numbered in reality less than 7,000 soldiers, certainly not many more, and Harold's army was still weaker, 4,000–7,000.

Even the armies of the Crusades, which were surely the largest of the Middle Ages, are comparatively small — we may estimate the highest number of cavalry who fought in one battle in Palestine at 1,200, that of foot soldiers at 9,000[22].

The largest army which the Middle Ages surely saw was that which Edward III pulled together at Calais in 1347. It consisted of 32,000 men — as Delbrück adds to his calculation[23], an "armed force unheard-of for the Middle Ages". And we must still consider with these numbers that these large armies could only ever be kept together for quite a short time.

In contrast, the modern armies appear for us already at the end of the 18th century, up to which point we are following their development here, to have grown into the gigantic.

The *strengths of the standing armies of all the European states* in the second half of the 18th century are given by the well-informed contributor to Krünitz et al (1773, 50:746) — whose articles over the armed forces, filling volumes 50 through 53, are distinguished by great expertise — individually on the basis obviously of the best sources, right down to Mecklinburg-Strelitz, whose armed forces amounted to 50 men. Accordingly the number of troops in the four great military states amounted to:

Austria in peace...........................297,000 men
Austria in war..............................363,000 men
Russia, regular troops.................224,500 men
Prussia...190,000 men
France..182,000 men

b) The Fleets

i) The Italian States

In the 13th century the greatest sea power of Europe was the republic of Genoa. Its war fleet was at this time even by current standards not small, and for medieval circumstances quite improbably large. The numbers are, however, hardly to be questioned, they awaken trust through their imprecision. The source is the Annales Januenses. Even the conscientious Heyck[24] assumes that they correspond to reality.

Already around the middle of the 12th century (1147–1148) 63 galleys and 163 other vessels were sent against the Spanish Saracens. In 1242, 83 galleys, 13 tarides, and four large cargo ships fought against the Sicilian-Pisan fleet. In 1263, 60 Genoan war-galleys crossed into Greek waters. In 1283, 199 galleys even, calculated on the smaller squadrons, were put into service. If we consider that a galley had 140 oarsmen, then thus for 199 galleys there would have been 27,860 oarsmen (not counting soldiers!) There we will have to assume that the 199 galleys were manned and sent out one after the other. We are, however, also informed over the size of the crews — in 1285, the republic placed into service 12,085 men from its area on the riviera, consisting of 9,191 oarsmen, 2,615 marine soldiers, and 279 mariners (*nauclerii*). They were divided amongst 65 galleys and one galleon.

ii) Spain

The Grand Armada which was defeated by the English in 1588 consisted of 130 sailing ships and 65 galleys when it left Lisbon (two ships fewer arrived at the battle). These ships had a tonnage of 57,868 t. and a total crew of 30,656 men, "excluding volunteers, priests, and other civilians"[25].

iii) France

The French war fleet was raised up to its imposing size especially by Colbert.

At his death (1683), the total number of already finished warships had risen to 176[26], to which 68 were still to be found in construction, so that the result was a total complement of 244. Of these there were:

of the first rank......................................12
of the second..20
of the third...39
of the fourth to sixth...............................71
auxiliaries..44

iv) Holland

The Dutch war fleet also developed within a few decades during the great 17th century from small beginnings into what was at the time perhaps the preeminent and strongest fleet in Europe.

In the years 1615–1616[27] the Dutch sea power still consisted of only 43 mostly tiny ships, of which four had a crew of 90 each, 11 between 50 and 80, 9 with 52 men each, whilst 19 were even smaller. That results in 2,000 to at most 3,000 men crewing them. In the year 1666, the United Netherlands opposed the English with a fleet of 85 ships and a total complement of 21,909 officers and men.

v) Sweden

Sweden was a significant sea power in the 16th and 17th centuries. Its war fleet had its beginnings under Gustav Vasa in the year 1522. In the year 1566 the ships register already exhibited a complement of 70 ships. They then underwent a new upswing at the beginning of the 17th century — in 1625, 21 new ships were built and 30 galleys made ready for service[28].

vi) England

The quick rise of this greatest of European sea powers has its equal only in the sudden development of the Prussian armed forces. The development[29] started perhaps in the time of Henry VIII.

Towards the end of our epoch, the complement of the English marine was the following (31 May 1786 according to the registry of the Admiralty):

> 292 warships, of which
> 114 ships of the line,
> 13 5-cannon ships (similar to ships of the line),
> 113 frigates,
> 52 war sloops.

The ships of the line had crews of between 500 and 850 men. In constant pay stood 18,000 seamen, comprised of 14,140 sailors and 3,860 marine soldiers.

The total tonnage was in 1749 already 228,215 t.

The strengths of the war fleets in the European states at the end of the 18th century (Krünitz et al. 1773) was the following:

> Great Britain..............................278 warships
> (of which 114 ships of the line)
> France...221 warships
> United Netherlands........................95 warships
> Denmark and Norway............60 armed vessels
> Sardinia...32 warships
> Venice..30 warships
> Both Sicilies..................................25 warships
> Sweden..............................25 ships of the line
> Portugal...24 warships
> Papal States..................................20 warships
> Tuscany......................................"a few frigates"

II. The Principles of Equipping the Army

The *organisation of the equipping of the army*[30] forms a part of the administration of the army. It sets as its task the providing of the army with all the tangible goods necessary for its existence and its proper functioning. These tangible goods are:

1. weapons;
2. means of transport, thus particularly horses and wagons;
3. means of upkeep, thus food, clothing, and shelter.

To the extent that it concerns the obtaining of this or that category of tangible goods, the problems arise of:

> arming,
> mounting (transporting),
> feeding,
> clothing, and
> housing the army.

The most important branches of the equipping of armies have shown the following development:

1. Armaments

The soldier of the Middle Ages, whether he be knight or footsoldier, in the rule brought along his own weapons and armour.

That had to change, and indeed at first from purely technological, external reasons when the firing of cannon with gunpowder had been learnt. With the best of wills, the individual soldier could not bring weapons of his own like *these*. We thus see early on cities and states taking care of the obtaining of the big guns. The outward expression of this care is found in the construction of armouries or arsenals in which the cannons were stored which were put at the disposal of troops as needed. In the beginning, they were city arsenals, later state arsenals. Thus in the 15th century the city of Paris had a magnificently endowed armoury[31], just as did the cities of Mons and Bruges[32].

In the 16th century the princes endeavoured to construct numerous arsenals. Foremost were the two great military powers of the future, France and Brandenburg-Prussia.

What an expansion the armouries had obtained in all the European states up to the end of the 17th century is taught to us by a look in the "Das neueröffnete Arsenal" [*The Newly Opened Arsenal*][33] which gives us in four sections a catalogue "of the places where cannons and ammunition are finished, kept, and used".

Now it is to be noted here though that in the arsenals and armouries in no way was it just the "big guns" which were stored, but that in them rather were stored also armour and protective weapons of every sort. The fact is thereby demonstrated that the total work of armaments in the period from the 15th to 17th century was gripped by a tendency towards nationalisation, since of course the weapons piled up in the armouries were there to be delivered to soldiers free of charge or for hire, it makes no difference which.

The demonstrably first provision of soldiers with weapons by the state took place with the contingent of the population left over after the old call-up, when a war had broken out[34].

Then the system of weapons provision by the state gradually extended to all troops. In the 17th century, during which so many new things came into the world, the transformation was completed. We can in that time still distinctly observe the various states of transition which can arise from the transformation of the private provision to a state provision of weapons:

1. The soldier brings a part of the weapons, the others are delivered to him by the state[35]. A deduction of pay was the usual form of charge.
2. The Colonel obtains the weapons for the unit and deducts the sum from the men's monthly pay[36].
3. The weapons are either delivered in kind or the soldiers receive a special pay for weapons[37].

Besides that, however, the full delivery of weapons by the state also occurred throughout the entire 17th century[38].

But the new order of armaments will only then be comprehensible to us in its entire characteristic significance when we discover that in connection with the nationalisation there was at the same time a standardisation in the form of weapons, a *making uniform* of the entire nature of weaponry.

55

Up into the 16th century weapons and armour had been different for each individual soldier from that of others — with knights of course, but also with footsoldiers, even with the new violent mobs of the Swiss who still carried all sorts of short swords, battle axes, spiked maces, and above all halberds, and even still when firearms came in — "calibre, form, and name are down to the preference of those who buy them or have them made" ("Calibres, façons et noms étant selon la volonté de ceulx qui les acheptent ou les font faire"), it states in La Treille[39].

The first example of a uniform arming of larger mobs is probably offered by the long pikes of the mercenaries in the 16th century[40], whose unity followed immediately from the basic idea of the modern body of troops aiming at a mass effect. De-individualisation here as there.

But then of course firearms signified a new, as it were technological cause for standardisation. At the end of the 16th century, the Augsburg gunmakers offered Wilhelm V, Duke of Bayern, 900 hand cannons, "every one fitted for a ball"[41], which was yet unusual.

Now *the concept of calibre* made its entrance into the world of weaponry[42].

2. Feeding

We will do well to examine land and marine forces separately, since the provision of food to their troops shows too many internal differences to observe them as one.

Through the entire Middle Ages until deep into the modern age it was the rule with *land troops* that each soldier took care of his own upkeep himself or that those closest to him provided him with means of upkeep in kind, quite regardless of whether it was cavalry or footsoldiers, whether conscripts or mercenaries.

It is the state which still reigned in Wallenstein's time[43].

With the progressive nationalisation of the army, the regulation of the work of provision was also gradually recognised to be a responsibility of the state[44].

Everywhere, as far as I can see, the authority of the state begins the regulation of the work of provision with a sort of *indirect care* — the officials of the king or the other authorities keep an eye out that the food needed for the upkeep of the troops is at the disposal of the purchasing soldiers in sufficient quantities, at a good quality and for a civil price. We learn of such care in the 15th century with the Swiss contingent which we have already discussed[45]. We hear of it still earlier in France[46]. It is encountered by us with the armies of the Thirty Years War[47].

But early on the involvement of the state in the feeding of the troops became in essence a helping role. The prince had since time immemorial had a bodyguard for whose physical upkeep he himself provided. He furthermore had to supply the fortresses with provisions. He had to equip the troops he sent overseas with food. Thus we see once again in the Middle Ages the King of France at work having bailiffs and seneschals buy up food which he used for the purposes mentioned above[48].

In addition we find early on public bodies of the state tasked with looking after the upkeep of the troops — the ordnance companies of Charles VII were served in kind by the provinces[49].

With the increasing strengthening of the idea of the state, it could not fail to happen that the prince hit upon the idea, after he had nationalised his army, of also nationalising the entire work of provision. It seems as if the system of *provisioning of the troops by the state* first reached its full development in Spain during the 17th century. From here it also spread to other states, like in Brandenburg-Prussia. Here we see it in practice up to the time of the Great Elector in the form of "providing meals", that is, the provisioning through the host of the billet.

This system of complete provision by the state, however, did not hold out for long. The difficulties of implementation, with the associated detrimental effects for the regions quartered in, already induced the Great Elector to put aside the feeding of the army again, and put monetary payment in its place. Frederick William I sought still more to limit the fiscal administration of natural produce — placing the regiments, companies, and individuals on fixed monetary incomes which they had to get by on. Thus in the course of the 17th and 18th centuries in most states a sort of mixed system

developed which rested fairly uniformly on the following basic principles — the state provisioned the soldiers entirely on
the march and in the field; in the garrison it left it essentially
up to the individual as to how he got his meals with the pay
that he received. In the individual states this or that component of the soldier's upkeep was administered by the state or in
kind by the billet host (in the form of the so-called Servis).

As soon as the state undertook some provisioning for the
upkeep of the soldier, thus in particular as soon as it delivered
him bread — be it always, as in France, be it occasionally, as
in most German states — it had to take care of the storing of
provisions, and especially for the stockpiling of grain.

That happened through it setting up magazines, if possible
strewn across the entire country — in France this was already
happening under Henry IV, then under Louis XIII to a wide
extent[50]; in Prussia especially under Frederick William I (in
1726, 21 war magazines were constructed)[51]; of the other German states, Saxony, Bohemia, and Württemberg had already
been advancing in the same direction since the 16th century[52].

***

The situation with the marine is different to that with the
land army in so far as the self-provision of the crew is hardly
practicable for any of the larger types of ships and longer
journeys. You can imagine that on a warship a few hundred or
thousand men are excluded for weeks or months from all intercourse with the external world. They must be provided
thus in any case with large *stores* of food. To leave the procurement of these stores to the individuals, to stack them up
and guard them individually in the ship, and then to also have
them consumed individually would be extraordinarily
troublesome. This sort of self-provision also seemed to have
occurred on ships, probably in small situations[53].

The large seafaring states, thus particularly Spain, Holland, France, and England, seem to have never known the
system of self-provision for their ships' crews. What was configured differently was only the form in which the collective
procurement of food for the ship's crew took place. Here, so
far as I can see, two systems were used in the course of the
centuries — one which you can call French, in which the
ship's captain is responsible for the provisioning of their ship,

and an English one in which the state takes care of the provisioning for the ship's crew[54].

3. Clothing

a) The Clothing System

In the beginning clothing was also here the self-responsibility of every soldier. The mercenary brought his outfit with him as far as it suited him. But even the soldiers in the ordnance companies of Charles the Bold (1471), thus already a sort of "standing army", had to sort out there clothing (just as with their weapons) themselves[55]. We encounter the same situation in the English fleet at the time of Elizabeth[56].

When a higher instance begins to worry about the work of clothing, then it sometimes happens, similarly to what we have already been acquainted with in the provisioning of food, in the form of an indirect support — it is still left to the individual soldier to equip himself according to his own discretion and at his own cost, but attention is given that he finds good and inexpensive wares for purchase.

The English government proceeded thus for their fleet in the 17th century[57].

But in the main, as the individual bodies of troops themselves solidified and were welded together into a uniform army, the collective satisfaction of needs took the place of individual provision.

The military entrepreneurship which reigned in particular during the 16th and 17th centuries brought about by itself that the authority to whom the clothing of a body of troops fell, when the individual provision had already ceased, became the colonel of the regiment or the company commander.

This system of regimental or company-wise procurement of clothing reigned probably in all military states from the beginning of the modern army up until into the 18th century[58].

Early on, however, *the state* also then intervened in the work of clothing in that it participated in the outfitting of the army itself. At first *next* to the other authorities, be it that it fully clothed a part of the troops, be it that it took on itself a part of the provision of clothing for all troops.

In this case it either placed the raw material for the cloth-ing at the disposal of the colonels and commanders, thus in particular the cloth for the uniforms, for a corresponding pay-ment. That happened for example in Brandenburg-Prussia[59].

Or the prince delivered a part of the clothing, the officers the rest[60].

The other way which the prince took part in the clothing of his troops led him to the complete provision of a part of the army, so that in this case the army diverged into the state-clothed regiments and those clothed from elsewhere.

From the beginning the prince had probably looked after the equipping of his bodyguard. And the main efforts then re-mained directed at its ample and expensive outfitting even when it had later considerably expanded and, in France for example, had grown into the "troops of the royal house". In addition, the prince gave other troops uniforms according to their need and his abilities[61].

In the 18th century the nationalisation of the provision of clothing was then completed in all military nations.

The *Austrian* Uniforms Commission established in 1768 became exemplary for the organisation of the provision of military clothing, and had the aim of "providing all the parts of the army in both peace and wartime with the required uni-forms, fittings, leatherwork, objects of horse equipment, and field requisites of all types", and which also at the same time had to take care of the procurement of infirmary utensils and bed furniture[62].

b) The Uniform

The changes which the form of clothing underwent, which are especially important for the economic problem, are very closely connected with the changes in the clothing systems.

When each soldier had to take care of clothing himself ac-cording to his discretion and means, then with a large troop a great motley look arose, similar as we saw with the arming of troops. The image of a mob of mercenaries appears before the eyes, in which each individual confers his own odd expression of taste to his clothing[63].

The modern uniform[64] is a through and through rational object — it was born from a series of quite intensive and quite subtle considerations of functionalism. Considerations of functionalism which in the first place were of a *military nature*.

There was the purely external reason — that by a uniform you could more easily recognise a troop and more easily differentiate it from the others. But to this external reason were joined significant internal reasons which arose from giving a uniform to an army — the uniform lends the wearers, so it is said, a *feeling of solidarity* which they do not possess without the same garb.

Related, but not identical with this consideration was the other reason which the great organisers of troops later employed — when they suggested the uniform leads to the good discipline of an army. Here it was as it were a heteronomous submission of the individual to the goals of the whole which was expected from the provision of the uniform. *Without uniform, no discipline* — Frederick the Great expressed this thought when he described the state of the army of the Great Elector[65].

These, as I call them, military considerations of functionalism were now, however, complemented by the strong reasons of *economic rationalism*, which then likewise pushed for the provision of uniforms — the uniformity creates the possibility of mass purchase and mass production, and this confers numerous advantages, of which the most important is the lower price.

The uniform spreads to the same extent and at the same pace as the nationalisation of the system of clothing.

To the extent now that the prince provides the troops entirely with clothing, he also uniforms them. So that we can follow during the 16th, 17th, and 18th centuries the progress of the state systems of clothing in the progress of the uniforms — until the complete victory of both principles[66].

Chapter 23: Mercantilism as a Whole

Sources and Literature

As *sources* for the study of mercantilism, it is worth considering the laws, regulations, etc. along with their establishment. They are gathered together for all nations in easily accessible collections.

A complete overview of all *English* sources is found in Cunningham (1907, App.).

For *France*, most worthy of consideration are Jourdan et al (1822) (see the index and categories Manufactures, Mines, etc.), and then for more comfortable use the special collection *Recueil des règlemens généraux et particuliers concernant les manufactures et fabriques du royaume* (France 1730) where you will find collected all the laws from 1660–1730 which refer to large industry. The *Code du fabricant* (France 1788) was not accessible to me. Also see the list in Appendix 2 of G. Martin (1899, 360 ff.) of regulations from 1650–1715 which apply to manufactures.

For *Spain*, see *Recopilacion de las leyes destos reynos* (Spain 1640).

For *Holland*, see *Groot Placcaetboek (Cau 1658)*.

For *Austria*, see Kropatschek (1804), Wekebrod (1799).

For *Germany*, Senckenberg and Schmauss (1747). For *Brandenburg-Prussia*, see Mylius (1737), Riedel (1838), and the *Acta Borussica* (Preußischen Akademie der Wissenschaften 1892).

Next to the legislative material, the correspondence, etc. of the princes, the great statesman, and the higher officials can be consulted, of which we possess in fact a series of good collections for *France*, like Vol. 3: *Affaires de Finances — Commerce – Industrie* of Depping (1850), de Boislisle (1874), Clément (1861) (the second volume refers especially to industry). For *England*, see Carlyle (1902).

Works which handle mercantilism from a general viewpoint are, if we leave aside the pure works of literary history, not numerous. The most important are Bidermann (1870), Heyking (1880) (for the date of its appearance a quite excellent text), Schmoller (1884b; 1902), and Sieveking (1907).

All the more numerous are the depictions of the mercantilist epoch in the individual nations, which I will name in the following chapter.

The uniform characteristics of the mercantilist economic policy are best understood, as it appears to me, when you realise what ideas and principles were adopted from the earlier (city economy) period and which innovations had to arise by necessity from the altered interests of the princes.

Mercantilism is firstly in fact nothing more than *the economic policy of the city extended to a larger territory*. As the city had formed the central focus of the world with its interests, to which obviously all other interests were subordinate, this now becomes the area ruled by the princes — politics remains egocentric in its basic conception. But the old idea of community also continues in the general idea of the state unto its last consequences — the welfare of the whole takes precedence over the individual; the entire population, even if represented by the absolute monarch, stands together as one[67]. From this basic conception there also follows at first a far-reaching care of the absolute state for the economic consumption of its citizens — the "supply policies" of the medieval cities is continued by it in all its components in the most conscientious way.

The *"supply policies"* of the cities had followed the aim of providing the residents with the necessary foodstuffs (grain, cattle). Hence the striving to draw as much as possible of these goods into the city, which you sought to achieve by forbidding exports from the countryside, obligating the producers to bring their products to markets, prohibiting the preemptive purchase of goods, inducing passing traders to "store", and laying in stockpiles in case of need. In all these points the princes were continuing the policies of the cities.

In *Spain*, we encounter royal export prohibitions for cattle and bread in 1307, 1312, 1351, 1371, 1377, and 1390; and for grain and flocks in 1455, flocks and cattle in 1502 (Spain 1640, 2:102 ff., 2:198 ff.).

In *France*, the supply policies of the kings begin with Philip IV's ordinances of 1305 and 1307 — in them the export of grain is forbidden, sending to market decreed, buying up prohibited, and prices for foodstuffs established. These principles remained in force for all the following centuries — in 1577 the export of grain is only allowed with a permit; the tariffs of 1614 contained tolls on grain exports (22 livres per muid[*]). The regulation of the grain trade becomes still stricter in the 17th and 18th centuries — tenants shall not have their grain longer than two years in the granary; cities shall stock up for three years at a minimum; merchants shall not buy grain within a radius of more than 2 miles (3.2 km) around any city, or of more than 7–8 miles (11–13 km) around Paris; foreign traders must bring and sell their grain in person, etc., etc. See,

---

[*] [Tr.: a *muid* was a measure of capacity of varying amounts — originally a wagon load.]

for example, the *Ordonnance du Roy sur le faict de la police générale de son royaume* (France 1578). A quite detailed portrayal of this legislation is given by Boissonade (1900, 1:Livre II, Ch. 1), the main regulations having their origins in the 17th and 18th centuries. Cf. Afanassiev (1894).

In *England*, the welfare policy of the kings begins with Henry III. It comes likewise to a prohibition on grain exports (as long as the price does not sink to 6/8 per quarter[†]), as well as very strict regulations over preemptive purchase and the wholesale trade of foodstuffs. See in particular 5 & 6 Edw. 6 c.14 (Forestallers Act 1551) and 13 Eliz. 1 c.25 (Continuance of Acts 1571).

From the time of Elizabeth I, the regulations over grain exports became somewhat milder — that had its natural cause in the increasing consideration which the kings had to take of the grain and cattle producers, and made itself noticeable at the same time in all lands. A sort of compromise is reached between the interests of civic consumers and country producers, which mostly culminated in that grain exports were fundamentally allowed, but could be banned again in times of high prices. Like in France in the 16th century as was already mentioned above. Thus in England after 1571 the export of grain was allowed, and only in times of rising prices could the magistrates forbid it. Bans on preemptive purchase, price taxes, and supervision of purchase and sale, however, also remained in force after this time. See, for England, Faber (1888).

The principle follows from it furthermore that the individual economic subject derives his right to produce goods or to conduct trade from the community — that this community, which was now represented by the monarch, at its discretion lends him as many rights and confers on him as many duties as it considers in its own interests to be right — all economic activity is "privileged".

And it follows finally from that basic conception that the individual is obliged to fit his behaviour strictly to the directives of the authorities, and that the latter have oversight of economic activity and are responsible for its careful exercise — to the extent that they are obliged to accompany any action of the economic subject with a reprimanding directive, all economic activity is "regulated".

This firmly established system was now faced by the prince with his special interests. We know that he founded his power above all on two institutions — the mercenary army and the professional civil service — and know also that both these in-

---

†   [Tr.: an English weight, 1 quarter = 12.7 kg.]

stitutions were established at the outset on a monetary economic basis. In order to maintain the army and bureaucracy (to which the expensive court joined itself), the prince needed thus above all money, yet more money, and yet still more money. (Only later did the lack of people in individual lands make itself felt and lead to the population policies in, for example, poor Prussia.)

The prince obtained the money he needed for his purposes through taxes or through loans. But so that taxes could be raised and loans taken up, a *minimal stock of precious metal* had to be stored up in the nation, a stock which had to be that much greater, the less the forms of credit had developed.

We can see here from the vantage point of the historian how thus a specific minimal quantity of precious metals also had to be *produced* on earth in order to satisfy the demands of the modern principality. And we could add that the strong expansion in precious metal production during these centuries — of which we will convince ourselves more precisely in Section 4 — signified a substantial advancement for the development of the modern political system. When a good expert on army history makes the remark once in passing, "its [Saxony's] armouries and armies grew from the silver mines of Schneeberg"[68], we can thus give this sentence the general formulation that the modern state arose from the silver mines of Mexico and Peru, and the gold pans of Brazil. Or put another way, as much silver (later gold) — as much state! Obviously only in the sense of being required — *without* such an ample production of precious metals as appeared after the discovery of America, the modern principality would also not have arrived at such a quick and general development.

Obtaining money thus became the central problem of princely statecraft, and it is only too well known that all the ideas and measures of mercantilist policies were camped around this striving for money. While it had been the most assiduous endeavour of the city authorities to supply their city well with consumables, (you could say) it became the core endeavour of all great statesmen of the ancien régime to bring exchangeable value in the form of money into the coffers of their princes, and to this end to bring it about that money in the lands subject to them streamed directly or indirectly into the state coffers. *The city's policy of supplying goods became the state's policy of supplying money.*

"Je crois que l'on demeurera facilement d'accord de ce principe qu'il n'y a que l'abondance d'argent dans un Etat, qui fasse la différence de sa grandeur et de sa puissance" [I believe that we will easily agree with this principle that there is only the abundance of money in a State which makes a difference regarding its size and its power][69] — with these words Colbert expressed in fact the conviction not only of his time, but of the century which preceded it, and the century which followed it. This striving for increasing money lay at the basis of all mercantilist politics, and at the basis of the mercantilist theory and likewise its practice. What changed in the course of time or in distinguished individual cases was only the different conception of the most expedient way in which you could obtain the desired money most easily and abundantly. In England, we see the battle of opinions in the 17th century fought between the bullionists, who insisted on the direct influence of the inflow and outflow of precious metals, and the mercantilists, who considered an indirect regulation through the direction of the stream of goods (balance of trade!) to be more expedient, and we then see how in the last years of the Stuarts that conception came into general acceptance which above all expected the expansion of money stocks by the development of industry. One of the first to represent this idea in England was the writer of *Britannia Languens*[70].

We will hence win an overview of the colourful world of mercantilist politics most easily when we make it clear that the individual expressions of this politics are no less than attempts to realise the highest aim of statecraft, as far as it was of a material nature, and when we group them according to the differences in the method of achieving the stated goal. We will thus have to remind ourselves again and again of the fact which we were able to establish above — that the mercantilist statecraft sought to achieve its particular goals essentially in the ways which had already been used previously by the city governments.

The most assiduous striving of all mercantilist politics must of course have been directed at *seizing money in direct ways*, be it by endeavouring to retain the gold and silver present in the land, be it by endeavouring to produce precious metals in one's own land.

When the kings forbade the export of coinage from their states — we find such bans on export in France already in the years 1303 and 1322, as well as in England (under Edward III) and in Spain, amongst others — then they were thereby only walking in the footsteps of the city governments, as we will see more precisely in another connection.

The production of precious metals had also been carried out by the cities — admittedly only in isolated cases. From the 16th century, however, the tendency emerged now more and more distinctly within the state administrations of taking silver mines under their own control in order to not have the stream of precious metals in their own land dry up[71]. It even became a basic principle of mercantilist theories — that precious metal production also then brought economic benefits when it was carried out with reward[72].

But the main thing was that the yearning for possession of their own silver mines or gold fields drove the states over their borders "to India", the magical land, and that from this pursuit of gold, in which all states took part during those centuries, the great colonial empires of the European peoples arose. I will, however, speak in detail about their origin in context in Chapter 27.

The way in which colonial policies were meant to serve indirectly mercantilist ideas is expressed in classical form by the following words from one of the best authorities on colonial history:

> [The disciples of the Mercantile system] have carried into execution, in this branch of policy, the most elaborate, and the most violent of their artificial schemes, for pouring into the nation an abundance of the precious metals. Colonies have not, indeed, always furnished, directly, those precious supplies; but they have been used as means of obtaining the supplies from other markets, and of unlocking the money-chests of different nations in Europe: Their produce has been engrossed, as a weight, by which to procure, in other countries, the great object of the Mercantile system — a favourable balance of trade.
>
> (Brougham 1803, 1:5 f.)

In exactly the same way, I mention here in passing only briefly, in order to return to it once more later, that from the striving to supply the princely coffers with the greatest possible quantity of money in a direct way the entire elaborate

68

construction of the tax and credit economy naturally arose, and that the same striving led to specific mint and currency policies which were of great significance for the shaping of economic life.

But then the state itself became an entrepreneur in order to obtain the missing money by way of profit — we will meet it in this character when we follow the construction of the capitalist economy itself and take a look at the economic subjects of the early capitalist epoch (see Section 1 of the following volume).

Here above all those components of mercantilist economic policy are to be thought of in which the striving of the state to indirectly reach its goal — the obtaining of money — becomes visible. These roundabout ways lead it, however, into a sort of *partnership with the aspiring capitalism*, and the conduct of this partnership is actually really that which is generally thought of when one speaks of mercantilism.

We must remind ourselves that the prince and the capitalist entrepreneur in those centuries were natural confederates because they followed for a good part the same interests. Above all they were both brought together by their common opposition to the medieval civic feudal powers. Just as it was this which threw obstructions in the way of the expansion of princely rule over a large area, it was also this which placed the fetters of guild and toll barriers on the aspiring capitalism. But both the new powers had a mutual interest in the greatest expansion possible of the stock of precious metals in the land. Thus it happened quite by itself that the two stuck together; that in particular — as concerns us here — the absolute state became a promoter of and assistant to capitalist interests, thus in the first line of the capitalist industries and of the large foreign trade — the *Arts et manufactures* must be furthered, it says in the preamble to Henry IV of France's edict of August 1603, "pour estre [...] le seul moyen de ne point transporter hors du royaume l'or et l'argent, pour enrichir nos voisins" [to be the only way not to transport gold and silver out of the kingdom, [or] to enrich our neighbours], and "money is sanguis corporis politici [blood of the body politic] and to not only rein in, but rather to retain such requires no other means than that foreign goods are either not admitted

into a land or, when they are unavoidably and generally necessary, are to be produced in the land itself per naturam vel
industriam [by nature or hard work] and obtained that way;
always such things form occasio et causa movens cessat [a
delay to the occasion and motive of the actor] for making the
money leave the land."[73] The wealth of precious metals in the
land promoted industry, as Colbert suggested, "quant l'argent
est dans le royaume, l'envie étant universelle d'en tirer profit,
fait que les hommes lui donnent du mouvement" [when there
is money in the kingdom, the universal desire to profit from it
makes men move it] — and through that the state's coffers
profit in turn, "c'est dans ce mouvement que le Trésor trouve
sa part" [it is in this movement that the treasury finds its
share]. But in order to reach that favourable effect, it requires
above all the development of foreign trade, "il n'y a que le
commerce seul et tout ce qui en dépend qui peut produire le
grand effet d'amener de l'argent; il fallait l'introduire en
France où ni le général ni même les particuliers ne s'y sont jamais appliqués" [there is only trade alone and all that depends on it which can produce the great effect of bringing in
money; it had to be introduced in France where neither the
general populace nor even individuals have ever applied it]
(Clément 1861, 7:233).

The other side of the problem, of how the capitalist industry was of
use to the aspiring state, I will not pursue here. It may only be highlighted that, apart from the indirect support which the development of
capitalism granted to the prince and his land, the state coffers took a
direct interest in the progress of capitalist undertakings through appris-
ings of the most various sort. The privileges to be mentioned below
were mostly only granted for a fee. With many undertakings, particularly of the great trading companies, it was usual that the entire share
capital or even a significant part was put at the disposal of the state as a
loan — the (new) English East-India Company, for example, lent William III £2,000,000, Anne £1,200,000, together £3,200,000, "what
may properly be called the capital stock of this company" (Postlethwayt
1774, 1:644 § East-India Company). In the year 1744 it gave £1,000,000
at 3% in return for the extension of the privileges for 14 years (Macpherson and Anderson 1805, 3:239). The South Sea Company was founded in the ninth year of Queen Anne's reign to discharge a debt of
£9,471,325 which the government had taken on (Macpherson and Anderson 1805, 3:19 ff.). In 1715 a sum of £822,032 4 s. 8 d. was added to
it. In return the company received the right to the income from the duties on salt, candles, etc. (Postlethwayt 1774, 2:765 § South Sea Company).

The French Mississippi Company was founded and privileged so as to eliminate an amount of 60 million livres owed by the state — the first 60 million in capital was subscribed in government stocks; then the state increased the capital to 100 million.

The Dutch East-India Company paid the government 1,600,000 florins for the extension of its privileges in the year 1643, and once again each time it extended, e.g. 3,600,000 florins in 1729 .

Or the companies were taxed directly during their existence — 4 Will. & Mar. c.15 (Taxation Act 1692) taxed the East-India Company with £5 on every £100 of stock, the Royal African Company with £1 per share, the Hudson Bay Company £5 per share, etc. (Macpherson and Anderson 1805, 2:652). The government accepted quite naively that the economic activity in the land would also always at the same time be carried out in the best manner for the state's coffers. Thus the Charter of Leeds in the year 1626 states that this city had fabricated cloth for a long time "for the fame and to the best for the income of the English Crown"; in 1661 a new constitutional charter bemoaned the cheating of the wool industry which not only redounded to the detriment of the industry, but also to the public income, etc.

The reader will find countless examples of an undisguised granting of privileges for the payment of a fee in the specialist works named in the following chapter.

Chapter 24: Trade and Commercial Policies

Sources and Literature

I have already named the *sources* in the previous chapter. The *literature* is immense — next to the history of guild and city charters, no branch of economic history is as strongly developed as the literature over the mercantilist trade and commercial policies. As much learning as it has brought us over the events in the state *administration*, it has though (similar to what we have seen with the literature on the history of the cities) held up the actual *economic* history research in many cases — they thinks they are writing economic history when they are writing administrative history, which is certainly not the same thing though. I have in the following put together a small selection of writings which are suitable for a first introduction.

France.

1. Commercial Policies: (up to 1851) Eberstadt (1899); for the 17th and 18th centuries: Fagniez (1897), Des Cilleuls (1898), Mosnier (1898), G. Martin (1899; 1900). Of course, Levasseur (1900) is the very best to have at hand.

2. Trade Policies: Gouraud (1854). From the literature over the great trading companies, see Bonnassieux (1892), Kaeppelin (1908), Pigeonneau (1887) (up to Richelieu), and Levasseur (1900).

Paris in particular: Frégier (1850).

Also belonging here is the large literature over Colbert. The main work is Clément (1892).

England.

1. The commercial policies are treated in numerous monographs on specific industries, inter alia: James (1857), Burnley (1889), Duchesne (1900), and Lohmann (1900).

2. General works: Held (1881), Hewins (1892) (chapters 1 & 2 deal with trade policy), Unwin (1904), Price (1906), and H. Levy (1909).

3. Trade Policies: Schanz (1881) (deals above all with the reigns of the first two Tudors), and Hewins (1892).

Also a good guide directly into matters of economic *policy* is Cunningham (1907). Distinguished by its clear and correct judgement is the book, still readable today, of Ochenkowski (1879).

Spain. Ustáriz (1753), Ulloa (1753), Colmeiro (1863), and Bonn (1896).

Holland. Laspeyres (1863), Pringsheim (1890).

Austria.

1. Commercial Policies: Přibram (1907, Vol. I), covering the period 1740–1798, is an excellent, extraordinarily content-rich and instructive book. Standing comparison next to it are the earlier texts by A. Beer (1895), Waentig (1898, 7–47), and Rizzi (1903) (whilst the title indicates a focus on commerce, it deals in essence with commercial policy). A broad overview is given by Adler (1903). The portrayal of Slokar (1914) extends beyond the mercantilist epoch. The work extends the earlier ones. It is probably a product of the especially strong bureaucratisation of Austrian economic policy that its history has found so many — good! — treatments.

2. Trade Policies: A. Beer (1899), Landau (1906) deals in essence with the internal trade policies, Srbik (1907) is likewise a good book.

Brandenburg-Prussia. Schmoller (1884a; 1886; 1887a; 1898a). Other relevant works in Schmoller (1898b). See also Schmoller and Hintze (1892), Rohrscheidt (1898), and Matschoss (1912), Freymark (1897), Meinardus (1891), and Fechner (1907) (pages 1–453 deal with economic policy).

Germany in general. Below (1900). Naudé (1896) extends it to various states.

Somewhere in between literature and sources are the great merchant lexicons by Savary, Postlethwayt, Schatzkammer, etc., in which abundant materials can be found. Much information is also contained in the various volumes of the *Encyclopédie méthodique* which deal with manufactures and commerce (Platière 1785; Bandeau 1783).

I. Overview

The following sketch of mercantilist policies will bring nothing new in detail to the expert. What I am aiming at with it is to furnish proof that these policies (despite considerable national differences) were formed similarly in their essential features in all the European lands. This compilation of the legislative measures of the most important states that are conformant in their nature is also perhaps welcome for those who have a complete knowledge of the individual national systems of administration. My overview shall serve the others as an introduction to the studies. But it must not be lacking in this place, because it forms a necessary part of the entire structure of my historical synthesis.

When we now look at the measures in detail which the state took up in the interest of the capitalist economic elements, we see that it really did at base nothing other than apply the maxims of civic economic policy to the entire state and further develop its specific aims correspondingly in detail. That is, the mercantilist economic policies did not go beyond the policies of the city in:

(1) the granting of privileges;

(2) the regulation of production and trade, in order to then admittedly add an important new complex of measures which we could summarise best of all under the description of:

(3) unification.

The following sections have the aim of reminding the reader by a few examples of the sense and significance of these policies.

II. Granting of Privileges

Under the granting of privileges I understand here quite generally the application of governmental instruments of power to the aim of calling into life for the first time the economic activity of private persons or, where it is already practised, of shaping it in a profitable or more profitable way. Here it concerns obviously only the "granting of privileges" to capitalist enterprises whose rise, as we have seen, modern states were also primarily interested in. If you want to specify it precisely, then you will have to say that the governmental instruments of power were applied either to promote capitalist interests that were already present; or to develop capitalist interests which were demanding to come to life, but were only slumbering in a germ-like state; or finally to plant the germ of such interests for the first time. The granting of privileges also served in many ways to make possible the capitalist economic manner despite the opposition of the exclusionary laws of the craftsmen's guilds.

The entire idea of governmental "granting of privileges" is expressed, however, in the following letter of Henry II (from 13th June 1568):

Nous voulons [...] accroistre le désir à tous et chacuns de nos subjetz et les exciter à s'exercer à choses bonnes et prouffitables au publicq de nostre royaume, et s'occuper et employer, en recongnoissant et authorisant par

dessus les autres par priviléges et bienfaits les personnes vertueuses et industrieuses en tous artz.
[We want [...] to increase the desire of each and every
one of our subjects and to excite them to practice good
and profitable things for the people of our realm, and to
occupy and employ themselves, by recognising and au-
thorising over others, via privileges and benefits, virtu-
ous and industrious people in all arts.][74]

The "granting of privileges" assumed now many different
forms, according to which they shall be grouped in the following for the purpose of a better overview.

1. Monopolisation

Monopolisation played a very large role in the mercantilist
system. It consists fundamentally in the exclusion of others;
and thus is, as you could say, a sort of negative granting of
privilege[75].

In its historical derivation, the right of granting a monopoly probably goes back to the old ideas of feudalism — the
king is holder of all power and all rights derived from it, and
confers it, to the extent he judges proper, on his attendants,
who themselves hand down the rights conferred on them entirely or in part to others. This feudalism often throws light
with wonderful clarity on the conferring and sub-conferring
of quite modern industrial monopolies. The immediate predecessors of the princes had here also been the cities — "The
city as a whole conceives of the sale of traded products within
its environs as a sort of fief. A few branches of this fief were
freed to all citizens as such, others reserved exclusively for the
town council, but most were given as it were as sub-fiefs to
the guilds." (Roscher 1874, 16)

How the royal prerogative then developed by a slow transformation into the post-medieval period's corresponding legal
form of the princely exclusive warrants is not depicted here,
because it is of no importance for the goal being pursued
here[76] — it is enough that the modern prince ascribed to himself the right to permit and to forbid any economic activity, to
allow its exercise by specific persons, and to deny it to others.
Occasionally the monarch had his sole right of disposal over
commerce or trade expressly declared; thus we encounter in

Frederick's Constitutions of Melfi (1231) already a monopoly of the king over the trade in grain, salt, iron, and raw silk; thus in the 15th century the entire trade in the Italian states was "monopolised" by the prince[77]; in the 16th century the entire spice trade in Portugal became a monopoly; in France under Henry II trade and commerce was declared domanial by right, etc. The important thing, however, was just that all monarchs — with or without such express declarations — thus acted as if they were the solely entitled ones.

Some have wanted to distinguish the modern form of granting privileges from the medieval form, thus the capitalist from the craftwork form, by characterising the guild monopoly as corporate privileges and the governmental (royal) monopoly as private privileges[78]. That does not apply in all cases though. Rather the capitalist monopoly also appears as both corporate and personal privilege, and this may even form the rule. We see, for example, how in England the control over other guilds, e.g. in silk and pin manufacturing, was transferred to particular corporations during a period in which this commerce had already long since been organised capitalistically[79]; or we find the communauté [community] of the traders of Paris in the exclusive possession of the right to trade specific goods[80] — or we learn that a number of coal traders in the year 1600 obtained the right to an incorporated guild and with it the right to sell coal to the ships which sailed the River Tyne[81], and so on.

When a corporation was awarded the right, it could at the same time be bound with the right to limit the number of members. This right, the *numerus clausus*, could also be missing — most of the "regulated companies" in England during the 16th, 17th, and 18th centuries were examples of such a sort of privileged (i.e. endowed with a monopoly) incorporation[82].

The monopoly which is granted to a person or corporation could extend in principle to any arbitrary profitable activity — we encounter production monopolies just as often as trade or commercial monopolies.

Production monopolies were of course essentially industry monopolies. They were either (that is, with already existing businesses which were to be converted into a capitalist organ-

77

isation, mostly in the presence of a new procedure which offers the opportunity for monopolisation) realised in the
already active way that an individual corporation obtains control over the entire business, or so that a national monopoly
was created at the outset — the rule with newly founded industries, like perhaps the glass, salt, or wire industries in
England.

Occasionally the privilege of producing goods of a specific
type was also granted to a city or a region — that is, to all the
persons who were producing at the time in that place. Thus
Lyons received the exclusive right to produce stockings from
black coloured silk.

The monopoly could be received for eternity, or for the
lifetime of the first receiver, or for a specific number of years.
In this last form, it nears the modern patent, and as such it
already appears frequently in the *England* of Elizabeth I — in
1565 a monopoly-patent (for twenty years) for the production
of salt; in 1567 (for twenty-one years) for the production of
window glass, etc.[83] In France we also encounter early on such
time-limited monopolies — thus the very first monopoly
which Henry II granted in 1551 for the erection of glassworks
in S. Germain-en-Laye was limited to ten years[84].

In *Austria*, we can distinguish two epochs — in the beginnings of
mercantilist policies (under Leopold I) the legal basis of the new economic forms was formed by the *privilegium exclusivum* which secured
individual enterprises the sole right of sale in bulk in the entire region
of the Austrian home territories for their products. Under Maria
Theresa their place was taken by the "factory warrants", which were of
two types. "Simple factory-type warrants", which contained the recognition of the usefulness of the enterprise, the freedom from any guild con-
straints, and the right to combine all sorts of industrial workers in the
operation, were distinguished from "national factory warrants". The latter contained recognition of the "special importance and solidity" of the
enterprise. They were entitled to use the royal eagle and to hire and re-
lease apprentices, which with the other class was reserved for the
guilds.

Or the monopoly was *a trade monopoly*. Then it embraced
either the right to conduct trade exclusively with specific
goods or a type of good — such a monopoly was possessed by
the Newcastle coal merchants during the 17th century, by the
privileged merchants in the Solingen knife industry[85], and by
the society whom Louis XI had already granted the privilege
of spice importing[86]. Alternatively, the monopoly could be

78

granted to a place instead of a person — where, for example, all silk which was traded in France had to make its way through Lyons.

Or the monopoly contained the right to conduct trade exclusively with a specific region or with a specific land — where the Merchant Adventurers (still in the 17th century) alone had the right to export all sorts of cloth wares to Germany and the Netherlands[87]. The geographic monopolisation of which you can speak in such cases found its most significant sphere of use with all the great *overseas trading companies*. In the rule the land which the company was allocated for unlimited exploitation was expressly named in the charter — the most famous of them, the English East-India Company founded in 1600, was called "The Governor and Company of Merchants of London trading into the East Indies" and acquired the trade monopoly for all lands in the Indian and Pacific Oceans between the Strait of Magellan and the Cape of Good Hope. The French Compagnie des Indes, formed out of three other companies, was "chargée de tout le commerce colonial de la France" [charged with all the colonial trade of France][88].

Such monopoly policies now, as the examples by which I have made the various forms of monopoly recognisable already show, were used by all states since and in so far as they entered into the course of promoting capitalist interests — also in this they were heir to the civic economic policies.

In the one land the inclination for the monopolistic form of economic life was perhaps stronger than in others; in this land it slackened off earlier than in another land; here it grasped all branches of economic life equally, there a few stronger, others weaker — but in the fundamentals the policies were the same everywhere. Whilst in France the industrial monopolies experienced in the 18th century the greatest extension and their end, whilst they were preserved in the German states in the form of the concessions system until well into the 19th century, this form of monopoly had already vanished in England after 1687. For all that, in no land were the trade and commercial monopolies operated as rigorously up until the 19th century as in Great Britain — only in 1813 was the Indian trade opened to outsiders; only in 1796 was the shipping monopoly, which, as we will see, dated back to Richard II and, as is well known, obtained its final form in Cromwell's Navigation Acts (1651), broken for the first time, and only in 1849 were the Navigation Acts repealed.

What a writer in the 1770s wrote about Austria could have applied to all states:

> "Les monopoles dans nos provinces sont innombrales, partie ignorés, partie tolerés et partie legalement autorisés par le Gouvernement. Presque tous nos fabriquants, manufacturiers et gros négociants sont monopoleurs."
> [The monopolies in our provinces are countless, part ignored, part tolerated and part legally authorised by the government. Almost all our factory owners, manufacturers, and large merchants are monopolists.][89]

2. Trade Policy

One form of privileging capitalist industry, which basically also leads to the granting of a monopoly at the least for an entire branch of industry, is the artificial influence of the market for goods through measures promoting or hindering the in or outflow of goods. The same aim is sought to which monopolisation strives — achieving the excluding or limiting of competition in an indirect way instead of directly. To which then certainly a series of other effects of trade policy measures newly arise.

The trade policy of mercantilism did on the other hand grow in a straight line from the civic trade policy as we have already had opportunity to establish when we recalled the "supply policies". The goal which the princes followed in their states had remained the same as that which the city authorities had striven to fulfill — the commercial producers should have ample raw materials at their disposal and be protected against the competition of foreign products. Thus the means then also remain the same in the beginnings of the trade policy of the states — the export of raw materials (and intermediate goods) is forbidden just as is the import of finished products.

In *Spain*, the export of (foodstuffs and) raw materials was already forbidden during the 14th century by the kings, e.g. of Aragon. In 1462 Henry IV determined that, with the export of wool, at the wish of native producers a third was to be left for them at a reasonable price — this privilege was extended by the laws of 1551, 1552, 1558, and 1560. In 1537 the export of iron ore was prohibited; in 1548, 1550, 1552, and 1560 the export of leather was forbidden.

In *France*, the oldest ordinances in which the kings take up the exclusionary policies of the cities go back to Philipp II who in 1278 had already forbidden the export of native wool. The ordinances in which this ban was renewed and extended to other raw materials and intermediate goods, like flax, dyes, thread, raw cloth, etc., were then numerous in the following centuries — we encounter them, for example, in 1305, 1320, 1567, 1572, 1577, and so on. To them were joined early on the ordinances which forbade the import of finished products, particularly of the textile industries — in 1469 Louis XI forbade the import of Indian linen, in 1538 Francis I forbade the import of cloth from Catalonia and Perpignan, in 1567 that of Flemish *sayetteries* [woollen cloth]; in 1567, 1572, and 1577 the import of *draps d'or, d'argent et de soie* [fabric of gold, silver and silk] was forbidden.

In *England*, the Oxford parliament was already in 1258 forbidding wool exports, and Edward II the export of teasels. Then these export prohibitions were forgotten for a time as wool exports attained a great economic significance for England. But towards the end of the 15th century the old prohibition was again taken up — 4 Hen. 7 c.10 (1488), 22 Hen. 8 c.1 (1530), and 37 Hen. 8 c.15 (1545) contain bans on wool exports; and 2 & 3 Edw. 6 c.26 (Exportation Act 1548) contains the prohibition on the export of white ash. Under James I, the export of unfinished woollen goods was forbidden; in 1648 and 1660 the prohibition on wool exports was repeated. The prohibition then remained in force until 1825. Even in the last quarter of the 18th century the efforts to hinder wool exports were particularly lively. See James (1857, 301 ff.). Cf. also Bonwick (1887, 14 ff., 167 ff.).

Just like the export of wool, the export of hides was also prohibited (1 Eliz. 1 c.10 (1558); 18 Eliz. 1 c.9 (1575)) (a compilation of the laws related to leather is found in the pamphlet "Leather: A Discourse tendered to the High Court of Parliament" (Sparke 1903, 331 ff.) (first printed in 1629), also the laws about horns (4 Edw. 4 c.8 (1464); 7 Jas. 1 c.14 (1609)); and about metals (21 Hen. 8 c.10 (1529)).

And on the other side numerous finished products were still excluded during the 15th century from being imported into England — 33 Hen. 6 c.5 (Importation Act 1455); 3 Edw. IV c.3 (Importation of Silk Act 1463); and 22 Edw. 4 c.3 (Importation Act 1482) prohibit the import of silk and various silk goods; and 3 Edw. 4 c.4 (1463) prohibits the import of almost a hundred articles from all branches.

The matters were quite the same in other lands — numerous export bans for raw hides and pelts, and for oak bark in the various *German* states (overviews of both in Bergius (1775, 4:25 ff.)); in *Holland*, export bans for ships' materials (Laspeyres 1863, 154).

Whilst the principality was just continuing the import and export prohibitions of the civic economic policy, it developed in due course into a means of trade policy as well, something which the earlier time was unfamiliar with, and with respect to which the entire mercantilist trade policy was often described as a complete renewal — the *protective tariff*.

To raise duties from physical goods found in transport had been common right through the entire Middle Ages — originally these duties had the sense of a commission, then they had gradually becomes a source of taxes for lords and cities. It was a brilliant idea to make these financial tolls, as we would call them today, serve the purposes of industrial protection. We cannot say with complete certainty when this transformation took place[90] — perhaps, or even probably, the reorganisation of the financial toll system into a protective tariff system took place quite gradually as a work of casuistic policy.

As far as we can see, protective tariffs emerge in greater quantities in France and England during the 16th century — in England you can speak of the first protective tariff as being the tariff of 1534; in France the tariffs of 1564, 1577, and particularly that of 1581.

It is well-known that the system of protective tariffs then experienced its full systematic development in Colbert's tariffs of 1664 and 1667 — high export tariffs on raw materials, high import tariffs on finished products, import relief for raw materials, export encouragement for finished products — these were the principles of the policy which we describe on account of the man who perfected them as Colbertism, and they, just like the policy of monopolies, dominated all lands until deep into the 19th century — in England, the "land of free trade" par excellence, the first breach in the high tariff system which had existed until then was placed by the trade agreement which Pitt concluded in 1786 with France. Despite the reforms of Huskisson in 1824 and 1825, Peel's tariff reforms of 1845 still found tariffs on 130 various articles to abolish.

***

Now, however, the trade policy of mercantilism was only very imperfectly implemented, if you want to leave unmentioned a measure by which the capitalist interests received an especially strong support — *the lifting of the internal tariffs*. The boundary of the city's outskirts was now as it were pushed out to the country's borders — but the area which was enclosed by this was supposed to be integrated and not split

82

up into individual parts by any customs barriers. The internal tariff systems were especially strongly developed in France and Germany. In France, Colbert (1664) succeeded in lifting at least a portion of the customs barriers — those which existed in the 20 "provinces des einq grosses fermes" [provinces of the five big farms*], so that from then on Normandy, Picardy, Champagne, Burgundy, Touraine, Poitou, Anjou with Île-de-France and Paris were merged into a very similar whole. The French Revolution completed the work, whereas, as is well-known, in Germany at least the state border tariffs (which corresponded somewhat with the French provincial tariffs) were only lifted by the customs union (1834).

3. Premiums

Next to the granting of monopolies and the protection by the artificial influencing of goods movements, however, yet other means of privileging capitalist interests were present in the arsenal of mercantilist economic policy.

You can describe them all together as "support" or "premiums" by whose granting you either wanted to make people inclined towards acting as capitalist entrepreneurs, or, if they had already made the decision to engage in an industry or trade or some other gainful activity, inclined towards making profits.

Savary lists in his *Dictionnaire* all of the privileges which the state bestows on entrepreneurs and workers in the royal factories[91]. They are the following:

1. The entrepreneurs receive:
    • hereditary title (the most significant);
    • the permission to be naturalised (when they are foreigners);
    • remission of import tariffs or export tariffs which apply to raw materials needed by them or goods finished by them;
    • interest-free loans for several years;
    • annuities (whose size is measured according to the success of their undertakings);
    • permission to purchase salt at wholesale prices;

---

* [Tr.: i.e. tax farming operations.]

- permission to brew beer for themselves, their dependents, and their workers;
- building sites for their workshops;
- the right of "committimus"[†];
- freedom from trade controls;

2. The workers receive:
   - freedom from taxes;
   - master's rights.

The main thing for the entrepreneur was of course the subsidies which he received in cash from the state treasury. They were, especially under the rule of Colbert, in France quite substantial sums. It has been calculated that between 1664 and 1683 1,800,000 livre was given out for the founding or subvention of industrial enterprises — excluding the state factories, which alone cost 3 million livre, excluding the purchases which Louis XIV made from privileged undertakings, and excluding the pensions granted to the entrepreneurs. Guiffrey (1881) arrives at a total sum of 5½ million livre which was given as direct support to the textile industry — 2 million for pensions and subventions, 3 million for orders of carpets and fabrics. In addition, the provinces and cities were induced to finance industrial enterprises, and numerous Etats provinciaux [provincial assemblies], particularly those of Languedoc and Burgundy[92], and cities like Lille, also then actually supported industries from their means. "All inventions were assisted by privileges and protections, the King's purse stood as it were in markets and on streets and awaited those who had at their command some invention in order to reward them" (Heinrich Laube[*]).

The princes in all places sought to promote capitalist industry, perhaps not with the same enthusiasm and the same sacrifices of money, but in essence with the same methods. In particular, the rewards for the export of finished goods were especially favoured in England[93]. Or opportunity was found in other ways to make donations to industries — in that, for example, the right of preemption which the crown was entitled

---

†   [Tr.: exemption from justice in lower courts.]
*   [Tr.: Sombart does not cite which work of Laube, and I have been unable to locate the quote.]

to was ceded to capitalists, this was the way the English kings acted after Elizabeth I with the right to preemptive purchase of ore which they had with regards to the tin mines in Cornwall[94].

The same measures recur in all lands. From the middle of the 1760s, 50–80,000 florins were expended annually in the way of support and advances in Austria[95].

II. Regulation

Just as the first fundamental idea of medieval economic life — that nobody should work without receiving authorisation from above — was taken over by the principalities, so no less strictly was the second — that every man has to arrange his (economic) behaviour in accordance with the instructions of the authorities. I called the first fundamental idea that of privilege, and the other that of regulation, under whose compulsion the entire early capitalist epoch likewise stands.

What you could surely describe as the "excess rule" innate to the absolute state — in it the power of this idea of regulation finds expression, from Frederick II and the Italian princes of the trecento[+] in the beginning to the Stuarts and Louis XIV or Frederick the Great. What was taken in the beginnings of the absolute principality to be ones duty and was striven for as an ideal — we hear Burckhardt on this — became a reality in the 17th and 18th centuries in the most ample abundance. We hear what the government in the still least "regulated" land — England — concerned itself with (admittedly during the time of the Stuarts — I choose as an example the year 1630):

- silk shall have been badly dyed — ordered that only Spanish black is accepted for dyeing;
- grain is short — ordered that no bread is to be eaten on Friday evening, nor on other fast days;
- the fishery is not thriving — ordered that a commission be appointed for investigating;
- exported cloth shall occasionally have had defects in length, breadth, and weight — ordered the appoint-

---

†   [Tr.: Italian 14th century.]

ment of commissions for Somerset, Wilts, Gloucester, and Oxon which shall supervise the inspectors;

- the wool industry needs support — ordered that cloth material is only to be produced from native wool;
- false dyeing occurs — ordered that no logwood or blockwood is taken for dyeing;
- too much foreign wire is used — ordered that no foreign wire is to be imported anymore, etc.;
- London threatens to be overpopulated — ordered that no new houses are to be erected in London or within three miles of it;
- the use of tobacco increases out of hand — ordered that in England no tobacco shall be planted, etc., etc.[96]

Here we are interested only in the order of economic activity, in particular that of commercial and trade activity (so far as it is not already contained in the granting of privilege), and in the following pages an attempt shall be made to establish what the essence of this order consisted of in the absolute state — what was taken over from earlier times, what was newly added.

There we then have to establish above all that which was already given in the introduction, *that the economic constitution of the Middle Ages as expressed in the guild order remained in its fundamental ideas unchanged in validity during the entire early capitalist epoch*. The commercial law remained thus fundamentally a bound one.

Which now certainly does not rule out that the absolute principality made essential changes to the old economic order, about which more shall be spoken in the following.

At first in the centuries of the absolute state *the guild order was tightened in numerous points and its validity was generalised*. The ordinances of the *French* kings from the end of the 16th century introduce the compulsory guilds everywhere properly for the first time, and carry out the enforcement of the guild strictly — above all the two most important ordinances: Henry III's ordinance of December 1581 and Colbert's ordinance of 1673. And when many guilds then renewed their statutes in the middle of the 18th century, it happened with the express intent of strengthening the spirit of exclusivity through the new publication. The assembly is useful, suggested e.g. the boilermakers, "surtout quand il s'agira d'avoir affaire à des marchands ou maîtres de différentes communautés qui entreprennent continuellement contre le commerce de la dite communauté au préjudice de ses droits et des différents arrêts et sentences obtenues" [especially when it comes to dealing with merchants or masters from different communities who continually undertake against the trade of said community at the prejudice of their rights and the various judgments and awards obtained][97].

Even the *English* guilds, which were newly founded during the 16th to 18th centuries, are partly more exclusive and narrower in their principles than those of the Middle Ages[98]. Likewise it is known that in *Germany* the guilds became more rigid and sombre during the 17th and 18th centuries[99].

The number of guilds also increased considerably in this period — in Paris there were in 1672 60, shortly after enactment of Colbert's industrial laws 83, in 1691 already 129[100]; in Poitiers there were in the middle of the 16th century 25, in 1708 35, in 1717 43 sworn crafts[101].

This intensification of the guild tendencies now surely primarily concerned craftwork, and it probably originated for the most part from the great difficulties in which many crafts were thrown by the progress of capitalism. But to a not inconsiderable degree *the capitalist interests were also hit by the innovations* — thus, for example, all those regulations of the statutes which referred to the supervision of the business, thus concerning themselves with the goods of the factory, the orderly arrangement of the business, etc., had directed their closest attention directly to the capitalist industry. We hear the lively interest in its regulation from the words of Colbert in which he introduced the *French* industrial laws of 1669 (in which 150 earlier special regulations were absorbed!):

> Nous désirons remédier autant qu'il nous est possible, aux abus qui se commettent depuis plusieurs années aux longueurs, largeurs, force et bonté des draps, serges et autres étoffes de laine et fil, et rendre uniforme toutes celles de mesme sorte, nom et qualité, en quelque lieu qu'elles puissent estre fabriquées tant pour en augmenter le débit dedans et dehors nostre royaume que pour empescher que le public ne soit trompé!

[We wish to remedy as much as possible the abuses that have been committed for several years to the lengths, widths, strength, and goodness of sheets, serges, and other fabrics of wool and thread, and to make uniform all those of the same kind, name, and quality, wherever they may be manufactured, both to increase the flow inside and outside our realm, and to prevent the public from being deceived!]

He said another time "Il n'y a de plus important" [there is nothing more important] than to enact regulation[102].

In the 18th century the regulations became ever stricter, ever more meticulous — they were listing up to 100 and 200 articles, and contained more and more instructions for production — the legislation became more and more complicated. Up to 1683 the number of regulations amounted to 48, from 1683 to 1739 we count 230 "édits arrêts et règlements sur les arts et métiers" [edicts, rulings and regulations on arts and crafts][103]. "A madness has seized contemporaries which you would never have considered the human spirit capable of", Platière cries in horror, having to examine industry for the Encyclopédie[104].

In the other lands the matters were not much different — the *English* textile industry had been placed in close fetters since time immemorial (except for the cotton industry which developed in a somewhat freer manner). The laws of 1329, 1469, 1484, 1585, and 1593, inter alia, regulated the dimensions of the pieces; the laws of 1515 and 1518, inter alia, regulated the production process, the marks, etc. To this end the implementation of the laws consisted of a strict enforcement, likewise right into the 18th century — in 1806 a commission of investigation into the wool industry found 70 laws of regulation still in force.

In *Holland* we find in the 17th and 18th centuries quite exact regulations over the manner of production, the manner of sale, the government controls, etc., not only as a leftover from the Middle Ages, but frequently renewed and increased — "in the second half of the 18th century the authorities sought more than ever the help of the trade in its governance" (Laspeyres 1863). Ban after ban on adulteration followed — of hops (1721), milk and cheese (1727), butter (1725), indigo (1739), etc. In one branch of industry after the other the production process was regulated ever anew — in woollen weaving (1724), dyeing (1767), preparing hemp (1770, 1790), the making of warp for sailcloth (1759), etc.

In *Austria* the same picture[105] — laws over yarn, cloth, linen. "The Austrian policy of the 17th and 18th century strolled entirely along the path of Colbert's. The terms regulation, state guardianship, and police oversight describe in short the system by which the government sought according to Colbertian custom to influence the trade in an educational manner; the *reality* of production was to be ensured by strict control and standardisation of work"[106].

Regulation was of course most popular in the standard industry of that time — the textile industry. But even in other branches of commerce production was subjected to strict rules — thus the *German* sheet metal work ordinances contained exact regulations over the number and size of the hammers, over the size, length, breadth, cutting, adornment, etc. of the sheet metal[107].

Likewise we possess very meticulous regulations for the paper industry[108], etc.

If these regulations struck capitalist industry (and also capitalist trade) in many cases because it was commerce and trade (not because it was carried out in a capitalist form), then there was yet an abundance of regulations, a number of measures which were newly struck with regard to the capitalist character of trade and industry, which signified directly a *breakthrough or turning around or further training of the craft-like order* with which the absolute principality was in turn eager to serve the capitalist interests — in many cases at the cost of craftwork.

I am thinking primarily of the elimination of all those restrictions of the guild-based commercial law which had the goal of hindering the expansion of the business — thus the restriction on the number of assistants or tools of production (weaving looms, etc.) Either the new industries were expressly liberated from these laws or these restrictive regulations were removed from the commercial law itself — thus the Statute of Artificers of Elizabeth I indeed still contained the prescription of a minimum apprenticeship of seven years, but no restriction anymore on the number of apprentices, provided that they stood in a correct proportion to the number of workers.

III. Standardisation

An essential demand of the capitalist interests was signified, however, above all by those measures of mercantilist policy which can be described as *nationalisation of the guild order*, by which all the hindrances which the medieval cities had erected in local interests were to be pushed aside, and by which above all the commercial law was standardised for the entire land where possible.

This nationalisation was achieved either by the state stepping in as organ of oversight or control in place of the city or guild; or by forming the guilds into national associations; or calling into life national guilds for newly emerging branches of industry. In accordance with the reconstruction which the economic form experienced in that period in countless businesses — from handcraft to home industry — the new national guilds received at the outset the character of *home industry ordinances* — of that type of state-managed commercial association which emerged newly and in mass in all lands during the 17ᵗʰ and 18ᵗʰ centuries and lent the commercial structure of that time its particular character. It is not the place here to follow these transformations in detail — they are put in an especially bright light by a series of good books and are absolutely familiar to anyone who has occupied themselves with the early capitalist epoch. I will only give for the sake of completeness a few indications to some of the most important laws and regulations.

The *nationalisation of the guilds* begins in England and France, in accordance with the strong tendency to standardisation reigning there, already during the Middle Ages; under the last of the Plantagenets and the first Valois — the ordinances of 1307, 1351, and 1383 took the first steps. They were completed in both lands approximately at the same time — in the second half of the 16ᵗʰ century — in *England* through the Statute of Artificers and the Statute of Apprentices under Elizabeth I; in *France* through the ordinances of Henry III in 1581 and Henry IV in 1597. The content of these laws was essentially the same — the guild constitution was confirmed, but its local character stripped. In the *English* laws national guilds were expressly established, in part on the ruins of the local guilds, whose competence consisted in the oversight of business and was derived from the Kings. In the *French* ordinances flexibility within certain bounds was expressly preserved — each master can settle in his business also at another location in the same bailiwick or Sénéchaussée without further ado — just not in Paris; Parisian masters can settle without further ado anywhere in the realm.

The guilds in the remaining lands, particularly in *Germany*, had this degree of standardisation like in France and England before the introduction of freedom of trade was achieved.

At any rate the imperial guild law of 16 August 1731 (proclaimed in *Austria* as General Guild Patent on 16 November 1731) attempted to act in an equally unifying sense as the corresponding West-European laws, whilst the larger individual German states (*Brandenburg-Prussia* 1668) ordered the guilds independently, that is, as you might describe it, they endeavoured to nationalise.

The most important measure, however, for bringing the guilds into harmony with the demands of capitalist organisation, was the *creation of new, specific associations for the arising home industries* or the home-industry-like work arrangements which often stood midway between craftwork and capitalism. Such home industry structures were in turn called to life in great abundance in France and England almost simultaneously — in *France* there belongs here the furrier ordinance of 1583, the trouser-makers of 1575, the belt makers of 1575, the glove makers of 1656, but above all the Lyon silk weavers ordinance which had its culmination in 1700. For the Paris trade, the 3rd volume of Boileau (1879) is to be consulted; for the Lyon silk weavers the specialist literature over the silk industry, within which Godard (1899) stands out. Cf. also du Bourg (1885), and Hauser (1903, 376 ff.).

In *England* we have as a corresponding structure the Clothiers Company, the guilds of tanners, goldsmiths, haberdashers, tailors, ironmongers, saddlers, cutlers, cabinetmakers, pewterers, etc. — all approximately at the same time, the age of Elizabeth I. An especially informative example for the new guilds on a capitalist basis is the Company of Stationers in which publishers and printers were united to a common work. Unwin (1904) has now spread new light over the associations of English home industry.

We find quite the same associations then, however, in other lands too — in *Holland* the bedsheet weaver and silk ribbon weaver guild was founded in 1752, the lacemakers guild in 1756.

In *Germany* the most well-known example is the Solingen sword makers and cutlers, the Worsted Trading Company of Calw, the Franconian hosiers, and the producer associations in the Sonneberg toy industry. In addition to the named writings, the following works can serve for orientation over the German conditions: Thun (1879, 2:); Troeltsch (1897); Schanz (1884); with it Schmoller (1887b); Bein (1884); Schmoller (1891, 1 ff.); and Dressel (1908, 55 ff.).

A similar development in *Austria* is depicted by Přibram (1907, 42 ff.).

Chapter 25: Transport Policy

Literature

There are numerous monographs which I will cite in a subsequent volume with the depiction of the system of transportation. A summary treatment has been given for a at least a few parts of the transport policy of the absolute state in *France* in the excellent source work of Vignon (1862). Also many of the writings named in the previous chapter occupy themselves with transport policy.

I. Measures for the Promotion of Private Entrepreneurs

The mercantilist transport policy makes use of the same means in part as the trade and commercial policies to achieve its goal of "increasing commerce". The most important measures of this sort are the following:

1. Monopolisation and Granting of Privileges

Monopolies over transport create benefits granted to national shipping (as a whole) — when perhaps the carriage of goods between specific places, especially the transport into the harbours of the country are reserved for ships of their own country.

The mercantilist shipping policy, which on the other hand is only a continuation of the civic shipping policy, bears everywhere the same strongly protectionist trait. Most distinctively, as is well-known, in *England*, where the tendencies towards monopolisation were already beginning under Richard II — 5 Ric. 2 c.3 (Confirmation of Liberties; Charters and Statutes, Exportation of Gold, Silver, Leaving the Realm, etc. Act 1381) determined that "none of the Kings subjects should bring in or carry out any merchandise but in English ships." A further development of this policy occurred under the first Tudor, then it experienced a few setbacks, but was taken up again from Elizabeth I (banning coastal shipping for foreign ships!) and reached its high point in Cromwell's Navigation Act (1651), at which it remained until into the 19th century. The famed Navigation Act determined, however, that:

1. goods of Asian, African, or American origin, be it from British colonies or from other areas, were only permitted to be imported into England and Ireland on ships which belonged to British subjects and were manned by a majority of such;

2. the goods originating from European lands were permitted to be imported only on English ships or ships of those lands from which the goods came;

3. the fisheries were reserved for English ships;

4. the coastal shipping was reserved for English ships.

Similar measures in France — according to the ordinance of 8th February 1555, Frenchmen were only permitted to load cargo onto French ships; in 1659 the "droit de fret" [freight fee] was introduced — a differential tax of 50 sols per ton on foreign ships; in 1670 the traffic with the colonies was reserved for French ships, etc. See the summary in Lexis (1901a, 549 ff.).

On the path of monopolisation and granting of privileges they also strove, however, to bring about a quicker evolution of the transport institutions.

Transport on roads and waterways was — especially the postal traffic — declared early on to be a Royal prerogative in most states.

2. Granting of Rewards

All seafaring states have made the greatest effort to promote national shipping by means of an elaborate system of rewards. Already in the Italian states, then in Spain (law of 1498), in France and particularly in England we find the granting of rewards for shipbuilding as a permanent institution — Elizabeth I and James I paid 5 s. for each tonne with ships over 100 t., Charles I (1626) paid the same sum with ships over 200 t.[109]; and Cromwell continued this policy which remained in practice through the entire 18th century.[110]

3. Unification

The transport policy of the absolute state made it its task to order the public *transport law* in an integrated manner and to fit it to the needs of a transportation which was becoming more active — the market and fair laws, the system of measures and weights, in part too, as we will see, the mint and money system were newly formed by the state for its entire sphere.

II. Automatic Promotion of Transport Interests by the State

The particular nature of transport and its conditions had the consequence that the state, when it wanted to promote the development of the transport system, saw itself compelled to itself often have a hand and create transport institutions on its own initiative. Thus the modern princely power directed its special attention to the *improvement of roads and waterways* and took care of the first *organisation of transport* in the interior of the land — the beginnings of government postal systems fall in this period.

Above all the *French* kings from Philip the Fair (1268–1314) onwards, who had already made the Seine navigable as far as Troyes, achieved great things in this area — since Henry IV (1553–1610) the transport system had been centralised by the establishment of the office of Grand Surveyor of France, whose first representative was Sully. Expenditures for the building of roads and bridges appeared now regularly in the state budget — they amounted already in the time of Henry IV to around 400,000 livres per year[111]. In addition to that were the expenditures of the provinces and the cities.

In the year 1609, 870,000 livres were expended for making rivers navigable, exactly as Sully reports to us in his memoirs, "pour divers canaux, pour rendre communicables plusieurs rivières, comme Loire, Seine, Aisne, Velle, Vienne et Chin" [for various canals to make several rivers communicable, such as the Loire, Seine, Aisne, Velle, Vienne and Chin]. Under Sully the first canal building in France was begun[112] — the Briare Canal, which was not only meant to serve to relieve the supplying of the capital, but also meant to connect the Mediterranean with the ocean (for the time being the Seine and Loire). 6,000 troops were occupied in the building of it. The work begun in 1605 was completed in 1642.

Under Colbert this policy was continued with determination — the roads were improved; rivers corrected; the great canal between the Mediterranean (Rhone) and the Atlantic Ocean (Garonne), the Canal du Midi, was constructed (1666–1681) under the management of Riquet. The expenditures amounted in the years 1666–1683 to[113]:

for bridges and roads	4,860,489 livres tournois
for the plaster of Paris	1,436,641
for canal construction	9,619,315
for improving the waterway	15,916,445 in total

In the years 1737–1769, for which we possess the exact lists, the expenditures for the named goals wavered between 2,297,001 livres and 4,011,125 livres, but kept in the last years close to 4 million livres.

In *England* the care of the roads was left to the inhabitants, that for the building of artificial waterways was left to private capital[114]. River correction was carried out by the government[115].

In *Germany* it was a few of the West German territories which pursued road building from the beginning of the 18th century; and it was above all Brandenburg-Prussia which from the time of the Great Elector pursued canal building by the state.

Since, however, the state's concern for transport touched very closely on the endeavours of private concerns, and since a judgement cannot be given over the management of a positive transport policy without going into the actual form of the transport conditions, and since these have other non-state conditions for their development, I have thus reserved a closer investigation into the measures of state transport, policy as well as an appreciation of their success, for the portrayal of transport systems in a later volume. *I refer the reader there* for whom the overview given here appears all too sparse. There he will also find an in-depth handling of the postal institution, whose organisation in many lands emanated from the state and hence, considered closely, forms a part of the state transport policy or transport governance. Such a strict separation of the various sides of one and the same complex of facts, as would correspond to the requirement of a cleanly carried out arrangement of the materials, is often out of the question for objective reasons.

Chapter 26: The Monetary System

Preliminary Remarks

The chapter over the monetary system occupies a special place in the framework of this section. As the reader knows, this section is essentially dedicated to the portrayal of those expressions of the life of the modern state which signify a promotion of capitalist economic ways. That certainly does not now apply, however, to a large component of state monetary policy, which must rather be seen as "hindrances" to capitalist development, although they (unwanted by the law-giver) have contributed quite frequently indirectly to the evolution of a directly capitalist existence. Now, however, this component is not to be weeded out from the whole of state monetary policy without making difficult the understanding of the remaining measures which were also present and favoured the evolution of capitalist existence. Yes — to fundamentally understand the significance of state mint and currency policy, it is even unavoidable to have to sketch the *actual form of the monetary system* itself, at least in a few especially prominent occurrences, whereby reference must be made back to the time of the Middle Ages. On the other hand now, however, the area of monetary systems remains a province of state administration and appears to the economic world as a given, and remains in its entirety "foundational", for which reason it cannot be relegated like the transport system to the portrayal of the flow of the economic processes which is given in a later volume.

The outcome of all these considerations is the following sketch which (after a short orientation over the theory) portrays an attempt to describe the *course of monetary history in the period of early capitalism*. A part of this history — the transformation of precious metals into minted money — I can, however, only deal with when I mention the realisation of the value of precious metals and their connection with price formation, namely in Chapter 35[*].

That it is thereby always only focused on the emphasis of a few main points is understandable in itself. I would like to make my own for the characterisation of the type of this "Outline of Monetary History" the expression of one of the first mint researchers who introduced his masterful "Overview of the History of the German Monetary and Coinage

---

*   See page 253.

Systems and the Current Sorts of Coinage" (Grote 1857, 1:137 ff.) with the nice phrasing: "I don't want to be a swimming teacher, but rather a signpost with the inscription: 'Shallows'." The closest attention is also directed here to the evidence for *uniformity of development* in the main countries of Europe.

Sources and Literature

I: *Circulating Money and State Money*. It suffices if I on the one hand refer to the book by G. F. Knapp (1905; 1924), and name from the older literature Marx (1859; 1904). Marx can be made representative of all modern 'metallist' monetary theorists, who all (like, for example, Knies and Menger, to name the two most significant) walk in his tracks.

II: *Metallic Money*. Literature and sources are of two sorts here. Into consideration come works of both coinage history and monetary history. In quantity and quality the two groups are extraordinarily different. The *literature on coinage history (numismatics)* is (as far as I am able to judge) in a brilliant state — specialist treatments are just as numerous and good as summary portrayals. A series of excellent journals provide for a methodical treatment of specialist questions. For our purposes it suffices if I name here the two newest publications which will also probably for a long time represent a high point of the scientific development — as a collection of materials, the great work of Engel and Serrure (1891; 1897); and as a systematic treatment the distinguished book by Luschin von Ebengreuth (1904), where I admittedly would like to place the emphasis on the numismatics, since it is this which that masterful treatment has to instruct, whereas the monetary history part of that book is entirely left behind in worth next to the other part. Nevertheless you must also accept with thanks that portrayal of *monetary history* by Luschin, because it hardly has the like as a general summary treatment of the subject even for modern times. What the economist in particular will miss in it — the firm background of monetary theory and with it also the specifically economic formulation of the problem — he will find in the articles in Lexis's dictionary on precious metals (Lexis 1900b), the dual standard (Lexis 1900a), gold (Lexis 1900c), silver (Lexis 1901b), and coinage systems (Lexis et al. 1900). They probably portray the highest point which science has achieved to date in the systematic examination of the area of monetary history. Only that they perform this function in a broken-up and aphoristic manner (and — unfortunately! — are immeasurably hard to read). Apart from those articles, from the newer works of a general nature (since the books of Alexander del Mars in the area of monetary history fail completely because of their uncritical nature), those worth considering are A. Wagner (1907) as well as Shaw (1895) — a certainly also highly merited, irreplaceable achievement. Only that Shaw only treats in essence just one problem of monetary history (even if one of the most all-important) — the struggle between state and commerce over money (as you can state it in brief). Cf. also the introduction to the book of Nübling (1903). Other good works of monetary history of recent years deal with smaller parts of the great whole — individual epochs of finance in Cologne,

98

Brandenburg-Prussia, Pomerania, Florence, Vienna, in Alsace, in England, etc. The thorough work of Cahn (1911) deserves special emphasis, in addition the depiction of the Prussian finances in the 18th century in the *Acta Borussia* (Schrötter 1904); as well as the book by Schmidt (1914).

There is on the contrary, unfortunately, so far as I can see, an entire lack of usable and comprehensive publications of *source documents on monetary history*, so that we must still fall back on the older, in part quite old collections. A discerning publication of the most important mint regulations, ordinances, parliamentary commissions, etc. concerning the finances of all European states would be a commendable task. For the time being the following works probably give the best information:

- over *France*: Le Blanc (1690), and Saint-Maur (1746).
- over *Italy*: Argelati (1750) contains in addition to the dissertation a rich collection of documents.
- over *England*: Ruding (1840), and Shaw (1896) contains treatises, no statute material.
- over *Spain*: Heiss (1865) provides in addition to the coinage descriptions valuable documentary evidence for the history of coins and money.
- over *Germany*: Goldast (1620), and Hirsch (1756). All sorts of interesting material, mostly from the Ulm council records, is found in Nübling (1903). For Brandenburg-Prussia there is the aforementioned publication in the *Acta Borussia*.

III: *Bank Money*. Marperger (1717) describes (amidst the citation of bank laws) in chapters 7–10 the four well-known banks of his time.

Ludovici (1741) likewise informs us about them under various headings. Cf. also Hübner (1853) (who, however, confuses all sorts of "banks"), and Ehrenberg (1899).

Over the *Amsterdam* Wisselbank, see especially L'Espine (1710, 1–12), and Ricard (1722, Ch. XXVI, 467-471).

Over the *Hamburg* Girobank, Halle (1891).

I will yet cite other specialist literature in the text.

IV: *Paper Money*. Sufficient, since the theme will not be discussed in-depth here, is the reference to the various essays under the keywords "Banken" [Banking] and "Papiergeld" [Paper Money] in Conrad et al. (1898, 2:132 ff.; 6:15 ff.), where the historical development is also portrayed in its main features, and to the literature named there.

I. Commercial Money and State Money

For the problems being discussed in the following, the sharp conceptual differentiation of the two types of money in the heading is an essential condition. Knapp (1905; 1924), when he considers money to be a state institution, a "creation of the legal system", is certainly right; but Marx, when he defines money as a "general commodity equivalent", is quite certainly too. That means *that we are denoting two quite distinct things with the word money*, as the following reflections will show.

Agreement reigns over which "functions" in the circulation economy are exercised by that thing which we call money, but which we can also describe as M or X. It serves to:

1. measure "exchange value" — it is the expression of all exchange value;
2. mediate acts of exchange — it is a general means of exchange and commerce;
3. translate exchange value — it is a general means of payment;
4. store exchange value — it is a means of building wealth.

The argument begins where it concerns the establishment of what this "something" is; of what its "nature" consists.

Now this question of the "nature" of money does not seem to be very felicitous for me, so that I would prefer to set in its place another: what (which authority) causes that indefinite something to exercise the functions which we actually see it exercise; from where does its "competence" derive?

For it is only this question whose answer falls in the area of interest of the social sciences. Just as the public administration theorist on the question of what is a policeman is only interested in the alternatives of whether he is an organ of this or that authority.

When we place the question over the "nature" of money thus, then it turns out that two entirely quite different things are described by the word, because that something derives its absolute power to be the expression of all exchange value, general means of exchange, etc. from two quite different sources. In one case, it is the silent consensus of all persons participating in a commercial association, and in the other case, it is the arbitrary act of law-giving power (the state) which lends the something that authoritative position; and by which we can now describe as per the origin that "money" as *commercial money* or *state money*.[116]

Whilst in the end the sphere of the functions of commercial money is the same as that of state money, it arises though from two quite different points — commercial money takes its

point of origin always from the function of measure of exchange value or of mediator of the act of exchange, which
only a consumer item with its own value, which has become a
good, can ever exercise — *in the beginning it is a physical
good (or a valuation)*. State money, by contrast, comes into
the world as a means of payment which ventures to exercise
from then on the remaining functions of money — to exercise
its initial function it is enabled by being provided by the state
with the power to settle legal commitments, being declared to
be the *"legal"* means of payment — *in the beginning it is an
act of state.*

What the state (in the way of currency) declares to be
money, that is thus only ever the thing to which it confers
legal power of payment, is (formally) completely up to it —
whether old hats or paper notes or metals. "Why shouldn't
pieces made from any material be treated as cash?"[117]

It can be seen that money in the commercial sense and
money in the state sense are concepts very distinct from one
another. In reality, however, the two phenomena frequently
touch one another, often even outwardly coinciding. That is
the case *when the state recognises the commercial money as
its money or conversely commerce accepts the state's money*.
But the sphere in which both monies can coincide is always
defined locally by the state's sphere of power, and thus spatially restricted. Though even within the state's sphere money
in the state sense and money in the sense of a general commodity equivalent can quite well be very distinct from another. That happens when perhaps (as was surely the case in
the Middle Ages) the commerce plays out on the basis of
"cash currency", without worrying about what the state (the
city) has declared to be money, or when foreign coins circulate in a land without being themselves recognised by the
state.

The dual nature of the concept of money, however, plainly
becomes visible regularly in that international commerce for
which no state law can create compelling norms. This knows
money only as general commodity equivalent, as a symptom
of commerce which obtains its right to existence just from the
silent consensus of all. And if all the states on earth today
pass over into cooking pot currency — money in international

commerce would (for the time being until it were replaced by another commercial item, which is of course thinkable) just be gold.

(The extent to which the currency *policy* of the state is bound to the choice of commercial money for state money, and is dependent on the creation of state money from commercial money, is something we do not have to decide here.)

In this observation the fact is given due attention that a developed commerce is capable of creating money out of its own necessities without state assistance and even against it. And on the other hand connected with it are a series of so-called "laws", better called developmental tendencies, which control the nature of money in all its stages as soon as it is first grasped by large commerce. I mean:

1. the "law" that a metal used by several in a land as money, and which is undervalued by law, vanishes from commerce;
2. the "law" that coins which are overweight likewise vanish, and in this case the lighter money remains.

Both tendencies find, taking into the consideration their causes, that the people who seek their advantage (and know where it lies) will rather settle their obligations with lesser values than with higher.

Both "laws" are incidentally also summarised into one — if in a land "good" and "bad" (that is, superior and inferior) money circulates with the same power of payment, then the "good" money has a tendency to vanish from circulation. For all monetary history, to which we now turn, the efficacy of this tendency has been of overwhelmingly large importance.

II. Metal Money

1. The General Basis of the Nature of Money from the 13th to 18th Century

The period which we now survey, the early capitalist epoch, begins with the first stirring to life of a greater, inter-locale commerce (with which a "history" of the nature of money has its beginnings more than ever) and closes with the effects of a series of significant events in the 17th century — minting technology on one hand; the Coin Act 1666 (18 Cha.

2 c.5 — 6th session of the Cavalier Parliament), the founding of the Bank of England, and the development of paper money on the other hand, and the writings on monetary theory on another.

But what was to be decisive for the forming of the nature of money in this period were above all the following factors:

1) A great *imperfection of knowledge and ability* in technical as well as economic areas.

The *technology of mint production*[118] was primitive and experienced almost no change at all during the entire period (since the steps forward in minting technique, mentioned below on page 193, only came into use in England from the 18th century, and in other lands even later). The entire labour from the preparing of the cast to the minting rested on a purely empirical-craftwork-like foundation; it was performed from beginning to end by craftsmen who made use of no other tools than the necessary pans, ambosses, and hammers. A number of craftsmen worked in concert (if you will, you can discover in the mint workshops already early on the beginnings of manufacturing processes)[119]. Goldsmiths (1) seemed to have concerned themselves with the engraving of the mint dies (but probably in their own workshops). Besides them (e.g. in the so-called Vienna Mint Law of 1450), iron diggers (2) are mentioned who likewise had the "Eysen" (die) to produce. The mint casting was examined by the tester (3) and the retester (4); after the testing the founder (5) cast the supplied material into metal strips; these were hammered out by a master (6) into the required coin thickness and then cut into pieces by another type of master (7) by means of special shears. The cut-out pieces are now levelled by hammer blows (8) and then handed over to the setting master (9) who has to manage the setting of the strike. The striking itself is dealt with in the following way: the die is fixed in a wooden or stone block which has to be large enough and firm enough to cope with the vibrations induced by the hammer blows. The coin plate is placed on this die, and the upper die is placed vertically on it; the latter is held by a worker (10) while another worker (11) performs the blows with a heavy two-handed smith's hammer as needed. Later (to which can also be inferred, Ernst suggests, the conspicuously smoothly hewed upper end of the dies still preserved today; for France it has been expressly confirmed) a sort of drop hammer was surely used instead of the freely swung smith's hammer to be able to make the blows with greater certainty. But even then the minting remained a protracted, wearisome activity, as our overview of the course of the work process reveals. The significant consequences of this imperfect minting technique were these two: *that the production of coins was expensive and inexact*. Expensive — the cost of minting amounted with gold coins to 0.6%, with large silver coins to 1.5–3%, with the smaller coins 8–25% of the minted coin[120]. Inexact — since they neither possessed sufficient knowledge of chemistry to confidently achieve a specific content in the casting; nor above all the required weighing instruments to produce coins of exactly equal weight. The differences in the weight of one coin from another of the same type could come to several grams.

For example, the weight differences of the English coins at the end of the 17th century were the following[121]:

	Value of the lightest pieces				Value of the heaviest pieces			
	s.	d.	d.	d.	s.	d.	d.	d.
Crowns	4	9	10	11	5	1	2	3
Half-crowns	2	4	5	0	2	7	8	0
Shillings	0	10½	11	0	1	1	2	0
Sixpence	0	5	5½	..	..	..	..	..

No better than the technology was the *socio-economic knowledge* of the nature and function of money[122]. Still in the 14th and 15th centuries even the men of the Italian trading cities stood as if before a miracle — when they saw all the silver suddenly going out of the land or perceived that their fellow countrymen did not want to take their own land's coins in payment. And half droll, half stirring are the ever repeated complaints of the French ordinances over the irrationality or the malevolence of the common folk who wanted the abandonment of any worsening of the coinage. Summarised in a sentence — the insight into the difference between state gold and commercial gold was still lacking in authoritative circles.

Thus even with the best of will it would not have been possible for the time to create a (in our current mercantile sense) perfect money. But what now marked that epoch as well is this:

2) That that *will of the state — to create a, to mercantile understanding, good coinage and currency system — was not even present*, that instead the monetary policy of the states, in parts into the most recent period (France, Germany), but everywhere deep into the 17th century, was exclusively fiscally oriented. That is, the princes saw in money nothing more than a source from which they could always fill empty cash boxes with riches. It is, speaking of financial history, the period between the epoch purely built on state-owned possession and the modern epoch of public credit of which I am speaking. Since the insight into the commercial necessity of money was still missing, the public authorities (incidentally the trading cities of Italy — even the governments of Venice and Florence — did not act completely free of error, as we will yet see, even if more free than those princes of other lands who were cut from feudal wood) treated money only as a state institution which they were in the position to arrange according to their discretion. The theorists of the time busied themselves with formulating the "State Theory of Money" corresponding to this conception — one reads the writings of the monetary theorists of the 15th and 16th century which Budelius compiled in his work (Budel 1591)!

But we must not imagine that "commerce" accepted this arbitrariness without further ado. That had surely been the case in the early Middle Ages until into the

12th and 13th centuries when trade had still played out to a quite modest extent in a purely craftwork-like manner. With the growth period in the 13th century when the Italian cities began to climb to the heights of their commercial power, that altered fundamentally. "Commerce", and above all of course international trade, the wholesalers of goods and (particularly) money in the Italian republics *began to rebel against the arbitrariness of the state authorities*. In various ways they strove for those aims natural to every trade (above all of course to any capitalistically aligned trade) — to have a secure general commodity equivalent in money. If you are to understand that century of the genesis of money properly, then you must not make too small an estimate of the international nature of the commercial relations at the time at least in their intense effects. We must rather keep in mind that at least from the 13th century on a regular mercantile control of finance took place in the various lands, a control which gave cause for an exact registration of the "piece" rate and on the strength of that to a lively business of arbitrage and a regular international movement of money and precious metals. The market on which the rates for all Europe were established was from the 13th to the end of the 15th century Florence, then it became Antwerp, until London took its place (from the end of our epoch)[123].

That the finance which built itself on these foundations had to bear the mark of uncertainty, inconsistency, and disorder is clear from the start. The following portrayal shall prove it in detail by a few striking symptoms in order to then show the beginnings of an improvement, that is, an adaptation to capitalist interests.

2. The Formation of Coin and Money Relationships

a) The Spatial Ambit of Coinage

The Middle Ages had developed the principle that the heller* was only valid where it was minted. And for an essentially local commerce in which a foreign trader turned up out of the blue only now and then, this principle proved itself well. More than anything else, weight was placed on the familiar coinage which the native money alone provided. The minter naturally had a lively interest in maintaining this principle. When it applied, the sphere of influence of pure state money was assured. Even "the commerce" could be reassured by it, so long as the content of the coins remained the same everywhere. Then the international trader incurred only the trouble, only the cost of exchange (which in the rule was also seen as a profitable statutory right practised, leased, or otherwise awarded by the authorities). The situation changed, however, completely when the coinage system developed in various directions, when above all "good" and "bad" coins, coins of higher and lesser metallic value began to become more differentiated. Then it was considered as advantageous and expedient to pay with coins other than those of the land. And indeed — as paradoxically as it sounds initially — either because the foreign coins were better or because they were worse. In the former case they offered the greater guarantee and offered the greater security; in the latter case they enabled the settlement of a debt with a lower (metal) amount.

For one or the other reason, foreign coins hence always flowed into the land's coinage. And it is absolutely a characteristic of our epoch that *the means of circulation bore a strongly international stamp*. And it is the eternal struggle between state and commerce over the purity of the land's currency which fills the centuries. And the eternal monotony of hundreds of orders and laws — complaints over the getting out of hand of foreign coins, bans on their use which obviously remained in most cases ineffectual, as we may conclude from the frequent repetitions, and partly also the allowing of foreign coins.

---

*   [Tr.: a heller was an old coin of very low value.]

A few arbitrarily selected examples will confirm the correctness of these statements.

In *Florence*, we learn that the wage labourers in the 14th century were paid with bad foreign coins (Rodolico 1904, 467). In the year 1382 all foreign coins — they are then *eque bona vel melior* [equally as good or better] than the Florentine — were forbidden (Archivio di Stato, Balia, reg. n. 19, cited in Rodolico (1904, 467)). Bans on foreign silver coins were frequently enacted in Florence — in the period 1534–1660, 13–14 times (Shaw 1895, 93).

In *France*, one ordinance after another forbade the circulation of foreign coins. Under Philip the Fair (1309) it was the sterling and golden florins which were banned. Further bans took place — 1355, 1577, etc. (Le Blanc 1690, 227 and elsewhere). Cf. Sully (1747, 4:6 ff.) for 1601. The edict of 10th March 1500 allowed the circulation of Venetian, Florentine, Sienese, and Hungarian ducats; of English "angelots, lions, saluts et nobles"; of Spanish and Portuguese cruzados.

The *Austrians* complained of bad Bavarian coins which had penetrated into Austria and had called forth many nuisances there (Karajan 1838, 293; Eheberg 1879 Doc. LXXXI).

Germany: At the parliament for Nuremberg (1522) — complaints over the unusable, false, and devalued coins which were circulating in the land in place of the gold guilders and good silver coins.

A coinage edict of Ferdinand I from the year 1559 determined that half a year after enactment of the edict, "no foreign money struck outside the German nation shall be given out or accepted in the empire, then only subsequent pieces which have their weight regulated", until then all other guilders "as now come and go, are given and taken" shall be permitted. But the gold coins permitted for the following period and regulated with a statutory rate (in "good Rhenish gold guilders") were these:

- All Castilian, Aragonian, Valencian, Navarrese, Sicilian, Milanese, or French *double ducats*;
- All Spanish, Castilian, Aragonian, Neapolitan, Münsterberg, Polish, Genoese, Venetian, papal, Boulogne, Breslau (both episcopal and civic), Liegnitz, Weid, Glatz, Florentine, Milanese, Salzburg, Augsburg, Kaufbeuren, Hamburg, Lübeck, and Portuguese *ducats*;
- All Burgundian, Dutch, French, Spanish, Castilian, Valencian, Milanese, Sicilian, Genoese, and papal *crowns*. (Goldast 1620, 148 f.)

At any rate a quite nice number of foreign types of coins!

Cf. also the coinage ordinance of Charles V of 1551 (Goldast 1620, 162 ff., 188 ff.), where a few dozen silver coins are listed which circulate in the empire and shall be "put out of circulation" after a year. Obviously the ban had no effect. For all sorts of inferior silver coinage also crept later incessantly into the Holy Roman Empire. In the Speyerish Decrees of Maximilian II from the year 1570 it stated "that one must see and have in the Holy Roman Empire instead of the well tried imperial coins nothing but bad foreign adulterated coins. Which then also not the least causes the persistent increase in all victuals and commerce" (Goldast 1620, 178). Cf. the entire titles XLV and LIV in Goldast (1620).

In *England*, the English merchants complained in the year 1346 that the good money was going out of the land and false Lusshebournes (Luxembourg) which were only worth 8 s. in the pound were being brought in. In 1401 parliament complained — Flemish nobles were so common in England that you could not receive a sum of 100 sh. without finding three or four such nobles amongst it; and they were though worth about 2 p. less than the English nobles (Shaw 1895, 44, 55). For the 17th century this was characteristic, for example Mun (1895 Ch. VIII and following). How numerous in the 18th century the Portuguese gold coins were which circulated in England has already been mentioned.

We find express recognition of foreign coins, for example, in *Spain*. In an ordinance of Charles of Navarra (1356) it states:

> "nos place y queremos que toda manera do mercedores tanto de nuestro Regno como de fuera puedan traher, poner y sacar fuera y allober en aqueil todas maneras de monedas francament y sin arrest o empachamiento alguno"
>
> [we like and want all manner of merchants both from our realm and from abroad to be able to bring, give and receive, and utilise in that way all forms of coins openly and without arrest or any seizure]
>
> From the "Doc. ined. del Reino de Navarra ec." in Heiss (1865, 3:231).

The replacement of one's own coins with foreign ones could go so far that the foreign coins threaten the place of the native ones. Thus the Constitutio volgare di Siena (from the beginning of the 14th century) contains the express command to take the land's coinage in payment: "che neuna persona scusi la moneta senese" [that no one excuses the Sienese money] (Arias 1905, 150).

b) Currency and Coinage Systems

When we ask first about the *substance of the currency*, about the metal or the metals which at the time served as monetary goods, then we must do altogether without a quick answer like that we can demand to receive for that question today. Of the concepts like gold currency, silver currency, bi-metallism — in the sense that by law to one of the two or both is ascribed expressly the character of legal means of payment, the other granted limited power of payment or, in the case that both possessed full power of payment, a relation between the two is established and — which is the main thing — all that would be closely maintained — of those there was no talk at all in those centuries. Instead everything here is wavering, everything empirical, everything casuistic — without even the attempt at fundamental and systematic ordering of those relations. Hence you cannot say that currency regulations were there; though you cannot say either that they were not there. I would like, for example, in view of the numerous regulations over the suitability of a specific metal to serve as a means of payment, to disagree with Shaw when he utters the opinion that from the 13th to 18th centuries there had never been talk of expressly establishing or limiting the legal power of payment — be it to gold or silver (Shaw 1895, IX). Shaw himself offers in his book the directive of Edward III from the year 1346 (Shaw 1895, 45) — whereby all goods should be paid for in gold, also no arrangement may be made over the type of payment, but in the case that an arrangement already exists, nevertheless the buyer shall have the right of the option between gold or silver. He could also have recalled 2 Hen. 6 c.12 (The Thames*, 1423) and 19 Hen. 7 c.5 (Coin, 1503). But even in the Italian laws similar regulations are frequently to be found. Only we need not believe in their effectiveness.

In reality things probably turned out thus: gold and silver during the entire period from the 13th to the 18th century were in use next to each other as money; one of the two metals was *preferred by the trade of the day as proper money* — in the 14th and 15th centuries probably gold, in the 16th and 17th centuries again silver more, which in economically backward states remained the principle money metal up into the 19th century, whereas England in particular turned more and more to gold from the end of the 17th century.

The *value relation between the two metals* was partly established by the lawgivers (then in the rule deliberately false), partly by commerce — exclusively (if the legal relation was perhaps lacking) or alongside the legal standardisation. More and more relationships arose thus in this period:

- one according to the prices which the minters paid for the raw material, and which they sought to impose by

---

* [Tr.: Sombart may have intended 2 Hen. 6 c.9 "Currency" or c.15 "The Mint" or c.16 "Price of Silver", rather than c.12 "The Thames" (all 1423).]

all means on commerce — the mint price relation, as Lexis calls it[†]; and

- then the relation which arose from the quantities of precious metal which were contained in coins of the same nominal amount — the nominal value relation.

(The first and second relation would have had to agree if the seignorage had been the same with both metals; in fact it was, however, higher with silver coins.) These two relations, which (as it can be expressed) depicted a pure state money relationship ("an artificial arbitrary mint rate", as Shaw describes it[‡]), now faced as a third relation that which formed itself in commerce — the commerce money relation. It occurred or rather was portrayed in the elevated exchange value of coins which were produced from the preferred (legally undervalued) metal.

The consequences of this situation are easy to think of — constant exchange fluctuations of the coins of one metal expressed in the coins of the other; incessant movements of quantities of money and precious metals — from one land to another or from the minted form to the bar form; finally frequent divestitures from a land of the one metal — as perhaps happened in Florence in 1345, from which at the time all silver, because undervalued, had vanished[124].

The unrest which came over all finance as a result was now, however, increased even more by a series of peculiarities which the coinage systems of that time demonstrated as such, independently from the choice of the one or the other metal.

The first of these peculiarities is the *debasement of individual coins* continuing almost unbroken through centuries, be it through reduction in their fineness, be it, which is by far the more important case, through reduction in their weight, always with unchanging nominal value. This development took place as follows.

As European economic history made a start, finance was also arranged anew; it created the pound system of Charlemagne — 1 pound of silver was divided into 20 solidi, 1 solidus into 12 denare, hence the pound was divided into 240

---

†   [Tr.: Sombart does not specify which of Lexis's works this refers to.]
‡   [Tr.: Sombart does not specify which of Shaw's works this refers to.]

denare. This Carolingian coinage system spread into almost all Northern and Western Europe, and reigned as the calculation system for finance for almost a millennium — everywhere they calculated in pfund, schillingen, pfennigen; livre, sols, deniers; libbra, solidi, quattrini; pounds, shillings, pennies, etc., whilst the actually minted coins underwent their own development. From the coins of the Carolingian system at first only the pennies (den.) were minted — corresponding to the small size of the turnovers. For several centuries they sufficed with pennies — numismatically the period from the end of the 8th to the end of the 12th century is described as the age of pennies. Then, with increasing commerce, they also began (about the middle of the 13th century) to mint the solidus, which until then had only existed as a calculation unit. The 12 penny pieces, the silver solidi in specie, were the large coins, the nummi grossi, and since they were first minted at Tours, they were called grossi turonenses, gros tournois, tournosgroschen, tournosen. Almost about the same time they also went over to minting the pound (in gold), of which the talk will be later. For the present we must occupy ourselves somewhat more exactly with the pennies and the thick coins and seek to establish what type of coins they were now.

According to the system of Charlemagne, as we saw, 240 d. went to the pound. Its weight has not yet been established. Grote (1857) sets it at 326.6 g; according to more recent research it shall have been 409.32 g in weight[125]. However the decision might turn out, the solidus was always a silver piece of the size of our taler* and above; the penny contained a silver content of 25–30 pfennigs in our current currency. But how did these coins look a few centuries after the time of Charlemagne? They had become smaller and ever smaller — like the bread roll from bakers in inflationary times, and had, like those, always depicted the same "amount of value" (arithmetically) — it always remained that pennies = 1/240 of a pound, and solidi = 1/20 of a pound. As they began to mint the solidi, then it, thus 12 d., depicted only one silver piece of

---

*   [Tr.: the taler was a German coin with a diameter of about 4 cm and a weight of 25–30 g.]

the size of perhaps a present-day franc — thus the penny was already devalued, that is, was minted worse and lighter. And yet the period of foreign currency devaluation only really actually began with the grossi, the thick coins which now shrivelled up again themselves, soon becoming thin coins again. But they always remained 12 d. worth and always went 20 to the pound, thus the pound also depicted an ever smaller amount of silver. To enliven the image, I share the numbers for a few coinage systems, from which this outrageous devaluation can be read without any trouble. It is a general phenomenon in all lands; only the size and tempo of devaluation varied from land to land.

1. *Germany*:
a) in *Hamburg-Lübeck* from 1 Mark (ca. 24 g) of fine silver the following were constructed:

	Mk.	Sch.	Pf.		Mk.	Sch.	Pf.
1226	2	2	0	1398	4	15	2
1255	2	9	5	1403	5	1	11
1293	2	9	8	1411	5	12	5
1305	2	15	5	1430	8	8	0
1325	3	0	9	1450	9	12	2
1353	3	10	11	1461	11	8	10
1375	4	3	0	1506	12	8	0

b) in *Strasbourg*:

Year	Number of pfennigs to the raw mark	Weight of pfennigs
12th century	240	0.979 g
1313	480	0.487 g
1319	490	0.476 g
1321	494	0.473 g
1329	510	0.455 g
1340	516	0.453 g
1362	540	0.432 g

(Cahn 1895, 44)

2. In *England* a silver penny weighed in Troy grains:

1300	22	1351	18
1344	20¼	1412	15
1346	20	1464	12

3. In *Spain* the following number of maravedi (a billon* coin) were minted from the Cologne mark:

1312.....................130		1390.....................500	
1324.....................125		1406..................1000	
1368.....................200		1454..................2250	
1379.....................250		1550..................2210	

4. In *France* from the silver mark were minted:

	Livres (Tournois)	Sols		Livres (Tournois)	Sols
1309	2	19	1561	15	15
1315	2	14	1573	17	0
1343	3	4	1602	20	5
1350	5	5	1636	23	10
1361	5	0	1641	26	10
1381	5	8	1679	29	11
1422	7	0	1693	33	16
1427	8	0	1713	43	7/11
1429	7	0	1719	69	1/8
1446	7	10	1720	98	2/11
1456	8	10	(then the value climbed		
1473	10	0	again somewhat, until it was		
1519	12	10	fixed by the law of 1803 at 222		
1540	14	0	2/9 francs from 1 kg silver).		

To also be noted with all these numbers is that they did not perhaps depict the only changes which the currency experienced in the course of the centuries, but rather only indicate the great stages of the reduction. Between the years listed here the coin value often went up and down countless times. The French coinage is especially rich in these incessant changes in value. For example, in the year 1348 the coins were changed eleven times, in 1349 nine times, in 1351 eighteen times, in 1353 thirteen times, and in 1355 eighteen times. Within these short periods of time the exchange rate of 4 livres (to the mark) went up as far as 17½ livres and sank down again to 4⅜ livres.

What were the *causes of this abrupt and entirely general devaluation of money*, we ask.

The blind pursuit of profit or, if you want rather, the growing financial needs of the princes gives us the answer. And doubtlessly they contributed their good part to this strange monetary policy. In a time in which public credit was only a little developed, in which paper money was still unfamiliar, I have said it already myself, this way out must have appeared extraordinarily fortunate to money-needy princes — for 3 or 4

---

* [Tr.: billon is an alloy of gold and silver with a large proportion of copper or other base metal.]

gold pieces which they accepted and collected, 5 or 6 (nominally) of the same value could be given out. But to me this reference to the financial need of the government does not seem to suffice to make this quite enormous phenomenon understandable without anything left over to be explained. Whence this spread to all lands? Were all governments equally needy, all equally unscrupulous?

No — I believe you must yet look around for other causes. And other causes have already been named. Shaw, for example, suggests that the monetary devaluation of the 14th and 15th centuries was connected with the increase in the value of silver in that period — the cities and states would, in order to check the consequential lowering of prices, have reduced the silver content in the way described. Certainly this consideration must have often at least motivated the measure of devaluation on the face of it[126]. But was this reason generally distributed? And what explains then the fact that the devaluation was continued after the precious metal stock had long since increased again and prices had experienced an abrupt rise?

I believe on the contrary that a tendency towards devaluation at first already lay in the technical nature of the finance of that time, that, however, as soon as the coinage system of *one* land had been devalued once for whatever reason, this fact forced the others almost to plan likewise to artificially devalue their own coinage.

From the imperfection of the minting technology, next to which certainly in numerous cases a consciously fraudulent counterfeiting went on, followed, as we were able to already establish, an often very considerable *difference in coins by size and weight*. Thus any quantity of a land's coins contained from the outset heavy and light, good and bad coins. But this offered the dealers (they were probably mostly goldsmiths or usurers [Jews] who busied themselves here) a welcome opportunity to make profits by pulling the good pieces out of circulation and either melting them down or taking them out of the country to where they could exchange them advantageously.

That this practice was exercised in all periods — for this we possess an entire series of documentary proofs — see, for example, the oath of the *Viennese* cooperative members, that they will not pick through money obtained through exchange, and not melt down the heavier, but trade thereby unselectively (Karajan 1838, 321 LXXI & LXII).

The *Strasbourg* coin law of 1470 begins with the words: "As minters searched for [...] advantage in all silver coins, picked out the heaviest and best of the others and had them melted down and the silver sent away and also had some cutlery made out of it." (Eheberg 1879, 200, cf. 206 No. 16).

We even learn who knew how to obtain that "advantage" and how much it amounted to — up to 80 marks of silver were melted down by individual residents of Strasbourg and sent out of the city. Especially at the Frankfurt fair, which at the time supplied many mints of the Rhineland with precious metal, silver was being sold in secret. The older heavy engelpfennig was generally picked out by the money-changers and melted down — "Clein Rülin Lentzelin also saw that you always bought the odd engels ... and have melted them down and sold the silver and also saw that it resulted in scarcity." (15th century) (Cahn 1895, 60).

Similar complaints are frequent in the royal decrees — for example, the Frankfurt decree of Maximilian II from the year 1571 (Goldast 1620, 41).

England — in a law of Charles I from the year 1627 it states:

> "some of them [i.e. goldsmiths] have grown to that licentiousness that they have for divers years presumed, for their private gain, to sort and weigh all sorts of money current within our realm to the end to cull out the old and new monies, which, either by not wearing or by any other accident, are weightier than the rest; which weightiest moneies have not only been molten down for the making of plate etc. but even traded in and sold to merchant-strangers etc., who have exported them." From Rymer (1727, 18:896) cited in A. Anderson (1787, 2:324).

Over the conditions in England at the end of the 17th century, a contemporary writer instructs us as follows:

> "But tho' all the pieces together might come near the pound weight or be within remedy; yet diverse of 'em compar'd one with the other were very disproportionable; as was too well known to many persons who pick'd out the heavy pieces and threw 'em into the Melting pott, to fitt 'em for exportation or to supply the Silver Smiths. And 'twas a thing as last so notorious, that it 'scap'd the observation of very few." (Haynes 1700, 63)

Any history book will instruct over the rapid devaluation of silver as a consequence of trimming in the years 1672 ff. which led to restamping in the year 1696.

The well-known events in *Germany* during the years 1621 to 1623 which have accorded these times with the description of the "*time of clippers and trimmers*" (see the vivid, if also probably somewhat literarily exaggerated description of Gustav Freytag (1859, 3:152 ff.)) were only an acute outbreak of an entirely general, creeping evil, similar to the English clipping period at the end of the 17th century. Almost the en-

116

tire epoch of early capitalism was a "time of clippers and trimmers". The phenomenon also bore an absolutely European stamp.

Thus the money of a land at first became worse entirely by itself — its coins after some time did not contain as much metal anymore as their nominal value specified.

Now when these undervalue coins came into a land where full-value coins still circulated, the former drove out in turn the latter which now for their part threatened to vanish from circulation. But that would have to induce the governments to likewise reduce the currency of their own land so that they could withstand the competition of foreign coins and keep their currency in the land. Now these devalued coins themselves passed into other lands and acted there in the same way that those of the foreign state had previously acted on them themselves — they drove out the good coins from circulation and forced the rulers to a devaluation, and so on.

The development could, however, also run directly in reverse and yet produce the same end result — the compulsion to deterioration of money. While in fact in the just observed case the bad foreign money drives out better money from its own land (because it contained a smaller amount of silver with the same nominal value, thus that the same price in coins could be settled with a smaller amount of silver), it was just as well possible that the good money in a land with devalued coins flowed out in order here with its higher metal content to be represented in a greater number of inferior coins of a land. In the one case the same nominal value was of use to the bad money, in the other case its higher metal value was of use to the good money. This dual application explains why we read in the evidence that sometimes bad money, sometimes good money flows out. But the tendency always occurs that the good money vanishes from circulation, and as a result the necessity was produced to reproduce in one's own land the devaluation which a foreign land had started.

Providing evidence in detail that the events actually played out in the described manner is unnecessary — not only in that monetary history is full of examples; you can directly say that in and outflows of gold stocks from one land to another, that constant disappearance of good money, that necessity for devaluation of a land's coins produced thereby — that that *is* the monetary history in the period of time examined by us.

For the other characteristic of finance in those centuries which I have in mind is also very closely connected with those events just described — I mean the *bimetallism system* which became established in all European lands from perhaps the 13th century and with the following explanation.

It is apparent that this spatial muddle of variously valued coins of all leading nations, as must occur as a consequence of the flowing across of masses of money; this temporal exchange of value of one and the same coins, as must arise by necessity from the habit of the coinage masters of setting the value of a coin as often as they like and as high as they like, was fit to bring about a state of the most irksome uncertainty which must appear all the more intolerable the more regular and numerous the international commercial acts became, and the more the capitalist nature demanded evolution. "Commerce" had to think of a remedy. And it found means and ways to take off at least the sharpest edge of the evils. One way out which it adopted to save itself from the ever worsening muddle of coins was *the return to purely stateless commercial money* — it needed the precious metal again without consideration for its coinage form or in unminted form as money. *In short,* paying by means of weight. It did that when it weighed the coins and based the agreement on effective (rather than the account-like fictive) weights ("defined method of payments with use of weight"); it did this when it left the precious metals in bars or transformed them into bars. Thus, for example, the payments to the English exchequer were conducted for a long time *ad scalam* — that is, by weight[127] (the treasury knew their way best around how it stood with the coins!); just as in Germany for a period the denare was accepted by weight[128]. The practice of using bars, however, likewise spread particularly in Germany during the Middle Ages — we encounter it on the Rhine and in Swabia, Bavaria, Austria, and Silesia from the beginning of the 13th century; in Lower Saxony, Angria, and Westphalia during the entire 14th century[129].

In the long run, however, commerce could not be content with this means of replacement for a decent monetary sys-

118

tem. It also had to strive to obtain respect for its interests in the area of state money, so that it at least protected *one* type of coin from the "plague" of devaluation[130]. In fact it succeeded in creating a coin, at first in the Italian city states, *whose metal value remained once and for all the same* (or at least approximately the same), and which now became the fixed pole in the flight of appearances: it was *the golden "pound"* which first saw the light of the world in Florence as "fiorino" in the year 1252.

The Florentine *guilders* had in fact an unheard-of constant value for that period — it was minted for centuries quite finely and weighed for centuries 3.519 g. This characteristic soon made it the most favoured coin for trade, which was happily accepted everywhere and now also found imitations in other states. The model of the Italian gold pieces (Venice still minted in the 13th century its sequins or ducats, Genoa its genovinos) forced the governments of other lands to likewise create an unchanging gold coin, if they wanted to avoid the Italian gold guilders remaining exclusively in circulation. They even preferred to mint their own coins outwardly in the image of the fiorino — a proof of the sort of distribution this coin must have found and in what standing it must have stood with traders. For they obviously wanted with the imitation of the imprint to make their native coins so similar as to be confused with the fiorino.

See the illustrations of those imitating the florins in the supplements to the treatise by Dannenberg (1880, 146 ff.). The history of gold minting in the Middle Ages is portrayed best by Shaw (1895). For comparison, see Inama-Sternegg (1895).

This ideal of unchangeability was certainly not achieved entirely outside Italy. Thus the guilders, for example, deteriorated in *Germany*, from the 15th century less in size than weight. They differentiated from then on the Hungarian (Italian) guilder and the Rhenish guilder — so called because the four Rhenish electors endeavoured with success to stabilise it. From the end of the 15th century the metal content of the Rhenish guilders was likewise quite stable — it worked out to about ¾ of the value of the ducats.

The following overview instructs us over the fate of the Rhenish guilder (Cahn 1895, 154):

Year	Weight (carats & grains)	Weight (grams)	Gold content (grams)	Gold value in current (1916) money
1391	23 ca.	3.542	3.396	9.48 marks
1402	22 ca. 6 gr.	3.542	3.322	9.27 marks
1409	22 ca.	3.542	3.248	9.06 marks
1417	20 ca.	3.542	2.953	8.23 marks
1425	19 ca.	3.507	2.777	7.95 marks
1464	19 ca.	3.405	2.696	7.52 marks
1477	18 ca. 10 gr.	3.372	2.647	7.39 marks
1490	18 ca. 6 gr.	3.278	2.547	7.05 marks

Now (from the middle of the 14th century) as a result, however, *the gold guilder also became the common coin of account — you calculated in the great trading world in guilders*, whilst the calculation in pounds remained for local commerce. The guilders were then rated according to the state of the pound reckoning[131]. There was thus always two types of money whose relationship to one another constantly wavered — the guilders type and the type of (pounds, which were often omitted) shillings and pennies.

This situation remained approximately unchanged until the end of our epoch. What changed was only the metal substance and the name of the guilders — from gold it turned to silver, from guilders to talers (piasters, Louis d'argent, etc.).

This transformation was connected with *the increase in silver production from the end of the 15th century*[132]. Silver was used up to then for the minting of groschen and pfennigs, which had sunk ever more and more into "token coins". When now at first in Germany and Austria suddenly so much silver was being obtained, this could not all be placed as token coins. Hence they fell on the idea of minting courant coins (the guilders) likewise now in silver. Thus around the turn of the 16th century the large silver coins arose which with a weight of about 32 grams [2 Lot] and a fineness of about 240 grams [15 Lot] according to the rate for silver at the time represented actually one guilder in value. Because previously no silver coins larger than the groschen had been known, the new coins were called guilder-groschen until a new description, (Joachims-)taler, arose. But, just the same as with the German silver, the American silver then demanded the production of large silver courant coins — these were the piasters in Spain and similar large silver pieces in other lands.

Ever more and more did silver seize back in this way its leading position in commerce which it had possessed three centuries previously, and which it then kept up until modern times (in England until the beginning of the 18th century, in the other lands until about the middle of the 19th century).

The old relationship, however, of the full-value, "good" courant coins to the smaller, still deteriorating shillings and pennies remained in existence.

In *France*, the breakdown of the coinage only really reached its high point in the 17th century, after the unfortunate financial speculation of the government. Even in *Germany* little changed until about the middle of the 19th century. "Depiction of the fruitless struggle which perhaps ten ignorant counterfeiters lead against the gradually developing world trade is the same as the history of German finance during the previous three centuries." (Grote 1857)

In the place of the (accounting) pound, a new accounting unit appeared in a few lands — in Germany, the accounting taler which now, just like the pound before it, received a changing accretion of discount against the species taler (so-called because present "in specie") or the piaster or the Louis d'argent, etc. Next to them the gold pieces remained likewise in circulation and helped to increase the confusion. From the 16th to the 18th century contracts were concluded partly in gold, partly in silver money, or with specific businesses the one or the other metal was conventionally used. Of course that in turn gave rise to two different prices, which just like the setting of rates for courant coins was still established by commerce — despite all legislated setting of rates and all prohibitions (e.g. in the imperial coin law of 1509) — in accordance with the market conditions.

The pfennigs were occasionally limited in their ability to serve as legal means of payment, so were declared to be token coins[133] with consequences that remain to be seen.

A new epoch of finance started to develop during the 18th century in *England*, especially as a result of the fact that the English government began to be the first (and until the end of the 18th century the only) to treat finance from a rational mercantile point of view. The law 18 Cha. 2 c.5 (Coin Act 1666), whereby the seignorage was lifted, made the start. When the strong devaluation of silver money then started at the end of the 17th century as a result of the acutely arising clipping and trimming, the state resisted the temptation to reduce the silver content of the coins correspondingly, stepping rather to a reminting in the interest of commerce. It then kept watch over the new currency in that it introduced a minimum weight for acceptance, and kept it fairly intact thanks to the simultaneous advances in minting technique. On top of that, from the beginning of the 18th century *the gold currency* was introduced firstly de facto, then de jure. This — an immediate effect of the opening up of the Brazilian and African gold fields, as we will yet see — introduced the new epoch, that of high capitalism, the golden one. Its beginnings fall in the epoch of early capitalism and are denoted by the following stages:

1. Declaration of the free mintability of (silver and) gold by the law of 1666;
2. Filling up of the public accounts with gold, since this for the time being was alone subject to the acceptance obligation;
3. Declaration of the obligation to accept for everybody in the year 1717;
4. Outflow of silver in consequence of the overvaluation of gold (21 s. the guinea);
5. Declaration of silver as token coins in the year 1774;
6. Lifting of the free mintability of silver in the year 1798.

III. Bank Money

The bad confusion of coins particularly in the 16th and 17th centuries led to an institution which — similar to the "golden pound" — was meant to serve to obtain for the commercial trade a means of payment unaffected by the incessant fluctuations in rates, thus in a word a constant means of payment, or more precisely, to make possible payments which fulfilled those conditions of certainty — that was the institution of bank money. It consisted in merchants depositing metal money of prescribed coinage in a "bank" where this sum was booked in an accounting money created to this end (or even in the firmly accepted coins of the land). The depositor could dispose via instructions over this sum, which corresponded thus to a quite specific quantity of precious metal, and which remained untouched in the cellars of the "bank". Since most of the business people of the places where these "banks" existed had an account with them, the payments could take place by way of giro, from which a second essential advantage arose.

That these institutions had nothing to do with what we understand today under the term bank is clear. Nonetheless they were called at the time "banks", indeed in the 17th century they understood by "banks" exactly those giro accounts.

Thus: "A bank is according to the present day [...] in the common idiom that place, or the laudable organisation, in which large and small sums of money can be deposited for safekeeping, but [can] be again demanded and withdrawn by their owner at any time if he so desires" (Marperger 1717). They are introduced "to be free of lots of counting money". The was surely only the second reason — they were principally called into life to escape the misery of insecurity of coins.

And the definition in Ludovici (1741, 1:362) goes:

> Banco, banque or bank means with merchants a house, established and privileged by public authority, in which they deposit their money in part for safekeeping and more security, in part for convenience (to be free of much disbursing), and thereafter have written off from their account to those whom they owe certain sums of such money, and on the other hand have written to them thus in such a way also what they have demands on from others, and this they call a giro.

The historical description of the banking system has (similar to the postal system) suffered a lot under the fact that at the time something quite different was understood by the term bank (as with the post). I will come to speak of that in the portrayal of economic life in the period of early capitalism in the next volume.

In the contemporary literature at most four such bank money institutions are named, namely (in the order of their years of founding):

1. Banco di Rialto (1587), from 1619 Banco del giro, in Venice;
2. Amsterdam's Wisselbank (1609);
3. Hamburg's Girobank (1629);
4. Banco publico in Nuremberg (1621).

But, as far as I see it, still more institutions bore the same or a very similar character, namely:

5. the Bank of Lyon[134];
6. the Casa di S. Giorgio in Genoa (from 1586), which in 1675 the Banchi di moneta corrente joined[135];
7. the Banco di S. Ambrogio in Milan (from 1593)[136];
8. the Banco di deposito in Leipzig[137];
9. the Bank of Rotterdam (1635).

The most famous of these institutions is *Amsterdam's Wisselbank*, over which I want thus to report in somewhat more detail. It was erected on 31st January 1609 on the strength of a privilege of the gentlemen of the States General as well as the Mayor of Amsterdam, under whose care the money deposited in the bank stood. It describes in its statute the aim of its founding: "om alle steygering ende confusie in 't stuck van de munte te weeren, ende den luyden, die eenige specien in de koopmanschappe van doen hebben, te gerieven" [to avoid all confusion of coins and to create for those who have money to dispose of a comfortable payment facility]. "It is", writes a contemporary who was competent to judge, "of such a great comfort for the trading world that you do not consider it possible if you have not lived and done business for some time in this city, that you can pay with its help millions daily by means of simple payment instructions which they call bank notes."* Hence, there were also very few merchants in Amsterdam and the neighbouring cities who did not make use of it, that is, who did not have a bank account. This you acquired:

1. by purchase of bank money at the exchange;
2. by acquisition of a bill of exchange which was payable in bank money;
3. by sale of goods to be paid in bank money;
4. by deposit of coins.

The bank accepted:

1. gold ducats;
2. rigksdalers;
3. piasters;
4. Louis d'Or.

All to a specific rate standing below the value of the metal. Bar gold or silver could not be deposited. You could (except on three days a year) only dispose over a committed sum on the following day. The minimum amount of a payment order was 300 fl. You had to personally hand over the payment orders, up to 3 o'clock in the afternoon (after 11 o'clock in the morning on payment of a special charge), and personally accept the payments. All bills of exchange over 600 fl. had to be in bank money.

I will also share the judgements of two especially well-informed foreigners, from which you will see best of all the character of this institution:

---

* [Tr.: neither of these quotes are referenced by Sombart.]

Cette banque est proprement la caisse générale, où châcun serre son argent, parce qu'on le juge là en plus grande seureté et l'on en dispose plus facilement, tant en payant qu'en reçevant, que si on le tenait en ses propres coffres. Et tant s'en faut que la banque paye interest de l'argent que l'on y depose que mesmes celuy qui y est, vaut plus que la monnoye courante, dont les payements se font manuellement; parce que l'on n'y apporte point d'autres especes que les meilleurs les plus approuvées et les plus générale-ment connues tant en Allemagne qu'à un Pais-bas.
[This bank is properly the general cashier, where everyone keeps their money, because it is judged there to be more secure and it is more easily disposed of, both by paying and receiving, than if it were held in one's own coffers. And so much so that the bank pays interest on the money deposited there, as even that which is there is worth more than the current currency in which pay-ments are made manually; because no other specie is brought there but the best, the most approved, and the most widely known, both in Germany and in the Netherlands]

(Temple 1685, 97)

The proper definition of this bank is not a bank of current money, to be received and issued daily, like those of London, Venice, etc., but is purely a deposit of money, the credit whereof passes from hand to hand daily, by signed tickets [...] But al-though it be, without doubt, an excellent institution for safety, ease, dispatch, and record, yet it cannot be said to increase the general quantity of circulation of money, as some other banks certainly do" (A. Anderson 1787, 2:237).

Since it is always the full sum which a businessman disposes over which lies *in the bank in cash*. Cf. also the well-known depiction and as-sessment of the Amsterdam bank by Adam Smith (1776, 2:219 ff.).

Figures on the size of its turnover are not known to me. It would be very instructive to give us an idea of the extent of Dutch trade in its hey-day. The contemporaries call it consistently the "richest" bank. Temple (1685, 131) suggests the treasure accumulated in it was the largest of all those known, "reels ou imaginaires" [real or imaginary]. Well-known is the estimate which Adam Smith made: 2,000 accounts at 1,500 pounds = 3 million pounds or 33 million fl.

By comparison we happily possess precise statistics for the *Ham-burg* Girobank from its last period, which I convey here:

Bank funds	1772	3½ mill. marks
	1799	38½ mill. marks
Number of ledger pages used	1774	7,570 pages
	1799	24,151 pages
Total turnover	1774	230 mill. marks
	1799	1,506 mill. marks

(Baasch 1900, 166)

IV. The Beginnings of Paper Money

You will only comprehend the character of finance in the period of early capitalism if you remind yourself fully that everything we describe with the terms paper money or paper currency was foreign to the spirit of that epoch, that thus these forms of money, where we find them perhaps at the time, are not to be seen as normal components of economic life in its entirety (with *one exception*).

What characterises the history of paper money in the early period of capitalism rather is:

1) the inability of organs of state to handle this dangerous tool,

2) the deep distrust of the public towards this form of money, which first really began in particular in the 18th century (as a consequence of the fraudulent manoeuvres in the first "period of founding".

A touch of romanticism still played about the concept of paper money; it was still seen by the princes as a new way of making gold; they still had not understood the inner conformity to laws of this form of money; it was still regarded as "devil's work", as a work of magic. As all that was indeed shown in its classic portrayal in the emperor scenes of "Faust".

Hence you must, however, also see Law's[*] bank enterprises as the essential form of all attempts at the time to introduce paper money. It is known that this episode, which amounted in the end to the issuing of 2 billion francs of banknotes, was of very short duration — everything stopped in 1720, and only half a century later did they begin to think again in *France* of creating a bank of issue. But that the time of paper money had at the time not yet come is shown by the fate of the assignats[†].

Not much differently, if also less dramatically, ran the experiments which were made with paper money during the 18th

---

[*]   [Tr.: John Law, as Controller General of Finances for France, created the Banque Générale Privée (later the Banque Royale) in 1716, which developed paper money and was involved in the Mississippi Bubble which burst in 1720.]

[†]   [Tr.: assignat = banknote issued during the French Revolution.]

century in *Denmark* and *Norway*, in *Sweden*, in *Russia*, and in the *American states*. Everywhere the outcome was the same — the undertaking ended everywhere with a heavy devaluation of paper money — in most American states, for example, the devaluation amounted to at least 100%, in individual cases up to 1,000%, in one even 1,400%, so already almost assignat conditions.

The distrust of the population and in particular the business world towards paper money was thus understandable.

It will only have been the expression of the general mood when a Hamburger wrote in the year 1782:

> You see that only our bank alone is structured for safety, comfort, and the correctness of our business; that it is consequently distinguished from all credit banks, which are so often only kept together and preserved by all sorts of artificial financial projects, and from which you chase into the world so many beautiful copper-engraved banknotes which are meant to represent the clinking coins — as a result of which then, however, credit can also in the end be weakened so much and the business of a land brought so much into disorder [etc.] [138]

The exception of which I spoke above are *the notes of the Bank of England*. Since here the right to issue notes was limited to the amount of the bank's capital, a misuse of the paper money presses could not occur like in other lands. We also thus hear only of tiny devaluations of the notes of this bank, which we have to imagine rather as a part of the normal money supply of England in the 18th century. Yet I would also like in this case to warn against now assuming perhaps that the paper money or the banknotes in England already had during the 18th century also approximately the same meaning as perhaps today. They remained on the contrary even in England until the beginning of the 19th (or at least up to the last decade of the 18th) century entirely a minor phenomenon which was without considerable significance for the English finances as a whole. We may conclude this on the one hand from the way in which the notes were issued, and on the other hand (and above all!) from the insignificance of the quantity of notes brought into circulation.

At first the notes had to be endorsed; until 1759 only notes of 20 pounds or more were issued.

Up until the middle of the 18th century the notes of the Bank of England had to struggle for their money character. Even in the year 1758 it was first established only by decision of the highest court that a testamentary disposal of a man over all the money in his possession also included possible notes of the bank because these notes were money just as good as the guineas. Receipts over the acceptance of notes of the bank were synonymous with receipts over the acceptance of money. With bankrupts too the notes were treated as money. (Schmidt 1914, 170–71)

The sum of issued notes, however, for the longest time in the 18th century amounted to not much more than 2 million pounds (corresponding to the size of the bank's capital). Even in 1780 only 8.41 million pounds, in 1796/97 only 9.67 million pounds in circulation.

We must contrast these figures with the quantities of hard money which circulated in England at the time. That was, however, as we will establish more precisely, approximately 100 million pounds. Paper money was to hard money in England during the first decades of the 18th century by quantity in a ratio of perhaps 1 to 50, a relationship which then gradually moved in favour of paper money until the close of the century, so that it finally stood at about 1 to 10. But that is still a fundamentally different relationship to that of today. Today we have (even in a land like Germany which has a strong preference for metal money) in normal times only perhaps double as much hard money in the land as paper money.

Chapter 27: Colonial Policy

Preliminary Remarks

Taken exactly, the founding of large colonial empires, as we see them since the days of Venice and Genoa during the Middle Ages and the more recent period, forms a part of the mercantilist trade policy and would thus have had to have been handled in Chapter 24 if the taxonomy of the structure would have done it full justice. That I likewise dedicate a special chapter to the colonies or, more properly, colonial policy has its cause above all in the extraordinary force with which this current has directly burst from the mercantilist waters into history; but then also in the many peculiarities which attach themselves from all sides to the colonial endeavours and lend them a quite independent significance which drives them into a quite specific evolution. This special position of the colonial problem has also been acknowledged since time immemorial in the literature in so far as an extraordinarily rich specialist literature has always occupied itself with it — a final reason for also discussing the problem in this portrayal separately from the general mercantilist politics. The taxonomy of the work is, however, preserved in so far as this chapter fits into the section which is concerned with the state, so that thus everything which is said here over colonies and the founding of colonies is only ever that which stands in an immediate connection with the state — conquest, organisation, administration. (Whereas the significance of the colonial *economy* is acknowledged in various other places of the book.)

Finally there is a need for a word of explanation — about why I begin my sketch of the modern colonies with the Italian colonies, and depict these directly in an especially detailed way.

The first matter has an inner cause — I really believe that the turn from the Middle Ages to the new period started with the seizure of the Levant, at least for Italy, and that Dante's age is to be seen not only intellectually but also economically and in particular governmentally as the beginning of the new historical epoch — not least directly *because* of the colonial expansion of the Italian city states. We will see that colonisation also started at first entirely in the forms of medieval life, which indeed, however, as we can establish, applies to all the policies of the modern state; that then, however, in the colonial endeavours there arose one modern institution after the other, one modern thought after

the other. But above all the work of colonisation of the cinquecento*
would also be in its inner structure utterly incomprehensible without an
insight into the founding of the Italian colonies of the Levant. That I
then dedicate to them such a correspondingly large space in my depiction has the outward reason that so little is known of them — of all the
professional works over the history of the colonies only the Italian
colonies have found in the most recent period a consideration worth
mentioning, namely in the book of Morris.

***

Sources and Literature

As sources, for the most part those from which we take our know-
ledge of mercantilist policy in general come into consideration. Of col-
lections of material which refer especially to colonial history, the
following can be added to those named in Chapter 24:
- For the *Italian* colonies (other than Tafel and Thomas (1856)):
  Noiret (1892), and Mas Latrie (1852).
- For *Spanish* colonisation: Pacheco et al (1864).
- For *Dutch* colonisation: De Jonge and Deventer (1862).
- For *English* colonisation: Calendar of State Papers: Colonial
  Series (Public Record Office of Great Britain 1860).
- For *North American* colonies in particular: O'Callaghan and
  Fernow (1853).

Much primary source material is also published independently in
newer monographs as I will note in the relevant places.

In addition to the "documents", the *travel reports* in particular also
come into consideration as sources for the older colonial history. I will
content myself with naming the two most important collections of travel
reports from the cinquecento: Ramusio (1550), and Hackluyt (1598).

The *literature* over the history of the colonies is extraordinarily substantial. I will at an appropriate place cite the works used by myself and
hence name here only the quite *general depictions*. Of a more colonial
policy nature, but also of historical nature are: Brougham (1803), and
Merivale (1861) (both works still belong among the best books over the
policy of colonisation); Roscher (1856); and A. Zimmermann (1905) (of
predominantly historical character). Essentially historical portrayals:
Raynal (1775), Leroy-Beaulieu (1886), A. Zimmermann (1896), Morris
(1900). The latter, newest depiction of colonial history is also the most
complete. It contains in the appendices a very well compiled bibliography to which to refer to as well. A comprehensive bibliography of the
entire colonial literature (at 156 octavo pages!) has been published by
Griffen (1900).

The works of *historical geography* serve as a supplement so far as
they have the origin of the colonial empires as their object. The beautiful work of Peschel (1858) belongs among the classic works of the Ger-

---

*   [Tr.: 16th century as a time of Italian art and culture.]

man literature. The most important appearances of more recent times are Ruge (1881) and Supan (1906). Both magnificent works deal a lot also, relative to their task, with the (external) colonial history. Both limit themselves to the period since the 15th century. Supan's depiction is *chronological*. A comprehensive survey is given by the brilliant sketch of Ferdinand Tönnies (1915).

A special branch of the general literature on colonial history which is of quite special significance in connection with this work is formed by the *literature over slavery and slave trading*, which I will provide information about further below.

I. The Idea of Colonies

When you, as happens in this book, observes the politics of absolute states in its outward forms as a continuation and culmination of the politics of medieval cities, then it suggests comparing the colonial area which lies around all these states with the "countryside" over which at a minimum the economic sphere of power of the medieval city extended — the state steps into the place of the city, as we can follow in countless examples, and creates now in the colonies an area which it can exploit just as the city exploited the countryside, in that it forced it to deliver its products to it exclusively and to take the products of the state in exchange. There is no doubt in fact that this basic relationship between city and countryside repeats in the economic relations between mother country and colony.

Let us though summarise the colonial economic policy of most European peoples in the following sentences:

1. The colonies may only deliver their produce to the mother country — "no sugar, tobacco, cotton-wool, indigo, ginger, fustic and other dying woods, of the growth or manufacture of our Asian, African or American colonies shall be shipped from the said colonies to any place but England, Ireland, or to some other of His Majesty's said plantations, there be landed"[139] — the right of passage!
2. The colonies may only obtain products, particularly manufactured ones, from the mother country — the market right!
3. The colonies must not themselves produce products which the mother country produces — the right of exclusion!

4. The mother country reserves for itself the monopoly over transport.
5. The goods which come from the colonies are charged duties when they leave the ports of the colonies and when they enter the ports of the mother country.

But then, with a closer look, numerous deviations are also found though, and the colonial relationship demonstrates essential differences from the old relationship of countryside to city. If you want to connect the conflict which exists between both with the conflict of the great economic ideas, then you can say that the need for expansion of the medieval city was accompanied and controlled by the idea of sustenance, that of the modern city-states and large states by the idea of acquisition. The old city wanted to have as much land at its economic disposal as it needed for its upkeep, which itself was defined by the quite constant number of inhabitants according to extent and sort. The modern state already from its origin does not know this natural limitation — it is a fact unfamiliar to us that precisely an innate peculiarity of the modern state (to which we must always assign the large Italian city-states) is made perceptible in the unbounded striving for expansion. And this tendency towards enlargement then really becomes evident in the colonial expansion. That this was a limitless one found a special cause then in the goal to which all states strived with their thieving raids — gold. Once this happened and because this enticed them all especially over their European borders, the same frenzy for unbounded possession seized them which seized the economic subjects and slung them out of the narrow circles of the ideal of sustenance.

This urge then led the states onto the same paths almost everywhere and caused similar forms of colonial rule to unfold everywhere.

II. The Origin of Colonial Empires

How the individual colonial empires were formed over the course of the centuries, how the various states and city-states disputed with one another over the regions of the earth, how sometimes this, sometimes that power possessed preeminence in the contested land areas — that is in general well known and can here only be told in outline.

The history of the modern colonies makes its start with the Crusades and the settlement of Europeans in the Holy Land.

The *Crusader states*[140] themselves were not colonies in the modern sense, but they surely offered the first opportunity for the Italian cities to penetrate into the pores of the foreign populace and lay with it the foundation for the later colonial economy. Of the 1101 and 1104 conquered cities of Arsuf, Caesarea, and Acre, Genoa received a third part of each, and likewise a part of the surrounding areas. Pisa and Venice followed it, the latter participating in battles from 1100, being awarded in 1110 a third of the wealthy Sidon, and in 1123 a third of Tyre[141]. A large countryside always belonged to the cities; the Venetians alone though possessed in the region around Tyre some 80 estates[142].

From then on all the thought and actions of the large, leading city communities of Italy was directed at the expansion of their colonial possessions in the Mediterranean areas. And colonial empires then also arose of a massive size (in comparison of course to the size of the mother city) like those which world history — despite Rome and England — has surely never seen a second time.

Venice's colonial possessions experienced, as is well known, a sudden expansion in consequence of the dividing up of the Byzantine Empire, by which the lagoon city received three eighths of the enormous area[143]. With that the lands of Epirus, Akarnania, Aetolia, the Ionian islands, the Peloponnese, the islands of the archipelago lying to the south and west[144], a number of cities on the coast of the Dardanelles and by the Sea of Marmara, Thrace's landlocked cities like Adrianople etc., Pera, the suburbs of Constantinople, Heraklion, and soon afterwards also the important Cyprus. This region was then in the course of the centuries continually rounded off by acquisitions in Armenia, by the Black Sea, etc.

But here the preeminence of Venice had its most dangerous rival — *Genoa*[145]. The Genoese possessed extensive estates in the Crimea as well as on the mainland. Kaffa, in which they ruled from 1266, formed the centre point of their colonies on the Black Sea. This city is supposed in the 14th century to have numbered 100,000 inhabitants(?). But then to be found in the hands of the Genoese were the lucrative islands of Chios, Samos, Icaria, Oinousses, Panagia, parts of Cyprus (Famagusta), Corsica (until 1768), and Sardinia, which Genoa then lost to the Kingdom of Aragon, possessions in Spain, in Greece[146], on the Armenian coast, in Syria and Palestine.

Next to Venice and Genoa's colonial empires, those of the Italian cities pale in comparison. Although the colonial possessions of *Pisa*[147] and *Florence*[148] were not insignificant either. Both cities had been settling in Syria and Palestine since the 12th century; Pisa had early on got a foothold on the African coast, and Florentine families were ruling in Greece[149].

When then after the discovery of America and the sea route to the East Indies new, large colonial empires arose on the other side of the ocean, it was, as you know[150], other nations which founded them — in the 16th century above all Spain and Portugal; in the 17th and 18th centuries France, Holland, and England, whereas the German states stood to the side and only tiny Brandenburg made a few vain attempts to act like a great state too.

The *Spaniards* were temporally the first of the modern colonial powers. Their possessions stretched in the 16th century already over all of South America (except Brazil), Central America, and the southern part of North America from California to Florida, as well as over a few smaller stretches of land in Africa and the South Seas — an area which they possessed up until into the 19th century.

In the 16th century standing as an equal at Spain's side was *Portugal*, which at the time ruled over the west and east coasts of Africa, the coasts of the Arabian Sea including the west coast of India, individual coastal spots in Southeast Asia, the Moluccas, and above all the great Brazil. These possessions, however, were already being heavily diminished in the 16th century and still more in the 17th century by the advancing of the other states.

Among them *France* took the leading position during the first half of the 17th century. Creator of the French colonial empire was Richelieu (1624–1642). When he entered government, France possessed only Quebec, at his death: Canada, Martinique, Guadeloupe, Dominique, and the other Antilles.

In 1682 Louisiana was founded, and France also took a firm foothold in Southeast Asia. The collapse of this great French colonial empire followed at the end of the 18th century when Canada fell into the hands of the English and (in 1803) Louisiana was sold to the United States.

In the 17th century then the two greatest colonial empires of the more recent period arose next to the French possessions — the Dutch and the English.

The *Dutch* in part displaced the Spanish and Portuguese from their settlements and took root in the course of the 17th century in Brazil, Africa, and the East Indies, where up to then the Portuguese had settled. But in addition they acquired the area around the Cape of Good Hope and above all the Sunda Islands.

The *English* followed in the footsteps of the Dutch, taking away from them a part of their spoils — New York, Ceylon, the Cape of Good Hope — while taking from the Spanish several of the West Indian islands, from the French Canada and the Indian peninsula, in order to then be left as the last with their rich spoils.

The colonies were acquired by each state in lengthy, hard, and merciless struggles — *they were conquered.*

The colonies were conquered in struggle with the natives, conquered in struggle with the envious, competing European nations. Certainly here and there diplomatic skill may have helped to obtain for a land an advantage in trade with a foreign folk; we know of numerous treaties which were concluded with native princes, and in which the European nation received an assurance of privileges of all kinds. Especially in the Levant's colonies, where you had half and fully civilised peoples to deal with, the concluding of treaties was frequent. And they also occurred in the Asian and American areas. In French such treaties are called "firman" [edict], in which (as, for example, in the firman from the year 1692 which Destandes obtained for the French East India Company in Chandannagar from the Mogul) was perhaps agreed the following:

- the company paid the Mogul 40,000 coins, 10,000 immediately, 5,000 in annual instalments;
- the French received the right to trade freely in the provinces of Bengal, Odisha, and Bihar; with the same privileges and also the same practices as the Dutch;
- they paid like the latter 3½% duty.

But as excellent as such arrangements were, it was certainly not the end of it. Already in that they were kept by the natives, an expansion of power of the land concluding the treaty was presumed, an expansion to infuse the princes over there with sufficient respect. And then there still remained always the rival European state which was ready at any moment to fight for its place with sword in hand.

Thus the colonial history of the Genoese and Venetians is already a history of eternal wars. A large part of the book by Heyd (1879) is dedicated to the enumeration of such struggles. Also here already those states which appear most formidable receive good treaties:

> During these struggles the republic [Venice] limited itself essentially to placing its quarters in the city of Negreponte in a good defensive state. This probably contributed to them in the year 1272, when a treaty for two years with Michael Palaiologus was concluded, in obtaining more favourable conditions. (Heyd 1879, 1:479)

And no less than those of the Western European nations since the 16th century — expansion of power by warlike appearance also remained the solution here, as shown by a memorandum of the directors of the French East India Company from the year 1668:

> Il faudrait envoyer des vaisseaux du Roi afin de les faire voir sur les côtes et surtout n'épargner ni poudre ni boulets, et c'est d'une grande conséquence afin d'abattre l'orgueil des Hollandaise [...], fomenter la guerre entre Anglais et Hollandais et secourir toujours le plus faible [...]; la Comp. étant établie une fois, il ne tiendra qu'au Roi d'être le maître des Indes.
> [It would be necessary to send the King's vessels in order to show them on the coasts and above all to spare neither powder nor cannon balls, and this is of great consequence in order to bring down the pride of the Dutch [...], to foment war between the English and the Dutch and to always come to the aid of the weakest [...]; the Comp. being established once, it will be up to the King to be master of the Indies.] (Kaeppelin 1908, 322)

It is known that from the 17th century it became common to transfer the rights of the state, above all the means of war, to the privileged trading companies, to whom the conquering of the colonies actually properly fell to as a result, and between them the battle over the feeding trough (as far as it was decided outside Europe) came to a resolution. That in this struggle the size of the state instruments of power decided things in the last analysis, and that victory was obtained not by peaceful merchants, but by agile business people and brutal naval heroes is quite obvious.

The always clear-headed G. Martin reported home:

> L'on connaîtra par là qu'il faut que les personnes qui sont à la tête des Compagnies dans le Indes, aient d'autres qualités que celle qui regarde la fonction simplement d'un habile marchand: c'est un service mêlé, où il est nécessaire de savoir un peu de tout.
> [We will know by this that it is necessary that the people who are at the head of the Companies in the Indies have other qualities

than that which regards the function simply of a skilful merchant: it is a mixed service, where you need to know a bit of everything] (Kaeppelin 1908, 63)

And that applied to all nations — the most brutal, most ruthless carried away the victory in the battle and finally the war.

An especially good, because extraordinarily transparent example of the sequence of events in the acquisition of the colonial possession are delivered by the history of the African trading companies.

Firstly Africa was possessed by the Portuguese. Next to them the English also achieved a firm foothold — Queen Elizabeth I privileged a company. The English then built their first fort on the Gold Coast, then on the Gambia River, at the time of the Stuarts. In 1621 the Dutch West Indies Company was established, with the right to take possession of all the land on the African west coast and the American east coast; as well as the sole right to carry on trade there. Since the Portuguese had already taken possession of the places which were important for the company, collisions were unavoidable, and they also appeared soon enough — in 1637 the Dutch conquered the first Portuguese fort in Africa, soon all the others which were awarded to them in the treaty of 1641. But now the English were still in the way, and the Dutch now took up the right of sole trade against them too — they constantly had two warships crossing by the coast, which were meant to make chase of English trading ships arriving — the names of the captured ships are in Postlethwayt (1774, 1:927). It had now become clear:

1. that English private merchants could not prevail against the combined might of the Dutch West Indies Company;

2. that little worth was to be placed on a treaty between the involved states (Southeast Asian experience!);

3. that there was only one means to set against such an opponent as the Dutch West Indies Company — to also amalgamate the English merchants similarly into a company and to give this all the powers and privileges which it required.

The result of these considerations was the founding of the "Company of Royal Adventurers of English trading into Africa" in the year 1662.

Now began a well-ordered struggle between both companies — the English positioned forts now too, armed warships as well, etc. What outlay came into question is shown by the following figures: for the building and upkeep of forts on the African coast the company spent in 1672–1678 £390,000, in 1678–1712 £206,000, in 1712–1729 £255,000, thus altogether £851,000 in these 57 years! But the English were now also not disturbed anymore in their possession. Postlethwayt, who gives this report from good contemporary sources, adds: "For 250 years past, it has been the constant policy of all such European nations [who have discovered foreign lands] to build and maintain forts and castles; and in virtue of such possessions to claim a right to whole Kingdoms and to tracts of land of a vaste extent and to exclude all other nations from trading into or from them." (1774, 1:725).

Only in the course of our epoch, in the 18th century, did the "treaty" begin more and more to obtain significance as a means of power — force gave way to cunning as the predominant category of subjugation, and it surely the English above all who developed this new form. But for the greatest part of the early capitalist period it was the force of weapons which decided the fate of states in Europe and the colonies. Thus the validity of the sentence: in the beginning was the army.

The history of the colonies is thus for the most part *military history*, and most history writers are even of the opinion that it was *only* a military history — since you find in the general works of colonial history mostly an extensive depiction of the wars of conquest. To add to this, I add the following writings which occupy themselves especially with the battles for the colonies: the book by Heyd (1879) is particularly worth mentioning for the Levant colonies, it exhausts itself almost entirely with the enumeration of diplomatic and military actions.

Quite especially thorny were the paths of the pioneers in the course of time naturally, thus in the east the *Portuguese*. Their experiences are reported innocently by Saalfeld (1810). A very in-depth portrayal of the struggles of the Portuguese in the East Indies has been provided recently by Bokemeyer (1888, 45–79). Of the older descriptions, de Veer (1864) is still worth checking.

The *Spanish* colonial history (as a history of conquest) has been portrayed in an unsurpassed manner in the two works by Prescott (1843; 1847). A very useful book even today is that of Helps (1855). Of the newer works, to be highlighted are the works of Häbler (1899; 1907).

The struggles of the *Dutch* are treated again in-depth by Saalfeld (1812) without, however (and very much to distinguish it advantageously from most other colonial histories), leaving the economic side unconsidered. A detailed military history of the Dutch colonies is found in Klerk de Reus (1894, XI–XLVI). For comparison, see Dubois (1763).

Much material over the struggles of the *French* is contained in the often cited Kaeppelin (1908).

The last decisive battles, however, were not even fought in overseas waters, but were fought in Europe. Most of the countless wars which filled the 17th and 18th century quite distinctly had trade and colonial policy causes which, particularly after England obtained decisive ascendancy, became more and more exclusively so: "The heroic religious war of liberation of the Netherlands from the Spanish yoke is to be seen as an almost hundred year long war of colonial conquest in the East Indies and a pirate war just as long against the Spanish silver fleet and the Spanish-American colonial trade" (Schmoller 1884a, 52). The war which the United Provinces conducted from 1652 to 1654 with England was caused by Cromwell's Navigation Act; when conversely England in the year 1664 declared war on the Dutch, this was the answer to

138

the hostile behaviour of the Dutch West Indies Company in Africa. Louis XIV, whose wars in general were certainly based more deeply than on mere trading interests, invaded Holland in 1672 though to punish the Dutch for the inordinately repressive measures which they had taken against the tariff duties of Colbert. The Spanish War of Succession, just like the War of the Grand Alliance of 1689 to 1697, was in the first line a battle of England and Holland against the danger which threatened from France and from the unification of the French trade with the Spanish colonial power. Finally in the 18th century repeatedly, finally and with decisive results, a duel was fought between the two great colonial powers, England and France. That England remained the victor in the wars of 1756–1763 decided its position of supremacy in world trade and in colonial possessions.

III. The Use of Colonies

Of course the use turns out differently depending on whether it concerns the mere establishment of foreign trading posts or carrying on plantations or settlement. Settlement indeed at that time only came under consideration essentially in the northern of the North American colonies, whilst all the others — both the Levantine and the later overseas colonies — were "trade" or "planting" colonies. That use took place once again in various ways depending on the system of administration which the states brought into operation. We distinguish two of them — the direct state administration and the handing over to colonisation companies. We find the former with the Venetians and later with the Spanish and Portuguese, the latter with the Genoese and then with the colonies of the Dutch, the French, and the English.

The earliest form of colonisation company was the Genoese Maona. The most famous *Maona* is that *of Chios* which came into existence in the year 1347 as follows. A fleet equipped by private shipowners for other purposes had conquered Chios. On its return they desired, as was the condition, 203,000 livres compensation from the government. Since the government could not pay, on 26th February 1347 this debt was transformed into the Compera or Maona Chii. For security and for interest on the debt the creditors were provided with Chios and Phokaia. For two centuries then the Maona was in possession of the dominium utile [beneficial ownership] not only of Chios and Phokaia, but also the islands of Samos, Nicaea, Oinousses, and Panagia, and for a long time possessed the monopoly on the mastic trade of Chios and the alum trade of Phokaia (Hopf 1859, 316 ff., 327 ff.). In 1374 the Maona Cipri was founded, in 1403 the Maona nuova Cipri; in 1378 Corsica was handed over to a Maona; later also the Crimea. Cf. Sieveking (1898, 1:177 ff., 2:99 ff.).

From the 16th century the great trading companies appeared which we have already met in another connection and will meet again in yet another.

But at core the colonial system in all the centuries from when the Italians seized a firm foothold in the Levant up to the decline of the great trading companies and up to the abolition of slavery had been the same though because it rested on the following foundations:

I. the *granting of privileges* which experienced its highest expression here in the colonies. When a trading company was granted the sole use of a colony, the form of the privilege was clear as day. But even where we encounter no privileged company, we find the system of granting privileges in operation. In the beginnings of the Italian colonisation, but also in that of the Spanish and Portuguese even, the old feudal system was used without further ado in order to equip individual persons with prerogatives — as it were "enfeoffments" took place with specific territorial parts of the colony. Later the investition of the royal prerogative took its place, and individual persons received in exchange for a specific rent the right to exploit the prerogatives.

Over the feudal-like allocations in the Levant, see Beugnot (1854); Noiret (1892); and Heyd (1879, 1:336 ff.).

In Spanish America the "fiefs" were called *encomiendas*, the population belonging to them *repartiementos*. Helps (1855, 3:99 ff.) deals with the encomiendas in the most detail; also found there is the famous definition of the repartimiento according to de Leon (Helps 1855, 3:135).

In the Portuguese colonies they spoke of capitanias and sesmarias (Handelmann 1860, 47).

A special sort of personal bestowal of prerogatives was the so-called contracts of discovery. Such contracts of discovery were frequently struck by the Fuggers, the Welsers, and the Ehingers, amongst others. A detailed account of such a contract is found in Häbler (1897, 56 ff.). Cf. in addition Schuhmacher (1892), and Häbler (1894; 1903). As well as the critique by Eulenburg (1906). The rich literature over the relations of the Welsers to Venezuela is compiled by Hantzsch (1895, 18 ff.).

Quite modern privileges were already exhibited in great abundance by the administration of the *Venetian* colonies in the 15th century. On 16th March 1429 the exclusive right to obtain alum on the island of Crete was transferred to Petrus Quirino for ten years (Noiret 1892, 327–28); on

20th June 1465 the same for the construction of a mine for copper, silver, or gold ore went to Nicolao Genus (Noiret 1892, 495–96); on 3rd
April 1480 the same for the extraction of nitrium on the granting of a
credit of 300 ducats (Noiret 1892, 547); on 16th March 1445 an auction
took place for the ten year monopoly over the extraction of alum (Noiret
1892, 410); on 31st July 1442 the privilege for the introduction of the
mastic tree to Crete was granted to Thomas Quirino and his associates,
at the same time the sole right to the cultivation of mastic trees was
awarded to him for the next 20 years (Noiret 1892, 402); on 24th July
1428 the sole right to planting sugarcane on the island of Crete was conferred on Marcus de Zanono for the next ten years (Noiret 1892, 324–
25), etc.

II. The second governmental measure which lent all colonial
policy of the earlier period its peculiar stamp was the equipping of the colonists — it might be individuals or corporations
— with an extraordinarily *strong military apparatus*. We
must imagine all colonial settlements of those centuries
stocked with fortifications in which mostly a strong unit with
ample munitions had its permanent residence, in so far as the
merchants or farmers did not perhaps maintain themselves
the defence of the fort which protected them alone.

That applied in turn equally to the Italian colonies in the Levant as to those of the later period. To just select a few arbitrarily selected examples: "We must imagine as being very
significant the Venetian fortifications in Tana according to
the description of Giovanni Bembo. It was of course not just
the quarter occupied by the Venetians in the town itself surrounded with walls and towers, but the Venetians possessed
also their own castle with two towers and surrounded by a
large ditch, outside the town on a hill, to where they could
withdraw with their possessions if the town was attacked by
an enemy."[151] And the Dutch trading post in Bengal "looks
more like a castle, being incompassed with deep ditches, full
of water, high stone walls and bastions faced with stone and
mounted with canon. Their spacious warehouses are also of
stone and apartments for the officers and merchants are large
and commodious"[152].

The Dutch East-India Company kept as permanent troops (at
the beginning of the 18th century) 12,000 men in their Indian
possessions, whilst 100,000 natives were trained in the
weapons so as to find occasional use. The large companies
also had to keep their merchant ships on a war footing since

they just as often had to serve as warships. The fleet of the Dutch Indies Company consisted of perhaps 60 sailing vessels "fit for service", equipped with 30–60 guns each[153].

The outlay of the English East-India Company for civil and — principally! — military administration including fort construction in the province of Bengal amounted, for example, to £9,027,609 in the six years of 1765–1771[154].

The strengths of the military forces in the English colonies during the 18th century is visible from the following figures:

- Jamaica (1734): 7,644 white population, of which 3,000 man garrison; and 6 forts;
- Barbados (1734): 18,295 white population, of which 4,812 man garrison; 21 forts; and 26 batteries with 463 cannons;
- Leeward Islands (1734): 10,262 white population, of which 3,284 militia.[155]

III. But the main thing though was that the states which founded colonies deployed their instruments of power so that the work, which was to be performed in these colonies by native or foreign workers, and on whose exploitation, as Columbus recognised quite rightly when he had discovered America, all the worth of the colonies rested[156] — that the work in the form of forced labour was recognised by law, that is thus that *slavery* was permitted in some form as a system of work. The colonial economy of the Italians in the Levant just as much as that of the Spanish, Portuguese, French, Dutch, and English in Africa, America, and Asia rested on slavery (or serfdom). What is needed to be said about this is in Chapter 46, which deals with the colonial economy and is to be seen as an complement to the observations made here.

Chapter 28: State and Church

Preliminary Remarks — Literature

Through the various conduct of the state administrations of the day towards religious communities and religious denominations peculiar conditions for the development of capitalist existence were created, for which reason it becomes necessary to lay out here in its essential features the relations between state and church as they configured themselves from the conclusion of the Middle Ages to the end of the 18th century or beginning of the 19th century. (The significance of *religious conviction* for economic life is to be appreciated on the other hand in a quite different connection. See the relevant chapters in my "Bourgeois" (1913a, 282 ff.; 1915, 222 ff.) where I have attempted such an appreciation.) Now the relations of the state to the church, however, especially in the period surveyed by us, apply themselves to the form of economic life above all through a decisive influence that they exercise over the toleration or exclusion of various religious communities within the state's territory. What we thus principally have to follow, apart from the actual spread of the various systems of religion over the civilised peoples, is the rule of the principle of tolerance or intolerance in the individual lands at various times. Under this viewpoint I will also pick out from the large *literature* the most important works.

The books of Ruffini (1901; 1912) and Matagrin (1905) attempt to deal in a quite general connection with the *problem of religious tolerance* from an historical point of view; both good works which, however, in no way exhaust the topic — in addition their formulation of the question is predominantly too literary. The portrayal of Simon (1859, 2:285 ff.) is a sketch. The problem is treated in a more philosophical and rational way by Lecky (1865; 1873). The problem is discussed from a more dogmatic than historical standpoint by Troeltsch (1919; 1931). An overview is given by the article "Toleranz" in Herzog (1854, 16:201, 3:537-544) [Tr.: or Herzog et al (1877, 18:379-391)], and in Wetzer and Welte (1847, XI:72-81).

For the study of the real course of the thing, you have to rely still on the monographic treatments of the subject for the individual lands. You will find these in any general work of history as well as in any church history. From the specialist literature, the following works are to be named:

France: Polenz (1857) (only continued up to 1629), Schott (1885), Buckle (1864, 1:460-854), and Matagrin (1905).

Spain: Schäfer (1902) (the second and third volumes contain documents). This excellent work, which rests on thorough studies of the sources, contains in its introduction a critical overview of the relevant literature. In it a leading position has been held for decades by Llorente (1817), which first appeared in French in 1817 and was then often published and translated into many foreign languages — in German 1820–1822 in four volumes*. The work has been valid for a long time as an objective portrayal based on the sources, but is today recognised though as being heavily tendentious — see over this Schäfer (1902, 1:24 ff.). For comparison see from the non-specialist literature Buckle (1864, 2:1-155).

England and the English colonies: Buckle (1864, 1:306-459, 2:158 ff. (Scotland)). J. Anderson (1856) (very usable). Cobb (1902) serves as a supplement. Over puritanism in particular, see D. Campbell (1892) and Byington (1896) — both in their way excellent portrayals. One is often required even today to fall back on the work of Neal (1822). A good overview is now given by Clark (1911).

Holland: D. Campbell (1892). Ulbach et al (1884) contains three prize essays which are all quite meagre and cliché-ridden.

Germany: Landwehr (1894), Keller (1900) (an excellent work), G.A. Pariset (1897) (concerns mainly the organisation of the church), and Arnold (1900). Cf. also Hintze (1906).

Furthermore, the *history of sects* and the *literature over emigrants*, which I cite in another connection, belong here.

The place of the Jews is discussed in Sombart (1911a; 1913d).

***

I. The Rise of Intolerance

The spirit of tolerance which wafts towards us from the traditions of the Renaissance had though only grazed the few fine and educated intellects — it had not penetrated into the masses, but it had also not yet seized those powers from which the outer forms of human coexistence are created. It dispersed like a breath, it dissolved like a cloud in the sky.

The time for the idea of tolerance had not yet come. It was as if the spirit of intolerance should first once more be given full expression before it vanishes from history. The development of the states directly through the wielding of power, which had awoken to life during the Renaissance, pushed at first towards a sharpening of religious intolerance. The begin-

---

* [Tr.: the only English translation (Llorente 1826) is abridged.]

nings of this development lay already in the centuries of the Middle Ages — the Reformation then brought all the seeds to full fruition.

What brought about the reason for the increasing intolerance was at first that which we can describe as the secularisation of the state, which logically had to lead to the *establishment of a state church*. "The earlier relationship between the Church and the secular arm reversed into the opposite; religion as a valuable *instrumentum regni* [instrument of rule] had to place its powers in the service of politics" (Bezold, Gothein, and Koser 1908, 38) — that was the simple consequence of the idea of the absolutism of princely power — once all order was entrusted in the sovereign prince, the ordering of the church's affairs could not be withheld from him. The territory of the church and that of the state now coincided, just as church power and state power, and the religious and the political were united in the concept of a Christian society.

It is well-known that this movement had set in perhaps from the second third of the 14th century at first in Spain and France as well as in a few of the city territories of Germany. And it is likewise known that it was extraordinarily reinforced and animated and only really first directed to the goal through the processes of the reformation of the church — Lutheranism pushed with inner necessity towards a national religion[157].

From the type of church which characterised Lutheran teaching came the uniformity, unity, and general dominion of the church which with the impossibility of a European or German complete reform ended up finally in the establishment of unified national churches. "Lutheranism was based entirely upon the idea of an ecclesiastical civilisation, forcibly dominated by religious ideas [...]. Thus the concept of a State Church still remains at the centre of the social doctrines of Lutheranism". (E. Troeltsch 1919, 513; 1931, 2:515-516)

If now the state churches all carried within themselves the seed of intolerance[158], then this was brought to a rapid fruition by the refashioning experienced by *the religious experience itself during the 16th and 17th centuries*. What spread there in the way of new communities of belief was filled by a hard intolerance — one more like the other. And catholicism in the struggle with the heretics of course also gained in irreconcilability and harshness — Calvin and Ignatius von Loyola depict two sides of the same thing.

Lutheranism had perhaps in its beginnings, corresponding to its inner nature, possessed a tendency towards tolerance — Luther expected that the power of the word would bring about the universality of the confession. Since this hope had been deceived, however, he also had to grasp for measures of coercion which he, like the Catholic Church, had exercised not through the church, but through the state. The culture of Protestantism was just as much a "culture of compulsion" (E. Troeltsch 1919, 738; 1931, 2:660) as the medieval one. And so Luther demanded in the end the eradication with force by the government of all the heresies disturbing the order of the Christian polity. "It is not the church as such, which punishes the rebels, and gets rid of them by violent methods, but the ideal created by the Church of the universal dominion of the only saving Truth over Society, the absolutist objective conception of truth, and the universal idea of Christian society supported by it."[159]

We then find these same views again, only gloomier by a few nuances, with the other Protestant communities of faith — Calvin pursued with terrible earnestness the idea of strict beliefs and with it complete intolerance. After he had Michael Servetus burned at the stake because of dogmatic differences, he defended his actions in a text (1554): "ubi ostenditur haereticos jure gladii coercendos esse" [where it is shown heretics ought to be coerced by the law of the sword](Calvin 1554).

And the Calvinist spirit then lived on in the Puritans — they fundamentally declined any accommodation towards those of different faith: "A Toleration is the grand design of the Devil, his Masterpeece and chiefe Engine he works by at this time to uphold his tottering Kingdome; it is the most compendious, ready, sure way to destroy all Religion, lay all waste, and bring in all evill"[160].

Likewise for John Knox heresy is a crime to be punished with the death penalty.

As then too the state-approved Protestantism in England about that time had intolerance advocated by its official representative: "Liberty of conscience is an instrument of mischief and dissettlement [...]; to strive for toleration is to contend against all government." (Glanvill 1681, 26) So it went in a polemic by a high church official from the year 1681.

These last words indicate to us, however, another circumstance which makes the brusque intolerance of this age comprehensible to us. It seems almost as if the conflicts of belief alone, as much as we understand how there settlement must have spurred the clergymen on to fanaticism, would though not have been strong enough to bring about the long and embittered struggles with which all lands were filled in the 16th and 17th centuries. As if only the devouring of the religious by the *political interests* could have exercised that enormously dynamic effect. For that is indeed in any case the character of these centuries — that in the struggles of religion always embittered political adversaries stand opposite each other; as then also vice versa all great political movements of that time bear a religious or ecclesiastical character[161]. We cannot imagine at all that a man like Richelieu should have had so much animosity towards a purely religious community as he revealed in the suppression of the Huguenots, had he in this not fought above all against the rebellious, in strong places united for resistance, political party: "ce furent là les citadelles de cet Etat dans l'Etat que redoutait Richelieu" [these were the citadels of this state within a state that Richelieu feared] (Matagrin 1905, 251).

As then equally the tensions between Protestants and Catholics in Germany, between Episcopalians and Presbyterians in England could never have assumed those intensities had the parties not been formed just as much by political as by religious views.

But where intolerance had its roots was in the end of no consequence for the reality of life — for this it was decisive that for two centuries the policies of the states were applied to making a community of religion — the recognised state church — sole ruler and correspondingly suppressing all hereticism and forcing the heretics to emigrate, if not burning them at the stake.

Thus read the programme of both the Catholic and the Protestant states.

Spain had gone first with this policy — here the tribunals of the Inquisition had first displayed their effectiveness; here the exclusion of those of a different faith was pursued most ruthlessly — in the mother country as well as in the Dutch possessions.

In *France* the hostility towards the Protestants begins under Francis I, who had initially under the influence of his sister, Margaret of Navarre*, sympathised with the reformers. But from 1535 the era of persecution began which continued for one and a half centuries with short interruptions; still under Francis I in the struggle with the Vaudois, 3,000 men were killed, and towns and villages burned down, so that Voltaire could close his description with the words: "la contrée démeura déserte et la terre, arrosée de sang, reste sans culture" [the land remains deserted, and the earth, watered with blood, remains uncultivated]†. Then (under Henry II) the Inquisition came to the land; in 1548 the Chambre Ardente [fiery chamber] opened its sessions; in 1559 the Edict of Écouen was enacted, which forced the judges to condemn to death any Lutheran simply because of their confession. The time of Henry IV signified nothing but a short armistice in this struggle for life and death which under Richelieu and Louis XIV, not only on political grounds — of internal politics, as we saw — but also on the grounds of ecclesiastical politics[162], reached its high point — in 1681 the violent measures begin, the repeal of the Edict of Nantes (1685) concludes the series of measures which were meant to eradicate Protestantism in France.

In *England*, where the Reformation had made its entrance in 1532, the Acts of Supremacy and Conformity (1558/59) and the 39 Articles (1562) were the first steps to consolidation of the state church, against which the dissenters soon rose — we must set the origin of the Puritans in the years 1563–64 (from whom at the end of the 1570s the Brownists — later called In-

---

*   [Tr.: Sombart erroneously named Catherine of Navarre here.]
†   [Tr.: not referenced by Sombart, and I have been unable to locate it in Voltaire's works.]

dependents — detached themselves); in the year 1567 falls the first proceedings against the Non-Conformists[163], when more than 200 people were arrested during the religious service in Plummers Hall. The excommunication of Elizabeth I (1569) gave on the other hand cause for sharp laws against the Catholics[164]. The conflicts between the High Church and the Dissenters were intensified now, as is well-known, more and more under the Stuarts — the effectiveness of the Westminster Assembly of Divines (from 1643)[165] is a distinct expression of their intensity — climbing even further during during the period of the Commonwealth and remaining the same during the Restoration — in 1664 a law was enacted which punished all persons over 16 years old with prison or exile who attended a church service other than the High Church one[166].

The heretics were punished with exile — with exile to the colonies in which — partly at least — the Non-Conformists found some peace — in 1617–1619 the Puritans who had fled to Holland had arrived in America and had here, on the basis of a charter granted them by the Virginia Company, founded the colony of Massachusetts, on whose pattern then later Connecticut, Long Island, and other "New England" states were formed. So here the heretics driven out of England found a home, and here they could now exercise themselves all the intolerance under which they had previously suffered — the New England states were the most intolerant states there have been. All factions which did not conform with Presbyterianism were persecuted with dreadful severity. Thus the laws of 1652 and 1657 banned the Quakers — this cursed sect whose adherents, when they were apprehended, were sentenced to death[167].

In other English colonies in which the High Church was the recognised state church, the Dissenters were persecuted the same as in the mother country. Thus in Virginia, where in the year 1631 an Act of the General Assembly decreed: "that theire bee a uniformitie throughout this colony both in substance and circumstances to the canons and constitution of the Church of England as neare as may bee"[168], hence enmity towards the Puritans, who had at first been received in a friendly way, and finally a law which decreed the expulsion of all Non-Conformists[169].

In *Germany* we experience the same spectacle. Here the cities led with sharp decrees against un-churchlike behaviour and heresy — an immediate effect of the idea of the national church taking hold more and more.

Already in 1531 in the foreword to the laws for the territory of Lübeck the concern for the purity of the teaching and the worship was established as a duty of the government, whose neglect must bring down divine judgement on it (Richter 1846, 1:149 ff.). In the same year the church laws of the city of Goslar went ahead with the penalty of expulsion against the Zwinglian and anabaptist teachings in the names of the "mayor, councillors, guilds, and community" (Richter 1846, 1:154). According to the Strasbourg church laws of 1534 the "parish secretaries" have to exercise vigilance in the name of the magistrate against deviations from the Augsburg Confession, furthermore over church attendance and participation in Communion (Richter 1846, 1:231, 1:237). The regulations in other civic church laws sounded just the same.

But the principalities did not lag behind either.

Already in 1527 the Duke of Liegnitz saw it as his duty, and indeed to avoid the fury of God, "to apply all diligence to that which concerns the salvation of the soul, that his subjects are supplied with the pure, clear word of the Holy Gospel" (Richter 1846, 1:247 ff.). Similar words are contained in the church laws of Hessen, Württemberg, Brunswick, among others (Richter 1846, 2:). In the Electorate of Saxony's General Articles of 1557 it states: "where one or more teach differently [...] he or she shall not be tolerated in His Elector's lands any longer, but be suitably penalised according to the opportunity for error, temptation, and loss." Cf. also Hundeshagen (1861).

In close connection with the rise of religious feeling in Christianity is the hostile treatment which the *Jews* have tolerated again and again in various lands since the end of the 15th century. They were driven out of Spain (from 1492 onwards), Portugal (1497), and from various German and Italian cities (in the 15th and 16th centuries).

That this policy of intolerance and persecution, as we see followed in all states during the time of the Counter-Reformation in which capitalism was in a period of strong development, must have exercised a determining influence on the formation of economic life is to be assumed from the start and will be proven by me in the further course of this portrayal in the appropriate place. Here I only want to indicate the directions in which we must primarily look for the effects of the intolerance. I think these effects are:

I. *of inner nature*: the religious feeling is raised to the extreme; the religious fanaticism experiences its perhaps strongest development. In the conflict of the various dogmas amongst each other, however, the sense for the finer nuances of religious experience were also sharpened — we observe in England in particular an usurious display of sect formation — in part as the immediate consequence of the external struggle of various communities of faith. The English sects arose especially in the beginnings of the Civil War as a reaction against the behaviour of the Long Parliament and the Assembly of Divines — when the old worship was pushed aside, however, a new one was not yet ready — "during which time, no wonder sects and divisions arrived to such a pitch that it was not in their power afterwards to destroy them."[170]

The effects of intolerance are:

II. *of external nature.* Of such we can — in a most general way — follow three in particular which became of the greatest significance for the development of capitalism:

    a. hereticism as a social phenomenon;

    b. the migrations from land to land to which the heretics were forced;

    c. the wars to which the religious disputes during the 16th and 17th centuries gave cause in all lands.

To which is added an event especially significant for England:

    d. the abolition of the monasteries and the confiscation of Church property under Henry VIII.

II. The Development of the Idea of Tolerance

At the same time during which people were tearing each other apart because of trivial differences in divine confession, the *idea of tolerance* was continuing to glow under the ashes until it finally burst into flame.

The reasons which cause individuals to tolerate foreign ideas, especially a foreign belief, can be of a diverse nature and were obviously also of a diverse nature when the idea established itself in our historical epoch. If for Ficinis or Montaigne it was religious indifference which made them into tolerant men, then by many it was in fact religious conviction itself which led them to tolerating other religions — like in the

17th century perhaps Balzac*, or Milton, or Jeremy Taylor, or William Penn. Others, like Bayle, arrived by way of logical deduction to a broad minded conception. Men like the chancellor L'Hôpital, like the "politicians" in France, longed for a policy of tolerance because they perceived the heavy political damage which grew from the falling out of nations. Still others placed the economic viewpoints in the foreground when they stood up for the tolerance of diverse communities of faith — I am thinking of men like Vauban or William IV of Holland, but also of Cromwell when he let Jews in, or of James II who suggested in his Declaration of Indulgence (1687): "persecution was unfavourable to population and to trade", or to the Most Catholic Empress of Austria who decreed for the Old Catholics who could not settle in the land "to open the way to admit them into homeland trade associations, in such cases, however, [...] to allow them residence for the time being on account of their trading business."[171] Or the general interests of the state tipped the scales, as with Frederick William I when he granted refuge to the Protestants of Salzburg[172].

We can perceive clearly in the ways the idea of tolerance won recognition in reality which forces decided in the final analysis over the formation of this human world; we can follow quite precisely how this idea remained without effect as long as it only lived in the heads and hearts of benevolent friends of humanity, how it first established itself at the moment when it was supported and promoted by strong interests, be they governmental or be they economic; at the moment also, however, where it appeared as a necessity as a result of the contradictions in which the policy of intolerance had intertwined itself.

Here is not the place to pursue the genesis of the idea of tolerance and its intrusions into the politics of modern states. It must suffice if we call to mind the most important stages which describe this triumphal procession.

You will not go astray if you call William of Orange the first prince who fundamentally stood for the principle of tolerance, and describe the *Seven Provinces* as the first state in

---

*   [Tr.: Jean-Louis Guez de Balzac (1597–1654).]

which religious tolerance formed an essential component of the policy. William IV could justifiably declare in his *Propositie ter Generaliteit* [Proposition for Generality] that tolerance was from the start "de standvastige staatkunde van de Republiek, om deze landen te maken tot eene veilige en altoos verzekerde vrijplaats voor alle vervolgde en verdrukte vreemdelingen" [the steadfast policy of the Republic, to make these countries a safe and always assured sanctuary for all persecuted and oppressed foreigners][173]. So, as Bayle expressed it, Holland became an ark which took in the shipwrecked from everywhere. And barely a hundred years after the Utrecht Union, at a time when the rest of Europe still shone blood-red from the flames of the wars of religion, a clear-eyed observer described for us the conditions in the Netherlands as follows:

> Ainsi les Juifs ont leurs Singogues à Amsterdam et à Rotterdam, il n'y a point de secte qui soit connuë parmy les Chrestiens qui n'ait ses Assemblées publiques dans la première de ces deux places.

> [Thus the Jews have their synagogues in Amsterdam and Rotterdam, there is no sect that is known to Christians that does not have its public assemblies in the first of these two places.] (Temple 1685, 194)

> L'on a de la peine à s'imaginer, comment cette violence et cette aigreur, qui est comme inseparable de la diversité des Religions dans les autres païs, semble estre appaissée et adoucie en celuy-cy, à cause de la liberté générale, dont tout le monde joüit, ou par adveu ou par connivence.

> [It is hard to imagine how this violence and this bitterness, which is as it were inseparable from the diversity of religions in other countries, seems to be appeased and softened in this place, because of the general freedom which everyone enjoys, either by happenstance or by connivance.] (Temple 1685, 195–96)

Il se peut que la Religion fasse plus de bien en d'autre pays; mais c'est en celuicy où elle fait le moins de mal.

[Religion may do more good in other countries; but this is where it does the least harm.] (Temple 1685, 198)

From the mother country the idea of tolerance was also then carried over to the *Dutch colonies* — the first agreement with a colonial populace in which, next to the monopoly on purchasing spices, free exercise of religion was expressly made a condition was the treaty with the little republic on Banda from the year 1602[174].

But in another place, without any connection to the actions of the Dutch, a second source of tolerance opened up — in the *English colonies*, at first those in *North America*.

The latter showed in addition to the intolerant Puritan states and the just as intolerant High Church states a third type —that of the states with religions on equal terms or states that were at a minimum religiously tolerant. The first colony which took up the principle of tolerance in law-giving and administration was probably that of Maryland, founded by the Catholic Lord Baltimore, whose assembly (between 1637 and 1657) decided on the following form of oath for Governor and Council: "I will not, by myself or any other, directly or indirectly trouble, molest or discountenance any person professing to believe in Jesus Christ, for or in respect of religion."[175] An Act of 1649 affirmed this constitution, as a result of which now — similar to in Holland — a colourful mix of sects of all sorts gathered in this colony[176].

The first charter for Carolina from the years 1662/63 likewise contains in Article 18 the assurance of "indulgences and dispensations" for Non-Conformists[177], and the 97th Constitution of the second charter (from 1669) (whose author is generally know to have been Locke) determined that: "Any seven or more persons agreeing in any religion, shall constitute a church or profession, to which they shall give some name, to distinguish it from others."[178] The constitution of William Penn's settlement, Pennsylvania, rested from the start on an absolutely tolerant basis[179].

Then finally the idea of tolerance took hold in the mother country, *England*, in that the year 1689 brought the Toleration Act. This indeed contained in no way a fundamental recognition of Non-Conformist religious communities (retained rather "persecution" as the rule), but settled the open struggle against the Dissenters — it let the sects hold their services under specific conditions (signing of specific articles of faith, making of the oath of allegiance, etc.). (In Ireland the persecutions and oppression of Non-Conformists continued throughout the entire 18th century — only in the year 1782 did an Irish Toleration Act become law.)

Of the larger states during the 17th century, a certain measure of tolerance was exercised only by *Brandenburg-Prussia* under the rule of the Great Elector, whose ideas were strongly formed under the Orange influence[180]. Here the Edict of Potsdam (8th November 1685) opened the doors of the Elector's land to the fugitive French members of the Reformed Church; on 2nd February 1732 the Patent was enacted for the benefit of the Salzburgers.

The general acknowledgement of the idea of tolerance as an essential component of the constitution of the state occurs first at the end of the 18th century when the reforms of Joseph II and the French Declaration of the Rights of Man followed shortly after one another. With that the epoch of high capitalism was launched, which we do not need to address here yet.

Here a word must be given again to the *exceptional position of the Jews* in constitutional law.

The Jews were tolerated and enjoyed wider rights in Holland after the Declaration of Independence, in England from 1654, in a few American states and a few German cities from the end of the 16th century or from the 17th century. But even in those lands in which the Jews were only allowed in much later, the princes found out ways to enable the Jews — at least the rich amongst them — to practise their economic activity — through the system of granting privileges and particularly through the development of the institution of Court Judaism[181].

What the great significance of the somewhat isolated penetration of the idea of tolerance for economic life rested on does not require any special emphasis — tolerance of different communities of faith in one land exercises the same influence on migration (in the opposite sense) as the persecutions had exercised on it — adherents of specific communities of faith who would otherwise have emigrated were held back in the tolerant lands, or were drawn to them if they were forced to emigrate from other lands. What Keller says about the effects of the Edict of Potsdam, that it "led to migrations and transformations which were to permanently influence the power relations and cultural conditions of Central Europe"[182], applies absolutely to the ecclesiastical policies of those days.

Appendix: The Structure of Civil Law

The decisive and fundamental transformations of civil law — both in formal and in material connection — fall in the following epoch or at the end of the period of early capitalism.

Under the command of the absolute principalities only these reorganisations were carried out:

I. *Commercial Law*, which had rested up to the 17th century predominantly on common law, began to be codified. The first state codifications are the French Ordonnance de commerce (1673) and the Ordonnance de la marine (1681). In Germany up until the end of the 18th century only isolated commercial law institutions were regulated by national laws[183], while the first greater codification took place through the Prussia national law of 1794.

II. *Financial Law* especially was prescribed in numerous state and civic financial laws during the 17th century and adapted structurally to the demands of the time. In the middle of the 18th century there were 48 financial laws[184].

The decisive step which the new financial laws made was the transition to a general law no longer differentiated on social status.

Thus, for example, the *Brandenburg* financial law's Article 4 specified: "All those as undertake to write out a bill of exchange, whether they be alike of male or female sex, prince, count, baron, courtier, noble, academic, or military personnel, whatever condition, social status, and service they want, shall be bound just as firmly as the merchants by the financial law, without difference or exception".

If you want to properly grasp what took place here for the first time in the area of law formation, then you must discern in the new laws a *depersonalisation of the law as well*. But as stated, just as in many other areas of cultural development, we observe during the epoch of early capitalism only the *first beginnings* of the new culture.

III. A not inessential reorganisation which was intended to serve the interests of capital was experienced already during the period of early capitalism by the legal system in the *procedural area*. The main points were as follows: a) mercantile documents were granted an as firm as possible power of evidence and an as firm as possible effect of obligation (depersonalisation!); and b) the executive process or the executive power of the debt instrument was developed. Of course in the interests primarily of commerce, for which the ordinary procedure was unbearable. It was of the greatest benefit for commerce when it obtained by the clear presentation of a debt at least temporarily the enforcement against the debtor. The executive power of the debt instrument stretched from the trading cities of Tuscany and Lombardy over all Italy and further from the 15th century onwards. At the same time the executive process was also developing[185].

IV. That the *reception of Roman law* in *Germany* did not take place in the "capitalist" interest, indeed probably had little connection at all with economic events and demands, seems now more and more to be the view of the legal historians[186]. In fact, why would only Germany have performed this change from economic grounds, not France, not Holland, not England, who at the time had a much more highly developed economic life. Also to be considered is that the areas of law principally serving capitalist development — law of the sea, commercial and financial law, particularly corporate law — only arose to a very small extent from Roman sources, in any case their development was not thanks to a "reception of the Roman Law", but at most gradually took on Roman legal ideas.

Even for Italy they now seek to prove that the new (Roman) law school was for the longest time a purely academic movement — the revival of classical antiquity by the law scholars was begun in the 12th century from purely scientific interest, which after jurisprudence then carried on the scholasticism in the domain of philosophy[187].

Section 3: Technology

Chapter 29: The Spirit of Technology

We are accustomed to considering the centuries which include the Renaissance and Reformation, Counter-Reformation and baroque — despite or perhaps directly because they have achieved the greatest things in the area of formation of states and religions, in philosophy, poetry, painting and sculpture, in short all areas in which the human spirit can give full expression to itself — to be unfruitful in all things which were of a technical nature (despite Leonardo da Vinci!). *Because* they are so great — for we conclude (perhaps prematurely) from the experience with which our day provides us that periods in which technology collected "laurels" could only be small in other human endeavours. And we recall the sad fates which famous "inventors" had in those centuries — starting with Berthold Schwarz* who introduces our period, up to Denis Papin† who closes it, and believe that we can feel the hate therein which people of that time had against all technological innovators, or even the fear which they had of it. And in fact we find the aversion and the contempt of the time towards the inventors also expressed often enough in bare words. Like when Pascal summarised the mood of his contemporaries in the sentences:

Ceux qui sont capables d'inventer sont rares: ceux qui n'inventent point sont en plus grand nombre, et par conséquent les plus forts. Et l'on voit que pour l'ordinaire ils refusent aux inventeurs la gloire qu'ils méritent, et qu'ils cherchent par leurs inventions. S'ils

---

* [Tr.: Berthold Schwarz is a legendary alchemist credited with discovery of gunpowder and allegedly executed for it.]

† [Tr.: Denis Papin built a steam powered boat, which was then destroyed by a guild of boatmen.]

s'obstinent à la vouloir avoir, et à traiter de mépris ceux qui n'inventent pas, tout ce qu'ils y gagnent, c'est qu'on leur donne des noms ridicules, et qu'on les traite de visionnaires. Il faut donc bien se garder de se piquer de cet avantage, tout grand qu'il est; et l'on doit se contenter d'être estimé du petit nombre de ceux qui en connaissent le prix.

[There are but few that are capable to invent, there are very many that are not capable, and therefore by consequence the greater number; and 'tis commonly seen they refuse to the inventors, the Glory they deserve, and that they seek by their Inventions; if they go on resolutely and will have it, and go to undervalue those that cannot invent, all they get for their pains, is, That they are called by ridiculous Names, and are termed Dreamers: One must therefore take care of boasting of this advantage, as great as it is, and one ought to rest satisfi'd to be counted one of the little number of those that know the value of it.] (Pascal 1670, 315–16; translation from 1688, 241)

Or when Joachim Becher, who had to know, cautioned:

So that you should not consider all speculators to be dandies and fools, as those who have a screw loose, but you must know that by such people the world will be done a great service, and that they lose thereby their effort, time, and money just so that they might serve the commonweal. (J. J. Becher 1682, 94–95)

But as distinctly as the enmity of "public opinion" towards the "inventor" speaks from these and similar words, it would be wrong though to now conclude without further ado from them and other signs that it was a period poor in invention. Yes, in contrast, the tension which we can read from those remarks and from conduct in accordance with them must lead directly to the assumption that *strong currents of an inventive nature* passed through the period. And we then also find this assumption confirmed when we occupy ourselves somewhat more in-depth with the technical literature of those centuries. It is astonishing, for example, how many texts during

162

the 16th and 17th centuries contain depictions of the machines to be found and of their use. Just to offer the most important works of that old technical literature, I name:

- Biringuccio (1540; 1942);
- Agricola (1556; 1912), the well-known work which occupies itself for the most part with machinery;
- Besson (1578);
- Ramelli (1588; 1994);
- Zonca (1607);
- Zeising (1607);
- Caus (1615);
- Strada (1618);
- Branca (1629);
- Böckler (1673).

Then we have from the second half of the 17th century a series of texts which can be described as inventor books or books of inventions or even as collections of suggestions for new inventions.

The most famous of those I have already mentioned is that of Joachim Becher (1682). A few English counterparts to it are:

- Somerset (1663). Often reprinted, most recently in Dircks (1865).
- Hale and Petty (1691).
- White (1773) (17th century).

With regard to this literature, it is no wonder at all when we hear the contemporaries talk of an "age of inventors", a "projecting age" of which, for example, Defoe speaks in his well-known tract[188].

And really, when you take the trouble and pull together everything in the way of significant innovation which has been added to the stock of technological knowledge and practice from the Middle Ages perhaps to about the middle of the 18th century, then it results in a quite impressive series of truly important inventions and discoveries — the reader will find such an overview in the following chapter.

But we must on the other hand guard against equating those centuries perhaps with our own time somehow because of this wealth of inventions. Instead we must, if we want to assess properly the place of technology in the epoch of early capitalism, be conscious of the *deep difference* which prevails between the technology of that time and that of today — of course also of the difference which exists between the technology in the age of early capitalism and the technology in the pre-capitalist period. It appears to be an extraordinarily appealing task to work out the special peculiarities of the acquisition and possession of technological capability in the period of the Renaissance and the baroque — especially to follow the turns which the style of technology went through from the Middle Ages to the Renaissance and again from the Renaissance to the baroque; to follow how the peculiarities of this strange and great age were reflected quite distinctively in the technology just as in all the other cultural phenomena. The following lines contain a first, tentative attempt at tackling this task, but could of course only indicate the points which are essential to hold in view, and wants — like so many observations in this work — only to indicate the paths in which the researchers will have to travel in the next lifetime.

Above all, *the technology of those centuries was lacking the exact scientific foundation* in the same way that all earlier technology had lacked it. Certainly we have considerable starts at a scientific underpinning, but only starts though. We must not let ourselves be deceived by a phenomenon like Leonardo da Vinci[189], who admittedly, at least in his principles, was an altogether modern researcher and inventor. Modern in the sense that he "speculare", that is, that he wants to observe and understand, to investigate empirically and follow the causes, to look at the special cases and consider what is common in them. That he was in particular also striving for the quantification of all human knowledge. "No human investigation can be called true science if it is not given by mathematical demonstration," he taught. And: "anyone who spurns the extreme certainty of mathematics nourishes themselves on confusion and will never impose silence on sophistic sciences which produce nothing but an eternal clamour."*

Causal thinking is a strict precept for Leonardo: "Necessity is the mistress and guardian of nature. Necessity is the funda-

---

* [Tr.: Sombart gives no specific references for either these or the following quotes of Leonardo.]

mental idea and the inventor of nature and bridle for it and eternal law."

"Nature does not break its laws."

"Nature is under the compulsion of the rational principle of the law which lives poured out within it."

Leonardo, however, is also modern as a technologist and inventor in so far as he endeavours to anchor all his technical ideas in the natural sciences: "At first the theory must be written then the practice afterwards." "Those who love the practice without science are like the pilot who enters a ship without wheel or compass — which then never possesses certainty as to where it is going. Always the practice must be built on good theory."

He derided those who sought a perpetual motion machine just like those who practised black magic: "Oh researcher of constant motion, how many vain plans have you created in that same search. Join with those who seek gold thus."

But Leonardo sticks out as a quite singular man in a world foreign to him. Most other "inventors" did not want to take this strictly scientific path at all. And he himself also could not have fulfilled at all these high demands which he put forward in his teaching. For that the scientific insight into the relationships in nature was far too meagre. Now they were only beginning to lay the first foundations for the new world view; now they were only composing the first movements of the new world system — scientific mechanics was only founded after Leonardo's death. And the men who were putting together this massive edifice were only rarely concerned with practical technical problems. There are exceptions when we encounter in the 16th and 17th centuries theoretical researchers amongst the inventors, like perhaps Otto von Guericke or Christian Huygens. The paths of the natural sciences and technologists, which had crossed in Leonardo and run next to each other perhaps for a time (I think of men like Jacques Bresson amongst others), separated again for the next centuries — on the one wandered Galileo, Newton, Leibnitz, on the other Becher, Hautsch, Papin.

The world of technology, of inventors, was still the old, colourful, cheerful, scary world in which men had lived before the scientists reduced it to rubble. You still applied your own spirit and your own imagination to nature, and heaven and earth were animated for the mind of the observer. From these beliefs in the animateness of nature flowed all those mystical ideas and imaginative activities in which precisely the period which we are surveying here, namely the deeply religious 17th century, is so rich; that is even valid for those practical technologists who worked as court or town "engineers", and to whom we are obliged for the many collections of the technical discoveries of their time — the greatest "technologist" of the 16th century, Agricola, populated the mines, whose operations he described for us so expertly, with "demons" who preyed on the life and health of the miner. Many called their treatises "Magia naturalis" [magic of nature] and left a large scope therein for the miraculous. The great Kepler explained ebb and flow as the breathing, sleeping, and waking of the monster gifted with reason which he imagined the earth to be.

Magic is indeed nothing else but the expression of this belief in the animateness of nature, to which is adjoined the other, "practical" belief — that the living beings which are housed in nature, in particular also the lower nature demons, associate with men and can be influenced in their behaviour by men.

> "Now fills the air so many a haunting shape,
> That no one knows how best he may escape."
>   (Goethe 1832, 314; 1890, 491 Act V)

From the belief in the animateness of nature follows likewise the belief in the regulation of man by the position of the stars and the conviction that human fate can be read from the stars — astrology.

From the same belief grew the witch craze — the belief in women who had concluded a pact with the devil so as to inflict harm on their fellow men by all sorts of hocus-pocus.

Alchemy based itself on the same belief, and in the closest connection with alchemy stand the inventors of that time, and the technology which was created by these inventors.

From the medieval world was taken that mysterious veneration, that devout awe before all technical ability which we found in the handcrafts.

Also the busying oneself with firearms, that art whose development then actually really brought about the new age, and precisely this was considered in the first centuries to still be a secret art which was understood by a few much sought-after people. It is well-known what a circle of legends slung itself about Berthold Schwarz[190] because he was the first to know how to work with guns and how to prepare gunpowder. This unconscious awe before the mysterious was then brought by those who came later, as one can say, consciously into a system. And this system was then *the art of invention*. You must read a text like that of Joachim Becher, who lived at the end of the 17th century and was considered one of the greatest inventive geniuses of his age, to be able to perceive this peculiar magic with which they loved to clothe all technological processes and practices:

> "In particular the common fluid sand, as a womb for minerals, has great love for the metals, in such a way that they set about with it to always come out improved."[191]

> "The rising waters [...] have a warm spirit in themselves, on account of which they are called lively spring water; but the waters which fall there or must be raised are dead waters."[192]

Yet "fills the air so many a haunting shape":

> "thus I do not want though to dismiss the secret power of a few characters, words, and talismans. We have even in our time experienced the story of a physiologist in Vienna, by the name of Lutz, who stayed with General Heuster and in Padua dug for the famed great treasure, how far he got with it I read from his own hand, how he exorcised everything, except forgetting the sleep-devil who after that sent him sleeping to his death".[193]

That was the age of which it has been fittingly said that it "sought quintessences and preferred to venerate mysterious powers than study them"[194].

The important conclusion, however, which they now drew from this view was that the art of invention could not be learnt, that to bring about technological innovations you did not have to conduct scientific studies, that instead "inventing" is a mysterious process, and that you have to see the ability for it as a gift of the heavens.

Becher (in which we encounter the most perfect type of those inventors of the baroque) expressed these ideas in the preface to his "Närrischen Weisheit" [Foolish Wisdom] thus:

> Although dear God has placed various arguments and documents of his kindness, providence, and existence visibly in nature, the Donum inventionis [gift of discovery] though is not the slightest thing with humans [...] Here there is no respect for the person or profession: kings and peasants, learned and unlearned, heathen and Christian, pious and evil are gifted with it [...] The divine grace has also given me some of this gift, just as my writings demonstrate. (J. J. Becher 1682)

"Here there is no respect for the person or profession" — and in fact, if we survey the series of men to whom technology in essence owed its further development up until the middle of the 18th century, then we find among them the representatives of every class and profession, of which most had undertaken absolutely no "specialist study". But when one of the typical inventor types of that time actually "studied" "physics" or something similar, then you can be certain that his inventions owed their existence only for the slightest part to these studies — one thinks perhaps of men like Réaumur or Cornelius Drebbel.

I will name at random the following "outsiders" who during the 17th and 18th centuries made important inventions (added in brackets):

Princes: Uncle to Charles II of England, Prince Ruprecht (a metal named after him, raft engines, and lifting machines); Ferdinand II of Tuscany (condensation hygrometer); Leopold von Dessau (steel ramrod).

Nobles: Count de Lauraguais, de Montaney, Count de Milly (improvements to porcelain manufacture); de Montbruel (hydraulic water raising machine); de Lille (type of sickle); de Solages (steam engine — as one among many); Marquis of Worcester (see below); we also find adventurers like Cyrano de Bergerac among the inventors of their time.

High Officials, Officers, Scholars, Doctors, etc.: Gerard Desargues (theory of conic sections); Maurice de Sachse (chain boat navigation); Bon, President of the French Court of Auditors (improvements in silk manufacture); Rector John Beal (barometer variations); the philologist Johann Heinrich Schulze (light images); the student of theology Lee (knitting machine); the doctor Andreas Cassius (purple of Cassius); the doctor Eirini d'Eirinis (asphalt); Benjamin Franklin (lightning conductor); the Swedish colonel Christian Treuleben ("the art of going under the water").

Priests, Monks, etc.: the Jesuit Athanasius Kircher (magic lantern, aeolian harp); the Jesuit Bonami (enamel); the Minim Marinus Mersennus (submarine); the Capuchin Anton Maria Schyrleus of Rheita (terrestrial telescope); the monk Perignon (champagne!); the pastor Cartwright (mechanical loom); the abbot Soumille (the unwinding of silk); the curé Langruet (improvement of the silk mill).

Craftsmen, Workers etc.: the carpenter Perse (tidal mills); the worker Dugaure (the first odourless pit drainage); the worker Humphrey Potter (control of the steam engine); the barber Arkwright (spinning frame); John Harrison (marine chronometer).

Next to these pastors and barbers we must then of course also imagine the *technician* as inventor — that is, the clockmakers invented the new watch mechanisms, the dyers the new dying methods, the weavers the improvements of the loom.

Here then we must also name those men who we have looked on as the fathers of our professional engineers and professional chemists, and who united to a certain degree theory and practice — the "court architects", urban planners, the "war engineers" in the retinue of the great Condottieri, to whom the responsibility for all "technical" work was given, and who then wrote those treatises over war and fortress architecture, over machines and mining, over waterworks and "milling" structures[195], which we have already encountered frequently and which we will encounter again several more times because they actually form the best source for the history of technology. To what extent these practical technologists had themselves invented the structures and mechanisms and processes they describe in their books is in most cases unable to be established with certainty. In essence they will surely have been merely compilers, which a few of them admit to without further ado. Others, like the craftsmen in the individual trades, will have demonstrated already in the current sense so to speak "professional" — if also without much scientific ballast — improvements to this or that mechanism.

You can call them everyday inventors while the time was still characterised by those lucky persons to whom the donum inventionis was gifted through God's grace, and who now profited on their pound and dedicated their entire lives to inventing, who also did not limit their activity perhaps to a single branch, but invented wildly without hesitation in all areas. The inventor types actually quite characteristic for that time, especially for the period of the baroque, are though those inventors of a lot of things, a few of whom I have named already. It teems with them.

There is "a Swabian by name of Paul Weber in Vienna [...] he was a very ingenious man in all sorts of manufactures, particularly in varnishes and air pipes"; there is Isaac von Nickeln, a good lens grinder who understands the art of raising mulberry trees and silkworms; there is Fausto Veranzio (about 1617), a clergyman who published a dictionary in five languages and also turned his mind to and wrote about mills, bridges, grain cleaning, flooding, and the construction of Venetian fountains[196]. It is those people of which Neudörffer wrote of one (Hans Hautsch) that he was "an inventive and artful man" (Neudörffer 1875, 217). There is James Young, a writer in Edinburgh who invented an engine for writing in 1684, in the following year a new lock, a few years later a weaving machine ("an engine for weaving, never before practised in any nation, whereby several kinds of cloth may be manufactured without manual operation or weaving looms")[197].

This baroque excess of inventiveness then peaked in such peculiar phenomena as Somerset, Réaumur, Papin, and Becher.

Somerset, second Marquis of Worcester (1601–1670). He invented various types of seals, a new script (type of stenography), a type of telegraphy shooting with cannons at night, an unsinkable ship, a boat to travel against the wind and tide, a floating fortress, a garden on the Thames, artificial fountains, a brake mechanism, a water-powered weighbridge, a water clock, a lifting engine, a transportable bridge, a transportable fortress, a universal script, various alphabets, a fire lighter, an artificial bird, a cipher, a waterworks with the use of ebb and flow, a revolver ("how to make a pistol to discharge a dozen times without one loading"), repeating weapon, mitrailleuse, the steam engine ("an admirable and most fascible way to drive up water by fire"), a security (alarm) lock, a new weaving technique, the flying machine ("how to make a man to fly"), a clock that keeps going, a calculating machine, ship raising machine, etc., etc.

A. R. F. de Réaumur (1683–1767) we find equally strong as inventor of the 80 degree thermometer as well as innovator in the area of iron making, porcelain making, dyeing, and mirror manufacture; he also wrote, however, a promemoria [aide-memoire] over rigging and its durability, and over the methods to get hens to lay at all seasons and to breed large; he invented a process of conserving eggs, etc.

Denis Papin (1647–1714) invented or improved amongst other things the air pump, a powder machine, a diving ship, a stove heater, a water-raising engine, a centrifugal pump, ventilators, wind shelters, the high pressure steam engine, the steamship; was interested in the artificial forcing of flowers; presented to the Royal Society of Sciences in London (1685) a plan for a power transmission; wrote (1681) the *Traité des operations sans douleurs* [Treatise on Operations without Pain], etc., etc.

And then there is the most delightful of them all — the magnificent fellow, *Johann Joachim Becher* (1635–1682), from whose ingenium [innate character] the inventive thoughts sprayed and burst like sparks and flares. All the things he "invented"! An instrument to separate the raw wind or goat hairs from wool; a weaving instrument for weaving with two people in one day 100 ells of linen; a wooden instrument for knitting fine woollen stockings, a day a pair; a silk filature or spinning instrument which spins fine silk with few people in great quantity; the perpetual motion, physico-mechanical clocks which kept going in one place continually without being wound; invention to build watermills in all places; a new waterwheel for a ship mill; a fantastical salt, not acid and not alkali and yet both at the same time, also giving off when distilled a strange spirit and solvent of fantastical operations; making iron from common potter's lime; making tar from hard coal; an invention to keep a drink, be it wine, beer, or cider, in fermentation for quarter of a year; a world script; a world language; a sort of regiment piece ... which a man can carry and a horse can leisurely carry a number of, a species of musket; a thermoscope; a new stove which saves on wood ...

How such heads invented is easily imagined — in essence with help of their imagination, unsystematically, unfoundedly. Their imagination drove them to indulge themselves in all directions without proper sense and without actual plan:

> There are eight things over which scholars and the curious strive, namely:
> I. the lapis philosophorum [philosopher's stone];
> II. liquor alcahest [universal solvent];
> III. making glass soft;
> IV. eternal light;
> V. a linear hyperbola in a concave mirror;
> VI. finding the gradus longitudinis [degree of longitude];
> VII. the quadratura circuli [squaring the circle]; and
> VIII. the perpetuum mobile [perpetual motion].
> Whoever now has money, time, and desire can find occasion herein [...][198]

And all too frequently the path taken did not lead to the goal — because they suddenly had to come to a stop on it. Thus there were a number of inventions in that period which stood close to a solution which today any student of physics or chemistry would "fully invent" in a few weeks like schoolwork, and which yet at the time remained incomplete because their completion was dependent on the accident of lucky thought which did not want to occur. Or the attempts failed because some error was made in the construction of the machine of which the inventor was not aware — thus Papin suffered a lot that he was not a trained mechanic. His frequent failures often depended only on a triviality — too weak a screw or bracket. You must consider that to a man like Papin the theory of the firmness or load-bearing capacity of materials, etc. was still as good as unknown.

But obviously — what those men were lacking in scientific education and training they knew how to replace by a blossoming imagination whose creative power we can still barely imagine. Those centuries preceding the Enlightenment in which the epoch of early capitalism falls are indeed of an un-heard-of fruitfulness of invention and construction in all areas of human culture — it would be strange if this creative power had not also shown itself in the area of technology, since the age, as must be established now in conclusion, was actually filled by a strong and tenacious inventive will.

While the manner by which the pioneer develops his nature in the area of technology is still shrouded at base in medieval mysticism, this *determined wish for technological progress* is that which the intellects in the period of the baroque in particular described as peculiarly "modern", which likewise connects them with our time, just as their habit of thought made them kindred with the Middle Ages.

How was this inventive will given life? If *Defoe*, who had already as a contemporary tossed up this question at the time, gave the answer to it — because the business losses during the time of the Commonwealth and the Restoration forced many people to improvements of their efforts, to think of new pos-sibilities for economic existence — then this answer seems to narrow to me. Above all, I would like to believe that it con-tains in the last analysis an explanation only for a time in which new forces were already pushing for the improvement of technology — forces which burst forth from the tension of capitalist interests, and which then became right up to our day the actual driving forces for technological progress, but which in all the centuries in which we previously already saw the inventive will unfolding were not at all or not quite present embryonically, and which, as it appears to me, even in the late period of the baroque of which Defoe speaks, barely had the outstanding significance which they later ob-tained and to which we thus, even in this epoch, let alone in the days of the quattrocento* and cinquecento, can trace back the at the time indubitably already strongly active inventive wills.

We must thus ask what lifted the medieval traditionalism which not only did not want any technological innovations, but bristled against them with all its power — what lifted this

---

*   [Tr.: 15th century as a time of Italian art and culture.]

persistent traditionalism, which would never have been capable itself of furthering technology, above itself before the business interests, before the striving for profit inherent to capitalism pushed for its overcoming?

I see three *sources from which the inventive will could have arisen and had to have arisen*, even before capitalism generated it, all three of which on the other hand were fed from the fountainhead of the striving for eternity from which all life of the new Europe flowed. One source is the general urge of the age, at least the closing 15th and the 16th and 17th centuries, for knowledge of the world. It is *the Faustian trait of the age*, as you could also say: "Dr Faust stood as if shut out from loving what was not to be loved, he strove for it day and night, took on the wings of eagles, wanted to explore every ground on heaven and earth", it states in the oldest Faust book*.

> That I may detect the inmost force
> Which binds the world, and guides its course.
> (Goethe 1808, 34; 1890, 13 Act 1 Scene 1)

This striving leads one person into the heights of speculation, another into the valleys of experiments and the devil's arts. And here resided the inventors and discoverers, particularly when combined with every dark urge for knowledge was the indefinite yearning for reshaping, for new forms of life, new worlds — that yearning which found its expression as much in the journeys of discovery of those days as in the dreaming up of new governmental forms, as much in Drake and Raleigh as in More, Campanella and Vairasse.

But of course, real interests must come to the help of that pure ideal striving so as to give it the great penetrating power which it actually possessed. And there we hit now with closer examination on two points of interest from which even in the pre-capitalist period at the end of the Middle Ages an ardent endeavouring to subject nature, to control the forces of nature and with it an incessant search for new technological possibilities burst out ever anew and ever more powerfully with com-

---

*   [Tr.: Sombart does not provide any more precise reference.]

pelling necessity — I mean the interest in the possession of money and the interest in the successful conduct of war.

From the *urge for money* alchemy grew, which itself would again become the mother of numerous inventions and discoveries; from the same striving arose the significant reforms in the area of mining technology; the same striving for gold sent men out into the ocean and forced progress in the realm of navigation.

Likewise the *development of the armed forces* systematically promoted technological progress[199]. Here a sphere of human activity had emerged for which the fundamental striving for innovation and improvement likewise became a necessity, just like the fundamental persistence of the traditional was in all other areas of culture. We can quite distinctly follow how all progressive technology of that time set up camp around these two kernels — the alchemical texts, the fireworks books and other artillery texts, the mining books, and the seaman's texts are the first signs of the urge for a clear overview of the technical possessions and above all the yearning for expanding these possessions, for the improvement of the technological capabilities.

What arose from those endeavours in the way of important reshapings in the area of technology during the half millennium from the middle of the 13th to the middle of the 18th century, I will put together in the following chapter. We will learn there that the technological innovations essentially increased certainly only from the beginning of the Renaissance period and then quickly in number during the 17th and 18th centuries; that amidst these innovations there were a few of fundamentally great significance which gave the development of capitalism, already in its early period, a wider latitude, and a few to whose appearance the origin of the capitalist economy seems directly bound.

Here the *general nature of technology* during this time may be characterised to the effect that we establish that the technological capabilities and knowledge also remained during the epoch of early capitalism built on the same foundations on which they had rested up until then. That is to say that technology remains in this period still (1) empirical, and (2) organic.

The purely *empirical orientation and founding* of technological capabilities applies still for almost the entire 18th century, and indeed both for chemical and mechanical production processes. A few examples — I select the most important chemical industry, iron and steel-making, and the (next to the textile industry) most important mechanical industry, shipbuilding — may that suffice.

Iron and steel industry:

"Up to now the opinions of researchers are divided as to what actually goes on in the way of a change when iron is transformed into steel, whether merely the excess sulphur must be isolated or whether you must furnish the iron with several combustible parts if it is to become steel. In the first case you would have to get rid of the sulphur through alkali salts; in the last case, however, horn, bones of animals, coal dust, soot and other things which contain a lot of combustible material would have to be added to the iron in part". (P. N. Sprengel and Hartwig 1773, 5:187)

"You recognise a good coal by whether it is not too heavy or too light, when tapped or broken in two it gives a certain (!) clang, inwardly gleams and has more of a bluish-black than a moorish-black colour to it; which is all better recognised from experience than can be described." (Bergius 1775, 2:166)

"One has at Baruth found well by experience that it is better when the coals are lit by a fire made below, that the bellows are not started immediately, but the walls of the oven are warmed up to the thickness of three feet roughly in the following way". (Bergius 1775, 2:168)

"One names the following phenomena and conditions which show with the high ovens, and from which one can judge whether coals or ore are to be added" (a list of outward symptoms follows). (From the description of the iron works at Baruth.) (Bergius 1775, 2:170)

Shipbuilding:

The Jesuit priest and teacher of mathematics at the seminary in Toulon, Paul Hoste, writes in his *Théorie de la construction des vaisseaux* [theory of vessel construction] (emphasis added):

> You cannot deny that the art of shipbuilding so necessary for the state is of all arts the least developed. *Chance has so much to say with shipbuilding that the ship built with the greatest attention usually turns out very bad, while those ships which are constructed very casually are often the best.* Thus the great ships are mostly entirely unsuccessful, and amidst the merchant vessels you find more good ships than in the royal fleet. (Hoste 1697, preface)

In the year 1757 Daniel Bernoulli indeed published a note in which he scientifically established the conditions for static stability. Even 30 years later, however, English authorities in shipbuilding were incapable of fathoming the cause of the faulty stability of three of their ships. That lay in part because the theoretical treatises of the time assumed to high a mathematical and technical knowledge to be understood by practitioners — between these and the technological science a chasm yawned which would only be bridged in the next age. Thus it said in Euler's 1776 appearing *Théorie complète de la construction et de la manoeuvre des vaisseaux* [complete theory of the construction and manoeuvre of vessels]: "Although forty years have already passed since the mathematicians worked on this matter with some success, there discoveries were though accompanied by such difficult calculations that the mariners have hardly made use of them." (Euler 1776, preface) Cf. Ahrens et al. (1896, 9:600).

While technology was still based empirically as before, insofar as it was not built on the scientific knowledge of nature, it was though no longer absolutely traditional. Rather technology began categorically to become rational in our time period. When you grasp the concept of empirical knowledge as the opposite to scientific procedure (and not — as linguistic usage also allows — as the opposite of rational procedure), then you can say in summary that the technology of the Middle Ages was empirically traditional, that of the period of early capitalism was empirically rational, whilst modern technology is scientifically rational. The expression of rational technology is associated in our imagination most easily with agriculture. Here there was (from the middle of the 18th to the middle of the 19th century) a period of "rational agriculture" which likewise inserted itself between the periods of traditional and of scientific agriculture. Technology as a whole developed quite similarly. And if you want to characterise the period of early capitalism by form of technology with one phrase, then you must say it is *the age of rational technology.*

The persistence of early capitalist technology under the influence of living nature, whereby it preserves its *"organic"* character, is conveniently proven where I describe the material developmental tendencies of production and transportation technology.

Chapter 30: The Progress of Technology

Preliminary Remarks

In the following the attempt will be undertaken of pulling together those innovations in the area of *instrumental* technology which became of decisive significance for the course of economic life. This significance can come in many different ways — an invention can be important in that it transforms the production process in its outer forms and thus makes new forms of operation necessary, demands other types of labour, moves the site of production, and the like. Its effect can, however, also be indirect — in that it increases the degree of productivity, in that it in turn promotes an expansion of production, alters the division of profits, and the like. The effect of an invention can also in this respect be significant in a roundabout way when it is brought to fruition by other branches of production or non-economic processes are defined in a decisive way, which then itself is again of influence for the formation of economic life. In turn production technology can be influenced by other technologies, and vice versa — think perhaps of the close connections which exist between the improvement of iron production technology, the improvement of weapons technology, and the development of the modern state, or of the connections between measurement technology and transport technology. I discuss similar more distant relationships between technology and culture in Sombart (1911b).

Where the invention whose effect we observe originated from does not matter for our aim — it does not matter thus whether the invention is new, that is, has been made for the first time, at the moment in which it comes into use during our period; or whether it was already well-known for a long time on earth without being used by the European peoples. So if the Chinese 1,000 years before or the Arabs 500 years before had already employed a process which for instance came into use in Europe during the 15th century, then this process in our sense signifies just as well an innovation as a process of which perhaps the peoples of classical antiquity made use, but which only comes into use again in the period of the Renaissance.

The period of time which the following overview encompasses reaches from perhaps the end of the 13th century to the middle (or the end) of the 18th century.

The material for this overview was collected from numerous technological works — the value of the overview can also consist exclusively in
the proper selection of actually significant inventions. With the specific
revolutions which technology experienced in our time period, I will
name the sources explicitly from which I have drawn. In general there
is, however, no sense in my citing with each innovation I mention where
I took the information from. It suffices if I ensure that with each important occurrence I have compared various informants with one another and given the preference to the most trustworthy in the case
where no agreement arises. In addition it does not matter so much at all
for our aims to be able to date an invention exactly to the day and hour
— it is quite unimportant to know whether the rifle with flintlock was
invented in 1630 or 1640, or the ribbon loom in 1590 or 1600 — it suffices (in most cases) completely to be able to define the point in time
approximately, that is, within a stretch of two or three decades.

Sources and Literature

The *sources and literature* often merge into each other in this area
as in so many others — the older works of literature are our best
sources. It is a matter either of special treatments — then I will name
them in their place — or of *general portrayals of the history of invention* or of the state of technology at a given point of time. Of these I will
name the most important right here.

We possess one source of unsurpassable quality — of course in essence only for the inventions made in *England* from the beginning of
the 17th century — in the *collection of patents for inventions* which
reaches back to the first years of the 17th century. It has previously to my
knowledge only been exploited in individual English monographs for its
historical content. Its use is made easier by the index volume (specifications) which order the inventions to the number of many hundreds alphabetically by the trade and within the trade chronologically. A
complete example of the collection is found in Germany in the Library
of the Royal Patent Office in Berlin.

An important group of literary source works are formed then by the
old "Histories of Inventions". The fame of being the first "History of Inventions" belongs to the (otherwise of quite little use) work of Polydori
Virgilii, *Urbinatis De rerum inventoribus libri octo*; first published in
1499, then often, in the 16th century alone 39 times (I use Virgil (1576)).
Beckmann (1780; 1777) and particularly Poppe (1807; 1837) are not yet
to be surpassed for the older period — they are directly indispensable
for the period of time in question here, because the primary sources
from which they draw are in part not to be obtained at all. Fournier
(1877) contains a rich, if also disordered material. The value is occasionally restricted by the chauvinistic tendency of the author to trace back as
many inventions as possible to Frenchmen. Ahrens et al. (1896) also
contains many special investigations of an historical nature. The historical part is certainly the stepchild of this great work. Feldhaus (1910)
distinguishes itself through the effort to substantiate the origin of indi-

vidual inventions — mostly of a military or transport technology nature — by reference to sources.

In *lexical* form, which was very popular previously, particularly in the 18th century, the following works are drawn up: Macquer (1766), more a commercial lexicon, usable; Duchesne (1776), usable; Busch (1802), a sort of encyclopedia, as it contains all possible "inventions" even of a purely intellectual nature — astronomy, inscription, parades, evaporation, leprosy, etc. — often without critique. But quite usable anyway next to the other older works, since like those it references literature and sources which today have long since disappeared, and since it surpasses in wealth of material most of the other books with like content. By the same author, Busch (1797) is supplemental to his other work — a sort of annual report from the areas of chemistry, physics, and technology. Ure (1839) is usable for us in its historical introduction. Recently another alphabetically ordered lexicon of inventions has appeared, Feldhaus (1914), a source-critical, very valuable work. Now the best complete work.

A few compilations in *chronological tabular* form serve for a quick orientation: Feldhaus (1904), Darmstaedter and Du Bois-Reymond (1904), enlarged second edition, Darmstaedter et al. (1908), is the second edition of the same under a different title.

Then the *textbooks for mechanical and chemical technology* come into consideration, of which we possess a number from the 17th and 18th centuries. I will name them with the depiction of the nature of business in our epoch in the next volume.

A good bibliography of old technical and technological texts of the 16th and 17th centuries as well as the literature referring to them is found in the appendix to Dircks (1865).

I. Production Technology

1. General Developmental Tendencies

Even the technology of the period of early capitalism, we can already establish, bore the stamp of a transitional phenomenon. In general it continued to move on the same tracks along which it had run during the Middle Ages — its essential feature remained empirically organic. What differentiated it from earlier technology by comparison is not so much the fact that here and there attempts at a fundamental reshaping are found — first attempt at a scientific mechanical engineering!, first attempt with the coking process in the iron industry! — as rather the circumstance that the knowledge and abilities, that in particular the procedures which they had had at their disposal since time immemorial experienced in this epoch an extraordinary process of improvement up to the point where "the quantity changes into quality", that is, where a strong improvement of a technical principle had practically as good as an effect as a fundamental innovation.

An overview of the various elements of technological capability will confirm that.

The *material* which they made use of for producing goods remained essentially the same as before — just that it experienced an enrichment through the discovery of new materials in the lands of the newly opened-up parts of the earth. The material belonged as before almost exclusively to the plant and animal kingdom, and the most important material which was taken from the mineral kingdom — iron — remained closely related to organic material in as much as it needed for its production a great quantity of auxiliary material which in turn had to be delivered by the plant kingdom (wood).

A sentence like this, which is found in a recent historical depiction (Lindner 1901, 6:407), is absolutely misleading: "The iron industry had developed in Germany from the Netherlands (?) towards the end of the 15th (!) century so far that the true iron age had begun". Precisely *that* characterised the period of early capitalism, that it is absolutely not an "iron" age, but, if you will, a "wooden" age. Think, for example, that the rolling of the calender, that the first steam engines, that all ships, bridges, beams, girders, that most larger vessels were made of wood. In the middle of the 18th century in all of England something over 17,000 tonnes of iron was produced (as much as a blast furnace produces on average in four months today). In Germany it was not much different; not even in Sweden, the classic land of iron extraction at the time. I refer as well to my depiction in the next volume of this work. Cf. also Sombart (1903, 3–48).

Even the forces which were used for goods production and goods transportation remained for the time being the same as before — man and animal; water and wind. Since the use of steam pressure as the driving force (of which the machinery books of the time report) probably retained for the time being still the character of a playing around, and even the "weight mill", by which gravity had to take over the role of the usual forces (illustrations and descriptions of such weight mills are found in Böckler (1673, 6–8, Fig. XXIV-XXX)), were barely permitted to find a propagation worth mentioning. But what distinguishes our age from the previous one is the extraordinary improvement in the use of these forces. This improvement was at first effected by the increasing replacement of human and animal power by the elemental forces of water and wind; then, however, above all by the setting up of elaborate mechanisms which first made a better use of the forces possible. The most important technological innovations which we have to mention lie in our period thus in the formation of more perfect *processes*.

I. The *mechanical* processes continued to develop massively in the direction of the machine principle (which itself is as old as humanity) — above all the movement machines experienced in this period a fundamental further improvement, whilst in the area of work machines less success was achieved, which contributed to preserving the "organic' character of technology.

In order to make the progress of machines clear, I want to pick out from the confusing jumble of individual facts[200] two series of developments which seem to me to be especially important in the history of machines — the development of the mill and the development of power transfer.

1. You can describe our period, especially though the last two centuries, directly as the classic *age of the mill*, if by that you understand a structure which harnesses water power (to a lesser extent also wind, animal, and human power) for various uses through transformation into the turning motion of a wheel. The oldest form of factory, which certainly had significance next to the manufactory as a form of business in the period of early capitalism, is indisputably the "mill" (hence why the English for a long time even during the period of steam called their factories "mills"). The most popular force for driving a mill was, as already mentioned, water power, which you used either as the natural force of flowing water or as the force of artificially falling water after pumping it up to a higher point.

Thus, for example, in the city of *Augsburg* and in its surrounding area there was towards the end of the 18th century 137 mill wheels or "gears" present: 74 outside the city on the canals flowing from the Lech, 46 within the city, 17 on the Senkelbach — of them only 44 for grain mills. See the list in Nicolai (1783, 8:94-96 Beylage IV.14, Cf. 8:18).

In the absence of water, you harnessed the wind or instead you set up step treadwheels for animals or men or horses.

I will list here the most important types of "mills" operated towards the end of our period according to the aims which they served, and reserve for a special part of this overview going deeper into the processing machines or machine tools coming into use in these various "mills".

Grain mills: long known as water and windmills, experience in our period various improvements — the Dutch windmill appears in the middle of the 15th century.

Barley mills: first barley mill 1660 in Saardam.

Oil mills: as the so-called Dutch from the last half of the 17th century.

Sawmills: driven by water — with one saw already in the Middle Ages, with several from 1575 — driven by wind from the end of the 16th century; 1663 a Dutchman erected a sawmill driven by wind on the banks of the Thames, with whose help a man and a boy were capable of sawing as many boards as 20 men did previously; but — this method was later given up again: "lest our labouring people should want employment." (A. Anderson 1787, 2:354)

Turning mills: for turning of numerous objects, amongst others the metal goods of tin workers — driven by water already during the Middle Ages, 1661 improved;

Drilling mills: for drilling wood or boring metal tubes — already with Leonardo da Vinci and Biringuccio[*].

Hammer mills: for hammering of large pieces of metal — from the 15th century — I will yet speak about the trip hammer as well as the pounding hammer, which only depict special types of hammer mills.

Metal cutting mills: from the 16th century.

Metal grinding/sharpening mills: first (?) described by Zonca (1607, Fig. 360) — they existed though much earlier — according to Stetten (1779, 1:141) a grinding/sharpening mill was in use in Augsburg already in the year 1389.

Wire mills: the name Drahtmüller [wire-miller] appears in Nuremberg already before 1400; whether the machines for hand drawing wire were also called wire mills is doubtful; in any case the water-powered wire mills first come into use in the 15th century; in 1532 they are described by Eobanus Hessus (1532) as a marvel; Biringuccio describes a wire mill with water power (1540, 141; 1942, 380).

---

[*]   [Tr.: see page 163.]

Brass mills: thus were named those organisations in which both brass hammering and wire drawing were dealt with by water power; one spoke of "mill hammers" and "brass hammers" with which a "wire-wheel" was connected. The fate of such a brass mill in Thos by Fürth from the year 1484 is described in Nuremberg's Annalen. See Roth (1800, 2:76 f.). Cf. also the illustration of the "brass hammer" by Weigel (1698, 315).

Bellows mills: structures with waterwheel power in order to set bellows in motion (for metal smelting) — already mentioned by Jacobus Marianus (15th century), see Beck (1900, 289). Illustration of a "bellows mill" in the 17th century in Böckler (1673, 26, 146–47, Fig. 78).

Paper mills: 17th century; first (?) illustration of a paper mill in Zonca (1607, Fig. 376).

Powder mills: 16th century (Biringuccio 1540; 1942), roller mills were probably already using waterwheels for power in the 15th century.

Paint mills: by Leonardo da Vinci in his Codex Atlanticus, Fig. 682 fol. 60v, according to Beck (1900, 451).

Silk thread mills: first (?) in Zonca (1607); spread in Italy in the 17th century; see below.

Ribbon mills: from the end of the 16th century; see below.

Cloth mills: fulling mills from the 14th century — in 1389 a rolling mill in Augsburg (Stetten 1779); cloth cutting with water power from the 17th century — the first mill in England in 1684.

Mangel mills: from the 17th (?) century — description and illustration of a mangel mill in Böckler (1673, 20, Fig. 80).

2. The other moment in the history of machines which I want to pursue here was the *development of power transfer*, which in our period made a few quite extraordinary and fundamentally significant advances.

    a) The art of transferring power by "*translation*", that is, through the interlocking of several toothed wheels, was already well-known — it was, however, very much improved in the centuries of the Renaissance — the gearwheel mechanisms became more intricate and as a result more effective.

In our epoch now, however, fell the invention of a series of new and important kinematic installations — now the following were added to the previous mechanisms:

b) the *flywheel*: it is found in the technological works of the 16th century — with Leonardo da Vinci (the first?), Agricola (1556; 1912), Lorini*;

c) the *belt drive*: according to Beck (1900, 306), first by Vittorio Zonca;

d) the *line shaft transmission*, that is thus a device by means of which several processing machines are set in motion by the same engine. The invention of this extraordinarily important equipment falls in the period around 1500 — Agricola (1556, Bk. 8 Fig. 22; 1912, Bk. 8 Fig. 22) describes line shaft transmissions which had been in use by the Saxon iron workers for a long time already — how long, he does not say — Biringuccio, however, speaks of the transmission as a new invention, from which we may conclude (since Biringuccio was also quite familiar with German conditions) that the innovation falls in his lifetime.

II. The *chemical* processes remained at first the same as those which had formed the technology of the craftsmen and apothecaries during the Middle Ages and were enriched only by the fantasies of the alchemists who were developing a scientific chemistry. These, and with them the radical innovations which the chemical industries (in the broad, not the usual sense) experienced thereby, belong, however, to the following epoch. What chemical technology had to show before the middle of the 18th century in the way of specific, admittedly very significant achievements (in the powder, iron, and silver production in particular), I will list further below. Here I make do with pointing the reader to the few works from which he is capable of making out the general situation of chemical knowledge at the close of the early capitalist epoch: Justi (1760); and Kunckel von Löwenstern (1767).

---

* [Tr.: probably Buonaiuto Lorini (1545–1611), see Beck (1900).]

2. The Decisive Progress in the Individual Areas

a) Agriculture

The technological progress in the sphere of agriculture was very small in this period. The "paterfamilias literature" in which the knowledge was set down contains, apart from a few recollections by the farming writers of the elders, nothing but the learning of the Middle Ages. "The idea of the age, which sought quintessences and preferred to venerate mysterious powers than study them, also understandably dominated the farmers who were moreover richer in faith than other classes" — with these words Fraas concludes his portrayal of agriculture and forestry in this period[201].

At any rate we notice a few beginnings of more rational economic management at least from the 16th century — the insight into the significance of crop rotation begins in Italy about this time — in 1550 Bernard Palissy taught that soil becomes infertile through continuous cultivation, because all soluble material is thereby removed*. The Ricordo d'agricoltura (Tarello 1567) ascribes the "invention" of crop rotation to a certain Tarello.

In the same century fall the first attempts at a rational live-stock breeding — in Germany Fugger (1578) and Löhneisen (1609) were epoch-making.

The improvement of tillage begins with the invention of the seed drill which is traced back either to Giovanni Cavallina (1500) or to Locatelli (1663). The in this case extraordinarily widely differing information on the date of origin is presumably to be explained by the earlier year being the point of its first being mentioned, the later indicating the permanent use of the new process.

The writings of Olivier de Serres[202] portray a significant progress in agricultural science and agricultural technology. The creation of artificial meadows goes back to him; he was the first to deal with fruit farming in-depth; he is the first since antiquity to describe and recommend drainage again, etc.

---

* [Tr.: Sombart is possibly referring to Palissy (1580).]

But that all remains just beginnings. Even France, which at the time had the best agriculture, and which was envied by other nations for its agriculture[203], only begins in the second half of the 18th century to reduce the uncultivated land which up to then had taken up more than half the land, only then did they begin the cultivation of fodder plants, only then did they devote more care to the care of livestock when they began to concern themselves with fertiliser. All significant progress of technology in our period lie more in the area of industrial production.

b) Industry

i) Mining and Iron Making

Mining during the Middle Ages and up into the 17th century was in essence mining for iron, copper, zinc, and silver ore. Only towards the end of our epoch did coal mining obtain a greater significance. Both mining technology in the narrow sense and iron-making technology had been throughout the entire Middle Ages at an altogether primitive level. The general rule with mining was probably opencast mining or a simple tunnel mine. The means for obtaining the ore consisted of the usual hand tools of the pick axe, and for extraction buckets and carts which had to be carried on the back or lifted by means of a simple hand reel. This primitive technology remained fundamentally unchanged through the entire Middle Ages except for one advance — the *tunnel mine* which was developed in Bohemia in the 13th century and had become important there already towards 1300, whilst it first found widespread use elsewhere in the course of the 14th century. As is generally known, by a tunnel in this sense we are to understand horizontal or gently rising passages which are driven from below the mine face so that the mine water is led away from the points above and air supplied to the places.

All other important advances in the old mining technology belong to the 16th century or even only to the 17th century. Among them is the *introduction of machines*[204] which could be used for the raising of mine water, which was of decisive importance for the development of silver mining in particular (because they enabled its continuation to greater depths for the first time and thereby stopped the abrupt exhaustion of the deposit).

For driving these machines they made use from the 16th century on more and more of treadwheels and in particular the horse engine — the first horse engine used in mining was that for the St Andreas mine in Joachimstal[*].

The extraction machines of which Agricola gives us illustrations are already imposing structures. Important inventions in the area of mining technology then before the 18th century are:

1. the earth and mountain drills (Palissy 1580);
2. exploding with powder — in 1613 the first attempts are made with it. What is lacking is a safe tamper, which is found in 1687[205];
3. the tram and later railroads — tram roads, that is, hollowed out wood, stone, or even iron tracks, existed in German mines from the 16th century (described in Agricola (1556, Lib. 5; 1912, Bk 5)); wooden rails were first used in England towards the end of the 17th century — from 1671 in the Newcastle coal mining — "whereby the Carriage is so easy that one Horse will draw down [to the coast] four or five Chaldron[†] of Coals, and is an immense Benefit to the Coal Merchants."[206]
4. The invention of the ventilation machines is erroneously attributed to the 18th century (1721 or 1734) — Agricola already knew of three different varieties.

The processing of ore was also carried out up to the year 1500 in a primitive fashion: "they have pounded the earth in mortars with their hand to a coarse powder and ground this, with such handmills as they needed for grain, so fine that the silting and washing was possible. For washing the silt they made use of a sieve."[‡]

At the beginning of the 16th century (1512–1519)[207] the important invention of the (wet) stamping mill and the concen-

---

*   [Tr.: Jáchymov in the Czech Republic.]
†   [Tr.: a chaldron is an English dry measure used for coal, fixed by law in 1678 to weigh the equivalent of 2,670 kg.]
‡   [Tr.: not referenced by Sombart.]

tration of poorer ores through slurrying occurred. This invention was important for two reasons — it made human power superfluous and brought about a saving of ore.

The actual *smelting of the ore* now, however, experienced around the turn of the 15th century and in the further course of the 16th century a decisive transformation which became of far-reaching significance for all economic development — the production of iron underwent the transition to blast furnaces; and the production of silver experienced the introduction of the amalgamation process.

Up into the 15th century only the so-called direct *iron production* by means of the so-called bloomery process was known.

After that easily reducible limonite and siderite were smelted in an open furnace (the bloomery) with the help of blown air, and the iron clumps occurring by reduction were hammered hard so as to remove the melted down slag, then split into several pieces which were stretched out.

The important progress which was made in the 15th century consisted of the *invention of iron casting* and the *transition to blast furnaces* — that is, to the so-called indirect iron production by means of which pig iron was first produced and from this wrought iron and steel was prepared. The use of water as a driving force formed the starting point of both the invention of iron casting and the transition to pig iron production. Water power was put to use principally in two directions — for the movement of iron hammers in the drawing out of iron clumps — the so-called trip hammer[208] — and for the movement of the bellows (which were originally made of leather, from the 17th century of wood[209]). With the smelting of the ore the effect of the strengthened air supply was such that the iron was no longer received from the furnace as a tough, waxy mass which had to be wrought under the hammer, but as a fluid metal which, set, flew apart under the hammer. The insight gradually came that you could pour this fluid metal into forms, but that it could also, when it was smelted for a second time, and indeed in an open fire, be transformed into a soft, malleable metal which was more even and in many cases also better than the iron obtained since then in a bloomery[210].

The great significance of these technological innovations lies in the following:

1. through the blast furnace process the smelting of ores that were difficult to melt, like those which form by far the greatest part of the stocks on earth, became possible for the first time. But that meant, of course, an extraordinarily large expansion of the scope for production, which was increased still further by the greater size of the blast furnaces;

2. iron casting made possible a much quicker and cheaper production of larger pieces, which came very much into consideration particularly with the production of artillery which was only really beginning now;

3. the use of water power effected a restructuring of the location of industry — the iron industry moved from the heights of the mountains, out of the forests into the valleys;

4. this new process placed entirely different demands on the organisation of operations — in the place of numerous, small smelting fires, new stately furnaces with iron works buildings, waterwheels, bellows, stamping engines, and heavy hammers. All this can be seen more precisely in the next volume.

Towards the end of the 15th century the victory of the blast furnace operations over the bloomery operations was decided in principle. The naturalisation of the new process was not completed suddenly, however, but rather gradually — in France and Italy the blast furnace operations began to take root at the beginning of the 16th century, in Germany and England in the middle of the 16th century, in Sweden at the end of the 16th century. But the entire 16th century and also the 17th century are still fuller of bloomery operations.

The other material which was needed both for the production of pig iron and for the preparation of wrought iron and steel remained in our epoch wood.

Of no less importance for the course of economic development than the just described alterations in the technology of iron smelting was the revolution which the *technology of silver production* experienced around the middle of the 16th

century through the introduction of the amalgamation process.

The extraction of silver from ore was obtained up to then through the accumulation of silver in lead and its separation from it through the so-called forcing process.

The revolution consisted in the use of mercury for the purpose of separating silver by way of amalgamating, hence the name: amalgamation process.

The *amalgamation process* was invented in the year 1557 by Bartholomé de Medina in Pachuca, and came into practical use from 1566 on a greater scale. In 1571 it was transplanted to Peru. The process consisted (or consists — since even today a large part of the American silver is obtained by means of this cold amalgamation or patio process) as follows[211]:

i. The ore is reduced to a fine powder in an *arrastra* or mill.

ii. Then the powdered ore is spread out on the court of amalgamation, the "patio", which is paved with flagstones, and sodium chloride, sulphate of iron and calcined copper ore [*magistral*], and mercury are mixed in which it.

iii. The various components were previously (up to 1793) trodden into a mixture by people and are now trodden by mules.

iv. The reaction taking place in the heaps of ore forms an amalgam of silver which is later separated from the powder by washing.

v. The silver and mercury are separated by distillation.

The great advantage of this new process consisted in that it needed almost no equipment and above all no combustible material at all. *But it thereby made the processing of silver ores on the barren heights of the cordilleras possible for the first time.* Its disadvantages are certainly considerable. They exist in the very long duration of the process, which takes 3–6 weeks, and in the heavy use of mercury. The losses of mercury with this cold amalgamation amounted to 10 to 20%, on average one and a half times the obtained silver. The silver production was thereby dependent upon mercury production, as will be shown by figures in a fitting place (see Chapter 36 below).

But these disadvantages faded in importance opposite the advantages mentioned and could not hamper the quite enormous significance of this new process. The world owes to it, as we will yet follow quite precisely, the flood of silver, the strong reduction in the value of silver, and thus the great increase in prices of all goods, all of which contributed not the least to the quick victory of capitalism.

<u>ii) Metal Processing</u>

The *processing of iron* experienced a few important changes: wire-pulling developed into fine wire-pulling (16th century); the tinplating of sheet steel developed (first half of the 17th century); the rolling mill spread in the 17th century (after it was mentioned for the first time by Salomon de Caus (1615)); steel cutting works joined them; in 1738 John Payne invented the rolling of sheet steel, etc. With that a few innovations in iron processing arrived which at first and above all played a large role in the fabrication of weapons — the drilling machine for the boring of gun barrels had already been invented before 1500, it was described by Biringuccio.

We must observe also that there was already in the time before the 19th century a *hammering machine* which made possible the working of man-size blocks of iron as happened particularly in the manufacture of anchors[212]. The smithing of clumps of iron by trip hammers was succeeded by machine hammers which weighed 300–500 kg and performed two strikes a minute[213].

As important as these and other advances in the area of iron processing were, their significance disappears opposite the changes which the *processing of precious metals* underwent. I do not mean the fact that a new gilding technique as developed in the 17th century — Gouthière under Louis XV: "l'inventeur de la dorure au mat" [the inventor of matt gilding][214] — I am thinking rather of the revolutions which the processing of precious metals into coins underwent — in the 16th and 17th century they transitioned to mechanical coin minting. And indeed in the following stages:

1. in 1552, the drafting mechanism of the Frenchman Brulier[215];

2. in the second half of the 17th century, adjustment mechanisms;
3. at the same time, cutting machines;
4. at the same time, embossing units (minting presses);
5. in 1685, knurling and crimping mechanisms invented by Castaing, after an edge-embossing machine had already been in action in England under Cromwell.

What wide-reaching significance this transition to mechanical coin minting must have had is obvious — it first made possible an ordered coinage system, without which at least the high capitalist economy is unthinkable. Certainly I want to repeat here once more that the full effect of this revolution in minting technology falls essentially in the following periods, and that it belongs to those advances in technology which introduced the period of high capitalism — in addition, see Chapter 26 of this volume. I must mention these important inventions in this place, however, since they all fall in the epoch of early capitalism — perhaps their long ineffectiveness rests in the deliberate intent of influential authorities.

iii) The Textile Industry

Our economic historians still gaze as if entranced at the advances of technology which the textile industry was accorded during the 18th century whenever they concern themselves with technology. Now it should certainly not be denied that the technological revolutions which the textile industry experienced in the 18th century (and which we do not have to acknowledge yet at this point) became of decisive significance for the course of economic life. But they are still only to be considered and consequently assessed in connection with the other ground-breaking innovations at that time. On the one hand you should not forget that all the epochal inventions of the 18th century which have contributed to the revolutionising of the textile industry were already fundamentally made in our epoch — the three rollers of Paul[*]!

The *spinning process* was essentially perfected in 1530 by the fixing of the pedal device to the spinning wheel which had been turned up until then by hand. Other improvements to

---

[*]   [Tr.: Lewis Paul (d. 1759), inventor of roller spinning.]

spinning occurred in the 17th century[216]. Special machines for the unwinding of silk had existed since the 15th century. Becher[217] invented a "silk filatory or unwinding instrument" — better than that used in Bologna — simple, noiseless, "quite easy to move, thus that one person can quite conveniently at once unwind a thousand strands, on the other hand the Bolognese machine must be driven by water." (!)

Mechanical *weaving* was invented in Holland at the end of the 16th century (according to others in the year 1600 by Anton Moller in Danzig (Darmstaedter and Du Bois-Reymond 1904)) in the form of the *ribbon mill*. According to the descriptions which we possess of the ribbon mills from the middle of the 18th century, up to which point in time we learn of no improvement, it was already a complete machine which fundamentally was not missing any single component of the mechanical loom. It looked like a loom, but no shuttle is thrown through with the hand, instead the loom weaves itself — everything is performed through the movement of a wheel (gears). The ribbon mill can have 10, 12, 16, 20 and more gears. Here a single person works, and it creates at the same time 10, 20 and more ribbons, each of a different colour; "and the worker weaves without having to perform a single weft by hand, without understanding the ribbon-making, without making an effort."[218]

But even the *wide mechanical loom* had already been invented at the end of the 17th century. Our old friend Becher tells us that he invented a "weaving instrument for weaving with two persons in one day a hundred ells of linen". "And this instrument I thus invented on the type of Harmelen silk ribbon-mills, but this is the difference, that it can weave as wide a linen as you want and that it weaves it much righter than you can with your hands." (1682, 14 f.)

Of course, it seems as if these inventions remained unused in most lands for a longer time. Not the least because the authorities forbade by law their use in the interests of craftwork masters — the inventor of the ribbon mill was (so it is said) placed under permanent arrest by the *Dutch* general assembly, but the work not retained. In the years 1623, 1639, and 1661 the general assembly expressly forbade the use of the ribbon mill and all things made on it; the same ban was enacted by the government of the (at the time Spanish) *Netherlands* in Brussels. In *Germany* the ribbon mill was forbidden by the decree of 5 June 1685 in the entire German empire, and by suchlike of 19 February 1685 in the

Austrian lands. In 1719 these bans were renewed. The bans admittedly did not seem to have been strictly enforced: "thus the matter remained and the ribbon mills were retained *here and there* unhindered." In 1765 an edict in the *electorate of Saxony* recognised the status and expressly allowed ribbon mills, indeed allocating a reward for their installation (1775).

We are precisely informed over the history of the ribbon mill in *Switzerland*. Here a wool weaving master brought the first loom to Basel from Amsterdam in the year 1668. Already in 1669 Zurich noticed that the mill loom for ribbons had been introduced to Basel, Schaffhausen, and Chur. Soon the guilds' laments arose, from which we learn that the new invention had actually come into effect. "An unskilled person takes away the work of 16 masters", etc. See the in-depth documentary portrayal in Geering (1886, 609 f.). According to the expert opinion of a committee of enquiry which the Basel parliament appointed in the year 1670 to examine the complaints of the braiders' guild, the ribbon mill shall at the time already have been tolerated in Bavaria, Vienna, Chur, Schaffhausen, Feuerthalen, and Zurich.

The hand loom experienced a fundamental and practically significant improvement through the invention of mechanically moved *flying shuttles* by John Kay (in 1733)[219].

An entire series of mechanical arrangements existed for the *finishing of fabric* — there were fulling mills, as we have already seen, in Augsburg already in the 14th century; cloth cutting machines are described by Leonardo da Vinci (there were several systems for them); nap raising machines as well — both in da Vinci's Codex Atlanticus. Likewise we find descriptions of machines for scraping woollen cloth in Zonca (1607, Fig. 377). Mangles for smoothing fabric, driven by horses, likewise also existed in the 14th century (Stetten 1779, 143). That they were transformed in the 17th century into mill form, we saw above when we familiarised ourselves with the various types of mill.

The introduction of *printing fabrics* to Europe, however, became of quite special practical significance. You cannot call it an invention, since "the painting or printing of woollen fabrics à la Siamese had been practised in India and East Asia for centuries already when the East-India companies brought this Indian material to Europe at the beginning of the 17th century" (Geering 1903, 399). But here the use of this technique, which was also soon improved fundamentally by the introduction of the plate press, was something new. The imitation of the Indian fabric printing begins perhaps at the same time (towards the end of the 17th century) in France, in England, in Augsburg, and in Geneva — "the first demonstrable cotton printer in Europe of the Indian sort in indigo and madder was founded in the year 1678 by the merchant Jakob ter Grouw in Amsterdam"[220]. The great practical significance of this technological innovation, of which I spoke, lay in that (as we will see) the printing of cotton offered an especially favourable field for the activity of capitalist enterprises, that they quickly grew into large firms oriented to expansion *and through that* exerted a strong spur on the development of the basic textile trades — spinning and weaving.

Knitting also experienced at the end of the 16th century the decisive transition to purely mechanical technology through the invention of the stocking frame knitting machine. This machine of the theology student William Lee was already a monstrously complicated mechanism with hundreds of needles and has in principle not been overtaken as far as the present day. The later inventions were insignificant, "and primarily directed at production of new patterns and the so-called circular and tube looms on which tube-like knitwear without seams is produced (knitting machines)"*. The knitwear machine entered into use in the course of the 17th century — the first *Manufacture de Bas au métier* [manufacturer of stockings by trade] in France was established in 1656[221].

When we yet consider that during the 16th and 17th centuries fundamental changes in dyeing technology took place — in the middle of the 16th century indigo dyeing started[222]; in 1630 scarlet dyeing (nitric hydrochloric acid and cochineal) was invented — then you must admit that the technological innovations which the textile industry had already undergone before the 18th century were in extent hardly left behind by later ones, and that if the effect of the inventions of the 16th and 17th centuries were not as dynamic, this must have its cause in other circumstances. At any rate we will see that even the inventions of the early period offered cause for many an economic change, which in the textile industry at this time are hence always of quite special and general importance because it was the leading industry in the epoch of early capitalism.

---

*   [Tr.: not referenced by Sombart.]

iv) New Industries

A not unimportant influence on the shaping of economic life was exercised by technological innovations in our period, especially during the last two centuries, in that they provided the occasion for the introduction of entirely new industries or at least for such a decisive rearrangement of old trades that this came close to a new start. The newness of industry can lie in that an entirely new material is processed for end purposes which are already known, or in that new items of consumption arise, or finally in that an old consumer good with the same material is, however, produced in a fundamentally different form.

It suffices if I simply list here the most important of those new branches of industry whose founding falls in our epoch:

A special category is formed by those branches of industry which were connected to new raw materials imported from the colonies, amongst which the most significant were:

1. The *chocolate industry*. It develops at the end of the 16th century in Italy; spread towards 1650 into France — in 1659 David Chaillon received a privilege for the manufacture and sale of chocolate (E. Fournier 1877, 2:366 ff.). In England the first establishment of a chocolate house takes place in the year 1657.

2. *Production of sparkling wine*. It first became possible after the stopping of bottles with cork was invented. This invention which is connected with the making of sparkling wine is ascribed to the cellar master Father Dom Pérignon of Hautvillers Abbey around the year 1670. At the beginning of the 18th century champagne was already known in wide circles (E. Fournier 1877, 2:311).

A series of new branches of industry were started by the old core of the textile industry:

3. The *knitting of stockings* which was supposed to have been invented in Spain in the first half of the 16th century — Henry VIII possessed a pair of silk shirts which were a gift from Spain. In 1564 the first stocking maker in England is mentioned — William Rider. *How* quickly the knitting process itself was then improved again, we have already seen. Knitting was significant in that it was practised by women and children and displaced the old tailoring by men.

4. The *weaving of tapestries* had already been well-know for a long time when it was much improved at the beginning of the 17th century by Peter DuPont in Paris and brought to the highest degree of perfection in 1667 by the Gobelin brothers (Guiffrey 1886; Gersprach 1892; Fenaille 1903 was not accessible to me).

5. The *lace industry*. From the end of the 15th century braided lace (oldest bobbin lace) was domesticated in Spain, Italy, the Netherlands, and Germany. Proper development, however, first started in

the 16th century from Italy both for sewn and bobbin lace. In *Italy* (Venice!) the technology of lace making underwent in *punto a rilievo* [point in relief] its noblest development. One then sought to domesticate this relief lace made with the utmost delicacy in the other lands too — in 1664 Colbert had (as we will yet follow more precisely in another connection) Venetian workers come to *France* in order to raise the indigenous coarse lace making and thereby actually first founded properly the famed French lace industry.

In 1561 Barbara Uttmann domesticated the bobbin lace making in the Ore Mountains (Bury Palliser 1865).

6. The *underclothes industry* — arises in France from the 16th century. At the time the flat iron and a number of methods for making underclothes were invented. Very amusing are the countless "Livres de lingerie" [books of lingerie] which appeared between 1530 and 1597. Extracts from them in Fournier (1877, 2:212 ff.).

And then a motley quantity of various industries — firstly a few making use of wood:

7. The *piano industry*. According to the latest research Bartolomeo Christofori, instrument maker in Florence (1655–1732), was the inventor of the piano in so far as you see this as a new principle in the use of the hammer technique. The new invention was made well-known in 1711 in the Giornale dei letterati d'Italia.

8. The *coach industry*. What we today call coaches, that is a covered wagon whose box hangs on straps or springs is no older than three or four hundred years. The name coach is supposed to originate from the Hungarian village of Kocs, and wagons from there which bore the described features shall have first been put into use towards the end of the 15th century (Feldhaus[*]). According to others (Poppe) the first real "coach" is traceable to Spain in 1546, the first in England in 1580. According to a third (E. Fournier 1877) the coach on springs was a patented invention of M. Dufresny which came from the year 1686. In order to do justice to all opinions, we can say that there was certainly not a coach industry before the end of the 15th century, that it certainly developed quickly, however, in the 17th and probably already in the 16th century — in any case we already encounter many covered state coaches in the retinues of the great during the 16th century, whose production — whether "coach" or not — gave employment to a new industry.

In the 17th century we see the elegant coaches with large glass windows spreading everywhere. "In Münster the coach of the Duchess of Longueville had stood out and caused many German princesses to imitate it; they brought the Polish queens to Warsaw, and Christine of Sweden's travel procession, for the most part rented coaches which Louis XIV paid for, gave half of Europe cause to praise the miracles of glass, gilded wood, and damask cushions." (Gleichen-

---

[*]   [Tr.: Sombart does not specify which of Feldhaus's works. Likewise for Poppe in the following sentence.]

Russwurm 1911, 143) Cf. with the named informants in Beckmann (1780, 1:390 ff.).

9. The umbrella industry was a member of various branches of trade according to the material it handled. Its genesis falls in the beginning of the 17th century — in 1622 the umbrella was a novelty in Paris; somewhat later the parasol came into vogue. Around the middle of the century Evelyn noticed it in Montpellier; in 1675 it attracted the attention of the philosopher Locke on a trip to Paris (E. Fournier 1877, 2:228 ff.).

10. The *lamp industry* developed likewise from the 17th century — at that time the first lamps, the reverbierer [reflective] and soon afterwards the fontaine [fountain] lamps, were invented (Poppe 1837, 234 ff.).

11. The *mirror glass industry* took up the invention of the Frenchman Thevart for pouring glass sheets (end of the 17th century).

12. The *porcelain industry* is in Europe probably no older than two hundred years. The claim that porcelain was manufactured in Europe already in the 16th and 17th century, which is put forward by Fournier (1877, 2:331 ff.) (so as to also in this case again trace an invention back to the French), does not seem proven to me. It remains thus for the time being that Johann Friedrich Böttcher (also not Ehrenfried Walther von Tschirnhaus) is the inventor of porcelain, and that the founding of the first European porcelain manufacturer is set in the year 1710 at Castle Albrechtsburg by Meissen. An exact investigation over the beginnings of the porcelain industry in Europe which also addresses the question over the priority of invention is found in Doenges (1907, 13 ff.).

13. The *wallpaper industry* concerned itself at first with the production of leather wall coverings which were already made in *Spain* in the 12th century by the Moors. The leather wallcovering industry spread from the 15th century into all the European lands; it had during the 17th and 18th centuries its headquarters in *Germany* in Augsburg. The art of preparing paper wall coverings originates from China; it arrived in Europe probably during the 17th century, where wallpaper was demonstrably produced from the 18th century. In the beginning they painted the paper with the help of stencils, until in 1760 Réveillon replaced stencil and collage painting with the printing process used in calico printing. The wallpaper industry first came to proper development with the invention of continuous paper (1799), since until then the sticking together of long strips from rectangular sheets was very arduous (Exner 1869, 16 ff.). Further literature is also cited in Exner (1869).

II. Military Technology

The advances which weapons technology made in our period deserves a special mention. They are of great significance not only because of the influence which they have had on the transformation of organisational forms (the artillery and arms manufacturers and factories are, as we will see, the first large businesses of modern society); not only because of the enlivening effect which weapons manufacture exercised on other important industries (iron-casting and with it the entirety of steel-making experienced their greatest advancement through the development of gun technology); but rather those advances are above all naturally of such wide-reaching significance because of the momentous consequences which they brought with them for the entire reformation of the state.

I will content myself with compiling in the following the most important inventions in chronological order and refer for further detail to the *literature on the history of weapons*, of which I have compiled a selection in Sombart (1913b, 214).

The *invention of gunpowder* and its use in gun technology is veiled in an impenetrable darkness which, it seems to me, becomes all the more dense, the more the research occupies itself with the problem. It is now known that the scholars of the 13th century — Roger Bacon and Albertus Magnus — were already familiar with gunpowder, and it is accepted that it had also been used in Europe since the 14th century for the purpose of shooting.

The granulated powder is first mentioned in the "Feuer-werksbuch" [firework book] (1450). Rollers powered by waterwheels for the easier and safer grinding of the powder were probably already in use in the 15th, certainly from the beginning of the 16th century — Biringuccio (1540; 1942) knows of them already.

The portrayal of powder in larger quantities begins, however, probably only in the 16th century — until then you only had a small stock prepared by the roaming pyrotechnists and gunmakers when a feud directly threatened. The first powder mill is traceable to Spandau in the year 1578.

The *beginnings of firearms* likewise reach back to the 14th century — at the time they knew of and used already handguns (the matchlock gun) and artillery (cast cannons).

The advances in handguns are described by the following:
- in 1515 the German wheel lock;
- in the middle of the 16th century, rifled barrels;

- in the course of the 16th century, the musket, whose weight was reduced by Gustav Adolf (1626) to 5 kg.;
- between 1630 and 1640, the flintlock or so-called French lock; and
- about the same time, the bayonet.

Artillery technology developed in the following stages:

- in 1471 Louis XI introduced the iron ball in place of the stone ball;
- the 16th century brought the improvement of the gun carriage,
- the rear loading cannon;
- the cast cannonball;
- the bomb filled with powder (shells) (which were first thrown in 1588 into the city of Wachtendonk);
- the rifled cannon barrel (of which the first news originates from the year 1591);
- in 1627 the first use of cylindrical shells;
- in 1692 the shooting with shells from cannons was invented; and
- from the middle of the 18th century, the cannon barrels were fully cast (the 1740 horizontal drilling machine of Geneva's Maritz).

The change in the *technology of fortress building* since the arrival of firearms was also of not insignificant meaning for individual branches of commercial production.

III. Measurement and Orientation Technology

Again we stand before technological events whose entrance we must observe as essential for the fulfillment of the capitalist economic system when we think of the epochal inventions which were being made in the area of measurement technology from the end of the Middle Ages to the end of our period.

Of the three basic units which we measure — length, time, and mass — only the first two come into consideration here. Not as if the *determination of weight* was not likewise of the greatest importance for the development of economic life as well as cultural life in general — but in the period which we are surveying no really meaningful inventions were made in the area of weighing technology. The scales in both their forms, the spring and the lever balance, are ancient. And the refinement of the weighing mechanism which led to chemical scales or to precision scales falls in a later period. They belong again to those inventions which set up the transition to high capitalism, especially in that they made modern chemistry possible.

In contrast the technology for both time and length measurement showed very significant advances directly in the centuries with which we are occupied.

We call instruments for *measuring time clocks*[223]. Antiquity knew sun and water clocks (in part quite elaborate), the Middle Ages (from the beginning of the 11th century in the monasteries, those nurseries of rational lifestyles, mostly as night and alarm clocks) mechanical clocks. The clocks in their present-day form are, however, a work of the 15th, 16th, and 17th centuries. The year 1500 brought the invention of the pocket watch by Peter Henlein, that is, the timepiece built on the principle of the springiness of specific bodies — the spring-driven clock[224] which in the course of the next centuries would be essentially perfected. At the beginning of the 17th century the coil which had to correct the unequal pull of the spring; in 1674 the coil spring; in 1680 anchor escapement, around the same time cylinder escapement, equation clocks, and repeater watches. At the beginning of the 18th century, clocks with portable second hands.

The invention of the second form of clock fell in the middle of the 17th century — that which made a completely spring-free determination of time possible for the first time: the pendulum clock. It is accepted that Galileo invented them in 1641, but from fear of persecution did not make it known, while the invention was then made once more independently from Galileo in 1656 (1657) by Huygens and to a practical end.

The significance of the exact measurement of time lay in part that by it the production of goods as well as transport reached for the first time a higher degree of exactness and reliability, but above all in the influence which the exact determination of time exercised on the behaviour of the businessmen whose rationalisation in return can be measured by the advancing use of clocks[225].

If I also see the advances in the area of *measuring length* which fall in our period[226] to be of decisive importance, then that is explained in that I grasp the concept of measuring length in a somewhat wider sense and understand by it also the determination of place, whose technology was revolutionised above all during these centuries from the ground up. You will see what I mean — only the possibility of being able to orient oneself quickly and safely at any place on the earth made the globe accessible to mankind — only the possibility of travelling out into the open seas paved the way to America and the sea route to India.

The invention of the compass, similar to gunpowder, is lost in the darkness of the Middle Ages. You will find the first written news of the use of the compass in Europe in the writings of the Englishman Alexander Neckam (around 1195). The water compass, in which form the compass appeared at first, is described in detail in the year 1205 by the minnesinger Guiot. The compass was also frequently mentioned in the writings of the 13th century. For a long time Flavio di Gioia in Amalfi was recognised as the inventor of the compass, and his invention was published in the year 1305. The "Gioia legend" has been destroyed by recent research[227]. Its genesis proves, however, that the general use of the compass is not to be moved prior to the 14th century. Yes, other indicators speak in favour of it becoming established only much later — even in 1499 Polydorius Vergilius does not mention it at all in his book of inventions; in 1560 Cardano calls it the crown of all inventions, etc.

In any case the 16th century first brought the decisive advances above all in the use of the compass. On the 13th September 1492 Christopher Columbus entered the first observation of the declination in his ship's journal; in 1510 the declination was observed for the first time on land by Georg Hartmann from Nuremberg. Further improvements in the determination of the declination fell in the years 1525, 1538, 1585, etc. In 1544 Georg Hartmann discovered the inclination which in 1576 was observed exactly for the first time by the navigator Robert Norman. Important for the use of the compass is the invention of the universal joint (1545).

Next to the compass, the instruments of determining place on the sea are indispensable for an unhindered and safe navigating of the ocean. Their invention (which first made possible the journeys of Vasco de Gama and Columbus) falls in the last decades of the 15th century (if you leave out of consideration as imperfect the "Jacob's staff" invented allegedly in 1325 by Levi ben Gerson, which also served for geographic determinations of position at sea) — in the year 1473 Abraham Zacuto drew up his astronomical tables and charts (Almanac perpetuum) on the basis of which José Vecinho and the mathematician Moses in conjunction with two Christian colleagues invented the astrolabe — the instrument with whose help you can determine from the state of the sun the latitude of the ship[228].

The corresponding instrument for determination or measurement of longitude then had to wait a long time for itself — its invention was desired after with true passion — academies and governments established prizes in the 17th century for the successful solution to the problem.

After many futile experiments a prize competition was declared in 1714 in England by parliament on the expert opinion of Isaac Newton and Dr Halley — "for the Discoverer of the Longitude, if he determines it to one degree, or 60 geographical Miles, shall be £10,000, if to two-thirds of a Degree, £15,000, and if to half a Degree, £20,000." (A. Anderson 1787, 3:59) Only at the beginning of the 18th century did John Harrison succeed in inventing the marine chronometer which fulfilled those demands theoretically at least.

Harrison's invention did not seem to have yet sufficed for the practical requirements. At least the English parliament repeated its 1714 enacted prize competition in the years 1765, 1770, 1780, and 1781. In 1765 £1,000 was advanced to encourage a Mr Witchel, who submitted a marine table method for finding longitude, in order to put it into practice. (A. Anderson 1787, 4:71)

Finally we fit out the mariner with a *telescope* which for the first time completes his equipment — its invention is now, after the meticulous investigations of Professor Harting, placed in the year 1608[229].

Even the best instruments for determining position were of no use to mariners if they did not possess reliable sea charts. The oldest sea charts are those of Marino Sanuto (1306–1324) and Pedro Vesconte (1318). These charts were still so-called compass charts and consequently very incomplete. An important advance was signified by the introduction of the so-called Mercator projection which its inventor, the famed cartographer Mercator (1512–1594), first used in 1569 on his great world map. At the end of the 17th century Halley finished the first chart of air currents for the use of mariners; in 1665 the Jesuit priest Athanasius Kircher drew for the first time the sea currents on charts.

From the 16th century the helmsman's art was made the object of a special science — 'navigation'. In 1575 the first better work about ocean navigation appeared, the *Itinerario de Navegacion à los mares y tierres occidentales*[230].

As is apparent, the improved measurement and orientation technology served above all the commerce which now also developed its own special technology though.

IV. Transport Technology

It is an especially peculiar characteristic of the epoch of early capitalism that the advances in transport technology during this period were very few and apply in essence only to a single form of transport — the inland waterways.

Ocean navigation remained unchanged in its fundamentals. Ships were improved in some respects — ships' bottoms were shod with copper plates (important for the development of the copper industry!), here and there the ropes began to be replaced by iron chains (since they had been introduced in the year 1634 by Philip White); masts and sails were distributed better; the ship forms expanded in size — but neither the technology of shipbuilding nor that of navigation experienced any fundamentally significant change.

The *roads* were, as we saw, likewise improved; but no new road-building techniques were invented, they instead underwent their great reform only at the end of our epoch. The carriages were improved in that new types were created — the "coaches", the Berliners, the Journaliers, the Turgotins, the mail coaches, amongst others. That surely signified a furthering of the industries, as we could likewise already establish, but it exercised only a little influence on the shape of the transport. The most significant invention in the area of carriage building was probably making the front wheels swivel, which seems to have occurred in the 16th or 17th century.

We learn of one fundamentally new form of locomotion on land by means of the so-called *land yacht*.

Bishop Wilkins (1691, 155 f.) describes this type of vehicle and reports that it has had its greatest success in Holland. "That in some few hours space it would convey 6 or 10 persons 20 or 30 German miles, and all this with very little labour of him that sitteth at the Stern, who may easily guide the course of it as he pleaseth." Cited in Beck (1900, 3937).

But it surely only had a quite limited, purely local significance for Holland. In the other lands its spread would have been hindered above all by the pour conditions of the roads.

Even that arrangement which was destined to prepare for one of the greatest technological innovations in transport — the *track railway*, which we first find in the mines (the German mines already in the 16th century, the English in the 17th century) — only came into consideration for overland transport to a quite small extent.

The will to invent was concentrated for the time being still entirely on the transport by *inland waterways*. With the difficulties of land transport, the traffic was, as we saw earlier, carried out during the Middle Ages, so far as it occurred, by waterways. They remained a preferred means of transport during the early capitalist period, and the only inventions in the area of transport which we must grant a fundamental significance served for their improvement. They were:

1. The invention of *locks*, at first the flash lock, then the pound lock.

    When and by whom this invention was made, one has previously been unable to establish yet beyond doubt. According to Darmstaedter and Du Bois-Reymond (1904, 18), William of *Holland* had already in the year 1253 carried out the first known construction of a pound lock at Spaarndam. Others name Leonardo da Vinci, others L. B. Alberti, others Simon Stevin as inventors. A few see the first pound lock in that built by Viconti in 1439, a few in that erected on the Brenta by *Padua*. Only so much is certain: that the invention was known to its full extent at the end of the 15th century. This is spoken for by the numerous descriptions in Leonardo's works, and a place in Stevin to which Beck (1900, 317) draws attention, where he describes the pound lock as an installation "which has been in use for a long time". In 1617 an Englishman was granted a patent for improved locks — see the text in Forbes and Ashford (1906, 69).

2. The invention of the *dredging machines*.

We find with Leonardo descriptions already (with illustrations) of dredging machines which are quite similar to our own, only that they were driven by hand. We find dredging machines with Lorini (born around 1545)[*]. And we find them with Fausto Veranzio (1616). There it states: "One has many instruments for scooping the silt and sand from the floor of the sea (!), of which you see many in Venice, but these instruments are quite slow and cannot grab into the floor at depths of more than six feet [Lorini describes such a machine!], our one though can justifiably be used at any depth of the sea or river." (T. Beck 1900, 527). In *England*, John Gilbert was granted on 16th July 1618 a patent for a dredging machine as if the invention were quite new; the machine is described as follows: "a water plough, for the taking upp of sand, gravell, shelues, or banckes out of the river of Thames and other havens, harbours, rivers or waters" (Patent Office 1876, 1). Eighteen inventions for the improvement of waterways are recorded in Patent Office (1876) as being registered for patents in England during the 17th century. Cf. also Patent Office (1868).

In the year 1634 we find a so-called dipper boat bought in Holland in use in *Hamburg*, whose machines were "probably those of a so-called dipper" (Verein für Hamburgische Geschichte 1890, 101).

In the possession of both of these inventions, the first of which was above all significant in that you could now travel by water even over the mountains, one went energetically from the 16th century onwards about the construction of a network of inland waterways — be it that they made the river course navigable (in that they either "corrected" or "channeled" it), or be it that they constructed artificial waterways (canals). I will report on that in detail in the next volume.

V. Book Printing

Its mention suffices.

---

[*]   [Tr.: probably a reference to Lorini (1609).]

Section 4: Precious Metal Production

Overview

It is a basic idea of this work that modern capitalism as it has developed could only become thus because the historical "accident" led men to large, rich deposits of precious metals. And one of the tasks which this work sets itself is this: to provide the proof not only for the correctness of the claim that modern capitalism would absolutely not be there, could not be there without the uplifting of gold and silver treasure from America, Africa, and Australia, but also that it is defined in its entire character by the peculiar course of precious metal production. It is like a current of life which emanates from gold (which here is always used for precious metals in general when nothing special is noted) and helps capitalism in its development. Every time new sources of gold open up, capitalism raises and stretches to new growth; every time the stream of gold becomes weaker, a state of weakness befalls capitalism — its growth falters, its powers decline.

Thus the history of modern capitalism is (also!) the history of precious metal production — the names Kuttenberg and Goslar, Schwaz and Joachimstal, Potosi and Guanaxuato, Brazil and Guinea, California and Australia, Klondike and Witwaterstrand describe just as many stages in the development path of modern capitalism. The moods of precious metal production, which are like the moods of love in nature and with their innate irrationality stand in such strange opposition to the fundamental idea of capitalism — rationalism — it is them as well which define the two main epochs which we distinguish in the previous course of capitalist development — that of early capitalism and that of high capitalism — the former coincides with what you could call the silver age of capitalism, the latter with its golden age. For silver is the precious metal which during the entire Middle Ages and during the first centuries after the opening up of the New World was of outstanding significance. Gold, which in the 13th century shone out for a short time, then only entered world history decisively with the discovery of the Brazilian gold fields. The Brazilian and African gold introduced the golden age of capitalism, but were not powerful enough to bring about the development of high capitalism. For that the new, unusually strong flows which poured from the Californian and Australian gold fields around the middle of the 19th century were required.

All that shall be shown by the following portrayal. But so that it is capable of tackling this task satisfactorily, it is necessary beforehand to obtain insight into the course and conditions of precious metal production itself, which is also of importance for the various development sequences of capitalism, for which reason it belongs to the independent "foundations" of the capitalist economic system. It is advisable thus for reasons of the logical structure of this work to anticipate all references to precious metals and dedicate a special portrayal to them. In this section I will therefore deal in as many chapters with:

1) the course of precious metal production and the movement of precious metals;
2) the system of effects which the form of precious metal production was capable of exercising on cultural and economic life in general; and
3) the connection between precious metal production and price formation in particular, both theoretically and empirically/historically.

The portrayal will in essence cover the period from about 1250 to 1850, thus the epoch of early capitalism in its widest sense. Only in the survey over the course of precious metal production will I reach back further to establish the great historical connections.

Chapter 31: The Course of Precious Metal Production and Movement

Preliminary Remarks — Literature

We possess reasonably reliable statistics for precious metal production and precious metal movements only for the time after 1493. Giving numbers for the Middle Ages is in comparison very risky and better not done. The aims of this portrayal, however, also do not absolutely demand an exact numerical coverage of the absolute quantities of precious metals produced or moved. What matters for us above all rather is to learn whether during a period the stock of precious metals in Western Europe (for we direct our examination from here) increased or decreased (quickly or slowly), or remained stable. We can also establish that with some certainty, even if we do not know the absolute sums of precious metal production and movement — be it on the strength of the general history of production or from certain symptoms of various types.

Corresponding to our interest in getting to know above all the movement of precious metal stocks, I have also — contrary to the commonly preferred division of periods — differentiated the various epochs into those in which we perceive an increase or a decrease or a stasis of the precious metal stocks in Western Europe.

Of the comprehensive portrayals in which the history of precious metals for the entire period considered by us would be contained, we possess none from recent times which is capable of replacing the commendable, despite its great defects, work of William Jacob (1831; 1838). For the works of Del Mars (1880; 1886), as commendable and stimulating as they are, are based though — particularly for the earlier period — almost directly on the information of Jacob. Fortunately we have been well informed about the precious metal mining in Germany and Austria during the Middle Ages, over which Jacob and Del Mar are completely remiss, by a great series of thorough works in the last decades, so that, since Germany and Austria come into consideration almost exclusively for the supply of precious metals before the discovery of America (if we dispense with a numerical survey of the quantities), we can now form a quite clear picture of the course of precious metal production even before 1493.

With the year 1493 then, as stated, better statistics begin. The foundation for them is laid by the information of Alexander von Humboldt in his *Essai sur la Nouvelle Espagne* (1811; 1814). All the figures for the time after 1493 are compiled then in exemplary manner in Soetbeer (1879). The "present" in his title is the year 1875. I will speak about the continuation of Soetbeer's work in another place when I deal with the new times.

Soetbeer's numbers have obtained authoritative status which they also indubitably deserve. A few corrections which do not fundamentally alter Soetbeer's results are contained in the excellent study by Lexis (1879). Lexis calculates a somewhat smaller amount for the Mexican and South American precious metal production, namely in the period 1493–1800 2,420,000 kg of gold and 90,200,000 kg of silver, whereas Soetbeer correspondingly gives 2,490,000 and 101,400,000 kg. This higher estimate occurred in that Soetbeer calculated more for the actual Peruvian silver take. That the numbers are essentially correct in their extent is vouched for by the source from which they came — for the Spanish colonies, the shipping lists of the quinto[*]. Of course, all the numbers calculated on the basis of this authentic information must be "appraised", which has though happened with both the named researchers in an absolutely unobjectionable way. That differences are thereby possible is shown by the various figures of Soetbeer or Lexis. But that these two scholars shall have calculated nonsense figures that were in agreement would have been made unbelievable by their universally known meticulousness, even if one's own judgement would have to bear them out on examination.

And yet the figures of Soetbeer and Lexis would be simply nonsense if a recent Spanish author, cited by Supan (1906, 41), were correct. This author (Laiglesia y Auset 1904) comes to the following production figures, supported "by the account books of the Spanish crown revenues in America" (Archivo General de Indias, Seville):

1509–14:	995,925 Pesetas
1516–23:	624,210 Pesetas
1525:	2,121,460 Pesetas
1526–29:	943,152 Pesetas
1530–40:	3,110,896 Pesetas
1541–46:	2,419,840 Pesetas
1547–50:	1,225,312 Pesetas
1551–55:	10,145,760 Pesetas
1509–55:	21,559,555 Pesetas

That is 17,277,244 marks in present-day [1916] currency.

In contrast, Soetbeer assumes an average *annual* production as we will see:

---

[*]   [Tr.: quinto real = King's fifth, a tax on precious metal production.]

1521–44 of 90,200 kg

1545–60 of 311,600 kg

That is thus a total production of approximately one billion marks in this period, against 17 million marks according to the Spanish author. One of these two figures is naturally idiotic; I believe that it is the last named. To see this you need only perhaps refer to the following figures for comparison — the mine of Annaberg in Saxony produced in the middle of the 16th century (according to quite reliable information) around 40,000 pounds of silver per year, that is thus around 4,000,000 marks in present-day [1916] currency, thus in about four years as much as all the American mines shall have produced in their most productive years during a period of 46 years according to the views of Mr Laiglesia!

What nonsense the Spanish author has committed I am incapable of saying as I cannot get hold of his book. Perhaps he has confused pesos with pesetas, has mistaken the quinto for the entire yield, and taken into account only the figures of a mint.

When Supan (1906, 41) suggests the difference between the two figures (those of Laigelsia and of Soetbeer) is "quite considerable" — namely 17 million marks against 73 million marks, he makes the mistake of taking the figures of *Soetbeer* for the entire amount, whereas it is the *annual average*; the difference is thus, as we see, even "more considerable" — 17 million against 1,000 million! The errors in Strieder (1914, 4) are also to be corrected accordingly.

First Period: From the downfall of the Roman Empire up to the 8th century

During the Roman imperial times a great stock of precious metal had been gathered up in the centre of the world empire. Much was obtained in the course of the centuries through conquest and plundering — one thinks of the victories over Antiochus, of the loot from the Aetolian War, of Mummius's sack of Corinth, of Sulla's plundering of Greece, of Vera's plundering of Sicily, etc.

The incessant new extraction had, however, surely added even more — Rome had gradually brought almost all the mines of the famed peoples of antiquity into its possession — in Dacia, Illyria, Dalmatia, Thrace, and above all in Spain, whose silver mines and gold fields had probably formed the most hotly contested objects of struggle in the Punic Wars. If the estimates which Lexis gives are correct, the stock of precious metals in the Roman Empire at the time of Christ amounted to perhaps 10 billion marks in present-day [1916] currency — of approximately equal parts gold and silver.

Of this wealth now, the greatest part was lost to the Western Europe already in the last centuries of Roman rule, but still more in the following period.

At first from the time of Constantine the Great, the supply of new material from the gold sluices and mines diminished more and more[231] — whether because of the diminished supply of slaves or in consequence of the exhaustion of the stocks remains uncertain.

In the following centuries it then stopped completely as the barbarians took possession of the Roman Empire. In Spain, the most important production site of that time, we find still in 413 a Comes metalli [Count of mines] who undertook the management of the mining. Soon afterwards, however, the operations were completely stopped.

The existing stock, however, decreased quickly — not just through its natural decline, but rather more in that it streamed east, be it to the caliphate (by way of the certainly very small trade), or be it (above all!) to Byzantium — particularly in the form of taxes and tribute. We may assume that in the 8th century the lowest level of this movement was reached, that at the time, that is, at the time in which, as I have tried to show elsewhere, European economic history begins, Western Europe was bare of all but a few remnants of precious metals, that in particular precious metal in the form of gold had become vanishingly small[232].

Second Period: From the 8th century to the end of the 13th century

It is a time in which the stock of precious metals in Western Europe at first increased slowly, then — in the last two centuries — quickly again.

The first mines which were opened for use on a larger scale again were probably the Spanish ones. At least as far as they were subject to Arab rule. The rich gold sluicing of Leon certainly, which remained in the hands of the "barbarians", were only started up anew later. By comparison we learn that where the Arabs had settled — thus in Andalusia, Jaén, etc. — soon after their arrival the extraction of precious metals was taken up again[233]. That they delivered a considerable yield, we can see from the wealth of gold and silver which we find with the Spanish caliphs in the 9th and 10th century — the annual income of Abderahman I shall have amounted to 10,000 ounces of gold and 10,000 pounds of silver; that of Abderahman III over 100 million marks in present-day [1916] currency. In the year 938, they delivered to the caliphs 400 pounds of pure gold, a large quantity of silver in bars, 30 gold-embroidered garments, and 48 horse covers made of gold and silver[234].

But even elsewhere in Western Europe the old sites where precious metals were found came to life around that time once more — in Bohemia, Hungary, and Transylvania much gold was extracted. And then the discovery of more and more new sites now followed, particularly for silver, in quick succession — already in the 9th century in Alsace; in the 10th century (mentioned in documents from 1028) in the Black Forest and in the Harz Mountains (970 in Rammelsberg). But particularly rich in new workings of silver mines are the 12th and 13th centuries — in this blessed time falls the full blossoming of the Mansfeld, the Saxon (Freiberg, from 1167), the Bohemian (Kuttenberg*), and the older Tyrolian (Trent) silver mining; in the 12th century, however, silver mines were also worked of which no trace is present today anymore — e.g. in Westphalia[235] — at the same time (in the 13th century) gold extraction[236] began in the Goldberg, Löwenberg, and Bunzlau regions, and occurred to a greater extent in Hungary.

The lands of the German crowns were the Mexico and Peru of the earth before the discovery of America. But even in the other lands of Western Europe the production of precious metals was stirring — we learn of a silver mine in Italy during the 12th and 13th centuries[237], likewise in France[238].

From all that we know about the development of gold and particularly silver production in these two centuries[239], we may conclude that the stock of precious metals in Western Europe in that epoch increased comparatively quickly — assuming that the produced quantities did not perhaps flow elsewhere. The tendency for that certainly now always existed whenever the Western Europeans entered into trading relations with the East — for the Levant trade had been passive

---

* [Tr.: Kutná Hora in the Czech Republic.]

for Western Europe since time immemorial. And hence the words with which Peschel closed his outstanding investigations over this question are indubitably correct: "The distribution of metal yields among the peoples occurred from the earliest historical times according to its own rules. Culture pushed constantly westwards, gold and silver flowed always eastwards, and indeed the metals had to take their direction towards the east because culture had come from there."[240]

But I would like to believe that in the time which we are speaking of here the outflow of precious metals to the east was balanced by a returning current from there, which owed its existence to the Italian colonisation of the Levant[241]. The balance could have been perfect, indeed could have ended up in an overflow for Western Europe — because the extent of trade relations at the time was not yet very large, and because on the other hand the conquest of rich cultural sites fell precisely in that time, and this, as is well-known, tended to be constantly bound with theft and plunder. But as a result great quantities of precious metals suddenly came into the possession of the conqueror.

But that on the arrival of Western Europeans in the Byzantine and Arabian empires great quantities of precious metals were present is testified to us by the descriptions of contemporaries[242].

A considerable part of of these precious metal quantities now certainly flowed by the path of taxation, of gifts[243], and not the least through theft and loot into the pockets of the conquerors. That we are also incapable here of determining the amounts even approximately goes without saying. But considerations of a general nature also have here, as so often, good value as evidence, especially when we consult occasional reports of plundering, etc.

See the table in Del Mar (1880, 239 f.), and cf. the treatment of Soetbeer (1880, 114 ff.). The wave of gold had its origin firstly in the south of Europe and continued from there to Germany where it arrived half a century later (the consequence of (1) a favourable trade balance of the Hanseatic League with the Netherlands — Bruges — and (2) war aid on the part of England, where the shiny Italian gold pieces had flowed by way of lending traffic). It was then strengthened by the increasing productivity of the Silesian and Bohemian gold mines, and reached its high point in the short episode of German gold coin minting (1325 King John of Bohemia).

Such general considerations also provide the source of my conjecture that in consequence of the described processes a shift in favour of gold took place in the precious metal stocks of Western Europe. The goods of the Orient were paid for with (German) silver, and they carried off gold more than silver in the conquest of the Asiatic empires. Two facts speak for the correctness of my conjecture:

1. the minting of gold coins, which a series of Italian cities performed in the 13th century — in 1252 fiorino d'oro, in 1283 Venetian ducats, amongst others;
2. the movement of the relative value in favour of gold in the 13th and 14th centuries, which was permitted to vary during the later Middle Ages between 1:10 and 1:11[244].

Third Period: From the end of the 13th century to the middle of the 15th century

For the devaluation of gold, which was just spoken of, not only the more advantageous situation of gold, but also very much and perhaps still more the worsening of the production conditions for silver had an influence. For the distinguishing mark of the following period, which comprises the last two centuries of the Middle Ages (the last not entirely), is the *decline in silver production* in consequence of worsened extraction conditions. The stocks lying close to the surface which had been made accessible in the 12th and 13th centuries were exhausted, and the deeper lying ore was incapable of being extracted because they could not control the infiltration of water. Thus the mines frequently flooded[245], and almost everywhere we hear of a decrease in output. When King Wenzel II gave Kuttenberg its constitution (anno 1300), he said:

> With hands raised to Heaven we want to thank the Creator who has also made us happy here in that, whereas *in almost all kingdoms of the world the mine yield has dried up*, the absolutely fruitful Bohemia of our time refreshes us with its gold and silver.[246]

Aside from these references that are directly enlightening to us, we also know of a series of symptoms from which we may conclude that there was a strong reduction in precious metal and in particular silver production during the 14th and a part of the 15th centuries.

Here I take into account:

1. the bans on the export of precious metals which towards the end of the Middle Ages were enacted quite generally by cities and territories[247];
2. the decrease in the quantities of precious metals delivered to the mints for minting. Admittedly only one set of figures concerning it — that of the English mint — is known to me, but I think though that it may be seen as typical for the entire state of the market in precious metals. We know the quantities of gold and silver delivered to the English mint — for silver from 1272, for gold from 1345[248]. Accordingly I calculate an annual average (in present-day [1916] currency) of:

	Silver	Gold
1272–1377	£8,906	£2,538 (1345–1377)
1377–1461	£1,157	£1,845
1461–1509	£3,184	£4,338

Thus at the end of the 14th century a seeming plunge into the depths, and indeed much quicker and greater still with silver than with gold.

Keeping pace with the decrease in production, however, was in all probability the *draining away of precious metals to the Orient*. We may assume that this was at its strongest precisely in the centuries at the conclusion of the Middle Ages — because at this time the Levant trade was actually developing to its first blossoming — but on the other hand the causes effecting a backflow (which, as we assumed, made up for the outflow in the preceding epoch) no longer applied or were weakened in their effectiveness. What was obtained in the way of German and Austrian silver went at first in exchange for goods from the Orient and probably also products of the southern and western lands of Europe[249]; from there, however, it was exported to the Orient to pay for their goods[250].

Various circumstances combined thus to strip Europe more and more of precious metals towards the end of the Middle Ages. Then around the middle of the 15th century the crucial turn took place which would be decisive for the entire further course of European economic life.

Fourth Period: From the middle of the 15th century up to 1545

The turn by which the scarcity of precious metals was transformed overnight into abundance traces back to three different causal sequences:

1. the opening up of new sources of silver and gold in Germany and Austria;
2. the settlement of the Portuguese in the gold lands of Africa and Asia; and
3. the plundering of Mexico and Peru by the Spaniards.

1. The opening up of new sources of silver and gold in Germany and Austria

It is to be attributed partly to a fortunate accident, partly to an improvement in mining technology[251] that from the middle of the 15th century a series of new, rich mining sites of precious metals were opened up in Germany and Austria, and old mines were given new life, from which a previously un-heard-of quantity of gold and silver could be obtained.

The land of Salzburg produced gold. The heyday of its gold mining fell in the hundred years from 1460–1560. In Gastein they counted at the time 30 mine managers and many pro-spectors who opened 1,000 pits during this time. Around this time 4,000 marks of gold and 8,000 marks of silver were ex-tracted annually[252].

But it was above all new silver finds which gave the site its stamp — in Tyrol, in Saxony, in Bohemia. In *Tyrol* the *Schwaz* mines began to deliver significant yields just around the middle of the 15th century; when the most famous deposits — the Falkenstein — were tackled[253]. The yield was rising quickly towards the end of the century and even in the first decade of the 16th century, until it reached its high point in 1523 with 55,855 marks of fine silver[254]. (Then the crash starts. And in the year 1570 only 2,000 marks were still being obtained.)

After Tyrol — *Saxony*. Here the rich pits of *Schneeberg* were opened in the year 1471, those of *Annaberg* in 1496.

Schneeberg delivered from 1471–1550 an annual average of perhaps 5,400 marks of fine silver (in the second half of the 16th century at most 1,400 marks); Annaberg's average annual production amounted to:

1493–1520	22,145 pounds
1520–1544	31,180 pounds
1545–1560	39,700 pounds

And after Saxony — *Bohemia*, where they began in the year 1516 with mining the *Joachimstal* pits. Its yield again climbed quickly into the heights — from 2,064 talers in the first year to 254,259 talers in the year 1532. (From then on the production yield sank just as fast as it had risen, until at the end of the 16th century it had as good as vanished.)

Unfortunately it is not possible for us to make clear the rapid increase in precious metals production in the German lands during the 15th and 16th centuries by comparing it with the production up to 1450. For reliable figures only begin around this time. But that the growth was quite enormous is to be recognised from the information which I have just provided. But how large the increase in production even after the new finds was up to the middle of the following century is visible from the figures pulled together by Soetbeer for the time after 1493. The (Salzburg) gold production was certainly already reaching its high point around the turn of the 15th century with an average annual yield of 5.58 million marks during the period of 1493–1520 (on average, the years 1521–1544: 4.18 million; 1545–1560: 2.79 million). By contrast the total yield of the silver mines of Germany and Austria from 1493–1560 rose as follows (annual averages):

Germany:

1493–1520	22,145 pounds
1520–1544	31,180 pounds
1545–1560	39,700 pounds

Austria:

1493–1520	24,000 kg
1521–1544	32,000 kg
1545–1560	30,000 kg

2. The settlement of the Portuguese in the gold lands of Africa and Asia

The crucial event for Western Europe which separates two ages, from whose occurrence we rightly set the beginning of a new episode in history, was the ousting of the Arabs from their place mediating between between Orient and Occident — as is well-known, the work of the Portuguese. The reign of the Mohammedans in Africa and the East Indies was broken by force of arms — their ousting from Africa began with the conquest of Ceuta (1415), it was completed with the Battle of Alaçer Kebir; and with the conquest of Malacca (1511) the influence of the Arabs in the Indies was destroyed. The news of the irresistible force of the Portuguese spread over the entire land; from all sides, even from the kings in Siam and Pegu, envoys came to conclude alliances and trading treaties. Albuquerques's far-sightedness then recognised, however, the necessity of attacking the Arabs in their own land, of blocking the Red Sea and Persian Gulf, the link roads of Arabian intermediate trade, thus hitting it at its root. The conquest of Aden and Hormuz served this end. With this moment in fact a new cultural epoch had opened — Western Europe had finally taken up the inheritance of the caliphate.

What that meant for the further development of European economic life on the whole, I will attempt to show in another place. Here for the time being only the effects of the new circumstances on the supply of Europe with precious metals will be followed. For even in this respect the advance of the Portuguese proved to be extraordinarily significant — it helped to considerably increase the supply of precious metals, above all gold, particularly in the first decades after settlement.

The *direct connection with the East Indies* and the resulting rise in the European-Indies trade indeed increased at first the quantities of precious metals streaming eastwards, particularly silver. Silver was the usual cargo of ships departing Lisbon; usually each carrack carried 40–50,000 Spanish talers on the royal account for the purchase of peppers. Likewise the Dutch had to pay for a large part of their East Indies imports with hard money: "the export of other goods was not very significant."

But the direct connection with the peoples of the East also created on the other side a series of improvements for the backflow of precious metals. Once again the colonial settlement created above all the possibility of raising tribute, of plundering and extortion, of robbery and theft.

The advancing Europeans' system of plundering of course had all the more success the richer an area was in precious metals which had either already been extracted by the natives or now had to be brought to the surface by them. But it turned out that both the Asian mainland and particularly *the Asian islands were extraordinarily rich in gold* when the Portuguese were establishing themselves. This fact has fallen so much into oblivion today that our top specialists in precious metal statistics do not make a single mention of Asian gold[255]. And yet during the 16th century large quantities of gold must have been fetched by the Portuguese from their Asian possessions if such rich areas could be exhausted so quickly. For obviously those islands around the year 1500 were gold lands of the first rank, *although* we can follow how the Arabs at the time had already penetrated to all places of gold production and hat probably been drawing out gold from those lands throughout the entire Middle Ages[256].

But it appears as if the Arab rule was not anywhere near so fateful for the exhaustion of the area of precious metals as that of the gold-greedy Europeans — for what the former had needed centuries to do, the latter achieved in decades.

If this applied to the gold lands of Asia, it applied no less to the *gold-rich areas of Africa*[257]. These too, of which there were three, had been used during the Middle Ages for long periods by the Arabs without even having approached being exhausted when the Portuguese penetrated into them. Again it signified thus a strong increase in gold with which Europe was blessed when the European conquerors first arrived at the gold sites of the Senegal region and soon also at the rich deposits of East Africa on the coast of Sofala.

That a quantitative survey of the gold imports in that distant period is hardly possible, all experts have admitted. For if you could yourself ascertain the "produced" metal approximately correctly, the quantity of stolen gold and silver though would escape any realisation. Under this reservation, the figures which Soetbeer assumes for the gold exports from Africa may be given space here. These amount in the opinion of this scholar on average each year for the below periods to[258]:

1493–1520   3,000 kg or 8,370,000 marks
1521–1544   2,500 kg or 7,975,000 marks

For the supply from Asia, any quantitative statement is lacking.

3. The plundering of Mexico and Peru by the Spaniards

The stock of precious metals, which were mostly valued as adornment and treasure, was abundant in the lands of the old American cultures[259] in which the Spanish entered as conquerors at the beginning of the 16th century.

Putting into figures the quantity of precious metals brought to Europe by plundering these lands is extraordinarily difficult. The estimations (or calculations) of the best experts deviate so much from each other[260] that I would prefer to dispense with making a quantitative statement. That it is a matter of a large amount is spoken for already by the sums of individual hauls, of which I will quote a few further on below.

Fifth Period: From the middle of the 16th century to the beginning of the 17th century (1545–c.1620)

My report can be as short as the changes were enormous which were experienced with the production and the stock of precious metals during this epoch. For as was already noted, we enter with the discovery of America into the periods of useful statistical information and are also in the pleasant situation of being able to use the oft-mentioned work of Soetbeer to its full extent. The following numbers are taken from it where not especially noted otherwise.

What so transformed the situation with precious metals around the middle of the 16th century from the ground up was the opening up of the richest American mines (Zacatecas, Guanaxuato) as well as Potosis in particular on the one hand, and on the other hand the already acknowledged introduction of the amalgamation process (see page 192 f.). The sudden and strong increase in silver production during the second half of the 16th century is to be attributed to these two events. For I have in the previous section already proven with a few figures that in the same period the silver and gold sources of Germany and Austria dried up. But the (gold) yield of Africa was also declining from the middle of the 16th century — the newly discovered part of the earth had to compensate for all these losses and do so in an exuberant way, at least where silver was concerned. This precious metal entered with the opening of the American mines into the period of its absolute supremacy (which lasted until the discovery of the Brazilian gold fields) — while its share in the total value of precious metals production during 1521–1544 only amounted to 44.9%, it rose to 70.3%, 73.9%, 78.6% at the end of the 16th century.

The gold production of the earth remained during the entire 16th century at approximately the same level — it climbed from 7,160 kg annually on average from 1521–1544 to 8,510 kg annually on average from 1545–1560, but then sank to 6,480 kg and 7,380 kg annually on average in the subsequent two twenty year periods.

By comparison now the increase in silver production! It amounted on average annually to:

1521–1544	90,200 kg
1545–1560	311,600 kg
1561–1580	299,500 kg
1581–1600	418,900 kg
1600–1621	422,900 kg

Thus a tripling around the middle of the century and (after a temporary stagnation) a further climb up into the first decades of the 17th century — thanks, as stated, above all to Mexico and particularly Potosis.

The silver production of Mexico climbed in the above twenty year periods on average annually from:

3,400 kg

to 15,000 kg

to 50,200 kg

to 74,300 kg

to 81,200 kg

That of Potosis began straightaway with 183,200 kg on average annually from 1544–1560 and then sank to 151,800 kg in the following period, to reach in the years 1581–1600 its maximum of 254,300 kg.

But of significance for the development of European economic life in this epoch was not only the rapid increase in the quantity of precious metals, but just as much the transfer of its production locations — the source of economic life in Germany had dried up, in the colonies of the Western European nations it had sprung freshly to life. But it was not this now which was to be fertilised by the new stream of gold, which rather (to extend the metaphor) flowed off as if in an artificial pipe as it were over Spain (and later Portugal) into the economic areas of Holland, France, and England. I will treat that and the national shifts arising in connection with it later in detail. Here for the time being only the fact will be registered that Germany dried up because its own sources of precious metals petered out, but Spain remained likewise dry, despite its American possessions. The causes for why the American silver did not remain in Spain or even did not come to Spain at all to begin with are primarily the following:
1. a part of the production was held back in the colonies;
2. another part was lost through piracy[261], etc.;
3. much of it was withdrawn from circulation and transformed into expensive items, etc.;
4. most was used for payment of the Northern peoples, particularly the Dutch, the French[262], and the English, who delivered goods to Spain or the colonies[263]; and
5. the rest served for settlement of the interest obligations of the Spanish state.

About what quantities of precious metals being withdrawn in this way from Spain it concerned in particular, we can discern from a few figures which have been passed down from the time. Thus the value of the silver which the fleet of Philipp II brought to Antwerp for the Fuggers in the year 1577 (where it was then taken advantage of) was 800,000 ducats. In the year 1595, which had to deliver the yield of three years, 35 million scudi in gold and silver went over the bar of San Lu-

car, of which in the year 1596 not a real was to be found anymore in Castile[264].

With respect to these figures, we are capable surely of giving credence to the claim that a hundred years after the discovery of America, Holland, England, France possessed much
more precious metals, even in the form of gold, than Spain[265].

Sixth Period: the 17ᵗʰ century

In this period precious metal production sank somewhat at
first, to rise again rapidly during the last third of the century.
Europe's share in the silver production was vanishingly small.
Gold production increased. Here are the summary figures.

Annual production by weight (in kilograms):

Period	Silver	Gold
1601–1620	422,900	8,520
1621–1640	393,600	8,300
1641–1660	366,300	8,770
1661–1680	337,000	9,260
1681–1700	341,900	10,765

The wavering course which characterised this period appears even more distinctly before our eyes when we throw together the production quantities for both precious metals and
express them in (monetary) values. Then the total precious
metal production amounts namely to:

1621–1544	1,880.1 million marks
1641–1560	1,808.1 million marks
1661–1580	1,729.9 million marks
1681–1600	1,831.5 million marks

In the last two decades of the century the strong increase
in gold production made itself especially noticeable.

Seventh Period: the 18ᵗʰ century

A period of rapid and continuous increase in precious
metals production. From the beginning of the century up until about the middle it is the newly discovered Brazilian gold
which floods across Europe. Brazil, whose gold fields began to

give more abundant yields right around the turn of the century, delivered:

1701–1720	150 million marks of gold
1721–1740	490 million marks of gold
1741–1760	816 million marks of gold

Then (from the year 1764 on) the yield lets up, until at the beginning of the 19th century it has almost entirely stopped[266].

But right at this moment when the Brazilian gold begins to become more scarce, the strong increase in Mexican silver production starts — in the year 1760 the richest parts of the mines of Valenciana on the Veta Madre [mother vein] of Guanajuato were opened up by the work of the Spaniard Obregon; in the year 1765 the development of the bonanza in the concession of St Acasio on the Veta Grande [great vein] at Zacatecas[267]. Mexico produced annually in silver:

1721–1740	230,800 kg
1741–1760	301,000 kg
1761–1780	366,400 kg
1781–1800	562,400 kg
1800–1810	553,800 kg

In total the annual production amounted to[*]:

	Silver	Gold
1721–1740	431,200	19,080
1741–1760	533,145	24,160
1761–1780	652,740	20,705
1781–1800	879,060	17,790
1800–1810	894,150	17,778

The following table expresses it in terms of value and makes the rapid increase in precious metals production in this period — taken precisely, during the 18th century and the first decade of the 19th century — still more apparent. The total production amounted to:

---

[*] [Tr: Sombart does not give any units in this table, so whether he is adding the previous table amounts to the production of other countries is unclear, but the following table suggests this is the case.]

1701–1720	1,995.5 million marks
1721–1740	2,617.0 million marks
1741–1760	3,292.6 million marks
1761–1780	3,505.2 million marks
1781–1800	4,157.3 million marks
1801–1810	2,106.0 million marks

From these amounts which originated primarily from Spanish and Portuguese colonies the greatest part also passed the motherlands by or passed quickly through them to the economically more rapidly progressing lands of Northwestern Europe, now especially to England[268].

Eighth Period: 1810–1848

In this period such a strong and sudden decrease occurs in precious metals production, particularly of silver, as is hardly ever to be found in any other period. The cause — above all political disturbances in the American production regions (whereby, as will be shown later, the conditions of production worsened).

The silver yield of Mexico sank in a few years to less than half — from 553,800 kg on average annually during 1801–1810 to 312,000 kg and 264,800 kg during the following two decades. The American gold production declined just as much, and it was only thanks to the circumstance that with the third decade of the 19th century Russia delivered gold in rapidly growing quantities that the gold yield of the earth did not fall off at the same rate as the silver production. The increase in Russian gold production then became still greater in the 1830s and 1840s and contributed (together with the slowly recovering silver production of Mexico — 1831–40 = 331,000 kg, 1841–50 = 420,300 kg annual production) to the total value of precious metals production slowly rising again from the 1830s. The figures in summary are the following:

Year	Total production (million marks)	Silver (million marks)	Gold (million marks)
1801–1810	2,106.1	1,609.1	497.0
1811–1820	1,292.7	973.4	319.3
1821–1830	1,225.6	829.0	396.6
1831–1840	1,639.7	1,073.6	566.1

In the year 1848, however, the decisive turn took place which was to lead the history of the world in new directions — the golden age of capitalism unfolded. But its portrayal does not yet belong here.

Chapter 32: The Significance of Precious Metals for Economic Life in General

Literature

Of course numerous researchers have occasionally pointed out the significance which precious metals and the production of precious metals possess for economic life in this or that relation. Naming them here is unnecessary. By contrast a few works must be cited which occupy themselves fundamentally with this problem and have likewise made the attempt to capture the entire impact of precious metals. They are in particular the following books, strangely all books coming from Americans: Del Mar, from whose numerous works *Money and Civilisation* (1886) with its bibliography is particularly worth considering here; Adam (1895; 1907); and Fisher (1911). Cf. page 239.

Apart from the conviction that the influence of precious metals production on the path of economic life as well as the entire culture is an overwhelmingly large one, nothing connects me, however, with the researchers named above. The manner *by which* we substantiate the influence is different, just as we also see this influence operating in very different direction.

I. The Chimeric Significance of Precious Metals

Of gold and what an important role it plays in the life of humanity, the sagas of most peoples have a lot to tell — of the golden fleece and how it drew the heroes to death or victory; of unhappy Midas, for whom all things he touched turned to gold, and who thus, when this also happened with food and drink, was headed for a wretched death by starvation until he bathed in the river Pactolus which began to carry abundant gold from then on. In the German myths, however, the gold problem is grasped deepest of all, where all woe which seizes Gods and men is ascribed to the possession of gold, and where the solution to all misery is tied to it so that the gold ring brought up from the depths of the Rhine to wreak havoc is given back to the Rhine daughters. Here its says no more and no less than that the fate of Gods and of men is the fate of gold.

And from the folk sagas, we know, almost always a deep truth speaks to us. What is it which pronounces to us the many gold sagas? What does the history of humanity teach us? Did gold also have in it that great, towering significance which the myths ascribe to it?

Certain is this — that gold possessed in the *imagination* even of historical humanity always the highest of all values, and that humanity was always ready to dare great things in order to obtain possession of the noble metal. But as a result only gold has received a quite enormous significance in the course of human history — so that the desire for it became a powerful driving force for decisive events. Above all as the driving force for campaigns and wars of conquest, from whose outcome the fate of entire peoples, entire cultures often depended — Darius went after gold, likewise Alexander the Great; Romans and Carthaginians fought in the last analysis over the Spanish gold; Caesar hoped above all to find gold in Germania; many wars in the Middle Ages flared up over Bohemia's silver and gold treasures — the chronicler of the old times already knew, "quid est quod Cuthno fames avaritiae ac abyssus malitiae, diversa ac peregrina ingentiaque gentium genera ad contemplationem sui contrahit regesque ac principes exteros allicit, nisi quia in sinu suo, in terrarum abditis, fomentum avaritiae argentum nutrit?" [how and for what reason is Kuttenberg the abyss of avaricious hunger and of malice, that some diverse and peculiar and foreign people, and other kings and princes are attracted to come and invade it, save that in the bosom of the place, in the secret places of the earth, the warmth of the covetousness nourishes the silver]; the European states scrapped for centuries over American gold, and one of the last great wars owed its origin to the struggle over gold mines*.

But gold also became significant for cultural development in that important events began with that chase after the gold, events which nobody had thought of when they began the

---

*   [Tr.: presumably the Boer wars.]

chase, but which we must identify as the immediate consequences of the yearning for gold — the institution of slavery
reached its fullest development in the wake of gold mining:

> Sorglose Schmiede, schufen wir sonst wohl
> Schmuck unsern Weibern, [...]
> Wir lachten lustig der Müh'.
> Nun zwingt uns der Schlimme,
> in Klüfte zu schlüpfen,
> für ihn allein uns immer zu müh'n.

> [Carefree smiths, we usually created
> jewellery for our wives, [...]
> We laughed merrily at the effort.
> Now the bad one forces us
> to slip into crevices,
> to always strive for him alone.]*

In the search for gold, gunpowder was found, chemistry
was formed as a science; in the search for gold, America was
discovered, the modern great states were formed.

When, as you could put it, the *chimeric significance of
gold* for the development of humanity is surely beyond all
doubt, then with that nothing yet is said over its real significance; whether it has really exercised such a strong influence
on the path of cultural life, whether this was actually determined in its character and direction by the possession and use
of gold, and whether its extraction for the individual and the
community which strove for it was then now in truth a blessing, as all who strove after it imagined, or a curse, as the
myths pronounce to us in warning.

The last part of this question has a philosophical-meta-
physical sense and encapsulates the question over the sense
and significance of human existence; that is the sense which
does not come into consideration here. But beside it the
purely historical question remains — over the influence which
the use of precious metals, their increase and their decrease
actually exercised on the path of culture.

---

* [Tr.: From Act 3 of Das Rheingold by Richard Wagner.]

II. The Real Significance of Precious Metals

The foregoing portrayal has prepared the response to the question: what real significance did precious metals and the form of their production relations in quantity and type have for economic life. The answer itself will be contained in the following two chapters as well as in this work. Here for the present only a short indication shall be given to the many-sidedness and diversity of effects which precious metals are capable of exercising — their significance for economic life shall be expressed in a schematic form so that our attention from the outset is steered to the various connections in which actual effects of precious metals can appear or be hidden. For that the observation which forces itself on anyone who surveys the earlier attempts in a similar manner of describing the role of precious metals in the course of history is that as often as the question as to the significance of precious metals for economic (and furthermore cultural) life is made, its exhaustive answer still has not occurred, be it that they have not attacked the problem systematically enough, be it (which has occurred still more frequently) that they envisaged far too one-sidedly only this or that effect, indeed in the rule only a single effect of precious metals (for the formation of prices), and also not followed this one effect deeply enough in all its ramifications and all its nuances.

This work would like to avoid these errors. And hence it appear to me at first necessary at once to put up an as complete as possible scheme of the conceivable effects which precious metals could ever exercise (or have exercised).

I have said already, one mostly thinks only of the effect of precious metals on price formation. In contrast it is right now to be established from the outset that the significance of precious metals can also manifest itself without them at all exercising an influence on prices, or at least before they exercise an influence on prices, indeed before they have even been turned into monetary goods. We must thus distinguish:

1. effects of a *direct* and *indirect* sort, that is, effects of precious metals as mere consumer good and effects as money. When the effect follows from the last named path, then it can be of various nature;

2. according to whether it concerns a *mere quantitative influence on demand* or at the same time an *impact on price*.
   Of significance for the character of the effects is:
3. the *origin of the precious metals.*
   Here the following different ways are to be distinguished for how precious metals can be obtained (by the individual and in addition also by an economically active collectivity):
   a. *directly*: through theft, payment of tribute by subjugated lands, or own production; or
   b. *indirectly*: then the first possibility is that they come into the land through trade — as payment for delivered goods. There are still other ways though, above all that of the payment which a land has to make to another from debt obligations. A special case of such debt payments are war reparations.
   In so far as precious metals are produced through one's own production, the effects of precious metals will show great variety:
4. according to the *variety of their production circumstances*: who brings the precious metals to the surface — whether slaves, craftsmen, or paid labourers — who participates directly in the profits of production — whether the state (as owner of the mines or as sovereign power), whether little people, whether Spanish grandees or London businessmen. It will also be of significance how those entitled receive their shares — whether as interest on their capital or payment for their work; whether as regular, constantly flowing income or as sudden lottery-like contribution; whether they have become rich through mining or live in poor circumstances; whether they are becoming richer through it — from rich people to still richer, from poor people to rich. As is apparent, it is here the various ways in which precious metals production affects the formation of income which become significant for the formation of economic life.

In particular, in turn depending on the character of income formation will be:

5. the *variety of spending*, which is also influenced considerably by the manners of production mentioned under 4 above: whether necessary consumables, luxury goods, or production goods are bought by the surplus of precious metal production or from the profits directly made from it.

But now it is immediately clear that all those possibilities for effects which have previously been spoken of receive their peculiar stamp:

6. according to *the milieu in which the precious metals arrive*: in particular, according to the economic system in which they shall have an effect — whether this is the self-sufficient, the expanded self-sufficient, the craftwork economy, or capitalism, and in what development stage in turn the economic system finds itself. The effect in the early capitalist epoch is different to that in the high capitalist epoch; when the credit organisation in an economic area is scarce it is different to when it is highly developed — thus quite different effects 1750–1850–1900.

But how shall a portrayal do justice to all these infinitely variable possibilities of effect without losing itself in the chaos of a confused casuistry? I believe in only one way — the general significance of precious metals must be investigated *with regard to a single sharply defined* problem. And that will happen here. As I have already explained in the introductory remarks to this section, we want to strive to recognise the connection between precious metals production and capitalism, but first of all its *significance for the genesis of capitalism*. In this connection, we thus now add the various effects of precious metals while we again establish that:

7. they can be expressed in *four different directions*, in four different sorts.

These four directions are:

a. state formation;
b. mental formation;

c. wealth formation;

d. market formation.

We have already had opportunity to follow the effects gathered together in a. when we got to know the conditions for the growth of the modern state.

Precious metals exercise their influence on the *formation of the mind* by developing the various sides of the capitalist spirit when they either by sudden and strong increase in the urge for acquisition rise to a paroxysm of acquisition and develop the speculative spirit or help by their constant use as money in developing the calculative mind. This part of their effect is not portrayed in this work, in which the capitalist spirit is not *derived*, but rather assumed as given; I have said much more over that already in another place[269].

Precious metals possess wealth-forming power and have proved it in more than one direction — both with their obtaining and with their transformation into money. It is clear that this power must grow to the same extent as the production of precious metals is increased, and that the forms of wealth formation depend on the organisation of the mine and the value of the precious metal, for which reason it is thus important to obtain exact knowledge of these things. Next to this — as you could call it — direct wealth formation, which is tied to precious metals and which I pursue in Chapter 42, there is then yet another, direct manner of influence which precious metals exercise as formers of wealth — through the medium of price formation.

Finally precious metals appear as market formers. As such they express their effects in a fourfold way:

a. in so far as the transition to market-like production are at all first made possible — an effect which we have already traced earlier (see Volume I, Chapter 8, page 141 ff.);

b. in so far as they act as a constant demand for goods to expand the market precisely to the extent that the quantity of newly extracted precious metals grows;

c. in so far as they appear as a condition, so that the *extra demand* called forth by the increase in wealth can *be applied to goods*;

d. in so far as they *influence prices*, thus in the case of the effect of rising prices a general upward movement is capable of producing an upturn in the economy.

Most of the connections claimed here will be easy to perceive by mere appearance in the fitting place — to indicate them means already to uncover them, for they lie on the surface like panned gold which you can easily grasp. By contrast in one case a somewhat more elaborate process is required — to obtain the knowledge that precious metals are able to exercise and have exercised during the epoch of early capitalism an influence on prices and the consequences, be it on wealth formation, be it on market formation, and why. This knowledge is comparable to the gold which draws through the gold-containing ore in thin veins and which must be extracted with an elaborate apparatus.

The following chapters shall serve the goal of uncovering the connections between precious metal production and price formation — theoretical (Chapter 33) and empirical-historical (Chapter 34).

Chapter 33: Money Value and Price

Literature

The problem is dealt with in every textbook of political economy. Of German textbooks, those of Philippovich (1893) and A. Wagner (1907) are especially cited. A good overview of the state of the research is given by Altmann (1909), where the reader will also find further literature. For the history of dogma I refer still to the book of Hoffmann (1907).

From the latest literature the book by Fisher (1911) deserves to be highlighted, above all on account of the decisiveness with which the author again takes on the much blasphemed against quantity theory. Unfortunately I cannot find that Fisher — who stands in essence on the ground of the "naive" quantity theory, on the indubitably correct and important realisation that the quantity of money, in particular the production ratios of the precious metals, is of a determinative influence on the level of prices — has created new supports for it. You cannot do that with the arguments of the classical quantity theorists. — In passing, it is to be noted what an excellent scholarly example the contest over the quantity theory is for "the power of the word" in our science. Most writers connect with the *words* quantity theory the ideas of the old school and are thereby deaf to any new revival of the material.

I. The "Laws of Prices"

It cannot be my task in this place to develop a thorough price theory. Rather it must suffice to expose those points which seem to me to be of special significance for my argument.

I essentially stand on the foundation of the "classical" price theory and thus consider both the "law of supply and demand" and the "law of production costs" to be the best settings for the "laws of prices", over whose nature itself I would like expressly to make the following remarks in order to prevent misunderstandings.

The laws of prices whose formulation forms one of the most important tasks of the so-called "theoretical political economy" are aids to our thinking which we form for the goal of comprehending the empirical-historical price formation. They do not portray the real course of price formation, but rather give a schematic idea of how this *would* run under specific assumptions.

"Laws of prices" are conceptual ideas which are formed by us following *one* of the causes (motives) active in real life in its effects under the assumptions,

1. that these causes remain always the same and always equally strong;
2. that they work under the same conditions, which we likewise define.

The motive whose effects we are following is the striving to complete a purchase as advantageously as possible; the striving thus of the seller to sell as expensively as possible, of the buyer to buy as cheaply as possible. The conditions which we assume as given means are the following:

a) complete rationality of the buyers and sellers — they shall only be led by the cited motive in their dealings and shall know absolutely where they are to find their advantage, thus shall be constantly informed over the most favourable opportunities;
b) free commerce — the possibility shall exist for the buyers to also seek out at any time the best recognised opportunity, just as the possibility for the sellers to guide trade and production in a direction where the highest profit will be accorded to them;
c) that prices already exist. It is especially important to realise that *the price is an a priori of the laws of prices*.

The prices in reality never (or at most only by accident) follow the posited price rules, because the assumptions necessary for that just never occur to their full extent.

One or several of the following deviations are always appearing:
1. next to the striving for the greatest advantage other motives are in operation — the sense of tradition, if I remain true to a tailor because he was my tailor for 30 years; sympathy, if I give the old cobbler the boots to fix because he is old and frail; comfort, if I shop in the closest shop; considerations of standing, if I only shop in elegant shops; fashion addiction, if I frequent department stores; political principles, if I avoid Jewish businesses, etc., etc. (which in this case

is really not just one façon de parler [so to speak], since there are countless stirrings of the soul which determine the price);

2. rationality does not exist — we frequently do not know where the cheapest goods are to be bought; the seller frequently does not know where the strongest demand reigns;

3. freedom of commerce does not exist for the movement of goods — all sorts of artificial (legal!) and natural obstacles stand in the way of the owner of the goods who wants to bring his goods to the place which has the most favourable sales conditions;

4. freedom of commerce does not exist for capital and labour — production in reality cannot (or mostly not) always be expanded as quickly as our schema assumes; the price can also remain for a longer period above the rational price. Production is no more limited in the required measure when the prices sink below the "natural" price, because the structures should be made use of, the workers (craftsmen) cannot immediately retrain, etc. The price remains thus perhaps for a long time below the rational price;

5. one and the same seller of goods (producer, trader) frequently does not calculate his profit evenly from the entire goods which he sells, but rather sells some of them perhaps without profit, others even with a loss, because he earns so much more from others — the consequence is prices for individual objects which stand above, for others below their rational price (and yet in their totality have been formed in accordance with the laws of prices) — so-called related prices.

In summary: a chaos of various details. But — enjoying only some commercial freedom in one economic area — yet a certain regularity which is elicited by the motive at the base of the price schema always (as a constant) being in effect, the others not with the same regularity. The image of a storm-whipped sea whose surface is curled by thousands and thousands of waves and whose water is held though in uniform motion by quite large waves.

The "laws of prices" should serve at first only to describe the effect which is produced by alterations in the exchange value of goods. But since contained in the price now is an equation between the exchange value of money and that of the goods, you will not only have to seek to explain the changes in price from the side of the goods, but also from the side of the money. It is at the outset evident that changes can also occur in money values and that such a change — in the reverse sense — will be able to influence the price — when the money value falls, the prices must rise, when it rises, the prices must fall. It is precisely at this point that this influence of changes in money value on the price is to be looked into

241

since I judge it to be especially high historically. Hence I will in the following, departing from the previous approach, discuss in detail the *connection between money value and price*. I will answer directly as a result so many questions which have been directed at me in the criticism on this point.

II. The Application of the Price Laws to Money

An earlier, naive time accepted without much worrying, as something obvious as it were, that a connection prevailed between money value and price, and also knew how money value was determined — through the quantity of money present. They were the adherents of the teaching described by us as the *quantity theory of the old stamp*, which numbered in its ranks the best heads — Locke, Hume, Montesquieu, and others. They derived the price level from the quantity of money circulating in a land by simply dividing the sum of prices being paid into the total value of coins present. When its amount increased now, that is, the denominator became greater, whereas the divisor (the size of the sales of goods) remained the same, then in their opinion, which rests exclusively on the basis of simple arithmetic, the quotient, just the price of goods, likewise increased. And vice versa.

This way of looking at things appears so naive to us today that we are incapable rightly of comprehending how such outstanding thinkers, who saw clearly into all other things, could adopt it. The explanation may well lie in that the psychological explanation of all social and also economic events that is so obvious to us today lay distant from that time, and that they did not feel the grotesqueness which lies in the attempt to want to explain an act of will, like of price formation, without any reference to its mental basis. For us the mechanical process of division by the naive quantity theorists is utter mysticism and absolutely not worth a discussion.

Incidentally there were cases during the early capitalist epoch in which prices really came into being in seemingly purely mechanistic ways through the process of division. Such a case was the price formation at the market fairs of Vera Cruz and Portobelo at which, as is well-known, almost the entire exchange of goods between the European lands and the silver producing lands of South and Central America took place. Here silver producers and the sellers of goods thus met directly. The quantity of goods brought to the market fairs was of course a given, just as the quantity of precious metals obtained by the sellers. When all the goods were sold, and all the precious metals (money) brought along were handed over, the respective price complied with the (not predetermined, incidental) quantity of money which was in the hands of the buyers. This fact was made clear by Ulloa (1753, 2:101). Cf. also Ricard (1722, 528).

Of course a mental process also lay at the base of this seemingly mechanical price formation. But the effect was striking and could certainly provide cause for the establishment of the old quantity theory.

We know today that a social theory will be psychologically based or it will not be. To the psychologically based price theories belong those by which supply and demand determine the price. For behind the abstractions of supply and demand hides the needs of the seller and the desires of the buyer. Mental processes (defined objectively as always) lead to prices rising or falling. Hence we will have to listen after all more to those price theorists who want to use the law of supply and demand on money and to have it rise or fall according to the money value. As far as I see, it is the great majority of political economists who seek to establish in this way a connection between money value and price. Thus as Roscher writes: "It concerns here firstly the use of general laws of price. Thus the supply and demand of money."[270]

It is not hard to prove that this schematic transfer of the law of prices for goods to the formation of money value is inadmissible. From the very simple principle that there is for money absolutely no supply and demand in the sense with which we apply these concepts to general goods[271].

These considerations have then led many to now absolutely deny the possibility that an influence on prices can take place from the side of money.

That is, however, going too far. If an argument is recognised to be erroneous, what is being proven does not need to be false. I believe that changes in money value certainly do take place and can have determinative effects on prices. Only that the connections which prevail between money value and prices must be found in other ways that those previously attempted. Let us look at which ways.

Best of all if we take our starting point from the producer of precious metals and his quite singular position in economic life. He is the only one amongst all producers who does not need to sell his goods and yet can value them. With that, however, that he is the only non-seller, he becomes the sole only-buyer. He can buy — he alone — before he has sold. *His products represent no supply, like all others, but rather demand.* For they are simply exchangeable, simply marketable — in whatever quantities they are produced. From the depths of the silver mines, the gold mines, and gold-carrying streams swells thus unbroken a demand for goods which breaks forth as it were out of nothing, which, so long as it is there, cannot experience any interruption, which constantly creates a new world of desire — a source of economic life as cannot flow anywhere else.

Should not the value relationship between precious metals and goods be able to be influenced decisively from this position? I think yes. And yet we will have to imagine the connections thus.

III. The Conceivable Influence on Prices of the Quantity and Value of Money

A change, say an increase, which changes the production of precious metals, in the assumed case increases the demand for goods, be it means of production, be it consumer goods. As soon as the product of the gold producers comes into circulation, it just works as demand. Thus, when the quantity of extracted gold increases, the prices of goods will at first rise in the producing areas settled by the gold producers. And each rise in prices effected here means of course a rise in demand on the other side of the first group of producers which must manifest in a rise in prices in the second production zone. With a decrease in precious metals production the process is reversed.

We will thus safely be able to put forward the:

1ˢᵗ *Proposition: Every increase (decrease) in production of precious metals (money) has the tendency to raise (lower) the prices of goods.*

Whether this change in price is now permanent and whether it becomes general, that is, is thus reflected in a devaluation of money, depends on a series of special circumstances. I would like first of all to put forward the following proposition:

2nd Proposition: An influence on price of an alteration in the production of precious metals **can** *only ever happen when this alteration is accompanied by a corresponding change in the conditions of production, that is, by a reduction or rise in the costs of production of the precious metals.*

We assume that by a strong increase in gold production a strong and far-reaching rise in the prices of goods has been effected — according to our 1st proposition — but the costs of precious metals production has remained the same. The consequence will be that in accordance with the general rise in prices for the means of production and rewards to labour its expression as money rises. If the production of a pound of gold has cost say 1,000 marks, then with a rise in prices of 50%, if an equal quantity of machines and workers are used to extract the pound of gold, the sum transforms from 1,000 marks henceforth into the sum of 1,500 marks. A pound of gold, however, is as before equal to 1,392 marks — its producer thus instead of earning [392 marks] pays out with each pound 108 marks. The result will be that he withdraws his capital, closes the business. But with that it drops out as a source of demand. If the demand on the side of gold producers decreases in such a way, a tendency arises of making the prices of goods fall. When the fall has progressed far enough, production will again be rewarding for our gold producers, he is established again, demand increases, and it produces the tendency for an increase in the prices of goods, etc. Here the schematic is the same as with the formation of prices through alterations on the side of the goods.

Thus, a lasting influence on prices through a shift in the production quantities of precious metals *can* absolutely only occur when at the same time the production costs have changed — *must* it then also occur, however, or *when* must it then occur?

Answer: that will be dependent on the size of the production of precious metals and on its relationship with the size of goods production. Proof is given somewhat as follows. An initial rise in price (to begin in turn with this), which takes place in accordance with our first proposition, of course has the effect at first of increasing profits, but at the same time also increasing production. The goods desired more and at higher prices will be provided and produced in greater quantities. As a result (according to the familiar schema for goods prices) the countermovement is introduced — prices will begin to fall until they have reached the "natural" price, that is, that at which the average profits are obtained. If now at this time the production of precious metals is not increased further, the final result will be that the producers of precious metals (if we assume that their production conditions have not worsened) receive an above average profit which finds its cause in the proven monopoly character of their products. If in the meantime the production conditions have worsened, then the entire rise in prices was an episode.

But when the case now occurs that the production of precious metals stops for a long time for favourable or more favourable conditions; that the production of the goods desired by the precious metals producers cannot increase anymore as quickly as demand requires, then the effect will be produced that the prices climb up out of the first zone — the first gainers will (thanks to their extra profits) also pay higher prices to their suppliers, they to theirs, and so on. Capital and labour will not have cause to flow away into the first favoured sphere of production, but will find favourable conditions of utilisation where they are. When this process has lasted long enough, however, when the rings formed by the stone thrown into the water have spread across the entire pond — plain speaking: when all branches of economic life are caught by the rise in prices — then the cause for a countermovement which can lead to a fall in prices — that is an increase in production of a category of goods over and above the demand — no longer applies, since no sphere demonstrates an above average profit anymore, *the profits rather having levelled out on the basis of the general higher prices*. Then a general fall in the value of money has become in reality a general (and lasting) rise in prices.

In the same way on the other hand in reversed sense, a worsening of production conditions for precious metals would be effected. Only that this would surely express itself more quickly in a fall in prices. The process would be that the demand of the precious metal producers decreases, in consequence of which the prices fall for the first suppliers and the jolt would now be passed on by them. As will be shown later, the effects must vary here according to the general organisation of economic life — different in a craftwork economy (15th century!); different in a capitalist economy (1880s). Common to all, however, even for this case, is that the proposition is valid which we can now put forward as:

3rd Proposition: The generalisation of price changes depends on the proportion of precious metals production to goods production.

There is no need to specially mention that the schema of money value formation developed in the foregoing pages is entirely of just as ideal a character as the schema of price formation is; that *in reality the same irregularities* disturb the schematically pure development here as there. But what still deserves to be emphasised and noted is this: that for all the conditions influencing the formation of prices "in an incidental way", a series of irregularities are to be added which are peculiar to the formation of money value. They originate entirely from the special manner in which the procurement of precious metals takes place, and are principally the following:
I. The assumption that the production of precious metals must yield the average profit applies not much more frequently than with the production of goods. Because precisely with it, it is especially often continued to be worked without any profit in the hope for future gain. It is well-known that most seekers of gold go under; it is just as well-known that among the gold and silver mines at any time a large (mostly the greatest) part are worked without gain.

In Joachimstal (to clarify by a few examples what has been said) there were (Sternberg 1836, 1:426):

in the year	returns	out-payments
1525	125	471
1535	217	697
1545	120	452
1555	83	312
1565	63	237
1575	34	128

Likewise the idea of a commerce-free regulation of production under the point of view of the average yield is messed up again directly by the frequent use of unfree labourers in the production of precious metals;

II. In reverse it is surely possible only with precious metals that large quantities of them are brought into circulation having incurred no manufacturing cost at all when they are obtained in the way of theft and plunder;

III. Precious metals are eliminated at times from the ranks of increasable goods; if perhaps all the familiar mining locations are exhausted or the business at the familiar locations cannot be continued (from technical causes — flooding!). With that they become monopoly goods, and all statements over their conditions of production are invalid;

IV. Also as long as they are increasable, the production costs which determine their exchange value are not always of the same nature. Sometimes it is the production costs of the most productive mine, other times those of the most unproductive mine which have a determining influence on the price.

***

Now with the candles which we have lit in these schematic observations we descend again into the darkness of history and examine whether we are capable of showing in the course of it the meaningful connections as we have been visualising them up to now.

Chapter 34: The Formation of Prices during the Epoch of Early Capitalism

Sources and Literature

The following works instruct us about the facts:

Italy: Carli (1804). Cibrario (1839, Vol. III).

France: Saint-Maur (1746). D'Avenel (1894). From it, an extract by the same author: D'Avenel (1895). Leber (1847). Hanauer (1876) (Denrées et salaires [staples and incomes].)

England: Fleetwood (1745) (the best edition). Fleetwood was the main source for most of the discussions of price history by Adam Smith. Rogers (1866). Rogers himself, as well as his son, have made several extracts from the great work. Tooke and Newmarch (1838; 1862).

The Netherlands: Hubert van Houtte (1902).

Germany: the oft-mentioned works of Lamprecht (1885) and Inama-Sternegg (1879). In addition, Wiebe (1895).

Then a number of local history investigations come into consideration: Kius for Thuringia, Falke for Saxony, Hildebrand for Hesse, etc., which I will, however, refrain from listing.

The remaining literature is to be found listed in Lexis and Sommerlad (1901); there the overviews and individual figures for prices can be compared for all lands in the various time periods.

The best information over the difficulties of medieval price statistics is in Inama-Sternegg (1879, 2:427 f., 3.2:487). The unfortunate problem of the "purchasing power of money" has been dealt with once and for all by Held (1871). Cf. Sombart (1903, 438). Recent works dealing with the topic: Walther (1912). Walther correctly dispenses with measuring "money value"; he would like to "illustrate" it by establishing a scale of incomes "in which the organism of economic stratification comes to a living unity". Of course, there is nothing against that — it is then that which I asserted in Sombart (1903) (which Walther unfortunate is not familiar with): that the shifts in the *quality* of consumption make any comparison of different epochs impossible.

***

What the study of goods prices in the past has brought us up to now is above all the certain knowledge that a good num-

249

ber of interesting things will *not* be established with certainty. We will probably dispense for all time with general price statistics, but just as much also have to free ourselves finally from the madness of being able to establish the "purchasing power" of money for a specific time or even to express in a figure the change in the "purchasing power" of money in the course of the centuries.

Fortunately we are not dealing with this problem here, but with a question to which there very surely is an answer.

We can namely establish something in the area of price history with some certainty and reliability even for distant time periods. And it is — happily! — that which especially interests the economic historian in the history of prices, I would like to say that which should interest him exclusively, because it alone is of significance for the knowledge of the great connections — I mean the *movement of prices* — their change in the course of the centuries. To obtain from it a reasonably clear picture, the material on the history of prices which has been collected for all lands in the course of the last lifetime is sufficiently complete. And to give a sketch of the general movement in prices from 1250–1850 is the exclusive goal of the following portrayal which makes full use of the results of the great collections of material without perhaps providing new discoveries of its own.

The study of these works lets us recognise the following course of prices during our periods.

The time around 1250 like the entire 13th century falls in the period of *rising* prices which had already begun earlier, especially clearly from the 12th century. This rise in prices continues up into the 14th century — according to some until the middle, according to others (e.g. D'Avenel) until the second third of the century.

Prices fall from then on until about the year 1500. That is the result which all price historians arrive at.

Rogers advocates in two different places two different opinions. In his lectures (J. E. T. Rogers 1898, 191) he maintains that for England the nominal price in pounds sterling, shillings, and pence remained admittedly approximately the same from 1300 to 1500 and countered the objection that they had thus fallen, since the metal content of the pound in this period was reduced (see the figures on page 113), with the claim that most price fixing would have rested on the actual weighing of the coins. But this practice was surely not so general as Rogers seems to as-

250

sume. And then even in England (which is to be assumed from general causes) prices in reality would have fallen in the 15th century. Rogers also has this view in his main work (J. E. T. Rogers 1866, 4:715 ff.) where he expressly remarks: "there is a marked decline in the price from the average of 1261–1400 to that of 1401–1540."

From 1500 on prices begin to *rise* to an extent, as is well-known, which has never occurred a second time in history. If the earlier assumptions — that prices had increased five-fold, seven-fold, even ten-fold[272] during the 16th century — have also proven to be exaggerated, scientific examination of the facts shows that certainly a rise in almost all prices from about 100% to 150% occurred. A few goods, e.g. grains, experienced still far greater increases. Thus grain prices rose in the 16th century, for example, in:

> England........................c. 155%
> Paris............................c. 165%
> Orleans........................c. 200%
> Strasbourg..................c. 280%
> Saxony........................c. 300%
> Spain..................c. 453–556%

The researchers are in agreement also in the view that the greatest part of the price rise is to be allotted to the second half, particularly the last decades of the 16th century (Spain from 1586–1598).

From the end of the 16th century on the results of historical price investigations are not as uniform as up to then. That has its main cause probably in the different development which from then on both the different lands and the different categories of goods experienced.

In general it may be said that a part of the 17th century was a time of *price stagnation*, but that from the end of the 17th century and then in the 18th century — probably already in the first half, certainly in the second half — prices in general in Europe had the tendency to *rise*. This is on the other hand a generally observed fact. In the second decade of the 19th century a stagnation or fall in prices then occurred which lasted until the 1840s.

In order to better impress on the eye the main features of the price movement from 1250 to 1850, I have compiled the information just given into the following table:

1250–1350 Rising.
1350–1500 Stagnation. Falling.
1500–1600 Abruptly rising.
1600–1700 Stagnation. Uncertainty.
1700–1750 Uncertainty.
1750–1815 Rising.
1815–1850 Stagnation. Falling.

An extended schematisation, in which the very latest, quite general movements in prices from 1500 to 1800 are essentially correctly expressed, was carried out by Aupetit[273] in that he summarised the index numbers to which the investigations of D'Avenel, Leber, and Hanauer offered the foundation into a single average. Then, if you set the price level of the year 1800 equal to 100, a change in the price level in the years 1500–1800 is expressed in the following figures:

1500......................................35
1600......................................75
1700......................................90
1800......................................100

Which graphically looks thus:

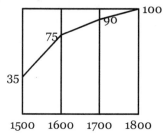

What share, our question thus now reads, do the precious metals have in this rise in prices which was decisively important for the entire course of European economic life; was and — if indeed — to what extent was the rise in prices called forth by the peculiar production circumstances of precious metals during the epoch of early capitalism?

The following chapter attempts to give an answer to these questions.

Chapter 35: The Influence of Precious Metals Production on Price Formation

Preliminary Remarks

The proof for the *actually occurring* effect of money value on prices is divided into two parts:

- first of all is to prove that a change in money value precisely in our time period, *if* it occurs, can be expressed especially easily in prices;
- secondly that changes in the exchange value of money occurred which corresponded to the movement of prices.

The first part of the proof again consists of the proof of characteristic formations of circumstances for goods production on the one hand, for money on the other hand, from which the correctness of the claim put forward arises. The circumstances of goods production have already been described, where the craftwork-like organisation of the economy was described, and will in the further course of the portrayal (for the early capitalist period) be described still further (in the next volume). The essential feature being considered here is the low development of productive forces and the consequentially low capability for expansion of production. In contrast the other side of the problem must be examined more precisely.

As strange as it sounds, an attempt to produce the empirical proof of a connection between the course and formation of precious metals production and the course and formation of prices has (as far as I know) not been undertaken at all up to now. Hence there is also *no literature*.

***

I. The Value Realisation of Precious Metals

Under value realisation of precious metals I understand here the totality of conditions under which their transformation into money takes place — seen under the viewpoint of the interest of a possessor of precious metals who would like to know how to shape this transformation into money as far as possible to his needs.

The value realisation process of the extracted (produced) precious metals (and we only need to consider these here) begins at the moment when the ore is brought to the surface, or the gold dust (with panned gold) separated from the sand and scree. While those only small changes up until its use as coinage are yet to be carried out now, the ore must — in our period only silver ore is concerned — first be smelted in a lengthy process. The producer of the ore thus cannot immediately realise the value of his product as coinage — he must first produce the finished (pure) precious metal. For him value realisation thus signifies at first the *sale of the ore to the smelter*.

Only in the case that he is at the same time the owner of the smelter does he need like the gold producer to first think of value realisation when the metal is ready for the mint. This combination of the silver mining and the silver smelting in one hand took place more frequently in Europe towards the end of the Middle Ages, in the American areas of production it probably always formed the rule (I have not been able to find an explicit confirmation of the correctness of this assumption anywhere).

In contrast, it was the rule throughout the entire European Middle Ages for mining and smelting to be two absolutely separate crafts. That is thus, the producer of the ore had to "sell" his product (if we disregard the case, rare for that time, that he had the ore smelted for a fee) in order to realise its value. The price for the ore was privately determined at the market. As buyer either the smelter owner himself appeared or, which (as it appears) formed the rule, a special class of intermediaries — "ore buyers", as they were called in the mining and smelting laws (in the Kuttenberg law, for example, the 22nd chapter concerns them). These ore buyers were necessary with the structure at the time of the mines, where thousands of workers, each after his own gain, were working. The smaller works had no smelter — what were they meant to do with their ore? Thus then every week the extracted ore was "bid for" in the presence of an official. The miners brought their carts of ore to the specified place where the ore buyers haggled with them over the price[274].

The state of affairs which developed as a result seemed now to have been the same everywhere, as far as we see, as in all places the ore buyers were the stronger party who dictated the price to the miners. Quite frequently at least we hear complaints over "exploitation" of miners and see the authorities endeavouring to protect the miners against the overly powerful ore buyers. In the Kuttenberg law there is talk of their "detestabilis conspiracio" [hateful conspiracy] which sets out to suppress the price of ore through arranged underbidding.

Likewise the Tyrolean miners opposed on repeated occasions the price-depressing "preemptive sale" of ore, that is, even opposed the intermediaries who bought the ore from the miners cheaply and then made an unseemly profit with smelting. For such complaints Duke Frederick* in his mine letter for Gossensaß forbade preemptive sale[275]; it was followed in that by the mining law for Schwaz of 1468[276].

The desire to regulate the evils, which grew out of the miners susceptible situation, was then one of the reasons which towards the end of the Middle Ages moved many of the rulers to take the silver smelting business into their own control. Thus the Tyrolean rulers erected their own silver smelters in Innsbruck; the Bavarian dukes founded in the second half of the 15th century the great smelter at Brixlegg which was managed by officials and which smelted not only silver from the neighbouring ducal mines, but also drew silver ore from various Tyrolean territories and even from a great distance for smelting[277].

In order to understand the particular conditions under which *the transformation of mint-ready precious metals into gold* took place, we must bear in mind the general features which treasuries and mints bore in our epoch — above all their pronounced fiscal character. The entire treasury was meant to be subservient to the interests of the royal household. Thus too — and indeed to a quite especially outstanding extent — the mints. The minting of precious metals did not take place to serve the private interests of the possessors of gold and silver, nor to tend to economic interests — rather as

---

*   [Tr.: most likely Frederick IV "of the empty pockets", Duke of Austria.]

good as exclusively to open up an income source for the ruler of the mint. The mint was thus in all earlier times directed to the making of profit. It turned then, however, directly into a commercial undertaking if it was not managed by the ruler on his own account but by private interests to whom the exercise of the minting prerogative was handed over, was run "at one's own expense and risk". And it formed, as is known, the rule during the late Middle Ages in most lands — whether it concerned a short-term lease or security contract between the ruler and a number of business people (a form which we meet frequently in Italy especially), or whether the mints are ceded as a permanent right to a body furnished with various favours, the mint cooperative (as in the larger German states)[278].

For if private persons run the mints for their own profit, then their striving must be directed to not only (as was constantly the case whether it concerned state or privately run operations) "strike" out the seignorage — that is, the tax for the ruler of the mint — with the minting, but to obtain the highest possible surplus over the expenditures.

From this situation now arises, however, two guiding principles for the conduct of the business of the mint in our time, principles which were of decisive importance for the realisation of the value of the precious metals. Obviously all striving of the minter must in fact be directed at:

1. minting as much precious metal as is possible; and
2. obtaining the mint material (the precious metals) as "cheaply" as possible.

And indeed, the (objective) *right to mint*, as you can name the totality of legal conditions under which the transformation of precious metals into (minted) money takes place, is uniformly defined in its character by these two guiding principles during the entire period which we are surveying, and indeed in all lands, as far as I can see.

Its content is in its main features as follows.

I. the by-far most important right of the possessor of precious metals for our purposes: to deliver and have minted by the mint any arbitrary quantity of precious metal — whether gold or silver — was at that time regarded so natural that in most minting laws it is not even explicitly mentioned at all. Where there is mention of it, it is only that whoever delivers precious metal to the mint for minting shall receive so many of the land's coins for the weight unit of silver (or gold?).

Examples: *Florentine* law of 19th August 1345 (Shaw 1895, 19 ff.) — *Strasbourg* minting law of 1470, No. 9 (Eheberg 1879, 201) — *French* edicts of 1329, 1332, 1350, among others — *Joachimstal* minting law (after nationalisation of the mints!) (Sternberg 1836, 1:322 ff.) — *Bohemian* state law of Ferdinand I from 1534 (Goldast 1620, 103 f.) — *Spain* (Spain 1640, p. tit. XXI, Ley X) — *Brazil* (Eschwege 1833, 192 ff.).

It is quite incomprehensible when Del Mar claims that the unlimited freedom to mint (in the sense understood here) first dates from the English law of the year 1666. It is not even right that at the time a minting "at cost price" occurred for the first time. The three named French edicts pronounce, for example, the renunciation of any seignorage; only that the reason was a different one from that in the law of 1666.

A legal limitation of this right to unlimited free minting of an arbitrary quantity of precious metals — which thus we call these days the *freedom to mint* — has not become known to me from the entire period of 1250–1750.

This state of law follows, as stated, directly from the spirit which dominated the minting policy of those centuries.

II. To this "freedom to mint" (in our sense) corresponds now on the other side a very extensive restrictiveness in the manner in which this "freedom" could be exercised. The possessor of precious metals was in fact forced to have it minted at the place where it was extracted. Everywhere we encounter legal determinations which forbid the export of precious metals from the area of production and prescribe the delivery to a specified minting office — that applies equally to Silesia[279], to Saxony[280], to Bohemia, and indeed to both Kuttenberg[281] and Joachimstal[282], to Tyrol[283], and to Mexico[284]. Only for Brazilian gold was I unable to locate any mint obligation (even if occasionally gold ingots were banned) and above all no export ban.

III. If the export bans had been strictly carried out, then precious metals would have not been able to be found in unminted condition outside their areas of production — the coins of the cities and lands in whose domain no precious metals would have been extracted would have had to become desolate because they received no material for minting, or would have had to limit themselves to smelting foreign coins and converting them into their own land's coins[285]. But we know now that this was not the case. We know that at all times during our epoch a market also existed for unminted metal, that thus precious metals came into free circulation.

Firstly the bans on private gold and silver sales, which on the other hand were a general phenomenon of the European Middle Ages, let us infer that. As in fact the rulers in the production regions sought to secure for themselves the purchase of the precious metals produced by forbidding their export and desiring the delivery of the entire production, the rulers in all other regions endeavoured to acquire as much minting material as possible by requiring everyone who was offering gold or silver for sale to offer it first to the mint for purchase: "quicunque argentum vendere voluerit, ad monetam debeat illud presentare nec ad nundinas nec alias presumat deferre" [whosoever wishes to sell silver, ought to present it for money and not presume to bring it to market or anything else], the King had pronounced to the Archbishop of Worms as the law of the realm[286], and then numerous cities and rulers adopted this law as their own[287].

But that a market for precious metals existed, we also gather from other evidence — thus we learn, for example, of the Viennese mint cooperative members who went to distant markets to buy precious metals for their coins[288]; we see the foreign precious metal dealer come to the Strasbourg mint and offer his material for minting and see him, without having agreed terms, leaving again "without quarter"[289].

Now you could assume the material for this trade in precious metals only delivered old precious metal — breakages, utensils, jewellery, old coins, or all that in melted down state. From numerous places in the sources we can conclude, however, that newly produced silver and gold was also indubitably traded. And we would also be permitted to believe without such evidence that it was so. Because we on the other hand possess numerous evidence for the fact of a breaking of the export ban. We know that this breaking happened in two ways:

a) through smuggling;

b) through contract.

That always, where trade in precious metals is restricted, smuggling is practised, appears so obvious that it hardly needs any special confirmation. We possess in abundance, however, both for the European Middle Ages and for the American silver lands a quantity of evidence which allows for the conclusion of extensive smuggling. Their listing is unnecessary since the facts do not permit any doubt.

In addition, we know of numerous contracts, particularly from the period of the 15th and 16th centuries, in which specific dealers were permitted to export precious metals. Rich moneymen bought freedom from the export ban often with high sums. Thus the rich mining company member Antony von Roß undertook in the year 1486 to make the payment of a lump sum of 4,000 florins to the sovereign prince for permission to be able to freely trade his silver for a year wherever he wanted, even if the exchange for his silver would not have been so high[290]. Similar contracts were concluded by Augsburg merchants with the King of Bohemia (16th century)[291], and by the Fuggers with the King of Spain[292], etc.

As easily as we are able to see that there were means and ways of bringing precious metals into commerce despite the export bans, the fact is as conspicuous on first glance that there could be a *trade in precious metals*, since both, as we have seen, were freely mintable. According to our present-day ideas there could have thus been at the time only ever a trade in gold or in silver when the one metal was bought with the other. Indubitably these purchases — gold with silver, silver with gold — also then formed a considerable part of the trade in precious metals. But we will also have to assume that even silver was bought with silver (coins) and (even if to a smaller extent) gold with gold coins.

The explanation for this conspicuous phenomenon lies again in the well-known characteristic of money and coinage of that time which had the effect that between the precious metals in the form of ingots and in the form of coins large and constantly fluctuating differences in value prevailed, and that in consequence in the market quite surely a silver price determined by supply and demand could form in silver, and a gold price in gold. Those large and fluctuating differences in value between ingots and coins (which have today as good as vanished from freely minted metals) occurred through the following circumstances:

a) size and fluctuations of transport costs;
b) size and fluctuations of seignorage (possibly of the mine contributions — smuggling of untaxed precious metal!);
c) size and fluctuations of minting costs;
d) fluctuations of the silver content of groschens and pfennigs, thus also of the exchange value of the pound.

IV. With these statements — and they were made for that reason — the important question, however, is now answered at least in part: in what circumstances did the mint buy gold and silver from the possessor of precious metals. The answer must in fact according to what we have learnt about the marketability of precious metals obviously be that the mint paid the possessor of a specific quantity of precious metal — although this was "freely mintable" — a price. In other words, *there was no ratio fixed for all time between a land's coins and the weight of metal*, a transfer of an equally large sum of value did not simply take place, a change in form did not simply take place. Rather, the quantity of a land's coins which was paid for a pound of silver (or gold — although for this these remarks apply to a much smaller extent) could be of various amounts, even if never *higher* — salvo errore monetarii [except for monetary error] — than the same silver coins less all costs (for minting, seignorage, etc.). If we assume this would have amounted to 25%, then the deliverer of one pound of silver could have received silver coins at most to the amount of ¾ of a pound of fine silver as reimbursement. This amount, however, could be higher *or* lower from as many causes as variations in the factors determining the size of production costs are possible. It could furthermore be so much *lower* when the mint succeeds in raising its profit. The price fluctuations are doubled by the fluctuations in the ratios of value of the two precious metals against each other.

How was this fluctuating price determined now? In two different ways: on one side through a directive of the ruler or the mints; or contractually through special arrangement between them and the possessor of the precious metals.

Example for the first form of fixing the price are offered by almost all mint rules. Exactly like today a mint law determined at the time the mint's rule — how many of the land's coins were paid out for a certain quantity of precious metal. But what outwardly distinguished those fixings in essence from modern standardisations of similar content is just the constant fluctuation of the amounts.

A few arbitrarily selected example will make that clear:

The *Florentine* mint paid for one pound of silver:
* according to the law of 19th August 1345:
  132 grossi and retains 2 grossi minting fee;
* according to the law of October 1345:
  140 grossi and retains 2 grossi minting fee;
* according to the law of 1347:
  111⅗ grossi and retains 5⅖ Guelphi grossi minting fee.

In *Breslau* to the mark of fine silver applied:
* 1532–1547 between 6 fl. 3 g. gr. (34 g. gr. = 1 fl.) and 7 fl. 7 g. gr.
* 1547 between 7 fl. 10 g. gr. and 7 fl. 18 g. gr.
* 1558 7¼ talers (for 36 white groschen).

In the law of 1534 Ferdinand I set the "price" for the "mark of fine silver to less than a quintlein* of Nuremberg weight" payable to the miners at all mines of *Bohemia*, to 7 guilders Rh. 54 (obviously a printing error for 14) white groschen and 6 white pfennigs (Goldast 1620, 96).

According to the Bilder-Kodex of 1556, the redemption price of one mark of fine silver was:
* under Duke Sigmund: ....5–6 guilders
* under Maximilian I: ....8–10 guilders
* under Ferdinand I: ....9–12 guilders

The fluctuations *could* only arise from the changes in value of the land's coins — but they could just as well owe their existence to differing sizes of profit from the coins.

Now it seems, however, almost as if in most case this shall we say "legal" price was not paid at all, but you far more frequently agreed the price each time first. Thus we frequently encounter contract-like price fixings.

Again a few examples:

In 1449 Duke Sigmund agreed with *Schwaz* and *Gossensaß* that he would pay them 6½ fl. for one mark of silver, less 2½ fl. exchange fee; sources in Worms (1904, 129).

---

* [Tr.: a Quintlein (or Quäntchen) was a quarter of a Lot, which was a unit of mass of around 14–18 grams.]

In 1488 a contract was concluded with the Fuggers whereby they would receive 8 fl. per mark — 5 fl. for the smelter, 3 fl. for themselves (Worms 1904, 65).

In 1476 a payment was promised to the new mines in *Freiberg* of 8 fl. for 8 years instead of the old 6 fl. for 6 years (Ermisch 1883, 2:217). The profitable mines in Saxony were mostly paid somewhat less than the loss-making mines by the silver office.

In *Silesia* Margrave Georg Friedrich in Tarnowitz (16th century) paid "according to circumstances" for the mark sometimes 6 talers 33 g. gr. and often with 7 talers 8 g. gr. (Steinbeck 1857, 2:233-234).

We have already learnt about the *Viennese* and *Strasbourg* mint co-operative members who had to buy their silver privately.

And what in the end was it that determined the price — be it legislated, or be it contracted? Of course, the power situation of both parties, since we may assume without further ado that both wanted to conclude their business for the most advantageous conditions.

Where we find legislative standardisation, its figure will have been defined more by the political situation, but also by the situation in the market for precious metals. When precious metals became scarce, then you fashioned the conditions for minting more favourably. Thus, for example, the French ordinances of the 14th century contain formal business recommendations — the mint paid back the full amount of the delivered silver; only the minting cost was to be held back, etc.

With the contractual fixing the economic situation was of course quite decisive, be it general — proximity of another sales area, etc. — or be it specific — difficulties of the ruler (whom the silver producer had advanced money), difficulties of the silver producers — as we have seen, the silver dealing in Tarnowitz paid "according to circumstances" sometimes more, sometimes less. And we also learn what sort of circumstances these were — those mines which received advances had to hand over their silver more cheaply[293].

Whether what Carl Schalk claims in his extremely commendable investigation over the standard coinage content of the Viennese pfennig is correct — that the market price and the legislated price were never very different from one another — is doubtful to me. The assumption would naturally be correct if you (as Schalk assumes) could actually acquire the silver elsewhere at all times, that is, if you had not delivered it but exported it instead. But frequently enough this possibility was lacking, be it for legal reasons (export ban!), be it for real causes — all those given above, in addition to which a further consideration remains to be taken into account — the length of time which elapsed before you received the coins, and which of course in a time of undeveloped commerce would be felt far more irksomely than today.

Pulling it all together, we must come to the result that the earlier time probably possessed minting freedom de jure, but that its content was of a different nature to today's — that it did not exclude a changing precious metals price, that the possessor of the precious metal thus — even if with significant deviation in his favour — found himself in the situation of any other possessor of goods — indeed he did not need to seek a sale for his goods (which was assured to him for all time), but he was yet in uncertainty — how high would they pay him — and thus saw himself compelled to haggle over a reasonable price. "Circumstances" of all types will have decided over its final figure.

It is perfectly clear what significance the peculiar realisation of the value of precious metals, as I have just portrayed it, must have had for price formation. *To the extent in fact that possessors of precious metals were sellers of their products, any change in the exchange value of precious metals had to convert far more quickly into the price than in a time of completely mechanised freedom of minting like our own.* Precisely this schematic and automatic transformation of money goods into an always completely the same amount of coinage must necessarily have weakened the influence of changes in money value on price formation. So that thus in the earlier period this weakening was less, the impact more direct.

When the money value thus rose, the possessor of precious metals could soon obtain a higher price for his goods; when it fell, he had to suffice with a lower one — all within certain bounds, as the forgoing portrayal has shown. So that we now would only have still to investigate to what extent the money value changed in our period. Earlier observations showed that mere changes in the quantities of precious metals produced could not exercise an influence on their exchange value,

263

rather that this was exclusively — or more correctly, in the end always — determined by the production costs. Hence the following discussion will occupy itself with the question of what changes in the production costs of precious metals are to be shown for the period under our consideration.

II. The Production Costs of Precious Metals

If I were to describe a *single* problem of political economy and economic history as the most important, I believe I would say that it is the extent of the production costs of precious metals. For if I see it rightly, the structure of the entirety of economic life stands for a good part in a somewhat closer or more distant connection with this. And precisely this central problem of two sciences was up to now only quite rarely made the object even only of discussion[294]; let alone then that it was solved in any satisfying manner. For the past usable information is almost unable to be gotten hold of at all — you are reliant for the most part on a symptomatic knowledge. Only in the present has the interest of technologists and capitalist entrepreneurs directed at precious metals production provided us with a richer material from which we can calculate the production costs with adequate certainty. But that is still no use to us now when we survey the period 1250–1850. What can be stated over the structure of production costs in that period is, as stated, little and to be obtained by deductions from general circumstances. In part it was already contained unspoken in the explanations which I made over the course of precious metals production in Chapter 31, and to which I now refer. But I want to present here in context what we know more precisely over the production costs of precious metals in our period.

In the 12th and 13th century fresh sites of silver were opened up whose mines indubitably depicted a degree of richness unknown until then. Panned gold was found. Imposing amounts were brought without any cost (as loot) by the Italians from the Orient — a lowering of money value is probably. We do not know anything more exact.

In the 15th century precious metals became scarce — the sources leave no doubt over that. The image which the time offers us is quite distinctly this — all the rulers (whose fiscal

interests, as we saw, desired a rich supply of precious metals)
are tugging at the silver blanket that has become too short.
Whether the silver also became "dearer" in that time by
reason of raised production costs? We may assume it, since
the mines of the old lodes were being worked, but new finds
had not yet been made. But even without this assumption
enough cause is present to conclude on an increase in the
value of silver. Obviously in fact silver entered in this period
into the category of absolutely unincreasable goods. For the
old pits could for the large part not continue to be kept in use
since they did not have the water under control — production
thus stopped completely. That silver was becoming "dearer" is
a constant complaint of the minters. The general coin devaluation which was especially strong directly around that time is
likewise confirmation that the money value had in fact risen.

That it fell from the end of the 15th century on is without
doubt, both for gold and silver. Gold was found as panned
gold in ample quantities in Salzburg areas and as (unpaid)
loot brought home by the conquistadors from America.

But that, both with the new precious metal finds in Germany and Austria and with the opening up of the American
silver mines, silver experienced a quite fundamental reduction in its exchange value — and indeed as direct consequence
of a strong diminishment in production costs — we may assume likewise with certainty.

Already the silver mines of Joachimstal and the Schwaz region were considerably more productive than those of Saxony
and the Harz. Considerably more productive again then, however, were the silver mines of Mexico, Peru, and Bolivia. The
character of the production conditions give adequately secure
grounds for the correctness of this claim. We possess in addition a statistical confirmation in a comparative table of costs
by Alexander von Humboldt for a Freiberg and a Mexican
mine — of course from the time when he was composing his
work over New Spain, thus for the end of the 18th century. At
this time, however, the conditions lay comparatively less favourably for Mexico than for Saxony, compared with the
earlier time, because in fact at the time when Humboldt was
making his observations the Mexican mine workers were
clearly already for the most part free, very highly rewarded

265

workers — he calculates their daily earnings at 5–6 francs, against 90 centimes[*] in Saxony! Whilst in the first centuries the Mexican, like all American silver mining, was established on the use of slaves. The in any case extremely instructive comparison of Humboldt's is found in the following[295] (translated):

Comparative table of the mines of America and Europe

Average year at the end of the 18th century	America: Mine of Valenciana, the richest of the Mexican mines (at surface: 2320m above sea-level)	Europe: Mine of Himmelsfürst, the richest of the Saxon mines (at surface: 410m above sea-level)
Extracted silver..............360,000 marcs		10,000 marcs
Total production costs................	5,000,000 livres tourn.[296]	240,000 livres tourn.
Net profit of shareholders................3,000,000 livres		90,000 livres
Silver content per metric ton of ore.........	5.7 g	8.5–10 g
Number of workers.......	3,100 Indians and Mestizos, 1,800 of whom are in the interior of the mine	700 miners, of whom 559 are in the interior of the mine
Daily earnings per worker......................	4–6 livres tourn.	18 sous
Cost of powder............	400,000 livres tourn. (nearly 81,280 kg)	27,000 livres tourn. (nearly 13,720 kg)
Amount of ore brought to amalgamation or smelting......................	36,576,000 kg	711,200 kg

---

[*]   [Tr.: 1 franc = 100 centimes.]

Comparative table of the mines of America and Europe

Average year at the end of the 18th century	America: Mine of Valenciana, the richest of the Mexican mines (at surface: 2320m above sea-level)	Europe: Mine of Himmelsfürst, the richest of the Saxon mines (at surface: 410m above sea-level)
Veins of ore..................	....A vein frequently divides into thin branches of from 40 to 50 metres of extent (in clay slate)	Five principal veins, from two to three decimetres of extent (in gneiss)
Water..........................	...... No water	Eight cubic feet per minute. Two hydraulic wheels
Depth of the mine...........	...... 514 metres	380 metres

To these eminent advantages of natural mining conditions which Mexico's mines had over those of Europe was added now also, as we saw already earlier, from the end of the 1550s the so much more productive *process of amalgamation*. Its costs stood, as I have already highlighted in another place, in close connection with the *price of mercury*, for which reason a few things are to be noted here over the development of the latter.

The production of mercury has in the world always been small and was limited since time immemorial to a few locations. When the amalgamation process was invented, the only two mercury mines of significance were Almadén in Spain[297] and the just then opened Idria in western Slovenia[298]. Their yield had been insignificant up to then though. Only by the newly created need did the production experience an uplift. By chance, just around the same time as the amalgamation process began to spread in Peru, a source of mercury was discovered there which in the first century supplied more mercury than any of the mines previously in use; that was the mine of Huanvelica in the Santa Barbara mountains (in use from 1567)[299].

The following figures give information over the share which these three main production areas had of the total mercury production in the first centuries after the introduction of the amalgamation process[300]. Mercury was produced:

in	from	up to 1700 t	1700–1800 t	1800–1850 t
Almadén	1564	17,860	42,141	37,642
Huanvelica	1571	30,424	18,756	2,608
Idria	1525	19,795	21,002	8,357

Now only a little is said with these statements, however, so long as we do not know how the *price of mercury* was formed under the new production conditions. Hence then it is now the fact of decisive importance that the supply of mercury was practised up into the 19th century as a monopoly by the Spanish government. The latter also established the price quite arbitrarily so that not the natural structure of the mercury production conditions, but rather the greater or lesser insight of the viceroy in the Spanish colonies had the decision over the height of the mercury price and as a result to a very large degree over the fate of silver production. According to the information of Humboldt[301], the price for a hundredweight* of mercury amounted under the viceroy Don Luis de Velasco II in the year 1590 in Mexico to 187 piasters. In the year 1570 the hundredweight cost 82 piasters — whether and what changes the price experienced from 1590 to 1750 is not given by Humboldt who cites as his only source a manuscript without date[302].

We may assume that the price reductions took place at the beginning of the 18th century, and that they probably occurred under the pressure which the import of mercury from China and the East Indies (as ballast!) exercised on the European mercury market. According to recent investigations[303], the price of mercury in fact fell suddenly in the open trading on the Amsterdam exchange in the first years of the 18th century (from 1704 to 1710) from 64 to 48 and 41 stivers† per pound.

---

*   [Tr.: 1 hundredweight = approx. 50.8 kg.]
†   [Tr.: 20 stivers = 1 guilder.]

From the middle of the 18th century, mining at Almadén
then also experienced a complete transformation which obviously was connected with a reduction in production costs.

At the end of the 1750s the main shaft which caught fire in 1755 was
brought into operation again. The government let German engineers
and workers come. A regular system of mining was introduced, the
compass gained recognition, and usable pit plans were drawn up. The
mining was done through step and ridge mining. The deposits increased
in magnitude with depth, served up though greater difficulties for mining — but these were (in the 1760s evidently) removed by the reformer
of mercury mining in Spain, Diego Larrañaga, so that now the extraction of the deeper lying ore became not only possible, but even more rational and economic (Nöggerath 1862, 365). Cf. Kuss (1878).

In consequence of all these improvements, production rose abruptly
in Almadén; it amounted in the years:

- 1646–1757 to 429,560 hwt 55 lb 13½ oz [~21,821,672 kg], thus
an annual average of 3,835 hwt 17 lb 6½ oz [~194,826 kg];
- 1757–1793 to 460,442 hwt 74 lb [~23,390,487 kg], thus an annual average of 13,155 hwt 26 lb 7⅓ oz [~668,286 kg][†]. (Hoppensack 1796, 155)

This increase in the supply of mercury and the reduction in
the cost of mercury production complied now also with the
increase in the use of mercury in the silver mines:

Year	Price per hwt [50.8 kg] of mercury	Use of mercury
1762–1766	82 piasters	1,816,100 kg
1767–1771	62 piasters	2,133,600 kg
1772–1777	62 piasters	2,692,400 kg
1778–1782	41 piasters	2,997,200 kg

We recall from Chapter 31 how this increase in the use of
mercury was reflected in the increased silver production during the last third of the 18th century. But we are able to draw
the conclusion from this fact that to a very high degree the
mercury producers in that time had as it were *their hands on
the crank by means of which they were capable of enlivening
or shutting down the entire development of civilisation.*

---

† [Tr.: Sombart miscites and thus miscalculates here. The first figure was
for the period of 46 years from 1754, thus the annual average should be
around 10,009 hwt. or 508,457 kg]

But how was the *exchange value of silver* influenced by the processes described? To answer this question, we must recall the characteristics which the production conditions of precious metals exhibited in our period, since these were of determining influence on the formation of the exchange value of the precious metals.

All signs indicate that the fall in the production costs of silver must in the course of the 16th century have already been very considerable. It found its first expression in the immediately brought on (subjective) *devaluation of precious metals* which piled up *in the hands of the producers*. In *Bohemia* and *Tyrol* (where for a short time at least probably a similar reduction in the cost of silver production occurred), it was in part still craftwork-like firms which formed the first intermediaries between the silver mines and the markets. That the sudden enrichment, however, triggered at all times the same mental processes in people of such sort is evidenced by the following description which a chronicler of that time (it is the 15th century) left behind for us:

> In Rotenberg vallis Oeni inventa notabili minera argenti, ex omnibus terris multitudo confluxit mercantium, tot et tam variis contractibus, ut *vix pecunia amplius aestimaretur*; adeoque homines illi ad ditandum avidi fuerunt, ut sine ratione et prudentia pecunias suas effuderint.

> [In Ratemberg of the Oeni valley there was found a notable silver mineral which the multitude flocked from all the lands to buy, so many and such various contracts that there is *scarcely any more money to be considered*; and so people who were eager to get rich would squander their money without reason or prudence.][304]

In *America* and *Spain* the rich stream of silver flowed at first into the pockets of the Spanish grandees — they too were a human species who tended to spend the new possession quickly on consumer goods — by rise in splendour and refinement of the conduct of life, as we will follow in Chapter 48. What we possess in descriptions from the 16th century of Spanish existence confirms the correctness of this judgement — everywhere quickly rising prices, in particular also of lux-

ury objects; an ell of cloth, for example, rose in price in a few
decades by more than three times what it had cost at the beginning of the 16th century. In Granada velvet cost 28–29
reals, but the Indian demand drove the price in 14 days to
35–36 reals. It was similar in Seville (Mercado 1569, 178).

Thus at once a massive boom in prices as the direct effect
of the new precious metal finds on the first possessors. And
what is specific now to the circumstances in the 16th century
— the incessant stream of so much cheaper precious metals.
It is not a short episode, like the development of new rich
gold deposits — it is a constantly strong enormous stream
which rolls through the centuries. Reason enough — especially when we keep in view the undeveloped state of the
goods production of the time — that the opening up of the
American silver mines — and up to now only them — could
call forth that price revolution.

Towards the end of the 16th century then, the price increase
seemed to have approximately fitted itself to the drop in the
value of silver; but a counter-movement could still not start,
for that the extent of the constantly extracted American silver
was too great. Thus a price stagnation then arrived in the 17th
century which, however, as we have seen, in the second half
of that century and in the next century soon transformed itself again into a boom in prices.

What had happened? The enormously rich *gold deposits of
Brazil* had been discovered and began their impact. I have
already spoken about their productivity. We learn from the
reports of contemporaries how the lucky finds immediately
drove the price up in the surrounding area. In Brazil the following items cost at that time[305]:

2 cats (owing to rat and mice trouble).........1 pound of gold
1 dairy cow..1 pound of gold
1 metze of maize....................................6–30–40 oitavas[306]
1 metze of beans......................................8–10–30 oitavos
1 plate of salt...4 oitavos
1 hen..6 oitavos
1 pig...28 oitavos
1 pound of dried beef or bacon..............................2 oitavos

But gold is a risky guest as long as it is only panned gold. The alluvial deposits mostly exhaust themselves so quickly that they are incapable of bring about any lasting fall in the money value and thus also cannot permanently keep the price at its level. Hence perhaps even the effect of the Brazilian gold on the money value would only have been a passing one.

But that this also sank further was taken care of again by silver.

We know in fact already from the earlier portrayal that this metal experienced from the 1760s once more a revolution in its production conditions — mercury went from 82 piasters in the years 1762–1766 down to 41 piasters in the years 1778–1782. The result of that was a rapid increase in silver production — but obviously also a lowering of production costs, of which the at the time still solely used cold amalgamation process made up a quite considerable part of the use of mercury.

At the end of the 18th century the price fitted itself again to the changed production conditions of silver, which then once more worsened fundamentally at the time of the Mexican wars of liberation. The fall or at least stagnation in prices after the Napoleonic Wars until the 1830s and 1840s occurred at any rate together with a considerably reduced silver supply from Mexico.

In summary, despite the little information which we possess about the production costs of precious metals, we are able though for the period of 1250–1850 of quite generally bringing the price movement into connection with the development of the production conditions of gold and especially silver.

Section 5: The Origins of Bourgeois Wealth

Chapter 36: Wealth-Power and Power-Wealth

If we want to follow in this section how the "bourgeois wealth" "originated", we will have to clarify beforehand what "bourgeois wealth is (Chapter 36) and what "originate" means (Chapter 37).

"Bourgeois wealth" is obviously a special type of "wealth", which is meant here in the sense of a condition associated with a person (the word signifies something else when we speak of the "wealth of nations", or of "national wealth"). Wealth, however, in this sense is either, if we take the word in its neutral meaning, the same as "means", or (as it is frequently used) so much as an elevated means. We come most easily to a deepened understanding of the word wealth when we strive to comprehend the sense of the word "means".

In splendid obviousness the German word for means here, Vermögen, expresses a number of different *states of power* — it encompasses all possibilities of which someone is capable. It approaches in our mind the manifold ways of having power which are separated from each other in foreign languages — pouvoir, power — fortune — and forces us thereby to the common origin of all these types of power and at the same time to the hidden inner sense of otherwise more detached circumstances. It tells us that we are dealing with the same primary phenomenon, whether we say it does not stand in my means, or this man has great means (plainly: in the sense of wealth), or he has great means of domination or imagination, or he is lacking means, whereby we leave in doubt whether we want to say he cannot do anything or has nothing.

We see best of all everything that is expressed by the word means when we recognise the individual meanings in their essence and strive to distinguish them from each other.

Then it results above all in that two entirely different types of means must be differentiated from each other first of all according to the last source from which the one or the other sort arises.

There is a means which is reliant completely on ourselves and our utterly personal power, and next to it a means which is conferred on us by society, a means whose existence is thus built on the latter's power. I call the former individual means, the latter social means, and mean thereby the following.

The *individual means* arise from the power of personality and are bounded by its capabilities alone, reaching thus as far as the power of an individual reaches which is not secured or supported by any societal (state) guarantee. It can rest in a personal *ability*, when we call it our *means of performance* — to climb a mountain, or drink three bottles of champagne, or hold a good talk, or sing a high C, etc. Or it rests in a power of disposal over people or things — when you could describe it as *means of command*.

I say a power of disposal over people and things; note: it has as its only source the power of the personality.

Thus when a person is capable of reigning over others, of forcing them to achievements or omissions, of making them subservient, only by the power of his beauty, his personal greatness, his goodness, his strength. Like the hypnotist has a purely physiological capability over others. By direct influence from person to person. Someone has individual tangible means when this itself is thanks to the purely individual power of his being; thus it does not rest perhaps on some legal title, be it even the most meagre right of possession (when it would thereby become social means). Such a form of tangible means are naturally very rare — Fafner had the hoard of the Nibelungs in his individual means. Or a thief has a stolen or concealed thing (but as soon as he redeems a stolen piece of jewellery for money and then pays for something with the money, he has obtained a social means).

The *social means* is in contrast guaranteed by society and *always* includes a legal relationship. That there would be a social means of performance may not be denied theoretically. Practically it is meaningless. Practically social means is on the contrary always a means of command (for even, for example, patent protection, protection of intellectual property which is thus meant to protect an individual means of performance, is founded always on a social means of command in so far as it hinders others from doing something).

Again the means of command can refer directly to persons or to things.

Persons command socially, whom society (the state) authorise to do so. In the sphere of public law the social means of command underlies all official relations, all military discipline, all policing; whilst in the sphere of civil law today the purely personal means of command is heavily restricted. In the age of slavery it could extend arbitrarily to all people and all their life functions; today it is frequently only found still in regards to family law — all parental authority (so far as it does not arise from an individual means of the parents) rests on the social means, on the means of command between parents and children which has been sanctioned by society with its instruments of power. In contrast the real area of social means is command of things. Here it thus appears as *social tangible means* and rests in the power of disposal of a person over tangible goods which is guaranteed by society (the state).

It is that variety of "means" which we think of when we (without further ado) talk of large, middling, and small means, which foreign nations describe with a special word (fortune, riches), but which (as follows from my explanations) portrays in fact nothing essentially different from all the other meanings of the German word for means. This man has great means signifies that this man can on the basis of some right in law dispose over large quantities of tangible goods and is in this protected by the state. And we call such a man "rich" (in the material sense). His wealth extends as far as the circle of tangible goods over which he can dispose; which society permits him to dispose over.

The content of this power of disposal is very diverse now. By far its most important component is the power which the wealthy person exercises on the strength of his tangible means over other people. It is a different power to that arising from individual means; it is also a different one to that flowing from the private social means (e.g. power of a ruler) — it is *always mediated by a tangible good* with whose help the performance of other persons will be "paid" or "bought" (these expressions used in the widest sense). I can "buy" someone's love or thankfulness through a gift, I can "pay" someone for performed service by the transfer of a tangible good (service in fief!); I can have an acting troupe play for me in return for proffering tangible goods; I can secure the service of a lawyer or doctor in return for "payment"; I can finally "buy" the work products of others by exchanging for my own goods. *That the other people must be active for me first gives to all wealth its sense and meaning.* Indeed Robinson can store up goods; he can collect "means"; but they remain individual means. And social means shrivel up into individual means when perhaps for some reason that mysterious effect of tangible goods which amounts to my "means" stops causing other people to take action — perhaps in consequence of a war, during a revolution or a difficult crisis. If in such cases I cannot "buy" anyone's service (or work products) anymore with my tangible "means", my means reaches only so far as I am capable of influencing with my person — be it directly on things (in that I work my fields with my own hands), be it indirectly on other people (in that I, for example, move others through force of persuasion, or by threats, or by goods to work for me). Or, however, my social personal means must continue to help me. My *social tangible* means has stopped to exist though — I possess only individual or personal social means.

In what form a means is portrayed is of no importance for the concept of means. It can be demands; it can, however, also embody my means in tangible goods — these are plots of land, when we speak of real estate as means, it is chattels, when we speak of mobile means. Money means is just a special form of mobile means. It is means in abstract form, in so far as all goods are portrayed symbolically in money. It is means in its most effective form, in so far as the symbol "money" in commercial economic organisation (in normal times) is happily accepted by anyone, and consequently: pecuniam habens habet omnem rem quam vult habere [he who has possession of money has everything that he wants]; more properly: the possessor of money can dispose over any performance of work by another.

Relationship of the Concept of Wealth to Legal Categories

Social tangible means are portrayed juristically in the most varied legal categories, not just in property. All legal circumstances of the law of property as well as of the law of obligation belong here. For overall it always concerns in the end a person having the power of disposal over a specified quantity of tangible goods (or disputes another's right, or only tries to obtain, or wants to transfer to another, or to exchange for a different complex of tangible goods, or to have established a passing power of disposal over them for himself or others, etc.).

(That in the end, even legally, in the control of a "thing" only a control of persons lies, every lawyer knows. Also a law of "things" is not founded on a legal relationship between a person and a thing, but between persons. Understandably.)

What distinguishes the concept of "means" from all legal relationships is this: that the power of command based on "means" grants to the entitled person the *final* disposal over the command of the subjected quantity of goods. To that extent the "means" encompasses the ability to stand as one likes in a legal relationship to the object, whatever it is, but also in a physical relationship to the object, whatever it is. By virtue of the authority enclosed in my "means", I can also concede rights to the thing as much as it suits me to third parties — of the property itself without relinquishing my means. That happens, for example, by necessity in the legal form of the loan. Here the debtor obtains property by the money which belongs to the means of the creditor. The extent of our means is thus established by the reach of our right to property, plus our claims, minus our debts. (When I have spoken here of money and credit, it occurs of course only to choose examples familiar to everyone. The facts of the matter explained with the examples can be realised in any form of economic life, thus belonging to the elemental phenomena.)

When we now examine the *historical development* of means, it is apparent that the individual means must always be there first. On it the social means is then built. The people equipped with special powers, might, abilities — medicine men, priests, army leaders — receive social "recognition", are equipped with social instruments of power by society — at first with mere power of command, then also with tangible means. The mighty become the rich — to them falls prey the conquered land and the conquered booty to a larger extent. They are rich (in tangible goods), and have a great tangible means, because they were mighty, by virtue of their com-

279

manding position in society — such wealth I will call *power-wealth*. It was the wealth as we find only with the European peoples at the start of history, as it predominated still through a greater part of the Middle Ages. It is the wealth of kings, of large estate owners, of the church. This wealth bears a strong feudal imprint, and we can hence (not quite exactly, but fittingly) describe it as *feudal wealth*. It consisted partly in estate ownership, partly in chattels, *also* in money.

Money now brought about that the wealth transformed itself imperceptibly in its innermost essence. The possession of money, as the abstract form of tangible means, bestowed as such, to anyone who had it, power. *This* power stemmed from nothing other than the fact that someone disposed over a sum of money. And this power derived from (tangible) wealth now in time appeared equal to the power flowing from relationships of command, so much so that it finally created these state relationships of command entirely from its own power. It came about that the rich became the mighty. Such a power which stems from wealth, I will call *wealth-power*. This wealth-power now grew more and more stronger in the European states from the Crusades on. Its bearers were the nouveaux riche, the gente nuova, the homines novi, quos fortuna e faece tulit [new men who made fortunes from the dregs] — they stand at first outside the nexus of feudal society (in which they penetrate at most by virtue of their wealth). We can hence describe their wealth as *bourgeois wealth*.

That is now also the great world-historical change which we want to follow in its stages — *how the wealth-power was developed from power-wealth*. It is the problem of the origin of bourgeois wealth.

Once again: it is not so much the bearers of wealth who establish the deep difference — this lies in the essence of both types of wealth themselves in their different derivations, in their different spirits.

"What are you?", one asked previously. "A mighty man." Thus you are rich.

"What are you?", one asks now. "A wealthy man." Thus you are mighty.

It may yet be noted that the concepts wealth or means are not at all to be equated with the concept of capital. It was a crude mistake of the first edition of this work that it did not differentiate sharply enough between means and capital, and consequently also between means formation and capital formation. We will see how these two developed differently in European history. First, however, we will address only bourgeois means (wealth), *not capital*. Its origin is a great event of a quite peculiar stamp, which is of singular importance not only for the problem of capital formation, but even for the origin of capitalism.

Chapter 37: Towards the Theory of Means Formation

After we have now clarified what "bourgeois wealth" is, we must still, before we pursue its origins, recall what is then to be understood by "origin" of wealth (or "means" in the established sense).

We possess two methods of portraying means formation — the *subjective-biographical* and the *objective-sociological*.

By the former, the path is investigated which has led the one person, and yet another, and yet another to wealth.

Apart from the objective circumstances, the subjective characteristics above all are shown which made this or that person into people of means. You endeavour to attribute the success to the particulars; you attempt a partitioning of the obtained wealth into the two categories: luck and merit. You attempt, so as to express it in the terminology displayed here, to prove what connection prevailed in the individual case between individual and social means.

Whether such a task is doable in the frame of a monograph may remain to be seen. Mephisto has in epigrammatic form already pointed to the enormous difficulties, and Friedrich Albert Lange has produced in the famous third chapter of his "Arbeiterfrage" (1910, 97 ff.) a strictly scientific proof that "chance" has the greatest part in any scientific success.

But if you wanted, however, to consider even for the individual case the proof to have perfectly succeeded that a specific means is seen to be the result of quite specific personal efforts and gifts, then still very little would have been won for the knowledge of an entire social condition. For to generalise those particular circumstances without further ado, to see the fate of the individual as typical, and to conclude from it for the remaining cases, is of course not permissible. You could at most attempt an inductive proof in that you investigate a greater number of "typical" cases to derive from them general conclusions. These general statements could then always only refer to two things — to the objective possibilities of obtaining means, and to the subjective qualities which are especially suited to exploit those objective possibilities. At the same time, however, you would already have left the ground of the subjective-biographical method and would have placed yourself on that of the objective-sociological. For this consists simply in that you suffice with the establishing of the object-ive possibilities and the enumeration of the characteristics most conforming to them, knowledge of which you can arrive at in numerous ways other than the biographical investiga-tion of individuals. (The economics of this work means that this fifth section is dedicated almost exclusively to the proof of the objective possibilities of means formation, whilst proofs of a subjective nature appear only occasionally in this section, but are followed in detail later in the utilisation of yet other viewpoints.)

The drawing up of a *general theory of means formation* has to my knowledge never been attempted. Except for the few remarks in the Pantschatantra (Benfey 1859), nothing at all has been seen by me which would have undertaken to draw together systematically the theoretical possibilities and prerequisites of means formation. I give the schema here.

The question over the circumstances of means formation is:

I. the question over the *sources* from which the means flow.

In accordance with that, the formation of means is:

a) (*formally*) either *original* or *derived*.

To understand this especially important distinction cor-rectly, it must be said first that this view should only ever be concerned with the origin of "larger" means, that is, of such means as encompass more tangible goods than are found in the hands of primitive, equally situated economic subjects, so that the problem of means formation is in a certain sense equated with the problem of means differen-tiation, with the origin of "wealth".

The means formation is *original* on the other hand in a double sense: in the economic or in the geographical sense, as I want to say straight off. I call original means formation in the *economic* sense that which takes place in the circle of people of equal means — where thus both the small means of all people first forms, and larger means grow from nothing or from these small means of approximately equally placed people; *derived* means formation is by contrast that by which a larger means forms through transmission of already present larger means. In the case of derived means formation the means is already heaped up in one place — it only changes its possessor. That can play out in the frame of one and the same economic system or this transmission of means can at the same time be about a change in economic system, if perhaps feudal means are transformed into bourgeois means, or if some day the "expropriators are expropriated" with the transition from the capitalist to the socialist social order according to the wishes of the socialists. (The entire evolutionary theory of Marx is founded on the opposition between original and derived means formation in the sense struck here.) Also any "nationalisation" or "civic appropriation" belongs here. Means formation is original or derived in the *geographical* sense according to whether it takes place within a specific, spatially bounded area (e.g. a land), or jumps across from one land to another. As far as, for example, the formation of the English great means occurred within England, I call them original, when they rest on the transfer of means which had previously already formed in Spain, Italy, Holland, etc., then derived.

b) (*materially*) means formation follows either with *stable wealth*, or with *growing wealth*, or with *sinking wealth*, whereby I use the word wealth this time in the sense of national wealth. The national wealth grows when the productive forces grow — these, on the other hand, grow either extensively, when the population increases, or intensively, when the work is made more productive by better organisation or improvements in technology. When a formation of means takes place under stable conditions of wealth, then it can of course only occur at the cost of other means; it can thus then only be seen as a movement of means. In the other case, new means can arise next to the old. A formation of means with sinking wealth means in the rule rapine, be it that the ground is sucked dry, or be it that the people are. To be "sucked dry", that is, to be used so that a renewal (reproduction) of its strength does not take place, thus is consumed from the substance and not just from the yields. Quite commonly then the formation of means is the reason for rapine.

The problem touched on here can also be paraphrased thus: means is either formed from the consumption goods or production goods already present (which then just change owners — formally "derived" means formation); or it is formed from the work yield of a new production period. If this is so strongly used for means formation that a reproduction of the social wealth is not possible, then rapine appears.

The problem of means formation (in so far as the sources from which the new means arise are considered) is thus both a production problem and a distribution problem — production decides over the total tangible goods available for means formation, distribution over its accumulation in specific places.

II. The *methods* by means of which means are formed are of course extraordinarily numerous. The most important groups can be differentiated in the following ways:

a) according to the *type of activity* (or conduct) which leads to means formation — whether it is economic or extra-economic activity; whether it concerns acts of production or consumption; whether means are thus increased through surpluses in business or through "saving" (or, of course, through both); whether an active doing or a passive toleration is the cause of the means formation; whether theft or inheritance perhaps allows means to arise.

b) according to the *form* in which the means formation occurs. Means formation can take place in the frame of existing laws and customs, or under the disregard of law and custom; it can thus be "legal" or "illegal". It can rest on one-sided force, or on agreement. It can rest on payable or free exchanges of value, to the extent that you take away value from it, give back this value (entirely or in part), or not.

III. An important difference is finally that accorded to the *tempo* — whether means formation takes place gradually or in leaps. Gradually so that during a long life or only during several generations from small beginnings does a middling, then a larger and great means form; in leaps so that in a few years gigantic means shoots from the earth like mushrooms. This difference is hence so important because these two ways of means formation exercise a quite different effect on economic life — because the gradual means formation leads to the slow growth of new forms, as it were the development from internal to external; whereas the arising in leaps brings about a rapid, mechanical bringing about, as it were influencing the development from external to internal.

***

From all these theoretical considerations, however, now arises the view above all that the *problem of means formation is an historical problem*, that is, that the way in which means arise — the sources, the methods, the tempo of means formation — are defined by the historical circumstances. The general propositions have in this connection also just the sense of making the empirical phase of means formation to be described now — that in which bourgeois great means, thus bourgeois wealth arises — easier to understand by bringing out the point of view under which we will conveniently consider the individual phenomena.

The structure of this section is now this: in the following chapter (38th), I give an overview of what we will call feudal wealth, that is, that form of wealth in which wealth is a result of social might — to that belongs all wealth of the (feudal) great estate owners, the wealth of kings and princes and all public bodies.

In the subsequent chapters (39th to 47th) the manner of origin of bourgeois wealth is described — it is shown how much (from feudal wealth) it deviated, how much it is of original source; when it occurred abruptly and in leaps, when gradually; with what methods it was obtained finally. Since now all the distinguishing features for organisation of the material cannot be used at the same time, a feature must be selected as the topmost organising principle. I have chosen for that the *method of means formation*. In accordance with it the portrayal is structured according to the following scheme which I have not repeated in the outer arrangement in order to make the organisation into chapters easier. The individual chapters thus stand in relation to the order of higher, lower, and equal importance as given by the following overview of the entire disposition:

A. Means formation outside the capitalist economy:
  I. The bound forms of means formation:
    1. The means formation in the craftwork-like economy — Chapter 39;
    2. The means formation through money-lending — Chapter 40;
    3. The accumulation of civic ground rents — Chapter 41;
    4. The direct formation of means — Chapter 42.
  II. The free forms of means formation:
    1. Betrayal, theft, embezzlement as formers of means — Chapter 43;
    2. Robbery — Chapter 44;
    3. Forced trade — Chapter 45;
    4. The exploitation of colonies through forced labour — Chapter 46.
B. Means formation in the frame of the capitalist economy — Chapter 47.

Chapter 38: Feudal Wealth

I. Large Estate Ownership

I have already recalled in another place the well-known fact that in the course of the Middle Ages a quite considerable part of the lands of Europe massed together in the hands of estate owners into more or less large properties.

This property, which in the beginning was indubitably an almost exclusively natural one and which had its entire significance in essence in the possibility of allowing a greater number of people to live, was gradually, as we may assume, more and more "mobilised" the more the tribute of the indentured serfs was levied in money or the harvest yields brought to market by the owners themselves.

At the same time the yields to land ownership experienced a constant rise thanks to the advances in agricultural technology as well as the denser settlement, a rise in which the estate owners took part to the extent that they succeeded in preserving the duty of tribute at an equal height or even raising it.

To ascertain the "value" of land ownership in earlier times is of course an almost unsolvable task. We must thus be satisfied if a few researchers have calculated some approximate values which at base have no other significance than to lend a self-evident fact an expression in figures.

For individual parts of Germany, Lamprecht has put together such calculations. He assumes that it occurred in the first half of the Middle Ages that for the absolute first time a somehow noteworthy land price was formed, and that correspondingly a rise in land prices from the 9th to the 12th century came about in a ratio of 100 to 1,184.3; the price then rose up until the 13th century to 1,671.3; until the end of the 14th century to 3,085[307].

The still vaguer figures which D'Avenel[308] gives for the Middle Ages set the price of a hectare of ploughable land at:

- for the 9th century at 70 francs
- for the 12th century at 93 francs
- for the 13th century at 135–261 francs
- for the 16th century at 317 francs

It is to be assumed that a not inconsiderable part of this rise in value, which of course continued in the following centuries, benefited the large estate owners in the form of higher rents. Perhaps too the development exhibits here in the various lands a different direction — in particular it seems almost as if in Germany from time to time at least the rising land yields would not have translated into rising rents, indeed as if from the 13th century in many parts of Germany the tribute of the farmers would have become smaller because it (with the hereditary leases which though formed the rule) was fixed and hence fell — as money interest in consequence of the coin devaluations running riot since 1250, as grain interest in consequence of the fall in the grain price (from 1400?)[309]. But in all the lands, and that was most of the Western European states, where the estate owners succeeded in initiating time-bound leases, the additional yield of the land flowed for the greatest part to the estate owners and raised their incomes.

What sums did these incomes and means of the estate owners amount to?

A clear insight into the structure of medieval society would only grant us statistics on income and means for the named circles. And it would probably be a thankful task for skilled economic historians to write for once a history of landed wealth in the Middle Ages as a counterpart to the numerous portrayals of civic rates of income and means. It does not seem to me to be an unworkable plan, to follow perhaps from the Domesday Book and the polyptiques* of the 10th and 11th century the development of the means of the temporal and spiritual lords. The essential thing here will also be the for-

---

* [Tr.: polyptique = inventory of the resources of large landed estates, especially monasteries.]

mulation of the question. What we possess for the time being in the way of knowledge is certainly only sparse and incomplete. At any rate it suffices to obtain approximate ideas of the conditions of wealth in the countryside during the Middle Ages. There now the fact is surely to be assumed as established that (even for so-called "mobile" means, in particular precious metals) the large private means were to be found until deep into the Middle Ages, even until after the Middle Ages only with the secular estate owners, abbeys, and monasteries. Cities like Lübeck and Hamburg in their heyday certainly did not have the incomes which a great English lord drew from his properties or which flowed to a rich monastery from favours and rents. Quite apart from the half princely great estate owners like the Dukes of Burgundy, the Counts of Flanders, or the Margraves of Tuscany[310]. We may well surely imagine the transition from the royal means to those of the greats in the countryside to be not so sheer during the Middle Ages as today. The grand seigneurs in fact claimed for centuries a position similar to the princely.

We possess for various lands figures which confirm the correctness of what was stated above. I will choose a few from the time of the late Middle Ages and the first centuries after the Middle Ages because these epochs are naturally the most important for the formation of means.

In *England* the average incomes of the various grades of noble have been frequently estimated by knowledgeable individuals, and the various estimates help to increase each other's credibility by the sizeable agreement in their figures.

According to one such estimation for the period of Edward IV[311], the incomes were:

- duke...£4,000
- marquis......................................£3,000
- earl..£2,000
- viscount....................................£1,000
- baron...£500
- baronet......................................£200
- knight..£200
- squire...£50

Of course individual greats had a multiple of this income — thus the annual income of the Duke of Buckingham in the

15th century was estimated by the Venetian envoy Giustiniani at 30,000 ducats[312].

Well-known is the estimate of income by Gregory King[313] for the 17th century. According to it, the average incomes amounted to:

- secular lord...................................£3,200
- baronet...£880
- knight...£656
- esquire...£450
- gentleman......................................£280

Whilst according to the same informant, average incomes amounted to:

- larger merchant............................£400
- smaller merchant..........................£198
- retailer...£45
- craftsman.......................................£38

The *Italian* nobility were extraordinarily affluent. We hear of the Orsini and Colonna that in the 15th century they took in annually 25,000 florins[314].

We are often informed of the rich possessions of gold and silver items of the Florentine noble families in the earlier period[315].

The Milanese nobility stood out for its wealth. They numbered some five families who had between 10,000 and 30,000 ducats in income. In the 16th century the Medici of Marignano, the Sforza of Caravaggio were calculated to have rents of 12,000 ducats, the Borromeo family of 15,000, the Trivulzio family of 20,000, the Serbelloni of 30,000. In contrast, there was a tremendous number of such dynasties that had incomes between 2,000 and 4,000 ducats[316].

In *Spain* the greatest part of the land belonged to 105 lords secular and spiritual in the 15th century. The Dukes of Infantado and Medina de Rioseco, of Escalona, and of Ossuna possessed about 100,000 ducats, the Duke of Medina-Sidonia 130,000 ducats in annual rents; some had 30,000 families subject to them[317].

We are especially well informed about wealth in the *French* nobility by the events of the great revolution. Those who belonged to the nobility in the year 1789 were indeed not all old nobility, thus not all of "feudal" origin, but rather for

the most part already a product of bourgeois means formation — but at any rate the state at the eve of the revolution
gives an approximately true reflection of the feudal wealth at
the outbreak of revolution because the legal character of the
formerly knightly land had remained preserved so that you
can establish exactly how great its extent had formerly been,
even if it had now already arrived in the hands of the nouveaux riche. This wealth incidentally preserved, as long as it
was equipped with privileges, a part of its old feudal character
even during the bourgeois period. It is calculated that at the
time the number of nobles in France amounted to 140,000,
and that an entire fifth of the land belonged to them[318]. That
will have been the state in which it had developed in the
Middle Ages.

And the *princes and lords of the Church* competed with
the secular grandees. The two English archbishops, says
Stubbs, kept house like the dukes; the bishops lived on the
heels of the earls. That the monasteries during the Middle
Ages arrived at princely riches is a well-known fact.

A sort of "accumulation" of wealth followed in the 14th century with
numerous prelates through the accumulation of benefices: "et quae uti-
que abominatio, quod unus tenet ducenta, alter trecenta beneficia eccle-
siastica" [and it is of course an abomination that one holds two
hundred, another three hundred ecclesiastical benefices] (from "Decla-
ratio compendiosa defectum virorum ecclesiasticorum" in Gerson
(1483, 2:314) cited in Andre (1887, 282)). Urban V said in a bull that individual benefices possessed "in numero detestabiliter excessivo" [in excessive detestable number] (André 1887, 282). There was a formal
"stock market" in benefices with boom and bust speculation, agents,
brokers, etc. The possessors of money bought the sinecures as annuities. Other figures are in Müntz (1899, 5 ff., 20 ff.).

And indeed with these "great estate" means and incomes it
is also in the earlier period in no way about — I must emphasise that — just property ownership and obtaining produce.
We will have to think rather that after the downfall of the Roman Empire up until the late Middle Ages the greatest part of
the total *stock of precious metals* flowed together into the
treasuries of the estate owners, the abbeys and monasteries.
"In a time when money was a great rarity, the monasteries
possessed almost entirely, thanks to the oblatory donations of
the faithful, the inestimable advantage of disposing over
ample gold reserves."[319] Often enough the congregating pre-

cious metal certainly changed its form and was transformed from money form to decoration and utensils. Only thus do the reports become comprehensible to us of which we hear from the Middle Ages over the enormous wealth of gold and silver things in churches and monasteries[320] or in the households of secular lords[321] when we leaf through their inventories.

The land ownership of the Church seems to have remained at the same level for almost a millennium. When we learn that at the time of the Merovingians a third of *France* was supposed to have been in the clergy's hands, we need not strike off so much at all from this figure to bring it into harmony with the information which we have about the Church's possessions in revolutionary France. For that the latter comprised about a fifth of the land is quite certainly proven. The value of Church property at the time has been estimated at 4 billion francs which brought in a return of 80 to 100 million. If you add to this still the 123 million of tithes, then the incomes of the French clergy at the eve of the French revolution number to around 200 million francs[322]. The enormity of these means appear still more distinctly when we recall the possessions and incomes of individual churches and abbeys.

The 399 Premonstratensians estimated their income at more than a million, their means at 45 million. The Dominicans in Toulouse had 200,000 livres in pure income. "Non compris leurs couvent et leurs enclos et, dans les colonies, des biens fonds, des nègres et autres effets, évalués à plusieurs millions" [Not including their convent and their enclosures and, in colonies, property, Negroes, and other effects, valued at several millions]. (Here we note incidentally how the feudal wealth had already transformed in part into capital!) The Benedictines of Cluny had 1,800,000 livres in revenue; those of Saint-Maur estimated the chattels of their churches and houses at 24 million, their pure income at 8 million, "sans compter ce qui retourne à MM les abbés et prieurs commandataires" [without counting those returns to the abbots and priors in charge]. Dom Rocourt, Abbot of Clairvaux, had 300,000 to 400,000 livres in rents; the Cardinal of Rohan, Archbishop of Strasbourg, more than a million, etc. See the sources in Taine (1875, 1:19 f.). These figures appear low when we compare them with the quite precise estimate which we possess for the wealth of the Church in the time of Louis XIII — at the time the total income shall have amounted to 104.5 million écus — according to an official drawing up from the year 1636 (manuscript in the Bibliotèque Mazarine, cited in Griselle (ed.) (1913, 390–91)).

The means situation of churches in the other lands was not much different. We learn something of the wealth of the monasteries in *England* with their being dissolved in the 16th century. Unfortunately the sources differ too much from each other to be able to form a clear picture of the means of the monasteries in the England of that time — only that it was very significant is without doubt.

The lowest estimate of annual incomes for the monasteries at the point of their dissolution is £131,607 — it is cited by Hallam (1832, 1:75) who, however, himself considers it to be too low; Lingard, with reference to Nasmith's edition of Tanner's Notitia Monastica, assumes £142,914 (Lingard 1820, 4:486; cited in Hallam 1832, 1:75); the most well-known estimate, which Hume (1754, 4:182) also adopts, is that of Lord Herbert, namely £161,100 (Herbert et al. 1706, 2:218). If these estimates were approximately correct, and if Hume's estimate of the total income for England in that time is likewise correct (£3,000,000), then the incomes of the monasteries would have amounted to about ½0 of it. Now, however, both the estimate of the total income is considered to be too high and that of the monasteries to be too low — so that perhaps the author of Harmer's Observations of Burnet comes closer to the truth when he assumes the monks possessed a fifth of England, which certainly would have represented only a tenth of the value of all land (Hallam 1832, 1:75). We know in any case (according to the information in Camden's Brittania (1586)), that 643 (645?) monasteries were dissolved and that some of them were very rich. According to the estimate in Speed's Catalogue of Religions Houses (by Collier, Appendix p. 34, cited in Hallam (1832, 1:75 note)) 16 abbots had an income of more than £1,000. St Peters, Westminster, was the richest with £3,977, Glastonbury had £3,508, St Albans £2,510, etc.

Cf. also C. Anderson (1845, 2:65) and the literature cited in it.

Recently the question of the extent of the English Church's possessions at the time of the confiscation has been thrown up again and an attempt has been made by Savine (1909) to answer it on the basis of a broader source material that has come to light in the meantime. The result is not so much different from the earlier assumptions. Savine assumes an income for the monasteries from property amounting to £100,000, of which a tenth was obtained from their own farming, whilst the rest came as leases.

II. The State Budget

The state budgets are the other point at which the pre-bourgeois means crystallised to a greater extent; where especially larger amounts of money regularly flowed together. But it is always, as we will yet see more precisely, directly of special significance for the bourgeois formations of means.

I cite first two states which became important in that they were the first which fashioned themselves even in the early Middle Ages into the nexus for a large circulation of money, to then get to know the dimensions of the most important of those state budgets which preserved its preeminent status through all the centuries.

1. *the Camera apostolica.*

If you called the Camera apostolica *mater pecuniarum* [mother of money][323], then you would be expressing the indubitably correct thought that the earliest massing of larger means in cash in the Middle Ages is to be traced back to the papal financial operations. Up until the 9th century the treasuries of Christianity extended to all lands by means of the Peter's pence*; and already in the 13th century the papal finances had formed into the imposing system which we know from later times. The beginnings of papal finance go back, as is well-known, to the measures of Innocent III (1198–1216). From this time the general ecclesiastical contributions emerged more and overtook the estate property receipts and the feudal tenure census in significance for the accounts, so as to grow towards the end of the Middle Ages into that "ecclesiastical fiscal policy" which finally led to the revolution.

What gives the papal finances great historical significance now, however, is above all the circumstance that the finances of the popes promoted in an outstanding way the tendency toward monetisation of larger flows of means. We can distinctly follow how it is the accumulation of numerous contributions and payments created by the papal taxation which forced by necessity the transformation of originally multiple presentations of natural produce into money. Thus we find the tithing in its beginnings to have developed everywhere as natural produce — that was absolutely appropriate for the mostly natural produce income of bishops, monasteries, etc. — "the transition to centralisation caused the pure money economy. How would it otherwise have been possible in all the world to erect papal tithe barns, tithe cellars, tithe granaries, and similar costly structures"[324]? In 1217 Honorius III gave the Hungarian bishops the order "ut vicesimam fideliter redigant in pecuniam" [that they faithfully bring a twentieth in money][325]. Later in Central and Southern Europe deliveries

---

*   [Tr.: Peter's pence was an annual tax of one penny from every householder owning land above a certain value, and paid to the papal see.]

of natural produce are quite rare, whilst they remain for a long time yet in the north. But even here they attempt to contrive with all their strength for monetisation, as great as the difficulties were often enough. Then gold or silver utensils probably had to be melted down to create the missing amounts of money[326]. (Importance of increased precious metals production!)

We observe thus how the papal taxation pressure in the midst of an essentially in-kind economy stamped larger sums of money as it were out of the earth and had it gathered in the little sacks and chests of the papal collectors into considerable quantities. We are also informed over the *extent of the amounts heaped up* in such a way; at least we can conclude from the accounts which are available for individual years the sums coming in regularly. In general it can be said that the earlier assumptions about the enormous amounts over which the popes had to dispose were greatly exaggerated. Nevertheless it concerned for that time very respectable sums.

The greatest yields were delivered probably by the so-called "Crusade tithes" which were raised from the end of the 12th century in periodic recurrence sometimes even for other aims than those for which they were originally meant to serve. The best expert on this material estimates the height of the papal tithe yields in the 13th century for all of Christendom at about 800,000 pounds tornese[327]; that would be thus perhaps 15–20,000,000 marks in metal value in present-day [1916] currency. The sums regularly commanded by the pope were considerably smaller that that tithe's yield, and still smaller were the amounts which actually collected in the treasury of the Holy Seat. These revenues figured in the 14th century at about 200–250,000 gold guilders (each 9–10 marks) annually and in the next century did not rise considerably above this amount either. To this sum are perhaps 100,000 ducats also to be added which flowed not into the main accounts, but that of the Curia, so that its total income ran to about 400,000 ducats. The rest of the revenues did not go to Rome[328]. Nevertheless the effective incomes of the popes were significant enough to at least allow a few of the successors of St Peter the gathering of greater means. Thus Clemens V left behind a treasury of 1,000,000 gold guilders, John XXII (1316–1334) one of 775,000[329].

Nonetheless the revenues of the popes were quite considerably outstripped by the amounts which:

2. *the orders of knights* were in a position to store up in their headquarters[330]. Here it is in the first instance about land rents which actually flowed most directly to those orders from their enormous possessions. These extended, as is known, almost over the entire known earth. The estate possessions of the Templars lay strewn from Greece to Portugal, from Sicily to the Eider and as far as Scotland, and after the dissolution of the order were granted to the already enormous possessions of the Knights of St John. The number of manors of the Templars amounted in the 13th century to 9,000 and rose in the period up to 1307 to 10,500; those of the Hospitallers were reported to already be 19,000 in the 13th century. From each of these one knight could equip and maintain themselves, which would correspond to a year's rent each of 200 Byzantines. Consequently the annual rents of the orders would have had a metal value of 36,100,000 francs; whilst those of the Templars is estimated to have been no less than 2 million pounds.

Of the secular powers, two interest us here above all — for the reason that their budgets belong among the oldest and are likewise preserved through the centuries in unbroken development, and because they are in addition the largest, so that they can stand as an exemplar for the countless other budgets of emperors, kings, and princes. I am meaning the kings of France and England.

I will list what we possess in the way of figures for the appraisal of the size of their finances.

3. the *King of France.*

Philip II Augustus left behind at his death 893,000 marks of silver (thus c. 38,000,000 marks in present-day [1916] currency)[331].

In the year 1238 the gross income amounted to the sum of 235,286 liv. 7 s.; in 1248 to 178,530 liv. 12 s.9 d.[332]

At the end of the reign of Philip IV the Fair, the oldest French budget calculated the regular income at 177,500 pounds tornese[333].

For that time the Parisian livre may be replaced with 22 to 23 francs, the pound tornese with 16–17 francs of metal value in present-day [1916] currency. Then the revenues for the 13th and the beginning of the 14th century result in amounts of 4–5 million francs in present-day [1916] currency. The revenues of Charles V (1364–1380) were thought to amount to 1,600,000 livres, those of Charles VII in 1439 to 1,700,000 livres, in 1449 to 2,300,000 livres[334].

According to the (probably somewhat too high) estimates of the Venetian envoy, the revenues of the King of France numbered (in present-day [1916] currency):

- 1497.....................16,306,000 francs
- 1535.....................28,750,000 francs
- 1546.....................46,000,000 francs
- 1554.....................57,500,000 francs
- 1563.....................69,000,000 francs

For the period from the end of the 16th century to the beginning of the 18th century, the conscientious figures of Forbonnais[335] stand at our disposal. According to them the (gross) revenues of the King of France amounted to:

- 1574.......................8,628,980 livres
- 1581......................11,491,775 livres
- 1595.....................23,000,000 livres
- 1620.....................16,000,000 livres
- 1649.....................50,294,208 livres
- 1661.....................84,222,096 livres
- 1670.....................96,338,885 livres
- 1685....................124,296,635 livres
- 1690....................156,740,783 livres
- 1715....................165,576,792 livres

(The metal value of the livre was at the end of the 16th century about three times as much as the franc now, in the first third of the 17th century about twice, up to 1700 about one and a half times.) The cost estimates by Necker (1789*) set the revenues at 475,294,288 livres.

4. the *King of England.*

---

*   [Tr.: possibly a reference to one of Necker (1781; 1784; 1788), although I have been unable to locate that figure in any of them.]

We know his revenues quite precisely from William the Conqueror on. They amount at the death of each king to[336]:

- William the Conqueror....£400,000
- Richard I............................£376,666
- Edward III..........................£154,139
- Henry VI............................£64,946.4
- Mary..................................£300,000
- Elizabeth I.........................£500,000
- James I..............................£450,000
- Charles I (1637–41)...........£895,819
- Charles II.........................£1,800,000
- James II............................£2,001,855
- William III (1701)...........£3,895,205
- Anne.................................£5,691,803
- George I............................£6,762,643
- George II...........................£8,523,540
- 1770................................£9,500,000
- 1780................................£12,255,214
- 1788................................£15,572,971
- 1800................................£36,728,000

Thanks to the role which the cities played before the rise of the modern principality, they must be mentioned at this point for completeness, even if only to make clear their distance from the powers looked at previously.

5. the *city budgets*. We may assume that during the Middle Ages probably only the city budgets of Venice, Milan, and Naples had even only approximately as large an income as pope and kings. According to a manuscript whose value I cannot judge, in the year 1492 Venice shall have possessed income of 1,000,000 florins, Milan and Naples each 600,000 florins[337]. In contrast, it is reported from another work that already in 1395 Gian Galeazzo Visconti, the first Duke of Milan, collected 1,200,000 florins[338]. I know one reliable figure for Bologna. There the revenues in the year 1406 ran to 320,611 lira 18 s 11 d[339]. For Florence, as is generally known Villani cites 300,000 florins[340]. None of the other Italian cities will have reached this sum. At most Paris, London, Barcelona, Seville, Lisbon, Bruges, and Ghent, later Antwerp, could yet rival the Italian cities. The German cities remained far behind those named. The revenues of one of the largest (Nuremberg)

in its heyday (1483) numbered only 421,926 pounds 19 shillings 8 hellers, that is, thus to something more than 60,000 florins[341]. Cologne in 1370 had an income of 114,780 marks in present-day [1916] currency, in 1392 of 441,397 marks. And then our "great" maritime cities: Hamburg had incomes in 1360 of 35,440 marks, in 1400 of 102,104 marks; Lübeck in 1421 received 96,617 marks, in 1430 87,576 marks, all calculated in present-day [1916] currency[342]. The same will have applied to the great number of French and English cities. They will have had the income of middling baronies.

Chapter 39: Means Formation in the Craftwork Economy

If you take a good look at the character of the craftwork-like organisation, be it that of the commercial production, be it that of trade or transport, you shall consider it out of the question that in times like those of the Middle Ages and even of the following centuries means could be accumulated by the economic subjects of this economic system to a somehow considerable extent. The smallness of the extent of the operations seems to speak against it, and with goods trade in particular the expense of transport and other expenditures.

We must though make the following considerations.

The elevated prices depicted the gross profit of the trader; if we want to ascertain the net profit which he made from the business in question, then we must — commercially speaking — deduct the expenditure accruing to it from the amounts struck. This must not be unfamiliar. But we know now that the expenditure in those times with which we are preoccupied was extraordinarily high by today's notions. They were composed of:

a) the quite considerable transport costs;

b) the no less considerable tolls;

c) those expenses or losses which arose from the insecurity of the roads. These demanded either expensive escort or led to frequent robberies and losses, in any case making transport more expensive, even where transport security had penetrated somewhat, which then of course naturally had to work for a very high reward.

I make statements about the height of transport costs in the third part of the next volume. I point the reader to both that and the information in Sombart (1902a, 1:222, 1:278). For the proof conducted here, statistical evidence of the uncontested fact that transport costs in the Middle Ages were high is unnecessary.

The high expenditure indicates low rates of return.

But we also must not assume that the *rates of profit* had been much higher. Since these were determined with a given rate of return by the frequency of turnover of business means in a year, it is not to be understood how a sizeable increase in the rate of profit above the rate of return could have been obtained. For what we learn about the turnover times of business means in Middle Ages trade indicates that this was turned over *at most* twice a year.

The western Flemish squadrons of Venice regularly travelled to Naples, Sicily, Tripoli, Tunis, Algiers, Oran, Tangiers, Morocco, Spain, Portugal, the French coast, London, Bruges, and Antwerp, and returned via Cadiz and Barcelona. This journey lasted on average a year. Even in commerce with the Levant the one-time journey of the Italian trading fleet was the rule (Heyd 1879, 1:453). This long turnover period is absolutely probable where it concerned predominantly agricultural produce. A Hanseatic merchant made the trip from Talinn or Riga over the Baltic Sea twice a year (Stieda 1887, CXVII). Further information over the length in time of voyages in the Middle Ages (which indeed decided over the length of the periods of turnover) is in Götz (1888, 515 ff.) and Rogers (1866, 1:134 ff.).

The point now, however, is that the extent of the rate of profit did not yet decide over the possible and actual *extent of accumulation*. This was instead determined, as is apparent, by the extent of the rate of accumulation, that is, the ratio of the capitalised to the consumed part of the profit on the one hand, by the amount of profit on the other. Now the extent of the rate of accumulation and the amount of profit stand in direct relationship to each other — the greater the amount of profit which falls to the individual, the greater the amounts which he personally does not consume, thus accumulates. Which is all self-evident. But here now it is to be established, through recalling the smallness of the means which were applied in craftwork-like trade by itself or, in consequence of the splitting of the total profit which a larger — because established cooperatively — trading enterprise showed among the members that, even at high rates of profit, only very small rates of accumulation and correspondingly low amounts of accumulation are too be assumed. The idea that the medieval professional merchants had obtained riches through their trading activities seems entirely out of the question. When we

304

take into consideration all the circumstances which characterised trade in the old style in craftwork-like settings — smallness of turnover, length of journeys, and the residence in foreign parts — then we will have to come to the conclusion that the traders could have been happy if, aside from what they had personally spent on the journey, they still brought home enough to preserve their families' livelihood and pay the rents for their cottage to the landowner.

What is said about trade here applies to *all other branches of pre-capitalist economy* in a corresponding way, thus above all also to the commercial handcrafts.

> Min dynge mach ick recht eñ slecht,
> Daerum blif ic een arm Knecht
> [My things I do good and bad,
> That's why I remain a poor lad]

So went the poem of a tool maker on a copperplate engraving of Israel von Meckenen (15th century — Vienna, the imperial collection of copperplate engravings, B. 222).

The normal craftwork master of the Middle Ages was nothing more than a simple trade worker who was barely distinguishable from his journeymen. According to the calculations of Rogers, the income of the master (in the building trade) was perhaps 20% higher than the wages of the journeymen[343].

And yet! In this seemingly firmly closed chain of reasoning a link must be brittle at some place which brings it to tear apart — the historical reality does not agree entirely with the results to which our theoretical considerations have led us — in the framework of the craftwork-like economy means *were* built up, commercial craftsmen and craftwork-like traders *did* obtain wealth in the course of the Middle Ages.

Certainly we must not make the thing too simple like most historians. We must not draw the conclusion yet from the fact that in the Middle Ages there were rich people engaged in trade and in particular rich merchants — for that the numbers which I myself have shared over means and turnover in medieval craftwork offer sufficient evidence — that — thus! — the craftwork-like activity *indeed* possessed the power to form means. That would be entirely inconclusive, for firstly the people whom we see in particular conducting trade could be rich already before they conducted trade. In fact that is then also to a great extent in reality the case with that trade which I have described as opportunistic trade[344].

Secondly our craftsman could have become rich through something other than his activity as a craftsman — be it through a rich marriage, an inheritance, a lucky land speculation, or some other "stroke of luck".

But even if we do not want to draw such strokes of luck into the area of our considerations — we know that in numerous cases those conducting trade and in particular merchants during the Middle Ages ran alongside their craftwork businesses to which they could very well owe their wealth (and as we will see in the following — in fact probably also mostly owed it). I mean their participation in mining, particularly in gold and silver mining, and the activity of money-lending.

I think of Hænsa-Thorir[*]. He was a pack carrier who went from place to place. He earned so much that he could buy himself a piece of land. He farmed there for a few years until he became such a man of means that he had large sums lent out to seemingly everybody. His means grew even more; he became one of the richest men ...[345]

Or I think of Andrew Bate, the butcher of Lydd, who, one of the "leading" and richest men of his place, was just as well-known through the encroachments of his great cattle herds, as through his hunger for land and his speculation in it, as through the ruthless way with which he extorted tolls from the "Western men"[346].

Or I think of the Zurich tanning master and iron trader, later mayor, Hans Waldmann, who died a very rich man and of whom we know that he ran an extensive money-lending business and made great sums as a "pension lord"[347].

Or I think of Hagenel, the master butcher in Orléans, and his wife Hersent, who:

> "se sont, au dire d'un trouvère [...] si fort enrichis par le prêt sur gage et à intérêt, qu'une grande partie des maisons de la ville leur est engagée et qu'ils achètent aux nobles fours, moulins et châteaux"

---

[*]   [Tr.: see end note 185 in the previous volume.]

[have, in the words of a troubadour (J. Normand and Raynaud 1877, v. 2656 ff.) been so much enriched by pawn and interest that many of the houses in the city are mortgaged to them and they buy the noble's ovens, mills and castles][348]

Or I think of the means of the Baumgartners, the Gossembrots, above all the Fuggers.

And ask in all these and hundreds of other cases in vain whether now the carrying of packs or the butchery or the tanning or the weaving[349] or even the money-lending or farming or land speculation or mining activities made these people rich.

But I also think of the excellent investigations of Kulischer (1908) who, as it appears to me, produced the conclusive evidence that in the Middle Ages *the goods trade was always connected with money changing* so as to arrive after all that at the result that a craftsman becoming rich still proves nothing for the means-forming power of craftwork.

But I would like though to make concessions to the earlier historians and do not want to deny at all the fact that in reality the craftsman arrived at a part of his means through his craftwork (and as I will show in another connection, also personally rose to become a capitalist entrepreneur). Then of course the problem arises for me of *how in all the world was that possible?*

Of the three possibilities for producing high surpluses, as we saw, two were closed to the craftsmen of the Middle Ages — reducing the production (transport) costs and acceleration or expansion of the turnover. The third possibility remains — high margins on the purchased or finished goods. More precisely, to produce as high as possible a gap between the purchase price and the sale price.

The figures which stand at our disposal to establish the actual *extent of price mark-ups in the Middle Ages* are extraordinarily sparse. The most important information known to me which is beyond question is the following.

Wool trade: in the famous example which Uzzano (1440, 118) cites from the English-Florentine wool trade, 100 pounds of wool (gross) at the places of production in England cost 10½ florins, 200 pounds net (which corresponds to 300 pounds gross) was sold in Florence for 76–

88 florins. According to another list in Uzzano (1440, 186–87) for 11 bales of English wool in Calais 612 florins was paid at purchase (after at least 50% expenses had already arisen), in Milan at sale 1,315⅘ florins.

Cloth trade: the five packs of Flemish cloth whose fates Tölner (1885) reports to us show at sale the following mark-ups on the purchase price: 26%, 27%, 21%, 19%, 30%, thus on average 25%.

Entirely in agreement with that are the price mark-ups which we know of from the cloth trading of Vicko von Geldersen. They run in the years 1370–1376 to 15, 9, 18½, 19, 21⅗, 29⅗, 25⅛, 22³⁄₁₀, 12, and 22½% respectively (Nirrnheim 1895, LXVIII).

Johann Wittenborg could in one case (1356) mark-up Bruges linen 70%, another time (1353) though could only mark-up 5% on the purchase price of 32 pieces of Poperinge linen (Mollwo 1901, LXXI).

Hildebrand Vecklinchusen bought (1409) serge in Cologne for 2¼ ducats for which he obtained in Venice 3 ducats (Stieda 1894, 110).

20 pieces of cloth (panni bianchi de Cadix [white cloths of Cadiz]) were bought in Cadiz for fl. 256. 13. 4., and sold in Florence for 395 fl.; another item of 35 pieces of cloth was bought for 207.6 fl., sold for 408 fl.; a third bought for 262 fl., sold for 300–350 fl.; with a third item the piece cost 20 fl. at purchase, at sale 26–28 fl.; with a fifth respectively 21 fl. and 32–34 fl. (Uzzano 1440, 123–30).

Trousers: Hildebrand Vecklinchusen bought a dozen for 4 marks 5 shillings and sold them for 6½ ducats (Stieda 1894, 111).

Caps, which formed the objects of the Flemish-Florentine trade in the 14th/15th century, were sold in part with enormous mark-up; fine caps per dozen purchase price 1½ fl., sale price 15 fl. (!); medium-fine respectively ⁹⁄₁₀ fl. and 6 fl.; ordinary (tonde a orrecchi [round to ears]) respectively ³⁄₂₀ and 2–2½ fl. (Uzzano 1440, 128 f.).

Iron in ingots was bought for 12–13 florins per thousand (1 migliaio = 980 Florentine pounds), and sold for 17–18 florins; another time the thousand, which was sold for 47 Venetian lira gross, cost at purchase 42 lira (Uzzano 1440, 168, 4).

Pewterware (Stagno lavorato [tin products] = piatelli [plates], scodelle [bowls], salsieri [gravy boats]) had a purchase price in London of 8 florins and was sold in Florence for 13½ to 13⅔ fl. (both prices calculated for 100 English pounds which was the same as 133⅓ Florentine pounds).

In the 13th century:

100 kg of pepper cost:	the same amount of wax cost:
in Marseille (1264) — 481 marks	in Piedmont (1262) — 335 marks
in Lombardy (1268) — 512 marks	in Champagne (1262) — 420 marks
in Champagne (1262) — 602 marks	in England (1259–70) — 530 marks
in Champagne (1265) — 629 marks	
in England (1265) — 683 marks	
in England (1159–70) — 796 marks	(Schaube 1897, 5:279, 5:282)

A pipe of **oil** cost:

	at purchase	at sale
in 1374 c.	£22 5 s. 6 d.	£23
in 1375 c.	£17 8 s.	£21

(Nirrnheim 1895, LXII)

At any rate, these figure suffice to give us the impression that in fact goods in the Middle Ages were often traded with quite considerable markups. Carrying out the same calculation for the price markups with production is quite impossible. But if we recall the extraordinarily high price which in the Middle Ages was paid in the rule for commercial products, and compare it with the low prices of raw materials, then we must draw the conclusion that obviously even here the gap between purchase and sale price was quite large.

But, we must ask further, how was it possible to produce this large gap; why did one buy so cheaply or (and) why could one sell so dearly?

The immediate answer to this question is because traders and producers found themselves in a *monopoly situation*. For wealth to arise, some monopoly must always be present. The monopoly might be artificially created — privileges of trade! guild orders! a family's right to dispense wine! — or it might simply be based on the natural situation.

The commercial producers, particularly the skilful amongst them, had a natural monopoly in times of such poorly developed productivity as the centuries of the Middle Ages.

The monopoly position which specific cities or regions obtained through the *production of some highly desired soil (or water) product* seems, however, to be of particular significance to me for those times. You can characterise some cities according to their most important (monopoly) product — as wine cities: Pressburg, Cologne; beer cities (on account of malt and hops!) like perhaps Hamburg; as herring cities: Lübeck, Wismar, Rostock, Stralsund, Greifswald (by which up to the 12th century the herring passed in such thicks masses "that in summer you only had to immerse the basket in the water to pull it out full" until it moved to the coast of Schonen and to the Norwegian shores, and the Hanseatics were entangled in bloody wars with the Danes, the masters of the northern beaches, with the English, Scots, and Dutch); above all, however, as salt cities. Famous "salt cities" include Lüneburg, Danzig (salt trade!), Hallein, Halle, Salzburg, and Venice.

In part it was of course probably the estate owners who took the main profits from the salt production; or their creatures who became well-known under the names of "salt junkers" or "panners". In part, however, even small craftwork-like existences, be it as producers, be it as traders, seemed to have worked themselves into prominence with the help of salt. I am thinking of the Hallenses or Hallarii in Salzburg, but also of the Venetians. "The lagoon residents were [NB. so far as they were not something else, like for example estate owners!] fishermen, like the present-day residents of Chioggia, and obtained sea salt, which for the rock salt poor Italy is so important that a region which produces salt almost by itself, like the lagoons, must have great importance."[350] If it is true that in the Kingdom of the Lombards in two generations a rich, estateless merchant class developed — one concludes that as is well known from the Lex Aistolf[351] — it was then owed in essence to the salt works of Commacchio. All of upper Italy was supplied with salt by the salt works of Commacchio; the salt trade of Commacchio was at certain times the trade of the Po in general[352].

Now, however, as you must know, no monopoly position in the world, be it yet so exclusive, is of use in actually trading goods now with high mark-ups. For this to be possible, once more quite specific conditions must be fulfilled, in other words the economic nature of the sellers and buyers must be quite special. The latter must namely either be peoples with whom you can practice exploitation, as was the case with the residents of colonial areas (which shall be treated in context in another place), or they must be "rich" people, that is, persons who do not live from the work of their hands. As such, however, in the Middle Ages almost *only drawers of land rents or receivers of taxes* come into consideration, and only if we consider the outstanding significance of this category of sellers and particularly buyers are we then capable of making comprehensible within the cultured lands themselves the (occasional) means-forming power of medieval trade and commerce.

With the drawers of land rents you could *buy* especially cheaply. The English monasteries, for example, from whom the Florentine and Hanseatic traders drew their wool[353], were not bound in establishing prices to any firm lower bound like is necessary for any independent producer. They indeed sold wool delivered free of charge (i.e. by their bondsmen), a product thus which cost them nothing at all, and which they sacrificed with joy even if they received only a relatively tiny sum of money for it. If you want to insist on describing the work embodied in a product as the "value" of the good, then we would say those entitled to the rents could ceaselessly, without experiencing a loss, sell the goods coming into their power of disposal below their value. Put another way, what the buyer of these goods added onto the purchase price was up to a certain amount the returns to work of indentured bondsmen.

This fact, that medieval trade particularly in its early period was for a large part trade with drawers of land rents, only now obtains its full significance, however, when we take account of it directly for the *sale* in particular of costly items. It is surely not saying too much when one claims that three quarters of all colonial products and all commercial produce which were sold by pre-capitalist trade had as buyer drawers of rents — namely princes, knights, churches, monasteries, abbeys.

There are of course no statistics on buyers with information on their social position. But what we learn about the quality of buyers, however, from the occasional information of the business books especially — the almost only reliable and usable source for the older trade history — confirms the assumption that a very large part were drawers of rents.

Above all it is the products of the East which probably found their purchasers exclusively in the higher spheres of society. You encounter them in great quantities in the castles of the great and at the courts of the princes. The Church especially also appears as a purchaser capable of paying for oriental products which it required for the furnishing of its buildings, for the adornment of its servants, and for the glorification of its rituals. To this end it was asking constantly after magnificent garments, hangings, tablecloths and carpets, pearls and precious stones, incense and fragrant sub-stances[354]. Also for relics, real and supposed, the highest sums were paid — one recalls the precious little story which a monk of the monastery of St Gallen tells us of the sale of an embalmed mouse, of how for this faked animal relic the rich prince of the Church offered the Jew a fortune[*].

In addition, some commercial products, particularly armour, weapons, and fine cloths, found easy sales at any price with the rich estate owners. We see precisely the tailors rising often and fully to standing and wealth in the cities. And we can imagine how they arrived at their wealth. "The tailor not infrequently took entire villages and estates in exchange for the quantities of expensive cloths which he — perhaps on the occasion of a wedding celebration — delivered to a house that was great, but not at all times rich in ready money."[355] For the foreign cloths, particularly the Dutch, belonged to the most desired luxury articles — as material for beautiful clothes, and as drapery for festive rooms. That the increasing luxury here contributed to his own luxury, increasing the demand for such goods more and more, is self-evident. The furrier's craft also offered opportunity to enrich oneself in the same way[356].

Up to now I have only cited examples from the world of commercial craftwork. But of course cases can also be thought of in which perhaps a *transport craftsman* understood how to obtain wealth through adroit exploitation of a rich clientele. Such a case, which even became of great historical significance, was the exploitation of the Crusaders by the Italian municipalities, particularly Venice, which took the poor fellows' last groschen when they wanted to travel over the sea. That here real usurious prices were demanded is vouched for by a series of printed figures. We learn, for example, that the Venetians were paid for the ferrying of a knight with two squires, one horse and a stable boy 8½ marks of silver (= 340 silver marks = 200 Austrian florins in present-day [1916] currency)[357], whereas today for the journey from Trieste to Constantinople you pay for the Austrian Lloyd in first class 124.4, in second 85.6, and in third 37 florins.

---

[*]   [Tr.: for this tale see Koegel (1897, 1.2:246 f.).]

Thus it was "rich" people or public bodies alone with whom profitable business could be closed in the Middle Ages (as forming means by craftwork is at all times tied to these preconditions).

I place the greatest weight on this fact. Its recognition is an indispensable prerequisite for understanding medieval commercial relations. For obviously all price-formation was influenced by it. It caused everyone to buy the named goods as well as the raw materials below their "value", so they could be sold above their value. *Could be* — the emphasis is to be placed on that. For they were paid with shares of rents, and thus for the level of their prices any specifying of limits above had become pointless. It did not cost the knight a solidus more if for a Milanese armour he paid instead of the yearly rent of two or twenty peasants that of four or forty; just as the abbot of the monastery did no damage to his physical or spiritual well-being if for a costly chasuble or a few pounds of pepper he paid the yield of two or three more fields that owed tribute. Thus what the traders added on to the purchase price at sale here were in turn land rents (or taxes).

But the means which a commercial producer or a small trader perhaps formed in commerce with these rich people of the Middle Ages was a "derived" means — it resulted from the massing together into larger amounts in the hands of craftsmen parts of the (already present) feudal wealth.

Thus it explains why despite all "rational" consideration here and there means could form even in the framework of the craftwork-like economy.

Certainly, I would not like to attach an excessively large significance to means-forming from goods trade and production profits in the Middle Ages or even later on. Perhaps that a larger number of middling means were constantly formed in the framework of the craftwork-like economy — they may have brought about that imperceptible transformation of craftwork into small capitalist undertakings which we see for a millennium and which was of course also of significance for the genesis of capitalism. If we want to grasp the great phenomenon of the genesis of a new, bourgeois wealth in its entire extent, then we must survey other places where wealth could form during the Middle Ages to a larger extent.

Chapter 40: Means Formation through Money-Lending

I. The Spread of Money-Lending

The struggle lasted for more than a millennium between the ideas of money which finally gave birth to modern capitalism and the old feudal powers in state and society, the struggle which it is fundamentally the task of this entire work to describe, but which at this point we are only pursuing on a specific side — how it led to the formation of larger means outside the circles of feudal wealth.

During the entire course of the European Middle Ages there was probably no time in which a need for cash did not arise in this or that place and above all — to which we direct our attention here alone — within feudal society, with nobility or clergy, with princes or churches. Even in the 9th century, which in its economic structure was the most distant from all monetary economy and credit-like relations, in which the principles of self-sufficiency had gained the deepest and most general recognition — even in this most money-shy of all centuries of the Christian era, we encounter money-lending as an in no way isolated phenomenon. I need only bring to mind the Capitulare de Judaeis (814) or the Liber manualis (814–844) to prove the correctness of this claim[358].

From the Crusades onwards the financial difficulties of the nobility or at least of a large part of the nobility surely became a chronic suffering. From then on we also hear everywhere that the nobility have fallen into debt, lost a part of their possessions, and the like.

I content myself with making a few references to the sources and literature from which this generally well-known fact is to be seen.

For the extortionate lending to the *Crusaders* in particular, see Heyd (1879, 1:159), Prutz (1883, 364 ff.), Schaube (1898, 605 ff.), Cunningham (1907, 1:191), and Piton (1892, 1:21).

Italy. In the region of Florence we observe how already from the end of the 11th century the high nobility begin to fall into debt and become impoverished (Davidsohn 1896b, 1:284 f., 1:795 f.; 1896a, 158 f.). For the Tuscany of the 13th century, Davidsohn (1896a, 4:281 ff.) again provides a wealth of material. We hear of an impoverishment of a part of the nobility in the 12th century also in Venice: "Multos nobiles, qui ad paupertatem devenerunt" [many nobles who fell into poverty], confirmed the Doge Ziani, who himself "possessed enormous means". "You see how an obviously not small part of the nobility, unable to adapt to the features of the time, sank into poverty" (Lenel 1897, 46). Obviously the estates of these nobles had to have thus previously passed into the hands of others; and they could also only have been financiers. For *Savoy*: Sella (1887, 229 ff.).

France. "Gentilshommes et usuriers, ayant un constant besoin les uns des autres paraissent vivre [...] en bonne intelligence." [Gentlemen and usurers, having a constant need for one another, seem to live [...] in good understanding.] (D'Avenel 1894, 1:109 f.). An interesting document is the testament of the richest Parisian usurer in the 13th century, the famed Gandulphus de Arcellis (Gandouffle), who (as it frequently happened), tormented on his deathbed by fear, listed all the victims of his work whom he had refunded the "usurae" received from them. The list contained almost exclusively lords spiritual and temporal. Printed in Piton (1892, 161 ff.).

> Mes peres fu francs hom et de grant parénte: [...]
> Puis kei en malage et en grant poverté,
> Et engaga ses terres, petit l'en fu remés.
> Cis hom ert par usure en grant avoir montés:
> A mon pere fist toute se tere racater;
> Puis m'i dona a feme [...]
> [My father was a Frenchman and of great parents:
> Then fell into illness and into great poverty,
> And pawned his land, little by little.
> This man had by usury a large mountain to climb:
> My father chose to bring everything back to earth;
> Then my woman and wife ...]
> (J. Normand and Raynaud 1877, ll. 7113–7120)

Cf. also the chronicler Rigord (Guizot 1825, 22) and Davidsohn (1896a, 3:No. 139). In all the troubadour poetry the noble tormented by creditors plays a large role. Cf. Herrmann (1900, 31 f.).

In *England* we first encounter the Jews, then the Lombards as financiers of the large estate owners. "The Jews obtained forty percent by lending money to extravagant or heavily taxed landowners." (Cunningham 1907, 1:189 ff., 1:328). In 1325 the King and most of the prelates were debtors of the Lombards, so that the Archbishop of London wanted the latter expelled, which the Pope forbade (Piton 1892, 216). Cf. Madox (1769, 1:222 ff, 1:249 f.).

For the usurious lending to the great estate owners in *Flanders* a wealth of material is to be found in des Marez (1901, 165, 174, 183, 195, 254 f.). Cf. also Vanderkindere (1879, 223).

For Guy of Dampierre, for example, the moneymen, especially the Italians, sat like fleas in a fur coat. A nice characterisation of that splendid, genuinely seigneurial type, who never had money but always all the more debts for it, is found in Funck-Brentano (1897, 76 ff.).

For *Germany* and *Switzerland* Schulte (1900, 1:290 ff.), Lamprecht (1893, 233 f.), and Janssen (1874, 1:444), as much as their views deviate from one another otherwise, concur in the judgement of the nobility. Over the usurious lending to large estate owners by Jews, see Stobbe (1866, 117 f., 240 f.).

As rich as the *Church* was and remained throughout the centuries, there were though times, were especially always individual churches and monasteries, and individual clergymen who had a strong need for money and sought to cover this need for money by way of loans (if not the sale of all they owned).

Such a time in which the Church fell victim to an extensive indebtedness in which a part of the Church's estates passed into secular hands seemed to have been the 11th and 12th centuries when that mighty tendency towards secularisation overcame the clergy. At the time the Church's estates were "squandered on the high life", the churches and monasteries had to sacrifice a part of their possessions to be rid of the debts. A legend of the 13th century, reported by Cesarius, tells: "l'on voit l'argent d'un usurier mis dans un coffre avec l'argent d'une abbaye le dévorer comme une proie; de sort qu'au bout de peu de temps on ne trouve plus rien dans le coffre" [we see the money of an usurer put in a safe with the money of an abbey devouring it like prey; it is fate that after a short time nothing can be found in the safe]*.

Exaggerations — certainly. But in it there is a real grain of truth. Aside from that it is a familiar thing.

What then later once more entangled the spiritual lords so much into debt were, as is well-known, their obligations to Rome, the payment of the Servitia communia. Hence their need for money was for a period a general phenomenon in all

---

* [Tr.: no reference given for Cesarius by Sombart.]

lands and thus, particularly for the solvent possessor of money, the outlook to quickly enrich themselves was a very good one.

Through the investigations of Gottlob (1899), Schneider (1885, 50 ff.), and others, and through the absolute wealth of material collected by Schulte (1900, 1:235 ff.), we are now informed down to the smallest detail over the relations between the prelates seeking money and their creditors. We know that it was again above all Italian houses which even outside Italy made business with the spiritual lords.

At the same time it concerned quite enormous sums. If we use as a basis the conversion which Schneider (1885, 53) has carried out, then the following houses loaned the bishops in the years 1295–1304:

Mozzi	282,460 marks metal value
Abbati	525,868
Chiarenti	706,280
Ammanati	942,274
Spini	1,629,465

When we consider now also what a large and growing need for money the princely and civic budgets had as they developed into *public accounts*, we will be able to imagine what a powerful embrace the lending activity must have already assumed in a relatively early period — say during the High Middle Ages.

So much is in any case certain — that the value turned over in trade vanishes into insubstantial appearance as soon as we compare it with the figures of the credit activity in the same period, and that the highest thinkable profit from trade is left behind at a still greater distance by the sums earned exclusively by lending. You will perhaps recall that approximately in the same epoch (middle or end of the 14th century), when the value of the *entire export trade* of a city like Reval amounted to 1–1½ million marks, that of Lübeck to 2–3 million marks in present-day [1916] currency (according to Stieda's calculations), a single Florentine banking house (the Bardi) had lent the King of England over 8 million marks in present-day [1916] currency (900,000 gold florins), and another (the Peruzzi) over 5 million marks[359]; that at the time when the entire Hanseatic merchantry bought wool in England for 5–600,000 marks, the Italian for 1½–2 million marks in present-day [1916] currency (end of the 13th century), a single

318

Parisian usurer (Gaudouffle) paid tax on a turnover of 546,000 marks, all the Lombards in Paris, however, on one of 61,440,000 marks in present-day [1916] currency[360]. What in contrast even would the turnover of a million ducats in the Fodacio dei Tedeschi signify, even assuming it was correct! Or consider what it means that the Genoese and Pisans lent the Crusaders before Acre in the 12th century 26,400 marks of silver, 2,220 ponds tornese and 930 ounces of gold[361], thus about 1½ million marks of metal value in present-day [1916] currency; that Louis IX of France raised a loan from merchants of 102,708⅔ pounds tornese, thus of more than 2½ million marks in present-day [1916] currency[362]; and that in 1390, when the Jewish debts were rescinded in Regensburg, they amounted to about 100,000 gold guilders, thus about 1 million marks. "And how much the Jews of Regensburg might have lost to out-of-town debtors!"[363].

Money-lending was an important sideline of goods traders during the entire Middle Ages, as is shown by Kulischer (1908). I would like to add for completeness that it remained a profitable business activity of goods traders *up to the conclusion of the epoch of early capitalism*, that is, up until credit negotiation was organised in banks and cooperatives. When we look, for example, at the means formation of a rich Hirschberg merchant in the 18th century, we are astonished by the many-branched money-lending activity of such a goods trader. The testament of the "great" Christian Mentzel exhibits a long series of loans, the largest of which were given to noble lords, but which were also given to poor bourgeois debtors down to amounts of 12 talers.

The outstanding loans amounted, next to owed interest, to 109,635 talers, 4 silver groschen, 5 pounds, whereas the value of the stores and the trading activity was estimated at 121,038 talers, 26 silver groschen, 11 pounds[364].

II. The Profits from Money-Lending

That on these large sums large returns were also made, we may look on as a given. It is vouched for already by the *highness of the interest rate* during the long centuries of the Middle Ages. It is known that 20–25% was about the usual amount for which loans were given out, that this amount in rare (for the debtor favourable) cases fell to perhaps 10%, but quite frequently also climbed to a height that is dizzying for our comprehension[365]. One tends to consider some of the "legally" standardised interest rates to be the result of fantasy — thus when you learn that a statute from 23 May 1243 established for the Jews of Provence an interest rate of 300%, the Jewish privileges of Frederick II (1244) one of 173%, a regulation of the Prince-Bishopric of Freising (1259) one of 120% — but you are forced to believe in such possibilities, as sufficient evidence is at hand that in reality interest rates which hovered around 50% were no rarity — in the eight sea loans which a shipowner in Venice concluded in the year 1167, the lowest interest rate amounted to 40%, the highest 50%[366]. A sum of 20,000 marks (856,000 silver marks), which Richard Lejons of Winchelsea (1375/76) lent the King of England, yielded interest at 50%[367]. That just to cite a few examples from quite different circumstances in the Middle Ages.

Even in the centuries following the Middle Ages the interest rates for money-lending remained high — Louis XIV had to pay 15% for his borrowing.

Likewise the *commissions* which the 'bankers' were paid for their service were considerable. Thus, for example, the commission of the Campsores [money-changers] of the camera apostolica amounted in the cases known to me[368] to 8, 11, 12¼, 24, 25, and 35%.

On top of that, the medieval laws on right of lien and mortgages granted the creditor much greater powers than our current laws. The mortgaging amounted, in many cases at least, to an alienation whose coming into effect was tied to the delayed condition of non-fulfilment of the contract. It amounted mostly to a contingent purchase. The sale document was given to the lender as a security; a clause was added to the sale contract that it became invalid if principal and interest were paid by the agreed date, otherwise the alienation became effective without further ado, the creditor became owner of the mortgaged property. "All the property of nobles as well as monastic foundations hence stood constantly in danger of falling into the hands of usurers."*

---

*   [Tr.: this quote not referenced by Sombart.]

As example, in a document from 1287: Günther von Schwarzburg mortgaged a property to a Jew "tali pacto, ut si termino statuto non redimeremus, quod tunc sibi absque contradictione maneret et titulo proprietatis liberae suum esset" [such an agreement that if the term of the statute were not redeemed, at that moment it remained without hindrance and the title to the property of the woman became one's own] (Stobbe 1866, 240). With the limitations on the rights of Jews to own land, the granting of the loan took place mostly for them with the pawning of jewellery, precious items, silver and ornaments. Examples are given in Stobbe (1866, 240).

Another trick which the lender (under the pressure of the canonical ban on interest) tended to use against his client consisted of a sort of betting contract by which, for example, a pilgrim received the travel money on the condition that his inheritance or certain goods, in the case that he did not return, fell to the one who had provided the money[369].

The main reason, however, for why in all earlier times — that is, during the entire Middle Ages until the end of the 18th century — all money-lending, particularly to the small and large holders of public power, brought such extraordinary profits was the custom, generally common in the past, of providing the creditor with satisfaction through the transfer of specific revenues — like taxes, tolls, fees, mine duties, etc. — of revenues which in the beginning mostly flowed from the absolute power of estate owners, but were gradually attributed to specific rights of the state as their source. This custom corresponded to the earlier practice of the state of bestowing all public authority with the character of alienable value and relinquishing it as such as need arose.

The creditor, who with the lesser lords often also became asset manager, with the greater princes the court banker, mostly appears as "leaseholder" of the various sources of income from which he was remunerated at his discretion, be it for his interest, be it for his capital — understandably to an extent not disadvantageous to his interests. We can describe thus what dominated the finances of those centuries as a *clientele economy* — it has its beginnings in the early Middle Ages (Roman legacy?) and reaches its high point in the establishment of the French fermiers généraux* or the "Partisans" of the 18th century.

---

*   [Tr.: a tax farming system.]

How generally spread this conduct was is shown by the following, certainly very incomplete collection of evidence which
I have compiled:

Leasing of Tax Revenues, Toll Differences, etc.
(with exclusion of mines and mints)

Popes. We encounter a mortgaging or pawning of tithes very often.
You can find precise information in the already mentioned works of
Kirsch (1894), Gottlob (1892; 1889; 1899), and Schneider (1885), whose
results Schulte (1900) has portrayed in summary with the addition of
numerous further details.

The *Campsores camerae apostolicae* achieved a particular fame
which old Pagnini (1765) points out to us and whose fate has been made
familiar to us in a quite especially endearing way by numerous thorough
special investigations.

We now know precise information about the way in which the popes
directed by means of an elaborate collection system the money streaming to them from the four corners of the earth into their central accounts. We can follow the head collectors, collectors, and sub-collectors
on their wanderings, know the little sacks and caskets, possibly with
their signatures, in which the money tended to be kept before it was delivered to a higher centre. We know thus now also what is of interest
here — that already from the 13ᵗʰ century merchants were entrusted
with the collection and conveyance of papal money — we meet the first
"bankers" of the curia under the papacy of Gregory IX (1227–1241).

The earliest document which confirms the use of merchants in the
papal administration of finances is a letter of Gregory IX from the year
1233 in which he gives receipt to "Angelerium Solaficu quondam Camp-
sorem nostrum & eius Socios Mercatores Senenses de omnibus rationi-
bus, quas in Anglia, Francia, et Curia Romana, vel etiam alibi nostro vel
Ecclesiae Romanae nomine receperunt" [Angelerio Solaficu, formerly
our money-changer, and his associates the Sienese merchants, those
amounts which are received in England, France, and the Roman Curia,
or even elsewhere in the name of the Roman Church] (Muratori 1738,
1:889 Diss. 16).

But then in the 14ᵗʰ century, especially after the abolition of the
Knights Templar order, which during its existence had been used a lot
for the collection of money, the institution of the Campsores camerae
apostolicae developed its great significance. If to begin with merchants
of the various Italian cities, like Lucca, Pistoia, and especially Sienna,
were used for such functions, so with time the Florentines won ever
greater influence over the Holy Seat, until they finally monopolised the
banker business almost completely. The Spini and Spigliati, the Bardi,
the Cerchi, the Pulci, the Alfani, they considered it a particular honour
to take care of the money business of the Holy Father, until the Medici
overtook them all, being the bankers of the popes par excellence during
the 15ᵗʰ and 16ᵗʰ centuries — the Rothschilds of the Italian Renaissance.
Cf. Meltzing (1906).

We find *the orders of knights* likewise in connection with merchants who served them as bankers or even (with the enormous revenues this seems almost unbelievable) being of use with advances. At least this applied to the Knights of St John of Jerusalem whom we find in 1320 in the debt of the Bardi and Peruzzi (Bosio 1621, 2:28). Apart from the aforementioned Italian houses, there were money-changers in Montpellier and Narbonne whom we encounter as bankers to the Knights Hospitaller. Cf. Heyd (1879, 1:576).

Italy, Venice. When in the 12th century a number of citizens raised the money for creating a fleet, "promissum fuit civibus, restituere mutuatam pecuniam eis obligantes redditus communis" [it was a promise by the citizens to restore the money lent, binding on the common revenues] (Simonsfeld 1878, 137). Thus in turn the revenues of the salt monopoly, the money of the tithes, and the ground rents of the terra firma were mortgaged to the state's creditors (Ferrara 1871). Cf. Lattes (1882, 232). In the year 1169, the Doge Dandolo mortgaged to a certain Mairano for six years all buildings, taverns, carriages, and weights, measures for oil, wine, and honey to be found on the Riva in Constantinople (Cecchetti 1870, 38; Heynen 1905, 102).

Genoa. Mortgaging or pawning of numerous tolls and duties, of the salt monopoly, the mint, etc., from the 12th century. "Mortgaging of taxes forms the leading system of raising taxes until the end of the republic." (Sieveking 1898, 1:41). Genoese were in possession of a third of the harbour tolls in Acre (Prutz 1883, 378).

Pisa. Davidsohn (1896b, 685).

Florence. In 1329, the mortgaging of the village of Gabella by the Acciaiuoli family and associates (Davidsohn 1896a, 3:186).

In *Naples* we frequently find civic offices mortgaged to Florentines (Davidsohn 1896a, 3:XVII).

Occasionally the tax farmers in the Italian municipalities obtained considerable sums for the taking over of the rights by prior issue of share certificates, imaginary quotas, so-called portiones of the mortgaged object. The purchaser of the portiones were called portionarii, partionarii and participes, their relationship to the undertaker partecipatio. We find the same phenomena later with the French Partisans again (Lastig 1879, 24, 425).

England. A comprehensive examination of the object has already been carried out by Bond (1840). The institution of the Sheriff, to whom the collection of the taxes was entrusted in each county in exchange for the granting of fixed rents, is ancient (Sinclair 1803, 1:55). See the interesting work of Turner (1898). Round (1888) and Maitland (1907, 204) have recently dealt with the Firma burgi[*] magnificently. The first king who made use of foreign merchants would have been John; under Henry III their use became entrenched. From 1276–1292 we find Lucchese as takers of tolls; in 1294 ten different trading houses from

---

[*]   [Tr.: Firma burgi = lump sum provided to an authority in lieu of other irregular fees due.]

Lucca and Florence are involved in wool transactions. At the beginning of the 14th century we see the Frescobaldi gathering up in their hand as security for their lending to the English Crown almost the entire wool revenues of the Kingdom. See Pagnini (1765, 2:70), where the English source is cited. Cf. also Toniolo (1895, 563), and Stubbs (1874, 2:561). Further evidence is contained in Fox Bourne (1886), and the extraordinarily interesting essay of Law (1895). Law furnishes the proof that after the Bardi and Peruzzi, who in the year 1340 were still in possession of the ninths of six counties, came a series of English houses who ran their business entirely in the way of the Italians. "They undertook the *ferm* not only of the customs, but even of the war subsidies, and in return for the ready-money payments they made the king they were allowed to take not only the legal custom of 40 s. a sack, but any additional impost they might be able to extort from the extremities of the other wool merchants" (Law 1895, 63). New light over the participation of foreign and English money-lenders in the public revenues is propagated by the very thorough work of Terry (1914). But even in the 17th century the custom still existed of mortgaging to creditors of the king public revenues; thus with the loan which Sir William Courten provided the king in 1625 to the extent of £27,000. (Rymer 1727, 18:156; Macpherson and Anderson 1805, 2:336). In the "funded" loans are to be found the last traces of this drinking at the trough. In the same century we also still encounter the gifting of sinecures, the ancient custom of anticipations[*] to the government, etc. A good, though not entirely clear portrayal of the contemporary conditions is in the article "Monied Interest" in Postlethwayt (1774, 2:284 f.).

Germany. In 1187 the burgrave of Cologne mortgaged the revenues from his castle (Ennen 1863, 1:102; Inama-Sternegg 1879, 2:447). Danzig and Worms (from the 13th century), Nuremberg from 1360, and other cities mortgaged their revenues (M. Neumann 1865, 538 f.). Lüneburg mortgaged in 1372 the Kalkberg ('chalk mountain'), in 1375 the city scales, in 1381 the salt revenues of the city (Volger 1872, 2:765, 2:857, 2:961). Cf. Inama-Sternegg (1879, 3.2:491). In the 14th century Archbishop Wilhelm of Cologne mortgaged the tax office with the beer brewery to Johann Hirzelin for 4,450 gold guilders; and to the same man the mill and gate tolls in the city to which the Archbishop was entitled for 9,000 gold guilders (Hegel, Cardauns, and Schröder 1875, 3:CXXVI). During the 14th century we frequently encounter Italians as leaseholders of the princely tolls in Central Germany (M. Neumann 1865, 377). Cf. also Kostanecki (1889, 32 f.), and the ample collection of relevant data again in Schulte (1900, 1:328 f.): "Italians at German Customhouses".

Over mortgaging of tolls, etc. to Jews, see Stobbe (1866, 116 f.).

But the classic land of the customhouse economy appears to have been France. Here we encounter the leaser of taxes from the earliest Middle Ages through to the most recent times. Around the year 584 we

---

[*]   [Tr.: anticipation = prepayment of a debt.]

encounter a Jew Armentarius to whom was offered for a loan to a Viscarius and a Count Eunomius of Tours debt contracts over the public revenues (Aronius, Dresdner, and Lewinski 1902, Reg. 47).

Pigeonneau (1887, 1:266) tells of wealthy receivers of interest in the 12th century:

> "Ces bourgeois sont chargés d'encaisser les redevances du domaine et chacun d'eux a une clef des coffres ou sont déposés les deniers royaux, au trésor du Temple"
> [These bourgeois are responsible for collecting the dues from the estate and each of them has a key to the coffers where the royal funds are deposited, in the Temple's treasury].

"Lombards" during the 13th century were "receveurs" [tax collectors] in France. Evidence in Piton (1892, 1:36). The well-known hero of a novella by Boccaccio, Signore Ciapperello da Prato[*], was receveur de la baillie d'Auvergne [tax collector of the bailiwick of Auvergne] from 1288 to 1292. (Piton 1892, 1:69). In 1295 there were also other tax collectors under Philip IV the Fair. The brothers De Bonis were also collecteurs de tailles [collectors of taxes] (14th century) (Forestié 1890, 1:XXVII). Ordinances from 1323 and 1347 prohibited the employment of Italians, but without success. Cf. Clamageran (1867, 337).

> "Les banquiers se chargeaient aussi d'opérer la recette des grandes propriétés seigneuriales; ils faisaient, en quelque sorte, fonction de régisseurs ou d'intendants. Tel est en ce genre à la fin du XIV. sc. Digne Rapponde, Lombard en vogue, qui a des comptoirs à Paris et à Bruges. Il est l'homme d'affaires du duc de Bourgogne, du comte de Flandres, d'Yolande de Cassel, du sire de la Tremoïlle et sans nul doute de cents autres."
> [The bankers were also responsible for operating the receipts of the great seigneurial properties; they were, in a way, enacting the function of stewards or factors. Such a sort at the end of 14th century is Digne Rapponde, Lombard in vogue, who has offices in Paris and Bruges. He is the businessman of the Duke of Burgundy, the Count of Flanders, Yolande de Cassel, the seigneur de la Tremoïlle, and undoubtedly hundreds of others.]
> "Des domaines sont donnés aux Lombards par de puissants princes, 'en reconnaissance de leurs bons services.'"
> [Domains are given to the Lombards by powerful princes 'in recognition of their good service.'] (D'Avenel 1894, 1:109, 1:110).

Cf. also Marx (1903, 1:709-710 n.229; 1906, 1:816 n.2). In the years 1403–1411 an Oddonius Asinerii Domicellus is creditor and castellan of the Count of Greyerz in the lordships of Aubonne and Coppet (Amiet 1877, 251 ff.).

---

[*]   [Tr.: or at least the real person of that name who may have inspired the character.]

The 'partisans' or 'traitans' then became famous (and notorious) and experienced their greatest flourishing in the 17th and 18th century — they were the bankers who advanced the government the sums of money which they needed and were allocated in return specific payments which remained left to them to collect themselves. They received their name from the 'parti'; what was thus called "une opération financière qui avait pour but d'avancer au Roi des fonds soit sur la création de nouveaux impôts et de nouveaux offices, pour en percevoir en suite soi-même le produit; soit sur la recherche des impôts impayés, des fonds royaux divertis, des non privilegiés qui avaient réussi à se soustraire aux charges publics" [a financial operation which aimed to advance funds to the King, either on the creation of new taxes and new offices, in order to subsequently collect the proceeds oneself; or on the search for unpaid taxes, diverted royal funds, or non-privileged people who had succeeded in evading public charges]*. Just as well known is the establishment of the *ferme* [tax farm], the position of the *fermiers généraux* [farmers general].

The *sale of offices* had a special significance for France in particular during the last period of the ancien régime. All somewhat tangible services, from the highest to the lowest, from the position of a first president of parliament to that of a wood measurer and a hay seller, were raised to offices which were sold to private individuals. The holder of these offices then received the authority to collect the taxes and revenues bound to the office to their own advantage. (I will come to speak of this establishment of the sale of offices in yet another connection where I will share further particulars.)

The main source for the study of the French customhouse economy in the more recent period is the contemporary pamphlet literature. See, for example, Froumenteau (1581), la Barre (1622), Bourgoin (1625), Loyseau (1610), Gourville (1838), Moreau de Jonnés (1867), Tallemant des Réaux (1910), etc. Since these texts are almost unobtainable, particularly abroad, we must greet with thanks such works which share them in excerpts. Deserving of mention among these are above all Thirion (1895), and Normand (1908). Alongside them Forbonnais (1758) is to be treasured as a rich source of numerous details. Good overviews are also given by Ranke (1856, 3:50 f., 3:192 f.). These things have recently been depicted in a splendid and exhaustive way in the very valuable book by G. Martin (1913).

How *lucrative* the business of tax farming must have been in all periods emerges from the complaints which we also hear about them and their oppressiveness in all periods. What the seigneur de Joinville tells us in the year 1269:

Je fu moult pressé du roy de Navarre moy croisier. A ce respondis-je que, tandis comme j'avoie eté [...] outre-

---

*   [Tr.: not referenced by Sombart.]

mer [...] les serjans an roy de France et le roy de Navarre m'avoient destruite ma gent et apouroiez si que il
ne seroit jamès heure que moi et eulz n'en vausissent
piz.

[I was much urged by the King of France and by the
King of Navarre to take the Cross. To this I replied, that
all the while that I had been [...] overseas [...] the Ser-
jeants of the King of France and the King of Navarre
had destroyed and impoverished my people; so that I
and they should be the worse for it for all time to
come.][370].

And what is confirmed by the ordinances of 1254 and
1256[371] repeated the despairing complaints against the partisans and fermiers généreaux in the 16th, 17th, and 18th centuries:

La pluralité des officiers font autant de roytelets en
telle monarchie, plus dévotionnez à establir et conser-
ver une je ne sais quelle damnée tyrannie, ambition et
avarice, par le moyen de la quelle de jour en jour ils se
font plus tost riches, qu'à rendre la fidélité du service
qui'ils doivent à Sa Majesté et soulagement de ses sujets.

[The plurality of officers make so many kinglets in
such a monarchy, more devoted to establishing and preserving a certain damned tyranny, ambition, and avarice, by means of which day by day they make
themselves richer, than to render the fidelity of the service which they owe to His Majesty and the relief of his
subjects][372].

Publicanus mala bestia, tyrannus populorum et regnorum.
[The tax collector [is] a ferocious beast, the tyrant of
nations and kingdoms] (Guy Patin*).

A French saying which was in vogue up until the 18th century was: "l'argent du roi est sujet à la pince" [the king's silver
is subject to the pincer], and just as meaningful is the comparison which was drawn between the financiers of the time

---

*   [Tr.: Sombart does not identify which work of Patin this is from.]

and the angels who guarded the Ark of the Covenant: they have four wings, of which "deux dont ils se servaient pour voler et les deux autres pour se couvrir" [two they used to steal and the other two to cover themselves]˙.

These complaints appear well founded to us when we hear of the *enormous earnings* which the tax farmers made. With the tax farm in the year 1348 the businessmen of the agreement were accused of having earned 60%[373].

In the 17th century it was claimed that only the fifth part of the tax haul came into the government's hands[374]. We find just the same calculation in the particular case of the well-known "Anti-Financier" in the 18th century[375]. And even if that is exaggerated, we possess though figures sufficient to verify which, for example, put the amount of raised taxes at 80–90 million francs, and the paid out taxes at 30–35 million francs. In the examples which Forbonnais provides us of Traités extraordinaires [extraordinary treaties], the partisans in one case earned on 14 million 3,653,333 livre, in the other their profit amounted to 107,513,861 livre, whereas the king received from them from the same contracts 329,691,513 livre[376].

In a certain sense the profits also belong here which, for example, the Fuggers received for the lease of the Spanish Maestrazgo† (although they in part concerned the profits from mining, of which I will speak in more depth in another place). The lease revenues of the Maestrazgo amounted in 1538–42 to 152,000 ducats annually, the average yield though to 224,000 ducats, whereas in the years 1551–54 a mere 84% pure profit was obtained. During the 40 years of 1563–1604 the Fuggers earned from these leases a straight 2,127,000 ducats. During the years 1551–54 the average yield of the Maestrazgo was 114,646,370 maravedís‡. For the years from 1563 to 1604 the following profits were obtained:[377]

---

*   [Tr.: not referenced by Sombart.]
†   [Tr.: Maestrazgo = area of Spain; the Fuggers leased the revenues paid from there to the Spanish crown by three knightly orders along with those of the mining ventures, including those of the mercury mines of Almadén.]
‡   [Tr.: approximately 380 maravedís = 1 ducat (Häbler 1897, 80)).]

1563–1567...............ca. 200,000 ducats
1567–1572...............ca. 570,000 ducats
1572–1577...............ca. 490,000 ducats
1577–1582.................ca. 167,000 ducats
1582–1594...............ca. 400,000 ducats
1595–1604...............ca. 300,000 ducats

That now, however, the money-lending in the sense described here also possessed real *means-forming power* in the grand style, is something our understanding would tell us even if we did not have numerous explicit confirmations of the great productivity and lucrativeness of these dealings.

A first grounds for assessment is granted by the reports of *business profits* which we possess from well-known money houses. They are quite considerable in all periods[378]. But only entirely conclusive are reports which we can make about really successful means-forming by people who were predominantly occupied with money-lending. Those exist, however, also in ample fullness. I content myself with selecting as especially conclusive the groups who pursued all the various forms of money business, but all three could serve equally well as examples for the means-forming power of money-lending (and indeed in essence even outside the capitalist nexus), and over whose fate we are also sufficiently informed: the Jews, the rich Augsburg families of the 16th century, and the French financiers of the 17th and 18th centuries.

1. The Jews

That the Jews during the Middle Ages always had people of means amongst themselves is put beyond doubt by the information we possess over Jewish wealth, and that these means grew almost exclusively from money-lending is something we may conclude from the general conditions. As is well-known, the wealth of the Jews never lasted long because the princes and cities squeezed the sponge whenever it became full enough. But it is astounding though in what quick time Israel knew how to replace again the taken property; it is astounding what large sums it was occasionally a matter of with the plundering. It suffices if I give a few instances:

Germany. For their privileges the Jews in Speyer paid the bishop 3½ pounds of gold annually (1084). In 1096 the Jews of Cologne and Mainz gave the leader of the Crusade, Godfrey of Boullion, 1,000 pieces of silver. In 1171 two Jews in Cologne were ransomed for 105 pieces of silver. In 1179 the emperor received 500 pieces of silver from the Jewish community, the archbishop of Cologne 4,200 pieces of silver from the Jews of his territory. According to tradition the archbishop Dietrich of Cologne built almost all the buildings of the castle of Godesburg from the money which he extorted from a captive Jew[379].

In 1375: "in the times then those from Augsburg caught all their Jews and placed them in prison and assessed them at about 10,000 florins."

In 1381: "they caught all the Jews and they had to give the city 5,000 florins."

In 1384: ditto, 20,000 florins etc.

By the appraisal in Nuremberg in the year 1385, individual Jews paid 13,000 florins, Jekel of Ulm and his two sons 150,000 florins[380].

In 1414 King Sigismund appraised the Jews of Nuremberg and Cologne at about 12,000 florins, the Jews at Heilbronn had to pay 1,200 florins, one at Windsheim 2,400 florins, and one at Schwäbish Hall 2,000 florins[381].

England. Evidently the Jews in England arrived in the course of the 12th and 13th centuries at great wealth. We find many of them in possession of castles and landed seats, which were then occasionally taken off them, and understandably above all of a great wealth of cash. An insight into the means of Jews in England at the time (in 1290 they were expelled as is well-known) is obtained again by the amounts of taxes and the numerous fines which were applied to them.

In 1140 the king placed on the Jews of London a monetary fine of 2,000 marks[382].

In 1168 Henry I expelled the rich Jews from England and left them in exile until such time as their fellows paid 5,000 marks.

In 1185 Jurnet Judaeus de Norvico paid the king 2,000 marks; soon after the same paid 6,000 marks; in the same year another paid 3,000 marks, another 500 marks; in 1189 another paid 2,000 marks.

In 1210 Isaac, the "man trading for himself", paid £1,336 9 s. 6 d. in taxes (thus about 60,000 marks in present-day [1916] currency), etc.

Total appraisals: in 1210 = 66,000 marks (ca. 2½ million marks in metal value); in the 28th year of Henry III[*] 20,000 marks (fines), about the same time 60,000 marks (taxes).

The same picture in *France*: "Les juifs [...] se trouvérent tellement enrichis, qu'ils s'étaient appropriés près de la moitiè de la ville" [The Jews ... found themselves so enriched, that they had appropriated nearly half of the city] suggested the chronicler Rigord already at the end of the 12th century. And that they really had arrived at great wealth during the 13th century is confirmed in particular by the reports over the value of their confiscated (in 1306 and 1311) estates, of which we possess a few. It may be assumed that it essentially concerned landed property, about which alone we hear in the sources. The barons reclaimed from the king the Jewish properties gathered up in their areas. The king made an agreement with them and shared. Thus the Vicomte of Narbonne received for his part 5000 pounds tornese, several rows of houses and pieces of land[383]. In the the bailiwick of Toulouse the auction resulted in (non compris les bijoux [not including jewellery]) 75,264 pounds tornese.[384] In eleven places of the bailiwick of Orléans it amounted to 33,700 l. 46 s. 5 d. (excluding jewellery and silver utensils)[385], in the city of Toulouse 45,740 pounds[386]. In 1321 persecution and seizure of property again. The king is supposed to have profited thereby by 150,000 pounds[387].

I limit myself here intentionally to information from the Middle Ages, since in the later centuries the origin of the Jewish means from money-lending is not as indubitable as in the earlier period. In another place in this work[388] I have compiled some material from which the wealth of the Jews in the 17th and 18th centuries can also be seen distinctly. That it likewise arose in this period for a very large part from money-lending is of course to be assumed without further ado.

---

*   [Tr.: 1243–1244.]

2. *The People of Augsburg*

We are as informed about the fate, and in particular also the means, of few other groups of business people of the closing Middle Ages as precisely as over the Augsburg merchants of the 15th and 16th centuries — thanks to the excellent sources which Augsburg offers for this period (the tax books!) and thanks to the outstanding treatments which they have recently found, and thanks above all to the absolutely foundational book by Jakob Strieder[389].

We can follow precisely how the means of individual citizens were formed from about the middle of the 15th century to the middle of the 16th century. We see how in this time the means of Augsburgers experienced a sudden increase and can also establish essentially what this abrupt growth in wealth stemmed from.

The development of the "great means" in Augsburg (i.e. those over 3,600 florins) took the following course during that critical century:

Year	Number of possessors	Sums of means	
1467	39	232,209 to	464,418 fl.
1498	99	956,168 to	1,912,336 fl.
1509	122	1,295,867 to	2,591,734 fl.
1540	278	5,110,783 to	10,221,566 fl.

The sources from which this great wealth flowed were primarily (if not exclusively):
1. the colonial economy;
2. mining;
3. money-lending.

That these, which alone concern us for the time being, also had in particular a principal share in the expansion of means is shown most clearly by the investigations of Strieder, alongside which those of Richard Ehrenberg of course always stand in a complementary way.

The Gossenbrots, Bimmels, Mentings, Höchstetters, Herbrots, Kraffters, etc., and above all the Fuggers are expressly mentioned as money dealers, and in part their wealth was obtained in immediate connection with the money-lending conducted by them in the grand style.

3. The French Financiers

Whereas with the just mentioned Augsburg trading houses the share which money-lending alone had in the origins of their entire means cannot be established, we can trace back the origins of numerous great means in France during the 17th and 18th centuries with fair certainty to a single cause — the participation in the public revenues through adroit financial operations, particularly also by means of tax farming[390].

Diderot asked a young ambitious man, "Savez-vous lire? — Oui. — Un peu calculer? — Oui. — Et vous voulez être riche à quelque prix que ce soit? — A peu près. — Eh bien mon ami, faites-vous secrétaire d'un fermier général et continuez dans cette voie." [Can you read? - Yes. - Calculate a little? - Yes. - And you want to be rich at any cost? - Nearly. - Well my friend, become the secretary of a farmer general and continue on that path.][391]

Contemporary judgements confirm sufficiently that this instruction of Diderot's was correct. In a petition to the Assemblée des Notables from the year 1626 it stated: "on les voit devenir riches" — namely the "officiers de finances" etc. — "et opulents en peu d'années" [we see them — the financial officials — become rich and opulent in the course of a few years][392].

A pamphleteer wrote: "Il ne suffit pas aux tresoriers de gaigner cent mille ecus en un an, ils veulent faire leurs commis et partisans aussi riches qu'eux" [It is not enough for treasurers to earn a hundred thousand crowns in a year. They want to make their clerks and supporters as rich as they are][393]. "Cela fit beaucoup de personnes extrêmement riches" [This created a lot of extremely wealthy people], judged the circumspect and always well-informed Gourville (1838).

We also possess enough pieces of evidence to be able to verify the correctness of such general remarks.

Examples from the 17th century:

Bullion in 1622 had 60,000 écus in annuities; in 1632 he became Surintendant [Superintendent]; in 1640 (at his death) he left behind annuities of 700,000 livre.

Fouquet, whose wealth became proverbial, was the grandson of a grocer in Nantes.

La Bazinière, son of a farmer in Anjou, came to Paris, became a lackey (the most favoured beginning!) to President Gayan, clerk for a prosecutor ("excellente école pour les fonctions de financier telles qu'on les comprenait alors" [excellent school for financial functions as they were then understood]) then deputy, finally treasurer — died very rich.

Bordier, son of a candlemaker on the Place Maubert, became Intendant of finances and built himself amongst other things a palace for 400,000 livre, gave his last daughter a dowry of 800,000 livres, bought an office of 800,000 livre, and had yet more estates which were worth six times as much.

Galland, son of a farmer, became in a few years so rich that a head magistrate married his widow.

Lambert, son of a public prosecutor, left behind 4,500,000 livres.

Camus, from nothing, left behind to each of his nine children more than 400,000 écus.

Catelan, beginning as a lackey, became rich under Bullion.

Marin, son of a farmer, left behind to each child one million.

Tabouret, son of a secondhand clothes dealer, gave his daughter 600,000 livre as a dowry and left behind for her just as much.

Piardière, poor boy from Loches, possessed more than one million livre; Marin, 2 million; Rambouillet, 6 million; Vidal, more than one million.

To which can yet be added dozens of names. The above examples are taken from the best source from which we can learn about the rise of French financiers in the 17th century — the "Catalogue des partisans" (Moreau 1853, 1:113-124).

Other examples in G. Martin (1913, 1:162). Very relevant material is to be found also in Boissonade (1902, 37 ff.).

Examples from the *18th century*: the lord de Saint-Foix inherited a means of 60,000 livre from his father. After he was treasurer of the navy and in particular of the Count of Artois, he had at his disposal an *annuity* of 80,000 livre, residents and furnishings in Paris and Neuilly which had a worth of two million, possessed 30 horses in Paris, 10 in Neuilly, etc., bought an office for 300,000 livre. "D'où vient une pareille future?" [Where does such a future come from?], asked our informant. (Thirion 1895, 290–91)

Nogaret, likewise an employee of the Count of Artois, had in the year 1757 nothing but a pension of 800 livre. In 1763 he married a girl without means. But he had meanwhile acquired the office of treasurer with the Count of Artois for 800,000 livre, the post of a secretary of the king for 110,000 livre, and a country house for 300,000 livre. In Paris he possessed a house with expensive furniture, likewise in Versailles, in Compiègne, and in Fontainebleau. He lived in a grand manner. "Encore une fois, d'où coule cet argent?" [Once again, where is this money flowing?]

Bourvalais, the richest Parisian of the Regency, began as a servant of the partisan Thévenin, then Bonnet (Thirion 1895, 8).

A quite excellent overall view of the wealth of the French financiers is provided by the lists of those "Gens d'affaire" [men of affairs] assessed for punishment because of dirty deeds in the year 1716. The list[394] shows 726 names which were assessed together at 147,355,433 livre in penalties. The individual sums swayed between 2,000 livre and 6,600,000 livre, to which the maximum amount was raised from the well-known Antoine Crozat (in reality only a small part of the treasure — one assumes perhaps 20 million — flowed into the accounts of the king). An apportionment to individual tax grades produces the following image. The number assessed at each level was:

> under 50,000 livre..........................298
> 50,001–100,000 livre......................105
> 100,001–200,000 livre...................127
> 200,001–300,000 livre...................68
> 300,001–400,000 livre...................42
> 400,001–500,000 livre...................26
> 500,001–1,000,000 livre................40
> 1,000,001–2,000,000 livre.............13
> over 2 million livre............................6

✱✱✱

All this means formation, the source of which was money-lending (and the business associated with it), was diverted means formation, resting on the transfer of already present means or in the diverting of a stream of value which had already developed to a proper breadth (where it was about the participation in public revenues). The strong accent of this circumstance, that it in all previously observed cases was about diverted means formation, should waken or sharpen the appreciation of the fact that in times of undeveloped commerce means formation in the grander style is only ever possible through a high degree of intensity in the relations of exchange (whereas later the intensity can also be replaced by a greatly increased extension).

Consequently I also bestow on the lending business which limits itself to commerce with "little people" only a subordinate importance as a means-forming factor (even if I obviously do not want to deny that in specific cases it became the source of larger means)[395].

But when we occasionally hear that men who carried out small scale usury arrived at wealth, we must always first check whether they perhaps did not mainly enrich themselves through the big men.

That applies, for example, to the typical usurer of the 16th century in England, as Hall shows in Mr George Stoddarde, who began small, but earned his wealth through profiteering off gentlemen[396].

Of the forms of original means formation, as far as I can see, in essence only two come into consideration for those times — the accumulation of ground rents in the hands of civic estate owners, and that which I call direct means formation, the means formation from the mining of precious metals, to which — as a variation — the means formation through the profit in coinage is connected. The following two chapters concern these two.

Chapter 41: The Accumulation of Civic Ground Rents

It corresponds to the character of the medieval cities and their development that a considerable part of the land and soil which the city was spread out on found itself over a long period in the hands of a not very large number of mostly very old families.

In the case that it was about the growth of a village into a civic borough, these were the old village comrades, the owners of holdings, the fully entitled landlords, "ceux qui ont entre leurs mains une portion du sol communal" [those who have in their hands a portion of the communal land]; "coloro che partecipavano a questi medisimi beni" [those who participated in these same goods]; "the people settled on the land and soil of the town's district", "those who lived in the town district and farmed their property themselves", the burgage* tenants. If the right of these landlords to the land and soil of the district was restricted at the start of the city's development by all sorts of encroachments by the owners above, we must assume that they soon knew how to free themselves from those restrictions. "The development of the city as a municipality consists in essence precisely in putting aside as far as possible the dependence of the municipality and giving back to the latter the state in which it found itself before the formation of the great estate owners, thus perhaps to the pre-Carolingian period."[397]

But where perhaps the town's district had gone over into the full possession of the emperor, the count, or the bishop, then it was achieved by way of the gifting or enfeoffing into

---

*   [Tr.: land or property held in a town in return for service or rent.]

the hands of the ministers who now obtained full citizenship by means of their land ownership and with it became the forefathers of the civic families.

Where finally we see town districts develop on virgin territory, in the colonial regions, the estate owning families are those famous "business people" to whom, as we have already seen, rural property, ownership or participation in large holdings was converted above all of course into the running of a farming business by the estate owner.

These original civic property owners were certainly in most cities only a small number of families and understandably since the running of an independent agriculture, which we may assume with their progenitors, must have limited their number to the given expanse of the city's farmland.

Everybody who later settled in the city, the whole retinue of merchants and craftsmen, the marchands et manouvriers sans héritage [merchants and workers without inheritance], in a word the entire civic population — so far as they did not find lodging in the space of the town or on the possessions of the churches and monasteries — settled on the land and soil of these few families. We must at the beginning of the civic development think of the entire working population as ballot men [*Losleute*'], as vassals of the few land-owning families; hence also at first as citizens of lesser rights, at any rate before they became homeowners, in economic dependence on the full citizens, the estate owners with whom they, as is known, entered frequently into a client relationship even[398]. The conflict thereby created between the two components of the civic population (the estate owners and the vassals in their charge, that is all tradesmen, the "guilds"), from which then first that of the constitutional influence was derived, was so powerful that it made all differences of civic development take second place in the cities of the Middle Ages, and led everywhere to the great tension which found its outlet in the class struggles of the 13th and 14th centuries. The uniformity of civic development, as we observe it in all West European

---

* [Tr.: In East Prussia, newly reclaimed land was allocated by lot [*Los*]. These plots were not large enough to support a family, so the tenant hired himself out as a labourer to others.]

states, would be completely inexplicable if we were not able to trace it back to the formation of land ownership conditions which took place uniformly in all cities, may the found constitutional structure of the city or the haphazard origination of the city be whatever it was.

But what now interests us at this point is something else — it is the fact which arises already without further ado from the preceding statements, that *the greatest part of the civic ground rents* must have accrued as "unearned increment" to the few land owning families of the city. The documentary confirmation of this enlightening statement is contained in every land register, every collection of civic private documents which has passed down to us from the Middle Ages[399]. It is sufficient for our purposes if I emphasise the following points.

1. The *use of the land and soil* which found itself in the hands of the families took place not only through supply of the necessary building sites for residences to the working population, but also through the construction and conferring of workshops, shops, and the like for a charge. In these instances it was of course especially profitable. Each land owner might lay out streets and markets on his land and build on it whatever he wanted — private houses, but also shops, stalls, market halls, etc. — and for whose use a payment in some form was obtained. Thus, as we may assume and as is also reported to us from various cities[400], many old families had ownership of butcher's benches, bread tables, granaries, mills, and the like which they provided to the craftsmen for a fee. A yet more intensive utilisation of property possessions was made possible finally by the use of privileged rights attached to specific sites, like the right to brew beer, to pour wine[401], to operate a mill[402], and the like.

2. The *form of utilisation*[403] was originally predominantly the lease, be it as hereditary lease, be it as temporary lease, in that case for a lifetime[404] or for a specific term, for example, 100 or 200 years[405]. This legal form of supplying as a loan corresponded to the low productivity of labour in the early period and the low efficiency of working people associated with it, as Arnold (1854) has quite rightly explained. This utilisation of the land, particular for the older period, is, how-

ever, economically thereby especially significant because it allowed the land owners to profit from the increase in ground
rents. For even with the hereditary leases we may assume
both a raising of the rents from time to time[406] and also an occasional surrender of the lease and frequently or mostly a
right of first refusal on disposal[407].

Certainly simple *rent* was also widespread in the medieval cities; see
for *Constance* Beyerle (1900, 76). Also here it is the case that you must
not conclude from the rarity of the documentary sources the rarity of
the occurrence of this legal relationship. According to the older German
conception, as is well-known, rent lacked real effect; it was not considered at all in any real sense to be a legal business, but rather a sort of
legally binding agreement. Hence in most cases it lacked the documentary setting down (Brünneck 1880). For long lists of craftsmen who
resided for rent in the England of the 13th century, see Brewer (1879,
1:117 f.); for the like for the 14th century, see Lappenberg (1842, §39 and
elsewhere).

In this case, as well as everywhere that we find a setting of
time limits on leases, the land owners thus assured themselves of the possibility of demanding higher rents or selling
the land more advantageously. But it was thereby brought
about that the property ownership remained in the hands of
its original owners up until a time when its value had risen to
an enormous level compared to its earlier value[408].

3. That the actual *increase in ground rents* in the medieval
cities was quite considerable, as was indicated in the last sentence, we would have to assume without further ado, even if
we had no source evidence for it. I believe that (comparatively) the growth in civic ground rents during the Middle
Ages, particularly in the period from 1200 to 1400, only experienced the like again in the cities of the 19th century, apart
of course from antiquity.

The rapid increase in population, the considerable rise in
the productivity of labour, and the cramming together of the
residents caused by the ring of walls worked together to drive
the price of ground rents quickly up and cause it to arise to a
point which astonishes us. It is not easy to believe that the
square metre of building land in Florence at the end of the
13th century cost in a large complex (500 m^2) 5–6 marks in
present-day [1916] currency, in small parcels (one sold five
square feet) even 10–20 marks, and yet it emerges from a
great number of sale documents with certainty, as we will yet

see. If to reach such a price there was a need for the entire wealth of the quickly growing Arnostadt, we learn also from other cities that during the 13th and 14th centuries the ground rents rose enormously high and the building sites were soon "sold at unbelievably high prices"[409]. And if, for example, in Frankfurt am Main the price of a rent of 1 mark (at purchase of the rental) amounted to[410]:

1304..................................14–15 marks
1314/18.............................16–17 marks
1323/27..............................18 marks
1333.....................................19 marks
1358.....................................24 marks

then this increase surely infers an approximately equal growth in the price of land.

4. With increasing commercial development in the cities the *sale* of land took the place of leasing more and more — the period of turning ownership of property by the leading families into cash arrived, and with it growing sums of money began to congregate. This influx was strengthened though so that in individual cities, like Lübeck[411], already from the end of the 13th century, in other cities later — in Vienna in 1360[412], in Munich in 1391, in Landsberg in 1392, in all the Lower Bavarian cities in 1420, in Worms in 1366, in Ulm in 1388, in Zurich in 1419, in Frankfurt am Main in 1439, in Basel in 1441[413] — the replacement of interest and rent took place and was completed for the most part.

When we look from the legal titles of the purchases (possession of land) at the sources from which this wealth arose, it is "surplus value" of civic labour which in the centuries long process of development could be taken and accumulated step by step with the increasing productivity of labour.

It thus concerns in this case for the first time that which I call an original means formation, and hence this form of means formation appears of special interest.

The *high level of civic ground rents* which we see forming the means here depend essentially on the attraction which a city is capable of exerting on the working population of the surrounding countryside. The more settlers, the higher the sums which can be deducted from their labour. Of course, other conditions play a part — above all the degree of productivity which the commercial work in a city is capable of reaching. When a city created perhaps a blossoming export trade, then it is apparent that the property owners were in a position to direct greater amounts of value into their pockets than if that were not the case. A fitting example of to what extent such fortunate conditions were capable of accelerating the accumulation of ground rents in a city is Florence. It then depended no less on how a city was placed topographically — the narrower the space in which a population must squeeze itself, the higher the surplus value taken from them in the form of ground rents — Genoa, Venice, Constance, and many Flemish cities (because of the boggy surrounds!) are examples of this. It is not undreamt of that the rapid formation of large means in their walls also traced back to the character of their situation.

***

What *statistical significance* this form of means formation had is just as hard to establish as it is for us to be able to ascertain those very means with certainty which directly arose only through the accumulation of ground rents. But that must not stop us from recognising the important role which the "farming community of millions" played in the genesis of bourgeois wealth.

After the attention of the economic historians[414] was excited by my somewhat provocative treatment of the object and the all-too sharply pointed problem formulation in the first edition of this work, the significance was only first properly made clear by a series of excellent investigations which were devoted to the form of means formation treated here. Since it would run counter to the conception of this book to deal in-depth with this theme, which in itself is very interesting, but in context only of minor importance, I have contented myself with enumerating at the conclusion of this chapter the most important texts which have dealt with my "ground rents theory" so that the specialists can immerse themselves further in the material.

Below (1903).

Strieder (1904).

Detailed discussion of this text is provided by Koehne (1905) and Rietschel (1905).

Nuglisch (1904).

Heynen (1905).

Flamm (1905).

Bothe (1906).

Häpke (1905).

Caro (1906).

Schipper (1907).

Sieveking (1904; 1909).

Davidsohn (1896a, 4:268 ff.).

Vetter (1910).

Maliniak (1913).

Voltelini (1913).

Neubauer (1916).

Chapter 42: Direct Formation of Means

I call direct means formation the means formation through money production. Money production comprises mining for precious metals (gold and silver, in some cases also for copper), the smelting of the ore, and the minting of the metals. To the extent a means formation is tied to the exercise of this activity, I call it "direct means formation", because it indeed concerns the accumulation of *money* without the requirement of an exchange or a change in the form of the manufactured product.

This form of means formation was of quite special significance for the origin of capitalism.

Firstly because here large means could grow out of nothing over night. Even the smallest craftsman can become a rich man in a short time by mining gold and silver, thanks to the aleatoric character of this branch of the economy. If he pans a pound of gold a day, he becomes a millionaire within three years. That is a priori possible in theory. That it also occurred in reality, we will yet see.

But then the means formation through money production is thus so significant, it hence deserves our attention quite especially because it is one of the means by which the precious metals exercise their decisive influence on the course of economic life. The strong means formation in times of abundant precious metal extraction — and of course the direct means formation is then at its strongest when new and productive stocks of gold or silver ores are uncovered — forms the component of an entire complex of phenomena which all lead back to the increase in precious metal production, and in their totality are suited to strongly promoting the development of capitalism. Direct means formation is above all also the cause of the rapid formation of greater means in other economic spheres, and all the forms of means formation previously acknowledged by us are more or less dependent upon the course which the direct means formation takes.

The great epochs of direct means formation are also the great epochs of "economic booms" — the periods of rapid increases in gold and silver production — the 13th century, the second half of the 15th and the first half of the 16th century, the first half of the 18th century, and then the various times in the 19th century which already fall in the period of the economic epoch of high capitalism.

If we want now to also apprehend direct means formation statistically by a few examples at least, like with the other types of means formation, then we must remember the peculiar organisation which precious metals production possessed in the Middle Ages and the following centuries, and recall that the stream of gold and silver divided into many branches.

Those who shared in the "mine blessing" were mostly:
1. the sovereign of the mine,
2. the estate owner (and besides him occasionally also 2a. the land owner),
3. the mining company (or other possessors of mines),
4. the smelters,
5. the mint owner,
6. the mint master,
7. the minters.

Of course the size of the amounts which fell to the individual depended for the first three groups on the productivity of the mine on the one hand, and from the size of the share which each was entitled to draw on the other hand.

That even in the Austro-German silver mines occasionally (especially when the smelting was included) they were able to obtain very high sums is revealed to us by legend. What we hear about it from old chronicles is of course not established fact. But it has value as an expression of the common opinion, which will have had its reasons. Anyone who in 1363 had in the mine at Eule a thirtieth share had at the time, so the chronicles tell, a yield of 50,000 Hungarian guilders for the quarter[415].

In Annaberg once, soon after the opening of the mine, a thousand guilder quarterly return appeared on a share certificate[416]. And from Schneeberg we hear that "on a share certificate about two or three thousand guilders shall have been obtained and thereby made the Römers of Zwickau rich. For you at once had a hundred marks of silver and six hundred gold guilders directly allotted to a share certificate."[417]

That the American silver mines granted still far richer returns, I have already established in another connection. Humboldt shares a few figures[418]. According to him a single mine brought in an annual profit of five to six million francs.

And that gold production, particularly as long as it appeared as gold panning, occasionally brought in fable-like profits is a well-known fact — the Kingfu mine in Alaska delivered for years a return of 2500%. And there is no reason for assuming that it should have been any different in earlier centuries with the mining of gold deposits.

Thus it is explained how even where the returns from mines were dissolved into many shares often quite considerable sums fell to each of those entitled to a share.

In Germany and Austria certainly the *sovereign (and the estate owner)* were best placed amongst all the participants up until more recent times. It is assumed that even in the 16th and up into the 18th century their incomes from the mines were about equal to the mining companies[419].

You only have to look at Prague, Meissen, Dresden, and Salzburg, which were for the most part built on the gold and silver from the surrounding land, to properly assess the lucrativeness of the mining prerogative in the earlier period. But even for the American silver, we know Spain's rulers drew large sums in the form of the quinto, and likewise the Portuguese government from the Brazilian gold, of which even only 30% shall have remained with the gold diggers[420].

But quite often now the stream which flowed from the mining of precious metals into the treasuries of the princes and kings was diverted into the pockets of those who advanced to them with willing hand the missing ready cash as loans and demanded the *mortgaging or leasing of a mine* (or the rights resting on it). Here it is about a variant of that business which we have already got to know well enough in the chapter on money-lending, only the mortgaging of a mine creates quite special opportunities for enrichment for the mortgager thanks to the aleatoric character of the mining activity. The custom of mortgaging mines lasted through the entire Middle Ages and up into more recent times.

King Wenceslaus II of Bohemia prescribed in 1305 in his testament that the seventh part of the income from the *Bohemian* mine at Kuttenberg should be given weekly in payment of his debts to his creditors, and King Rudolf also paid from the debts left behind by the late kings 1,000 marks of silver weekly from the income of Kuttenberg. See Hájek (1596, 492), cited in Gmelin (1783, 82).

In 1429 King Sigismund prescribed to the council and citizens of the town of Eger the mortgage of the district of the village Weß in the county Bechin with all the mines above and below earth against a loan of 18,000 Bohemian groschen (1783, 94). (60 Bohemian groschen at the time = about 19–20 marks in present-day [1916] currency.)

For the mortgaging of the *Silesian* mining prerogative, see the documents in Steinbeck (1857, 1:105, 2:134 and elsewhere); for *Saxony*, see Ermisch (1883, 2:XLVI).

The mortgaging of *Schwaz's* silver to the Meuttinger company in Augsburg by Archduke Sigismund in the year 1465 is reported in the pages of Wolfstrigl-Wolfskron (1903, 32).

For the silver from the Tyrolean mines, Christoph Scheurl had also handed over to the emperor Maximilian (1494) a "brave" sum of money which was to deliver for him, Scheurl, and his partner Heinrich Wolf annually at least 12,000 marks of silver in order to have it minted into imperial coinage (Scheurl 1884, 17).

In the 16th century the prerogatives of most modern states were already mortgaged to rich money-lenders. Over *Hungary*, for example, see Dobel (1879, 43 f.). The numerous mining contracts of the Fuggers with the Archduke of Tyrol, by means of which the Fuggers in part obtained the transfer of the taxes due to the lord from the works, and in part obtained the right to their own mine works, date from 1487 (Dobel 1882, 198 ff.; Wolfstrigl-Wolfskron 1903, 32 f.).

Just as the Tyrolean and Hungarian mines were transferred to the Fuggers as security, the *Reichenstein* mines belonging to the Dukes of Münsterberg-Öls also came into their possession, from which they likewise drew great profits (Fink 1894, 309 ff.). Originally it was only the transfer of legal rights which connected these houses with the mines; gradually they then extended further and either brought the works into their dependence or themselves became mine operators.

With that we have already arrived at the *mine owners themselves*. It is well-known that in the beginning silver mining in Germany and Austria was carried out by craftsmen (if not by estate owners). So far as this was the right to shares in the yields, any fortunate dig could lead from nothing to riches. And even the shareholders of the earlier period, even where they already did not have a hand in it themselves, were at least occasionally probably small people, craftsmen in the

348

towns who obtained a share with their savings, just as they would have otherwise bought a pension[421], farmers who sold their claim to land compensation for a number of shares[422], or they possessed as members of the mark the right to pan for gold[423], and similar elements with whom likewise a by-chance rich yield of a mine meant nothing other than the new creation of means. And what such sorts of considerations of a general nature suggest is confirmed for us by occasional reports from small estate owners who became rich. "In fact," it says in the first chapter of the third book of the Kuttenberger Bergordnung (around 1300), "between two miners who do not possess so much as to be able to say where they will be laying their heads the following night or where they will find sustenance the next day there often occurs an argument over a bestowal which can amount to several thousand marks of silver." (Sternberg 1836, 2:120) The Absalons in Todtnau and the Kreuz family in Münster had risen up from the mining workers and obtained means which moved them close to the nobility, in consequence of which their daughters became desired matches for the sons of noble families who had to put store on a new gilding of their escutcheons[424]. It was likewise expressly reported[425] that a number of citizens arrived at wealth with the Eyler mines. From the history of his own dear "Thales" (Joachimstal) the amiable pastor was able to tell us[426] "how a poor miner himself dug with his wife and worked at the face until he had extracted a hundred thousand golden groschen".

Even in the year 1539 the permission to mine the — from the start very rich (in 1552 it was already delivering 22,913 marks of silver) — mine at Rörerbühl in Tyrol shall have been applied for by Michel Rainer, a poor miner, together with two comrades who had discovered the ore on their travels[427].

The means of the Weitmoser family were established by Erasmus Weitmoser (died 1526), the son of a poor faceworker in Gudaunen, who with the help of an advance of 100 talers developed rich veins of gold at Radhausberge[428].

But in those times it was yet predominantly other circles whom the rich spoils of the newly developed mines benefited. Already from the 14th century we see the shares in the older silver mines slowly pass from the hands of the estate owners or poor shareholders into the possession of the prosperous townsmen. And we mostly find the newly developed mines of the 15th and 16th centuries already in advance in the hands of rich trading houses, so that you must identify them already (as I will later establish more precisely) as early capitalist enterprises.

It is thus these already prosperous businessmen to whom a great wealth then flowed in the 15th and 16th centuries from the "mine blessing".

It can be followed most distinctly with the mines of *Tyrol* and *Hungary*. Here compete "the most wealthy of the foreign merchants over the bet of having a share in the mines, and they consider themselves fortunate who are taken into the mining cooperative at Schwaz"[429]. Here we encounter among the mining companies in the 16th century the Fuegers, the Lichtensteins, the Firmians, the Tänzels of Tratzberg, the Jöchels of Jöchelsthurn, the Stöckels, and other notables of the land who obtained great riches through the exploitation of mines[430]. But we also encounter the Links and Haugs, the Scheurls, the Fuggers, etc. from Augsburg, and can follow numerically what enormous sums flowed from the "mine blessing" each day into the pockets of the already wealthy merchants[431].

The four main companies of the Schwaz mines (apart from the Fuggers) — the Andorfers, Tänzls, Hofers and Fuegers — had a yield in the years 1470–1535 of about 350,000 marks of smelted silver. This figure is shared by Peetz (1883, 49). Sigismund Fueger, the son of Hans Fueger, left behind at his death a means of 200,000 florins. The dowry of a "little daughter of the mines" amounted to 80,000 florins with the Lichtensteins, the Tänzls, even more with the Jöchlins (Peetz 1883, 50).

The assets of the trading company Link & Haug rose in Schwaz from 60,262 florins in the year 1533 to 193,547 florins in the year 1563; in Neusohl and Testhen they amounted in 1560 (first year) to 5,020 and 8,853 florins respectively, in the year 1562 to 10,191 and 54, 503 florins respectively (Hartung 1898, 39).

From their Hungarian mines the Fuggers and Thurzos drew in the years 1495–1504 a dividend of 119,500 Rhenish florins, from 1504 to 1507 142,609 florins. The Fuggers alone calculated their pure profit from the "Hungarian mine business" (in which admittedly the mortgaged crown revenues had been included) at 1,297,192 Rhenish florins (Dobel 1879, 33 ff.).

In direct connection with the development of silver mining stood the enormous lucrativeness which mining had *on mercury*, since after the invention of the amalgam process mercury became the most desired object next to silver and gold. Again it was the Fuggers who collected enormous riches through the monopolised exploitation of the mines of Almadén which had been mortgaged to them. Their profit amounted to 85 and 100%; in one five-year lease period they earned 166,370 ducats, from 1572 to 1582 around 300,000 ducats, 1582 to 1594 636,000 ducats, 1595–1604 around 600,000 ducats (Häbler 1897, 102 f., 156, 169, 176 f., 193).

Likewise we encounter in this period everywhere the traces of large trading houses participating in mining — in *Silesia*[432], in *Saxony*[433], in *Bohemia*[434], in the *Black Forest*[435].

And we find confirmed what I further claimed above — that the riches of the Upper German trading houses did not flow from money-lending so much as from mining.

It suffices to follow in detail the means-forming effect of *overseas* gold and silver mining. It is obvious that riches were produced here in still greater style by individual persons. The Spanish conquerors, who certainly for the most part, as we will yet see, in the beginning simply confiscated the already accumulated masses of gold and silver of the natives, could already offer Charles V 8 million ducats as a loan[436]. A few notes about the riches of American mine owners are found in Humboldt[437], who summarises his judgement therein: "The mines have undoubtedly been the principal sources of the great fortunes of Mexico" (Humboldt 1811, 2:28; 1814, 1:227); the Count de la Valenciana drew from his silver mine some years up to 6 million livres in rents; whereas in the last 25 years of his life those rents never fell below 2–3 million livres. A single vein of ore which the family of the Marquis of Fago-aga possessed in the district of Sombrerete delivered in 5–6 months a pure profit of 20 million francs. In Peru there was according to the same informant not such great riches as in Mexico — rents of 80,000 francs were "quite rare". A probably typical case of rapid enrichment through extraction of precious metals from a later period (1855) is shown to us by the fate of Pedro Romero de Terreros, later Count of Regla[438]. When you take into consideration the enormous quantities of gold and silver which have been taken out of America since the middle of the 16th century, you must also estimate their means-forming power so many times higher than the much smaller production quantities of the German and Austrian mines which were yet already so significant, as we have seen.

Aside from the people directly participating in mining, however, we also see other people enriching themselves in gold production — the smelters, who were often the stronger economically — already in the Kuttenberg mining ordinances their "detestabilis conspiracio" [hateful conspiracy]* had been censured, it aiming at depressing the price of ore by arranged underbidding — and of whom it was claimed[439] that they often made much greater profits than the miners; but above all the minters and holders of minting prerogatives.

We also find the mints, as a profitable prerogative, in the Middle Ages and everywhere as a rule mortgaged or leased.

In *Germany* we frequently encounter the mining cooperatives as leasers of the mints. In 1296 Bishop Konrad of Lichtenberg leased the Strasbourg mint for four years to seven townsmen (Wiegand et al. 1879, 2:201 f.). In the middle of the 13th century, the archbishop of Mainz mortgaged his mint to the minters for two years in exchange for a loan (Kirchhoff 1870, 168). In 1221 the mint of Trier was mortgaged, in 1237 that of Kreuznach (Beyer 1860, 3:174; Lamprecht 1885, 2:373). The Regensburg mint was also frequently mortgaged (Muffat 1868, 217 ff.). Mortgaging of the Bohemian mines in Sternberg (1836, 2:56 ff.). In the course of the 14th and 15th centuries many times the officers of the prerogative and the minters had brought the best mines and smelters for themselves, they demanded, in part badly paid, mine shares and gifts from mining companies and workers (Sternberg 1836, 2:184). For Jews as mint masters, see Schipper (1907, 52). Over the extraordinarily numerous Italians in German mints, see the detailed portrayal in Schulte (1900, 1:328 ff.). We also find Italians quite often in these positions. Italians as mint masters in *France* in Piton (1892, passim); in 1278 a contract between the King of France and the universities of Lombardy and Tuscany. A Frescobaldi was called to the head of the *English* mint under Edward I (Pagnini 1765, 2:74). The running of the mints in the *Crusader States*, in Syria and Palestine, was mostly in the hands of the Venetians (Prutz 1883, 373). Sale or mortgaging of the mint in the *Italian* cities: in Venice in 1112 (Lenel 1897, 40, cf. 42 f.); in Genoa from the 12th century (Sieveking 1898, 1:41). Cf. also Alexi (1890), and Arias (1905, 158 f.).

The rich profits which the mints produced were assisted above all by the constantly repeating debasements of the coinage. Every year, sometimes more than once a year — mint master Heinrich von Salza the younger called up the denar seven times in the year 1308 in the city of Görlitz![440] — the coins were stamped anew at a higher denomination. And that

---

* [Tr.: see page 255.]

was evidently done a lot[441]. Added to that was the monopoly on money-changing which the minters likewise possessed in many cities, and which must have been no less lucrative.

The minters were also mostly already affluent people, but who quickly arrived at wealth in their positions as mint masters. In the Middle Ages they were described as "monetarii opulentissimi" [monetarily opulent]. And we read about the Saxon mint masters of how they enriched themselves through the discharge of their office so much that they bought castles in the countryside[442].

Evidently the complaints of the doctor in William Stafford's "examinations" were not plucked out of thin air, but rather certainly drawn for a good part from a proper observation of reality. "And even when they [the mint officials] convince the prince that the profit for all that was to his benefit, then does not most of the profit stick to their fingers? [...] most of the pure profit falls to them just as it previously tended to fall to the alchemists and gold makers. And that is shown distinctly in how those who carry out this business or have carried it out suddenly became rich as if they, as the saying goes, had found the ring of Gyges*."[443]

The significance which the extraction of precious metals and the production of gold have as formers of means would certainly not have been anywhere near so great as it was in reality if the means formation evoked by them were limited to the previously discussed direct participation in the returns to mining and the profits from minting. I have already indicated, however, that precious metals production and money making also — and indeed to a very considerable extent — *in a roundabout way "indirectly" applied their means-forming power*. You can distinguish here the profit which was caused by the quantity of money produced from the profit which you were able to draw from the specific *forming* of money.

The quantity of precious metals produced led (not only directly, as we previously established, but also) indirectly to the wealth of individual persons to the extent that the derived

---

* [Tr.: In Plato's *Republic*, Gyges was a shepherd who discovered a ring of invisibility, enabling him to murder the king and take control.]

means-forming of course had to be fostered fundamentally in all its forms by them.

If from the end of the 15th century the *public debts* developed so quickly and massively, and with it one of the strongest sources of private means formation appeared, that not least had its cause in the extraordinary increase which precious metals production had experienced[444].

A strong revival was, however, also experienced by the means formation in the *goods trade* through the sudden and large accumulation of quantities of gold and silver in the hands of the first (or even later) possessors.

Well-known (and typical) are the profits which the merchants of Seville made directly from the opening up of the American silver mines — in 9–12 months they obtained 100 to 500%. While the value of exported goods amounted to 8, 10, 15 million pesos, that of the imported goods amounted to 20, 30, 40 million pesos[445]. Individual merchants in Seville drew the entire silver of the returning fleet to themselves[446], a single silver fleet often brought back for them more than 1,000 maravedis in coins (ca. 300,000 ducats) from America[447].

With respect to these figures you are tempted to agree with those who claim that the greatest benefit from the increased production of precious metals was had not by the producers, but rather by the merchants delivering goods to them — as such good authorities as Handelmann[448] and Eschwege[449] assume with reference to the Brazilian gold. You only have to recall the prices for foodstuffs, tools, etc. which the Brazilian gold prospectors had to pay to find that comprehensible.

The traders (and producers), however, did not only profit by this sudden increase in prices, but rather just as much and perhaps for a longer time *by the price differences* which occurred as a result of the lasting fall in the exchange value of the precious metals between the prices at the beginning of a delivery or production period and its close. Naturally this state, that prices in particular constantly rose from the 16th century, must have benefited above all the means formation of the farmers — thus many leaseholders who still paid their ground rent in dated money values may, when all the agricultural products rose in price, have been quickly enriched[450];

thus inversely though, which was certainly the more common case, landowners obtained considerable monetary means because their ground rents or the price of agricultural products rose without their doing anything.

The other way in which precious metals production and money production also led to the riches of those not immediately involved in them was the *adroit exploitation of the particular mint and currency relationships* during the Middle Ages and during the entire period of early capitalism, of which I have spoken in detail in Chapter 26. The side-by-side existence of gold and silver currency on the one hand, and the dissimilarity of mintings on the other hand offered ample opportunities for an extensive and, as it appears, very lucrative currency trade or (to talk in modern financial markets jargon) arbitrage business.

"But now the merchants have tasted the profits of the mint, they leave the business they lead and carry money from one land to another — *when they feel the unjust profits from it are enormous*", complained Emperor Sigismund[451].

These profits must have climbed beyond measure when silver experienced its sharp drop in the 16th and 17th centuries. "There are so great abuses of late yeeres groune by the corrupt dealing of sundry Merchants and Brokers as well strangers as English upon bargaines of exchanges and re-changes of Moneyes to be payed both out and within the Realm", it states in a proclamation from 20th September 1576, and we learn of many rich financiers in England who formed their means with the help of this "arbitrage business"[452]. Just on the other hand again, the Dutch enriched themselves in the same way on the English (in the 16th and 17th century)[453].

Chapter 43: Fraud, Theft, and Embezzlement as Formers of Means

We have for the description of what I call the "free" forms of means formation in part no other expressions but those taken from criminal law. What should actually be expressed is the freedom of the connection, be it through law or custom, be it through a contract with a responsible partner. Perhaps you could also call these free forms one-sided and contrast them with the contractual forms. But it is not so much about the correct description as the precise registration of the real facts of the matter. And there no doubt can reign as to what is meant in the particular case.

When I list fraud, theft, and embezzlement as special forms of means formation in earlier times, then I am thinking thereby not of the enrichment which happens to the particular private individual in these ways. These would never be able to form a special "social category", but rather must appear as accompanying symptom of the other forms of means formation. When we thus learn that trade and commerce was conducted in all earlier centuries with a strong element of fraud, then this method of enrichment (even if it must be recognised that frequently enough only the *dishonest* conduct of business possessed means-forming power) would though fall under the category of profit from business or commercial activity.

There are rather special cases in which the named forms of enrichment achieved special or independent significance. I would like to say that it was everywhere that a position of trust was taken advantage of to obtain unlawful advantages of means and then also where this unlawful enrichment was not limited to exceptional cases, but rather belonged as it were to the business activity as such.

You see what I mean — *the fraudulent discharge of office.*

The dishonesty of officials seems to be a general phenomenon — you might almost say — which is only confirmed in its generality by a few exceptional cases — like namely Prussia. In any case, it is in all earlier periods the rule.

We know from the Middle Ages that the governing families in the *cities* frequently enough filled their pockets from the public means[454]. We learn of enormous means which *state officials* left behind in those times — in *France*: Pierre Remy, général des finances [finance minister], left behind at his death (1328) a means of 1,200,000 livres (52 million francs in present-day [1916] currency); the chancellor Duprat left behind one of 800,000 écus and 300,000 livres[455].

In *Germany* as in France — Aeneas Silvius described the chancellery personnel under Frederick III as a rabble before whom he felt disgust, as a hungry mob who used every opportunity where there was something to be earned. The chancellor Kaspar Schlick, the first chancellor of bourgeois origins, advised a friend that you had to demand 6,000 in order to receive 3,000[456].

Special opportunities to obtain rapid wealth were namely offered everywhere also by the positions in the administration of mines.

"Towards the end of the 15th century (1496) the officials placed over them, who were visibly enriched thereby, disloyally took significantly from the royal revenues coming from the mines at Kuttenberg (Bohemia)."[457]

From the *Spanish Naples* of the 16th century we hear of officials whose salary amounted to 600 ducats, but who nevertheless accumulated great riches[458].

How open to bribery the officials in *England* were during the time of the virgin queen is well-known — the judges had fixed rates for acquittal of guilty criminals, etc. Even in the 17th century the government of the United Kingdom was described to us as "utterly corrupt"[459] — in 1621 Bacon was convicted of bribery, in 1624 Cranberry; in 1621 the treasurer for Ireland, Sir George Carey, was taken to court, having during his time in office embezzled £150,000[460]. Norreys wrote to Sir

John Coke over the condition of the English fleet in the year 1603: "To say truth the whole body is so corrupted as there is no sound part almost from the head to the foot; the great ones feed on the less and enforce them to steal both for themselves and their commanders".[461]

That in America, both in the north and in the south, stealing was at all times the actual function of officials goes without saying.[462]

A fertile soil for lucrative embezzlement then were the *half-public great trading companies* of the 17th and 18th centuries; just as much as the administration of the colonies. The administration of distant provinces was not always entrusted to the most capable and honest; the governors mostly set a good example for their subordinates and accumulated riches through embezzlement and extortion. They also knew how to counter complaints with bribery of the judges.

The same picture in the Portuguese colonies[463] as in the Dutch Indies where the officials of the East-India Company stole like ravens — a financial official who died in 1709 left behind after 3–4 years of activity a means of 300,000 talers; the governor Walkenier (1737–41) brought home on his return to Europe 5 million florins which he had stolen[464]. A good yardstick for the extent of embezzlement which the officials of the company committed is formed by the remittances to banks in the motherland, which in the course of time became more and more frequent. In the year 1705 no higher than 274,434 florins, this amount climbed by the year 1746 to 1,209,586 florins, and by the year 1764 to 1,333,419 florins. Individual bearers remitted quite significant amounts. In the calculations for the year 1746 a treasurer returning to the fatherland deposited 55,386 florins into a bank; to the orphanage masters in Amsterdam were transferred 74,808 florins, those in Utrecht 117,766 florins, in the Hague 37,839 florins, in Delft 33,253 florins[465].

An office to which at all times and with all peoples the stigma of a dishonest practice was attached is the *war ministry*. Here we ourselves hear from the most proper milieu — the Prussian — complaints over deceitful conduct in office — "Nothing is so desired by a commissioner or official than to be entrusted with the administration of a magazine or a cash box. If he was previously poor as a beggar, one month already makes him capable of putting himself in a comfortable state. And two, three, and several months make him into a great, wealthy, and significant man who keeps his coach or chaise, horses — often 10 or 12 — and servants, who appears in nothing but magnificent clothes, with two gold watches, several rings on his fingers, and similar precious things, [...] in short, he makes an outlay as if he were a servant of the Great Mogul and as if he has several thousand a month to spend [...] Clever people [...] judge: he must be really cheating the king". Consequences of the various activities by which the unfaithful servants help themselves[466].

If it was like that in Prussia, then it must not astonish us if we learn of much worse in other lands.

Chapter 44: Robbery

As high or as low as you may estimate the significance which fraud, theft, and embezzlement had for the origins of bourgeois wealth, that of the free art of acquisition being considered here, robbery*, was certainly much greater. Of it we can even say decisively that it was really very large.

To what origins robbery traces back, and to what fundamental conception of life and its preservation it corresponds will not be assessed here. For our aims, we suffice with the statement that the violent removal of goods belonged during the entire Middle Ages through to the 18th century to the common forms of means formation, that it was in no way a rare criminal act universally condemned by criminal law and public opinion, but rather an occasionally punished, but then an ever again half or entirely accepted custom widespread even amongst upright people and which formed a component of the "tradition" of those times[467]. (Even if not always the tradition of the land, though quite certainly that of the class.)

Robbery also did not everywhere and always have a significance for the origins of bourgeois wealth. The entire large phenomenon of the *robber barons*, for example, is barely worth considering by us. As much as this, as is well-known, oddly influenced throughout centuries the entire economic life, particularly in Germany, — already, for it to produce the companion being from itself, trade and exchange had to be directed along very specific paths — it could contribute nothing to the origin of bourgeois wealth because its bearers at all times placed themselves in a defiant opposition to all bourgeois existence[468], and even looked down derisively on the

---

* [Tr.: robbery is being distinguished from theft here by the presence of violence.]

Werner Sombart

money grubbers in the centuries in which elsewhere the
landed nobles who had become rich were slowly becoming
bourgeois. How proud did the "manger knighthood" [*Krip-
penreitertum*]* appear in which the robber barons were finally absorbed!

"And when the money grubbers in the cities had even so much jewellery hung around themselves, the townsman looked though every
time" ... "My heart wanted to burst from my body when I saw these
people in the city prancing around in such magnificent clothes and jewellery on golden carriages. Prance, I thus then thought, as you will, and
if every day you guzzle pearls instead of wine, so you are yet bourgeois,
remain bourgeois, and will never bring it about to be like us." In this
way the wives of the "manger barons" conversed over herrings and
potatoes and weak beer at their wretched manors towards the end of the
17th century. From the story "Der Edelmann" which the Silesian Paul
Winckler (died 1686) left us (Winckler 1697).

How entirely apart the manger knight stands from the currents of modern economic development at the same time as
the English "gentleman" was helping found a tin mine or a
glass factory with the money which perhaps even his father or
grandfather had only obtained by quite customary sea piracy.
The plundering raids of the Normans and Saracens also do
not concern us here. Likewise we need not in this connection
bother with the admittedly quite extensive brigandage which
appeared in France as a consequence of the religious wars in
the 16th century[469].

In contrast robbery in the *Italian cities* also contributed
during the Middle Ages to a wide extent to the formation of
bourgeois means.

It is known that above all Genoa[470] and Pisa owed their
wealth in no small part to sea piracy (to which often enough
an extensive land piracy was attached). But robbery and plunder must also come into consideration as important sources
for the origins of great means in Venice[471]. Above all Venice
had taken the greatest share in the plundering of oriental cities, particularly Constantinople.

That was, however, so meaningful because it concerned
here great quantities of gold and silver which fell as loot to

---

*   [Tr.: Krippenreiter were (often impoverished) nobles who led a life as
     wandering guests, riding "from manger [*Krippe*] to manger", sponging
     off their hosts.]

the robbers. But only then did robbery and plunder become properly lucrative and obtain their independent great significance as formers of means. I have already tried to establish in another connection that really significant amounts of precious metals were gained by the Italians and particularly the Venetians from the Orient[472].

But the sums looted by the Italians vanish when we place them against those which stood at the disposal of the robbers of later centuries once the gold and silver treasures of America were opened up to European nations. The free forms of means formation also grow quite considerably in significance when precious metal production booms, its means-forming power manifesting itself here again in a quite new connection.

In the 16th, 17th, and 18th centuries it is the Spaniards, Portuguese, Dutch, French, but above all the English and North Americans who use robbery as an important means to build wealth.

We encounter the *Spaniards* and the *Portuguese* occasionally as sea pirates, but above all as conquerors in the newly discovered South American lands which they were the first to plunder. Like predators, it has been said, the Spaniards roamed the new lands, like predators searching for prey[473]. Treachery and deceit, brutality and violence altogether in sequence had to help in bringing the treasures collected here over centuries into the possession of the new lords. They extorted ransoms from the princes, opened the graves, tore the gold plate from the temples, and stole the jewellery from the bodies of the inhabitants.

But we also know that this plundering dealt with quite considerable amounts and could in some cases even directly result in the accumulation of means thereby in the hands of individuals.

When Afonso de Albuquerque plundered Malacca in the year 1511, he carried off a million ducats, of which the king received 200,000 as quinto[474]. On an expedition into the interior of Venezuela, a Welser expedition (1535) carried off 40,000 gold pesos from graves, residences, or ransoms; on another expedition a tribe was deprived of 140,000 pesos of pure gold and 30,000 pesos of inferior gold[475]. One took a treasure from Montezuma which, poured into ingots, had a value of 162,000 pesos, whilst the smaller pieces of jewellery were worth 500,000 ducats[476]. The loot taken and melted down after the conquering of the capital city of Mexico was reported to be 19,200 ounces or 131,000 pesos. Cortez brought home on his return to Spain in the year 1528 gold to the amount of 200,000 gold pesos and 1,500 marks of silver[477]. A letter of the Bishop Zumarraga from Mexico on 17th August 1529 mentions that with Salazar, the deputy of Cortez, when he was arrested, 30,000 pesos of fine gold were found — the balance of the gold sent to Spain. Other officers had extorted some 25 to 30,000 pesos. From the captured cacique of Michoacán they desired as ransom 800 gold discs weighing about half a mark and 1,000 silver discs of about one mark in weight. In a further letter from April 1532 there is mention that a certain Uchichila extorted from the natives in Michoacán pieces of gold jewellery and melted them down into 15–16 ingots of gold, but only declared two[478]. In the Registro del Conjeso de Indias is found the information that in 1535 in four ships from Peru gold and silver to the value of 2 million ducats reached Seville. This was the loot which fell to the Spaniards with the destruction of the empire of Atahualpa[479], or more precisely the amount of Athualpa's ransom which amounted to some 1,326,539 gold pesos, and 51,610 marks of silver[480].

Of this ransom, the allocation was[481]:

Recipient:	Marks of silver:	Gold pesos:
the governor	2,350	57,220
Hernando Pizarro	1,267	31,080
Hernando de Soto	724	17,740
the padre Juan de Sosa	310	7,770
Juan Pizarro	407	11,100
48 knights	ea. ca. 360	ca. 9,000

The remainder of the 170 participants received about half these last amounts.

We are also precisely informed over the amounts of gold and silver looted in the conquest of Cuzco in the year 1535, *so far as they were handed in,* since the original records are still held in the Archivio de Indias[482]. According to that the loot ran to 242,160 gold castellanas and 83,560 marks 5 ounces of silver. Ransom of the Inca and the loot in this one city amounted together thus to over 33,000,000 marks in our money. Those are the figure of which you hear. What enormous amounts must have fallen besides to the humbler conquerors as loot from robbery to robbery!

The "taxation", *raising tribute,* was only a somewhat veiled form of robbery, of which too the conquerors of America made the most far-reaching use. The private persons received here the corresponding share through pay or they were directly enfeoffed with the revenues of larger areas. The estates with which the Spanish officers in Peru were enfeoffed shall have yielded up to 150,000 and 200,000 pesos annually[483]. The Cortez family received as marquisate the valley of Oaxaco with a population of 17,700 inhabitants[484] who had in Cortez's time 60,000 ducats to pay in tax. The governor of the Portuguese colony of Mozambique usually had at the end of his three year rule a return of 300,000 crusados[485].

In the following centuries robbery was organised professionally in the *sea piracy* to which all seafaring nations uniformly paid homage. Sea piracy was advanced as a manner of earning a living by the constant wars which raged during the 16th and 17th centuries in particular, and in which privateering played a prominent role in the maritime law applying at the time. Privateering and sea piracy constantly merge into each other though — the privateer becomes a pirate, as the latter again finds use as a leader of privateers in the service of the state.

We hear often of *French* sea piracy in the 16th century[486], but learn that it had reached a high degree of development in the 17th century. We are especially well informed over their state and their extent because we possess two different reports[487] which Colbert, because he drafted the plan of uniting the sea pirates of Dunkirk into a squadron and placing them (under the command of Jan Bart) in the service of the king, had written over the most well-known sea pirates, the "capitaines corsaires" [corsair captains]. The reports refer to 33 captains commanding 15 frigates and 12 large barques.

We also learn something about the extent and profit of this sea piracy business. Thus we hear, for example, that the most famous of all pirates of his time — Jan Bart, son and grandson of similarly famous pirates — seized a Dutch ship on each of the 1st, 2nd, 3rd, 4th, and 5th of January 1677, and that he released the five ships for 10,600 livres in Dutch currency. Another ship was bought from him for £480, a third had 80,000 livres in gold dust on board, etc.[488]

It has been calculated that French pirates in the time of William III took prizes from English ships to the extent of £9 million in a time period of three years[489].

Likewise the buccaneers or freebooters who conducted their mischief particularly in the waters of the Spanish colonies, by Jamaica, Haiti, etc. in the 17th century, were originally of French stock[490].

A picture of Holland around the same time: the Dutch West Indies Company equipped itself from 1623 to 1636 with an outlay of £4,500,000 with 800 ships — but they captured 540 ships whose cargo amounted to close to £6 million; to this they added £3 million which they had taken from the Portuguese through robbery and plunder[491]. In the profit and loss calculations of the great companies one sum is regularly found — profit or loss from privateering or sea piracy.

The booty which *Tuscan* galleys obtained in the 16th century when they attacked an Ottoman trading fleet on the African coast is supposed to have been worth 2,000,000 ducats[492].

The sea pirate nations par excellence in the 16th and 17th centuries, however, were England and the New England states in America.

Around the middle of the 16th century the coasts of England and Scotland teemed with *English* sea pirates — according to a report of Sir Thomas Chaloner in the Summer of 1563 there were over 400 sea pirates in the channel who in a few months had captured 6–700 French ships[493].

In an entry in the Privy Council Register of Scotland from the year 1546 it states: "Forasmuch as there is a peace taken and standing betwixt our Sovereign Lady and her dearest uncle, the King of England, who has written to her Grace, showing that there are certain Scottish ships in the east sea and other places, that daily take, rob and spoil her ships and lieges of his realm passing to and fro" etc. We encounter such entries frequently in those years[494].

One also recalls the descriptions which Erasmus drew up in his Naufragium [Shipwreck] of the dangers of sea piracy in the channel[*].

The English writers of history attribute this sudden expansion in piracy to the Marian persecutions — at the time a number of the best families had participated as sea pirates, and their hordes, increased by unemployed fishermen, also stayed together after the accession to power of Elizabeth I[495].

Within a few years in any case England assumed the same position as land of sea pirates in the North as Algeria in the South. Piracy became a fundamental component of the English national character. In a memorandum which Cecil drew up at the start of Elizabeth I's reign, three means were cited for the development of a fleet — among them the cultivation of sea piracy.

In fact those historians are right who claim that England's seapower was built on it. It not only provided the land with excellent sailor material, it also produced that great series of bold adventurers and sea heroes who were so abundant in Elizabethan England and who by their bold campaigns of conquest raised up the English nation in a short time to power and esteem.

All the famous sailors, and discoverers, and founders of colonies of that time were at base nothing other than sea pirates and yet were revered as heroes. Sir Francis Drake, on whose pirate ship the queen took breakfast at his return after his memorable voyage of pillage (1577–1580) and personally knighted him, was called by Hentzner, who saw the ship in 1598, "that noble Pirate, Sir Francis Drake"[496]. And when the queen knighted the highest of the sea pirates, the court could not punish sea piracy itself as a crime. "The present practice of pardoning notable crimes, of pardoning piracy especially, ought to cease", demanded an address to the queen from the year 1579[497].

We are familiar with the names from this time of only two or three of these sea pirates — apart from Sir Francis Drake, perhaps Sir Walter Raleigh, John Hawkins, and a few others. But even the preeminent among them, who undertook great

---

[*]   [Tr.: not referenced by Sombart.]

voyages of pillage, number many dozens and hundreds. You need only perhaps leaf through the third volume of Hakluyt's accounts of voyages (1598) to be astounded over the great number of enterprising pirates who sailed out of English ports in those days to capture treasure. John Oxham from Plymouth, Andrew Baker from Bristol, Christopher Newport, William King, Robert Duddeley, Annias Preston, Sir Anthony Sherley, William Parker, and many others were all cut from the same cloth.

But how numerous only must those have been who conducted their piracy in the vicinity of the homeland! "Nearly every gentleman along the western coast [...] was engaged in the business" (D. Campbell 1892, 1:391).

The operation of sea piracy was business-like and well arranged. The ships of the pirates were fitted out by well-to-do people who were called "gentlemen adventurers", behind whom then often others stood who advanced them the means for fitting out in return for high interest. The high nobility participated in part in such undertakings. When the Earl of Bothwell undertook sea piracy in the time of Queen Mary of Scotland, he thus did nothing other than take on a lucrative and absolutely normal profession for his time[498]. At the time of the Stuarts, we see the Earl of Derby and other royalists outfitting numerous sea pirates[499].

And the business was rewarding. Especially, of course, when you were so lucky as to run into the stream of gold or silver which constantly poured out of America. If we follow Sir Francis Drake on his great journey in the years 1577 to 1580: on the Spanish coast of South America he plundered the coastal cities; then he looted great quantities of silver which had just arrived from the mines of Peru; then he captured a treasure ship with a rich load of gold, silver, pearls, diamonds, and thus it continues until his ship carried "a cargo such as the world had never seen before and never has seen since his day"[*]. Of the yield, Drake himself received a rich share, 100% returns were paid out to shareholders, the rest went to — the queen (Froude 1858, 11:428).

---

*   [Tr.: not referenced by Sombart.]

In 1592, the "adventurers" — that is, just the outfitters — received back from an expedition which Raleigh had undertaken 10 for 1, making thus a 1,000% profit[500].

John Hawkins himself declared his booty, namely in gold, silver, and precious stones, to be £1,800,000. We hear of individual prizes which brought in 60,000 ducats, 200,000 ducats, etc.[501]

In the year 1650, the Levant Company complained that they lost through piracy in the space of two years various large ships which amounted to a value of at least £1 million[502].

How the sea pirates themselves also came to wealth and affluence is told to us by contemporaries. It is reported of a famous sea pirate, Mr Cavendish, that, "The passing up the river of Thames by Mr Cavendish is famous, for his mariners and soldiers were all clothed in silk, his sails of damask, his top cloth of gold, and the richest prize that ever was brought at any time into England."[503]

The *American colonies* then became learned students of the motherland. The expansion which sea piracy won there, particularly in the state of New York, would appear unbelievable if it were not proven by an abundance of impeccable evidence. Above all, the reports of the Earl of Bellomont to the Lords of Trade contain vivid descriptions of the sheer unbelievable conditions under Governor Fletcher who went for trips with the worst sea pirates, gave releases for the sailors being recruited — $100 per head — on a whim, and received gifts of entire ship's cargos which he then sold for £800, etc. We learn of quite large sums which the pirates looted, and that it teemed with them in New York and Boston, where many old 'buccaneers' also lived in comfort and esteem[504]. According to the evidence of the Colonial Secretary of Pennsylvania, James Logan, in the year 1717 1,500 sea pirates cruised the coast of Carolina alone, of whom 800 had their base in New Providence[505]. In the 17th century, "nearly every colony in America was in one way or another offering encouragement to the pirates."[506]

We hear of an Indian pirate of the 18th century, Angria, who was descended from an old family of sea pirates, that he had possessed an entire fleet, that he had fortified many islands by Bombay and had made his own a territory of 100 miles in length and 60 miles wide[507].

***

I do not know where else but this chapter, which handles the means formation through robbery, I should mention the origin of those bourgeois means which owe their existence to *the dissolution of monasteries* and the *confiscation of monastic and church property* by the state. This type of acquisition had a great significance especially for *England.* Over what amounts it dealt with, I have already reported[508]. It merely suffices here to state that the king made use of his booty to set up his favourites, and that the latter set about with an absolutely bourgeois sense of business the exploitation of the land gifted to them[509].

Chapter 45: Coercive Trade

I call coercive trade those actions whereby those unable to judge or without will have objects of value taken from them by trick or force in the manner of a seemingly free-willed exchange, and as far as possible for nothing. Coercive trade in this sense describes almost all goods exchange between the European peoples and primitive peoples, at least in its beginnings and in the manner in which the foundation of the European colonial economy was applied, but also all trade with the civilised peoples of the Indies in the first centuries was robbery, fraud, or theft.

Anyone today who reads the sources will be astounded over the shameless matter-of-factness with which the people of that time, above all of course the English, saw the exploitation of the subjected peoples as God-willed and trade as exploitation. Thus one of the most circumspect publicists of that time wrote about the state of things in the East Indies, "Instead of that incertain and precarious State in which our Commerce remained here for many years, we enjoy now the most certain and ample security from the Nature of our Fortifications, and particularly the extensive and highly improved Fortress at Calcutta, the large Body of Troops that we maintain and pay", etc. (J. Campbell 1774, 2:613)

It is only being English if the same writer establishes shortly afterwards that the company acquires its riches "without either Fraud or Oppression" (J. Campbell 1774, 2:613), and that the English in India reigned according to the "Principles of Equity and Indulgence" (J. Campbell 1774, 2:614).

The greater the superiority of the European state, the more lucrative this process naturally turned out. During the Middle Ages this colonial trade for the Western European was kept within relatively narrow bounds. Unresisting peoples for exploiting as you liked only existed in the Russian empire, in the north of which the Hanseatic League had extended its tentacles and in the south the Genoese. Between the peoples of the Orient and Western Europe in contrast the Arab trade pushed its way in, which faced the European trade in essence as an equal adversary. For a thousand years the Arabs have exploited the Oriental peoples in *their* interest, and have made use of the wealth of the Orient as a massive girder for their gleaming culture[510].

The discoveries and conquests about the turn of the 15th century put the European peoples now in the position of going around the Arabs as middlemen between them and the East. In order to gauge what it meant to direct the middleman's profit of the Arabs into European pockets, you must know of the enormous mark-up in prices with which the Arab traders had sold on their goods. A calculation by English merchants which has been passed down to us from the 16th century shows that the goods of the East Indies in London cost half as much as in Aleppo, but that the prices of the goods bought directly in the East Indies versus obtained via Aleppo were as follows:

Price of goods in the East Indies		Price in England, bought in Aleppo
1 pound pepper	2½ d.	20 d.
1 pound cloves	9 d.	5 s. – d.
1 pound nutmeg	4 d.	3 s. – d.
1 pound mace	8 d.	6 s. – d.
1 pound indigo	1 s. 2 d.	5 s. – d.
1 pound raw silk	2 s. – d.	20 s. – d.

Malynes (1623), cited in A. Anderson (1787, 2:304).

According to another list of prices which we owe to an anonymous companion* of Vasco de Gama, a hundredweight† of ginger cost 11 ducats in Alexandria, whereas in Calicut the bahar, which held 5 hundredweights, cost only 20 ducats. A hundredweight of incense cost 2 ducats in Alexandria, exactly as much as the bahar in Mecca (Velho 1838, 115; cited in Peschel 1858, 27).

If, through the displacement of the Arabs, they had come in the East into direct contact with the defenceless peoples,

---

*   [Tr.: later attributed to Álvaro Velho.]
†   [Tr.: roughly 50 kilograms.]

Portugal had already opened up during the second half of the 15th century a stately area of exploitation on the west coast of Africa, and to that was now added an entirely new, yet untouched part of the world which the Western European commerce could now draw into the circle of its activity.

That this activity, however, could become so profitable relied on the assumption that you attached fantasy prices to the European goods for the peoples with whom you "traded", and on the other hand bought the products of the natives for next to nothing. As a result then that enormous margin opened up between purchase and sale price which we consider today to be barely possible.

Prices in Coercive Trade

The Corregidor* allocated European goods to the Indies without consideration to need. According to Bodin (1586), old boots cost 300 ducats, a Spanish coat 1,000 ducats, a horse 4–5,000 ducats, a cup of wine 200 ducats. The unfortunate natives often received things whose use they did not remotely know. They might make representations as much as they wished, the "seller" refused to take anything back. Often they barely earned enough for the upkeep of themselves and their families, but they were supposed to clothe themselves in silk and satin, and decorate the bare walls of their dilapidated huts with mirrors; they were given lace, ribbons, buttons, books, and thousands of other pointless things, and all for the most absurd prices. Distributions of European imports of this sort were called ripertimentos [divisions] in Spanish America. Cf. the depictions in Scherer (1852, 225 ff.) and Bonn (1896, 111), where sources are also given.

The Hudson Bay Company exchanged (in 1743) for one beaver pelt any of:

> 4 pound copper kettle
> 1½ pounds of gunpowder
> 5 pounds of coarse grain
> 6 pounds of Brazilian tobacco
> 1 ell of baize
> 2 combs
> 2 ells of garters
> 1 pair of trousers
> 1 pistol
> 2 hatchets

Since in the same year 26,750 beaver pelts were sold for £9,780, a beaver pelt was worth 7–8 shillings. From the polemics between Mr Dobbs and Captain Middleton, cited in A. Anderson (1787, 3:230 ff.).

---

* [Tr.: the Corregidor was a local administrator in Spain or its empire.]

With the discovery of the Altai, the natives gave the Russians as many sable pelts for the iron kettles, etc. as could be stuffed in them. You could easily receive for 10 rubles in iron 5–600 rubles in pelts (Storch 1797, 2:16; C. Ritter 1822, 2:577; cited in Roscher 1856, 238).

"Tariffs" by which the Negroes were deprived of their precious produce, like ivory, gold dust, etc. See Labat (1728, 4:242-256) 242-256. "[Les] marchands ont la politique de les laisser [the Negroes] presque toujours dans la disette, afin de leur faire acheter plus cher ce qu'ils leur portent" [The merchants have the policy of leaving them [the Negroes] almost always in need, in order to make them pay more for what they bring to them] (Labat 1728, 4:44).

The bahar of cloves which cost 1–2 ducats in the Molucca Islands, was already paid for by 10–14 ducats in Malacca, and 50–60 gold escudos in Calicut (Ramusio 1550, 1:323 f.). Antonio Pigafetta tells of similar purchases at ridiculous prices on the island Gigolo — one purchased a bahar of cloves for 10 ells or 15 ells of bad cloth, for 35 glasses of water, etc. (Ramusio 1550, 1:366B).

The Dutch East-India Company bought pepper at 1½–2 stübers per pound and sold it in Holland for 17 stübers; the Portuguese paid 3–5 ducats for a hundredweight of pepper in the East Indies, for which they made 40 ducats in Lisbon. See Saalfeld (1810, 1:148, 1:258, 1:282, 1:290); there you will yet find numerous other price calculations which incidentally mostly apply to the end of the 18th century. You may assume that the differences between purchase and sale price at the start of the Indies trade were much more considerable.

In the year 1663 five ships brought a cargo to Holland whose purchase price amounted to 600,000 florins, and whose sale price amounted to 2,000,000 florins; in 1697 one such amounted to 5 and 20 million florins respectively[*].

In 1691 with the French East-India Company, they amounted to:

	Purchase Price (livre)	Sale Price (livre)
White cotton & muslin	327,000	1,267,000
Silk material	32,000	97,000
Pepper (100,000 lbs)	27,000	101,600
Raw silk	58,000	111,900
Saltpetre	3,000	45,000
Cotton thread	9,000	28,500
A few smaller items:		
In total	487,000	1,700,000

See Kaeppelin (1908, 224).

---

[*]   [Tr.: the reference from Sombart here is simply "Lüders", and I have been unable to narrow this down further.]

Profits

The "trading" profit of the Welser expedition amounted to 175% (Frensdorff, Lexer, and Roth 1865, 5:279).

The *Dutch East-India* Company distributed in the 198 years of its existence an average of 18% per annum.

In the first years:

1610/11 (first payment) — 162½% (in gold and spices)
1619 — 37½% in gold
1623 — 25% in cloves
1625 — 20% in gold
1626 — 12½% in gold
1628 — 25% in gold
1630 — 17½% in gold
1632 — 12½% in gold
1633 — 20% in gold
1634 — 20% in gold
1635 — 12½% in cloves

In the 17th century and in the first third of the 18th century about 25% on average.

See the exact figures in Klerk de Reus (1894, app. VI).

From 1605 to 1728, the amounts were:

smallest dividend	= 12½%
highest dividend	= 75%
average dividend	= 24%
total dividends	= 2,784½%
	= £18,000,000

(on an original capital of £650,000).

To be accounted for in addition:
1. the amounts paid to the state (for renewal of the privileges);
2. the means earned by the officials;
3. the profits achieved for the company and production with the facilities.

In Ceylon the profit of the Dutch East-India Company on the items of trade which were imported and sold was on average 142% in 1746 and 145⅛% in 1783; in Suratte and Malabar on average 176⅞% was obtained in 1764, and in Malacca on average 52½% in 1647 and 40½% in 1784 (Bokemeyer 1888, 278).

Even with indirect trade Usselincx (at the beginning of the 17th century) calculated that the Dutch obtained on average 20% (de een tyd min en d'ander tyd meerder [sometimes less, sometimes more]) for the goods which they sent via Spain to the West Indies (Laspeyres 1863, 66).

The first eight voyages of the *English East-India* Company are supposed to have brought in a pure profit of 171% (Coulsom 1818, 5).

In a memorandum from the year 1733, the *English South Sea Company* worked out for the ship which it was permitted to send to the

West Indies as per the trade agreement the following calculations of cost and profit:

Cost of purchase of cargo	£200,000
Cost of wages and upkeep of crew	£25,000
Cost of officials and gifts	£10,000
Cost of commission for super cargo	£20,000
Cost of two years interest for the capital invested in cargo	£16,000
Expenses at home, share for this business	£5,000
Total cost	£276,000
Proceeds from cargo	£350,000
Profit	£74,000

In direct "trade" with *Spanish America*, at the beginning of the 18th century you still calculated on profits of up to 300%, while such profits of "at least" 100–200% formed the rule (Savary des Brûlons and Savary 1723, 1:1233).

The *English Levant Company* made a 300% profit at the beginning of the 17th century. A testimony of its contemporary: "the author of the Trade's Increase, published in the year 1615, says, 'That at first this company's ordinary returns were three to one; and this has generally been the case in newly discovered trades.'" (A. Anderson 1787, 2:225)

When you measure the strong means-forming power of coercive trade correctly, then you must, as I have already frequently indicated, take into consideration alongside the dividends of the trading companies the often quite handsome profits which *the officials and other personnel* made *on the side*. Precisely these profits were sometimes the only reason why outwardly a company seemingly did not thrive and possibly shut down with losses. An example for that is provided to us by the closing of accounts of the *French East-India* Company.

From 1681 the French merchants were allowed to transport goods on the ships of the East-India Company on their own account. Whereas now the East-India Company through its great expenses for wars, because of lost ships, etc. — and despite ample profits in the traded goods (14 ships had returned with 3,400,000 livre in gold and goods, and 8 ships whose cargo had cost 1,870,000 livre had sold it for 4,370,000 livre) — did not make excessive profits, the personnel profited — they transported, for example, on two ships goods for a purchase price of 232,000 livre and returned — after deduction of the freight — 400,720 livre, having thus almost a 74% profit (Kaeppelin 1908, 142, 144).

In a memorandum of the *English South Sea* Company from the year 1733, it states with reference to their trading license: "the companys factors and agents in America [...] got large estates in a very few years,

and some of them in little more than one year, whilst the company continued to be such great losers." (A. Anderson 1787, 3:197)

The private "trade" of the employees of the *English East-India* Company in India was quite general and of considerable extent (J. Campbell
1774, 2:104). Over the extortion of employees of the great companies,
particularly the British East-India, Büsch (1784, 72 ff.) contains valuable information from contemporary sources.

Chapter 46: The Slave Economy in the Colonies

Literature

Levantine colonies. We are informed about slavery in the Middle Ages in context by Langer (1891); Cibrario (1868; 1860, 301–6); Lazari (1862); Zamboni (1897); and Wattenbach (1874). Cf. also the literature named on pages 130 f.

Slaves from the colonies were also used in *Italy* during the Middle Ages and the Renaissance. The evidence has been recently put together by Tamassia (1910, chap. XII). In the 13th and 14th centuries the Venetian and Genoese ships brought large loads of slaves from the coast of the Black Sea, the Crimea, from Africa, and Moorish Spain. Cf. Livi (1907). Frati in the 13th century counts 5,807 slaves in 403 families in Bologna (Tamassia 1910, 359). According to a ruling in Bari in 1127, the members of the Slavic race were slaves "iure sanguinis" [by right of blood]. The Florentine statutes declared slavery to be legitimate for all unbelievers.

Transoceanic colonies. Over the *yellow* slavery, see Saalfeld (1812), Bokemeyer (1888, 275 ff.), and Day (1904). — We are informed about the exploitation of the *East Indies by the English* in particular in the travelogues of Buchanan (1807) and R. Martin (1838); as well as the parliamentary reports over India from the last decades of the 18th century, for example the ninth from the year 1783. Recently the first usable, even if sketchy economic history of British India also appeared — Dutt (1908).

Over the *red* slavery, see Helps (1855), Häbler (1899; 1907, vol. 1, chap. 15), and Handelmann (1856, 5 ff.); over the red slavery in particular in the *North American* colonies, see Steiner (1893), Bassett (1896), and Cooley (1896).

For the history of *black* slavery we are also still reliant on the older works like Sprengel (1779), Hüne (1820), Clarkson (1786), Falconbridge (1788), Buxton (1840), Moreau de Jonnès (1842), and Cairnes (1863) (the most important theoretical work over slavery). — Amongst the *more recent* works, these stand out: Wilson (1872), Knapp (1891), Häbler (1896), Peytraud (1897) (containing a first general description of the slave economy of an area from the sources of the colonial archives,

it is also, however, rich in views on the overall development of this institution), Williams (1897), Spears (1900), and Scelle (1906, vol. 1).

We have only in the last decades been informed fundamentally by a
series of excellent works over the significance of the *white slavery* in
particular for a few of the North American colonies. The works to which
we owe much of our information are — apart from the above mentioned
works by Steiner, Bassett, and Cooley — Ballagh (1895), and McCormac
(1904).

We are informed over *all three types of slavery* in the English
colonies in North America by Waltershausen (1894). All encompassing
but scanty is the work of Ingram (1895).

As far as "trade" was conducted with the inhabitants of the
colony, their exploitation was already described in the preceding section. But one wanted though as far as possible to
achieve more with the military apparatus which one used to
overthrow foreign peoples than just an exploitation of the inhabitants in the way of coercive trade, which only ever extended as far as the voluntary goods production of the natives.
One wanted to induce them to work so that their labour, in
which according to the claim of Columbus the entire wealth of
the colony lay, was fully taken advantage of. Thus one arrived
at the forcing to work of the natives (or those brought in),
that is, one arrived at the slave economy in its various forms.
It cannot be emphasised often enough now that bourgeois
wealth both in the Italian city-states and in the great cities of
Western Europe before the full development of the capitalist
economic system above all owed its origin for a quite considerable part to the slave economy in the colonies. An attempt
shall be made to prove this in the following.

We will in this regard first have to obtain an overview of:

I. The Fact and Type of Slavery
in the Various Colonies

1. Slavery and Serfdom in the Levantine Colonies

What the Western European encountered on the flat land
in the regions up to then under *Arab or Turkish* control was a
half submissive population obliged to provide tribute and undertake services and which had remained in this state of de-
pendance for centuries. The reports which we possess over
the behaviour of the new rulers make it probable that the position of the peasants under Frankish-Italian dominion got

rather worse. They sank down often to the level of slavery. "A trace of inhumane harshness goes through the Frankish arrangements in this region; barely another example is to be cited of such a pitiless exercise of the hard rights of conquest, which here hit not merely the defeated enemy, but also the companions in faith of the victor [...]. Accordingly you will with reason not be able to assume anything else but that almost the entire rural population of the countryside captured by the Franks simply ended up in slavery." (Prutz 1883, 327)

In agreement with that, Beugnot (1854) remarked, "Le servage sous le Francs ne paraît avoir eu d'autre règle que la volonté absolue, illimitée des propritétaires" [Serfdom under the Franks seems to have had no other rule than the absolute, unlimited will of the owners]. In 160 villages which the Templar lords possessed in the region of Safed, we find no less than 11,000 slaves employed (Prutz 1883, 327). The form of grant was: "all rights and possessions in men, women, and children" was carried over. Cf. also Prutz (1877, 60).

But what applied to the lands of Arab-Turkish rule, we may also assume for the regions of the *Byzantine Empire* in which the Italians settled — and that they, stepping into the place of the old rulers, received at their disposal a peasantry heavily burdened with taxes and services and mostly tied to the soil, and certainly understood how to harness them not less, but rather more than their predecessors[511].

Where the sources tell us in more detail about the type of settlement, this view is confirmed by them. Thus we learn precisely about the establishment of the Venetians on Crete. Here after the first uprising of the Cretans the property of the "rebels" was first systematically "confiscated" and then shared amongst the Venetian nobles. The hamlets were passed into the hands of the Venetian colonists along with their entire property "in cattle and slaves". Each colonist received as first ration 25 "Villani" (thus probably serfs) for the cultivation of his land[512]. On Chios the Paroikoi (Villani) were bonded serfs of the Maona* or of the individual shareholders of the Maona. Their position was so oppressed that many sought to save themselves by fleeing the island[513].

What the legal situation was in which the *commercial population in the cities* found themselves before the arrival of the

---

*   [Tr.: *maona* = joint-stock company.]

Italians, or that in which they later found themselves, I am unable to clearly see. According, however, to what we have learnt about their composition and organisation[514], the conclusion seems to me admissible that a large part stood in a slave-like relationship to the ruling classes, but in a large measure at least were obligated to pay taxes and provide services. Had that not been the case, that is, had the rulers of a town not drawn advantages from its citizens, then the sharing out of entire parts of a town, as is well-known to have been the rule, would have been without any meaning.

Now we must, however, in order to gauge in its fullest extent the field of exploitation which the Italians developed in the Levant, take into consideration that during the entire time of their colonial rule the labour material was increased constantly by a continued strong supply of slaves. The Byzantines and especially the Arabs had already conducted a booming *trade in slaves*. In the Caliphate both black and white slaves were imported annually in many thousands. They were drawn from Zawyla, the principal town of Fezzan at that time, where a main market for them existed, from Egypt, or from the east coast of Africa, "and indeed in such masses that several times dangerous slave uprisings took place"; the white slaves came from Central Asia or from the Frankish and Greek lands[515]. What we know about the actions of the Italians, however, lets us conclude without further ado that they did not reduce this supply of slaves, but rather certainly increased it; just with the difference that they now, in place of Christians captured in war, led into slavery Muslims captured in war.

Even if we did not possess so much specific evidence over the use of slaves and the trading of them from that time, the spirit of the laws and ordinances in the colonial areas would have to convince us that there it concerned an economic institution which based itself more and more on the use of slaves and which differed in no way from those which the Portuguese, the Spanish, and the Dutch later introduced to their colonies.

There are firstly in large quantities utterances of the government of the motherland from which the concern about the maintenance and increase of the stock of slaves emerge. Premiums were offered for increasing the supply of slaves, which equalled amounts which were previously advanced to those who had previously declared themselves ready to increase the stock of horses: "de conducendo ad dictam nostram insulam Crete majorem quantitatem sclavorum masculorum qui sint ab annis quinquaginta infra" [on hiring to our stated island Crete a greater number of male slaves who are of the age of fifty and under], the Venetian government advanced a loan of 3,000 hyperpyrons (about 500–700 ducats) (Noiret 1892, 54). Or slaves and prisoners of war were sent to the colonies by the government itself. Thus, for example, the population figures for Crete rose thanks to such imports under Venetian control from 50,000 to 192,725 [Tr.: exact reference by Sombart is unclear, but may be Haudecouer (1896)]. On the 15th January 1447 the government of Crete sent to Sudan of Babylon a ship with 44 slaves out of gratitude for his making trade easier (Noiret 1892, 416).

There is, however, no lack of those decrees which an economy based on slavery makes necessary in such rich abundance — penal laws for the case of runaway slaves, protective measures against slave uprisings, etc. — "si aliqui ex hominibus quos habebit ad suum stipendium sive salarium *pro coquendo seu laborando dictos zucharos* fugerent, possit et liceat sibi hostales fugitivos ubique in terris et super Insula intromittere et capere et illos ponere in manibus Rectorum nostrorum qui fugitivi tractentur et puniantur eodem modo, quo tractantur faliti galearum" [if any of the men whom he will have for his wages or salary *for cooking or labouring* on the stated sugar plantation[?] should flee, he can and may himself find and take the fugitives from anywhere on earth and on the island, and place them in the hands of our rulers, that the fugitives are treated and punished in the same way as galley slaves are treated] (Noiret 1892, 325). You could think here of "free wage labourers". But then the work of those would in reality have been just as much very forced labour as that of a common slave. — General penal threat of 11th March 1303: to anyone who takes in fugitive slaves[*]. "Item concedatur sibi et quinque personis apud eum licentia armorum de die et de nocte, in omnibus terris et locis Insule Crete pro securitate personarum et rerum suarum" [Likewise, license of arms is granted to him and to five persons, day and night, in all land and parts of the island of Crete for the security of their persons and property](Noiret 1892, 325) was enacted in favour of an industrialist.

Anyone who has leafed through the collections of these decrees will be fundamentally cured of the opinion which is still heard often today, that during the Middle Ages it was merely about a more or less patriarchal house slavery. No — the slave economy in the Levant was in no way "more comfortable" than the later one in America and the Indies.

2. Slavery in the Trans-Oceanic Colonies

With all the multifarious forms by which one helped themselves in the seizing of possession of the new areas, the constitution of work also ran everywhere here to slavery, if you

---

[*]   [Tr.: not referenced by Sombart.]

see its core and essence in forced labour. Within this wide concept of forced labour there were then certainly quite considerable gradations of bondage, but which for their economic effect were of subordinate importance.

a) The Procurement of Labour Material

The labour material was procured for the various colonies and also for the same colony in various ways:

1. the Dutch and English in their Indian possessions were able to make use of the yellow population resident there during all the centuries — the result: the *yellow slavery*;

2. the American colonies were at first likewise worked by the natives, thus the Indians — the result: the *red slavery*. But it is known that the red race proved itself unsuited to slavery — the Indians died out, be it because of the pressure of the work which they had to do was too heavy for them — "se mueren los pobres como animales sin dueño" [the poor things die like animals without an owner], wrote an eye witness, Brother Domingo de Santo Tomas, in a report over the mines in Potosi* — or be it from despair exercised in mass suicide or abstaining from sexual intercourse. To that can be added that early on philanthropists took an interest in them, who were able to put through a sort of "Indian protection". Enough — the native population did not suffice for the demands of the plantation owners for long — hence, the missing labour material had to be obtained from outside. That happened in two ways — on the one hand, through the import of Negroes from Africa:

3. *black slavery* began its world historical mission[516]. Not that it would have occurred for the first time. But its outstanding importance now arrived for the first time. Central America, Brazil, and the West Indies at first delivered the scene for it. With astonishing quickness the slavery of Negroes expanded in these regions. In 1501 we notice the first imports of Negroes, in 1510

---

* [Tr.: not referenced by Sombart.]

the trade from Lisbon for mining work begins, between 1513 and 1515 falls the start of the sugarcane cultivation on the Antilles, in 1530 the ban on Indian slavery arrives, but already in 1520 on Santo Domingo the Negro slaves were so numerous that the European settlers weighed with trepidation the possibility of an uprising of the Blacks. The situation was similar in Puerto Rico. In the year 1535 there were already 30 sugar factories. In August 1690 the first slave ship landed on the coast of Virginia with 20 Negro slaves — from that day the black slavery in the North American colonies began to expand.

State and Church contributed substantially to the development of Negro slavery — the Church because it had pronounced through its servants that the Negro was a creature more suited to slavery than the Indian whose soul was yet rescued from damnation when you granted him in slavery the possibility of conversion — the state when it at first had the legality of Negro slavery proven by its jurists as follows: "Porque en estos vamos con buena fé de que ellos se venden por sa voluntad o tienen justas guerras entre si en que cautivan unos a otros y à estos cautivos los venden despues à los Portugueses, que nos los traen, que ellos llaman Pombeiros ò Tangomangos como lo dizen Navarro, Molina, Rebelo, Mercado i otros Autores" [Because in this we act in good faith that they sell themselves by will or have just wars amongst themselves in which they place each other in captivity and then sell these captives to the Portuguese, who bring them to us, who they call Pombeiros or Tangomangos, as Navarro, Molina, Rebelo, Mercado, and other authors say][517]. Furthermore, however, the state also contributed to the maintenance of Negro slavery by concerning itself with the obtaining of the necessary material from Africa. The slave trade was declared a prerogative, and the right to practice it, with which, however, at the same time the obligation to deliver a specified number of slaves was bound, was transferred in return for payment of an emolument to a private individual or a company.

The contracts which were concluded in such ways between the Spanish crown and the slave traders carried the name assiento (Spanish: asiento [seat]). In 1517 Charles V for the first time granted Flemish ships the privilege to supply America with 4,000 Negroes a year; in 1580 the Genoese received it, who exploited it through a British company. In 1702 the assiento was concluded with the French Guinea Company, and in 1713 in the Peace of Utrecht the assiento was through the agreement between France and England ceded to England — England, that is, the English South Sea Company, undertook during the next 30 years to deliver at least 144,000 Negroes to "India" — that is an undertaking, but, as stated, also a monopoly — nobody else was permitted to supply Negroes to "India" (article XVIII of the treaty which is found, for example, verbatim in Postlethwayt (1774, 1:131 f.)). Later another special contract between the King of Spain and a company of English merchants was concluded for the delivery of Negroes to Buenos Aires (Postlethwayt 1774, 1:134). (The actual slave trade was, as we will yet see, much more extensive than was provided for by the assiento contracts which interest us here where we are occupied with the activities of the state.)

4. The other way in which the necessary labour power was arrived at, after the natives had failed, and which was used especially by the plantation owners of the North American colonies, was the import of indentured labourers from Europe, which led to a work system which you can call for the sake of conformity of expression *white slavery*.

The forced labour of white workers was the basis on which most *North American* colonies, above all of course the planter colonies, developed during the 17th and partly also during the 18th century as the black slavery was already experiencing a greater expansion. Virginia, for example, had in 1671 about 2,000 Negro slaves next to 6,000 whites in forced labour; in 1683 their number had climbed to 12,000, that of the Negroes still only amounted to 3,000.

The "white slavery" emerged in various ways:

a. through voluntary acceptance — poor people obtained by it the possibility of emigrating without having to pay in advance the at first very high

price of transportation — at the beginning of the
19th century it still amounted to £80;

b. through persuasion, deceit, in the way of so-called
kidnapping — by false promises, etc.;

c. through force. Numerous criminals had been since
the time of the Stuarts forcibly sent to the colonies, particularly also political criminals; likewise
prisoners of war.

Of the Scottish prisoners who were taken in the battle of
Worcester, 610 were sent in the year 1651 to Virginia; in 1653
100 Irish Tories were deported; in 1685 a number of adherents
of Monmouth; in 1666 many of the rebels; and many of the
prisoners of Dunbar (Ballagh 1895, 35; McCormac 1904, 92
ff.). As punishment in the colonies, forced labour was imposed
for running away, for marrying slaves, etc. (Ballagh 1895, 57)
But then the white indentured labourers were complemented
many times by children and vagabonds who were simply "appointed" to the colonies. McCormac (1904, 9) reports on it
from good sources as follows: "The practice of apprenticing
poor children to the Virginia Company began as early as 1620.
In that year, Sir Edwin Sandys petitioned Secretary Naunton
for authority to send out *one hundred children* who had been
'appointed for transportation' by the City of London, but who
were unwilling to go. By making use of the *apprenticeship
statute of Elizabeth this difficulty was removed* and both children and vagrants were *regularly gathered up* in London and
elsewhere and contracts made with merchants for carrying
them to America."

Certainly here the support which the state accorded
the interested parties with its instruments of power is
obvious — they owed it alone not only for the possibility of being able to employ workers forcibly, but also
for the actual obtaining of the labour material.

I talk about related methods for the obtaining of labour material in Europe as well in Chapter 54.

b) The Various Forms of Forced Labour

I have said all European colonies were developed on the
basis of forced labour; but this exhibited in the various times
and the various places quite different forms:

1. *full slavery*, with which thus the ownership is associated with the person of the slave, was only that of the
Negro slavery;

2. the other forced labourers lived in a *form of serfdom:*

a. the Indians were mostly only subject to corvée. They had to put themselves at the disposal of the European masters for 8 to 9 months in the fields or gold panning, and were permitted during the rest of the year to farm their own fields at home[518]. Or alternatively they were required to deliver specific products. The encomiendas, for example, which were allocated in 1499 by Columbus, mention over 10–20,000 sprigs of cassava root. The cacique was then obligated to have these fields cultivated by his people. The natives, however, did not dare escape these obligations, for the Spaniards tracked down the fugitives who, if nothing worse happened, were permitted to be sold as slaves[519].

b. A similar system was introduced by the Portuguese in their *African* colonies, where they, like on St Thomas, mainly farmed sugarcane. Already at the start of the 16th century we find plantations here with 150–300 workers: "fra negri et negre, liquali hanno questa obligatione, di lavorar tutta la settimana per il patron, eccetto il sabbato che lavorano per causa di vivere" [between negroes and negroes, who have this obligation, to work all week for the patron, except on Saturdays they work for their own livelihood][520].

c. This system of indirect forced labour or compulsory supply then became famous in the *Dutch* colonies under the name of the system of van den Bosch. We encounter it in the collecting of spices in the Molucca Islands, in the coffee and sugar cultivation on Java, with the production of cinnamon on Ceylon, and with the cultivation of the nutmeg tree on the Banda Islands, etc.

d. The system of exploitation of *India* by the English, that is, thus in essence by the English East-India Company, was particularly sophisticated. Sophisticated because — under the appearance of complete freedom and the use of correct and cheap principles of government — the Indian people were drained *twice*. The "system" was as follows:

1. under all possible pretexts oppressive taxes were raised, amongst which the land tax was the most important — this was not actually a tax, but rather approached a confiscation in so far as it diverted in many cases half or more of the farmer's return into the pockets of the conqueror. According to a drawing up of costs by Buchanan, for example, the land tax for a field of bad soil class was 14/; the production costs amounted to 19/; to the farmer remained 7/8; for a field of the best soil class: land tax 17/; production costs 19/; net proceeds of the farmer £1 s. 6¾;

2. with the returns of these "taxes" now (after all the costs of the company had been covered by them), the commercial products in the countryside were "purchased" — you "invested" these amounts in trade goods, the expression went — the "investment" was thus the sum used. This "purchase" now consisted again in a robbery. The commercial producers, particularly the weavers, were namely called together, they were informed that one wanted to see such and such product made by them, for which one will pay them such and such — there was no contradicting these determinations. Producing for anyone else was forbidden. That the "arrangements" were kept by the weavers, that is, that they delivered a specified quantity of obligatory labour (for a payment, as we will yet see, which did not even always protect them from starvation), was taken care of by the Company appointed overseer who was equipped with a rattan cane(!). The law gave the customer full freedom to take his goods. The statements which the witnesses made before the committee of inquiry in the year 1813 over the process of "investment"

make it clear that the purchase of commercial products was a case of naked forced labour[521].

Likewise, with the money which was extorted from the Indian *farmers*, they held down the Indian *commercial* serfs.

3. in addition, indigo and tea plantations as well existed in India with an unconcealed forced labour[522].

e. The system of forced labour of *whites* became well-known under the names "white or indentured˙ servitude". The forced labourers themselves were called "indentured servants". With this description the character of the work relationship is also indicated — it was in fact a type of serfdom in which these forced labourers lived. They were obligated to the performance of "reasonable service" — be it in the plantations (tobacco farming!), be it in the house of the farmer, be it as craftsman, teacher, or such like. Their obligation extended in most cases only to a specified number of years (seven). Their payment consisted of food and clothing as well as the delivery of specific natural produce (later also in the paying out of money at the end of the bonded period of service).

II. The Expansion of Forced Labour

For the *Italian* colonies we do not possess any comprehensive statistics of either the production or the employed slaves. We are thus reliant on deductions from some conclusive situations or on occasional reports. We may make a deduction on the extent of the area of exploitation from the descriptions which we possess of the rich production opportunities in the Levant.

Palestine and *Syria* had blossomed into a true paradise under the blessings of the Arab culture at home there for half a millennium. The contemporaries of the Crusaders were unable to find sufficient words to describe the overflowing

---

*   [Tr.: Sombart uses the term "intented" servitude in English in this section, which I have changed to "indentured".]

wealth of the land. And added to that was a model cultivation all around. In the gardens grew an abundance of tropical fruits — lemons, oranges, figs, almonds, especially in the surrounds of Tripoli and by Tyre. In many places wine and olive oil was obtained; in addition they cultivated sugarcane and cotton, bred silkworms, and planted indigo and madder. In the mountains, however, the cedar and cypress forests rustled, and the herds of the nomadic Arabs grazed[523].

The same abundance on the *mainland of Asia Minor* and above all on the *islands of the Aegean Sea*, which still abounded with fertility when the Italians began their work. Pearls amongst them were Cyprus, Crete, and Chios, the latter above all renowned for its mastic plantations, but also rich in wine, olive trees, mulberry trees, figs, etc. Whereas Cyprus next to salt, wine, cotton, indigo, laudanum resin, colocynth, and carobs, delivered above all sugar — they not only cultivated sugarcane plantation-like in grand style on most of these islands, but also extracted the sugar on-site. In the region of Limassol the Venetian family Cornaro possessed an extensive and lucrative sugar plantation which Ghistele called the epitome of Cyprus's sugar; at the time when the Italian Casola saw the estate (1494), 400 persons were occupied there in the preparation of the sugar.[*]

We have for this time also a few credible numbers — in the year 1489 the Venetian Senate had the quantity of sugar produced on Cyprus surveyed. It was 2,000 quintals (at 250 kg each[†]) of single-boiled sugar, 250 quintals of zamburri (an inferior by-product), and 250 quintals of molasses; in the year 1540 the same figures according to Attar amounted to 1,500, 450, and 850.[‡]

But what lent the Italian possessions their high value was above all the circumstance that everywhere the population already possessed a significant degree of commercial acumen and hence *industries in the high style* could be operated. Among these in turn *silk manufacturing* stood out. It blos-

---

*   [Tr.: not referenced by Sombart.]
†   [Tr.: a quintal was a hundredweight (~100 lbs), at which 2,000 quintales would equate to over 90,000 kg.]
‡   [Tr.: details of the source not provided by Sombart.]

somed in Antioch, Tripoli, and Tyre. One of the reviews in which the Burchardish description of the Holy Land is contained gives the number of silk and worsted weavers in Tripoli at 4,000 and more. Tyre in particular produced expensive white material which was exported widely[524]. But also on almost every island the Italians found a silk industry in full bloom, particularly also on Cyprus[525], or they themselves instituted manufacturing, as in Sicily and Morea. In addition to the silk industry, the *cotton industry* was carried on, for example, in Armenia[526], and the *glass and pottery industry* in Syria[527], amongst others. Finally, however, the mines delivered high returns, especially the *alum mines* which were in operation on the peninsula of Phocaea in particular. Here the Genoese House of Zaccaria plundered the land through several generations. Manuele Zaccaria (died 1288) had obtained riches "which escaped estimation" through the extraction of alum. In the year 1298, for example, 250 hundredweight of alum were sold for 1,300,000 (?) lire[528], whereas the annual yield amounted on average to 14,000 (?) hundredweight[529].

That slave work in the colonies of the *Portuguese, Spanish, French, Dutch*, and *English* found its use mainly in the plantation economy is well-known — in the east it was the cultivation of spices, in the west the cultivation of sugarcane which first established the prosperity and wealth of the new colonies; later tobacco, coffee, cocoa, indigo, and cotton joined them as the most important products of slave plantations.

Even if we can follow the growth in production in the slave colonies quite precisely (so that a summary portrayal of the colonial economy would well reward) with the sources accessible up to now, which in part exploit an excellent specialist literature[530], it appears advisable to me though for the aims of this portrayal to establish the extent of the slave labour in the modern colonies in a direct way through the ascertaining of the number of slaves, since serviceable figures for this are available in great number and an overview can be given more easily than by a survey of the many individual production and trade figures.

Certainly the *total number of slaves* in the European colonies is first obtainable in a somewhat accurate way for the beginning of the 19th century. For the earlier period we are reliant on occasional information. Therefore we may assume that the highpoint of the slave business was only reached shortly before the abolition of slavery, and that only in the last half century before the abolition was the increase an especially rapid one[531].

The total stock of slaves in all slave lands in the 1830s numbered 6,822,759, allocated thus:

```
France...............................275,808
Great Britain.....................728,805
Spain...............................321,182
Holland.............................72,963
Denmark and Sweden.........46,500
Brazil.............................1,930,000
Cape of Good Hope.............36,096
USA (1830)....................2,328,642
                              5,739,996
To which add the freed...1,082,763
                              6,822,759
```

In the USA the black population then climbed still further until emancipation of the slaves, almost to double the stock in the year 1830; namely too:

```
1840...............................2,873,648
1850...............................3,638,808
1860...............................4,441,830
```

These quantities of black slaves must, since the black population did not increase in natural ways, have been achieved by the regular import from the Negro lands. That gave cause for a highly developed slave trade.

Over the *extent of the slave trade* there exists a quantity of widely varying information. The well-known calculation which Buxton[532] drew up is the following:

Fetched annually from Africa were
by the Christian slave trade   c. 400,000 Negroes
by the Muslim slave trade   c. 100,000 Negroes
500,000 Negroes

Of the 400,000 objects of the Christian slave trade, 280,000 perished in being captured, in transport, and in the first year, so that only 120,000 slaves finally remained at their disposal. This number, in view of the total demand for slaves at the beginning of the 19th century, hardly seems too high and is confirmed in its correctness by the official figures that have become known recently. Thus we learn, for example, that in the French Antilles during the years 1780–89 on average 30–35,000 Negroes were imported annually. If we set the total number of slaves who were kept at the time in the French Antilles at 240–260,000, then the annual imports amounted to $1/7$–$1/8$. But if finally there were 6–7 million slaves in total, then 120–150,000 slaves as total annual replenishment seems rather too small than too high.

But it does not depend so much at all on an exact statistical survey of the slaves traded as goods. It suffices perfectly for our aims to establish that it concerned in the end many tens of thousands per year and during the entire period during which the slave trade was in operation millions of humans who (that is the only thing which interests us here) offered cause for good business.

The nations which one after the other played the leading role in the slave trade, without thereby excluding the other nations, were the Jews[533], the Venetians[534], the Genoese, the Portuguese, the French, and the English. These last four nations were those which one after the other had the monopoly on the Negro trade in their hands. The share of the various dealers in the slave trade in its heyday is evident from the following figures.

In the year 1769 the numbers of Negroes taken away from the coast of Africa (from Cap Blanc to the Congo River) was[535]:

> Great Britain.........................53,100
> France...............................23,520
> Holland..............................11,300
> British America.......................6,300
> Portugal..............................1,700
> Denmark...............................1,200

Indubitably Great Britain during the entire 18th century, thus in the most important epoch, was the centre of the slave trade, and in Great Britain itself the centre in turn was Liverpool — of 192 English slave ships departing in the year 1771, 107 departed from Liverpool, 58 from London, 23 from Bristol, and 4 from Lancaster.

III. The Profitability of the Slave Economy

That so many people found use as slaves is now of course no proof that here a source of enrichment flowed for slave traders and slave keepers. Prominent men have often enough attempted to prove[536] that slave labour is unproductive, and consequently unprofitable, that slavery means a "restriction of profits", and has the tendency to bring the latter to a quite low level. From which then by necessity the consequence must arise that the Europeans over long centuries essentially needlessly sacrificed so many millions of human lives, that is, without achieving the aim of inflating their means with high profits.

With respect to such a conception it does not appear to me superfluous to prove the profitability of the slave trade as fact.

First of all we have to assess for itself:

1. The Slave Trade

That this now was a very lucrative business at all times is not to be doubted. That was already very well-known in the Middle Ages. *Hence* above all the ardent efforts of the Venetians and Genoese to get a foothold on the Black Sea, to displace the Byzantines, in order to completely dominate the slave markets present there. And Venice especially was damaged much more by the displacement from the lucrative slave trade to Egypt, as happened in consequence of the conquest of the region of Asia Minor by the Turks, than by the loss of the Levant trade.

How highly the business of the Negro slave trade was valued is well-known — England, when in the Peace of Utrecht (1713) the right to supply slaves to the Spanish colonies was promised to it, considered the achievement to be one of the most significant which the Utrecht treaty had brought it[537].

The *reasons* for *the lucrativeness of the slave trade* are, however, not hard to establish. The human manpower with which the "trade" here was carried on is a "good" at whose purchase firstly every relation to its production costs is at once cancelled. The prices of slaves can be set as low as you like, they are constantly irrational and depend merely on the greater or lesser violence or trickery which the dealer has at their disposal. It is mostly about pure coercive trade — in the beginnings of the modern slave trade, rum, gunpowder, cloth, etc. were the gifts in return. Where the slaves were definitely not bought, but rather were enslaved, this state of affairs appeared most distinctly. Enslavement, however, was the rule from about 1750[538].

With the particular nature of that good "manpower" to pay itself off through work, on the other hand then a relatively much higher price can be paid for it on the side of the purchaser than for any other good. When we finally take into consideration that the slave trade, where it does not enjoy a legal monopoly (which was the case during the longest period of its existence), also bears a certain exclusive character thanks to its quite peculiar nature, then we will comprehend how it was possible that here "trade" could be conducted for centuries with enormous excess profits, so that the slave trade was actually the most rewarding "trade" there has ever been.

We can now, however, establish precisely in an empirical way on the basis of statistical records the extent of the profits which the slave trade made for centuries. At the same time we must leave aside entirely the profits which were obtained in the beginnings of the Negro slavery when the chieftains did not understand at all how to assert their own interests. When one bought at the beginning, especially in the hinterland of Guinea, a young, well-grown and healthy man for a piece of linen to the value of 3 mithqāls[539], for an anker* of brandy; the Negro princes though at the time gave for a horse 10–15 men as the equivalent.

Travelogue by Alvise de la Mosto (1454) in Ramusio (1550, 99 verso). Certainly at the time the price for mature Negroes was also yet much lower than in the 17th and 18th centuries. Up to the end of the 18th century the sale price had increased seven to eightfold (Peytraud 1897, 127). I want to share a price list from the beginning of the 18th century. The Royal French Senegal Company had arranged with the chief Damel the following "equivalents" for a slave:
- 4 shotguns with 5 slugs, or
- 6 shotguns with 3 slugs, or
- 30 copper basins, or
- 9 ounces of coral, or
- 2 drums, or
- 100 lbs of yellow wax, or

---

* [Tr.: 1 anker = 34–42 litres varying on place.]

- 4 ells of red cloth, or
- 30 ells of coarse woollen cloth (*revêche*), or
- 100 pints of brandy, or
- 4 silk pinafores, or
- 30 bars (= 15 hundredweight) of iron, or
- 4 lbs of cloves, or
- 15 rolls of wallpaper, or
- 100 lbs of lead, or
- 1,000 flints, or
- 20 lbs of pepper, or
- 4 lbs of Valeriana celtica, or
- 100 pieces of linen (toiles platilles [flat canvases]?), or
- 4 pieces of Indian linen (Savary des Brûlons and Savary 1723, 1:1046).

But even for the later period we have enough evidence to show that the profit in the Negro trade amounted to hardly less than 50%, mostly much more, and in the last period up to 180 and 200%.

A Few Statistics on the Lucrativeness of the Slave Trade

A report of the Commandant Director and Inspector General of Guinea, M. Courbe, from 26th March 1693 contains the following figures: 800 slaves were bought for 29,200 livres and sold for 240,000 livres. He added, "au Sénégal on traite communément 200 captifs qui ne coûtent pas plus de 30 livres la pièce et sont vendus aux îles 300 livres au moins" [in Senegal, 200 captives are drafted commonly who cost no more than 30 pounds each and are sold to the islands for at least 300 pounds] (Peytraud 1897, 99–103).

The *French* slave traders are supposed (according to calculations drawn up on the basis of the Spanish export registers) to have brought to France 204 million piasters (N.B. already by the middle of the 18th century!) (Postlethwayt 1774, 1:134).

From the *Liverpool* trade, the ship 'Lottery' had 460 Negroes on board, sold 453 of them for £22,726, from which was deducted £2,307 10 s. for ship's outfitting, £8,326 14 s. for the transport, giving a net profit for the voyage of £12,091.

The net profit of the 'Lottery' amounted another time to £19,021.

The net profit of the 'Enterprise' with 392 slaves to £24,430.

That of the 'Fortune' with 343 slaves to £9,487.

That of the 'Louisa' with 326 slaves to £19,133.

That of the 'Bloom' with 308 slaves to £8,123.

In the year 1786 the Liverpool slave traders sold 31,690 slaves for £1,282,690 net. The price of the goods exported to Africa amounted to £864,895, the upkeep of the slaves to £15,845. The expenses for 'freight' which was also earned though amounted to £103,488. So that a net profit in this year of £298,462 would have flowed into the pockets of the slave traders. Also, however, to be taken into account is that with this calculation maximum amounts have been assumed for the expenses, and minimum amounts for the revenues. At any rate, with these net profits an annual income from £2,500 to £3,000 would have been allocated to each of the 100–120 shipowners (Williams 1897).

According to another table, we learn of the following numbers: in the year 1771 a total of 47,146 Negroes were exported from Africa, 29,250 of them by Liverpool traders. The profit made by them, was calculated after careful estimation, "according to moderate Computation", to be £1½ million, the usual profit in this trade being £500,000 (J. Campbell 1774, 2:633).

These numbers agree almost completely with the data which Nemnich (1800, 337) gives without reference: in 1783–1793, 303,737 slaves were traded by Liverpudlians. By this trade, £15,186,850 was *earned*. Each slave trader would thus have obtained on average in this decade a means of about 3 million marks.

Quite extraordinary profits, however, were first obtained in the slave trade when it was declared to be sea piracy and was thus treated as smuggling.

From the history of the *English* slave trade, the following cost calculations have been handed down to us. The ship 'Firm' (1838), according to a legal statement, brought in a total income of 145,000 dollars; the total expense for purchase, provisions, munitions, wages, etc. amounted to 52,000 dollars; the profit thus to 180%. A ship 'Venus' carried 850 slaves who cost it £3,400 at purchase, the food as far as the port of arrival ran to £2,500, the sale proceeds reached the enormous extent of £42,500 (Parliamentary Paper No. 381, p.37, in Buxton (1840, 222 f.)). Similar instances are known to us by the dozens. It is pointless to pile up examples in order to see what significance the slave trade possessed for means formation in the maritime cities of the European states.

A very informative and complete statement of calculation for a slave trading business is found in the autobiography of Captain Théodore Canot (1854, 101). He shows that with a ship which cost $3,700, and a total capital of $21,000, you could in six months obtain a net profit of $41,438.54.

Even in the trade with "white slaves" (or serfs) which, as we saw, was of great significance in the North American colonies for a long time, ample profits were made. Skippers, merchants, agents, etc. recruited a number of such indentured servants and sold the contracts to the highest bidder of the plantation owners in the colonies. A servant could be transported for £6–8 and sold over there for £40–60 (Ballagh 1895, 34, 38, 41). More precise information is given by McCormac (1904, 42), citing the Calendar of State Papers, Colonial Series, for September 28th 1670 (Public Record Office of Great Britain 1860, 7:94-110 §277).

2. Slave Labour

But it can now be no more doubtful that *production* with slaves or labourers brought in by force in another way — I want to be cautious and not say *is* also profitable, but rather — *was* also profitable for centuries. With that the thought should be expressed that it depends on specific external circumstances *whether* slave labour is profitable, and that these circumstances during the past centuries were suitable for making it profitable.

The conditions for its profitability, however, seem to be primarily the following:

1. *plantation operations* like those which actually ruled in the European colonies in question here — Cairnes (1863) places the greatest emphasis on the fulfillment of this condition;

2. a certain *high level of product prices*. Only when this could be squeezed by the employment of cheaper free workers did slave labour no longer provide any surplus value. This lowering of product prices first occurs, however, late — *that is*, whenever the demand for labourers is abundantly supplied[540];

3. *overworking of manpower*, that is, an outlay for the tending of the body which lags behind the minimum for physiological existence. The slaves are used *up* physically, not just used. It was lastly usual to work the slave in his prime to death so as to not have to feed him as an older man. That the slave population did not reproduce physiologically is well-known. Hence the enormous sacrifice in human lives, the enormous waste of human power which we recognise as the accompanying symptom of the colonial economy.

   Above all, the rapid *expiration of the red race* under the pressure of European domination is well-known, an expiration, as Peschel noted fittingly, "which comes quite close to the displacement of animal species in the geological period"[*]. When the Spanish came to the Bahamas, they found them thickly populated. When the English landed in 1629 in New Providence, no natives were there anymore. In 1503 the first Spaniards settled in Jamaica, and already in 1558 all the Indians had vanished (Andree 1867, 2:705-706). Española in 1508 (at the conquest) had 60,000 natives, in 1548 only 500. On Cuba

---

[*]   [Tr.: this appears rather to be a summary of this sentence in Peschel (1858, 547–48): "This farewell of entire races on the appearance of more refined and stronger peoples follows there [Sandwich & Society Islands] so visibly and yet so soundlessly that it reminds us of the events of geological periods where nature sweeps away with measured hand the spent forms of living beings."]

in 1548 the native population was already extinguished (Peschel 1858, 546 f.). Peru in 1575 (thus almost already half a century after conquest) still had about 1,500,000 inhabitants; in 1793 only 600,000 (Humboldt 1811, 1:319-320; 1814, 1:69-70). Häbler (1899, 310, 312) also talks about the dense settlement of Peru. Likewise in Mexico the population melted away. The orphans of the men and women who perished in the mines were after a few years as numerous "as the stars in heaven and the sand in the sea" — Quiroga to the Councillor of the Indies, Coleccion de Muñoz, ms. vol. 79, in Helps (1855, 3:208). Letter of friar Geronimo de San Miguel from Santa Fé on 20th August 1550: "para poblar 50 casas de Españoles se despueblan 500 de Indios" [to populate 50 houses of Spaniards, 500 houses of Indians are depopulated], Coleccion de Muñoz, ms. vol. 85, in Helps (1855, 4:390). "Daremos por cuenta muy cierte y verdadera, que son muertos en los dichos quarenta años por las dichas tiranias, é infernales obras de los Christianos, injusta y tiranicamente, mas de doze cuentos de animas hombres y mugeres y niños y en verdad que creo sin pensar engañarme, que son mas de quinze cuentos" [We will take it for a very certain and true account that they are killed in the said forty years by the said tyrannies and infernal works of the Christians, unjustly and tyrannically, more than twelve tales of spirited men and women and children, and in truth what I believe without being deceived in my thinking is that there are more than fifteen tales] (Casas 1552, 5).

But the *yellow race* also had to experience enormous sacrifices in human life. Banyuwángi, a province of Java, in 1750 still numbered over 80,000 inhabitants, yet in 1811 only 8,000. See Raffles (1817, 1:71), cited in Marx (1903, 1:717; 1906, 824). Precise figures over the reduction in population are not available; that it was present is a fact that cannot be denied. As circumspect a writer and excellent connoisseur of the subject as Bokemeyer summarises his judgement as: "The decrease in population (on the spice islands), the misshapen figures and skin diseases spreading from family to family among the islanders are the unmistakeable features of the centuries long oppression and suffering which rests as a curse on these beautiful lands" (Bokemeyer 1888, 293 f.).

But all that vanishes next to the hecatombs* of the Negroes who were sacrificed to the colonial economy — you may confidently say that an entire thickly populated continent was robbed in order to provide the necessary (and cheap because of its abundance) labour material for the plantation economy.

4. *Over-exploitation of nature.* This condition was also fulfilled to a wide extent in the European colonies, in

---

*   [Tr.: hecatomb = great public sacrifice.]

particular for a long time was most important in the sugar colonies — bleeding the soil of its powers, and the over-exploitation of the natural treasury of animals and plants was the regular accompanying symptoms of the colonial economy from the Middle Ages up to recent times.

That applies to the *Mediterranean lands* no less than for almost all colonial areas of the new period. *Over-exploitation* was the password here as there. We have seen what gardens the Franks entered when they landed in Syria and Palestine where it is desert today; we hear of the fertility of the islands of the Mediterranean, like Cyprus, where today more than half of the land is described as waste land (Unger and Kotschy 1865, 426 ff.). When Hans Ulrich Krafft travelled to the island in the year 1573 — two years after the end of Venetian rule — he found it deserted (Krafft 1862, 81 ff.).

Cypress forests on the island of Crete which fell victim to the axes of the Venetians (Haudecoeur [Tr.: possibly Haudecoeur (1896)]).

The same picture of desolation in the *trans-oceanic* colonies of more recent times. In the West Indies the sugar cultivation was so exhausting that soon almost all the better estates were unusable (Merivale 1861, 1:41 ff., 1:75 ff.). The same thing was reported from the provinces of Minas (Uruguay) and Bahia (Brazil) (Liebig 1878, 423); the same for the cotton cultivation of the slave states of the USA (Cairnes 1863, 56 f.).

Everywhere the magnificent forests fell victim to the European industrialists. Already in the year 1548 the landscape in the vicinity from San Domingo was so denuded of forest that you had to import wood from a distance of 12 miles (Peschel 1858, 559). About deforestation on Curaçao by the Spanish, see Friedmann (1860, 262). For forest devastation in Mexico, see Humboldt (1811, 1:301; 1814, 1:77). Here also belongs the systematic eradication of many plants, particularly the clove forests as the Dutch did on the Molucca Islands in order to secure their trade monopoly (Bokemeyer 1888, 117 ff., 179 ff.).

A schoolbook example for the rapine is offered by the activities of the Dutch East-India Company (Bokemeyer 1888, 275).

That the taxes extorted from the East Indies farmers by the English were so high that they damaged the agricultural operations, hindered the necessary expenditure, and finally exposed the population to death from starvation, is confirmed by all reporters. See the evidence in Buchanan (1807) and cf. Dutt (1908, 1:224, 1:231, 1:244, and elsewhere).

That the slave economy now, when these conditions are fulfilled, can in fact be quite profitable, and thus was through the centuries, is something for which we possess sufficient conclusive evidence, and I want to share some of that here for the strengthening of what has been said.

A Few Statistics on the Lucrativeness of Slave Labour

1. Negro Slavery

Towards 1700 a plantation in the French Antilles was estimated by Labat at 350–400,000 francs, which delivered 90,000 francs profit, thus about 25% (Labat 1742). According to another calculation, the following profit and loss statement arose for a sugar plantation (end of the 18th century), whose worth with land, buildings, and 220 slaves, inclusive of women and children, was estimated at £35,000:

Returns to production:	500 barrels of sugar at £20	£10,000
	rum and syrup	£800
		£10,800
Costs of production:	upkeep for buildings, slaves, etc	£1,200
Purchase of 12 new Negroes		£600
		£1,800
Total profit		£9,000

Which also again corresponds almost exactly to a rate of profit of 25% (Hüne 1820).

Another larger sugar plantation on Cuba needed (end of the 18th century):

650 ha. land
300 Negroes at 4–500 piasters
2,000,000 francs invested capital.

Annual production: 400,000 arrobas[*] of sugar, valued at 550,000 francs.

Net profit = 300–350,000 francs = 15–17%

There the alcohol produced from the molasses tended to suffice to cover the daily expenses (Humboldt 1811, 3:178-179; 1814, 3:10).

In general the profit that a slave brought in annually was calculated for sugar and coffee plantations at £30, for cotton plantations at £25, for rice at £20, for tobacco and grain at £15. The first two years tended already to pay back the purchase price of the slave, but then of course a considerable surplus remained over the cost of upkeep which was very low. Labat (1742) calculates them for a plantation with 120 Negroes at 6,610 livres, i.e. 55 livres per head per annum; Schoelcher (1842, 268–69 n.2) calculates 100 livres per annum. Spix and Martius (1823) arrive at similar results; cited in Nebenius (1829, 58). Nebenius himself makes some good remarks on it.

---

[*]   [Tr.: 1 arroba = 11–16 kg.]

For the beginning of the 19th century, a knowledgeable observer estimates the average profit at sugar plantations at 10%, at cotton plantations at 12–15%, and at coffee plantations at 15–20%. *All wealth*, he added, *heads as a result to the colonies* (Ouvrard 1827, 1:5).

For the first half of the 19th century and for the USA, an earlier slave keeper judged as follows: "Negro slavery was profitable in producing rice, cotton and turpentine. One good hand could thus make in rice from $300 to $400 a year above his expenses and in turpentine he could make as much as $1000 a year" (Bassett 1896, 86).

2. Forced Production in the Dutch Colonies

The Dutch Indies system consisted, as we know, of obliging the natives to deliver specific production quantities which were bought from them for a calculated price; the latter was then calculated thus that the sale price was always about 100 to 150% higher — for example, in the year 1762 the Governor of Java's east coast, Nicolaas Hasting, calculated:

the purchase price at 82,223.6 rijksdaalders
the sale price at 215,874.8 rijksdaalders (Klerk de Reus 1894, 213)

In order though to not have the natives, who liked handing over coffee at 10 stuiver per pound, get high-spirited, in 1724 it was determined that a quarter of the price would be paid in clothing. At the time they sold the coffee in Gamron (Persia) for 1 florin 14 stuiver, in Bassalor for 1 florin 11 stuiver per pound (Klerk de Reus 1894, 228).

3. Exploitation of British East-India

It would suffice for proving the profits of the English East-India Company to demonstrate the lucrativeness of the English system of extortion. But we also possess figures from which we can see clearly the absolute extent of profit obtained, which was not at all completely expressed in the dividends of the company. Thus the tribute raised from the inhabitants of the province of Bengal in the six years of 1765–1771 amounted to £20,133,579; a part of that was transferred to the Great Mogul and the Nabob, another part remained in the pockets of the company officers who looked after the collecting of it (charges of collection, salaries, commission, etc.), so that around £13,066,761 flowed into the accounts of the company. On that now again the civil administration and the army of the company lived, consuming £9,027,609. Remaining was a surplus of £4,037,152 (Great Britain House of Commons 1773, 335; cited in Dutt 1908, 46). This £4 million was the amount which was taken in for "investment", that is, served for drawing the commercial producers into coerced labour. The sums paid to the coerced workers were, as I have already stated, quite trivial, and probably did not suffice even in India to maintain the population who on the contrary either earned their upkeep alongside in agriculture or — died. What Buchanan (1807) informs us about "labour wages" appears barely believable — 40, 50, 60, 70, at most 80 shillings a year. So that the quantity of goods which were produced for the £4 million were quite considerable, and which was sold of course in Europe for multiples of the "price of manufacture". One author suggests for one and a half times as much, which seems very low. At any rate, that would be £10 million, 200 million marks *for which not a penny was paid*, which were rather — "without sending an ounce of Silver from hence", as J. Campbell (1774, 2:613) proudly suggests — simply "taken off" the natives. "The whole exported produce of the country, so far as the Company is concerned, is *not exchanged in the course of barter, but it is taken away without any return or payment whatever*." (Great Britain House of Commons 1785, 30, 45)

4. White Forced Labour in the USA

The servant produced according to the testimony of a contemporary (end of the 17th century) 2,500–3,000 lbs of tobacco on average each year (McCormac 1904, 33), and cost £12–15 (besides food). In the middle of the 18th century Governor Sharpe wrote, "the Plantar's Fortune here consist in the number of their Servants [...] much as the Estates of an English Farmer do in the Multitude of Cattle" (McCormac 1904, 35). Free workers are not to be paid. A planter must sell two oxen in order to pay his worker, and releases him because he does not know how to keep paying him. The worker: he might sell more capital; the planter: "but how shall I do [...] when all my cattle are gone? The servant replied, you shall then serve me, and so you may have your cattle again" (Winthrop 1825, 2:219-220; cited in McCormac 1904, 34).

The most knowledgeable people dealing with those epochs of the American colonial economy agree that white servitude was an extremely profitable form of labour (McCormac 1904, 111 ff.; Ballagh 1895, 89 ff.).

In view of so much evidence we surely must not doubt the means-forming power of the slave economy. To crown it all we know enough about the proverbial wealth of the planters, which I only want to reference by means of two arbitrarily chosen pieces of evidence.

A contemporary of the Dutch War, Brother Manoel de Salvador, reported of the luxury of the planter aristocracy in Brazil at the conclusion of the 16th century, start of the 17th century: "Anyone who did not eat with silver was considered poor; the women considered clothes of silk and atlas to be cheap if the richest embroidery was not added, and adorned themselves with as many jewels as if it had rained precious stones; the men for their part followed every new style, adorned themselves with expensive daggers and swords; none of the precious delicacies of Portugal or the islands was permitted to be missing from their table. In short, Pernambuco barely appeared to be an earthly land, so far as wealth and extravagance could make it so, it seemed an image of paradise."[541]

And the ever clear-eyed and well-informed Defoe wrote at the beginning of the 18th century: "We see now the ordinary planters of *Jamaica* and *Barbados* rise to immense estates, riding in their coaches and six, especially in Jamaica, with 20 or 30 negroes on foot running before there whenever they please to appear in publick."[542]

Chapter 47: Means Formation within the Framework of the Capitalist Economy

We have met means formation from entrepreneur profits in various places. In general, however, this section was meant to show that bourgeois wealth grows for a very large, if not for the largest part *outside* the capitalist framework, and occurs *alongside* the capitalist economy *so that it forms a "foundation", a "precondition" for the latter*. It surely goes without saying now though that from the first beginnings of capitalistically conducted trade and capitalist production, profit *also* served as a source of means formation. In order to establish it in principle, neither great acumen, nor excessively extensive historical knowledge is needed. I also would not have expressly mentioned it, if a few critics of the first edition had not noticed the absence of this category of means formation (or as it was called erroneously at the time: capital formation) and censured its omission. Thus for their sake the triviality is established here.

I have depicted schematically in another place already how the profit to capital forms (see Chapter 19). We know from that:

1. that all profit to capital arises through the contractual combination of the owners of capital and free workers acting for them in return for specific reward;
2. that thus all profit to capital rests in the surplus of the sale price over the amounts paid to the worker or, if you want to reduce both to the same denominator of the work effort or "labour value" incorporated in it, in the "surplus value" which the entrepreneur obtains in the product price over the "value" incorporated in the

labour wage. This establishing, which Marx racked his brains over so much, is, as Lexis has already worked out in detail, a tautology and does not exclude on the other hand of course that the goods amount incorporated in the labour wage would be greater than the goods amount produced by the isolated worker. Whether it is actually greater or smaller is a fact to be ascertained empirically and varying from case to case. The fundamental dispute over the "productivity of capital" is an idle one;

3. we know that the extent of profits is determined by numerous conditions which I have likewise already surveyed schematically on page 24 ff., and the empirical-historical establishing of which is one of the main tasks of this work.

I just want to add that the profits of the capitalist enterprises in the epoch of early capitalism was probably very high, in view of, on the one hand, the monopoly character which trade and production often bore (see Sections 2 and 6); and on the other hand, the low wages which resulted by necessity from the the general economic situation, and which the public body was also concerned about keeping down (see Section 7).

To what *extent the means formation* arose *from profit* is of course not to be established especially since we do not know even in the case of the individual entrepreneur whether he obtained his wealth in his business or outside it — we have got to know of various cases above which show that even in the 18th century, for example, money-lending was a quite common sideline of industrial entrepreneurs.

At any rate we will obtain the quantitative significance of these sources of wealth to some extent in flavour and in feel if we follow the progress which capitalism made in goods turnover and in goods production during the epoch of early capitalism. That occurs in the next volume of this work, which must be referred to here.

Section 6: The Reshaping of Goods Demand

Overview

Anyone who follows the developmental history of early capitalism attentively will of course perceive the influence on all sides which the reshaping of goods demand exercised on trade and production. They will, however, if they undertake to put the individual phenomena in order and endeavour to establish more precisely those places in which this influence made itself especially noticeable, arrive again and again at raising a number of consumer groups above the others and denoting them as those which by a reshaping of their demand effected in reality the transformation of economic organisation in so far as goods demand became of importance as a result. These *revolutionary groups* were the following:

1. the rich;
2. the armies;
3. the ships builders;
4. the citizens of big cities;
5. the residents of the colonies.

I have in another place already followed the first of these in its activity as a former of consumption. Both my "studies", on luxury and capitalism (Sombart 1913c; 1967) and on war and capitalism (Sombart 1913b), took on the task of uncovering the extremely large influence which the lifestyle of the rich and the growing demand of the armies (including the fleets) exercised on the reshaping of goods demand in a direction beneficial to the development of capitalism. I could refer the reader to these investigations and dispense here with a treatment of these problems entirely. But by that a tangible hole would arise in the structure of this work, for which reason I consider it necessary to repeat here, at least in a short summary, the findings I arrived at in the named books. That forms the content of Chapter 48 to 50.

This repetition is also justified in that I have in various places corrected and in particular augmented the earlier explanations. Chapter 50 gets more substance from these new pages in that I have extended the demand for shipbuilding to include that of the merchant marine.

The reshaping which goods demand experienced through the big cities and the colonies, by contrast, are portrayed by me for the first time here in Chapter 51 and 52.

**

For a better understanding of the *taxonomy lying at the base of this work*, I note expressly that I am treating in this section only the problem of demand formation, and not yet that of market formation. These two problem complexes are, as need not be explained any further, indeed related, but are in no way the same — they do not portray congruent problem areas, but rather crosscutting ones. Whereas on the one hand the formation of demand must be appreciated under different points of view than its significance for market formation (for example, in its relation to capital formation), on the other hand market formation is dependent on yet other conditions than that of demand formation, which appears rather as just one of several preconditions for it. Hence I am treating here, where I am discussing the general foundations of modern capitalism, capital separately from demand formation, whilst I will discuss market formation, which forms a necessary component of the actual economic organisation, in that place where I systematically portray economic life in the age of early capitalism, which is in the next volume.

Chapter 48: Luxury Demand

I. The Concept and Origin of Luxury

Luxury is any expenditure which goes beyond the necessary. The concept is obviously a relational concept which only receives a tangible content when you know what is "necessary". To establish this, there are two possibilities — you can anchor it subjectively in a judgement of value (ethical, aesthetic, or whatever type)[543]. Or you can try to find some objective standard with which you can measure it. As such, the physiological needs of humans or those which can be called cultural needs offer themselves. The former only ever differs according to climate, the latter always according to the historical epoch. You have it in your hands to draw the boundary of cultural needs or of the necessities of the culture arbitrarily (but it is requested not to confuse this arbitrary act with the judgement mentioned above).

Luxury has then, however, a double meaning — it can be arranged quantitatively or qualitatively.

Luxury in the quantitative sense is equivalent to the "squandering" of goods — if you keep a hundred servants where one "suffices", or if you strike three matches at once to light the cigar. Luxury in the qualitative sense means the use of better goods, means a demand for fine things. Luxury in the quantitative and luxury in the qualitative sense can combine (and are in reality mostly combined).

Refinement is all the preparation of goods which is superfluous for the necessary fulfillment of their aims. Refinement can occur fundamentally in two directions — in the direction of material or that of form.

When you grasp refinement in an absolute sense, the great majority of all our consumer durables belong to the refined

goods — for almost all fulfill more than the (animal) necessities. You will hence also have to talk about a refined demand
in a relative sense, in that you describe the refinement beyond
the average in a given state of goods culture only as refinement in the narrower sense. We then call the refined demand
narrowly defined in such a way luxury demand — the goods
which serve to meet it, luxury goods in the narrower sense.

Luxury in the sense of refined demand and its satisfaction
serves very different aims and can thus also owe its existence
to very different motives — whether I consecrate a gold-ad-
orned altar or buy myself a silk shirt, both times I am pursuing luxury, but you feel immediately that these two acts are
worlds apart. You can perhaps call that consecration an ideal-
istic or even altruistic luxury, the latter purchase a materialistic or even egotistic luxury, in that you likewise distinguish
thereby purpose and motive.

We see both types of luxury developing in our epoch. But
far mightier in that period between Giotto and Tiepolo, which
we call the period of early capitalism, was the development of
the current of *materialistic luxury*. Its sources lie above all in
the development which the life of the state took on the one
hand — so far as a necessary accompanying symptom of the
absolute principality was the court of the prince which, as we
will soon see, was the most fertile ground for an extravagant
luxury — and in the development of wealth and the amassing
of large private means in the formation of the big city on the
other hand.

II. The Princely Court as the Focal Point
for the Development of Luxury

An important consequence and then also again a decisive
cause of the transformations which worked through the constitution of the state and the army at the end of the Middle
Ages was the emergence of larger princely courts in the sense
in which we use the word today.

Predecessors and models for the later development here
too, as in so many areas, were the princes of the church. Perhaps *Avignon* was the first "modern" court, because here for
the first time both groups of persons met up permanently and
set the tone which in the following centuries formed that

which is called court society — nobles without any other profession than serving the interests of the court, and beautiful women "souvent distinguées par les manières et l'esprit" [often distinguished by manners and wit]˙ who really left their mark on the life and activities. The significance of the Avignon episode lay above all in that here for the first time around the head of the Church the clerical grand seigneurs of almost all of Europe gathered and displayed their brilliance, as John XXII brought home to us vividly in the decretal Etsi deceat[544].

Directly following on from the brightly lit Avignon epoch in our imagination is the heyday of the papacy in *Rome* under the rule of the great Renaissance popes, Paul II to Leo X, who, ever surpassing one another, developed a life full of fervour and splendour.

The courts of the other princes of Italy vied with those of the popes. Understandably the features of this life developed in *Italy* earliest of all, because here the conditions were fulfilled earliest of all — decline of chivalry, "municipalisation" of the nobility, development of the absolute state, rebirth of the arts and sciences, society talents, greater wealth, etc.[545]

But the development of a modern court in the so much larger and mightier *France* became of decisive importance for the history of court society, it then becoming from the end of the 16th century and during the following two centuries the undisputed teacher in all matters concerning courtly life.

For the history of courtly luxury (just as for the history of the court overall), the fact that the French king also took up the inheritance of the Italian princes in all things which concerned how life was viewed and conducted became significant — Catherine de' Medici was the mediator, though already before her the House of Valois had in Charles VIII and Louis XII been applying its strong inclination towards Italian culture to its entire politics, as one knows.

With the entry of the French court into history — that is the decisive event — the external possibilities for a development of luxury grew in circumstances, as France was larger than the Italian principalities. The last Valois's were already

---

* [Tr.: not referenced by Sombart.]

spending on their household considerably more than even the richer states of Italy had in total public revenues[546].

In the year 1542, the total expenditure of the King of France (according to the report of Matteo Dandolo in Alberi (1839, 4:42-43)) ran to 5,788,000 livres (the livre had in the period 1541–1560 the metal value of 3.34 francs in present-day [1916] currency). Of that, the expenditure on luxury was 2,995,000 livres.

From Henry IV on the expenditure rose year on year — in the last period of the reign of Louis XIV the development reached its peak. The budgets for the years from 1680 to 1715 show approximately the same picture. I will arbitrarily select one year (1685)[547]. In it around 29 million francs were used for the personal, that is, overwhelmingly luxury expenditure of the king, with a total budget (gross) of 100,640,257 livres.

The sort of gigantic sums which flowed under such conditions to luxury businesses becomes even more clearly visible when you take a close look at individual expenditures.

At the top of course sits *luxury construction*.

In total the amount expended for royal buildings during the reign of Louis XIV was 198,957,579 l. 14 s. 11 d. (Guiffrey 1881)

(That is, since in this period the livre stood at between 1.22 and 1.63, around 300 million francs in present-day [1916] currency.)

We can gather how the expenditure was allocated to the individual posts from the compilations which Guiffrey (1881) has made in a commendable way.

Of the total amount, the expenditures were, for example:
- for purchases of manufactures and from dealers:
  ....1,730,206 l. 10 s. 2 d.
- for purchases of Gobelin manufactures (furniture):
  ....4,041,068 l. 2 s. 7 d.
- for large pieces of silver jewellery:
  ....2,245,289 l. 14 s. 10 d.
- for purchases of marble, lead, and tin:
  ....3,790,446 l. 16 s. 2 d.

The actual constructions are given for the first epoch (1664 to 1680) in detail in the total figures and show for the palaces of Versailles, Louvre and the Tuileries, St Germain, Fontainebleau, Vincennes, Trianon, Clagny, and Marly the total amount of 43,537,491 l. 16 s. 6 d.

What wealth and *what splendour developed in the furniture* of the royal palaces, we see now from the publication of the inventories, which is also richly adorned with illustrations. A count up results, for example, in that just in complete large woven wall hangings (tentures complètes) there were 334 present in the palaces of Louis XIV, which contained 2,600 carpets and 140 individual pieces, and that 822 pieces or 101 wall hangings (tenture) had been delivered there from the factories of Gobelin.

A few commissions from the year 1669 show the luxury which was pursued in furniture fabric[548]:

To the gentlemen Duc & Marsollier, merchants, for 64 ells of gold and silver brocade, at 138 l. 10 s. per ell, and for 44 ells gold and silver brocade, at 133 l. 5 s. per ell, which they delivered to His Majesty:	16,545 l. 5 s.
To the same for brocade from Lyon:	22,155 l.
To the same 7,070 l., namely: 4,090 l. for 62 ells of gold and silver brocade, violet seating of Lyon make, at 66 l. per ell, and 2,979 l. 10 s. for 259 ells of carmine red damask of Turin make, at 11 l. 10 s. per ell:	
To Mr Reynon for gold and silver brocade:	70,716 l. 18 s. 11 d.
To Mr Marcelin Charlier for velvet and brocade:	5,572 l. 5 s.

The *splendour of the garments* which were worn for show in the palaces was in accordance with the furnishing. You read the descriptions of the celebrations in the "Mercure galant" where an L. P. of the 17th century describes every individual toilette of court society in detail! Louis himself wore a garment which contained 14 million francs of diamonds.

When Louis one day inspected the lace manufacturing in Paris, he bought lace for 22,000 livres[549].

The luxury of clothing at the French court continued to rise incessantly during the 18th century and reached its high point a few years before the revolution. We are precisely informed about the clothes budget of Marie Antoinette[550]:

In the year 1773 the wardrobe money of the crown princess at the time amounted to 120,000 livres. This sum probably remained even later the budget as it were which, however, was exceeded year after year by greater sums. The outlay for toilette amounted to:

1780	194,118 l. 17 s.
1781	151,290 l. 3 s.
1782	199,509 l. 4 s.
1787	217,187 l. – s.

From then on the outlay fell back.

It is no accident, but rather, as I believe I have proven in my study "Luxury and Capitalism" (Sombart 1913c; 1967), a matter of course arising by necessity from the character of the entire form of the early capitalist societal culture that the development of luxury in the Ancien Regime reached its high point in the extravagant life of the great mistresses of the king. Madame de Pompadour directly possessed a representative significance for her time. She became with her taste mistress of the entire fashioning of life — "Nous ne vivons plus que par Mme de Pompadour. Carrosses à la Pompadour, habits en drap couleur à la Pompadour, [...] éventails, étuis, curedents à la Pompadour" [We no longer live except by Mme de Pompadour. Carriages ala Pompadour, clothes in coloured cloth ala Pompadour, [...] fans, cases, toothpicks ala Pompadour], a contemporary wrote[551]. Her expenditure on luxuries, however, reached figures as had never been known before. She spent in the 19 years of her rule demonstrably 36,327,268 livres for her personal needs[552].

The Comtesse du Barry was a match for the Marquise de Pompadour. According to the conscientious calculations of Le Roi, she consumed from the moment of her rise 12,481,804 livres essentially in the satisfaction of an eccentric demand for luxury. Of that 6,427,803 l. 11 d. was allotted to the orders to pay which she wrote out for the banker Baujon during the years of her rule (1769–1774).

The original bills are found among the manuscripts of the Bibliothèque nationale de France, 8157, 8158. They are mainly published in Goncourt and Goncourt (1878). See the excerpts I took from it in Sombart (1913c, 89 ff.; 1967, 74 ff.).

***

Through a short timespan the brilliance at the *Spanish* court perhaps put the French court in the shade — say from the opening up of the silver mines of Potosi and Guanaxuatos until the reign of Philip IV, Madrid was the scene of an unheard-of development of splendour, and the Spanish style became, as one knows, from then on often the dominant one. The revenues on which this pompous form of life rested were still significant under Philip III. According to the estimates of the Venetian envoy Tomaso Contarini, they amounted to 16 million ducats (thus about 150 million francs). The correctness of this estimate is confirmed by the results of an inquiry which Henry IV had carried out (in order to investigate the sources of help of his opponent); this came up with a (net) income of 15,658,000 ducats, whereas about 5 million more landed with the viceroys, tax collectors, etc. Certainly, a quite considerable part of these sums served for the payment of interest on the state's debt (which, however, also essentially stood the development of luxury in good stead, as we will yet see). So that, according to a list by the Count of Lerma from the year 1610, only 4,487,350 ducats remained at the disposal of the king, of which not even a million was used for holding court[553].

***

(In Western Europe) *England* followed directly behind France and Spain. Here the reign of the Stuarts, who indeed saw in the French kings their model, formed the high point of courtly splendour. We have a reflection of the splendour of the court under these princes in the pictures of van Dyck, Lely, and Huysmans, who painted the dandyish men and the proud, beautiful women in the glorious brocade and atlas garments with the heavy baroque folds. The descriptions of contemporaries, like the journals of Pepys contain, correspond very well to the image of complacent lust for life which the paintings of these artist evoke in us. It reminds us of the great Louis when we hear of Charles I who outfitted 24 castles so completely that he could travel from one to the other without burdening himself with luggage, or of James I who spent £93,278 for the wedding of his daughter, whereas we then catch sight again of the difference to France when we learn of how Charles II wistfully and humbly swore a promise to the House of Commons to in future be less extravagant than before so that he might have enough with his civil list for once. The respectable citizens may in such moments have seen their chance — a new world, the world in which the spirit of adequate respectability should reign, announced itself. But even the House of Orange loved the splendour of its court[554], and the House of Hanover emulated them in its first two representatives.

The sums over which the English kings disposed did not reach as far as those which Louis XIV extorted from the land — they were nonetheless considerable enough for that time and portray a quite considerable demand for luxury articles[555].

***

To describe the quite similar conditions in the courts of the *German* principalities, amongst whom Saxony, Hanover, and Württemberg were the most luxurious, or even in the *eastern* lands, has no purpose, since these courts strove to imitate the western states where possible.

III. Luxury in Society

The luxury which the court exhibited spread gradually across all the circles which looked to the court for their ideal or which stood somehow in relation to the court; but that was, as we can say confidently, all rich people, who were now gripped by the same striving for worldly splendour as reigned in the courtly circles.

We can follow exactly how an urge for luxury emanated directly from the kings, particularly from Louis XIV, whose influence on society is reported to us by a, in this question certainly irreproachable, eye witness as follows:

"Il aima en tout la splendeur, la magnificence, la profusion, il la tourna en maxime par politique et il l'inspira à toute sa cour. C'était lui plaire que de s'y jeter en tables, en habits, en équipages, en bâtiments, en jeu [...] C'est une plaie qui, une fois introduite, est devenu le cancer intérieur qui *ronge tous le particuliers*, parce que de la cour il s'est promptement communiqué à Paris, dans les provinces et les armées, où les gens en place ne sont contés qu'en proportion de leur table et de leurs magnificences [...] Par la folie des gens, elle va toujours croissant; les suites en sont infinies, et ne vont à rien qu'a la ruine et au renversement général."

[He loved splendour, magnificence, profusion in everything, he turned it into a maxim for policy and he inspired it in all his court. It was pleasing to him to throw himself into it in tables, in clothes, in carriages, in buildings, in games [...] It is a plague which, once introduced, became the inner cancer which *gnawed away at all individuals*, because from the court it was quickly communicated to Paris, to the provinces and the armies, where people are talked about only in proportion to their table and their magnificence [...] By the madness of the people, it is always increasing; the consequences are endless, and lead to nothing but ruin and general overthrow.] (Saint-Simon 1857, 12:465; 1889, 2:369)

One looked, especially in France, at the king as if at a god — Louis became arbiter of taste for Paris ("Paris — pour l'ordinaire singe de la

cour" [Paris — for the ordinary monkey of the court], per La Bruyêre[*]),
for the provinces, for Europe. The way Mansard built, the way Le Nôtre
laid out the gardens, the way Lebrun arrayed the furniture, the way
Rigaud painted — that was the way everyone whose means permitted it
built their houses, laid out their gardens, arranged their furniture, had
themselves painted. Not only in France! One knows it indeed.

But the process of secularisation would certainly not have
taken place so quickly, the development of luxury would not
have grown beyond measure in such a short time, if next to
the court another important source had not sprung up, from
which pursuit of pleasure, lust for life, and vain splendour
poured out over the world in a broad current — if an entire intensive need for luxury by the *nouveaux riche*, whose development we have gotten to know, had not broken out like a
devastating illness. We must now follow their influence on
the reshaping of lifestyle, above all their collaboration in the
quantitative expansion of the demand for luxury.

***

In history the path of wealth is described by just as many
stages of the development of luxury — from the first emergence of bourgeois upstarts onwards.

Diderot did not observe rightly when he expressed the opinion that
the groups who had become rich previously lived modestly in seclusion
and had only put their riches on show in his time; even if he believed he
could put a name to the one who was one of the first to show off his
wealth through the display of luxury — Bonnier.[†]

In Dante's time we are already encountering the extravagant upstarts — like that Jacopo Sant' Andrea who threw silver and gold
utensils into the river or set buildings on fire in order to heighten the
festive mood, there were a number who lived similarly and formed a
whole society of spendthrifts — the brigata godericcia or spendericcia
[company of pleasure-seekers or spendthrifts] (Alighieri 1876, Canto
XIII; 1867, 1:Canto XIII; Kostanecki 1912, 8 f.).

Diderot was not even correct for France. Or should we not count as
spendthrift that Jacques Coeur in the 15th century, the investor made
rich, who possessed palaces in Paris, Lyon, Tours, and seven other
places, should we not count the Semblançay, should we not count
Thomas Bohier, the builder of Chenonceaux, in the 16th century? Do we
want above all to forget the 17th century scoundrels made rich who, as
Louis XIV himself said, indulged in a *barefaced* luxury? The words
placed in Louis's mouth are extraordinarily instructive — he speaks of

---

*   [Tr.: work not referenced by Sombart.]
†   [Tr.: work not referenced by Sombart.]

"gens d'affaires, qui d'un côté couvrant toutes leurs malversations par toutes sortes d'artifices et les découvrant de l'autre par *un luxe insolent et audacieux*, comme s'ils eussent appréhendé de me les laisser ignorer" [men of business who on the one hand cover their embezzlement with all sorts of artifices and on the other expose them with *an insolent and daring luxury*, as if they were apprehensive of letting me ignore them] (!) (Louis XIV 1860, 2:376; cited in Baudrillart 1880, 4:68)

Finally Fouquet, the supercrook, also belonged to this sort; he, who wasted 20–30 million francs for the purpose of luxury (of which 18 million francs were for his castle in Vaux alone), as Colbert (who, by the way, himself in no way spurned expenditure in the grand style) worked out with outrage in his expose over Fouquet*.

And had Diderot utterly forgotten the wonderful type who had a hundred years before him made his greater predecessor immortal in the 'Bourgeois gentilhomme'† first acted in 1670?

We can follow quite precisely the intimate connection between the rise of the commoners and the expansion of the demand for luxury if we keep in mind the stages in which the people, quos virtus aut fortuna e faece hominum extulit [whom virtue or fortune has plucked out of the dregs of men][556], appear in larger numbers. These stages form just as many layers in the construction of modern luxury — in which we can thus in that way distinguish in the history of wealth the Italian epoch of the 14th, 15th, and 16th centuries, the German of the 15th and 16th centuries, the Spanish-Dutch of the 17th century, and the French-English of the 18th century.

The enormous jerk forwards which the European peoples made in the direction of "prosperity" and above all good living always had the greatest significance for our investigation. The decisive change in European society probably just consisted in that at the time luxury caught hold in ever widening circles. We can, for example, see that from the housekeeping books, of which many are preserved from that time — one felt about the middle of the 18th century in the upper strata the distance from the 17th century just as distinctly in the rich lands as we Germans feel perhaps that of the present time to the years before 1870: "on a bien de la peine à s'entretenir aujourd'hu avec ce qui reste" [it is very difficult to converse today with what remains][557] — such complaints greet us often. And we will not wonder about the opinions arising in them

---

*   [Tr.: not referenced by Sombart.]

†   [Tr.: 'The Bourgeois Gentleman', a satirical comedy by Molière.]

when we learn that a large part of the great means which were obtained in that period[558] were wasted in luxury expenditure. D'Epinay spent 1,500,000 livres during 1751–1755. Roussel wasted 12 million, Dupin de Chenonceaux 7–8, Savalette 10, Bouret 40. The Count of Artois, neighbour of the rich Feventenès, suggested, "Je voudrais bien faire passer chez moi un bras de ruisseau d'or qui coule de son rocher" [I would like to bring to my house an arm of a golden stream flowing from its rock]. "On ne fit plus de capitaux" [We don't make any more capital]. One went in for "luxury" instead — in furniture, buildings, clothes. The warehouses of the Rue St Honoré, which at the time supplied the most beautiful materials to France and overseas, were emptied in a few days in the year 1720 when the golden rain poured down over Paris. "On n'y trouve plus de velours, d'étoffes d'or; mais on fabrique partout" [One no longer finds velvet, gold material; but we manufacture everywhere]. Du Hautchamp*, to whom we owe these descriptions, describes for us the view of the streets which were filled by dresses in the most various colours, decorated with glorious embroidery made from gold and silver fabric.

And everywhere the same picture. Thus Defoe tells us about *England*: "This is an age of gallantry and gaitey and never was the city transpos'd to the court as it is now: the play-houses and balls are now fill'd with citizens and young tradesmen instead of gentlemen and families of distinction [...] 'tis an age of drunkness and extravagances [...] 'tis an age of luxurious and expensive living"[559].

***

One point which seems to me to be of great and general significance for the development of modern society is the fact now that the rich upstarts who possessed nothing but their money, who had only the power of wealth and no other characteristic feature which they could display other than the ability to lead a luxuriant life with their great means; that these parvenus also shared their materialistic and mammonistic world view with the old noble families whom they thereby dragged with them into the whirlpool of good living. I have in

---

* [Tr.: Sombart provides no further details, but possibly from Marmont Du Hautchamp (1739).]

the section of this work which concerns means formation cited the impoverishment of the nobility as one of the sources of enrichment for the bourgeois investor and have shown there how this process of transformation of feudal means into bourgeois means took place incessantly after the Crusades in all the lands of Europe. Here it must be added now that one of the most frequent causes for why the old families became poor and why homines, quos fortuna e faece extulit [men whom fortune has plucked out of the dregs] took their place was the pressure to match those bourgeois show-offs in expenditure on luxury — this denial of the old, noble traditions led either to economic downfall of the old families or to the 'honteuses alliances' [disgraceful alliances] with the enriched barons of finance with which the period is filled — the connecting link in this development which interests us at this point was mostly *the secularisation, the materialisation of the noble families*. That the 'Subiti guadagni' [earnings immediately] of the Turcarets brought forth this effect — and they are above all guilty of this change which was certainly supported by the influence of the court, as we have already seen — it seems to me, as stated, to be an event of quite special consequence.

We meet this fateful inclination of the nobility to keep step with the moneybags in the display of luxury in all lands and at all times in which the bourgeois wealth suddenly increases in extent[560].

But to what extent now the entire upper strata of society, thus in essence the old and new nobility and high finance who were themselves as tightly bound with the nobility as the latter were with them, was gripped especially in the 18th century by a seeming frenzy of pleasure which expressed itself in the most insane display of luxury is indeed generally well-known. The judgements of contemporaries confirms it quite enough[561].

That and how luxury extended to all regions of the demand for goods is made apparent most easily by a few specific references which shall remind us of well-known things.

1. Luxury Dining

This was developed in *Italy* during the 15th and 16th centuries when a "culinary art" arose there next to the other arts. Previously there had only been luxury binging — now one refined this enjoyment and set quality in place of quantity.

Luxury dining also wandered from Italy to *France*, where it received its real cultivation from the end of the 16th century. To follow it in its development is barely possible without writing a long treatise over the preparation of meals which would not fit in the framework of this investigation.

A look in the "Gourmet Almanacs" suffices to recognise that at the end of the 18th century gastronomy had already reached its highpoint which it could not exceed anymore.

A great importance for the course of economic life was won by the increasing use of tropical products as *stimulants* — thus coffee, cocoa, tea, and with these and through them sugar, as well as tobacco. To begin with all these stimulants, perhaps with the exception of tobacco, remained limited to the circle of the well off who, however, quickly developed a great power of consumption until when, towards the end of our epoch, these goods entered more and more into the sphere of demand of the great masses.

The following figures give an approximately correct idea of the extent of the consumption of the most important stimulants in the past centuries.

The amount of *tea* consumed in *Great Britain* was:

1668	100 lb
1711	141,992 lb
1730	537,016 lb
1760	2,293,613 lb
1784	8,608,473 lb
1785	13,165,715 lb
1786	13,985,506 lb

The figures were obtained by extraction of the export figures from the quantities sold by the East-India Company according to the information in their reports. The sudden increase in use from 1784 to 1785 is connected with the reduction in the duty by Pitt from 119 to 12½ percent (McCulloch 1880, 1377 ff.).

The *coffee* consumption of *Europe* amounted (according to Alexander von Humboldt!) around the year 1800 to about 70,000,000 kilograms; the population of Europe ran (according to Beloch*) at the same time to about 120,000,000, thus at the time already about one pound of coffee would have been allotted per year to every living European; you could say that this stimulant began thereby to become a mass consumer item. In the year 1910 each German in the empire also consumed about six pounds of coffee annually.

Coffee use in *England* ran to:

1790	973,111 lb
1795	1,054,588 lb
1800	826,590 lb

See McCulloch (1880, 326). Admittedly, England has never been a land of coffee consumption.

22,500,000 kilograms of *sugar* shall (likewise by Humboldt) have been consumed in *Europe* at the time, 3–4 pounds per head of population.

The following figures resting on more precise investigations might serve to enlarge on Humboldt's estimate.

France in the year 1788 used 21,300 tonnes with a population of 23.6 million, that is 0.906 kg per head of population (Montvéran 1833, 96; cf. McCulloch 1880, 1337).

In *Great Britain*, sugar consumption rose during the 18th century as follows:

1700	10,000 t.
1710	14,000 t.
1734	42,000 t.
1754	53,270 t.
1770–75 on average	72,500 t.
1786–90 on average	81,000 t.

See McCulloch (1880, 1339). That would thus result for the end of the 18th century in a consumption of about 10 kilograms per head of population.

Tobacco consumption finally in *Great Britain*, for which we always possess the most reliable figures, had towards the end of the 18th century climbed to 8–10 million pounds — in 1789 8.2, in 1795 10.9, in 1800 11.8 million pounds (McCulloch 1880, 1397).

Luxury drinking of course kept pace with the development of luxury dining, and we can gauge that especially in the *consumption of wine* (in lands that did not produce wine). It may suffice to share the figures for *Great Britain* where the consumption especially of high alcohol wines (port! Cape wines!) took on a grand scale during the 18th century which was only overtaken late in the course of the 19th century. In the year 1789 there remained for home consumption:

French wine	234,299 gallons
other wine	5,580,366 gallons
in total	5,814,665 gallons

---

*   [Tr.: presumably in Beloch (1895).]

See McCulloch (1880, 1526–36). The yield from the duties to which this wine was subject amounted to £721,518.

The refinement of luxury dining had important consequences for the development of capitalism in that now an ever more refined *luxury in crockery and glassware* as well as in *tablecloths* and *cutlery*, etc. was conducted.

2. Luxury Clothing[562]

Luxury clothing was pursued in a way of which we can even today barely form a correct picture. It was a characteristic of seigneurial life which was popular even in the circles of the bourgeois rich that even the men clothed themselves with magnificent garments made of velvet, silk, gold embroidery, and lace, and that even the toilette of ladies was oversown to a far greater extent than today with precious things.

We are best informed about the luxury clothing of the 15th and 16th centuries by the wardrobe inventories of which a whole series are preserved for us — thus from that of Valentina and Elisabetta Visconti, of Bianca Maria Sforza, of Lucrezia Borgia, amongst others. Lucrezia, for example, had in her trousseau 50 dresses in brocade, velvet with embroidery and lace — 150 mules carried her dresses and linen when she left Rome (Polifilo 1903).

For all periods artworks offer us a good source to gauge clothing luxury, just as do descriptions of festivals, processions, etc. Thus, for example, Burcardus* in his diary of the entry of Prince Federigo of Naples into Rome (in 1492) draws the following picture: "The individuals rode absolutely magnificent horses, all dressed in gold brocade, gems of great value on the chest, on the birettas and hats. The prince wore a garment of purple velvet, the necklace of pearls and jewels at a value of 6,000 ducats, a belt along with sword of the same value, the entire reins set with pearls and precious stones to a value of 3,000 ducats, and the whole harness gilded front and back."

The Renaissance garb rose into the baroque garb, the latter refining itself into the rococo. We know how, for example, in England in the 17th century the elegant clothing of the cavaliers was seen precisely as a sign of class. At the time the reigning mode had an especially pronounced elegance — the tall riding boots were lined with expensive materials and set with lace. Even the clothes of men consisted for the great part of heavy silk and velvet materials. Van Dyck!

And what an outlay was made! The Duke of Buckingham possessed (in 1625) 27 expensive suits of velvet, silk, lace, pearls, etc., of which each had cost about 35,000 francs. The ceremonial suit in which he appeared at the wedding of Charles I had swallowed the amount of

---

*   [Tr.: probably a reference to Johann Burchard's *Liber Notarum*.]

500,000 francs. (Weiß[*]) A nobleman and his wife in the 17th century in France spent an entire third of their income for clothing; for toilette and equipage almost half — 5,000 livres of 12,000. From a letter of Mme de Maintenon to her brother from 25th September 1679; cf. Houzé de l'Aulnont (1889, 51, 116).

In the 18th century clothing luxury rose still further — it went more into finery, into refinement. The average price of the elegant gentleman's suit was 1,200–1,500 livres. Anyone who took pride in themselves had 6 summer and 6 winter suits. Festive clothes of men cost up to 15,000 livres. Fine gray cloth: 70–80 livres per ell (Barbier[†]).

Even the *luxury in fine underclothes* developed rapidly. "L'on doit avoir esgard à ce qui couvre le corps" [We must have regard to what covers the body], it said in the *Lois de la galanterie* [laws of gallantry] appearing in 1644, "et qui n'est pas seulement estably pour le cacher et le garder du froid, mais encore pour l'ornement. Il faut avoir le plus beau linge et le plus fin que l'on pourra treuver. L'on ne sçauroit estre trop curieux de ce qui approche si prés de la personne" [and which is made not only for hiding it [the body] and keeping it from the cold, but also for ornament. You have to have the most beautiful and finest linen you can find. One cannot be too curious about what comes so close to the person] (Sorel 1644, § 10). We are informed over the extraordinary extent of an elegant provision of underclothes in the 17th century by Garsault (1771). See the lists in Rogers-Miles (1910, 83 f.).

A quite special care was then dedicated, particularly in the 18th century, to "fashion accessories", thus hats, bonnets, etc. "La dépense des modes excède aujourdhui celle de la table et celle des équipages" [the expense of fashion nowadays exceeds that of the table and the carriage], writes Mercier (1782, 2:203).

The author of *The Complete English Tradesman* became very indignant over the common "beau" of his time, "our nicer gentleman", "the ordinary beau" wore shirts of linen at 10 or 12 shillings per ell and changed them twice a day! In his grandfather's day they were content with Dutch linen that was half as dear and changed their shirt perhaps twice a week (Defoe 1726, 2:328).

3. Residential Luxury

The development of residential luxury stands in close connection with the development of the big city. It is this which essentially fostered the luxury of residences and furnishings as became more and more popular from the Renaissance on, but particularly from the end of the 17th century. It did it on the one hand through the restriction of the living space which had to arrive by necessity in consequence of the massing to-

---

[*]   [Tr.: no further details on the reference provided by Sombart.]
[†]   [Tr.: no further details on the reference provided by Sombart.]

gether of large masses of people in one place; on the other hand by the restriction of the personally flavoured luxury which likewise had to appear as soon as the seigneur took up his residence in the city. These internal and external restrictions which the lifestyle of the rich people experienced in the city now led, however, if I may express myself thus, to an intensification of luxury which on the one hand was objectified and on the other hand refined. What luxury dining experienced — the raising by perfection of cooking technique — the residential luxury likewise experienced in the big city — in the place of giant, empty castles appeared smaller city residences, but filled with a growing quantity of precious objects — the palatial was detached from the palace.

This, shall we say, civic way of living now was then, however, transferred to the country — the country houses fitted out with civic elegance arose — the "villas" which are thus (just as in antiquity) the direct consequence of city life. With that luxury penetrated into the most distant parts of the land, which even at this point was subjugated to the big city and its conditions of life.

When we read the descriptions of the city and country houses of the rich people of perhaps Frances and England which their contemporaries in the 17th and 18th centuries drew up for us[563], we think at first that it is all exaggeration. Until we become aware through the amassing of numerous judgements all alike that residential luxury in that period must have actually reached an extent which, even seen from the standpoint of our showy time, was quite enormous. We recall then the remains of the glorious baroque and rococo furniture which we see for sale today with the antique dealers, recall the images of pieces of furniture from that time in art history and consider that all that which we see now only as individual items — reproduced or in reality — that all that once stood together and filled the spaces of the marquises and the finance barons of the Ancien Régime.

4. Luxury in the City

The big city raised the tendency towards luxury — the best observers of those days, like Montesquieu in France, Mandeville in England, confirm it for their time expressly, and we can deduce it from numerous symptoms.

How the big city with its luxury demand began to influence the people in the provinces at the time in their life habits quite decisively, to accommodate them to luxury expenditure, to "wind up" their living standard, is brought before our eyes vividly by a landed noble, Pierre de Cadet, in the following story which he wrote down in his housekeeping book: "Mon grand-père voulut aller à Paris et dans un an il dépensa 14,000 livres, ce qui fit dire à son père qu'une paire de lunettes, qu'il luy apporta en present, lui coûtoit 14,000 livres. Il y avoit déjà un équipage dans la maison et quatre chevaux blancs; mon grand père vint de Paris avec un grand goût pour les chevaux de main [...] Il avoit amené de Paris un valet de chambre, duquel son père disoit, en badiment, qu'il n'osoit lui demander à boire, le voyant mieux vêtu que luy." [My grandfather wanted to go to Paris and in a year he spent 14,000 pounds, which made his father say that a pair of glasses which he brought him as a present cost him 14,000 pounds. There was already a carriage in the house and four white horses; my grandfather came from Paris with a great taste for horses [...] He had brought from Paris a valet, of whom his father said, in banter, that he dared not ask him for a drink, seeing him better dressed than he was.] (Ribbe 1889, 167)

The reasons for this phenomena are easy to recognise if you keep an eye on the social structure of the big cities in the age of early capitalism[564].

When we ask what had made these cities big, then we still find in essence the same *city formers* at work as during the Middle Ages. Also (and particularly!) the big cities of the early capitalist epoch were consumption cities to an outstanding degree. The big consumers are well-known to us — the princes, the spiritual lords, the grandees — and to them now a new, important group was added: high finance (which you may with reason insert as "consumers", certainly without by any means wanting to do harm to their "productive" function in the economic organism). The biggest cities are thus so large because they are the seats of the biggest (and most of the) consumers; the expansion of the city bodies was thus essentially owed to a concentration of the consumers in the civic centres of the land.

The city formers, however, were almost all people who wanted to amuse themselves, for whom it was above all about spending their money in a way that increases the stimulus of life. Their condensed living together caused them to outbid each other in luxury and expense, so that an incentive to further extravagance grew from each extravagant action.

428

But the big city was significant for the development of luxury above all in that it created entire new possibilities for amusing and luxuriant lifestyles and with it *new forms of luxury*. It transferred the festivities, which up to then the courtiers had celebrated alone in the castles of the princes, to broad layers of the population who now likewise created their places where they regularly followed their pleasures. When at the end of the 18th century the Prince of Monaco after the death of the Duke of York at his residence came to London at the invitation of the king and saw in the evening the many lights on the streets and in the windows of the shops which were opened until 10 o'clock, he imagined all the lights had been organised in his honour — this anecdote reflects wonderfully the fundamental transformation which certainly only began to take place around that time — into the place of the strictly private display of luxury a sort of collective form of luxury stepped. The communication of lifestyle which is then quite peculiar to the following period of political economy begins — we take notice of that here briefly and establish that this significant effect of the big city — owing to which its mention belongs in this place — temporarily moved entirely within the bounds of luxury demand so that only the uppermost peaks of society were touched by the innovation.

What matters here is the following in particular:

1. The theatre, above all the elegant opera houses which were first built in Italy with the display of great splendour and then likewise found a place in the other big cities of Europe.

   The 1737 built theatre of San Carlo in *Naples* was epoch making in the history of theatre building. In *Paris* the opera, under the name of Académie royale de Musique, which from the death of Molière gave its performances in the Palais royale, existed from 1673; the Comédie française, which opened its new house in the Rue S. Germain des Prés on the 18th April 1689; and the Comédie italienne which played in the Hôtel de Bourgogne (with an interruption from 1697–1716) (Léris 1754, XX ff.). Cf. Du Casse (1862) (essentially literary history).

   At first it was mostly only court theatre to which outside the court itself only an invited audience had entry; the houses were gradually opened to everyone who paid their entrance money. But even then the better theatres were for a long time yet exclusively the rendezvous place of the upper layers of society to whom here a new opportunity was offered for flirting and displaying their position. For the *London* of the 17th century, see *The Character of a Town-gallant* (Anonymous 1675). Excerpts from that in Savine (1908, 130 ff.). Cf. also Zetzner (1913, 674).

Capon judged of Paris that the Royal Academy of Music and Dance, respectively the opera, was nothing other than a "maison publique pour gentilhommes" [public house for gentlemen].

2. The public *music halls and ballrooms* (as we would say today) which were first (it seems) erected in London with every expense and were admired because of their elegance by all Londoners and particularly by foreigners.

London must have been a true sink of iniquity in the 17th and 18th centuries. Already at the beginning of the 17th century it was full of the most luxuriant and lascivious public pleasure houses of the grand style. See, for example, the memorable descriptions of the above-mentioned Zetzner (1913, chap. 6). And during the 18th century it got even worse, as all travellers reported in agreement. Cf. also Defoe and Richardson (1778, 2:92-93).

Next to the theatres and concert halls lay:

3. The *fine restaurants*, the taverns — in the 17th and 18th centuries likewise still a speciality of *London* which, for example, was envied by the Parisians for these establishments.

In the excellent restaurants, and in the salons particuliers [private salons] which were connected to them, the expenditure was so great "that he as it were corrected the bon mot of the famed Beaumarchais who, as familiar as he also was with the feasting in Paris, was nevertheless astonished over the delights of London and claimed that in one winter evening in the brothels and taverns of London more would be consumed than the seven united provinces needed for their sustenance in six months (Archenholtz*).

Incidentally, fine restaurants were also by no means lacking in Paris in the 18th century — the "most chic" were those of the Palais royale, like Beauvilliers, Huré, or the Taverne anglaise. The situation in the Palais royale, the meeting point of the "playboy set", reveals their character.

4. The *luxury hotels*.

In *London* the Savoy Hotel, which stood in the same place where the well-known hotel of the same name rises today, was

---

* [Tr.: presumably a reference to one of the works of Johann Wilhelm von Archenholz, of which several concerned England.]

famous. What sort of thing it was, such a hotel in an aristocratic world, is indicated to us today by the Hôtel des Réser-
voirs in *Versailles*. The oldest luxury hotel in Europe was
surely the "Tavern of the Bears" (Locanda dell' Orso) in Rome
which had existed since the time of Sixtus IV.

There was now, however, yet another place where the
growing big city developed a public, open-to-all luxury, which was the place where the elegant world tended to buy its luxury goods; we must hence mention:

5. the *shops* to which from the middle of the 18th century
    more and more care was devoted, which from that
    time began to be embellished — a fact which called
    forth the head shaking of such stolid people as Daniel
    Defoe[565].

IV. The General Development Tendencies
of Luxury Consumption

The observation of the actual form of luxury in the various
centuries gives us the insight that luxury consumption underwent definite transformations which, because they, following
from definite, constant causes, took course in the same direction, we can describe as general development tendencies of
luxury consumption. Mind you, of the luxury in this quite
specific historical period, say from 1200 to 1800, is such as
there has only been a single time in world history. All endeavours to form general epochs of luxury, as perhaps Roscher attempted, will have to remain unsuccessful.

The causes producing those development tendencies lie
enclosed in the general structure of society and are well-
known to us. I attach a quite special significance to the increasing dominance of the woman or, as I have called the woman who has an effect here, the little woman. Next to that the
advancing municipalisation of lifestyle also exercised a determining influence precisely on the transformation of luxury
consumption[566].

The development tendencies which I single out, however,
are the following:

1. The *tendency to domestication.* Most medieval luxury
    was public, now it became private; it had also, how-
    ever, been displayed far more outside the house than
    in the house — now it was transferred more and more

into the house, into the domestic sphere — the woman brought it in for herself.

Formerly (still in the time of the Renaissance) tournaments, shows of splendour, processions, and public hospitality — now luxury in the house. With that, luxury lost its periodic character which it formerly had and became constant. Needless to say how much an increase in luxury demand was connected with this change.

2. The *tendency to objectification*. We can detect that the luxury of our period still bore a strongly personal and with it a quantitatively directed character, and can establish that here its seigneurial origin is to be recognised, since this strong valuation of numerous servants was a remnant of the old loyal retainers. the personal character to the display of luxury, however, had now indubitably become incessantly weaker since the Middle Ages. Formerly luxury exhausted itself many times in the contingents of numerous satellites, in catering to them and entertaining them with festivities, etc. Now the numerous servants was only an accompanying symptom to the ever growing use of tangible goods for the aims of luxury. In this objectification, as I call the process, the woman especially had an interest. For the calling up of numerous followers does you less benefit than the more splendid clothing, the more comfortable residence, the more precious jewellery. Economically this change is again extremely significant — Adam Smith would say you shift from "unproductive" to "productive" luxury because the former personal luxury occupies "unproductive" hands, the objectified luxury by contrast "productive" hands (in the capitalist sense — that is, wage labourers in a capitalist enterprise). In fact the objectification of luxury demand is of foundational significance for the development of capitalism.

Hand in hand with this objectification of luxury, however, went what was demanded by the little woman with particular energy:

3. The *tendency to sensualisation and refinement*.

As tendency to sensualisation, I see that development which has the effect that luxury serves less and less some ideal basic human value (like art in particular) and more and more the lower instincts of animality. When that process takes place which the Goncourts once described thus: "la protection de l'art tombe aux ciseleurs de bronzes, aux sculpteurs du bois, aux brodeurs, aux couturières" [the protection of art falls to chisellers of bronze, sculptures of wood, embroiders, couturiers]*, etc. They wanted thereby to mark the difference of the Du Barry epoch from the Pompadour time. It seems to me that this — pointless to say, economically on the other hand quite prominently important — change characterised more the passing from the 17th to the 18th century, thus the victory of the rococo over the baroque. This victory, however, signifies nothing more than the final and complete triumph of feminine culture. The victorious little woman radiates to us from all the creations of art and the arts and crafts of this time — from pier glasses and Lyon cushions, sky blue silk cushions with white net curtains, from pale blue petticoats, gray silk stockings, and pink silk dresses, from coquettes, dressing gowns trimmed with swan down, ostrich feathers with Brabant lace, which then everything, as Richard Muther, that incomparable describer of the rococo from whom the preceding words are taken, expressed it, composed a paternoster into a "symphony of the salon".

Standing in the closest connection with the tendency towards sensualisation of luxury was the tendency towards its refinement. Refinement means increasing the expenditure on living work with the production of a tangible good, means penetration, saturation of the material with more work (as far as the refinement does not exist in the use only of rarer materials).

4. The *tendency towards crowding together* — in time namely. Be it that much luxury was displayed within a given time — many objects were used, many pleasures

---

* [Tr.: presumably a reference to Edmond & Jules Goncourt.]

were tasted — be it that earlier periodic luxury events now became constant arrangements — annual festivals turned into regularly recurring festivities, processions on jubilee days turned into daily masquerades, feasts on sacred days and keg benders turned into everyday dinners and suppers — be it (on which I would like to place particular emphasis) that the "luxury goods" were produced in a shorter time in order to be able to serve their possessor more rapidly.

The rule in the Middle Ages was the long production time — years and decades were laboured on *one piece*, on *one work* — they were in no hurry to be completed. You also lived so long because you lived in a whole — the church, the monastery, the borough, the family would certainly experience completion, even if the individual person who had commissioned the work had long since rotted. How many families did building work on the Certosa of Pavia! The Milanese family of Sacchi had worked during three centuries, through eight generations, on the inlays of the altarpiece. Every cathedral, every monastery, every town hall, every castle of the Middle Ages gave witness to this bridging of the lifetimes of individual people — their origin stretched through families who believed in living for eternity.

Once the individual had torn himself out of the community which outlasted him, *his* lifetime became the measure of his enjoyment. The individual wants to live as if he himself experiences as much as possible over the change in things. Even a king has become too much for himself — he wants to reside himself in the castle which he began to build. And when even the lords of this world now transferred this world to the little woman, then the tempo in which the means for satisfaction of luxury demand were brought was quickened. The woman cannot wait. The man in love, however, not at all.

What a change in the character of life — Maria de' Medici had the Luxembourg Palace completed in the unheard-of short time of five years (Lübke 1868, 227).

The Palace of Versailles was worked on day and night: "Pour Versailles, il y a deux ateliers de charpentiers, dont l'un travaille le jour et l'autre la nuit" [for Versailles, there are two workshops of carpenters, one works during the day and the other at night], Colbert tells us himself (Clément 1861, 8:XLV). The Count of Artois had Château de Bagatelle rebuilt from the ground up so that he could give the queen a festivity there, and employed 900 workers day and night — when it did not go quick enough for him, he sent his bailiffs onto the country road to intercept stone and chalk wagons.

5. The *tendency for change*, which signifies thus the progressive *dominance of fashion*, that "general concept for a complex of temporally valid cultural forms", as Friedrich Vischer has fittingly defined it.

The *sources* for the *history of fashion* are very numerous. Most of the works about luxury come into consideration, since this has always been subordinated to fashion. A special source are the "fashion" magazines that appeared from the end of the 17th century — like the Mercure galant (later Mercure de France) from 1672, which admittedly was more a general magazine for the elegant world than a fashion magazine; the Journal des Luxus und der Moden [Journal of Luxury and Fashions], published by F.J. Bertuch and G.M. Kraus, from 1786; the Journal für Fabrik, Manufaktur, Handlung und Mode [Journal for Mills, Manufacturing, Trade, and Fashion], from 1794; the Leipzig Modemagazin [Fashion Magazine] for the latest in art, taste, fashion, the enjoyment of life, etc., published by Gruber and Berrin, from 1796; amongst others.

But also to be consulted are almost all comedies of manners, and the rich literature of memoirs. A rich source are works like The Spectator (1710–1714), and Mercier (1782), and the like.

The *literature* on the other hand is sparse. As far as I am able to judge, the best writings are those of the 18th century which you can almost still describe as primary sources. Unsurpassed to-date is the first part of Garve (1792), as well as the article on fashion in Krünitz's encyclopedia (1803). A series of essays on fashion and luxury in the Schlesische Provinzialblätter (Anonymous 1803) are also quite superb.

More recently the aesthetic side of fashion has experienced a stimulating treatment by Vischer (1888), and the social-psychological by Simmel (1905). I have attempted to illuminate the economic significance of fashion in Sombart (1902b). The literature stimulated by it, e.g. the content rich, rector's address of Walter Troeltsch does not belong here since it describes the role which luxury plays in the epoch of high capitalism.

A few contributions to the history of fashion are contained in Neuburger (1913).

For economic life, there are two necessary accompanying symptoms of each fashion which are to be primarily considered:

1. the changeability produced by it, but likewise what is commonly ignored,
2. the standardisation effected by it of the form of demand.

When we think of a form of demand which is independent of fashion, the length of use for the individual items of consumption would probably be longer, and the diversity of the individual consumer goods probably considerably greater. Each fashion always forces a great number of persons to standardise their demand, just as it forced them to change it earlier than the individual consumer, were he independent, would have considered to be necessary. Both, standardisation and change are relative concepts. When in particular the latter, for example, makes the "garb" turn into "fashion" is difficult to define precisely in time. You may say that every change in taste which leads to a transformation in demand during the lifetime of a generation is "fashion".

If we thus are taught that a population has "given up the customs of their fathers" and wears clothes and hair differently than them, then we can conclude from that with some certainty that in that time a "fashion" had not yet dominated. That was in the early and high Middle Ages probably the reigning condition, and the conclusions which Raumer draws from a source of the 11th century, as if at the time changes in fashion were already existing, appears to me inadmissible[567].

In contrast, fashion seems to arrive with the secularisation of lifestyles, with the increasing consumption of luxuries out of sensuous intention, as a necessary accompanying symptom. At least we already find it widespread in the Italian 15th and 16th centuries, even if still in battle with the "traditional garb" as far as clothing comes into consideration. Above all we are also told about a rapid change in fashion which shall have taken place many times in a year.

Pontano (1520, 1:71) writes of Italy, "quanquam mutari vestes sic quotidie videamus, ut quas *quarto ante mense* [!] in deliciis habebamus, nunc repudiemus et tanquam veteramenta abjiciamus" [nevertheless we see that our clothes are changed every day, so that we now reject those which we had in luxury in *four months ago*[!], and cast them off as old things]. Cited in Burckhardt (1860, 366; 1878, 2:125). See there for yet more evidence.

In the *France* of the Valois it did not look any different, as the sharp-eyed Montaigne lets us know:

> "nostre changement est si subit et si prompt en cela [cut of clothes], que l'invention de touts les tailleurs du monde ne sçaurait fournir assez de nouvelletez, il est force que bien souvent les formes mesprisées reviennent en credit, et celles là mesmes tumbent en mespris tantost aprez; et qu'un mesme jugement prenne en l'espace de quinze ou vingt ans deux ou trois, non diverses seulement, mais contraires opinions, d'une inconstance et legiereté incroyable."

> [our change of fashions is so prompt and sudden that the inventions of all the tailors in the world cannot furnish out new whim-whams enough, there will often be a necessity that the old despised ones must again come in vogue, and again fall into contempt; and that the same judgment must, in the space of fifteen or twenty years, take up not only different, but contrary, opinions, with an incredible lightness and inconstancy.]

> (Montaigne 1820, 2:174-175; 1842, 138)

Likewise in *England* at the same time, the change in fashions was already becoming a "social evil" which five statutes in the years from 1511 to 1570 were tasked with battling (Unwin 1904, 71 ff.).

A very droll lecture against the fashion devil, which was also at work in *Germany,* is found in the 1565 second edition of *Schulrecht wider den Hoffahrts-teufel**. There it says:

> "Who wants to or could surely number the various wondrous and strange patterns and types of clothing with men and women which have in 30 years risen and fallen again. Of coats, cloaks, furs, corsets, skirts, caps, cape collars, hats, boots, jackets, petticoats, doublets, Harz capes, shirts, collars, bibs, trousers, shoes, etc., etc. Then it would have to be Polish, Bohemian, Hungarian, Turkish, French, Welsh, English, Nuremberg, Brunswick, Frankish, Saxon,

---

* [Tr.: lit. "school rules against the haughtiness devil" — further details on this work have not been found.]

short, long, narrow, wide, simple, pleated, right for one and two, trimmed, adorned with frills, beaded, twisted, with fringes, with knots, entire, cut up, lined, unlined, stuffed, with arms, without arms, plucked, pushed, embroidered, with carvings, without carvings, with lost arms, colourful, creased, etc., etc."

The "correspondent" who offered this piece to the *Journal des Luxus und der Moden*, entitled their article "It was otherwise the same", and closed with the words: "C'était tout comme chez nous" [It was entirely like with us] (Anonymous 1787, 169 ff.). Nonetheless we will perceive differences not only between the 16th and the 20th, but also between the 16th and 18th centuries in the treatment of fashion — we need only open a "costume" book from the 16th century to see how at the time fashion and traditional costume were still fighting for dominance over clothing.

The actual age of fashion, I think, begins though really with Louis XIV who also made France the centre for fashionable taste for two centuries. It is probably only the expression of an inner development when in the year 1672 the first *fashion magazine* (the Mercure galant, the later Mercure de France) was founded, which was called to take the place of the former costume books in the literature. "La mode presse" [the fashion press], La Bruyère said of this time in which one fashion was already chasing after another. "Une mode a à peine détruit une autre mode, qu'elle est abolie par une plus nouvelle, qui cède elle-même à celle qui la suit et qui ne sera pas la dernière; telle est notre légèreté" [A fashion has scarcely destroyed another fashion than it is abolished by a newer one, which yields itself to that which follows it and which will not be the last; such is our fickleness][568].

And now just the 18th century! Its lifestyle was — take note always firstly of the luxury consumers![569] — in no way different from our own. "Une femme qui quitte Paris pour aller passer six mois à la campagne en revient aussi antique que si elle s'y étoit oubliée trente ans. Le fils méconnaît le portrait de sa mère, tant l'habit avec lequel elle est peinte lui paroît étranger; il s'imagine que c'est quelque Américaine qui y est représentée ou que le peintre a voulu exprimer quel-

qu'unes de ses fantaisies" [A woman who leaves Paris
to go and spend six months in the country returns as
ancient as if she had left herself there for thirty years.
The son does not recognise the portrait of his mother,
so foreign does the dress in which she is painted seem
to him; he imagines that it is some American who is
represented there or that the painter wanted to express some of his fantasies] – thus did the author of
the Lettres persanes (Montesquieu 1721, chap. 100)
describe at the beginning of the century the fashion
madness of his time which had reached a peak when
Mercier held the mirror to it. What the latter wrote
about the fashion of Paris at the time could pass for a
leader in any fashion rag today[570].

In close connection with the addiction to fashion
stands:

6. the *tendency for the consumption of foreign luxury
goods*. Once luxury consumption begins, we hear the
complaints of patriots (and regional interests!) over
this bad habit of rich customers preferring foreign
wares over domestic ones. Perhaps (or rather quite
certainly) this generally widespread tendency was
connected with the fact[571] that in the beginning of the
new European culture luxury consumption was *synonymous* with the consumption of *foreign* goods because the native soil did not yet produce any luxury
goods whatsoever. From where shall the dandies at
the court of Charlemagne have obtained their costly
clothes and their objects of adornment and their art-
fully worked weapons other than from the Orient?
And even the rich people of the time of the Crusades
were essentially reliant on foreign wares when they
wanted to pursue luxury. Thus the idea that fine
equals foreign was established in the heads of luxury
consumers and remained there long after it was out-
dated (we indeed experience the same in our own
day). Thus the Italians were already considering the
quattrocento an absurdity when their countrymen
only ever wanted to follow French fashions, since for
the most part fashions were first brought by the

French from the Italians who then again imported their own ideas and products from foreigners[572].

By contrast, it corresponds to the actual development stage of luxury production in the various lands when in the France of the 16th century the Valois, as we see, Italianised their lifestyle; and likewise the English beaus even in the time of the Tudors were surely right when they preferred foreign goods.

"[...] they must haue theire geare from London; and yet manye thinges thearof are not theare made, but beyonde the sea whearby the artificers of oure townes are Idle" (Lamond 1893, 126; cited in Unwin 1904, 71).

In the millinery shops which grew like mushrooms from the earth between Edward VI and 1580, there was for sale:

> *French* or *Spanish* gloves, *Flemish* kerseys[*], *French* cloth, [...] brooches, *Venetian* or *Milanese* aiglets, *Spanish* daggers, swords, knives, and girdles. *Milanese* spurs, caps, glasses, watches, painted mugs, tables, cards, balls, inkpots, penholders, puggets (?), silk and silver bottoms (?), fine china, hawks bells (?), salt shakers, spoons, and bowls made of tin [...]
>
> *Brief Conceit of English Poesie*, cited in Burn (1846, 252).

In Ben Johnson's comedy *The New Inn*, acted 1629, a beau says:

> "I would put on
> The Savoy chain about my neck, the ruff
> The cuffs of Flanders, then the Naples hat
> With the Rome hatband, and the Florentine agate
> The Milan sword, the cloak of Geneva set
> With Brabant buttons; all my given pieces.
> My gloves the natives of Madrid", etc., etc.
>
> Cited in Luard (1852, 76).

From the 17th century then, as we know, France became the master of taste, and from then on the preference for French fashion has remained. The early capitalist writers of the 17th and 18th centuries outside France looked on this development with very disapproving eyes — it spoiled indeed the entire concept of their nationalist economic policy. Thus — to single out

---

*   [Tr.: kersey is a rough woollen cloth.]

one instead of many — Hörnigk (1750, 18) gave vent to his anger over his fellow countrymen as follows:

> "Certainly, however, our forefathers were also in household economics quite different people to us. They did not send out every year just for the French rubbish three or four million guilders in cash from their homeland, like we do, but rather made do for the most part with what their own house produced. Their precious adornment was made of good solid gold, silver, and precious stones or sables and similar furs; which, if they were in part foreign could equally be bequeathed to children and children's children; but not in tearable French rags which were made unusable *every half year by changes in fashion*".

Likewise we find the dominance of Parisian fashion in other countries[573]. But the French were not content to dictate the rules of fashion to the other nations, they peered over (as they again do in part today) at England, and the 18th century ended with an *Anglomania of the Parisians.*

A very amusing writer of the time expressed himself over it with wit almost worthy of Heine, as follows: "In part we are avenged by the Anglomania. They meet everywhere in billowing riding coats in whose folds a frail, badly shaped, again half distraught being flounders, or in English carriages surmounted by a coachman from the family of the Titans who controls the chargers with a thunderous voice; on the back a pair of giants are also mounted, next to it not unusually a terrible dog leaps, and in a corner of the box you will see the baled up leftover of an old family — you feel pity for the pygmies surrounded by monsters.

At the same time it teems with the English here who want absolutely to be like Parisian dandies [...] I remain silent about my fellow Germans; their misshapen figures to not amuse me. It cuts too close to me to see many kitted out with the tinsel of all nations like a wild animal given the presents of Europeans [...] Many are draped with a general sample card and wear their history of travel around themselves, you can follow them from their hat to their boots from Italy through France to England". From the 7th letter by Helfrich Peter Sturz from Paris on 12th November 1768 (Sturz 1786, 1:201-204).

In *Holland* around the middle of the 18th century it was: "Les marchands en détail ont aujourd'hui leurs boutiques remplies d'étoffes étrangères. Tout ce qu'on porte, tout ce qui sert à l'usage et aux commodités de la vie vient de l'étranger." [Retailers nowadays have their shops filled with foreign material. Everything we wear, everything that serves for use and a comfortable life comes from abroad.] (Sérionne 1778, 2:228).

Chapter 49: The Demand of the Army

I. The Demand for Weapons

The demand for weapons which follows directly from what we have discovered about the development of modern armaments (see above pages 54 ff.) expanded. The enlargement of the armies and fleets pushed extensively as it were for their increase, and the ever better equipment of the troops worked intensively in the same direction — indeed the demand for artillery material, as we saw, arose entirely anew to join with the demand for weapons that was already present.

At the same time demand was standardised by the increasing use of uniforms and gathered together in ever greater masses in consequence of the advancing nationalisation of arms deliveries.

What we can thus see from general observations is confirmed for us by the statistical reports over the *actual extent of the demand* of which we would certainly like to have still more, and more precise and more comprehensive examples. But even what we possess in statistical information over weapons demand during the periods which we are considering gives us some hints and allows us to have quite certain conclusions on the total extent of the demand for weapons. Above all we can follow with sufficient clarity how rapidly and lastingly this demand expanded during the relatively short span of a few centuries or even decades; for the first decisive increase falls just in the 17th century.

What was already seen in the 16th century as the artillery demand of a small army (of 10,000 foot soldiers and 1,500 cavalrymen) is given by the following lists:

A rough estimate of what is needed in the way of guns for an army of 10,000 foot soldiers and 1,500 cavalrymen, from the year 1540 in the State Archive in Stuttgart, arrives at:

4 *Scharfmetzen* cannon, 4 *Nachtigallen* cannon, 4 short and 2 long *Sängerinnen* cannon, 4 large culverins, 8 *Falconen* cannon, 12 *Falconetten* cannon, 2 *Feuerbüchse* cannon, 2 large and 2 small mortars.

Total metal: 590 kg, costs.................9,440 guilders
Wheels and carriage.........................2,000 guilders
The cannonballs...............................2,315 guilders
300 kg of powder............................8,400 guilders
Together 22,155 guilders

"Schedule of notes on what belongs to a gun in a small campaign":
(70 lb) 200 balls 30 kg powder

		cannonballs	powder
3 *Scharfmetzen* cannon	(70 lb)	200	30 kg
4 quarter cannon	(40 lb)	250	50 kg
4 culverin extraordinaire	(20 lb)	300	45 kg
6 ordinary culverin	(11 lb)	300	24 kg
6 half-culverin	(8 lb)	350	18 kg
6 *Falconet* cannon	(6 lb)	400	12 kg
60 wall guns		10 kg lead	8 kg

All the cannonballs and lead together weigh 772 kg, and the total gunpowder weighs 446 kg.

For transport, 66 wagons and 330 horses are included. (Jähns 1889, 1:747 ff.)

In accordance with that, it is easy to gauge what was needed by large armies.

When Wallenstein's artillery was destroyed in Silesia (at the start of the second generalship), he himself, in a letter to Questenberg, set the needed sum for replacement at 300,000 florins (Hallwich 1879, 1:71; cited in Loewe 1895, 93).

Sully spent during his rule 12 million francs for arms and munitions (Sully 1747, 3:Ch. VIII; cited in Boutaric 1863, 363). And the arsenal still contained at his death 400 guns, 200,000 cannonballs, and 4 million pounds of powder.

An especially greedy consumer of weapons was the navy. The Spanish Armada took with it 2,431 cannon, of which 1,497 were bronze, 934 iron; 7,000 arquebuses, and 1,000 muskets (as well as 10,000 pikes, 6,000 half pikes, swords, axes, etc.). For the cannon, 123,790 shots (50 on average) were planned for (Duro 1884, Doc. 109; cited in Clowes 1897, 1:560).

The inventory of French ships' cannons increased seven-fold under the government of Colbert — it rose from 1,045 in the year 1661 to 7,625 in the year 1683, and indeed the increase essentially favoured the *iron* cannons, of which in 1661 there were only 475, in 1683 by contrast 5,619 (Sue 1835, 4:170).

The same massive growth is shown in the English ships' artillery. The inventory on the ships was (see the sources in Clowes (1897, 1:409, 1:421, 2:267)):

> 1548: 2,087 cannon
> 1653: 3,840 cannon
> 1666: 4,460 cannon
> 1700: 8,396 cannon

In the way of munitions, a ship like the Henry Grace à Dieu (so already a ship of the 16th century) carried 4,800 lb serpentine shot and 14,400 lb of coarse powder (Ms. from Pepys Library in Clowes 1897, 1:412).

The arming of the Sovereign of the Seas, the magnificent ship of Charles I, which consisted of 102 bronze cannon, cost £24,753 8 s. 8 d. (Public Record Office of Great Britain 1856, 374:30, 387:87; cited in Oppenheim 1896, 1:262).

II. The Demand for Provisions

The size and form of the demand of an army even for provisions is determined by the strength of the army and the particular nature of its system of catering.

The number of troops who are under arms always determines the absolute size of the demand; that is, it determines the number of mouths which want to be fed without their bearers lending a hand in the production of goods. For that is of course the economically important thing about it, that in the army just as many exclusive consumers are created as there are members of the military (or military families). The soldier has always had this characteristic of being exclusively a consumer, irrespective of whether he obtained his upkeep in natura or purchased it from a producer.

The system of catering then decides over to what extent a larger demand for provisions called forth by a larger army becomes a *mass demand*, which is to say, an agglomerated, unitary demand appearing as a whole. We consider that a large demand becomes a mass demand all the sooner, the further the centralisation of the satisfaction of demand has progressed. Further, if the centralisation only occurs in wartime, all the sooner, the longer the wars last. Finally (with ships), all the sooner, the further the journeys extend.

The necessity of provisioning *larger masses of troops for a longer sea journey* probably produced a mass demand for provisions first. And it was called forth at a time when the world still lived its life in dreams. It must have called forth massive upheavals in the blissfully dreamy people of those days when one day in Genoa the news spread that Philip II of France wanted to provide his army with provisions and horse fodder for 8 months and with wine for 4 months[574].

Or when the criers rode through the villages of France and announced what the bailiwicks were to raise in the way of provisions and deliver to Calais for the equipping of the troops embarking there.

We possess an overview of the individual requirements which the bailiffs were set in the year 1304. The numbers are of course not to be taken in full any more than that of a medieval list of provisions. The probably express no more than the hoped-for maximum quantity. At any rate, they give though an approximate idea of the quantities which had to be brought together at such an early time for the provisioning of an army. Its correctness is surely not to be doubted. The list is to be found in Reg. XXXV of Trésors des chartes No. 138 and is printed in Boutaric (1863, 278–79).

> Requisitions which were served in January 1304 to the bailiffs (for delivery to Calais):
> Bailiwick of Sens: 250 muids* of grain, 500 barrels of wine, 150 muids of oats;
> Bailiwick of Caen: 500 muids of grain, 500 barrels of wine, 500 muids of oats, 1,000 live pigs, 1,000 hams, 10 muids of peas, and 10 muids of beans.

And so on for 15 bailiwicks and seneschalties.

But then a proper and permanent mass demand for provisions naturally first occurred when the *modern* armies and fleets arose. In particular the *outfitting of fleets* demanded early on a regular heavy supply of provisions. The decisive transformation seems here to have fallen in the 16th century. At the time they switched to provisioning the ships in winter, and an English regiment established as a norm a provisioning of 4 months from 2 months. These higher demands on the catering system were connected with wanting to establish from the middle of the century quite different practices with the

---

* [Tr.: a *muid* was a measure of capacity of varying amounts — originally a wagon load.]

operation of warships. Up until the time of Henry VIII, the fleets had landed soldiers and returned; or they had struck the enemy and returned — now the era of long journeys began.

But what was already possible in the 16th century with regards to quantities of provisions with large undertakings is shown by the stores of food which the Spanish Armada took with itself in the year 1588. We are also informed quite precisely and reliably over it, and know that the 195 ships of this fleet took on board[575]:

> 55,000 kg of biscuit,
> 11,117 mayors (~255 litres each) of wine,
> 3,000 kg of pork,
> 1,500 kg of cheese,
> 3,000 kg of fish,
> 2,000 kg of rice,
> 6,000 fanegas (~55 litres each) of peas and beans,
> 10,000 arrobas (~16 litres each) of oil,
> 21,000 arrobas of vinegar,
> 11,000 pipes of water.

In the 17th century the opportunities piled up in which such large masses had to be raised in a short time — which first gave the whole its particular stamp. Thus we learn, for example, of a suddenly arising demand with the English fleet for 7,500,000 lb of bread, 7,500,000 lb of beef and pork, 10,000 butts of beer, in addition to butter, cheese, fish, etc., which was all to be obtained within a quite short time (the length is not given)[576].

The upkeep of their fleet in the year 1672 cost the Dutch 6,972,768 florins for 7 months[577].

Very precise lists for the provisioning of a ship or a fleet around the middle of the 18th century are found in Chennevières (1750, 1:238 f.).

You will perhaps now think the problem of provisioning ships is not at all a specifically military one, since indeed every merchant ship also must be provided with victuals for the crew. That is correct, but the extent of the provisioning was quite different with warships, and *only this expansion of the latitude for supply contained the problematic element.*

You must constantly keep in mind how minor the crews of merchant ships were in comparison to those of the warships. In the Middle Ages great masses of men were already perched on the warships — the galleys were the *warships* of the Italian sea powers, and galleys were *rowed* ships, and hence for that reason much more heavily manned than equally large sailing ships. Already in the 13th century the galleys of the Genoese republic had 140 oarsmen[578]. In the year 1285, 184 men came on a vessel. An equally large merchant ship had perhaps barely 20 men on board. Even when the merchant ships were equipped with soldiers for their protection, they exhibited in the 12th and 13th centuries only the following crews: 25, 50, 32, 85, 60, 55, 50, 45. The matter changed again immediately when the merchant ships, travelling with or without cargo, were mainly outfitted for war or piracy; then they were manned relatively more heavily; they were then called "armed", navis armata [armed ships], and then had the following crews: two ships in 1234 had 600 men, a Pisan ship in 1125 had 400 men, another ship of the same origin had 500, a Venetian merchantman had 900 men on board[579].

In the 16th century you reckoned for warships 3 men per 5 tonnes gross — a third soldiers, a seventh of the remainder for gunners, and the rest sailors — and with merchant ships by contrast only 1 man per 5 tonnes net — a twelfth gunners, the rest sailors[580].

From these crew proportions thus quite stately crews emerged on warships.

If you consider the number of ships which came together against the enemy, then it was easily about quite large masses of soldiers and sailors who were on board.

In 1511 Henry VIII promised to clear the channel with 3,000 men. In 1513, 2,280 sailors were enlisted for the English fleet (in addition to the crews of 28 cargo ships). In 1514, there were on 23 royal ships, 21 rented and 15 cargo ships, 3,982 sailors and 447 gunners, thus 4,429 men exclusive of soldiers (Oppenheim 1896, 1:74).

But even with *land armies* the quantity of demand understandably grew rapidly.

The 12,000 men of Brandenburg who in 1694 stood as reserve units on the Rhine and in the Netherlands received (aside from money of 38,180 talers per month) 2 pounds of bread per man per day. That resulted for 11,608 officers and NCOs in 23,216 pounds a day, thus in 31 days 719,696 pounds; 144 pounds bread calculated on about 50 kg of flour results in 244,900 kg of flour demanded per month (Hennert 1790, 15). In 1727, 200,000 talers were allocated from the treasury in order to buy rye for the military stores (Preußischen Akademie der Wissenschaften 1892, 2:285). In the 21 Prussian stores at the end of the reign of Frederick William I there lay about 19 million kg[*] — a sufficient supply for 200,000 men for one year (Preußischen Akademie der Wissenschaften 1892, 2:278). In Prussia in the 18th century, one reckoned on 2 pounds of bread per day per man, which amounted to about 166 kg per annum. The Prussian army thus needed already during the first half of the 17th century 12.5–13 million kg of grain, whereas the civilian population of Berlin in 1720 demanded only 3.7 million kg (Preußischen Akademie der Wissenschaften 1892, 2:297).

Similar figures are obtained for the armies of the other lands. Dupré d'Aulnay establishes for the middle of the 18th century the following calculation for France: the supply of an army of 150,000 men with wholemeal bread, that is 54 million rations per annum, demanded 300,000 sacks of grain at 200 lb each; thus 30,000 tonnes (Dupré d'Aulnay 1744, 165).

III. The Demand for Clothes

How large the demand for clothes of a modern army was can be easily calculated by anyone when they multiply the figures on the strength of armies which I have shared above with the quantities of material, ingredients, etc. which the individual soldiers needed, and when they look, as far as the clothes, cloaks, hats, boots, etc. are concerned, at the number of persons as the minimum number of the pieces thereby needed.

What belonged to the outfit of a soldier in the 17th and 18th century is seen from the following compilations:

> List of what was needed in clothing for 193 soldiers.
> 965 ells of London cloth for trousers, Cosiaken[†] and stockings each 5 ells,
> 965 ells of cloth lining each 5 ells,
> 2,316 ells of white, black, rough and stiff canvas each 12 ells,
> 1,158 dozen loops, each 6 dozen for trousers and Cosiaken,
> 193 lots[‡] of silk each 1 lot,
> 579 dozen iron buttons, each 5 dozen,
> 50 ells of bad 4th wire[?] to adorn the Cosiaken,
> 193 hats.

---

[*]   [Tr.: 45,000 wispels. Calculation was at 1 wispel = 1,200 litres, and 1 kg of rye = 2.32 litres.]
[†]   [Tr.: possibly a blue cloth item.]
[‡]   [Tr.: a lot was an old unit weight which varied, mostly from 10 to 50g.]

(Captain von Burgsdorff to Count von Schwarzenberg, Berlin, on 16th October 1620. In the State Archive in Berlin, printed in Kling (1906, 2:40 Anl. 16).)

Needs of an infantryman at the beginning of the 18th century:

		Talers	Groschen	Pfennigs
5	ells of cloth at 15 groschen	3	3	–
7	ells of baize at 4 groschen	1	4	–
1	ell of red cloth for cuffs	–	14	–
20	pieces of brass buttons at 4 groschen a dozen	–	6	8
1	lot of camel hair	–	3	–
2	pairs of loops of camel hair	–	6	–
1	hat with yellow edging	–	12	–
		6	–	8

(Hennert 1790, 12; in Richthofen 1839, 495)

The full clothing and outfit of a cavalryman including saddle and harness cost at the time of Frederick William I 73 talers and 2 groschen (Crousaz 1865, 1:45).
Each soldier of the Savoy Cavalleria and the Piedmont R[le] at the beginning of the 18th century cost 131.16 l., each D[ni] Genevois 110.14 l., each gunner 68.16 l. The outfitting of the horse of a cavalryman amounted to 75.5 l., of a dragoon to 67.4 l. (Prato 1907, 302) For the clothing of a regiment of English soldiers (in 1730), £1,570 165 s. 2½ d. was required (Grose 1786, 1:315).

If we now draw up a calculation for the material to clothe an army of 100,000 men, 500,000 ells or 20,000 pieces are required. Assuming a replacement of the uniform every two years, that amounts to an annual consumption of 10,000 pieces. Schmoller calculates the total consumption of the Brandenburg population at the beginning of the 18th century at 50,000 pieces of cloth (Schmoller 1898b, 514). Frederick the Great cites in his Brandenburg memoires the export of cloth from the Kurmark and Neumark at around 44,000 pieces (Friedrichs II. von Preußen 1846, 1:234; cited in Schmoller 1898b, 522).

In order to gauge the consequences of these figures, we must make clear that this large demand became a *mass demand of uniform objects* in that measure as the nationalisation and standardisation of clothing progressed. You may safely say without being guilty of exaggeration that such concentrations of demand as were already occurring in the 17th century with the supplies to the large armies had been entirely unheard-of at the time.

The people, even the business people must have been astonished when they heard that in a single contract the immediate delivery of 5,000 complete soldier's uniforms was insisted on, as was the case in the contract which the English government concluded in the year 1603 with Ury Babington and Robert Bromley (Hall 1901, 126).

Or when they read the figures as they appeared perhaps in the orders of Wallenstein. There it was, for example:

> Also have 10,000 pairs of shoes made for the lads so that I can distribute them afterwards to the regiments [...] Have the leather prepared, for I will soon also have a few thousand boots finished. Also have the cloth finished, perhaps clothes will also be needed.

Achserleben, 13th June 1626:

> [My cousin Max] will also have ordered that you shall have 4,000 clothes made for the servants, that is a skirt of cloth lined with linen, a pair of cloth trousers and a pair of cloth stockings.
> (Wallenstein to his provincial minister von Taxis, printed in Richthofen (1839, 439 f.)).
> The military paymaster is moving to Gitschin, shall have for 13,000 imperial talers shoes, stockings, and clothes [in a later letter an order of 40,000 imperial talers is added] made for the army; assist him diligently in everything. The 4,000 clothes, as you had made a year ago, that he paid you what they cost me, you will also take away the same as soon as he has paid", etc.
> (Wallenstein to Gerhard von Taxis, printed in Heilmann (1850, Beilage 4)).

On 26th September 1647, Conrad von Burgsdorf received the task of concluding the following contract with the merchant Eberhard Schlef in Hamburg for the delivery of cloth and baize. "He shall show for the Elector's army officers 1,512 Brabant ells of blue cloth like the sample, each ell calculated at 5 local imperial talers and for the common men 20,000 Brabant ells of blue cloth like the sample, each for 1 imperial taler [...] in addition 21,512 Brabant ells of baize, each delivered to Sgr. Date in 3 weeks after St. Martin's Day[*]." (Kling 1906, 2:211)

IV. Total Demand

The total demand of the army administration, which we can of course only express in monetary figures, is seen by us from the expenditure for military aims which we find recorded in the public budgets. It is well-known that these expenditures formed in earlier times a very much greater

---

[*]   [Tr.: 11th November.]

proportion of the total state expenditure than today, indeed that occasionally in the beginnings of the modern state finances they swallowed almost the entire income, but that they nevertheless grew at a rapid rate during the 16th to 18th centuries. The most important figures for the individual lands are the following[581]:

Piedmont, the military state of Italy, spent for army purposes:

     1580.....................................334,673 l. di Piem.
     1680.................................1,610,958 l. di Piem.
     1708/09...........................8,000,000 l. di Piem.

The army expenditures amounted from 1700 to 1713 to 77.72% of the total expenditures of the state.

Spain: spent 3,356,463 ducats in the year 1610 for army purposes (93% of all state revenue).

France: the army expenditure amounted to:

     1542..2,114,000 Franchi
     1601–1609..................ca. 6,000,000 livres (average)
     1639..........19,100,000 livres (60% of total spending)
     1680..........97,869,754 livres (74% of total spending)
     1784.......404,350,000 livres (66% of total spending)

Brandenburg-Prussia spent for army purposes:
— under the Great Elector:
     ....2,500,000 talers = 66⅔% of total spending
     1739/40......5,954,079 talers = 86% of total spending
— under Frederick William II (average of the last 3 years)
     ....12,419,457 talers = 75.7% of total spending
     1797/98.....14,606,325 talers = 71% of total spending

England: the total expenditure for military purposes (army and fleet) amounted in the century from 1688 to 1788:

     for the fleet to......................................£244,380,685
     for the army to......................................£240,312,967
     for the artillery to..................................£29,959,345

The wars against Napoleon cost England (1801 to 1814) £633,634,614, that is 13–14 billion marks or an annual average of £45,259,615, which is 900 million marks with a population of 10 to 12 million.

Chapter 50: The Demand for Ships

Shipping exercises a double effect on the formation of goods demand:

1. through the ships which it makes use of;
2. through the building materials which the ships make use of.

The ship was the first great "assembled" good which was desired next to the palace and the church, then the great house. I have dealt with the great house under the rubric of luxury demand because it in fact in all earlier times almost only concerned luxury buildings when the houses assumed a greater extent. Ships on the other hand are referenced here with reason since they are themselves not luxury goods and are fitted together from ordinary goods.

The effect which shipping exercised on the formation of goods demand is all the greater now:

1. the more ships are built, which indeed requires no explanation; but also:
2. the larger the ships are built. Again obviously the effect of size, provided that the same number of larger ships naturally produced a larger total demand for construction materials, is a larger demand for workers, etc. The size of ship, however, is also in and of itself significant — it brought about a stronger amassing of lively work and of demand for material and work tools — the shipyards had to be larger in order to be able to build larger ships in them; the quantities desired in one of wood, of ropes, of iron, etc. are larger only because the ship, an assembled good, creates a greater unit of demand.

What the size of ships brought about by its own doing can also now be brought about by the joining together of ship-building activity. You can hence say that the effect of shipbuilding on economic life was all the greater:

3. the more uniformly, the more crowded together, the more compressed the shipbuilding occurred — when 100 ships were built in a shipyard, a larger and more uniform demand arose than if the same 100 ships were built in 10 shipyards.

   Finally it is to be recalled that the sphere of influence of shipbuilding (which here of course appears no different to any industry you like to name) is all the greater:

4. the more rapidly the ships are built — when I place 100 men on a construction site, a ship of a certain size will be finished in — say — one year. If it should already be launched after three months, then I must increase the simultaneously active workers correspondingly. The same applies for acquiring material.

It will be shown in the following that the demand for ships expanded rapidly, that simultaneously the ships became ever larger, their production time, however, (comparatively) ever shorter. That through that, however, the demand for shipbuilding materials grew to a considerable mass demand which stood equally alongside the mass demand of the big cities and the army administrations.

I have in my already mentioned study on war and capitalism (Sombart 1913b) proven, as I believe, that the strong driving force in the development of the fleets in the period of early capitalism was the *military interest of the states* which pushed for the enlargement of the navy and above all the types of ships. This was the pacemaker and model for the merchant marine which experienced a — certainly also not insignificant — stimulus above all by the rapid expansion of colonial possessions and colonial trade. Next to the warship there appeared in the 17th and 18th centuries as its younger and smaller, but yet also strong brother, the East Indies merchantman.

In the following I will give a few statistics[582] which will both show the tendencies just described and also give an approximate idea of the size of the mass demand which shipping produced.

1. The Number of Ships

For the *16ᵗʰ century* we possess the following clues for assessing the extent of the *English merchant fleet*.

In his *Treatise of Commerce*, Wheeler (1601) suggested that about 60 years before not 4 ships (outside those in the royal fleet) in the Thames ports had been greater than 120 tons. The correctness of this judgement is confirmed by other information. In the period 1544/45 to 1553, ships departing over 100 tons amount to:

> Belonging to London.....................17 totalling 2,530 tons
> Belonging to Bristol......................13 totalling 2,380 tons
> Belonging to other ports...5

In 1577 a list demonstrates:

> 135 merchantmen of 100 tons or more, of which:
>> 56 were...............................100 tons
>> 11..110 tons
>> 20...120 tons
>> 7...130 tons
>> 15...140 tons
>> 5...150 tons
>> 656...........between 40 and 100 tons

In 1582 we find 166 merchant ships of more than 100 tons.

The fleet of Henry VIII, however, measured already at the beginning of his reign, as we saw above, 8,460 tons, at the end 10,550 tons; Elizabeth I left behind a naval fleet of 14,060 tons.

For the England of the *17ᵗʰ century* the following estimates are known to me:

In 1628 a stocktaking of the English merchant fleet in the Thames resulted in:

> 7 India merchantmen.......................................4,200 tons
> 34 other merchantmen.....................................7,850 tons
> 22 Newcastle coal vessels

In 1629 in all of England there were calculated to be 350 ships over 100 tons, that is, thus 35–40,000 tons capacity (Oppenheim 1896).

In 1642 the East-India Company had a fleet with a capacity of 15,000 tons. (According to the accounts of the East-India Company.)

In 1651 the merchants of Glasgow had 12 ships with a total capacity of 957 tons.

In 1692 there were belonging to the port of Leith 29 ships with capacity of 1,702 tons (Bremner 1869).

During this period the capacity of the King's ships amounted to 15–20,000 tons at least (1618: 15,670 tons; 1624: 19,339 tons; 1660: already though 65,294 tons) according to the sources shared above.

The *French* merchant marine shall, according to an official determination in the year 1664, have amounted to 2,368 ships, for which I calculate according to the scales described in that overview about 180,000 tons capacity. France in 1661 only had 30 warships, but at Colbert's death 244, as we saw, whose capacity we must certainly set at 80–100,000 tons.

For the 18th century we have for the *English* merchant fleet right at the beginning (1701) a quite dependable piece of information: the Commissioners of Customs had held a survey with the various harbour authorities. This produced for the entire English merchant fleet a total of 3,281 ships with a capacity of 261,222 tons and a crew of 27,196 men (Macpherson and Anderson 1805; cf. McCulloch 1880, 45–57 "Amsterdam").

For the year 1754 then an estimate exists by which it consisted of:

ca. 2,000	sea-going ships	with ca. 170,000 t. capacity and
ca. 2,000	coastal ships	with ca. 150,000 t. capacity
all up ca. 4,000		with ca. 320,000 t. capacity

These figures are also accepted by such an excellent connoisseur as Postlethwayt (1774, 2:254-255 "Middlesex") as being correct for his period.

That would be a believable increase over 50 years. To London alone there belonged (calculated according to the General Registry of the Custom House) in the year 1732 1,417 ships which together had a capacity of 178,557 tons.

In the 18th century the shipping statistics begin to become more precise, and they can also give us some information on the extent of the inventory of ships. We must assume for that period that for instance the ships coming into the English ports made the journey once or twice a year — for about two unique trips, one repeated occurs (Postlethwayt 1774, 2:335). Now, however, according to the General Registry of the Custom House on average for the years 1743, 1747, and 1749 for all English ports foreign ships came in with a total capacity of 86,094 tons. Whereas, for example, from the South England ports (1786/87) 233 ships left for the West Indies with 47,257 tons, likewise from London 218 ships went out with 61,695 tons, and likewise from the North England ports 77 ships with 14,629 tons. The total number of ships arriving in 1786/87 in the United States of America amounted to 509 with 35,546 tons, whereas in the same year 373 ships sailed from there with 36,145 tons (A. Anderson 1787, 4:659 f.).

The English merchant fleet then increased quite considerably in the last decades of the 18th century. According to the conscientious compilations of Moreau (1853) the totals were the following:

1788	9,360	ships with	1,053,610	tons
1791	10,423	ships with	1,168,469	tons
1802	13,446	ships with	1,642,224	tons

2. The Size of the Ships

We have already received an idea above of the size of the merchant ships during the 16th and 17th centuries. I will share a few more figures in order to have the picture appear quite distinctly.

In the already mentioned statistics of the *French* merchant ships in the year 1664, the 2,368 are allocated to the individual classes by size as follows:

10–30 tons	1,063
30–40 tons	345
40–60 tons	320
60–80 tons	178
80–100 tons	133
100-120 tons	102
120–150 tons	72
150–200 tons	70
200–250 tons	39
250–300 tons	27
300–400 tons	19
	2,368

The first fleet of the *French* Indies Company consisted of three ships each of 300 tons and one ship of 120 tons; the second was put together as follows: two ships each of 5–600 tons, two ships each of 300 tons, one ship of 250 tons, one ship of 200 tons, and four ships each of 60–80 tons. In 1682 one ship of 700 tons, and one ship of 800 tons set sail (Kaeppelin 1908, 10, 12, 137).

The ships which set sail during the 17th century from the port of Hamburg were on average 17–18 lasts of 2,000 kg each; in 1625, for example, 17.821 lasts on average. The largest ship in this year sailed to Venice and had a capacity of 200 lasts (thus 400 tons), in 1616 we find one with 150, in 1615 one with 130, in 1617 one with 120 lasts, etc. (Baasch 1894, 295 ff.)

In *England* Sir William Monson (1902; cited in A. Anderson 1787, 2:211) suggests that at the death of Elizabeth I (thus at the beginning of the 17th century) there were no more than four merchantmen of 400 tons capacity each. This would be correct, for even in the middle of the century the ships of the East-India Company (thus the largest in the land) only had 300–600 tons capacity.

The *Dutch* East India Company at the end of the 17th century was using ships of on average 300 lasts (Klerk de Reus 1894, 116 ff.).

Especially stately were the Indies-bound merchantmen of the *Spanish* fleet. In 1686 the fleet and galleons together included 50 ships with 27,500 tons (Álvarez Osorio y Redín 1687; cited in Colmeiro 1863, 2:404).

These sizes also remained common *during the 18th century* — large East-India merchantmen had 300–500 tons capacity, the European merchantmen 100–300 tons.

Thus of the already mentioned 1,417 ships which London possessed in the year 1732, there were:

130 between 300 and 500 tons; and
83 between 200 and 300 tons in size.

The remainder were smaller, and the famous ship of the South Sea Company had a capacity of 750 tons.

On 1st May 1737, Liverpool had 211 ships over 30 tons, of which:

1 with 400 t	2 with 340 t	7 with 160 t	13 with 120 t
1 with 350 t	2 with 200 t	15 with 150 t	6 with 110 t
1 with 300 t	2 with 190 t	10 with 140 t	16 with 100 t
1 with 250 t	4 with 180 t	5 with 130 t	135 with 30–90 t

(According to an especially cited list in A. Anderson (1787, 3:324).)

The foreign ships arriving in the English ports in 1749 exhibited the following sizes:

Dutch ships	62	with 6,282 t =	100 t
Denmark	292	47,382 t =	160 t
Sweden	71	8,400 t =	120 t
Hamburg	40	6,746 t =	170 t
France	24	1,289 t =	50 t
Prussia	26	2,420 t =	130 t
Danzig	16	2,748 t =	170 t
Portugal	26	2,100 t =	80 t
Bremen	16	1,975 t =	125 t
Russia	5	440 t =	90 t
Spain	16	940 t =	60 t
	594	81,740 t =	ca. 140 t

The largest ship was a Danish one with 510 tons; the smallest were the French barges — obviously ferrying from Calais to Dover — with a capacity of four tons. But also from Bremen a ship arrived with 35 tons, and from Danzig with 44 tons, etc. (Postlethwayt 1774, 3:317 ff. "Navigation").

At the end of the 18th century, the normal *Dutch* merchant ship had a capacity of 180–190 lasts; it measured 115 feet to the keel, 120 feet from stem to sternpost, with a breadth of 34 feet (Beckmann 1777, 3:739 f.).

To the inventory of the Royal *Danish* East India and Guinea Trading Company, formed in 1781 from the Guinea Trading Company, the Baltic Trading Company, and the Greenland Trading Company, there belonged 37 ships; of them *the capacities in commercial lasts* (of 2,600 kg) were:

50–60 lasts	10 ships
61–100 lasts	2 ships
101–150 lasts	21 ships
151–162 ½ lasts	4 ships
	37 ships

See § 4 of the octroi [Tr.: paid duties] of the company, printed in Beckmann (1777, 6:416 ff.).

If we now place opposite these figures the corresponding figures for the navy, we very soon notice that the navy is quite considerably larger than the merchant marine, that in particular the large types are much more frequently found among the former than the latter.

Already in the 16th century English warships (of the Tower) appear of 1,000 tons; in the list which Oppenheim (1896) compiled for the time of Henry VII, 9 ships appear of from 500 to 1,000 tons.

In the 17th century the warships increased in size rapidly.

It seems almost as if even in the 17th century the 1,000 ton type became the norm with warships. In the year 1688 we find them in the English fleet already with 41 ships, the largest of which was 1,739 tons. The size of the crews of these large ships swayed between 400 and 800, the number of guns between 70 and 100. This according to the lists in Pepys' diaries relating to the state of the Royal Navy in Clowes (1897, 2:244 f.).

3. The Speed of Shipbuilding

It is this above all which was influenced by the military interests. In order to recognise how hastily and often erratically shipbuilding was developing once the construction of warships became its main task, it suffices to bring to view the figures in which the increase in the inventory of the naval fleets was expressed. I have already provided them and refer the reader to them. For enlivening the image I offer a few especially striking examples from the history of shipbuilding in which the for its time unheard-of speed of construction is to be recognised.

In *England* in the year 1554 29 warships were to be found under construction ("in commission"), in 1555/56 38, in 1557 24, to which 8 more are to be added in December of the same year. But the speed becomes ever hastier. For that the following absolutely informative table contains the evidence:

There were in commission in the 22 years 1559 to 1580 and 1581 to 1602 in total 142 and 362.

And then indeed the great advance first comes in the 17th century in which all the military interests grew into the gigantic (into the baroque we could also say). Under the republic in England 207 ships were built in 11 years, thus almost 20 ships per year. In the one five-year period from 1690 to 1695 in England £1,011,576 8 s. 11 d. was granted for the construction of 45 ships (Charnock 1801, 2:462).

The speed with which the *French* fleet was enlarged in Colbert's time bordered on a paroxysm — Colbert found, as we saw, 30 warships on his entry into the government (1661); after a little more than 20 years he had made from that 244, but these mostly in much greater dimensions — thus annually on average 10–12 warships were launched.

4. The Demand for Shipbuilding Materials

This demand is expressed first of all by the costs to which the production of warships gave rise. Every such amount, in so far as it was not expended for the wages at the shipyards, signified a demand for shipbuilding materials.

An English warship of moderate size in the 16th century cost £3–4,000, under James I £7–8,000, under Charles I £10–12,000, at the beginning of the 18th century £15–20,000 (see the sources in Oppenheim 1896).

We possess a very precise setting out of the costs for the ships of various classes for *England* in the 18th century. They vary for the year 1706 between £3,138 and £78,581, for the year 1741 between £6,309 and £41,151 (see the sources in Charnock 1801, 3:126).

Now the sources only ever tell us something when we follow their application in detail, when we establish for what actually each of the expenditures was made. We want to attempt to see whether such a specification is possible.

The materials which mainly came into consideration for shipbuilding were:

1. wood, which had an outstandingly large significance for shipbuilding in all earlier times, as we will soon see;
2. tackle or the raw materials for it — hemp, flax, etc.;
3. sails or the semi-finished fabric or raw materials for them;
4. ironwork — anchors, chains, nails, wire;
5. tar and pitch;
6. brass, copper, tin-plated steel, tin.

In the 16th century already (on the "Henry Grace à Dieu") 56 tons of iron was used, whereas the timber that went into this ship weighed 3,739 tons. Conspicuously small are the quantities of oakum and flax, namely only 565 stones (1 stone of hemp = 32 pounds[*]) and 1,711 pounds, if we do not want to assume that the last figure signifies "ships' pounds" (about 125 kg) (Oppenheim 1896, 1:53).

We learn what was usually needed in the way of tackle on a ship in the 16th century from another well informed source (Marperger 1721, 142): there were on a 1565 built ship 2,280 kg or 456 ships' pounds, thus 114,600 pounds. The wood of the "Triumph", likewise built in the 16th century, cost £1,200 (with a total outlay of £3,788).

A cost for the construction of ten new English warships in the year 1618 looked as follows (of the ships, 6 were 650 tons each, 3 were 150 tons, and one was 350 tons in size (report from the year 1618 in Charnock (1801, 2:256)):

	£	s	d
Building with all materials (building of the hull)...43,425		–	–
Pulleys, mastheads.......513		6	8
Finishing boats and pinnaces.......320		10	–
Cordage (tackle).......6,716		1	6
Sails.......2,740		15	6
Anchors.......2,287		4	–
56,002		17	8

In the 18th century the demand for all material had been extraordinarily much greater again.

An English warship equipped with 100 cannon needed 3,600 ells of sail cloth.

---

[*] [Tr.: this appears to be a different measure from the imperial stone which equals 14 pounds.]

A French warship equipped with 100–120 cannons, a length of 170–180 feet, a width of 50 feet, required for its construction:

> 4,000 pieces of mature, healthy oak
> 300,000 pounds of iron
> 219,000 pounds of fixed rigging
>
> (Krünitz et al. 1773, 50:534 ff.)

According to an official (English) report the consumption of pitch and tar at the beginning of the 18th century amounted annually:

> in Britain and Ireland to 1,000 lasts (at 29 hl.)
> in Holland (for their own demand as well as for export to Spain, Portugal, and the Mediterranean) to 4,000 lasts
> in France to 500 lasts
> in Hamburg, Lübeck, and other German ports
> to 500 lasts
>
> (A. Anderson 1787, 3:17)

For further statistics, see Sombart (1913b, chap. 6).

Chapter 51: The Mass Demand of the Big Cities

When the army and shipbuilding had brought forth a mass demand so that many goods were needed by *one* economy, there the origin of mass demand had thus been a result of organisational developments. In the big cities a mass-like demand for specific goods originated through the external fact that many people were living together permanently in one and the same place, people who could not cover their needs anymore in the way of home production, and who thus had to purchase everything they needed.

I. The Growth of the Big Cities

Let us first recall the course which big city formation had taken during the period of early capitalism.

During the *16th century* the number of cities with 100,000 or more inhabitants grew already to 13–14. They were at first the Italian cities: Venice (1563: 168,627; 1575/77: 195,863), Naples (240,000), Milan (around 200,000), Palermo (1600: around 100,000), Rome (1600: around 100,000), whereas Florence in 1530 only numbered 60,000 inhabitants.

Then the Spanish-Portuguese cities: Lisbon (1620: 110,800), Seville (end of the 16th century: 18,000 hearths, thus about 100,000 inhabitants); and the cities of the Netherlands: Antwerp (1560: 104,092), and Amsterdam (1622: 104,961).

Finally Paris and London.

Paris, against whose expansion royal edicts had already been issued in the middle of the century (I will come to speak of this soon), fell back in consequence of the wars of religion evidently in the number of inhabitants, which in the year 1594 amounted to about 180,000.

London grew rapidly and showed at the end of the century all the signs of the over-populated big city, as we are able to perceive clearly from a decree of Elizabeth I from the year 1602. We must set its number of inhabitants at the time of Elizabeth I at about 250,000.

In the course of the *17th century* a few of the earlier big cities now fell back in terms of numbers of inhabitants: Lisbon and Antwerp sank below the 100,000; Milan and Venice likewise considerably.

By contrast Vienna (1720: 130,000) and Madrid climbed up newly to big cities.

Rome, Amsterdam, Paris, and London grew rapidly. Rome has 140,000 inhabitants at the end of the century, Amsterdam 200,000; Paris reached the half million, London passed it (1700: 674,350).

Whereas London gradually increased in size during this century, Paris evidently shot up. It had a boom especially during the reign of the first two Bourbons. We now frequently encounter those strange edicts which forbid the building of new houses in order to halt the growth of the city: "Reconnaissant que l'augmentation de notre bonne ville de Paris est grandement préjudiciable" [Recognizing that the expansion of our good city of Paris is greatly prejudicial]; "Attendu que l'intention de Sa Majesté a été que sa ville de Paris fût d'une étendue certaine et limitée" [Whereas the intention of His Majesty was that his city of Paris should be of a certain and limited extent]. (In these bans is expressed, you could say, a similar will as is acknowledged in the guild regulations: the resistance to letting an organic form grow without bounds; the resistance against the reckless tendency of the capitalist being towards expansion and quantification; the resistance of the old subsistence-like, corporative being against the limitless craving for expansion of the drive for acquisition.)

The bans naturally bore no fruit; despite them being repeated (1627, 1637), Paris grew enormously in these centuries. Between the Paris of Louis XIII and that of the League, a judicious writer of history (Baudrillat) suggests there was a greater difference than between the latter and the Paris of the Third Republic. How strongly the change felt to contemporaries is expressed by Corneille in his comedy "Le Menteur" written in 1642 (Act II, Scene V):

> Toute une ville entière, avec pompe bâtie
> Semble d'un vieux fossé par miracle sortie
> Et nous fait présumer, à ses superbes toits,
> Que tous ses habitants sont des dieux ou des rois.
> [A whole entire town, built with pomp
> Seems from an old ditch miraculously released
> And makes us presume, from its superb roofs,
> That all its inhabitants are gods or kings.]

The 18th century brought the following shifts:

The inhabitants of Moscow, St Petersburg, Vienna, and *Palermo (1795: 200,162) exceeded 200,000. Dublin remained not far from that (1798: 182,370; 1753: 128,870; 1644: 8,159).

Those reaching 100,000: Hamburg, Copenhagen, and Warsaw. Berlin climbed to 141,283 (1783), *Lyon to 135,207 (1787).

*Naples approached the half million (1796: 435,930), London the million (864,845), *Paris by the outbreak of the revolution had 640–670,000 inhabitants.

464

The figures are taken from the assiduous work of Beloch (1895, 55 ff.). Where I have added a * before the city names, the figures are borrowed from Inama-Sternegg (1899). I found the number of inhabitants for Dublin in Moreau de Jonnès (1837, 1:88). The last number for London is the official figure of the census from 1801; the number for Berlin according to the table by Normann which is provided in Mirabeau (1788, 1:278 f.).

II. The Extent of Demand of the Big City

In order to give a statistical idea of the extent of the demand of these cities, I want to share a few figures which we possess for a few objects of consumption in the two big cities of London and Paris. They shall simply serve for obtaining a closer understanding of a fact which is not easily provable in its measurable extent.

1. *London*: the driving of *slaughter animals* to London's Smithfield meat markets amounted to:

on average for the years	sheep	black cattle
1736–1740	599,466	97,548
1741–1745	531,134	85,892
1746–1750	655,516	80,878
1751–1755	610,618	80,843
1756–1760	616,750	91,699
1761–1765	730,608	93,480
1766–1770	632,812	84,244

Incidentally, these are confirmed by the figures provided by Anderson (1787, 4:156). A report to the House of Commons from the year 1795 contains in part different figures. But here it is only about quite rough approximate values. That the figures are correct in so far as they show none or only a tiny increase in the numbers at the London meat markets may be seen from the fact that at about that time (in the 1760s), just as with us in 1912, the expense of meat was complained about, which (a survey from the year 1764 gives information on this) was believed to be the result in specific respects to the deficient supply of cattle.

Of the brandy tax which amount in the year 1784 to £371,921 3 s 9 d, the payments in this year were:

London..£106,091 15 2
Surrey..£39,644 1 11¼
Hertford...£184,628 15 ½
London and surrounds..£330,364 12 1¾
The rest of England...£41,556 8 2

Admittedly, brandy production was concentrated in London and its surrounds, as is shown from the following figures from the official statistics on the gallons distilled from 10 September 1784 to 5 July 1785:

in	with distillers	with rectifiers
London	96,909	102,643½
rest of England	126,968	57,208½

The comparison of both figures, however, makes apparent that it was also about the so much greater *consumption* of Brandy in London.

Hard coal was already used as heating fuel in London in the Middle Ages — we hear already in the 14th century of complaints about the annoyance of coal smoke (Dunn 1844, 11; A. Anderson 1787, 4:701). Its use was supposed to be common since Charles I (Dunn 1844, 15). That signified a considerable demand in the big city. We are informed precisely over the quantity of hard coal brought into the ports of London. They numbered 6–700,000 chaldrons in the years between 1770 and 1790 (1779: 587,895; 1787: 764,272) (A. Anderson 1787, 4:321, 4:692), that is, since the chaldron comprised 36 bushels, it thus measured 1,272,265 litres, about one million tons. We may assume that these quantities essentially served the *London consumption,* since in that period only a little more than 100,000 chaldrons were exported from all of England, and we know from later evidence (parliamentary survey on 1829 in Dunn (1844, 74)) that at the time, before the introduction of gas lighting, 9 chaldrons per 8 persons were calculated for heating use in London. Since again according to other information the shipments to London, e.g. in the year 1776, amounted to over 68% of the total supply from Newcastle, you can say without further ado that the total coal demand of England rested for Tyne and Wear until almost the end of the 18th century on the mass consumption for heating purposes of London's population.

2. For *Paris* we possess for various years quite detailed consumption calculations which are absolutely usable for the aims being pursued here, as much as the individual figures might be able to be objected to in their absolute amounts.

Three official memorandums contain the imports of the most important foodstuffs for humans and horses. They were the following:

a) from the year 1634 a statistic which was provided in the orders of Michel le Tellier, the then Procureur du Roi au Châtelet, later Secretary of State and Chancellor;

b) from the year 1659 a table by Savary senior, who at the time occupied the Ferme du Domaine, Barrage et Entrée of Paris;

c) from the year 1722 a second table of the latter. The data in these three statistics refer to the consumption of salt, salted mackerel, salted salmon, dried cod, herring, coal, beef, pork, veal, mutton, grain, oats, hay, and straw.

The last source finally is:

d) the study by Lavoisier commissioned by the National Assembly in the year 1791 — Résultats extraits d'un ouvrage intitulé: De la richesse territoriale du royaume de France [Results taken from a book entitled: On the territorial wealth of the Kingdom of France] — in which he established with the use of official material (the taxation register) the consumption of the Parisians for a "normal year before the revolution" ("une année commune, prise antérieurement à la révolution") in almost all important foodstuffs and most commercial products. With respect to the sources from which Lavoisier draws, according to his own judgement the amounts of bread, drink, cattle, eggs, fish, fresh cheese, fuel, sugar, icing sugar, oil, wax, candles, wood, and building materials are exact and reliable; by contrast a "more hypothetical" character is carried by the figures for unsalted saltwater fish, metals, and "a few other types of wares".

At any rate it will be rewarding to share here the complete figures of Lavoisier's statistics, which are quite well-known, dispensing with an account of the much more incomplete statistics of the earlier years.

Lavoisier estimates the number of inhabitants of Paris at the time on the basis of births (19,769) which he multiplies by 30 to get a round 600,000. Then he establishes precisely on the basis of special levies which Turgot had made for the years 1764–1773 the quantity of grain and flour imported into Paris. We gather from it that at that time already the greatest part of the bread flour crossed the city boundary in a ground state (the picture with the many mills on the Seine that Paris offered in the 13th century had thus changed!). Annually between 1764 and 1773 the imports into Paris were:

     Grain.....................................14,351 muids[*]

     Flour......................................66,289 muids

Calculated in quantities of bread, that means that:

     in the form of grain: 14,330,880 pounds of bread

     in the form of flour: 165,457,344 pounds of bread

     arrived in Paris.

The working out of the cattle or meat consumption in the city then follows in Lavoisier's memorandum. Well-known is the number of driven cattle whose slaughter weight our informant sets as follows: ox 700 pounds, cow 360 pounds, calf 72 pounds, sheep 50 pounds, pig 200 pounds.

Accordingly the following annual consumption results:

Type of beast	Number	Slaughter weight
Oxen	70,000	49,000,000
Cows	18,000	6,480,000
Calves	120,000	8,640,000
Sheep	350,000	17,500,000
Pigs	35,000	7,000,000
Meat in slaughtered state	–	1,380,000
Total	593,000	90,000,000

---

*   [Tr.: a *muid* was a measure of capacity of varying amounts — originally a wagon load.]

The remaining objects of consumption and use to which Lavoisier's statements refer are then firstly provided by weight or number; in a second table he tried to establish their value on the basis of current prices. I will share the most important estimates and add an asterisk (*) as per the procedure of that author to those goods whose quantities could only be provided approximately.

Type of Good	Quantity	Value in Livres
Bread	93,440,000 kg	20,600,000
Wine	250,000 muids	32,500,000
Brandy	8,000 muids	2,400,000
Cider	2,000 muids	120,000
Beer	20,000 muids	1,200,000
Fruits & vegetables	—	12,500,000
Meat	40,820,000 kg	40,500,000
Eggs	78,000,000	3,500,000
Fresh butter	1,430,000 kg	3,500,000
Salted & clarified butter	1,220,000 kg	1,800,000
Fresh cheese	192,550 kg	900,000
Dry cheese	1,180,000 kg	1,500,000
*Fresh sea fish (Marée fraiche)	—	3,000,000
Fresh herrings	—	400,000
*Salted fish (Saline)	—	1,500,000
*Freshwater fish	—	1,200,000
Firewood	—	20,000,000
Wood in beams & for use	45,307 m³	4,000,000
Charcoal	700,000 cartloads (of 1.92m²)	3,500,000
Hard coal (? charbon de terre)	10,000 cartloads	600,000
Hay	6,388,000 barrels	2,100,000
Straw	11,090,000 barrels	1,980,000
Sugar & icing sugar	2,950,000 kg	7,800,000
Oil	2,720,000 kg	6,000,000

Type of Good	Quantity	Value in Livres
Wax & candles	244,000 kg	1,345,000
Coffee	1,130,000 kg	3,125,000
*Cocoa	113,000 kg	500,000
*Paper	2,720,000 kg	10,000,000
Potash & Sodium Bicarbonate etc. (Potasse soude et cendres gravelées)	1,040,000 kg	1,000,000
Copper	204,000 kg	450,000
Iron	3,630,000 kg	1,600,000
Lead	1,450,000 kg	960,000
Tin	159,000 kg	350,000
Mercury	8,200 kg	63,000
*Groceries (épiceries)	—	10,000,000
*Drugs	—	3,000,000
*Draperies (merceries)	—	4,000,000
*Haberdashery (quincailleries)	—	4,000,000
*Cloth	—	8,000,000
*Woollen cloth	—	5,000,000
*Silk and silk cloth	—	5,000,000
Linen	8,000,000 ells	12,000,000
Building materials (stone, tiles, lime, slate, cobblestones, etc.)	various, indiv. given	4,000,000
Various goods	—	6,857,000
amongst which soap	862,000 kg	—

Total Value: 260,000,000 livres.

3. For *Berlin*, Nicolai in his description of that city (1783, 1:234) made a just as detailed table of all the objects of consumption which was published and expanded by Mirabeau (1788, 1:2:148 ff.).

4. Likewise for *Vienna* in Nicolai (1783, vol. 3).

5. The statistics on consumption for *Dresden* in the year 1778 are to be found in Schlözer (1777, 4:287).

Chapter 52: The Demand of the Colonies

Sources and Literature

A *literature* which especially treats the problem of the market-forming power of the colonies in the early capitalist period is not known to me. It is touched on in works of trade history and industrial history — see, for example, for the United States Bishop (1868, vol. 1); Theodor Vogelstein[*]; Beer (1907); Taussig (1888); Rabbeno (1895); and Weeden (1890). Various things are also found in Bancroft[†].

For the other colonial empires see the writings named on 130 f. page above.

For *sources* and in particular *source literature*, various of the already mentioned works on colonial history come into consideration for the "problem of demand", such as Raynal (1775), Buchanan (1807), and others.

In addition, for the *entire British* colonial empire, see Campbell (1774, 2:586 ff.).

For *India*, see the "Reports [...] on the Administration of Justice in India".

For the *North American* colonies, see the report of the Governors to the Lords Commissioners of Trade and Plantation (e.g. for the year 1732).

For the *Spanish* possessions, see Ulloa (1753).

***

That the colonies and the related settlements of Europeans in the undeveloped and undiscovered foreign parts of the earth promoted quite significantly the "development of trade and industry", as per the commonly used colloquial expression, or more properly thus: the development of the capitalist

---

[*]   [Tr.: Sombart specifies loc cit as the reference but no previous reference exists – it could possibly be to Vogelstein's chapter in Leonhard et al. (1913).]

[†]   [Tr.: Sombart does not indicate which Bancroft or give any clues as to which work(s) are being referred to.]

economic system, is a view which the best experts have represented since time immemorial with all decisiveness and with every right. Above all their contemporaries were united over the colonies signifying an immeasurable value for the motherland, and that the wealth of the seafaring European lands was not least built on the colonial connections. We ourselves have likewise met the influence of the colonies on the transfiguration of European economic life already where we followed the origins of bourgeois wealth. And we must now establish here that the significance of the colonies in their influence on the reorganisation of demand is to be sought not the least in that it was exercised in various directions. Right there also where you do not immediately seek its effect. Thus, for example, John Campbell, one of the best experts on the colonial character of his times, showed rightly that the colonies had already thus become so significant for the sales of European goods because they *promoted shipping* and thereby produced a strong demand for the provisions for sailors and materials for shipbuilding:

> All the trades that are connected with building, rigging and supplying materials of every Kinds for ships and fitting out seamen are indebted to the same causes for their subsistence. The freight also both out and home is a matter of great consequence, amounts often to as much and sometimes more than the value of Goods. The provisions and other necessaries consumed by the Seamen in these long voyages, with many more articles which would be tedious to enumerate, concur to promote and to reward almost every species of industry exercised amongst us. (J. Campbell 1774, 2:566)

You will allow the correctness of these remarks without further ado if you recall that the Spanish fleet, but also all the large types of ships of the other seafaring nations as we saw them develop from the 17th century, almost entirely served the colonial commerce, and that of the English fleet a full fifth conveyed the trade with the West Indies alone, and that England (1769) supported 1,078 ships with 28,910 sailors just for the commerce with its North American colonies, etc. We will try to establish later more precisely in figures the large share of the colonial trade in the entire trade of the European states. Here I just want to bring attention to one of the side effects which the commerce with the colonies exercised on the market, and which is only too easily overlooked about the sales of goods to the inhabitants of the colonies themselves.

What Campbell explained for the demand from shipping and crews, he could have applied to another important category of demand which likewise experienced through the colonies an important expansion. I mean the *demand of the colonial armies* as well as all the expenditure which was made for military purposes in the colonies. We know how much the colonial undertakings were military undertakings, and what powerful garrisons and fortresses it was about. The building of forts and the upkeep of troops demanded large expenditures which were reflected in the form of a growing mass demand in the goods markets. It is useful to keep in view that, for example, in British India still in the second half of the 18th century the market which was formed by the demand of the army *was some five times as large* as that which arose from the sales of goods in India itself, as the following figures prove: in the years 1766, 1767, and 1768 the total value of goods imports to Bengal amounted to £624,375[583]; by contrast the civil and military administration in the same time period cost £3,971,836[584]. Since the military to administrative expenditure stood at about 5 to 1, £6–700,000 of that amount would be reckoned as the expenditure for the civil administration, so that the army demand would have amounted to £3–3¼ million — even that was five times the value of the goods imported.

But of course the goods sales to the inhabitants of the colonial regions *also* came into question. The overview across the international trade relations which the reader will find in part six of the next volume will provide information over the type and quantity of wares sold in the colonies. There we will see that it was about both the sale of many and valuable luxury goods and also a considerable mass sale of ordinary goods to the colonial markets. Here I would only like to mention what *the distinctive feature of these sales* seemed to consist of; and why precisely the colonies were enabled in such outstanding measure to take on goods in large quantities from Europe.

In order to give these questions a satisfying answer, we must without doubt examine the very different colonial regions individually and attempt to make clear for each their features as buyers.

But as different from each other as India and North America, the Antilles and Mexico also were — in a few points which are of special importance for their market-forming power, they demonstrate many concordant traits:

1. all had at their disposal an outstandingly strong spending power, as will yet be shown in detail, even if the sources of this power may have been quite different — here precious metals production, there rich fertility in desirable natural produce, there again the general wealth of an old civilisation;

2. in all of them the mother countries possessed a more or less complete sales monopoly, which again owed its origin to very different causes — natural or artificial;

3. the sales were agglomerated by the form of goods supply everywhere from the beginning, so that the supply had to take place from *one* place — the port of arrival, which was often also a market town (Portobello! Vera Cruz!) — in volume by necessity.

In particular the following picture arose.

The *Asiatic cultural realms* in which the Dutch and English especially nestled can be considered least of all to be sales areas for European goods. Both their low and high quality demand for consumer goods had been covered for centuries by their own production or by exchange amongst each other[585]. When the Europeans seized the Asian areas, they found, as is well-known, a blossoming trade being carried out between the individual realms, especially between Japan and China, between the Islamic and Chinese merchants. Even if they took away from them by violence a part of the trade, it did not yet always signify replacement of the indigenous goods by European goods. Certainly even here a more or less sensitive pressure was exercised on the population which was concerned with "convincing" them of the excellence of the European goods. "They [the Dutch] have brought the natives, where they have any influence, to cloath in the European manner, which has wonderfully [!] increased their commerce

from Europe thither" — i.e. to the Indies — declared Postlethwayt (1774, 1:304) enthusiastically. And we will see that the
European lords succeeded during our epoch in depositing a
few goods in their Asian possessions. But the actual conquering of the markets of the Indies, especially the British Indies
by the English, first occurs in the 19th century after the systematic destruction of Indian industry was begun from the
time of the Continental System*. First the famed commission
of inquiry of the year 1813 had to answer the fateful question:
how are we English to bring about forcing our trashy goods
on the Indians in place of their own excellent products?

The *American lands* were less capable of resistance than
the Asian, also probably having not as highly developed a
commercial production as the latter. To that was added that
in them more affluent Europeans had settled than in the
Asian colonies, so that they were considered in particular
more relevant as buyers of European luxury goods. A strict
ban on their own productive activity did not occur. The Spanish government declared with a certain air the principle: "Im-
porta menos que cesen algunas fábricas que el menos
agravios que puedan recibir los indios." [It matters less that
some factories cease than that the Indians may receive the
fewest grievances.][586] A certain sales monopoly created the
notorious institution of repartimientos†, about which we have
already heard in another connection[587].

In any case, we know that particularly in the 16th century,
soon after the conquest, a massive demand for luxury goods
emanated from those regions in which the Spanish had a
foothold, and that it was this which was benefited from at
first. In the year 1545 the Indian demand shall have been so
great that the entire nation would have had to have worked
ten years to satisfy it. Advance orders had arrived for six
years[588]. Velvet in Granada cost 20–29 reals, the Indian demand drove it in 14 days to 35–36 reals. The situation was
similar in Seville[589].

---

*   [Tr.: the Continental System was the economic blockade of Europe
against Great Britain led by Napoleon.]

†   [Tr.: system by which the houses and lands of the conquered population were distributed amongst those who took part in the conquest.]

The situation of the European possessions in the islands of the South Seas, the so-called *sugar colonies*, was entirely different. Here there was absolutely not an indigenous goods production which would have been capable of satisfying the demand of the white and black population for means of sustenance, objects of clothing, means of production, and luxury goods. But it was also entirely precluded that it could have developed to an appreciable extent — the natives had better things to do than farm grain or make boots and hats. They produced the strongly desired colonial products through whose supply they were put in the best possible position to obtain their entire goods demand, namely their demand for manufactured products, from abroad. Here a significant sales region for the motherland grew in which it could sell both luxury goods for the rich plantation owners[590] and mass-produced articles for the negroes. The uniform clothing of the slaves obviously produced a considerable demand for ordinary linen and cotton.

"Les habitans des Colonies de l'Amérique ont les mêmes besoins que ceux d'Europe, so on excepte les vêtemens d'hyver, que leur clima leur rend inutiles. Ils n'ont ni vins, ni eaux de vie de sucre, ni farines, ni salaisons, ni aucune sorte de manufactures. Il faut leur porter des étoffes légères, des toiles de toutes sortes, de la quincaillerie, des parures, des bas, des chapeaux, des meubles, des ustensiles de toute espèce, des armes et des munitions de guerre. Le commerce n'offre aucune branche qui embrasse une exportation si avantageuse et qui donne en même temps un retour si riche."

[The inhabitants of the Colonies of America have the same needs as those of Europe, with the exception of winter clothing, which their climate makes useless. They have neither wine, nor rum, nor flour, nor salted foods, nor any sort of manufacture. Light stuffs, canvas of all kinds, ironmongery, ornaments, stockings, hats, furniture, utensils of all kinds, arms and war munitions must be brought to them. Commerce offers no branch which embraces so advantageous an export, and which at the same time gives such a rich return.] (Sérionne 1768, 1:254-255).

The population assembled on the islands had already reached a considerable level towards the end of the 18th century, as the following figures show.

The population of the "sugar islands" (West Indies) amounted in 1793 according to Bryan Edwards (cited in Hüne (1820, 1:348 f.)) to:

	White	Black
Jamaica	30,000	250,000
Barbados	16,167	62,115
Granada	1,000	23,926

St Vincent..	1,450	11,853
Dominica...	1,236	14,967
Antigua...	2,590	37,808
Montserrat...	1,300	10,000
Nevis..	1,000	8,420
St Kitts...	1,900	20,435
Virgin Islands......................................	1,200	9,000
Bahamas...	2,000	2,241
Bermudas..	5,462	4,919
In total	65,305	455,684

There remained the *North American colonies* of England, which became an especially important market for the goods of the motherland. It is known that England here enacted a strict ban on manufacturing production and also, as far as we are able to judge, implemented it quite strictly. The English colonies in North America produced no manufactured products apart from a few coarse articles of demand. A few "manufactures" (e.g. of hats), which here and there operated in direct defiance of the ban, formed an insignificant exception.

The above-mentioned memoir from the year 1732 gives us a good picture of the state of manufactured production in the North American colonies. I will share some passages from it:

New Hampshire: "there were no settled manufactures [...] the people almost wholly cloathed with woollen from Great Britain."

Massachusetts Bay (New England): "in some parts of this province, the inhabitants worked up their wool and flax into an ordinary coarse cloath of their own use [...] the greatest part of both woollen and linen cloathing worn in this province was imported from Great Britain [...] there were a few hatters set up in the maritime towns [...] the greater part of the leather used in that country was manufactured amongst themselves [...] there had been for many years some iron-works in that province [... but] that province were not able to supply the twentieth part of what was necessary for the use of the country." From a later report: "Some other manufactures are carried on there; as the making of brown Hollands, for womens wear [...] they also make some small quantities of cloth made of linen and cotton, for ordinary shirting and sheeting. By a paper-mill, set up three years ago, they make to the value of £200 yearly."

"There are also several forges for making of bar iron and some furnaces for cast iron — and one slitting mill: — and a manufacture of nails. The governor writes, concerning the woollen manufacture, that the country people who used formerly to make most of their cloathing out of their own wool, do not now make a third part of what they wear, but are mostly cloathed with British manufactures [...] there are some few copper mines in this province but so far distant from water carriage, and they are so poor, that it is not worth the digging [...] they have in New England 6 furnaces and 19 forges for making iron [...] in this province, many ships are built for the French and Spaniards [...] Great quantities of hats are made in New England [the worst offence!] [...] they also make all sorts of iron-work for shipping. There are several still-houses and sugar bakers establishements in New England [...]"

But New England was also the painful child of mother England! And nonetheless, how tiny is the extent of manufacturing production even here.

New York: "they had no manufactures in that province that deserved mentioning"; in a later report: "the Company of Hatters of London have since informed us, that hats are manufactured in great quantities in this province."

New Jersey: "no manufactures here that deserve mentioning".

Pennsylvania: "having no manufactures established; their cloathing and utensils for their houses being all imported from Great Britain".

Rhode Island: "there are iron mines there; but not a fourth part iron enough to serve their own use."

What the later experts report to us about the state of manufacturing production makes us realise that this did not expand essentially in the North American colonies in the course of the 18th century[591]. In order to gauge how large an area of demand became accessible here for the motherland, we must bring to mind the *number of inhabitants* in the North American colonies around that time. Even if the estimate of the "Congress of America" from the year 1774 is obviously too high, namely 3,026,678[592], we may assume though that at the time of their secession the colonies were inhabited by more than a million people. I share here the quite consistent figures which two trustworthy informants openly give from good sources in their works[593]:

Colony	Per Campbell	Per Raynal	
New England	500,000	400,000	
New York	120,000	150,000	
Pennsylvania	2–300,000	150,000	whites
		30,000	blacks
New Jersey	600,000	50,000	whites
		20,000	blacks

Colony	Per Campbell	Per Raynal	
Maryland	100,000	40,000	whites
		60,000	blacks
Virginia	150,000	70,000	whites
		110,000	blacks
In total:	1,130,000	1,080,000	

Section 7: The Procurement of the Labour Force

Overview

Without a suitable labour force in sufficient quantity — no modern capitalism. Hence the "emergence of a class of wage labour" forms one of the necessary conditions of the capitalist economy. On closer inspection, it is revealed that the problem is twofold. It concerns on the one hand the question of how, when, and why a sufficient quantity of propertyless people (wageworkers in potentia) developed; on the other hand, however, as we will see, the far more important question of how the entrepreneur got hold of a sufficient and willing labour force (wageworkers in actu). The second part of this problem forms a part of the state *policy* in the mercantilist age. I said above on page 43 why I wanted to treat "labour policy" separately — because it demands for its understanding an investigation of the form of the labour relations themselves and because this is only possible in a later part of this work. This point has now been reached. In accordance with the particular arrangement of material necessitated by this special treatment, this section breaks into two separate components which are each represented by a special chapter — depiction of the objectiveness of the labour relations (Chapter 53) and depiction of the conduct of state power called forth by it (Chapter 54).

***

Literature

This part of economic history and politics is treated quite shabbily by the *literature*. Except for England, a summary of the specialist liter-

481

ature is not known to me. The numerous texts which occupy themselves with the "history of the working classes", even when they call it the "proletariat", are aligned entirely to completely different points of view, also most are kept much too general to be able to be of considerable use to us. Thus the problem posed here is barely touched on in well-known works like Bensen (1847), Baumstark (1853), Eccardus (1907), Var (1845) (which is essentially about the revolutionary movements of the labouring population, not about them themselves), and Villard (1882) (that author actually only acknowledges rural labourers and craftsmen up to 1789).

The labour relations and labour policy is mostly attended to by the researchers in the *depiction of the industrial policy* or in the general economic history (Levasseur even calls his book a history of industry and the working classes, despite it containing nothing especially interesting about the latter). Hence reference is to be made to those works which I named in Chapter 24.

To that is then added those writings which have the *history of the poor* as their object, since the poor and the working class (the poor, the labouring poor, Le Pauvre = wageworkers!) in those centuries touch closely on each other. I refer to the article on the history of the public care for the poor by Uhlhorn (1890) and the literature cited there. For our purposes, of the general depictions the following come into consideration: Gérando (1839), which is now superseded though by the great work of Lallemand (1902) whose four volumes cover the modern period from the 16th to the 19th century. The second book of the first part contains an exhaustive overview of the measures adopted in the various states against beggars, vagabonds, etc. Naville (1836) retains independent value alongside it because of its statistics. — From the recent, survey literature of the individual lands, the excellent book by Paultre (1906) especially deserves being singled out. I will be citing even more specific specialist texts in the course of the portrayal.

The history of *English* labour relations and English labour policy during the period of mercantilism has been the object of special portrayals several times. Three groups of authors can be distinguished, of which I name the most important:

1. the trade unionists: Brentano (1872); Webb and Webb (1894);

2. the historians of prices and wages: Rogers (1884); Steffen (1901) (the best depiction, but predominantly a history of wages);

3. the Marxists: they all trace back to the 24th chapter of Marx (1903, chap. 24; 1906, chap. 26) and paraphrase it without adding anything essentially new. Especially worth considering are Hyndman (1883); and Kautsky and Bernstein (1895). Marx's chapter over the "primitive accumulation of capital" was for its time an achievement of genius. Today its depiction is dated. We know that almost no word in it is "correct", that is, that it can be reconciled with the facts.

Indispensable for the study of the older English labour and poor policy is the work by Eden (1797). It contains:

1. still today the best, in any case most detailed historical portrayal of the topic, which is above all valuable through the long extracts from the hard to obtain pamphlets of the 17th and 18th centuries;

2. (the main content) a survey of the position of the worker and the state of the English poor in the 1790s;

3. furthermore in the appendix, all the important labour policy laws and regulations verbatim (Appendix VIII);

4. registers of *all* labour policy laws, regulations, etc. from 1 Edw. 3 c.7 (1327) to 36 Geo. 3 c.51 (1796) ((Appendix IX);

5. a bibliography of ca. 300 texts over labour relations and the poor in the English language from 1524 to 1797.

Studies corresponding to the state of our current knowledge over the origin of the wage labour class, over the position of the wage worker during the epoch of early capitalism, as well as over the mercantilist labour policy are urgently needed. I will yet name a few specialist texts which handle this theme in the further course of the portrayal.

***

Chapter 53: The Unemployed

I. Mass Misery and Mass Begging

The labour problem during the epoch of early capitalism is only to be understood if you bring to mind the strange contradiction which actually constituted the peculiar form of the labour market during the entire period — the contradiction that at the same time a surplus of labour power reigned and in many places a lack of labour power made itself noticeable. When I say a *surplus of labour power* reigned, it is to be understood by it that there was in all states from the 15th to the 18th century a great mass of propertyless, poor, fit for work people who did not find their sustenance through gainful employment or not in sufficient measure, and they as a consequence either begged or starved and in the end died of hunger. The *fact of mass misery* during all the centuries of early capitalism and in all the European lands is seen to be vouched for by a sufficient quantity of evidence.

France: Already in the 14th and 15th centuries we hear of an "almost general misery": Levasseur (1900) has summarised the sources in the second chapter of the first book under the title "Appauvrissement du pays" [Impoverishment of the country]*. I add that at the beginning of the 15th century, Guillebert de Mets estimated the number of beggars in Paris at 80,000 (!?). In Troyes there resided, according to a census of the year 1482, at the time 15,309 people "aside from perhaps 3,000 beggars" (Paultre 1906, 2 f.). Towards the end of the 16th century, the number of beggars increased alarmingly. In 1578 the lay judges of Amiens reported of 5–6,000 workers "estans à l'aumosne nourris par les autres habitans aisés" [receivers of charity fed by other well-to-do inhabitants]. The richest cities had the most poor, because all vagabonds streamed together there. In the last years of the century L'Estoile spoke

---

* [Tr.: that chapter is in fact titled "Appauvrissement du royaume" [Impoverishment of the Kingdom].]

of the "processions de pauvres qui s'y [in Paris] voyaient par les rues en telle abondance qu'on n'y pouvait passer" [processions of the poor which were seen there [in Paris] in the streets in such abundance that one could not pass] and told of how in the Hôtel Dieu "il mouriot près de six cents personnes par mois, la plupart de faim et de necessité" [nearly six hundred people died a month, most of them from hunger and necessity] (L'Estoile 1741, 2:269). In the year 1576 they erected in Paris "public workshops", "des ateliers publics" in order to occupy the beggars and vagabonds who filled the streets (Robiquet 1880, 653 f.).

Paris remained forever the main seat of misery and begging — in 1634 there were according to Talon (1821, 1:98 f.; cited in Moreau de Jonnès 1867, 217–18) 65,000 beggars there, which would have been a quarter of the population. According to another source, the number of beggars in Paris in the year 1640 was numbered at 40,000 (Histoire de l'hôpital général de Paris 1676; cited in Gérando 1839, 4:486).

In a memo to the governors of police in Paris in the year 1684 it spoke of the "misère affreuse qui afflige la plus grande partie des habitants de cette grande ville" [terrible misery which afflicts most of the inhabitants of this great city]. Confirmed by official reports. (Levasseur 1900, 2:333)

In a petition of the poor of Paris from May 1662, it says: "que les pauvres de Paris sont en très grand nombre et très grande nécessité [...] Leur misère est parvenue à son comble. Les hôpitaux sont si pleins qu'ils ne puevent plus recevoir" [that the poor of Paris are very numerous and in great need [...] Their misery has reached its peak. The hospitals are so full that they can no longer accept them] (Depping 1850, 1:654 f.).

The beggar in the grand style is deemed directly to be an unavoidable accompanying symptom of the culture and wealth. Thus Voltaire took the view towards a writer who had claimed that the more barbaric a land was, the more beggars were found there, that by contrast many beggars was a sign of the highest civilisation — for no city in the world is less barbaric than Paris, and in no city would there be more beggars than in Paris — "je pense qu'il n'y a point de ville moins barbare que Paris et pourtant où il y ait plus de mendiants. C'est une vermine qui s'attache à la richesse; les fainéants accourent du bout du royaume à Paris pour y mettre à contribution l'opulence et la bonté." [I think there is no city less barbaric than Paris and yet where there are more beggars. They are a vermin that clings to wealth; lazy people rush from the ends of the kingdom to Paris to contribute to opulence and goodness.] (Voltaire 1877, 22:361).

Mercier (1782, 11:340 f.) also suggested: "Les mendians vagabonds se multiplient dans les pays riches" [Vagrant beggars multiply in rich countries]. In addition, he ascertained a decline in the beggars in Paris — that "active and industrious poverty" (cette pauvreté active et laborieuse) had taken its place which alone constituted the wealth of the kingdom (!).

But not only in Paris, even in the countryside misery reigned and spread begging and vagabondage. Most of all in years of rising prices, like those of 1693 and 1694. On 15ᵗʰ January 1693 the bishop of Noyon asked the Contrôleur général to issue an order against the banding together of the poor — "La chose presse d'autant plus qu'ils menacent les curés, les religieux et les principaux habitans des villages de les piller s'ils ne font des aumosnes au-dessus de leur pouvoir" [The matter is all the more urgent as they threaten to loot the priests, the monks, and the principal inhabitants of the villages if they do not give alms beyond their power.] (Levasseur 1900, 2:351 f.).

"Les villes se remplissent de pauvres que les bourgeois ne peuvent plus soutenir. La calamité est encore plus affreuse dans les villages" [The towns are filled with poor people whom the burghers can no longer support. The calamity is even worse in the villages], wrote the intendant of Languedoc on 6ᵗʰ November 1693 (Levasseur 1900, 2:351).

The bishop of Montauban (16ᵗʰ April 1694): "nous trouvons presque tous les jours à la porte de cette ville 7 à 8 personnes mortes, et dans mon diocèse, qui compte 750 paroisses, il meurt bien 450 personnes tous les jours faute de nourriture" [we find almost every day at the gate of this city 7 to 8 people dead, and in my diocese, which has 750 parishes, 450 people die every day for lack of food] (Levasseur 1900, 2:351).

The intendant of Bourdeaux (19ᵗʰ April 1692): "il meurt tous les jours un si grand nombre de personnes qu'il y aura des paroisses où il ne restera pas le tiers des habitants" [so many people die every day that there will be parishes where less than a third of the inhabitants will remain] (Levasseur 1900, 2:351).

"Le menu peuple [...] est beaucoup diminué dans ces derniers temps par le guerre, les maladies et par la misère des chères années qui en ont fait mourir de faim un grand nombre et réduit *beaucoup d'autres à la mendicité*" [The common people [...] have been greatly diminished in recent times by war, disease and the misery of the dear years which have starved many of them and reduced *many others to begging.*] (Vauban 1851, 86).

On 4ᵗʰ August 1710, Fénélon wrote to the Duc de Chevreuse: "La culture des terres est presque abandonnées; les villes et la campagne se dépeuplent; tous les métiers languissent et ne nourrissent plus les ouvriers. La France entière n'est plus qu'un grand hôpital désolé et sans provision" [Cultivation of the land is almost abandoned; the cities and the countryside are depopulated; all the trades are languishing and they no longer feed the workers. The whole of France is nothing more than a large desolate hospital without provision] (Mothe-Fénelon 1825, 18).

In 1740 the bishop of Clermont to Fleury: "Our people live in terrible misery, there is a lack of beds and furniture, most do without for half the year of even the barley and oat bread which forms their only sustenance" (cited in E. Jäger 1890, 1:167).

An intendant wrote in 1772 to Terray: "La disette et la misère sont extrêmes dans divers cantons de la Bretagne" [Famine and misery are extreme in the various cantons of Brittany] (Levasseur 1900, 2:773).

In many provinces you could like in Le Berri speak: "de la misère extrème des dernières classes de la société" [of the extreme misery of the lowest classes of society] (Levasseur 1900, 2:785).

A pastor in Pas-de-Calais wrote in June 1786: "Je suis curé depuis trois ans; je n'ai pas encore vu la misère et la pauvreté montées à un si haut degré qu'elle est aujourdhui. Puis-je avec cinq ou six habitants nourrir trente-trois autres ménages nécessitaux?" [I have been parish priest for three years; I have not yet seen misery and poverty rise to such a high degree as it is today. Can I with five or six inhabitants feed thirty-three other needy households?]*.

I add to that a few texts from which the spread of the state of misery into the individual parts of France during the 16th to 18th centuries is to be seen: Hippeau (1870, 129 ff.), Sée (1906, 469 ff.), Chotard (1898), Valran (1899, chap. 3), and Feillet (1865) (the portrayal is tarnished by the liberalising tendency of the author).

A good overview across the French misery literature is given by Letaconnoux (1906, 418).

The expression "mendianisme" [beggary] arose in the 18th century.

The same picture in *England*: according to Harrison (1577–1587) there had been for about 60 years "many unoccupied beggars" in England; only recently had they become a real plague on the country; when he wrote (1580), he estimated their number at about 10,000 (cited in Steffen 1901, 1:462).

In the 17th century, begging in England increased rapidly. King (1804) estimated the number of those persons who were reliant on support at a quarter of the entire population, which he set at 5½ million. We can read off the state of the destitute existences as if from a barometer by the extent of the poor tax. But this already amounted in the year 1698 to £819,000 — that was perhaps a quarter (!) of the value of the export trade at the time. As if we today [1916] had to ante up 2½ billion marks in poor taxes. In addition, however, street begging continued to exist. Even in England begging seemed to have expanded with a preference for the capital city. At the end of the 18th century, you still encountered "an [...] enormous number of beggars on the streets in London" (Archenholtz 1787, 1:151).

As in England, so in *Scotland*: at the end of the 17th century 200,000 work-capable vagabonds shall have lived there (Fletcher 1698; cited in Mackintosh 1892, 3:255). The same source wrote: "many thousands of our folk die today from lack of bread."

And even in *Holland* it looked no different: "the entire land teems with beggars" (in the 17th century) (Pringsheim 1890, 61).

If the three richest European lands offered this image of mass misery, then it can be assumed without further ado that it stood no better in the other states.

In *Germany* one counted in the 18th century in the ecclesiastical territories for every 1,000 inhabitants 50 clergy and 260 beggars. In *Co-*

---

*   [Tr.: not referenced by Sombart.]

logne there shall have been 12,000 beggars (Perthes 1862; cited in Roscher 1854, 5:13). According to other reports, the number of beggars in Cologne shall in the year 1790 have even amounted to 20,000 (of 50,000 inhabitants) (Forster 1794; cited in Kuske 1914, 74). For the 16th century, cf. also Brant (1854, § 63). — In no way, however, did the beggar as a mass social phenomenon limit itself to the ecclesiastical or even only to the Catholic lands (as, for example, Friedrich Nicolai claims). Even in the Protestant states there was no lack of begging. Everywhere the begging mandates were the order of the day. The words of the legislator: begging increases "the longer, the more" are persistent formulae. In the Brandenburg-Prussian collection of edicts we count during the 17th and 18th centuries over 100 edicts against the beggar and vagabond state of affairs, of which a half were during the period from 1700 to 1789. In 1790 the Hamburg Society for the Promotion of the Arts and Useful Industry enacted a prize competition — for the expedient employment of the lazy and recalcitrant poor — stimulated by it (F. W. Wilcke 1792). Cf. also Frauenstädt (1897a; reprinted in 1897b).

Other source evidence on the begging in all of the German lands during the 17th and 18th centuries is given by Schorer (1904, 177 ff.). See also the literature cited with the mentioning of the workhouse problem and the problems with the origin of begging.

In the 17th and 18th centuries, idleness and begging also took on a threatening extent in *Switzerland* (Joneli 1907, 184 ff.).

Austria (in the 17th and 18th centuries): in Vienna the number of beggars was so great that faced with the siege by the Turks they grasped the measure of getting 7,000 of them out of the city. In Iglau there were, as in other cities, numerous citizens who, unable to get by as craftwork masters, served as day labourers. In the year 1719 the city numbered amongst 6,246 inhabitants 386 beggars. In the 1720s, when the Oriental Company in Upper Austria sought after workers for the Linz sheep's wool goods, the number of beggars in this land was estimated at 180,000 (M. Adler 1903, 49).

Italy (Piedmont): according to a hearth statistic of the year 1743, of 8,500 families of a district 3,162 were receivers of alms. A census in the following year resulted in numerous districts in "crowds of beggars" (Prato 1908, 331).

"The Origin of the Proletariat"

The *causes of the origin of this mass misery*, that is thus of these suffering masses, was questioned above all by Marx and his students. Since they had adapted their observations to England, that thus suggested that they make two events above all responsible for the origin of propertyless masses of people — the enclosures, and the abolition of the monasteries. Both rightly. Only you should guard against overestimating their effects.

(1) The first period of the enclosures falls in the time from 1450 to 1550. At the time in fact, community land was enclosed to a wide extent and arable land was probably also encroached on with the aim of extending the pastoral economy. Only you must not believe the hyperbole of Harrison and More* without further ado, but rather must attempt to present statistically how many farmers could perhaps be made propertyless by those enclosures.

In the first edition of this work (Sombart 1902a, 2:161 f.) I made the attempt to *calculate* the acreage that fell victim to the enclosures on the basis of wool export statistics, and arrived at the result that some 3% of the total acreage of England's arable land had been transformed into pasture by the end of the 16th century. Only subsequently did the publications of the Royal Historical Society become known to me, in which the results of the survey officially established in the year 1517 over the extent of the disclosures from 1488 to 1517 was worked out — Leadam (1897).

If I take the county of Berkshire as an example (for Berkshire and Buckinghamshire more exact information is available), then the following calculation results.

In the years 1488 to 1517, 0.59% of the total area of the county was transformed by enclosures into pastoral land (Leadam 1897, 1:515) — if we assume that this relationship would have remained the same from 1450 to 1600, then by the end of the 16th century 2.95% of the total acreage would have been transformed into pastoral land. My calculation would thus have proved quite correct. Naturally such an almost complete agreement is no more than a happy accident which rests in addition on a number of arbitrary assumptions. But what the figures of the survey prove with all desirable clarity is the fact that the correctness of my assumption, that the enclosures in the 15th and 16th centuries concerned a vanishingly small part of the total acreage, is absolutely confirmed. The acreage which was enclosed in the five thoroughly investigated counties from 1488 to 1575 amounted to 1.39 to 1.98% of the total acreage (Leadam 1897, 1:72). A large part of the enclosed land, however, was destined, the figures of the survey give this as well, not for pasture, but rather for arable purposes. We also learn, however, for two counties of the number of people displaced by the enclosures. They were, in the 30 years to which the survey refers, 670 in Berkshire and 1,131 in Buckinghamshire (Leadam 1897, 1:509, 1:579). Berkshire has now about 200,000 inhabitants, if the ratio is assumed to be the same as 400 years ago, thus perhaps 25,000, of that annually 22 to 23 people would have been driven from their properties by enclosures.

---

*   [Tr.: presumably a reference to William Harrison (1535–93) and Thomas More (1478–1535), both cited in Marx (1903, chap. 24; 1906, chap. 27).]

During the 17th and 18th centuries, the enclosures made only tiny progress towards the goal of an expansion of sheep pasture, just as up to the middle of the 18th century for those which shall have served the goal of moving to a more intensive arable farming. But this, which admittedly reduced the number of independent farmers, did not reduce at all the demand for agricultural labour.

"It was alleged that enclosed land gave employment to a larger number of hands than unenclosed." (Cunningham 1907, 2:555; paraphrasing T. Hale 1758, 1:208).

Conversely the commons was made directly responsible for the slowing population — most of the poor were in parts of the country where *a lot of* common land was, like in Kent. "Whether commons do not rather make poor by causing idlenesse, than maintain them" (Hartlib 1655, 43; cited in Cunningham 1907, 2:568).

The investigations of recent years, which furnish no new figures for the 16th and 17th centuries, do not come to any essentially different results, but do give a good overview — Tawney (1912, 113, 156 ff., 270 ff.) and Gonner (1912, 387 ff.).

Thus the enclosures certainly only delivered a quite small part of the propertyless and unemployed whom we meet in particular during the 17th and 18th centuries in England. From where else did they come?

(2) Was it the poor removed from their livelihood through *the dissolution of the monasteries* who now had to move through the land begging?

Indubitably this measure contributed much to increasing the number of unprovided for poor in England. Before the dissolution of the monasteries and when England was still Catholic, a third of the tithes served for the support of the poor which the monasteries and foundations devoted themselves to. Now 644 monasteries, 110 hospitals, and 2,374 chantries (houses of prayer at which most alms were dispensed) were dissolved, and all the poor provided for here — it has been calculated that there were more than 88,000[594] — saw the necessity now to obtain their livelihood in another way. They certainly represented a considerable contingent for the army of unemployed, beggars, and vagabonds. But even if we wanted to assume that all 88,000 monastic poor, which were actually only 35,000, had been turned into beggars, from where did the remaining hundreds of thousands come from who by all appearances were in the England of the time? We can only guess.

I think they originated both from the surplus population and the subsidised population.

(3) A *surplus population*, that is, a population which grows in excess of the sustenance available, must have arisen by necessity as soon as the land which farmers and craftsmen had possessed was settled, but the population nonetheless increased. That was now, even if to a moderate extent, precisely the case in England. The population of England (according to Rogers[*]) seemed to have remained towards the end of the 16th century approximately stationary, but then in the 17th century to have increased quite considerably. At the end of the 17th century, King (1804) estimated it, as we have seen, at 5½ million; in 1740 it amounted to 6, in 1750 to almost 6½, in 1770 to 7½, and in 1780 to 8 million.

But we will certainly always have to reckon in the epoch of early capitalism up front with the *subsidised population*, thus with such people who forfeited their economic independence, if we want to explain the great mass of unemployed. Only it is wrong, as Marx did, to see in both the mentioned methods of violent loss of property or income the only way to the creation of a propertyless proletariat. That does not even apply to England.

(4) Here we will rather have to see as at least just as significant as that sudden "robbery" the process of *gradual impoverishment* of independent agricultural or trade producers, if we want to explain the origin of the wageworker class. There were entirely natural processes of differentiation which eliminated from the farming community and the civic community of craftsmen in the course of the centuries non-viable existences which either sank down into begging or were at least needful of a subsidised income.

This gradual impoverishment of the old craftsmen existences is probably one of the most important causes for the origin of a class of workers ripe for capitalism. We will later follow exactly how these impoverished farmers and masters represented a very large contingent of the workers occupied in cottage industry. The fact is so generally well-

---

[*]   [Tr.: this could be a reference to Rogers (1866), or to Rogers (1884), or to Rogers (1898).]

known that it need not be proven first through source evidence. Particularly in the *textile industry* this sort of origin for the proletariat was especially common. See, for example, for *Italy (Florence)*: Doren (1901,
1:266 ff.); for *England*: Bonwick (1887, 403 ff.); for *Germany*:
Schmoller (1897, 77), Stieda (1889, 135), Zimmermann (1885, 56 f.),
and Troeltsch (1897, 22).

(5) Entire industries were shaken in their existence, their
representatives were suddenly ruined by *great sales stagna-
tions* which (as we will yet see) during the early capitalist
period were very frequent, but also already belonged to the
iron nature of the economy organised on a craftwork-like
basis. How can you even in England, in view of the centuries-
long development of a capitalist cottage industry, particularly
in the textile industry, want to attribute all of the propertyless
wageworkers to those two violent acts?

(6) We also must not forget that *the abolition of serfdom*,
which is already beginning in England in the 14th century,
now released existences which had formerly been sustained
on the great estates from the soil in which they had found
their nourishment up to then, and drove them into open begging.

(7) In the same sense, *the dissolution of fealty* made itself
noticeable here and there.

But how can you at all claim[595] that the English development represents a general rule?

Whereas both those events (enclosure and the dissolution
of the monasteries) doubtless played a role *together* in the
formation of the English proletariat (next to other, probably
more important causes), they do not come into consideration
for the other lands at all. What was it in these, especially in
France, the classic land of early capitalism, that produced the
propertyless or property-poor masses from which the wageworker class was formed? Above all of course again the causes
already acknowledged under (3) to (7). In the lands of the
European continent, these general causes are joined by:

(8) *war*, whose destructive and wasteful effects, particularly in France and Germany, are tangible[596];

(9) *the tax burden*, of which we may assume with certainty
that it in turn above all in France, but then too in a land like
Holland, destroyed numerous formerly independent existences. Anyone who knows the economic literature of France

of the century from 1650 to 1750 knows that the leading experts, like Vauban, Boisguillebert, and Melon, explained the impoverishment of the French people above all by the high and particularly badly assessed and partisanly levied taxes.

Here, as I have already said, comprehensive studies must be instituted which get beyond the class of mere guesswork that is certainly well-justified in more general considerations.

A nice start has been made by the repeatedly mentioned book by Kuske in which the origin of the civic trade and commerce workforce in Cologne is vividly described. "There were retailers and publicans, 'failed craftwork masters', furthermore craftwork journeymen who could not become masters, unskilled workers who came from 'dishonest' circles, etc." (Kuske 1914, 92 f.) More such monographic investigations over the origin of 1. the working, but also 2. the poor (beggars) must be carried out. *From this other side* light is spread by the interesting study by Detlefsen which I cited in note 596. It contains excerpts from an accounts book over the poor administration of the parish of Neuenkirchen an der Stör. It teemed with beggars from all over the world. Receivers of alms were: the war disabled, the wounded, the maimed, retired officers, former army chaplains, those dispossessed by fire, the shipwrecked, those impoverished by flooding, dislodged preachers, schoolmasters, organists, preachers' wives, wandering students, the blind, the lame, the possessed and other sick people, converted Catholics and Jews, etc. (Detlefsen 1901, 128). Similar investigations for a limited area have already been made by some older works like: Brückner (1856), and Pfaff (1857). Cf. also Leonard (1900, 14 ff.).

A fruitful, not yet at all exhausted source is the *contemporary poor literature*. I refer, for example, to Wagemann (1789b); furthermore to the informative article series in the Schlesische Provinzialblätter (Anonymous 1800), whose author describes with great expertise the various groups of beggars; and to Wilcke (1792).

III. The Lack of Labour Power and its Reasons

When you read through certain sources for the industrial history of the 16th, 17th, and 18th centuries — petitions by entrepreneurs, reports by officials, hearings by committees of experts or authorities, memoirs or stories by people familiar with industry — the lament always sounds through that there is no lack of work, there is a lack of workers. It will suffice if I share here a few random samples which let it be shown that the same phenomenon was to be observed in the various lands under quite different conditions and which only agree to the extent that it was about the demand for workers of rising capitalist industries during the last three centuries of the period of early capitalism.

In *Spain*, which is well-known to have experienced a rapid blossoming of industry in the 16th century, the Cortes* lamented in the year 1552 (pet. 120 cited in Colmeiro 1863, 2:93): "pues antes faltaban jornaleros que jornales" [since workers were lacking rather than wages].

France: in the year 1764 the woollen ware manufacturers of Vienne were complaining that the cotton ware manufacturers of Neuville were also having their cotton spun in the region of Dauphiné where the Viennese factories had brought in over many years work with much expense a core of good spinners ("Tableau de la manufacture de Vienne en Dauphiné" (1764 Ms.) cited in Kowalewsky 1909, 2:86). We hear the same complaint from the manufacturers in Sedan according to a memorandum written by Tricou, inspector of manufactures in Sedan (cited in Kowalewsky 1909, 2:88).

In Languedoc, the provincial representatives declared that there was a lack of workers in the countryside thanks to the development of the wool industry (Des Cilleuls 1898, 190).

In the Parisian Cahiers of the Estates General from 1614, the same complaint (Hauser 1903, 389).

"Les tireuses et les dévideuses deviennent rares" [Drawers and unwinders are becoming rare] — from a letter of the Intendant Letourneur to the head of the merchants in Lyon on 17th September 1745 (cited in Des Cilleuls 1898, 163).

In a letter of 20th November 1781, one of the factory inspectors of Montaurais mentions the question of whether and to what extent the boom which the cotton industry had experienced during the previous months had robbed the woollen ware manufacturers of their workers (Ms. cited in Kowalewsky 1909, 2:91).

There was a lack of workers in the iron industry of the South of France (Kowalewsky 1909, 2:104).

England: Defoe (1704) puts up as the first thesis: "there is in England more labour than hand to perform it, and consequently, a want of people, not of employment." Source references for the 18th century in Cunningham (1907, 2:529).

When Mr Dale wanted in the year 1784 to start his cotton spinning mill in Lanark, Owen (1813, 35) explained: "it was [...] necessary to collect a new population to supply the infant establishment with labourers. *This however was no light task.*"

Spinners were lacking in the cottage industry in the 18th century (James 1857, 252 ff.).

Germany: there was a lack of workers in Baden's iron industry (16th century) (L. Beck 1884, 2:702); and of mine and ironworkers in the Upper Harz (16th century) (L. Beck 1884, 2:794).

"Often the diligent countryman must share with these idlers from his sourly acquired stores just for a time, since he is incapable of getting

---

*   [Tr.: Cortes = Spanish legislative assembly.]

hold of any day labourers for his fieldwork even for a lot of money."
(Klein 1792, 131)

There was no lack of employment (Rochow 1789, 34).

The writer of the essay in the Schlesische Provinzialblätter mentioned above reported about begging labourers, "who with all the lack of workers in Silesia ran around though after a position" (Anonymous 1800, 32:203), and in another place about the "lack of workers growing from the begging" (Anonymous 1800, 32:237).

A lack of people in Baden (18th century) (Roller 1907, 337).

There was a lack everywhere of spinners (18th century) — in *Saxony*: A. König (1899, 83); in *Silesia*: Bergius (1775, 2:372 ff.).

Switzerland: in the Basel silk ribbon industry (17th century) (Geering 1886, 602).

Austria: a daily wage determination for craftsmen from 1686 resulted in a lack of journeymen (Quarient und Raal 1704, 2:324). A lack in the Moravian cloth industry (18th century) (Mises 1905, 235).

Sweden: see Krügern (1763).

When you ask about the reasons for *such a lack of workers*, which is an extremely conspicuous phenomenon in view of the fact of a general mass surplus of humanity, then you can distinguish external and internal reasons.

You may above all see the *external* reasons in the deficient understanding and connection which existed at that time between the individual regions of a land and between the individual industries. It thereby came about that an oversupply of labour power in one place could not simply fill in a gap in another place. This lack of an offset of labour quantities has persisted up into recent times and must obviously be assumed to have been active for the early period of capitalism to a heightened degree. It will also be allowed that this evil must have made itself especially tangible in a land like England whose poor laws fixed the unemployed artificially to a place, whereas elsewhere the limitation of freedom of movement existing everywhere contributed in its own way to hinder an even distribution of labour power across the entire land.

But to me the significance of the *internal* reasons which produced the lack of workers despite a surplus of workers seems to exceed that of the external reasons by far.

By internal reasons I understand the *character of the labour material* itself. We want to bring to mind that the mere physical existence of labour power yet in no way suffices for satisfying a specific demand for the performance of work. It can in fact very well be that those people who are physically

496

there and are also purely physically capable of work (those in-capable of work in a physical sense, like babies, geriatrics, the ill, invalids, etc., we naturally ignore when we speak of "la-bour power") either are *unable* to work or do not *want* to work. We may assume now, however, with the workers of that early capitalist period both shortcomings or one of them, and it was this shortcoming in the workers themselves especially which called forth the lack of workers.

They *could* not work because in most cases they did not possess sufficient preparatory training. The essentially still empirical technology of that time carried with it now, how-ever, the result that the skilful ability to work was bound up to a much greater extent than perhaps today *in the person* of the worker. Hence it could not, or not so quickly as you wished, be transferred to other persons. Industries which de-manded their own skill and own training could as a result al-most only be fostered or expanded in that you drew trained workers from other regions or lands. This technical character of industrial work which is completely different from the cur-rent one explains for the good part the fact that you could ex-perience in the midst of work-capable people a lack of workers, but also explains an entire, important group of measures of state labour policy, as will be shown in the next chapter.

We have been able to follow how in the Middle Ages during the craftwork-like epoch this *boundness of the capabilities to the person of the worker* was made tangible — in the lack of craftworkers, in the transplantation, alienation of craftworkers, etc. But now it must be es-tablished that this personal boundness of the technical means must have *continued during the entire period of early capitalism*, because indeed technology remained fundamentally empirical in its basis. An example: for centuries the hats of the Roman cardinals were made in Caudebec-en-Caux, a town in Normandy. When the hat makers emig-rated to England after the revoking of the Edict of Nantes, their craft emigrated with them — cardinals' hats could now only be made in Eng-land. In the middle of the 18th century a French hat maker, Matthieu, re-turned home to France and open a large hat factory in Paris — with that the secret returned to France (Cunningham 1897, 243). This depend-ency of production on the person of the worker lasted throughout the entire 18th century — in 1768 40 Frenchwomen were brought to Glasgow in order to weave fine thread (Cunningham 1907, 2:331) — and reached deep into the 19th century — in the 1820s the *machinery industry* in Germany could still only be introduced through the *import* of English experts and workers (Berger 1895, 153). Similarly with the *iron in-*

dustry — the first workers by means of which Remy* introduced the puddling process to Germany had been temporarily transferred by John Cockerill† of Seraing in the province of Liège (Berger 1895, 165). By contrast, Harkort (in 1826) fetched over again English workers for the establishment of a puddling and rolling steelworks (Berger 1895, 166).

A vivid picture of the difficulties in introducing the so-called Styrian scythes manufacturing to Remscheid is drawn by Eversmann (1804, 392 f.).

But now even this shall we say technical awkwardness of the workers would have been lifted much more rapidly — at least in the course of several generations — if another obstacle had not stood in the way of the training up of a class of workers suitable for capitalist production — an obstacle which was based in the mental state of mind of the people themselves. It is namely quite clear to see that the property-less or property-poor people of those centuries *did not want to work*, in any case did not want to work *in the way which* and *on what* the capitalist entrepreneurs desired from them. This shall we say natural laziness, idleness, indolence of the great masses was detected by every contemporary who expressed themselves over the labour relations of those centuries with a strange consistency in all the lands of the early capitalist culture. This judgement then solidified in the economic theories and the practical suggestions of reform into the claim that only with low wages were people to be moved to work, and consequently also of course, with everyone for whom it was about an expansion of the capitalist economy, to the demand for as small as possible a calculation of the reward for labour *so that* people would see themselves forced into regular work. These theories of wages and labour, even of poverty[597] are the outflow of a general opinion over the mental composition of the great masses and can thus serve us as a source from which we can draw the knowledge of the *views* at the times over labour relations (not so easily these labour relations themselves).

I will share a few especially representative utterances of practitioners and theorists of the 16th, 17th, and 18th centuries, in which are reflected:

---

*   [Tr.: German steel-making firm.]
†   [Tr.: a major Belgian steel-making firm.]

The views over the psyche of the worker of that time

Italy (16th century): "Voleno inanze stentare e morire di fame che lavorare per bon mercato e guadagnare la spesa" [They want more to struggle and die of starvation than work for a good wage and earn their expenses] (Bianchi 1862, a. 1528, a. 1534; cited in Tamassia 1910, 28). Cf. Palmieri (1909).

France: for France we possess above all in the remarks of Colbert and his officials an ample material for judging the labour relations at the time. They despaired over the idleness and ponderousness of the population who resisted them like a heavy, tough mass in their efforts to promote industry in the land.

In his letters, Colbert spoke of Avranches in which "le peuple est très fainéant" [the people are very lazy], of Bourges whose inhabitants were "d'une fainéantise sans pareille" [of unparalleled laziness]. He wrote to Basville in 1662 that he might make arrangements "de retirer les habitants de Poitiers de l'extrême fainéantise dans laquelle ils ont esté de tout temps et sont encore plongés" [to pull the inhabitants of Poitiers from the extreme laziness in which they have always been and are still immersed]. He recommended to the lay judges of Abbeville industry as the best means "pour bannir la fainéantise et réduire la mendicité aux malades et aux invalides" [to banish laziness and to reduce begging by the sick and disabled]. "Comme la ville d'Auxerre veut retourner dans la fainéantise et l'anéantissement dans lesquels elle a esté, mes autres affaires et ma santé m'obligent à l'abandonner à sa mauvaise conduite" [As the city of Auxerre wants to return to the laziness and destruction in which it has been, my other business and my health oblige me to abandon it to its bad behaviour].

In Chevreuse, the demesne of his son-in-law, Colbert tried to establish a woollen stocking industry: "Ils préfèrent emplir les cabarets" [They prefer to fill the cabarets], he wrote.

The reports of the intendants to Colbert are tuned to the same note. In 1669 the intendant of Bourges reported many communities had foregone introducing bobbin-lace making: "prétendant que l'application à cet ouvrage gastait la vue" [claiming that applying themselves to this work would ruin their eyesight].

The intendant of Bourges wrote another time: "La fainéantise est si grande dans la ville et le plat pays, que j'avance que je ne puis revenir de l'étonnement où m'a mis leur paresse et ce ne sera pas une petite affaire que de réduire ces gens-ci à travailler de la bonne manière" [The laziness is so great in the city and on the plains, that I say that I cannot recover from the state of astonishment in which their laziness put me and it will not be a small matter to get these people to work in the right manner].

The same laziness was reported from Saint-Flour, Auxerre, Avranches. (Depping 1850, 3:768, 3:770; Clément 1861, 2:209, 2:356, 2:515, 2:542 n.1, 2:589, 2:680, 2:714, 2:731, 2:760, 2:792)

The comprehensive attempts at education of Colbert had been incapable of solving the problem — the 'fainéantise' [laziness] remained (according to the judgement of contemporaries) even in the 18th century the basic feature of the French masses.

In the province of Dauphiné, the intendant Fontanien complained at the beginning of the reign of Louis XIV over "l'indolence espagnole et du génie des Valentinois, paresseux par tempérament et par éducation" [the Spanish indolence and the genius of the Valentinois, lazy by temperament and by education].

In Auxerre they spoke in the second half of the 18th century, as at the time of Colbert, of the necessity "de tirer le peuple de son inertie et de son assoupissement" [to pull the people out of their inertia and their drowsiness] (Levasseur 1900, 2:774).

From these observations then, the wage theorists and wage policy makers drew the conclusion that thus as little as possible must be given to the worker so that he goes to work. I refer to Bigot de Sainte-Croix (1788). Mayet (1786; cited in Godart 1899, 266):

> "Dans une certaine classe du peuple, trop l'aisance assouplit l'industrie, engendre l'oisivité et tous les vices qui en dépendent [...] Si la nécessité cesse de contraindre l'ouvrier à recevoir de l'occupation, quelque salaire qu'on lui offre, s'il parvient à se dégager de cette espèce de servitude, si ses profits excédent ses besoins au point qu'il puisse subsister quelque temps sans le secour de ses mains, il emploira ce temps à former une ligue"
> [Within a certain class of people, too much ease makes industry more flexible, engenders idleness and all the vices that depend on it [...] If necessity ceases to compel the worker to receive from his occupation whatever wages are offered, if he succeeds in freeing himself from this kind of servitude, if his profits exceed his needs to the point that he can subsist for some time without the help of his hands, he will use this time to form an association].

England: all the observers of the state of workers in the 17th century agreed that the worker only condescended in the most extreme case of need to work and only ever worked just as much as he needs for the most necessary livelihood. Hence he was all the lazier, the cheaper food and drink was (and the higher the wages).

"It is observed by Clothiers, and others, who employ great Numbers of poor People, that when Corn is extremely plentiful, that the Labour of the Poor is proportionably dear, and scarce to be had at all". William Petty, who made this judgement his own, added: "so licentious are they who labour only to eat, or rather to drink" (Petty 1755, 132–33).

We find this same view with Manley: "We have thousands of people miserably poor, yet will not work on such moderate terms the employers can chearfully afford them"[*]. With Temple; with Locke; with John Houghton, amongst others. See the evidence in Kostanecki (1909) and Schulze-Gävernitz (1892).

---

[*]   [Tr.: from a 1669 pamphlet by Delarivier Manley cited by Kostanecki (1909, 63).]

A competent judgement from the beginning of the 18th century: Defoe expressed himself in his well-known essay "Giving Alms no Charity" as follows:

> I affirm of my own knowledge, when I have wanted a Man for labouring work, and offer'd 9 s. per Week to strouling Fellows at my Door, they have frequently told me to my Face, they could get more a begging. (Defoe 1704, 12)
> Good Husbandry is no English Vertue [...] We are the most Lazy Diligent Nation in the World [...] there's nothing more frequent, than for an English-man to Work till he has got his Pocket full of Money, and then go and be idle, or perhaps drunk, till 'tis all gone, and perhaps himself in Debt; and ask him in his Cups what he intends, he'll tell you honestly, he'll drink as long as it lasts, and then go work for more. [...] I make no Difficulty to promise on a short Summons, to produce above a Thousand Families in England, within my particular knowledge, who go in Rags, and their Children wanting Bread, whole Fathers can earn their 15 to 25 s. per Week, but will not work. (Defoe 1704, 25–27)

Another writer:

> Every body knows that there is a vast number of Journy-men Weavers, Taylors, Clothworkers, and twenty other Handicrafts; who, if by four Days Labour in a Week they can maintain themselves, will hardly be perswaded to work the fifth; [...] When Men shew such an extraordinary proclivity to Idleness and Pleasure, what reason have we to think that they would ever work, unless they were oblig'd to it by immediate Necessity? (Mandeville 1723, 210-211 Remark Q)

(The great cynic then summarised his labour policy programme in the words: "where the Poor are well managed; who as they ought to be kept from starving, so they should receive nothing worth saving" (Mandeville 1723, 212 Remark Q).) In another place, Mandeville works out how necessary for a land which wants to become rich a large number of poor people are who must work because they suffer hardship (hence no charity for God's sake!): "if no body did Want no body would Work" (Mandeville 1723, 327).

Similar too is the impression which Arthur Young in the 18th century received of the working population in and around Manchester. The people are only industrious when food and drink is dear and they *must* work in order to not starve — when their livelihood is cheap, then the children of workers' families die, "for half the time of the father was spent at the ale-house" (Young 1770, 3:244). "The master manufacturers of Manchester wish that prices might always be high enough to enforce a general industry; to keep the hands employed six days for a week's work" (Young 1770, 3:249).

Holland: the following picture of the lifestyle of a Leiden weaver at the end of the 18th century was drawn for us: "Throughout the entire summer there were parish fairs alternating in the surrounding villages, for which a number of wagons stood ready at the gates to take the exuberant weaver with wife and child to the pleasant village. Arriving there, everything is joy and delight, and I need not say that the exuberant worker, after he had drunk and danced a decent amount, after arriving home had no or at least very little desire to work and would rather let everything lie than curb his desires" (Brender à Brandis 1786, 2:160; cited in Pringsheim 1890, 53).

Switzerland: it is to be noted "that most local subjects do not think of any saving of their earnings, but rather country-wise thus repeatedly overfill themselves with bread and nourishment as if everything had to go down the throat at once". From a report by the board of directors of the Basel merchants of 1717 (Joneli 1907, 191).

"The tiny amount of cotton spun by such people in this year proves that they would rather dedicate themselves to begging and idleness than useful work [...] a few have even had the audacity to sell the cotton delivered to them and the necessary equipment for the spinning and support themselves on the money." From a report of the poorhouse deputation to the lower parliament (in Basel) in 1761 (Joneli 1907, 205). The reason for the unemployment and the increasing street begging, it was said in another report of the same deputation from the year 1771, lay in many cases in a "bad money management and negligent performance", since many citizens "instead of diligently taking responsibility for their profession or business and taking care of the board and lodging of their families, would rather drink away what they have earned in their taverns and thereby leave their wife and children miserably going hungry" (Joneli 1907, 218).

The same thoughts return still more frequently in the reports which Joneli (1907) shares excerpts of.

For *Germany*, *Austria*, and other lands, the same thing is reported.

The question now is will we share these views as the contemporaries consistently expressed them? I think yes. We are brought to that firstly by the testimony of so many, in part completely disinterested men whom we must not expect to have seen the thing wrongly or portrayed it in a biased manner. They were too expert for that. The judgements only become skewed when they come from a doctrinaire mind. In order to cite an example: Mirabeau cited a remark by Normann over the laziness of workers in Germany whose meaning culminated likewise in that the people worked only so much as they needed to live; when bread is cheap, no thread was delivered anymore. To that the physiocratic doctrinaire remarked that that could not be correct, the free man and those who freely employ him have no need of such coarse motivations to work! But the men of the 17th and the early 18th centuries did not look with such glasses at the world, and hence they will surely have observed correctly.

We have, however, yet other reasons for believing in the indolence and laziness of the masses in the early capitalist period. I do not even think of *the numerous indicators* which lead us to conclude a comfortable and cosy state of mind, like perhaps the number of holidays which interrupted the work right up until in our stricter time. Of their extent, we have difficulty in getting a proper idea. Even in the 17th century, barely 100 8-hour work shifts were operated in the Carinthian iron industry. In Paris, when they wanted in 1660 to reduce the 103 holidays to 80, riots broke out and six more were added.

I think rather that we should recall that the state of mind of the great mass of workers at the beginning of the development of capitalism *could not have been any different* than those men whose voices we heard have described to us. The worker found himself still in the state of mind of any "primitive" man, and that *is* one of idleness or at least comfort. Above all the opinion also still reigned in him which we find widespread with the pre-capitalist economic subjects — that you busied yourself and worked in order to live, not lived in order to busy yourself, to work. Thus that you did not continue working when you had "enough". Even this idea of an "enough" is nothing other than ghost of the spirit of the pre-capitalist economic disposition — it is the same idea which in the idea of sustenance and of income befitting one's station returns in philosophical depth and programmatic emphasis.

That this "primitive", pre-capitalist economic disposition is no empty delusion, that it also then still survives in the economically dependent masses when the will for capitalism has long since animated an upper class, and that a characteristic of the early capitalist societal stratification is this conflict between individual economic subjects in which the acquisitiveness, the rationalism, the lust for enterprise is already active, and a mass of economic objects living still in the traditional craftsmanship — that is something a study of the economic conditions teaches us in such lands as are still in our lifetime making that transition from craftwork to capitalism. I once described[598] what difficulties even today (and perhaps always?) opposed capitalism in *Italy* in the population of many parts of the land which was resistant to all economic discipline and all specifically capitalist acquisitiveness. Even up until a few years ago, you could encounter the lazzarone* in Naples who only ever interrupted his dolce far niente† for a few hours or days in order to earn by work the few soldi which he needed for his modest livelihood, but whom no power on earth could have moved to work for even just one minute longer than was demanded for the acquisition of that minimal amount which he needed for the grace period of his life. Certainly, climate and national character contribute their own bit to bringing the type of the lazzarone to its full development. But the spirit of the lazzarone is the spirit of every pre-capitalist human, and it is nothing other than the state of the lazzarone which we encounter in all workers of the early capitalist epoch and which brought all the friends of "industrial progress" to despair — as it still today brings them to despair where it survives.

We will now look at how the modern state placed itself in respect to this problem, what it did to eliminate the split which was yawning between the character of the workers and the capitalist interests.

***

---

*   [Tr.: Italian for shirker.]

†   [Tr.: dolce far niente = sweet doing nothing.]

Chapter 54: The Measures of State Labour Policy

I. The Leading Ideas

Nowhere as clearly as in its labour policy actions did the basic conception of the absolute principality reveal itself.

That it took no measures under a different point of view than that of the welfare of the state (which had merged with the interests of the monarch quite spontaneously) goes without saying. All thoughts of the welfare of the individual, all "humanitarian" stirrings were missing. Only in the second half of the 18th century do they begin to win influence over the decisions of governments. The people of the early capitalist period were a hard race which was consumed by the struggle for objective ideals — be they religious, be they of the nature of the state — and which sacrificed its individual tendencies to serve the higher goal. The labour policy of mercantilism must above all also be understood from this idealist mood regarding the state. We must guard against setting about the interpretation of conditions and events in the epoch of early capitalism with the idea of class differences, economic interests, and other individualist categories like those which our time has developed.

Hence, investigations like those the economic historians of some schools employ (typical of which is, for example, the book of Faber (1888)), which would like to derive the measures of mercantilist policy from specific groupings of interests, fundamentally miss the mark. If it is already questionable in our time of the naked struggle of interests to explain at least for a land like Germany perhaps the agricultural policy as pure "interest politics", then the carrying over of the well-known game of questions of who has an "interest" in high grain prices, who in low grain prices (as forms the content of the cited book by Faber, which here only stands as a representative of an entire school) to the England of the 17th and 18th centuries, even if you take into consideration that this land at the time was already beginning to orient its policy to the point of view of the shopkeepers, that it already had a "parliamentary" constitution and mostly inferior kings, would be a crude mistake. Even in England at the time the "common interest" had still preserved a strong power and even decided over the economic and "social" policy measures.

What the welfare of the state demanded, however, was clear — the power of the state lay in its military power; this was thus above all to be preserved and strengthened. It is delightful to follow how even in a state like England even until up into the middle of the 18th century the military interests stood in the foreground with all economic policy considerations — read therefore the writings of Temple, Petty, Defoe, and the numerous pamphlets of the 17th and early 18th centuries about the poor, and you will be astounded, even with such a "progressively" (in the direction of commercialisation) minded man as Defoe, to hit again and again on the same idea: if you were to accept this suggestion, then your army and fleet would be strengthened by so many men.

From this basic striving indeed, as we know, the entire mercantilist policy was born — a lot of war demands many men and much money; many men are produced by the increase in the "manufactures"; much money is brought into the country by the export trade, when it is "active". Manufactures and export trade are supported by the up and coming economic elements — *thus* a community of interests resulted between capitalism and the principality — thus the capitalist interests had to be tended. Tending the capitalist interests meant, however, smoothing the way for the capitalist entrepreneurs. Thus — from well understood interests of state — the mercantilist policy received an "entrepreneur-friendly" stamp, and thus labour policy was also carried out under the viewpoint of enacting measures by means of which you could assure the entrepreneur of ample, industrious, efficient, cheap workers. Now where the interests of entrepreneurs and the interests of labour stood opposed, the interests of the entrepreneurs were unconditionally defended — the labour policy of mercantilism is as a result almost through and through a protection of entrepreneurs, not a protection of workers. Because the welfare of the state demanded it be so, for no other reason, absolutely not because they would have had more sympathy for the class of entrepreneurs as such than for that of the workers. Once more: such individualist stirrings were entirely foreign to that period. As soon as even once the interests of the entrepreneurs came into opposition with the interests of the state, the state legislation was also turned against them. That is proven by the laws for the protection of farmers, which even in England (where apart from that they saw the expansion of the pastoral economy fundamentally as a commandment for the state's welfare) was not lacking for a time[599]; it is proven by the approaches to that which we today call "worker protection" — like the ban on trucking and similar measures.

If you wanted to conclude from the events in England during the 18th century, where you turned away the workers who demanded a stricter enforcement precisely of the state's edicts of the 16th and 17th centuries and let the entrepreneurs calmly transgress those laws of Elizabethan times, that here obviously the "class interest" had been put ahead of the interests of the state, then that would be false. I believe rather that you can still explain that behaviour of the English government by its striving to perceive the contemporary interests of the state in contrast to the aged edicts of the same state.

But be that as it may, there can be no doubt about it that in the overwhelming majority of all cases the labour policy of mercantilism was defined to preserve *the interests of the entrepreneurs*.

It received its peculiar stamp now by the way in which the state understood how to bring into harmony this practical goal of its own with the moral and social views which had come down to it from the Middle Ages.

The basic idea of the medieval social doctrine remained even in this part of the mercantilist politics untouched — like all economic activity, it was also a matter of fitting the tasks and duties of the worker into the great cosmos of the human economy. The view that the sealing of a labour contract and the regulation of work conditions is a private matter which only concerns the employer and the worker would have appeared monstrous to that time. No — even these relations are to be ordered according to objective rules, and this order emanates from the authorities. The observation that the individualistic powers were already during the epoch of early capitalism rendering these objectively organic principles more and more irrelevant must not stop us from seeing the entire justification of the mercantilist labour policy dominated still by that medieval outlook.

Certainly, the material demands of the medieval social policy, which, as we have seen, was dominated by the idea of "sustenance" and of the livelihood befitting one's station, by the "just" price and with it also "just" wages, could be fulfilled by the state in its labour policy only to a limited extent. It still took as its starting point in its determinations these basic ideas; but it bent them in a direction in which no breaking off of its entrepreneur-friendly tendencies needed to happen — where the Middle Ages had the "just" reward for labour, be it determined by the demands of the traditional livelihood, be it determined by age-old customs, the modern state (like the modernising city governments already before it) indeed also established a "just" wage, but which now became a maximum wage, and (it is the advance of the law in 5 Eliz. 1 c.4 (1562)) which was adapted to the varying market prices — the autonomy of the morally commanded was thereby shaken for the first time.

II. Old and New Forms of Bondage

The most effective means which the public authorities had at their disposal in order to provide the missing labour power for the entrepreneurs existed at all times, as long as there were still no tribe of propertyless, free men, in that the compulsory recruitment of the worker and the external compulsion to work were legally permitted. This means also served the modern principality in so far as it on the one hand preserved for many centuries during its existence old traditional forms of bondage, and on the other hand where such were not preserved anymore, allowed or even developed new ones.

The *old serfdom of the countryfolk* existed up until the end of the early capitalist epoch in the Central European states, and to deep into the 19th century in Eastern Europe. It performed essential service to the upwards striving capitalism. Not only in the area of agriculture itself, where it is well-known that the modern large estates were built on the compulsory labour of farmers and the compulsory service of the farmer's children, but also in the sphere of industrial production. A great part of the mining and industry of Germany, Austria, Poland, Russia, in part even of Scandinavia during the early period of capitalism was being carried out with serfs, that is, with compulsory labour.

In *Germany* bonded workers had been used in the beginnings of capitalist industry surely to a large extent. Thus we learn, for example, that in the 16th century entire districts which were under the subjection of the Fuggers were *weaving* for them (C. Jäger 1831, 648). But even in the 18th century the subjects of the lords were brought in for *spinning* — particularly in *Silesia*. See the information in Grünhagen (1894, 242).

Likewise for labour in *mining* and the *coal and steel industry*. In a pamphlet from the 1780s the following was reported about *Upper Silesia*: "The great quantity of newly set-up ironworks and hammers have recently become a real detriment for agriculture in that you have the necessary handiwork and transport performed not by hard cash and your own oxen, but through compulsory labour. By that arose the essential disadvantage for agriculture that the handwork and oxen originally designated for its prosecution was withdrawn from it for the most part." (Anonymous 1788, 234).

The privilegium for the miners in *Nassau-Saarbrücken* from 25th January 1788 specified: "A serf, when he works in the mine, is free on payment of an imperial taler from levy in kind and having to participate as beaters on hunts." In Hue (1910, 1:338).

Austria: In the account books of many industrial enterprises, for example, the Oberleutensdorf cloth factory, no information is found in the 18th century over wages for labour — the serfs had to perform the work in the factory as obedient duty. This relationship lasted until into the 19th century (Schlesinger 1865, 139 f.). All the subjects of the Waldsteins spun for a long time for the neighbouring Royal Bolzasche cotton factory in Cosmanos (Demuth 1890, 331 f.).

In addition, see Grünberg (1893, 1:86, 2:181 ff.).

Poland: the employment of serfs in the rising industries of the 17th and 18th century was across the board. "The cloth factory (in Wengrow) sustained itself on the labour of the serfs who delivered finished thread. The foreign masters worked up this thread into cloth; all the preceding stages of the production process, like the combing of the wool and the spinning itself, were completed by the hands of the serfs. Thus the manufacturing industry still bore a fief-like character — the employer also used the serfs for industrial activity. This characteristic peculiarity became even more clearly evident in the industrial enterprises which the Polish magnates erected on their estates, and which almost exclusively rested on the exploitation of the gratuitous labour of the serfs." (Wobly 1909, 377 ff.).

Russia: it is well-known that the Russian industry during the entire 18th century, but also still beyond that rested on the employment of serfs who were placed at the disposal of the entrepreneurs in varying forms. The state's peasants who were employed in the works of the state (mining, iron) were likewise handed over to the private works. The number of male souls who performed such compulsory labour in the coal and steel industry alone amounted to:

	in the state's works	in private works	together
1741–43	63,054	24,199	87,253
1794–96	241,253	70,965	312,218

See Mavor (1914, 1:434 ff., esp. 1:441). In addition there was still compulsory labour in other branches of production, in particular also in the cloth industry (Mavor 1914, 1:489 ff.). See apart from that the detailed depiction in Tugan-Baranowski (1900, 24 ff., 51 ff., and elsewhere).

***

But the legislators also did not shrink from introducing there anew a sort of state bondage, as Steffen[*] rightly describes it, where the medieval serfdom of the country folk either did not exist at all anymore or was not effective without special state decree. This *new serfdom* was based on that in specific cases the compulsory recruitment of labour power was allowed in agricultural or industrial undertakings, even if the persons had not previously belonged to a poorhouse, indeed even if they had perhaps not taken up as beggars at all — their status of being propertyless sufficed to subject them to this compulsory labour.

Compulsory labour (state serfdom): in *Spain* already in the 16th century, in the time of the great boom in Valladolid, Zamora, and Salamanca, the beggars and vagabonds were forced to work in the factories (Häbler 1888, 59).

In *France* compulsory service existed for certain road workers (Paveurs) in the 16th century, which was not identical with the corvée (Vignon 1862, 1:19). But we also see how Colbert forcibly pulled in stoneworkers to work on the royal castles. Order from September 1682:

> "Il est ordonné à Antoine Thevenet, garde de la prévosté de l'hôtel et grande prévosté de France, de se transporter incessamment dans les villages de Herblay [...] et autres lieux et maisons particulières, où il trouvera des carriers en grès et les amènera

---

[*]   [Tr.: presumably Steffen (1901).]

aux carrières de Louveciennes et de Marly pour y façonner du pavé"
[Antoine Thevenet, warden of the provostship of the lodge and grand provostship of France, is ordered to travel without delay to the villages of Herblay [...] and other places and private houses, where he will find sandstone quarrymen and bring them to the Louveciennes and Marly quarries to shape cobblestones]

(Clément 1861, 5:302 n.2)

The *Dutch* had the children of those "who are too poor to keep themselves" (N.B. thus *not only orphans*) raised at public cost, and they were then delivered by the mayors as apprentices to the entrepreneurs (Davies 1851, 1:488; cited in Pashley 1852, 207).

Germany: frequently compulsory spinning — "at the complaint made by the cloth manufacturers that they lacked spun silk [...] at the beginning of the year 1761 in all their domains — i.e. Silesia — it was urged that they hold the persons of both sexes resident in their villages, old and young, who otherwise had no other profession or income and lay on the lazy bench [...] to spin wool for the cloth and other manufacturers in their region." Circular of 9th January 1761 on the subject of the soldiers' wives and children having to spin compulsorily. Circular of 6th June 1763 on the topic of the rural servants and such like. Cf. Regulation of 7th July 1765. See Bergius (1775, 2:372 ff.).

But even in other industries we meet the compulsion to labour, e.g. in *mining*. In the year 1616 the Landgrave of Hessen-Kassel ordered that "all strong beggars, beer drunks, those thus constantly lying in the taverns", and also "abandoned servants and gardeners, those endeavouring to exercise begging among our subjects", should be urged "to work at our mines for fitting reward", and if they refused, they were "to be thrown in irons and delivered to the mines" (Hue 1910, 1:336 f.).

Switzerland: in the town of St Gallen the authorities especially sought to hold the poor companions "stupid of face or even old persons unsuitable for other work" for spooling and spinning cotton — see, for example, the town council's minutes of 18th June 1773 in Wartmann (1870, 1:151 n.3).

Austria: the report of the Bohemian governor of 5th August 1717 expressed the expectation that the introduction of the finer cloth manufacturing into Bohemia would be possible especially with the help of a planned "poor, orphans, and workhouse". In a memorandum from 1721 the inner Austrian chamber suggested that the reigning misery and idleness could be helped by the erection of a cloth factory which at the same time would have to be a house of forced labour. Poor, work-capable people were present "in terminable surplus". It was necessary "to catch and to lock up" the requisite number of workers among the street beggars of Graz. The factory building had to be made of bricks and be surrounded with walls so that the worst rabble could not break out (M. Adler 1903, 89).

The governments also ordered the domains to place at the disposal of the factory owners "lively and capable heads of both sexes". From a circular of the county authorities to the masters of the Krems district from 2nd April 1767 concerning the provision of apprentices for the velvet factory of André Tetier in Krems (Mises 1905, 216).

The "state bondage" in *England* and *Scotland*, however, was developed into an artful system. The Magna Carta of bondage is described to us falsely, because much to narrowly interpreted, as a "law of apprenticeships". Statute of Artificers 1562 (5 Eliz. 1 c.4). Its expressed aim was "to banish idleness". To this end it made the following regulations:

§4: all unmarried persons under 30 years who had trained in one of the named industries (the most important) or practised it for three years, and were propertyless and without employment could (with cooperation of the authorities) be taken compulsorily into service by anyone who ran one of these enterprises;

§7: concerned similar regulations over the compulsory recruitment into agricultural enterprises;

§28: young people could be compulsorily taken into training (except for mercers, drapers, goldsmiths, ironmongers, embroiderers, or clothiers — there the parents of the young man must have a small property which bears at least 40 /).

Similar regulations were contained in the *Scottish* laws of 1617, 1649, and 1663. See the depiction in Mackintosh (1892, 3:249 ff.).

But even outside the area of application of those Elizabethan laws of compulsion various bondage-like conditions reigned in English and Scottish industry through the entire 18th century and up into the 19th century. It applied in particular to coal mining mainly in Scotland. Here circumstances had formed "by which the miners were just as definitely astricted to particular mines as villains had been to particular estates in the middle age". The laws 15 Geo. 3 c.28 (1775), 39 Geo. 3 c.56 (1799) attempted in vain to put things right. Even in the year 1842 the Commissioners of Staffordshire could report: "here in the centre of England slavery reigns which is as loathsome as any of the slavery in the West Indies."[*]

Next to this direct forced labour, however, a process now developed during the early capitalist epoch which consisted of bringing the remiss workers to work *in a roundabout way* in that you "educated them to work". From these efforts grew an artful system of compulsory labour which we must get to know more precisely in the following.

III. The Education for Work: the Workhouse System

From the laws and ordinances which were enacted from the middle of the 14th century in all lands almost with the

---

[*]   [Tr.: not referenced by Sombart, and translated from Sombart's quoted German (presumably translated originally from English).]

same words to control the begging and vagabondage, two different branches of internal political activity developed in the course of time. The one was formed by the large, ever expanding and deepening administrative area which we today describe by the words welfare of the poor. That is not our concern here.

The other branch died off towards the end of the 18th century. But it had the greater significance for the epoch of early capitalism. It was all the endeavours of the government to educate the people to work. We must now make ourselves conversant with these endeavours.

Already from the earliest anti-begging laws the complaints sounded of what a loss the land was suffering when so many people went idle. It was not the need to improve the miserable lot of the poor devils who were begging for bread which destined the legislators to step in, but rather — next to the efforts to establish order and security in the land — the wish to make use of the labour power present in the land.

This wish had to have been made especially strong and tangible in the first years after the great plague in which the beginnings of the vagabondage laws in many lands also then occurred — Spain in 1351; England in 1350: ordinance of Edward III; France in 1350: ordinance of King John. These laws proceeded consistently: the beggars should work, otherwise they were hit with heavy penalties — even for this a similar measure developed in all lands — in the first instance whipping, in the second mutilation or branding, in the third death or expulsion or forced labour on the galleys. It was believed you could break the will for idleness with these hard penalties. They were deceived — the laws remained mostly without success. Their frequent reenactment proves it.

Thus they then thought of another means to keep the idle population at work — the authorities placed the means of labour at the disposal of those who could employ the beggars.

This thought grew into the *workhouse system* by which all work-capable beggars were kept by the authorities at work which the state itself organised. Mostly the work in the workhouse was built on indirect compulsion — the beggars lost the right to support if they did not perform the work in the workhouse (so it was in the heyday of the English workhouse), or it

was forced labour in the actual sense (thus in the French dépôts de mendicité [depots of begging]).

There seemed to have been *workhouses* first in *Italy* — we find in
1539 in Albergo dei Poveri [lodge for the poor] in Genoa already 500
men and 1,300 women occupied with weaving. In 1582 (1618) the Albergo di Carità [lodge of charity] in Turin was opened, in which likewise
wool, flax, and cotton was processed. Other spinning and weaving
houses were found early on in Cannagnola, Novarra, Vigevano, Venice,
Bergamo, Florence, Sienna, and Rome (Gérando 1839, 3:538 ff.). There
was promotion of industry in the workhouses in Piedmont by Victor
Amadeus II (Prato 1907, 353).

Also in *Spain* the erection of workhouses had already been started in
the year 1545 by P. Juan de Medina (Gérando 1839, 3:580 f.).

In *France* they opened in the year 1576 in Paris "public workplaces"
in order to employ the beggars and vagabonds who filled the streets
(Levasseur 1900, 2:144). That workhouses at the beginning of the 17th
century were already present is acknowledged by the royal mandate of
27th August 1612. But their proper flowering was first achieved under
the government of Colbert. Through numerous edicts which began in
the year 1652 and whose most important was that of June 1662, the
"Hôpitaux généraux" [general hospitals] were created — institutions in
which all sorts of work-capable, idle folk were gather together and to
whom the prerogatives of small manufacturers were granted. Colbert
wrote on 22nd September 1667 to Maire and Schöffen of Auxerre:

> "D'autant que l'abondance procède toujours du travail et la mi-
> sère de l'oisivité, vostre principale application doit estre de trou-
> ver les moyens d'enfermer les pauvres et de leur donner de
> l'occupation, pour gaguer leur vie"
> [Especially since abundance always proceeds from work and
> misery from idleness, your main application must be to find the
> means to lock up the poor and give them employment in order to
> make a living.]

The Hôpitaux généraux expanded across numerous cities. Necker
founded 700 of them, whereas later by the Comité de mendicité [com-
mittee for begging] during the revolutionary period 2,185 were detected. In the year 1764 the Dépôts de medicité (maisons de force, de
renfermement, de travail [houses of force, of containment, of work])
were called into life, of which at the time of Necker there were 33 with
6–7,000 inmates (Necker 1784, 3:159 f.).

In *England*, which is described not unjustly as the classic land of the
workhouses, the development started only later.

In the year 1575 (through 18 Eliz. 1 c.3 "Poor Act" (1575)) it was regulated for the first time — Justices of the Peace were empowered to buy
or to rent in each county a house in which a supply of wool, hemp, flax,
iron, and other raw materials were to be made available in order to
thereby employ work-capable beggars. This thought, which was repeated in 43 Eliz. 1 c.2 "Poor Relief Act" (1601), seemed, however, to

have at first been carried out little or not at all. In any case, Sir Matthew Hale complained in his "Discourse" written in 1683 that there were no workhouses in England. The increasing begging then became the cause towards the end of the century for the erection of various workhouses, of which the first was that of Bristol (1697). The law 9 Geo. 1 c.7 "Poor Relief Act" (1722) then expressly declared that those beggars who did not go into the poorhouse were not to receive any support.

To the workhouses, which also spread in other lands, were then joined other institutions of compulsion, the *orphanages* and *foundling hospitals*. Frequently these were combined with the workhouses into integrated large institutions. One such model institution was the Pforzheim orphanage founded in 1718. Over that see the detailed depiction in Gothein (1892, 1:699 ff.).

In *Austria* we encounter the compulsion to labour (spinning) in orphanages, prisons, and poorhouses. In 1762 the directive occurred to erect workhouses in all provinces where none existed yet (A. Beer 1895, 61 ff.).

The best overview of the state of the workhouses in the second half of the 18th century is given by Howard (1777).

The men who recommended the workhouses and called them into life saw in them both the general remedy against begging and idleness and the nurseries possibly for entire industries, above all because the workhouses were an important institution for educating the people in keeping busy and accustoming them to discipline and order; to bring forth "the genius for commerce and industry in the dispositions of the children who will hereafter comprise the people"[600]. How consistently this view was shared in all European lands is proven by the following remarks:

"This would prevent poverty and in a little tract of time bring up hundreds to be able to gain their livelihoods [...] this course, within one seven years [...] brings people and their children after them in a regular, orderly and industrious course of life, *which will be as natural to them as now idleness and begging and thieving is* [...] By this means the wealth of the nation will be increased, manufactures advanced [...]" (M. Hale 1683; cited in Pashley 1852, 222–23).

"When land and city are provided with citizens and farmers, it is further necessary that you also do not forget the unmarried rabble and the craftspeople, both of which can be provided for by a workhouse. The first indeed, namely the single begging rabble, young and old, are a great burden and shame to a land if and so long as they are begging [...] To place such people now into work and to bring them honest plain sustenance there is no closer means than a general workhouse [...] All that I write here about beggars, you can also understand the same of orphanage poor, young and wandering rabble and journeymen who all can be put to work in the workhouse [...]

The appointment of a workhouse consists of a few points:

1. in the permission of the authorities;

2. in *the outsourcers of work*;

3. in good government inspection and *direction of the outsourcers of work*;

4. in consumption and handling of the goods and wares processed in them;

5. in good payment of the workers [...]

But how and what form the same workhouse can make appropriate use of *the outsourcers of work* is easily considered. If now a journeyman can thus sustain a master who generally does not work, but instead is a boss, along with wife, maid and child, then a hundred of them will, as God wishes, surely be able to sustain one." (Besoldus 1740, 957-958 Werck-Haus)

A land entered a boom "when the silk and wool manufacturers were well set up and only a prison is there through the fear of which the dissolute rabble are directed to diligence and work", and a note to that: "it is [...] certain that with prisons and orphanages newly established and starting manufacturers are absolutely incomparably and best of all to be linked with each other. A prison and orphanage should be by law a general craftshop and manufacturing house, indeed an economic craft and workschool [...] The aim is that such houses should be as it were nurseries of 1,000 good things and manufacturers for the entire land and all other cities." (Zincke 1746b, 165).

"In policy laws and institutions the paternal mind of the fathers of the fatherland strives to demand the positive best of the subjects and thus to make each capable of bettering themselves, and by all sorts of organised instruction, pleasant stimulus, earnest reminder and admonition, strict command and chastening punishment, just as if raising the children at home each according to their manner very wisely, cleverly, and carefully, which is to awaken a certain dexterity of disposition in them, by the power of which they do what their meagre and comfortable lives' livelihoods demand and leave off what disturbs it — this dexterity is then the characteristic of well-raised people who have discipline and are made into such people by good mild and strict discipline of institutions of instruction." (Zincke 1746a, 809 f.; cf. 1757, 713 f.).

The foundation order of the *Hamburg* workhouse and prison from the year 1622 had the motto: "labore nutrior, labore plector" [nourished by work, satisfied by work] (Bertheau 1912, 90).

These institutions indubitably operated educationally; not only directly by accustoming a — perhaps not at all even very large — mass of grown people to industrial activity, but rather directly by serving as a deterrent example and convincing many who would otherwise sink into public poor care to "freely" work in order to escape being taken into the poorhouse. The orphanages and foundling hospitals converted to workhouses were real nurseries for an "industrious" race. But the use of these workhouses for the rising industry expressed itself in a much more direct way by providing the entrepreneurs with the missing labour material.

Delivery of Labour Power by Workhouses and Orphanages

Italy: "nelle seconda metàdel secolo [sc. XVIII] è tutto un succedersi di tentativi per aprire negli ospizii, col concorso di abiti direttori, manifatture diverse." [in the second half of the century [i.e. 18th] there was a whole succession of attempts to open different factories in the hospices, with the help of resident directors.]

In 1759 the poorhouse of Mandovi rented to the cloth manufacturer G.B. Tempia a factory with the arrangement that he employed there at least 400 poor people of the city and surrounds.

In 1761 the congregation of Nizza erected a silk spinning mill which they leased to a certain Fo Vierne who worked there with the poor. Still more similar cases in Prato (1908, 340 f.).

France: an exact description of the industrial work in the Parisian workhouses and poorhouses in the year 1666 according to a contemporary depiction is given by Paultre (1906, 183 ff.). Complete manufacture based on the division of labour:

> "il y a dans la maison de Bicestre des drapiers pour les draps, pour les serges et pour les tiretaines; il y a des pauvres qui peignent, d'autres qui cardent, d'autres qui filent, d'autres qui sont sur les mestiers etc. etc."
>
> [in the house of Bicêtre there are drapers for sheets, for serges and for heavy cotton; there are poor people who dye, others who card, others who spin, others who are on the looms, etc. etc.]

Main industry: le tricot [knitting]. Contracts with four marchands bonnetiers [hosiery merchants] (Paultre 1906, 186 f., 188 f.). 1. Production for own account; 2. Production for cooperatives; 3. Production for outsourcers of work: these bound themselves for the giving of jobs; the Hôpital for delivery of a specific number of workers.

According to a table for this year, 6,000 people were working in the various houses of the Hôpital général for industrial purposes.

Lallemand (1902, 4.1:542) reports on contracts between enterprises and workhouses in the 18th century.

England: at the beginning of the 18th century 4,000 male and female workers were working in 48 workhouses for entrepreneurs at very low prices. See the individual contracts of the workhouses with the suppliers and traders in the text "An Account of the Workhouses in Great Britain in the Year 1732" (Anonymous 1716, 8 f., 25, 60). The 2nd and 3rd volumes of Eden (1797) give the desired information about the state of workhouses in England in the year 1795 and before. According to them there was a number of quite large workhouses with several hundred inmates which employed in total 11,142 people industrially.

In addition there existed the custom of delivering workers, particularly children, from such institutions to entrepreneurs in their factories.

A convincing example for this practice is the establishment of the cotton spinning mill by Mr Dade in the year 1784 which is described in detail in Owen (1813, 34 f.). It tells us how difficult acquiring labour power was ("was no light task"). "Two modes then only remained of obtaining these labourers: the one, to procure children from *the various public charities* of the country; and the other, to induce families to settle round the works.

To accommodate the first, a large house was erected, which ultimately contained about 500 children, who were procured chiefly *from workhouses and charities in Edinburgh*. These children were to be fed, clothed and educated [...]".

Holland: in 1683 the refugees in Amsterdam opened an orphanage in order to have silk spun there (Berg 1845, 1:160). In Middelburg the poor administration concluded a contract with a Frenchman according to which a number of orphans were meant to be employed in his cloth weaving mill (Coronel 1859, 120; cited in Pringsheim 1890, 55).

The "work and spinning house" in Amsterdam is described by Zetzner (1913, 17 f.).

Switzerland: in 1665/66 Basel erected a prison and orphanage, i.e. workhouse. The orphanage was then, as it appeared, lent in submission occasionally to those factories, no matter which branch, which were obliged to care for the upkeep of the children most extensively. In 1676 it was conceded to the stocking manufacturer Gernler. Gernler obtained the authorisation for erection of a "stocking factory" in the orphanage (Geering 1886, 608, 619).

Germany. Brandenburg-Prussia: in 1687 the prison and spinning mill at Spandau was established. Initially the prisoners were kept for wool spinning. In 1688 all the prisoners were handed over to the silk dealers Müller and Kopisch for silk spinning, for which weekly 8 groschen per person was paid (Schmoller and Hintze 1892, 1:6). The orphanage in Potsdam likewise delivered labour power to the silk factories (Schmoller and Hintze 1892, Nr. 94).

King Frederick William I arranged that 3–400 orphans were transferred to a factory of Leonischen Tressen for learning at its cost; for the construction of a weapons factory the entrepreneur received the right to take usable trainees from the orphanages in Potsdam and Berlin (Lenz and Unholtz 1912, 20 f., 34). In the Potsdam orphanage (1778) the Jews had lace made (Crome 1833, 69 ff.).

In the kingdom of *Saxony*, work and poorhouses and penal institutions were made serviceable for the production of yarn. The inmates produced above all the finer yarn (A. König 1899, 82 f.).

Hanover: the Gräzel factory in Göttingen delivered the combed wool to the workschool for spinning, likewise to the workhouse (Wagemann 1789c, 20 ff.).

Workschools in *Hessen* spun cotton for the factories in Elberfeld; there were similar schools in *Magdeburg*, *Strasbourg*, and Bohemia (Wagemann 1789a, 38).

Baden: the prison in Breisach had occasion "to lean on a factory. A Jew, Götz Offenheimer, *leased it* and erected a hemp and linen spinning mill" (18th century); an Italian, Fornaro, leased the prison at Hüfingen in the Black Forest where at first wool, later silk was spun (Gothein 1892, 1:756).

Austria: the "Relation" of 1756 reported about similar circumstances which were published in A. Fournier (1887). Cf. Demuth (1890, 293 ff.).

***

That was understood in the 16th, 17th, and 18th centuries under "education for work". It was approximately equivalent to compulsion to work. It referred almost exclusively to the moral side of the labour problem, almost not at all to the technical side. For the technical training of the worker, you did nothing at all until up into the 19th century; with one exception: in most states spinning schools were erected. This completely different orientation of the industrial education of the common people in the early capitalist period, which also did not link in the slightest with that of our days, was founded in the above-mentioned character of the workers at the time and the technology at the time. The main problem was that the workers absolutely first had to be educated to work. Their technical capabilities, however, could not be taught to them in theoretical ways. There it was about a practical transfer from man to man, there it was above all about an increase in the stock of technically capable workers. To solve this problem, entirely different measures of state labour policy were ordained — I will compile them in the following.

IV. The Struggle of the States for Trained Workers

That the naturalisation of the capitalist economic ways was for a large part the work of "foreigners", is one of the fundamentally important statements for the understanding of all European history. It is important in a two-fold sense: in so far as on the one hand the economic subjects (entrepreneurs) and on the other hand the economic objects (workers) of the new form of economy were to a large extent foreign immigrants. I will yet deal with that in another connection in detail — see Chapter 61 — here I will talk about what policy measures they initiated.

The peculiarity of empirical technology brings with it, as we have seen, that the technical capability adheres to the living person of the worker — introduction of a new process thus demands the introduction of people who are expert in this process. Hence the industrial policy of the Middle Ages was already filled by the striving to increase the craftsmen of a city through influx, and to hinder their moving away. The policy of the principality in turn tied itself to this policy of the medieval cities — in the first centuries of its existence it was above all about drawing proficient *craftsmen* into the land. A separation between entrepreneurs and workers had not yet taken place. Later, after this had occurred, it was about solving the two-fold task of getting entrepreneurs and (trained) workers. The measures taken to solve these tasks were in part the same; thus all those which we can summarise as religious or clerical policy measures and of which were already spoken of in Chapter 28. A different group of measures, however, bears the character of a markedly separate *labour policy*.

Similarly to how in the Middle Ages the individual cities struggled over the possession of craftsmen, we see the modern states up until the end of the 18th century waging a bitter struggle over trained workers. Naturally this struggle provoked on the one hand the striving to retain artisans and arts present in a land, on the other hand the striving to increase the supply of them.

In many states we encounter in the early period of capitalism the *bans on emigration* of trained workers.

Italy: Venice confiscated the property of any glassworker who left his fatherland. Even in 1754 it had Venetian workers who had settled abroad poisoned (Levasseur 1900, 2:258). The cloth makers in Milan still had to swear in the 16th century an oath to remain (Ranke 1857, 1:472). Bans on emigration for silk workers in Piedmont — edict of 28th August 1701. Cf. Prato (1908, 52 f.).

In *France* Colbert enacted several bans on emigration. An edict from the month of August 1669 denied the subjects of the king "de s'habituer dans les pays étrangers à peine de confiscation de corps et de bien" [working in foreign countries on pain of confiscation of body and property]. On 31st May 1682 the regulations were repeated, especially with reference to Protestants. It was not penalised anymore with the galleys, but with death (!) for "ouvriers qui sortiront du royaume" [workers who will leave the kingdom] (G. Martin 1899, 80 f.). Cf. also Dutil (1911, 294).

England: 5 Geo. 1[*] and 23 Geo. 2[†] placed under penalty the recruitment of English workers for emigration and taking work abroad: "if [...] any person [...] shall contract with, entice, persuade or endeavour to persuade, solicit or seduce any manufacturer or artificer, of or in wool, mohair, cotton or silk or of or in any manufactures made of wool etc. [...] or of or in iron steel, brass or other manufacturer, workman or artificer etc. to go out this kingdom". Cf. Postlethwayt (1774, 2:135).

In 1794 the emigration of all trained workers was forbidden once more (McCormac 1904, 109 citing Walsh's Appeal § VII & VIII).

An interim stage of development is signified by the ban on the *export of equipment and machinery* which we encounter in English legislation especially often in the 17th century. The proclamation of 15th January 1666 and 7 & 8 Will. 3 c.20 "Taxation Act" (1695) § 8 forbid the export of the stocking-frames invented under Queen Elizabeth I. The above cited laws under the first and second George forbade the export of equipment for the wool and silk industries. Other measures of similar content are:

1774. Ban on the export of utensils which find use in the cotton industry (A. Anderson 1787, 4:176).

1775. The same in the wool industry (A. Anderson 1787, 4:187).

1787. The same in the iron and steel industry (A. Anderson 1787, 4:668).

Austria: emigration bans were enacted in 1752 (pat. of 12 August), 1769, 1779, and often for the glassworkers of Bohemia, and for the expert weavers of Austria, amongst others (Kropatschek 1804, 1:316 ff.).

We find similar laws also in other lands.

This striving to hold down the trained workers in the land was now confronted with the assiduous striving of all governments to *draw in trained workers from lands*. To enliven the picture I cite a few examples below from the inexhaustibly rich material.

England: Cunningham (1897) treats the topic almost exhaustively. Since numerous refugees particularly from the Netherlands and France sought out England of their own free will, the policy of the English kings consisted essentially in taking in these efficient and technically well-educated elements and protecting them against the guild craftsmen. We will yet see that almost the entirety of English industry owes its origin to such foreign immigrants. Where the French and Dutch left gaps, there the English government thought to draw in the necessary labour power from elsewhere. Henry VI (1452) let Saxon, Austrian, and Bohemian miners come to England (Rymer 1727, 11:317; cited in Roscher 1854,

---

[*]   [Tr.: presumably 5 Geo. 1 c.27 "Artificers Act" (1718).]

[†]   [Tr.: presumably 23 Geo. 2 c.13 "Artificers, etc. Act" (1749).]

3:817). Henry VIII introduced weapons smithing into England with the help of almost only German workers. When in 1670 a society for the introduction of tinned plate was formed, German workers were likewise fetched in, etc.

France: already in the Middle Ages the French kings began to make an effort over the getting in of foreign craftsmen and trained workers. It was above all the welfare of the silk industry which drove them, and there was of course above all the Italian labour power which they were eager to draw into the land. In the middle of the 15th century Louis XI called Italian silk weavers to France, who settled in Tours (Eberstadt 1899, 317 f.). Catherine de' Medici erected a silk weaving mill in Orleans with the help of foreign workers. But even for other industries you needed Italian workers. Under Charles VIII they were already being fetched systematically and in the grand style: "une armée de parfumeurs, de joailliers, de brodeurs, de tailleurs, pour dames, de menuisiers, de jardiniers, de facteurs d'orgues et de tourneurs d'albâtre, qu'il installera au château d'Ambroise" [an army of perfumers, jewellers, embroiderers, tailors for ladies, carpenters, gardeners, organ builders and alabaster sculptors, whom he will install at the Château d'Ambroise] (Archives de l'art. franç. Doc. t.1 p.94 ff. cited in Pigeonneau 1887, 2:24).

Francis I had workers come from Flanders and Italy with whom he established a carpet mill in Fontainebleau. Henry II founded a glassworks in St Germain-en-Laye where the Italian Mutio applied the technology from Murano (Levasseur 1900, 2:34, 2:35). Henry IV drew in Flemish carpet makers in order to bring to life a haute-lisse carpet mill (Fagniez 1897, 147). Colbert carried on the import of foreign workers to a great extent — he fetched expert craftsmen and artists for the manufacture of Gobelin tapestries from Italy, Holland, and England; trained workers for carpet weaving, for the lace industry, for the silk industry, for the mirror industry mostly from Italy; for mining, iron-casting, and tar production from Sweden; for tin plate manufacturing from Germany, etc. (Depping 1850, vol. 3: Affaire de Finances – Commerce – Industrie; Clément 1861, 2:CCLX and table in vol. 8 'ouvrier').

Germany: we see almost all the German princes active in the same direction as the English and French kings. Above all it is Frederick II of *Prussia* who concerns himself keenly with obtaining the missing labour power for his land. Above all it was about spinners and weavers. Since the French wool manufacturers were lacking the spinners, Frederick obtained them from abroad and settled them in numerous villages (Weiss 1853, 1:201). In 1750 we hear of a complaint of the Dresden merchants that a royal Prussian senior civil servant by the name of Mentzel was travelling around Upper Lusatia in order to "entice, amidst all sorts of promises from His Royal Majesty in Poland, from local districts to Silesia" damask weavers and other manufacturers. From a memorandum of 24th January 1750, printed in Gerstmann (1909, 61–62). A rich material for the struggle over the trained workers in the silk industry is contained in Schmoller and Hintze (1892, vol. 1 Nr. 48, 52, 53, 93, 125, 128, 131, 139, 166, 233, 245, 248, 260, 283, 317, 363, 461, and elsewhere). But even industries other than the textile industry were supplied with foreign workers. Thus in 1763 leather workers were drawn to Silesia — see admonition on account of the benefits to the foreign leather manufacturers being set up in Silesia from 14th May 1763, printed in Bergius (1775, 4:20). Bergius gave very illuminating consideration to the problem in its fundamental significance in the following: "Without sufficient knowledge, science, and experience, no tanner will be in a position to prepare such leather which should deserve the name of a first-rate good and proper leather [...] If now no tanners are found in the land who possess this characteristic, then *no other means remains but to pull foreign tanners into the land.*"

Ironworkers were sought in *Baden*: "Like the Prussian weavers, emissaries of neighbouring factories draw through the land in order to get one another to part with the best workers through greater promises" (Gothein 1892, 1:779-780).

Austria also made an effort under Maria Theresa to draw in foreign workers. Already for several years, as the authorities reported in the year 1766, they had striven to use all serviceable means for the betterment of the domestic manufactures and did not allow any lack giving premiums and other support to efficient workers. Numerous branches of industry, however, were unable "*to be brought other than by the prescription of foreign artisans in the extreme.*" Thus the silk manufacturers would never "thrive to perfection if you had not attended to such skilled masters [as is well-known Fleuriet, Gautier, and Tetier] from France by means of a lifelong pension." For improvement of the steel industry, workers were drawn from England; Count Josef Kinsky owed the goodness of the linen and fine barchent produced by him to the circumstance that he had had the luck of a Saxon master coming over to him on the occasion of the last war (Přibram 1907, 149).

On the other hand the Kärtner representation of 4th July 1750 voiced that the ironworkers were emigrating. For that the emissaries of foreign potentates and iron companies were at fault, "some emissaries proceed incognito into these imperial hereditary lands and chat up the best workers secretly with promises of a large reward and earnings and capture per tertium et quartum [by the third and fourth], as has happened unfortunately recently." (Müllner 1909, 1:468)

By necessity conflict had to occur between the individual states who each wanted to hold back their workers and have any foreign worker. In fact we find constantly during the 17th and 18th centuries that *the governments are in dispute with each other over their workers*, we find entire systems developed on the one hand to secretly entice in new workers, on the other hand to guard over and hinder their recruitment and emigration. the struggle over the trained workers formed a regular topic of diplomatic negotiations of that time.

After *France* had become the classic land of modern industry, it also became the place of reference for highly quali-

fied workers. "Les étrangers sont fort empressés de nous enle-
ver nos ouvriers" [Foreigners are in a rush to take away our
workers], we read in a letter of Gournay from 22nd January
1753. Bigot de St Croix estimated that 10,000 trained workers
were taken abroad from France annually[601]. And after the
church policy of Louis XIV had driven a number of the best
workers from the land, the government during the 18th century gave double consideration to hindering the abduction of
French workers. Thus we can follow the peculiar labour policy
of those centuries especially clearly when we observe the
struggle which France fought with the foreign lands for its
workers. It is fortunate that already through the publications
of Depping and others, but in particular recently through the
two books of G. Martin, especially the second, such a wealth
of material has come to light for the illumination of these circumstances, which is not the case for any other land. I give in
the following, essentially by the use of those publications, a
sort of register for the theme:

France's struggle with foreign peoples over trained workers:
17th century:
In 1672 Colbert stuck a Swiss merchant in prison because he was
undertaking to recruit French workers.

When Venetian glassworkers wanted to return to Italy again, he had
them arrested at the border and imprisoned in the castle Pierre-Seize;
likewise with a Parisian silk weaver who wanted to emigrate to Spain.

In 1679 the Spanish envoy tried to export 30 silk workers, but was
prevented from doing so.

In Lyon a velvet weaver planned to settle in Florence — the Archbishop of Lyon learned about it and threw him in prison.

18th century:
Russia: in 1717 Russia lured 150 workers — clockmakers, gilders,
painters, coach makers, and smiths, amongst others.

Fugitive workers of the manufacturers of Sèvres helped found the
royal porcelain manufacturer in St Petersburg.

The patriotic society of St Petersburg set a price of 200 rubles for
the French tanners who betrayed their secrets.

The brothers Rullière received from the Russian government 2 écus
to 6 livre for each worker they delivered. There were special agents —
"emolleurs pour la Russie" [softeners(?) for Russia] — whom the French
government tracked down (like the girl traffickers today), and whom
they stuck in prison as soon as they were caught. Hence they resided
mostly abroad. Famed is a certain Fevrier, clockmaker of Paris, who occupied himself with finding good clockmakers in Paris and Lyon in order to take them abroad. When he was once again on his way with

several workers to Rouen in order to embark on a Dutch ship, they were all seized and imprisoned.

A formal spy service was organised to reconnoitre the ways which the emigrating workers took.

In 1767 the French envoy in Moscow complained that several draughtsmen from Lyon had gotten through to Russia where they were granted great advantages.

Patterns were sent in wine barrels in order to evade pursuit; even here the French authorities were after the malefactors.

Denmark: Schultze, secretary of the Danish legation in Paris conveyed cloth makers.

A Genevese man was arrested because he was the agent for the transport of dyers from Lyon to Copenhagen. Another recruited under the protection of the Danish legation file smiths for clockmaking and instrument making.

England: a female agent delivered over seven years young workers of both sexes regularly to England. In 1763 a troop consisting of Miss Buast, seven workers of both sexes and two children was stopped on the basis of a denunciation.

A resident of Beauvais had frequent meetings with the English envoys — he was supposed to establish a cloth weaving factory in London, similar to the one in Beauvais. He had committed to bring half the French workers to England. Discovered and imprisoned.

The brothers Grignon, workers of Gobelin, had determined to transfer to London; one succeeded, the other was imprisoned.

The same fate was shared by Jean Coillat, worker in the porcelain factory at Vincennes; the same for a fan merchant.

Austria-Hungary: in 1750 a Nicholas Français was arrested, who wanted to take cutlers to Vienna.

Germany: Hannong, a faience worker of ability, was obtained for the Saxon porcelain manufacturer. Workers from the Gobelin manufacturer the same.

A skilled draughtsman was already in Germany — when wife and child wanted to come after him, they were arrested and thus the father was forced to return.

Delegates of Francis II were traced in Strasbourg and Dunkirk, where they wanted to recruit tobacco workers. Cf. also Schmoller and Hintze (1892).

Similar dealings occurred between France and *Spain, Portugal, Belgium, Sweden,* and *Italy*.

The penalties which were imposed on the malefactors were often very hard. On 31 March 1751 two maîtres ouvriers [master workers] from Lyon were condemned to lifelong imprisonment because they had been guilty of enticing workers to emigrate. Their victims, ouvriers en soie, compagnons, mouliniers, and passementiers [silk workers, journeymen, millers, and braiders] received partly fines, partly imprisonment of two to five years.

In order to reach the goal, to go abroad, you grasped the most venturesome means — often a pilgrimage was feigned and similar. Cf. also Godart (1899, 202 f.).

V. The Regulation of the Labour Contract

You feel especially vividly the extent to which a systematic depiction of the labour or worker law in the period of mercantilism is necessary when you start putting together those regulations which governed the labour contract at the time — you find nothing but notes strewn here and there in the literature which never occupy themselves with the problem forcibly and separately.

What arises from a short study of the legal material is perhaps the following.

Before the state concerned itself about the workers, their activity was enclosed in the ordinances of the large estates or the guilds. Both now also remained during the early capitalist period objectively and locally partly in force. Everywhere serfdom had not yet been set aside, thus in as good as all lands, with the exception of Italy and England, the labour obligation of the vassals also existed in our epoch, from which, as we have seen, a not inconsiderable part of capitalist industry (and of course also agriculture) grew. Craftwork on the other hand, particularly in the cities, regulated its work as before through the guild ordinances which were here and there subjected to state oversight.

The state pushed in next to and above that with its specific labour law.

The state labour law of this time was now, when we grasp it as a whole, throughout still born from the same spirit as the earlier laws — it emanated like those from the basic idea of a labour duty which, as we have already been able to establish, frequently solidified into a direct compulsion to work. From this basic view now arose without further ado the essential features which distinguish the mercantilist labour law. They are the following:

1. The *duration of the labour* contract was approximated where possible to a lifelong state corresponding to the state of serfdom — the labour relationship was meant to be permitted only to change in the long interim;

2. accordingly the *changing of places of work* was made difficult where possible — long notice periods, bans on leaving incomplete work, or on leaving before the employer has a replacement; limitations on freedom of domicile; requirement of a leaving certificate, etc.;
3. the *duration of the work time* was determined by the authorities, just as:
4. the *amount of reward* was determined by the authorities;
5. the *personal freedom* of the worker was also strongly *limited* outside of work — frequently he must not leave the place of work at all, and of course he had no right to come to an agreement with his peers in order to improve his work conditions.

All endeavours of that sort would have been against the spirit of the entire law — accordingly the labour relations were indeed regulated by the authorities, it was a sort of civil service. But just as the right of association and of striking internally contradicts the concept of the civil service, so too in the early period of capitalism was all that which we today summarise under the institution of the industrial labour movement considered taboo.

More precisely, we encounter the following regulations.

We find the tied labour law already in the *Italian* industries of the 14th and 15th centuries, for example, in the Florentine cloth and silk industries which indeed still bore a half craftwork-like stamp — the worker had to stay the entire week, he had to finish his work, he had long-term contracts and had to give notice four weeks in advance — the "discipuli and laborantes" [disciples and labourers] of the silk guild were banned "from often changing masters".

Wage tariffs existed for spinning and weaving in the Florentine cloth industry in the 16th century, likewise for the silk industry. See the sources in Doren (1901, 1:232 f., 1:274).

England and *Scotland* then carried through the fundamental boundness of the labour law probably the most successfully and with zeal.

In England the labour law was, as we know, codified by 5 Eliz. 1 c.4 "Artificers and apprentices" (1562), which repealed 34 labour laws from the period of 1350 to 1560. That the compulsion to work was introduced by this law, we have already seen. Now had the worker entered his work of freewill or compulsion, numerous regulations bound him fast to this *one position* — as "apprentice" he was bound for seven years, that is, thus in bondage; but even the older workers had to serve out "their time". When this had run out, they could only leave their position a quarter of a year after giving prior notice (§§ 5–6), against a discharge slip (§ 10), and if they had completed any work started (§ 13).

The *wages* (maximum wages: § 18) were established by a Justice of the Peace. The English kings had enacted wage maximums numerous times since 1350 (Eden 1797, 1:30 ff.). The innovation of 5 Eliz. 1 c.4 consisted in that the wages were meant to be brought into harmony with the prices of food (§ 15). There are disputes over for how long the fixing of wages actually took place. Cunningham (1907, 44) assumes until Charles II. But the regulation of wages is recorded again later — in 1727 we find an exact specification of the piece-rate in Gloucestershire (13 Geo. 2 c.23 "Supply, etc. Act" (1739)); in 1756 a new wage statute was enacted (29 Geo. 2 c.33 "Woollen Manufacture Act" (1756)). The most recent worker on the topic, Tawney (1913, 337), gives the fixing of wages higher significance again than Cunningham, amongst others.

State *bans on unions* had existed since the 16th century. 2 & 3 Edw. 6 c.4 "Sherifs" (1548) & c.15 "Victuallers, etc." (1548) forbade all associations to influence wages and work times, with high penalties — with the second time £20 and the pillory; with the third time £40, loss of an ear and of good reputation. Bans from the 18th century in Steffen (1901, 1:505). Cf. Held (1881, 432 ff.).

A sort of actual *serfdom* existed still at the end of the 18th century in the English coal mines. We find in that time the typical slave advertising in the newspapers: "A run-away worker: anyone who gives the place where he stays receives £1 reward; anyone who employs him makes themselves culpable." (Jars 1774, 1:190 f.)

Labour relations in the Scottish coal mines and saltworks were regulated similarly. A law from the year 1606 specifies that nobody may recruit salt workers, faceworkers, or coal haulers without the agreement of their employer; if it happened though, the previous employer could fetch the worker back. The law was confirmed in 1661 and extended to water bearers, "as they are as necessary to the owners and masters of the pits as the colliers and the bearers". With the sale of mines and saltworks, the workers were sold along with them. Only in the year 1775 did a law of the British parliament abolish this serfdom, but it remained in effect in existence until 1799 since the workers could not fulfil a part of the conditions to which the setting free was tied (Mackintosh 1892, 3:291).

The beggars and vagabonds forcibly put to work, of whom we were informed above, were likewise treated as serfs.

The law of 1617 specified that the children taken into training "should be subject to their master's discipline in all sorts of punishments, except torture and death". (Thomson and Innes 1814, vol. IV).

In the law of 1663, according to which beggars could be taken into work by anyone, it stated: "The poor thus employed shall continue in the service of their employers, *under their direction and correction*, not only during the time which the parishes pay for them, but also *for seven years thereafter, receiving only their meat and clothing*." (Thomson and Innes 1814, VII:485-486; cited in Mackintosh 1892, 3:249 ff.)

France: Arrêts du Conseil [council judgements] of 1699, 1723, 1729, 1749, 1786. Lettre Pat. 1781. Law of 1791. Only on giving notice could the worker leave his position — he had to give notice early enough before that the employer had time to look for new workers.

It was forbidden to take on a worker without a discharge slip, which he did not receive as long as his work was not finished, advances not repaid, etc. That seemed to have been the usual treatment — where the worker was not simply bound to the firm, he was treated as a "servant" — the labour law then corresponded to our present-day servant regulations. An example of the execution: during the regency ribbon weavers of Saint-Lô left the Vicomté — a ban on leaving was enacted on those remaining, and a demand for the "fugitives" to return. Arrêts du Conseil of 22nd September 1722. A few years later a conflict broke out between cloth manufacturers and workers in Louviers — the workers demanded the right of freedom of domicile and went to Rouen. Arrêts du Conseil of 23rd September 1729: "ordre aux 'transfuges' de réintegrer les fabriques de Louviers sous menaces d'être réconduits par la maréchaussée" [an order to the 'defectors' to return to the factories of Louviers under threat of being returned by the marshal].

The workers of the royal manufacturers were subjected to an especially strict discipline — they owed their employers "loyalty" and could not leave at their discretion. The workers of the manufacturer de St Gobain could not distance themselves further than a mile for two years, with penalties of fines and imprisonment.

We encounter *wage tariffs* here and there. Thus the wages of porters (gagne-deniers, porte-faix, cocheteurs, hommes de peine, etc.) in Paris were set by the Prevôt des Marchands et echevins [Provost of merchants and aldermen] (Savary des Brûlons and Savary 1723, art. 'Gagnederniers').

Unions and strikes were forbidden. Specific industries: civic ordinances of 1712 for Parisian workers. General: Patent of 1749; repeated 1781, 1785, 1786; confirmed by the well-known Revolution law of 14th–17th June 1791 in which (already essentially from doctrinairism) any association of workers and any industrial combination was forbidden.

Germany: imperial and princely *wage tariffs* (Schönlank 1894, 135 ff.; Gothein 1892, 1:728 and elsewhere; Zwiedineck-Südenhorst 1900, 54 ff.).

Numerous wage tariffs of the 18th century printed in Bergius (1775, 3:176 ff.).

A special place in German labour law is taken up by the *mining and iron works ordinances* which were enacted by the princes or the "rulers" and in particular showed from the 16th century a strong tendency for the "binding" of workers. Thus they established for the most part long-term contracts and long notice periods; punishing premature stopping of work, requiring the "departure slip", etc.

At Rammelsberg by Goslar the duration of the labour contract "for all servants" was measured at one year, but at least half a year. Anyone who left service against the contract or was let go because of bad behaviour was not permitted to set up elsewhere during the remaining period. Similarly the Goslar mining ordinances of 1544. According to the Salzburg mining ordinances of 1532 only workers willing to serve should be employed who can prove with "passport and documents" that they were turned away elsewhere according to the regulations. Similarly the Hungarian mining ordinances of 1575.

The Upper Palatinate iron works ordinances of 1694 commanded the smith's lads who went into service for a year to hold out loyally; the Prussian iron works and hammer ordinances of 1769 prescribed for "all iron works and hammer people" "at least" one year contracts. Likewise the Hessen-Darmstadt mining ordinances of 1718, amongst others.

The new employment was in many cases made dependent on the agreement of the former wage master — see the Sayn-Wittgenstein mining ordinances of 1597; the mining ordinances for Nassau of 1559, for Palatine Zweibrücken of 1565, and for Hessen-Kassel of 1616. The Hessen-Kassel Patent of 1652 threatened miners who did not finish the work they undertook with loss of wages and being laid off.

A patent enacted by the mining authority of Zellerfeld in 1692 commanded that "local miners who take themselves off to foreign mines" should return, otherwise their houses would "be struck with heavy building money" or even publicly put up for sale.

The freedom of the miners to form unions was heavily cut, etc. Cf. Hue (1910, 1:260 f.).

Austria: far-reaching regulation of labour relations; wage fixing, especially for cotton spinning (normalisation of the so-called "spinning foot") (A. Beer 1895, 37 ff.; M. Adler 1903, 94 ff.). In the manufactures (quality) ordinance for silk wares of 16th October 1751 it specified: 20. "so that the wares made here are not made expensive by immoderate workers' wages, nor the journeymen also oppressed against fairness", wage tariffs would be introduced. Printed in Quarient und Raal (1704, Supp. V). Cf. Deutsch (1909, 67). Over serf-like labour relations in the Krain mines, see Müllner (1909, 1:318).

***

Section 8: The Origin of the Entrepreneurs

Chapter 55: The Birth of the Capitalist Entrepreneur

Capitalism is the work of individual prominent men, of that there can be no doubt. Any assumption of a "collectivist", as it were organic manner of emergence is false. Nobody knows who founded the village cooperative or the guilds. They really grew, arose "organically". Everyone and no one and anyone participated in their origin. Capitalism is different, coming into the world in the form of "enterprises" — in the form thus of rational, considered, farsighted forms of the human spirit. In the beginning, the "creative act" of the individual, of a "daring", "enterprising" man who spiritedly made the decision to step away from the tracks of the traditional economic approach and follow new paths.

We also therefore know many individuals by name who first busied themselves as capitalist entrepreneurs. The origin story of capitalism is a story of personalities.

It is natural to make comparisons between the capitalist enterprise and that economic enterprise which preceded it historically — the large estate and the socage economy. Certainly both economic forms have very much in common. In a certain sense the capitalist enterprise is the direct continuation of the large estate's enterprise. It continued the movement which that had begun. Both signify a lifting up of the economy from the tracks of the popular-collectivist economic approach. Both are aristocratic organisations which take the place of the democratic. The estate owner lifts himself just as much from the mob of peasant farmers as the capitalist entrepreneur does from the mass of industrial and commercial craftsmen.

But what distinguished the capitalist entrepreneur from the large estate owner as entrepreneur was this: that he operated to a much greater extent subversively and transformatively. The large estate owner had indeed also built new structures out of a creative spirit. But his mind had remained bound though to the old basic viewpoints of the great mass. The large socage estate was just a big farm. Like those it served for the production of goods for self-sufficiency, like those it was dominated in its entire orientation by the "principle of satisfaction of needs". The capitalist entrepreneur broke with the old traditions in that he gave his business entirely new aims. He consciously broke through the limitations of the old economic ways, he was a destroyer and constructor in one. And whereas the estate owner in his quiet forests had built up his new world untouched by the hustle and bustle of others, the capitalist entrepreneur seized with his activity entire lands, dragged away entire populations from their accustomed way of living. For the farmer whom the large estate owner made liable for interest or compulsory labour, his old ways of working remained preserved, whereas the capitalist entrepreneur created new ways of working for thousands. His sight was directed into the distance, he wanted to guide with his will the wills of many people, even if they lived and worked distantly from him.

Even if history does not confirm it for us, our insight into the essence of human nature would lead us to the conclusion that such doers-differently, such innovators, such disrupters, such creators were always only individuals, were always only a few.

Now it is, however, the particular nature of the *sociological* view of history that it always has an eye only for mass phenomena. And hence this expression of personal recall as it came to light in the creation of the capitalist enterprise also interests us only because we observe that it was actually a mass phenomenon. Our position with respect to the problem is therefore given: we do not have to describe the fate and the leadership of individual prominent personalities whom we acknowledge as the creators of the capitalist economic life, rather our task consists of taking notice of the bringing to life of a specific (the "new") spirit in numerous individuals and grasping these numerous individuals' striving and acting the same as a special type of biological-psychological disposition whose origins we are pursuing — I want to say: which we are attempting to comprehend as the result of a selection from the great mass of variously disposed individuals.

What sort this type is, we are easily capable of establishing when we recall the functions which the capitalist entrepreneur had to exercise[602].

An ample endowment with the gifts of the "intellect" must correspond to a fullness of "life force", "life energies" or however else we want to call this disposition of which we know only so much as that it is the necessary precondition for all "entrepreneurial" conduct — that it creates the desire for the undertaking, the *desire* for action, and then takes care of the carrying out of the undertaking in that it places the necessary *power* for action at the disposal of the person. There must be something demanding in the nature, something which turns the idle resting on the bench by the stove into a torment. And something heavy-boned — hewed into shape with the axe — something strong-nerved. We have the image of a person clearly before our eyes whom we call "enterprising". All those characteristics of the entrepreneur which are necessary conditions of a success — the decisiveness, the constancy, the perseverance, the restlessness, the single-mindedness, the toughness, the daring, the boldness — all are rooted in a strong life force, in a general liveliness or "vitality", as we are accustomed to say. More likely a restraint for its effect is by contrast a strong development of comfortable predispositions which tend to produce a strong emphasis on the feelings of worth.

Entrepreneurial natures, we can say in summary, are people with a pronounced intellectually voluntaristic talent who, when they appear as the founders of capitalist firms, possess a strong sense for the material worth, for the valuation of people in earthly works — being "practically active", as we can say quite generally, is averse to all introspective natures both of Homo religiosus and of the artist, as it is to all craftwork-like self-satisfaction and pleasurable comfort.

Such sorts of human dispositions are found now in all peoples who have made European history — certainly in varying quantities, also in varying forms, but they are found in Italy and in Spain, in Germany and in France, in short, all European peoples as well as that foreign people who has played such a strong part in the forming of the European-American history — the Jews. They are found, however, also in all social strata — among the kings as well as among the beggars, among the large estate owners as well as among the craftsmen — they are found in all professions — among the knights as well as among the peasants, among the merchants as well as among the tailors and cobblers — they are found in all religions — among the Catholics as well as among the Protestants of all shades.

What just distinguished these types of entrepreneurs, what divided them distinctly into two large groups, is *the variety of means* which served them for the carrying out of their plans — whereas the one made use of the instruments of power which their favoured position in the state had obtained for them, the others had to strive without such assistance to achieve their goals in that they made use of the arts of persuasion and temptation in place of the external instruments of power. Whereas the former developed more that side of entrepreneurship which made the entrepreneur appear as a conqueror, the latter shaped the commercial function of the capitalist entrepreneur to perfection. The former were the mighty, the latter the cunning, when we comprehend this contrast in a quite general sense. To the former belong those capitalist entrepreneurs who emerged from the ranks of the heads of state and state officials or from the ranks of the large estate owners, *when* they based their entrepreneurial activity on the instruments of power available to them from these positions; to the latter belong all those who originated from bourgeois circles, be they merchants or craftsmen, *when* they dispensed with direct support by the state. Obviously these two sorts merged into one another, but conceptually they can be distinguished from each other in essence with complete purity, historically also, as the following portrayal will prove.

It is a problem in itself whether and to what extent just like the capitalist variants in general either the conqueror variants or the trader variants are to be found stronger or weaker *in a specific people*, thus that you can distinguish capitalistically more or less gifted peoples and conqueror or trader peoples. I have looked into this problem in Sombart (1913a; 1915) and refer the reader to the investigations made there (Sombart 1913a, 266 ff.; 1915, 210 ff.). At this point I need not enter any closer into this question of national differentiation, since here it is for us about recognising the origin of capitalist entrepreneurship in its general significance. Here we can (and must) look away from the national variation in development to which I dedicated a wide space in Sombart (1913a; 1915), while we establish that despite all variations the same tendencies are to be shown in all peoples, which thus allows us to conclude the (even if perhaps variously strong) presence of all variants in all peoples.

But it is something else now when we strive to establish the *share of specific groups of populations* within the peoples in the development of capitalist entrepreneurship. It arises namely with complete certainty that individual groups of people were indubitably favoured by their character over others for delivering entrepreneurs, so that the contingents which placed themselves as lords over the modern economic subjects were in any case especially strong.

Such groups were predominantly the following:

1. the *heretics*, that is, the citizens not belonging to the state church, "those of a different faith";
2. the *foreigners*, that is, those who immigrated into a land, amongst which the religiously persecuted Christians were the most important from the 16th century;
3. the *Jews*, who take up a special place to the extent they are a special people, but also found themselves in a socially qualified position.

These three groups of capitalistically disposed people now do not of course correspond with the just distinguished groups of capitalist economic subjects in relation to the ancillary order, instead intersecting the various circles in multiple ways. Nonetheless it seems expedient to establish separately the significance which attached to each of these groups for the origins of capitalism. Hence I will attempt to describe in the following chapters one after the other the noteworthy types of capitalist entrepreneurship, while I strive to ascertain and at the same time establish their quantitative share in the forming of the capitalist political economy, what causes enabled them to play their special role, and what particular necessity brought them perhaps into the totality of the capitalist world.

***

Chapter 56: The Princes

We convinced ourselves earlier of what a lively interest the modern principality took in the development of the capitalist economic ways, how it saw in the representatives of this new economy very much actually the powers for preserving and advancing the state. The lively desire to bring the germ of capitalism to a quick unfolding led the princes and their servants in numerous cases to intervene with their own hands in the economic hustle and bustle, even to take part in the construction of the new economic form — even to be active as entrepreneurs.

To the eager wanting just as often corresponded a strong capability. In the early times of capitalism we encounter amongst the heads of state and state officials conspicuously many powerful personalities with a pronounced sense for the reality of economic life, with an unusual understanding for the new demands of economic practice; personalities full of the spirit of enterprise and entrepreneurial talents.

In creative ideas, in comprehensive knowledge, in scientific schooling — who shall have equalled the ingenious leaders of the modern states?

What a clever man said about *Gustav Wasa* in Sweden applies to all the significant princes of the Ancien régime: "He was the first entrepreneur of his nation; as he extracted the metal treasures of the Swedish soil and sought to make the crown serviceable, he showed the way not only by trade agreements and protective tolls, but also showed the way to his merchants through his own maritime trade in the grand style. Everything emanated from him."[603]

Behind numerous enterprises during the 17th and 18th centuries in England, there stood as the direct driving power, because interested with his purse, the king (or the queen). In

539

long dialogues Drake and Raleigh were induced by them to make new voyages — thus the last plan of Raleigh to sail once more to Guyana emanated from James I who was in need of money[604]; thus we see Charles I sending his agents about in the countryside in order to conclude profitable contracts with industrialists[605].

How much the heads of state in need of money actually really brought the capitalist world to fruition has been shown for the period of Charles V and Ferdinand I in *Germany* again now by Jacob Strieder with the use of much newly discovered material[606].

In *Austria* Francis I, the husband of Maria Theresa, was a true entrepreneurial genius whom Frederick the Great called the "greatest industrialist" of his time — a judgement which confirms Fürst's notes over the undeniable talent of the emperor for the economic subjects, his practical business spirit, and his fortune in acquisitions (Ranke[*]).

Amongst his fortunate estate purchases belonged the acquisition of the domains Pardubitz, Bresnitz, and Podiebrad in Bohemia. In 1748 he travelled around the province himself with his trusted paymaster Toussaint in order to look into the construction of linen factories. It occurred that the Brandeis establishment and the domain of Pottenstein were purchased for the same aim. Here then imperial bleaching facilities and a goods warehouse were erected under the management of Count Charmé who had moved to Austria from Prussian Silesia; suchlike also arose in Pardubitz, Wamberg, and Tetschkewald, etc.[607]

We recall the Prussian kings, we recall Peter the Great, and many, many smaller princes to find the judgement confirmed that in no social strata was so much effective entrepreneurship present as under the heads of state who had mostly arrived at independence and power in a hard struggle.

They were now surrounded by a crowd of select men who were active in the emergence of an early capitalist entrepreneurship either as executive instruments or on the other hand just as strongly as self-creative spirits — the government

---

[*]   [Tr.: Sombart does not specify the work, but presumably Ranke (1857).]

rooms were full of talents who at the time did not yet avoid the state administration. Colbert — the greatest of them — was a proper entrepreneurial nature — far-sighted, energetic, sober, ruthless, prudent, industrious. He said of himself and certainly with right that he "loses no time, has no pleasures and distractions, nor any other relaxation and by nature just loves the work too much." According to his own confession he possessed "a quite natural affection for work;" indeed it was directly impossible for him to withstand "idleness or even only moderate work". "My son [Colbert once exhorted] you should work in the morning *and* in the afternoon"[608]. But his mind was above all directed at the care of the economy, for whose building up in the capitalist spirit he did more than any private entrepreneur of his time.

To whom were also offered more perfect means for the execution of far-sighted, economic plans than the head of state and his servants? In times of insufficient capital formation often only the state possessed adequate means to be able to even begin a great enterprise.

Just as prominent was the organisational apparatus over which the state disposed. Again put yourself back to times in which there was still a lack of schooled personnel in order to gauge what a lead the state had in its bureaucracy over private entrepreneurs who had to first train their staff of people and supervisors.

At no point except with princes could the interest be focussed so much on the distant future and hence could have drafted and carried out quite extensive plans. What distinguished all capitalist nature was the long-sightedness of the enterprise and the persistence of the spiritual energy — it must have grown with state enterprises as if by itself from their nature.

Thus we understand very well the remark of a German cameralist who suggested that the betterment of the manufactures required cleverness, contemplation, costs, and rewards, and then came to the conclusion: *"Those are occupations of state; the merchant, however, stands by what he has learnt and to what he is accustomed.* He does not worry about the general advantage of his fatherland"[609].

The *manner in which* the princes took part in the founding of the capitalist enterprises was varied. In many cases it was only about "stimulus" or better "spurring", about guiding and leading.

It is the state which in many places pulled the private persons by the ear so that they became active as capitalist entrepreneurs. It pushed and urged them with force and persuasion into capitalism. The image of physical necessity which I use here is borrowed from the text of a cameralist writer of the 18th century who suggests there: "that the plebs do not depart from their old song until you drag them by nose and arms to their new advantage"[610].

A few examples may clarify the, for our present-day concepts, quite intimate sort of "encouragement" as it was accorded by the heads of state in earlier times to their "subjects".

The king of *France* (thus Colbert) announced to the authorities of Autun the mission of Camuset:

> "De par le roy, Chers et bien amez, envoyant le sieur Camuset pour établir à Autun la manufacture des bas d'estame au tricot nous avons bien voulu vous dire en mesme temps *que vous lui donniez toutes les assistances qui dépendront de vous* pour faire le dit établissement et pour cet effet que *vous obligiez ceux des dits habitans* tant hommes, femmes que les enfants depuis l'âge de huit ans qui sont sans occupation à travailler en la dite manufacture et que vous ayez à lui *fournier une maison.*"
>
> [From the king, dear and beloved, who is sending Mr Camuset to establish in Autun the manufacture of knitted woollen stockings, we were kind enough to tell you at the same time *that you would give him all the assistance that is required from you* to create the said establishment and for this purpose that you oblige those of the said inhabitants both men, women, and children from the age of eight who are unemployed to work in the said factory and that you have to *provide him with a house.*]
>
> From a manuscript shared in Levasseur (1900, 2:256).

The intendant of Bourges to Colbert:

> "J'ay parlé aux officiers de ville pour les inviter à chercher des bourgeois qui veuillent entreprendre ce commerce: ils demeurent tous d'accord de l'avantage qu'ils en retireroient; mais il n'y en a pas un qui veuille s'y engager. Cela m'a obligé, pour commencer à faire quelque chose, de m'adresser aux directeurs du grand hospital, afin de les obliger à commencer la manufacture de bas d'estam."
>
> [I spoke to the officers of the city to invite them to look for citizens who want to undertake this trade: they all remain in agreement on the advantage they would derive from it; but there is

not one who wants to engage in it. This obliged me, to begin to do something, to address myself to the directors of the large hospital, in order to oblige them to begin the manufacture of woollen stockings.]

(Depping 1850, 3:766)

A good, summary depiction of the Colbertian effectiveness as founder of new industries is contained in Boissonade (1902). It is interesting that Colbert favoured the joint-stock companies because he could exercise a direct influence on the conduct of business in them. The stockholders were mostly "fonctionnairs" [functionaries]:

"surtout des financiers, traitants, trésoriers, receveurs généraux, fermiers des droits du roi, tous placés plus ou moins directement sous l'autorité du pouvoir central."
[especially financiers, contractors, treasurers, receivers general, farmers of royal rights, all placed more or less directly under the authority of the central power.]

Especially richly coloured is the following report on the atmosphere from the reign of Frederick the Great of *Prussia*.

When the Hirschberg merchants did not want to condescend to support with their contracts the damask weavers drawn to Silesia by Frederick, the customs office blocked their own goods which were meant for export, and the minister Count Schlabrendorf wrote the following to them:

"I am making [...] it known to the merchant elders that if they do not buckle under soon and procure from the linen-damask-factory as per the example of the Schmiedeberg and Greifenberg merchants, military administration shall be placed on them and such shall remain on them as long as until they have condescended to comply with the royal will directed at their own and commerce's best interests, as their duty demands in any case. Up to now I have resolved on every degree of mildness with the merchants, only, since they show themselves to be refractory and even give notice by the conference that as long as it depends on them, the damask factory will never be accepted in Silesia, thus revealing themselves by their caprice and nothing remains but to show them that they are subjects who must follow the royal commands redounding to the land for the best [...] I am accordingly making it known to the merchant elders that they shall be held to get these chased-out damask weavers into the land again, to establish them in it, and to provide them with work".

And in his own hand as a postscript:

I will go there this summer and research everything and with further refractoriness I will take drastic measures as the situation demands and the merchants won't suspect [...]"

They themselves, however, the Hirschberg merchants, shall have made a great effort to adopt a better process for bleaching: "The start shall have been made with the bleaching. What is profitable in Holland and many lands is also in Silesia." Breslau, 11th June 1764. From the Archiv der Hirschberger Kaufmanns-Sozietät, cited in Gerstmann (1909, 85 ff.).

Other governments on the other hand took it upon themselves to promote their private entrepreneurs through their own activity. The officials of the *Austrian* government, for example, proceeded seemingly as travelling salesmen on the search for buyers of Austrian goods, took samples along, studied tastes and demand, recommended their articles, brought commissions home or treasured knowledge. These journeys went from out the Moravian Company in Brünn. The most well-known of these offical "trading journeys" is that of Count Haugwitz and the inspector of the Brünn manufacturing office, L. F. Procop, in the years 1755 and 1756[611].

Yet others founded enterprises at government cost and handed them over afterwards to private entrepreneurs; or they advanced considerable sums to entrepreneurs free of interest or they provided those private persons who founded factories with the means of production and workers[612]. Many of the measures which we have learnt to recognise as components of the mercantilist economic policy were indeed closely related to an actual entrepreneurial activity and hence have to likewise be brought to mind here[613].

Finally the states (and cities), as is sufficiently well-known, appeared as independent founders and leaders *of their own enterprises* and proved as such to be pioneers of the capitalist economic forms.

The *banks* erected from the 16th century to ever greater extent appeared first of all in many places as public (state or civic) enterprises. Here belong the state banks of Venice, Genoa, Milan, and Amsterdam; the Hamburg Bank; the Nuremberg banco publico; Law's bank; the Russian Assignation Bank; the Royal Bank in Berlin, amongst others. Since I speak about banking in another connection, this reminder suffices here.

A few *trading* companies also bore the stamp of the state.

The most important field of state entrepreneurial activity, however, was of course *industry*.

Here we encounter at first the striving to work on the private entrepreneurial spirit through the erection of state-owned *model institutions*. Such a model institution was the Manufacture royale des Gobelins called into life by Henry IV and completed by Colbert, which we will yet get to know more precisely; the manufacturing house on the Tabor in Vienna was though supposed to have been such a model institution[614].

The institution erected at the instigation of J. J. Becher in the year 1676 contained:

1. a large *chemical laboratory* for production of:
   a) the salts and alcohols necessary for the main chemical products;
   b) metallic colours (verdigris, malachite, white lead, cinnabar, etc.);
   c) gold and silver by means of alchemy (!);
2. a *workshop for the production of majolica crockery*;
3. a *pharmacy* in order to produce good medicine at a cheap price;
4. a *workshop for the production of good house utensils* (from a metal alloy invented by Becher);
5. the *silk factory*, run with three "ribbon mills";
6. the *wool factory*.

Apart from the main building in which these factories were placed, the "Craft and Workhouse" also encompassed:

7. the "house of residence of the director";
8. the Schnellenberg smelting works;
9. the Venetian glassworks.

The manufacturing house which Becher had also thought of as a sort of state apprentices' workshop (see Becher (1682, 120 ff.)), was apart from that an unsuccessful founding, so that it quite properly burned down in 1683, which does not interest us here though where we only have to assess it as an emblem of the state's entrepreneurial drive.

But the state firms extended themselves past the narrower circle of model institutions and became significant next to the private enterprises for a series of branches of industry. Those areas in which they won the most ground were mining and the essential war industries. Almost in all lands, but particularly in Austria, Germany, and Russia, we encounter here numerous state firms. A statistical survey of their share in the totality of enterprises is not possible, and also not necessary for our purposes. It suffices for us here to have established that under the creators and founders of modern capitalism the heads of state assumed a prominent position. Certainly, the enterprises called into life by them were not indeed "capitalist" in the strict sense. But they formed an important link in the development of capitalism, for which they served in many ways as a model, as pacemaker, from whose spirit they were born, and from which they borrowed essential features. These first enterprises also frequently passed from the one form into the other — state institutions became private enterprises, private enterprises were taken over by the state. It would thus have signified a severe hole in the genetic portrayal of capitalism had I not mentioned in this place the princes and their servants as types of modern entrepreneurs.

***

Chapter 57: The Noble Estate Owners

I. The Position of the Estate Owners towards the Commercial Economy

In and of itself the large estate owners conditions did not contain any chrematistic or even capitalist traits. Even the economies arising in the framework of the large estates, the socage economies, were by nature, as we know, not commercial economies, but rather remained for a long time economies of the satisfaction of needs, even after they were already (which occurred quite early) taking their surplus of production to market.

But in the course of time they stripped off their old character. The self-sufficient economy of the large estate owner was restricted more and more, and next to it a commercial economy developed within the sphere of influence of the estate owner which gradually grew into the capitalist economy.

The estate owner turned into the capitalist entrepreneur and did not contribute immaterially to the development of capitalism.

Thus what capitalism experienced in the way of advancement by the estate owners should be acknowledged here. Whereas all that which is portrayed as a burden perhaps of the capitalist industry by the estate owners lies far from our consideration, like the levying of fees for the granting of business licences, duties (weaver interest!), and the like of which the historians of trends thinks exclusively when they speak of the influence of the large estates on modern economic development.

What drove the lords who were burdening themselves with the effort and worry which was inevitable when they perhaps called an industry to life on their property?

Certainly it was often pure *neighbourly love*, it was the wish to raise their vassals bodily and intellectually which turned them into industrial entrepreneurs. In particular the churches and monasteries, when they founded industries, will have often been led by such motivations.

An example which can certainly pass as being typical of many cases: Benedikt Litwehrig, who was elected abbot of the the Ossegg monastery in 1691, saw that most of his subjects in Ossegg and the villages belonging to it, because they had no further employment outside the small amount of tillage, "for the most part snored away the long winter evenings in work-shy inactivity, and as a result had to live very meagrely". He considered means of helping and wrote to a certain Paul Rodig, a skilled stocking worker from Saxony, so that he would practice his trade in Ossegg and instruct the locals in it. Even before the close of the 17th century there were 50 trained stocking workers on the Ossegg estate who practiced their trade there and were not permitted to go abroad (Schlesinger 1865, 88 f.).

But such attempts will not have formed the rule. Rather the estate owner who was becoming the capitalist entrepreneur was also aiming at nothing other than what most of those who took this path wanted — he wanted to use his powers to extend his sphere of influence, to increase his wealth, and if he was an abbot or bishop to increase the lustre of his monastery or diocese. The spirit which drove the estate owners into capitalism was the same *spirit of enterprise with chrematistic justification* which animates all capitalist entrepreneurs. But how had the medieval seigneur, the martial feudal lord been able to carry out this change? We must attempt to answer this question first with reference to the generally valid fact, which I have already recalled above, that in any group of men of a specific population different variants are present, and that we must also assume capitalist variants among the knights and lords of the Middle Ages who could develop just as little in the medieval environment as now, when the conditions of the capitalist economy were gradually being fulfilled, they achieved more and more predominance. Even amongst the princes of the church such entrepreneurial types were not lacking. I think perhaps of some of the abbots of Rolduc in the Wurm valley on whose grounds the first (?) coal mining in Europe was carried out. Men like the abbot Haghen and particularly P. J. Chaineux who led the abbey in the 18th century differentiated themselves in no way from any "daring merchant" and industrial entrepreneur. That applies especially to Chaineux, under Haghen the provisor, that is, the administrator of the abbey's properties. He was considered one of the best mineralogists and mining engineers of his time, although he belong to the religious order from a young age. He induced his insightful predecessor, Haghen, to make investments in large measure in the mines of the abbey — up to 1771 over 669,000 francs were spent for subterranean apparatuses and a similarly large sum for surface mining. At the time 800 miners were employed underground in the mines and probably just as many above ground — a quite unusually high number for that time[615].

Amidst the religious estates, we will now certainly have to describe the emergence of such entrepreneurial types to be more "accidental", since the selection of the princes of the church took place under essentially different points of view than that of their business efficiency. With the secular estate owners we may already think of a sort of process of regeneration or adaptation to the gradually changing environment (which of course was forming itself under the influence of the new men themselves). We can imagine that from the feudal lords in time the commercial men were being selected.

But this process of organic selection of unfeudal elements would have been presumably a slower one, and it alone does not explain the rapid increase in capitalist entrepreneurs among the estate owners which we observe. This was rather the entirely natural consequence of another development which we see playing out in various lands from the 16th century; I mean the *nobility becoming bourgeois*.

We encounter this everywhere, in Germany and Austria too — among the Bohemian nobility, for example, there was an entire crowd of bourgeois upstarts, already in the 17th and 18th centuries, like the famous family of the Counts von Schlick. But this de-feudalisation of the nobility first became a general social phenomenon in the lands of Western Europe, France and particularly England, as it already had been before the 15th century in Italy. If capitalism had made so much more rapid advances here than, for example, in Germany, then the nobility becoming bourgeois indubitably contributed strongly to it. For that this led to a commercialisation of attitudes is obvious, just as much also as that with it the capitalist spirit spread more easily, was more easily able to penetrate all of society and the entire being of the state than in a land where the unmercantile or even anti-mercantile power of the old feudally and seigneurially disposed nobility was preserved for longer, like with us.

II. The Nobility Turning Bourgeois

The *nobility turning bourgeois* followed in two ways: either through the bourgeoisie becoming noble or through nobles marrying the daughters of the bourgeoisie. It will suffice if I describe this process of the nobility becoming bourgeois somewhat more precisely for England and France. (I have treated the topic in a more detailed way in Sombart (1913c, 10 ff.; 1967, 9 ff.)).

1. *England*: in England only the *upper nobility* formed (and still forms today) the aristocracy in the narrower sense. This was in essence newly born with the accession to power of the Tudors, more exactly with Henry VIII. After the Wars of the Roses the old families had been reduced to 29; also those who remained were in part still ostracised, weakened, impoverished. Henry VIII at first raised these old families to power and wealth again (and subordinated them to the Crown which from then on preserved its undisputed preeminence). The means for endowment was presented to the king by the confiscated church estates (which were thereby converted to a "worldly" use). The ranks of old families have now been supplemented though again and again since Henry VII and VIII by new creations. And these new peers who were placed entirely on a level with the old landed nobility were chosen by the king from amongst all the notables, above all also from amongst the rich bourgeoisie. James I even sold peerages. From Henry VII to James II 339 peerages were created.

After 99 peerages were extinguished under the Stuarts, from 1700–1800 339 peerages were newly created.

Naturally these elevations were not always from the bottom, i.e. emerging from the depths of the people like with the Russells and Cavendishs. Often (perhaps mostly) these peers had various preliminary stages to pass through — those of esquire, knight, and baronet. But we know that in numerous cases the family tree traced back to a wealthy Homo novus [new man] of the City. For evidence I will cite the following examples.

The dukes of Leeds were descended from Edward Osborne, who came to London as a poor merchant's apprentice; the dukes of Northumberland trace back to Hugh Smithson, who was an assistant in a pharmacy and married Lady Elizabeth Seymour; likewise with bourgeois ancestors: the Russells; the marquesses of Salisbury, the marquesses of Bath, the earls Brownlow, the earls of Warwick, the earls Carrington, the earls Spencer, the earls of Tylney (the first Earl of Tylney is none other than the son of Josiah Child!), the earls of Essex, the earls of Coventry, the earls of Dartmouth, the earls of Uxbridge, the earls of Tankerville, the earls of Harborough, the earls of Pomfret, the earls Fitzwalter, the viscounts Devereux, the viscounts Weymouth, the earls Clifton*, the earls Leigh, the barons Haversham, the barons Masham†, the earls Bathurst, the earls of Romney, the earls Dormer, the dukes of Dorset and those of Bedford; families whose peerages have in part been extinguished long ago, but who (as far as they are not of younger creation) blossomed in the first half of the 18ᵗʰ century. See the sources in Sombart (1913c, 10 ff.; 1967, 9 ff.).

But what above all gives the social structure of England its peculiar stamp, and gave it above all in the time in which we are interested, is the *gentry* — i.e. a group of persons who do not actually belong to the nobility and yet is noble — a sort of "lower nobility", but which according to the law is not noble. The uppermost strata of the gentry form the knights, amongst whom again the baronets assume the highest rank — a knight and baronet receive the prefix Sir placed before their first name. To the knights belong the holders of the knight's fiefs, who were originally the only knights; then the holders of specific orders, the Orders of the Garter and of the Bath (since Edward III and Henry IV‡) and a few offices; finally those who bought the knighthood — the availability for purchase of knighthoods (they were purchased on payment of £1,095) was introduced by James I in the year 1611. These knights by grace of the moneybag were called baronets — they were to have precedence over the old ones and ranked directly below the nobility. Many hundreds of such baronets came into being during the 17ᵗʰ and 18ᵗʰ centuries — by the middle of the 19ᵗʰ century they numbered 700. It is understandable that already in this way a great part of the rich commoners were being raised up into the nobility (which socially the knights indubitably were). The quite special peculiarity to the English gentry though is this now: that it cannot be delimited at all and certainly not from below.

With this peculiar concept it was given, however, that the affiliation to the nobility in England was determined as it were automatically through the transformation of economic relations which preserved for high-striving men of money access to the nobility always to the extent that their significance to social life grew. Since it belonged to the concept of the gentleman up until deep into the 18ᵗʰ century that he was a large estate owner, with that the interspersion of the landed nobility with bourgeois elements had become a necessary consequence of the growing wealth in the cities.

But the bond between nobility and wealth was tied even faster when the sons and daughters from both groups married each other and produced children. Such sorts of ties between nobles and upstarts belonged in England at least since the Stuarts to everyday phenomena. When Sir William Temple actually realised that it was according to his memory

---

*   [Tr.: perhaps the Cliffords, earls of Cumberland, were meant here, unless the *barons* Clifton were intended (see next note).]

†   [Tr.: Sombart erroneously gave the barons Havershams and Mashams as earls [*Grafen*].]

‡   [Tr.: the Order of the Bath was actually founded by George I.]

about 50 years since the noble families had married into the City "for downright money" (Temple 1754, 2:386), we could in view of the great authority of this quite distinguished observer place the beginning of this mixing of blood quite securely in the reign of James I. In any case, 100 years later, when Defoe was writing, the number of noble-bourgeois mixed marriages was obviously already quite considerable, for Defoe speaks of them like they are natural phenomena. Of course, it was no-blemen especially who married rich heiresses from the merchant class in order to gild their coats of arms anew. Defoe cited of such marriages only of high nobles with merchant's daughters 78 in particular, which there would be no point to individually name here; it is indeed at base all the same whether Lord Griffin married Mary Weldon, a merchant's daughter from Well in Lincolnshire, or Lord Cobham married Anne Halsey, a brewer's daughter from Southwark; these marriages interest us simply as mass phenomena, which they certainly had already become in the 18th century in England.

2. *France*: for France the turning point occurred perhaps towards the end of the 16th, beginning of the 17th century — at the time massive sources sprung up all at once from which new nobles emerged. The most important is that in 1614 the transfer of feudal property even into the hands of the commoners, which had take place since time imme-morial, was expressly recognised as legally allowed. This form of acquir-ing nobility had a quite especially great significance for France — in the 18th century it teemed with newly baked seigneurs who had arrived at their dignity simply through the purchase of a noble estate. The rich ad-orned themselves with seigniories like some do today with foreign or-ders. Paris Montmatre, the son of a small innkeeper in Moirans, signed himself at a baptism as Comte de Sampigny, Baron de Dagouville, Sei-gneur de Brunoy, Seigneur de Villers, Seigneur de Foucy, Seigneur de Fontaine, Seigneur de Chateauneuf, etc.

To the various ways of becoming a noble was added towards the end of the 18th century the purchase: in 1696 500 letter of nobility were sold, in 1702 200, in 1711 100 (Broc 1887, 1:353).

No wonder if in the end the French nobility consisted more and more of ennobled Turcarets[*]. It is no exaggeration when Chérin[†] says that what you called "Noblesse" in France in the 17th and 18th century was in essence "du tiers état enrichi, élevé, décoré, possessioné" [the en-riched, raised, decorated, and propertied of the third estate]; when the Marquis d'Argenson writes around the middle of the 18th century that with the easiness of purchasing the nobility for money there was no wealth which would not soon be ennobled.

---

[*]   [Tr.: Turcaret is a 1709 comedy by Alain-René Lesage in which the pseudonymous main character is a ruthless, dishonest, and dissolute financier.]

[†]   [Tr.: Bernard Chérin (1718–1785), genealogist and Historiographer of the King's Orders.]

The statistical evidence which we possess over the state of the nobility at the outbreak of the French Revolution confirms the correctness of these judgements, although they deviate from each other in details. According to Chérin there were 17,000 noble families; of them at most 3,000 had a title which was older than 400 years; at most 1,500 were "ancient nobility", i.e. descending from feudal fiefs; 8,000 families were nobles from officialdom, and 6,000 from purchased titles. According to other estimates there was a total at the time of 26,600 noble families, amongst whom 1,300–1,400 belonged to the ancient nobility (the "noblesse immémoriale ou de race" [immemorial or racial nobility]), whereas of the remainder 4,000 were nobles from officialdom. See the summaries in Boiteau (1889, 34; cf. Broc 1887, 1:350 f.). The share which high finance had in the composition of the French nobility now is, however, still far greater than these figures express, even if we here again draw attention to the extraordinary numerous marriages of noblemen to rich heiresses of common birth.

The process of fusion was obviously already in full flow at the beginning of the 17th century if we want to believe the genuine old nobleman, the Marquis de Sully, who made bitter complaints over it.

At the end of the 18th century Mercier (1782, 2:201) could write: "La dot de presque toutes les épouses des seigneurs est sortie de la caisse des fermes" [The dowry of almost all the wives of the lords has come out of the coffers of the farms].

I will tack on a few examples that speak especially clearly, in which you may recognise the peculiar social conditions of the 18th century (which in this respect is already quite similar to the nineteenth and twentieth).

The one son of Samuel Bernard, who is generally called "le Juif Bernard" [the Jew Bernard*], is the comte de Coubert, he married Miss Frottier de la Coste Messelière, daughter of the marquis de la Coste; the other bought an office as President with the Parliament in Paris and called himself comte de Rieur, he married Miss de Boulainvilliers. Through this marriage "the Jew Bernard" became the grandfather of the comtesses d'Entraygues, de Saint-Simon, Courtorner, d'Apchon, and the future marquise de Mirepoix.

Antoine Crozat†, whose grandfather was still a domestic servant, married his daughter to the comte d'Évreux from the princely house of the Bouillons. His third son, baron de Thiers, married Miss de Montmorency-Laval, and the second daughter of that marriage wed first the marquis de Béthune and then the marshal de Broglie.

The brother of Crozat married his daughter to the marquis de Montsampére, Seigneur de Glèves‡.

A relative of the marquis de la Vrillière married the parvenu Panier.

---

*   [Tr.: actually a Protestant artist.]
†   [Tr.: first private owner of French Louisiana (1712–1717).]
‡   [Tr.: neither of these titles appear to exist. Also Antoine's brother Pierre died childless.]

The marquis d'Oise married the two year old daughter of the Mississippian André (for a 20,000 livre annuity until the wedding and 4 million dowry).

The daughter of Berthelot de Pléneuf married the marquis de Prie — she was the most well-known mistress of the regent[*].

That of de Prondre was wife of the marquis de la Rochefoucauld.

Le Bas de Montargis became father in law of the marquis d'Arpajon, grandfather of the comte de Noailles and the duc de Mouchy.

Olivier-Senozan, whose father had still traded in old trousers, gave his daughter to the comte de Luxe, later prince de Tingry.

Villemorien married his to the marquis de Bérenger.

The comte de Erreux, d'Ivry, the ducs de Brissac, de Pecquigny — all, all walked the same heavy gait to the money boxes of the Turcarets.

The (excellent, but, as it appears, also seemingly unknown in France) major work over the bourgeoisification of the French nobility, which was only seen by me after finishing my own studies, is Bertin (1879).

III. The Distinctive Features of the Entrepreneurship of the Large Estates

The enterprises called to life by the noble estate owners received their particular stamp in that they all have *wealth of power* as their starting point and base. What above all enabled the estate owner to operate as a capitalist entrepreneur was the power of disposal which he had as property owner over important productive forces. He disposed over:

1. the land as producer of plants;
2. the treasures lying in the ground (minerals, etc.);
3. the production of the soil: wood, fibrous material, etc.;
4. the labour power subject to his power as an estate owner.

In that he used these productive powers for commercial aims, the various sorts of capitalist enterprises arose.

The power in the state which the estate owner can use to his advantage consists now, however, not only in the direct power of disposal over people and things, it also expresses itself in the influence which it can perhaps bring to bear indirectly in favour of an advantageous purchase or an advantageous sale of the products — through the obtaining of privileges, concessions, etc. Through that another, important

---

[*] [Tr.: actually of the Prime Minister, Louis Henry, Duke of Bourbon, who was a member of the regency council, but not the regent.]

variety of feudal-capitalist enterprise arose. We frequently find influential nobles combining with bourgeois moneymen or even poor inventors for joint action — the courtier then takes care of the necessary right of liberty or property rights, while the other participants provide money or ideas. We encounter such alliances in France and England in particular during the 17th and 18th centuries again and again[616].

The enterprises of the noble estate owners now, however, played during the epoch of early capitalism a greater role than you generally tend to assume. The share which they had in the development of capitalist enterprises does not of course show statistically because of the lack of any statistics in most cases. But you can probably get an idea of the significance of this type of entrepreneur in the earlier centuries if you imagine a series of cases of such capitalist enterprises by estate owners.

IV. The Actual Share of the Noble Entrepreneur in the Development of Capitalism

The *participation of the nobility* (be it the country or the city nobility) *in capitalism* stretches back into the earliest period. At the start of the development of capitalism it was more the *trade* which was directed by rich noble families (often at first) into the paths of capitalism. That applies to all lands; perhaps though most of all for *Italy*, where this oldest epoch of purely commercial capitalism appeared in classic form.

I have described in detail in the first edition of this work the role which the nobility played in the beginnings of modern capitalism. All the critics, as hostile as they might be, have not been capable of getting rid of the fact shown by me that *an extraordinarily large part* of the early capitalist wholesale trade, especially even the early money dealing, had lain in the hands of rich, noble, in part also landed families. I refer the reader thus for this early period to Chapter 12 of the first edition* and the list of names imparted there whose content was set right in individual points by this or that local historian, but was in no way shown to be essentially wrong. (See, for ex-

---

*   [Tr.: Sombart (1902a).]

ample, the ridiculously small corrections which Davidsohn (1896a, vol. 4) carried out on my list of Florentine noble families conducting trading and money businesses, and which really stand in no proper relation to the spiteful, brash tone in which he judges my work).

Here I want by contrast more to record the share of the property-owning nobility in the development of capitalism and hence I take into account more the northern lands in essence since the 16th century.

1. *England*: *mining* and the *steel-making industry* were carried on with pleasure by the estate owners. Carried on: not just taken advantage of as prerogatives. These pure rights of use are ruled out here entirely where we are tracing the entrepreneurs themselves. But even as such we encounter the estate owners frequently in both the mentioned branches of production. In the 15th century the "forges" of the bishops of Durham at Bedburn in Weardale already bore an outright capitalist stamp, particularly concerning the size of the staff (Lapsley 1889). In 1616 a courtier concluded a contract with the pin-maker guild over delivery of the necessary wire which he had thus produced himself on his properties (Unwin 1904, 167). In 1627 Lord d'Acre obtained a patent for sole finishing of steel according to a new patent (Rymer 1727, 18:870). From the 16th century the estate owners were setting up tin works on their properties, "clashmills", in order to process tin which they had obtained from their mines (Sélincourt 1908, 89). In 1690 numerous lords and gentlemen helped found the tin and copper mining association: The Mine Adventurers Company (A. Anderson 1787, 2:594). We also find numerous nobles participating in coal mining at his beginnings.

Textile industry: "Indeed the wealthy graziers were themselves very commonly clothiers also, in the sixteenth century; the wool grown upon their own land, they employed men and women of the neighbourhood to make into cloth, and then sold it to the London drapers or dealers"[*] (Ashley 1887, 80; cf. Gibbins 1897, 147).

The English estate owners ran the silk industry likewise. In 1629: "a grant to Walter, Lord Aston etc. of the Keeping of the Garden, Mulberry-trees and silk-worms near St. James in the County of Middlesex" (A. Anderson 1787, 2:335).

Or you founded any industry for the *utilisation of the cheap fuel* which you had on your property, like peat, etc. In 1637 Thomas Earl of Berkshire obtained a patent for a malt and hops kiln newly invented by him, just for the utilisation of his stocks of peat (A. Anderson 1787, 2:376).

2. *France: mining and steel-making industry*: the iron works in the province of Nevers, which was a key location of the steel-making in-

---

[*] [Tr.: Sombart actually quotes a literal German translation of Gibbins' summary of Ashley here. I have subsituted Ashley's original text.]

dustry, were up until into the 18th century in the hands of the old nobility; e.g. Villemenant was in possession of Arnault de Lange and Château-Renaud, who in the 16th century erected larger works; their neighbour was Seigneur de Bizy, who likewise ran an iron works and a blast furnace on his property; the iron works of Demeurs belonged to the gentlemen Gascoing, etc. (All these facilities passed in the course of the 18th century over into the hands of the rich Parisian bankers Masson) (Corbier 1870). But also in the Franche Comté we run into old nobles possessing iron works (G. Martin 1900, 115 ff.).

Of the 13 iron works in the Généralité de Tours, the owners were:

Marquis de Saucé	Abbess d'Etival
Duc de Villeroy	Marquis de Sourches
Duc de Vallière (twice)	Vidame de Vassé
Comte de Tessé	Duc de la Trémoille
Marquis de Béthomas	Duchesse de Mazarin
Créancier du Duc de Gesvres	Comte de Rhoné

(Dumas 1894, 168)

Even the iron working took place in part on the properties of the estate owners — the knight F. E. de Blumenstein erected (1715) near his castle a foundry; the duke of Choiseul was running at the same time a steel works; the lord of Montroger had a sheet metal hammer, etc. (G. Martin 1900, 110, 214 ff., 115 ff.).

To a high degree the nobility in France had participated in the spoils of coal mining. Henry II had granted the right of extraction to François de la Roque, seigneur de Roberval; the right passed to Claude Grizon de Guillien, seigneur de St Julien and another seigneur. Louis XIV then gifted the duc de Montausier the right to exploit all coal mines with the exception of that of Nevers over a period of 40 years. The regent obtained the right of mining exploitation in a company under the name of Jean Gobelin, sieur de Jocquier, who thus also bore a predominantly noble character. But nobles not only possessed the *right* of exploitation — the business itself was also frequently in their hands. At the time of Louis XIV the duc de Noailles opened a mine in the dukedom of Bournonville; the duc d'Aumont opened one in Bourbonnais; the duc d'Uzès another (Depping 1850, 3:LX); whereas the duc de la Meilleraye mined the deposits at Giromagny (G. Martin 1899, 318).

In the second half of the 18th century the cases pile up in which the nobility — be it on their own properties, be it elsewhere — obtained the right to conduct mining operations (coal!), thus:

Princes de Croy	Marquis de Luchet
Princes de Beauffremont	Marquis de Traisnel
Ducs de Chaulnes	Marquis de Gallet
Ducs de Charost	Marquis de Mondragon
Marquis de Mirabeau	Comte de Entraignes
Marquis de Lafayette	Comte de Flavigny
Marquis de Cernay	Vicomte de Vesins
Marquis de Villepinte	Baron de Vaux
Marquis de Balleroy	Chevalier de Solages
Marquis de Foudras	

(The information about the participation of the French nobility in coal mining is based, where I have made no other reference, on the excerpts from the files of the national archives in the good work of Des Cilleuls (1898, 59 ff., 210 ff.)).

Textile industry: it is also reported about France that the estate owners erected weaving mills on their estates in order to exploit the wool from their flocks or the cocoons of their silk worms. Examples from the 18th century: marquis de Caulaincourt erected a Manufacture des mousselines et des gazes de soie [factory for muslins and silk gauzes]; marquis de Louvencourt erected in Longpré a Manufacture de toiles [fabric factory]; marquis d'Hervily erected at his Château de Lanchelles a linen mill; duchesse de Choiseul-Gouffier erected a cotton spinning mill in Heilly; comtesse de Lameth had 100 wheels distributed in Hénencourt. Sieur Gaulme had a factory for fine cloth at the castle de Bas; de Ramel likewise; baron de Sumène silk spinneries; marquis d'Hervilly a tableware factory; sieur de Sel des Monts a cotton factory; the seigneurs Requin and Desbois cotton and flax mills; le sieur Marie de Perpignan a carpet mill; chevalier Pascal de Carcosonne fine cloth, etc. The number of noble textile industrialists in France during the 18th century was in fact very large (G. Martin 1900, 113 ff., 199, 244 ff.; cf. Calonne 1883, 111).

(The *glass works* of the noble glass makers [gentilhommes verriers] must not be reckoned with here. They were poor devils who had for a yet unexplained reason been ennobled in the 15th century and jealously preserved it, despite their poverty, on account of which they were looked down upon by nobility and bourgeois alike. See the nice study by Beaupré (1846).)

The participation in *trade* as entrepreneur, thus also openly appearing as a partner in business (it stood differently with participation in money matters) was derogated in general in France. Yet there were exceptions, particularly in the south. Thus we find the nobility participating on a large scale (also as named partners) in the coral companies of Southern France in the 16th century (Masson 1908, 19 ff.).

3. *Germany*: the *iron and copper industry* in Germany in many places owed its first development in capitalist guise to entrepreneurial estate owners. Thus we see the counts Stolberg in the 16th century eagerly active with the advancement of the iron making industry, foundries, etc.; count Wolfgang in the 16th century set up the iron works at Königshof, made Ilseburg into a centre of the iron industry, erecting there the first brass works, etc. The neighbouring count Julius of Brunswick-Lüneburg competed with him. An especially instructive example are the Gittelder iron works in the Harz, for which we possess the account books for the years 1573 to 1849 in the archives of the Oberbergamt at Klausthal. Beck (1884, 2:152 ff.) takes excerpts from them.

We are well informed about the entrepreneurship of the counts and dukes of Brunswick by Wilczek (Wilczek 1907, 8 ff.; cf. Möllenberg 1911, 19).

These "estate owners" were small princes and could just as well serve as examples of princely entrepreneurship as of the entrepreneurship of estate owners. Only they are better handled under the "estate owners" because the innate, personal tendency determined much more about their entrepreneurship than it did with the monarchs of larger states, with whom the state (represented by its bureaucratic apparatus) portrayed a super-individual instance which received its unchanging direction independently from the personal tendencies of the ruler. But with the smaller princes it was in fact purely personal initiative which pulled them onto the tracks of business entrepreneurship.

An especially instructive example is offered here by the well-known duke Julius of Brunswick-Lüneburg, the founder of numerous industries in his small land. An excellent characterisation of him has been drafted by P. Zimmermann (1905). We learn that the duke was weak, crippled, unsuited by nature to military service, but also his tendencies departed entirely from the context of his martial family. When his step-mother, the duchess Sophie, admonished him that for his relaxation — he was always working — he should occasionally also pursue hunting, he answered: "As other electors and princes are dependent on the hunting bug, we have the opportunity, as E. G. & L. know in part, to dwell on the mining bug" (P. Zimmermann 1905, 46). He proved himself just as gifted at turning to account his products: "he was without doubt the most significant merchant in his area" (P. Zimmermann 1905, 52). He pondered in all earnestness outfitting a ship himself which would transport his goods to Narva in Russia and there take other goods in exchange for them (P. Zimmermann 1905, 54). He canalised and corrected the Oker and other small rivers of his.

That the Silesian mining industry rested up into our time in the hands of estate owners is well-known.

Of 243 in Silesia (1785):
> 20 belonged to kings,
> 14 belonged to the duke of Oels, to the prince of Anhalt-Cöthen, and to the prince of Lobkowitz,
> 191 belonged to "the other counts, freiherrs*, and noble estate owners",
> 2 belonged to the Breslau merchants,
> 2 belonged to the religious foundations.

(Anonymous 1786, 206)

Other industries in Germany especially also owed the smaller princes for their origin or advancement. Thus the *glass industry*, the *porcelain industry*, amongst others. Stieda described to us vividly the founding of the porcelain industry in the monastery of Veilsdorf in Thuringia (in 1760) by prince Friedrich Wilhelm Eugen von Hild-burghausen. The prince was a counterpart to the Brunswickian Julius — treasured as a talented artificer and mechanic, an enterprising man always in need of money without being extravagant, "bourgeois" enough

---

*   [Tr.: Freiherr is a title below a baron, but often translated in English as baron.]

to appreciate the value of capitalist investments. See Stieda (1902, 176 ff.).

The nobility were also involved in the founding of the *textile industry*. Numerous examples in Gothein (1892, 1:751, 1:752, 1:791, and elsewhere).

But the German nobility also turned to the overseas *trade* which indeed still bore a half-adventurous stamp. A typical representative of such a type of mercantile interested estate owners is described by Kohl (1910). They organised voyages to Iceland.

4. *Austria*: the works in *mining* were originally often only, during the transition period to capitalist operations (16th century) predominantly, noble. Thus we find among the "lords and works of the imperial mines at St Kathrein" (mercury mine at Idria) from 1520–26: Gabriel count of Ortenburg, Bernard von Cles, cardinal bishop of Trient, Hans von Auersberg, lords of Schönberg, Sigmund von Dietrichstein, freiherrs of Hollenberg and Finkenstein.

Documents from 1536 — the lords were:

> Hans Jos. von Egg,
> Franz von Lamberg at Stein, furthermore:
> Niclas Rauber, freiherr at Plankenstein,
> Niclas, freiherr von Thurn.

Text from 1557 mentions:

> Anton, freiherr von Thurn,
> Wolf, freiherr von Auersberg,
> Leonhard von Siegersdorfer.

Documents from 1569 and 1574:

> Hans von Gallenberg,
> Franz Wagen von Wagensburg,
> Georg, count von Thurn at Kreuz,
> Herward von Hohenburg, etc.

(Hitzinger 1860, 13–14)

Likewise the *iron industry* in Steiermark preserved for long centuries its manorial character (L. Beck 1884, 2:620 ff.).

Over the estate owners' mining in Bohemia (counts Schlick, the founders of Joachimstal, Wilhelm von Pernstein, the Rosenbergs, amongst others): see Salz (1913, 62 ff., 405, and elsewhere).

An abundant source material and a series of proficient treatments provide us with valuable insights into the development of the *Bohemian* industry itself. Thus we also see the Bohemian estate owners especially clearly at work, we see how much entrepreneurial spirit and energy has become active in them. A quite outstandingly competent entrepreneur was Johann Josef, count von Waldstein, founder of the Oberleutensdorf cloth factory (1715). He drew Dutchmen and Englishmen to his domain who brought with them tools never seen before in the region and put the factory into operation. The residents had to first be trained for the work. Behind all that stood the count as the driving force, "who did not shy from any means or any costs". His investments, which were also kept up by his successors, thrived (Schlesinger 1865, 134 ff.).

For the development of big industry, particularly the *textile industry* in *Bohemia* during the 17th century, it became quite crucial that, spurred on by the example of the Konsess[*] president, count Joseph Kinsky, a series of aristocrats resolved on the introduction of manufactures to their estates. Already in 1762 Kinsky could give the empress the "gratifying news" that various lords in Bohemia, amongst them count Waldstein, prince Lobkowitz, count Bolza, "were also showing an inclination" to promote manufacturing on their properties (Příbram 1907, 1:127).

A list sent by count Kinsky of the factories founded by nobles from the beginning of the 1760s is in Beer (1895, 101).

5. *Russia*: the beginnings of modern industry in the time of Peter the Great were not noble; but then, from the second half of the 18th century the industry passed more and more into the possession of the nobility. (*Reason*: only the nobility held the right to employ serfs as factory workers, merchants were forbidden from purchasing them.)

In 1773 the factories belonging to nobles produced 1,041,000 rubles of 3,548,000 rubles in total.

Of 40 cloth factories, 19 belonged to them.

At the beginning of the 19th century (1809) of 98 cloth factories which delivered their products to the government, ownership was:

> 12 by merchants,
> 19 by the high nobility,
> 55 by simple nobles,
> 12 by foreigners and raznočinci[†].

(Tugan-Baranowski 1900, 35)

6. In *Sweden* many mines were formerly side operations of estates; the estate owner employed the miners as his statare-workers [agricultural workers receiving payment in kind]. Even today, after mines and agriculture have separated, the old relationship of dependency lives on in Dannemora. See Geijerstam (1897). I am indebted for the reference to a member of my seminar, Dr Bulle.

7. *Colonies*: the colonial capitalism is to be seen to a large extent precisely as the work of noble, frequently still quite feudally oriented entrepreneurs who appeared here almost as pure conquerors. That applied already to the "Franks" who exploited the Levant. It applies to the Spaniards and Portuguese who in the 16th century took root in the Americas and considered themselves there entirely to be estate owners — the descriptions encomiendas and repartiementos, capitanias and sesmarias indicate it already[‡]. See in addition the depiction in Chapter 27 of this volume.

But that applies in the end also to the first entrepreneurs to whom the southern states of North America were turned over for exploitation. We recall Lord Delaware who was the main participant in the Virginia

---

*   [Tr.: the Konsess was a regional representative assembly for the region of Breisgau.]

†   [Tr.: raznočinci were intellectuals who did not belong to the gentry.]

‡   [Tr.: see page 140 above.]

Company of London (founded 1606), of Lord Baltimore, the "founder" of Maryland, whose profit-seeking intentions are not to be doubted any-more today; we think of the eight proprietors to whom in 1663 the land between Virginia and Florida ("Carolina") was handed and find among them the Duke of Albemarle, the Earl of Clarendon, Sir William Berke-ley, and above all Lord Shaftesbury (Ballagh 1895, 17; McCormac 1904, 11 ff.). For a quick orientation, Jeffery (1908) is suitable, and for the set-tling of the Carolinas see page 64 of that work.

***

Chapter 58: The Bourgeoisie

I call bourgeois entrepreneurs all those who came from below and swung themselves up to be the leaders of capitalist enterprises on the strength of their good bourgeois nature. They are the commercial small producers, shopkeepers, and farmers who "worked their way up". They thus constitute as capitalist entrepreneurs a selection from the craftsmen.

What raised them up and out of the masses of their comrades was firstly their economic (bourgeois) virtuosity — they were more diligent, more frugal, and calculated better than the others. Their patron saints were L. B. Alberti and Benjamin Franklin, the canonisers of the doctrine of the "holy economy", the Sancta masserizia [holy thrift][617].

But with industry and frugality — those two cardinal virtues of the good paterfamilias — you have not yet become a leader of a capitalist enterprise, and especially not in the early period of capitalism where the goal must be set that the way be paved. Anyone who wanted to rise up from craftsman to capitalist entrepreneur had to also possess the characteristics of an entrepreneur. Only the far-sighted, but at the same time also energetic man detached himself from the masses of equally placed comrades; it was always "daring" merchants, "daring" craftsmen who took up the position of the new economic subjects. It is this daring which connected them with the previously described types of entrepreneur. But what now distinguished them just as much from the latter was the strong emphasis on the commercial side of entrepreneurship. They rose up above all because they were gifted "traders". Their strength was based on their skilfulness in the concluding of contracts — with the suppliers, with the workers, with the customers. For them money thereby stepped for the first time into the centre of their economic activity — from money it comes, to money it streams. They saw foremost in money the actual, indeed the only power factor, since they did not know any other power than the power of wealth. Through it the complete penetration of the economic process with the idea of money was first completed. They were quite properly foremost *capitalist entrepreneurs* because for them (money) capital became the indispensable prerequisite for their effect-iveness as entrepreneurs. Quite certainly they did not thus become entrepreneurs because they had money — that would be a bad mechanistic assumption. But rather they also be-came entrepreneurs because they were enabled to by the force of their personal characteristics. But their entrepreneurship was far less tied to the possession of money than that of the other types. Through them the bourgeois wealth, whose ori-gins we have been following, obtained its significance for the building of the capitalist political economy — they struck the fire from the stone. Bourgeois wealth, we saw, did not need to be transformed at all into capital. A quite considerable part of the bourgeois wealth which arose in the early period of capit-alism was lost to it because it ended up in the hands of extra-vagant people with a seigneurial bent. Only that bourgeois wealth which was also really acquired by "the bourgeoisie" could undergo its transformation into capital, and those un-der whose leadership it was called to play its role in economic life were precisely the bourgeois entrepreneurs who preoc-cupy us here. Not that they always possessed enough money themselves (although we may assume that in quite numerous cases) to call into life a capitalist enterprise — it was though again and again bourgeois wealth which they transformed into capital in that they united with other bourgeoisie for common activity, or had outside money employed in their own enterprises[618].

We find the bourgeois entrepreneur at work in all the branches of economic life. Yet the forms in which he performs his work are quite various, so that a whole variety of types of capitalist enterprises are called into life directly through him — we will investigate their inner construction later (in the next volume), here we are only following the varied form of entrepreneurship itself.

The foremost way in which the bourgeois person became a capitalist entrepreneur led *through the craft workshop run by them* — this was gradually expanded until it had transformed itself into a capitalist enterprise — which can happen with all sorts of "craftwork" — with rural, with industrial, with mercantile, with transport — in the first generation there arose what I call the petty capitalist entrepreneur.

This case of a gradual, step-wise enlargement with which the one economic form imperceptibly passes over into the other until finally the "quantity turns into the quality" was certainly a very common one (as it indeed occurs still daily today). A large part of the craftwork-like "*negotiatores*" became in the course of time capitalist entrepreneurs — they are the Florentine wool traders, the English tradesmen, the French marchands, the Jewish drapery dealers.

Just as frequently we encounter the *industrial* craftsman risen in the world. It is that entrepreneur whom the English called a "manufacturer", the French "fabricant" (in contrast to "entrepreneur").

In important industries, like the machinery industry, this type directly formed the rule in the beginnings of the development of capitalism.

Especially instructive is the story of the *Berlin* machinery industry. The small study of Dominik (1915) informs us about it in a vivid way. The main types of craftwork industrialists were the following:

1. Georg Christian Freund, born 1792, learnt the machinist's craft, made himself independent, supported by an investor, in 1815 in the Mauerstraße, "and began with good success and amidst adroit use of his own ideas to build steam engines";

2. Franz Anton Jakob Egells, born 1788, learnt locksmithing and founded, after long journeys in England, an iron foundry in 1821 in Berlin. Egells began working according to his own ideas without imitating English patterns;

3. August Borsig, born 1804 as the son of a furniture polisher, learnt furniture making. He *studied* from 1821–1825 at the commercial institute founded by Beuth, entered the Egells factory in 1825, was employed there in 1827 as "factor", and founded in 1837 with a sum of 10,000 talers saved in that job a factory by the Oranienburg gate in which he carried on foundry work and mechanical engineering with the most primitive means in simple wooden shacks;

4. Johann Friedrich Ludwig Wöhlert, born 1797, learnt joinery, started with Egells in 1818, became in 1837 an employee in Borsig's factory, and later made himself likewise independent.

(Carl Hoppe and Louis Schwartzkopf* each began as engineers.)

We find the craftsman type, however, strewn across almost all industries. Like in sugar refining where the "master servants" of the larger factories set themselves up as independent entrepreneurs[619]. Or in the metal mining industry.

Thus the chronicler (of the 17th century) writes of the Aachen copper masters, the owners of the copper yards: "This craftwork I have initially christened a trade, because the servants did the work alone, and the master could do nothing more than weigh in and out and keep books, hence also both women and men can practise this trade." (Nopp 1632, 1:111; cited in Peltzer 1908, 315)

The smaller and larger "cloth factory owners" also played a role in the textile industry.

The type was uniformly distributed in all lands. In large cities you found it especially frequently. For Berlin a good expert claims directly: "In the main, big industry grows from the craftwork in that capable, intelligent masters who have gone through the excellent school of the royal trade institute, acquired abroad and particularly in Paris the necessary technical capabilities to the fullest, and returned home, found factories."[620] Some approximate estimate of the numerical share is understandably just as impossible with this type as with any of the others.

Finally we find in some lands, like e.g. England, amongst the *agricultural* entrepreneurs many a one who had become big on a farm who himself or his father had guided the plough. The entire generation of middling capitalist tenants in England who advanced during the 18th centuries had for a large part emerged from the farmers' craft.

The other path to bourgeois entrepreneurship is the "*putting-out*", that is (as we will yet see more precisely), that form of organisation of production by which industrial workers are furnished by rich people with advances until they have become pure wageworkers in a capitalist enterprise.

In part it was richer "*colleagues*" who set themselves up as employers of the impoverished craftworkers.

Just to add a few early examples:

The Arte della Lana [wool craft, i.e. guild] in Pisa prohibited in the 14th century entrusting the "worker" with more than 25 pounds in the city, 50 pounds in the countryside. No lanaiolo [wool worker] of the city

---

*   [Tr.: both founders of Berlin engineering firms.]

of Pisa should erect a workshop in which he had weaving done for wages (ad pregio) outside of his own.

In the guild of wool shearers we find in England (1537) two loans of £100 and £50 which richer craftsmen lent to poorer. A series of disputes concerned these loans, from which we can extract that the poorer masters had to work off their debt. "Davy Ellys had commandement to worke with Humphrey Hitchcock or with Thomas Saunders untyll such tyme as they be both satisfied of their debts which is due to theym by the said Ellys". From the Clothworkers' Court Book, July 12, 34 Hen. 8 (1542), cited in Unwin (1904, 57).

In 1548 an English law forbade the rich masters of the leather guilds from supplying the poorer ones with leather; in 1549/50 the law was repealed on the grounds that without that it did not work. "Most of the artificers are poor men and unable to provide such store of materials as would serve their turn" (3 & 4 Edw. 6 c.6 "Leather" (1549)). Similar determinations were made in the *building trade*. Cited in Unwin (1904, 56).

In France the same picture around the same time — poor hat makers dependent upon rich ones. "Les maitres qui n'auront moyen de tenir boutique ouverte et qui travailleront chez les autres m^{es} ne pourront sortir de la maison de m^e où ils travailleront pour aller travailler ailleurs quilz ne l'en ayent averty quinze jours auparavant soutz les peines ci-dessus dernières dictes" [Masters who have no means of keeping their shop open and who work for other families may not leave the house where they are working in order to go and work elsewhere unless they have informed that family fifteen days beforehand of this, subject to the penalties dictated above]. Article 31 of the statute of the hat makers of Bourges, cited in Levasseur (1900, 2:163).

But much more frequently it was merchants, mostly intermediaries, who became the ones putting-out to craftsmen. This process is so common that it almost appears to be the norm: "ce sont ordinairement (!) les marchands en gros, qui entreprennent les manufactures" [it is ordinarily (!) the wholesale merchants who initiate the manufactures], Savary[621] suggested categorically. Its frequent occurrence has even blinded many historians so much that they simplify the problem of the origin of capitalist production enterprises into a gradual "crossing over of trading capital" into the sphere of production (Marx!). There is no talk of that now of course, as this book makes sufficiently clear. But that, as stated, the cases were frequent in which goods traders became the managers of production enterprises is subject to no doubt. Those trades in which this process played out especially frequently were:

1. (above all!) the textile industry, where in all lands certainly from the 14th century, perhaps even earlier, the members of the Calimala guild*, tailors, the clothiers, the marchands drapiers [merchant drapers], that is thus: the cloth dealers (just like the silk dealers) on the one hand, the thread dealers on the other hand, put out to craftworkers;
2. mining and iron works, to the extent that they did not retain the stamp of the estate owners; here the putters-out were the "ore buyers", the iron traders, etc.;
3. the branches of fashion accessories (rosary makers!);
4. dressmaking — at least in the 17th century "clothing manufacturers" developed in all the larger cities from the cloth dealers.

There remains finally *the new founding of large capitalist enterprises* in the area of overseas trade or industrial production or transportation, in which you likewise find bourgeois entrepreneurs active. Here they frequently take on a quite specific stamp which distinguishes them clearly from the previously described types of bourgeois entrepreneurship and that allows a quite new, peculiar type of capitalist entrepreneur to arise to which we must give our special attention — the following chapter is about them.

**

---

* [Tr.: the Arte de Calimala was the guild of cloth finishers and merchants in Florence.]

Chapter 59: The Founders

Even that type of entrepreneur which I describe as that of the "founders" can trace its ancestry back into an early period. Its ancestors sat in the noble guild of the projectors or project makers — those inventive heads whose careers consisted of forging all sorts of reform and reorganisation plans and winning over princes, great men, and the rich men of the land to their plans to move them to carry them out. Everywhere where there are influential people — in the courts, at the parliaments — we encounter such project makers; but even on the street and at the market they stand and sell their ideas. Since this phenomenon of the *professional project-making* is extraordinarily important, I want to share here a few details over the spread and the character of this strange breed of men who were called in their time "projectors"[622].

Already in the 16th century such projectors were emerging — we encounter them at the time in the courts of the *Spanish kings*. Ranke[623] reports as follows about one of them:

> There was still actually no science of public finance; there was a lack even of the knowledge, the skills which a comprehensive administration of the finances demanded — more individuals distinguished themselves who considered the outcomes of their contemplations to be a secret and only wanted to share them for special remuneration; adventurers and prodigals as it were, who ventured for good fortune in advance of the crowds of cameralistic masters and followers. They were for the most part Florentines. A certain Benevento who had already offered his services to the Signoria of Venice — "without taxing the people, without an innovation of significance, he wanted to considerably increase their

revenues; he demanded nothing but 5% of the benefits which he created for them" — was now at the same time respected; the emperor Ferdinand called him to his court; he also appeared at Philip's. To the latter he actually gave an advantageous suggestion. On his advice Philip bought back the privileges of salt preparation in Zeeland from the inhabitants, etc.

But the proper age of project-making seems to have been first the 17th century which was also so rich and blessed in all other areas. A fortunate accident has preserved for us a source from which we can determine for *England* quite precisely the time in which the project-making in any case obtained its greatest extent[624] — this source is the writing of Defoe over projects (Defoe 1697).

In it the author, extraordinarily knowledgeable as is well-known, describes *his* time directly as the age of project-making and names the year 1680 as the beginning of this "age" — "But about the Year 1680, began the Art and Mystery of Projecting to creep into the World" (Defoe 1697, 25). ("Mystery" here obviously has the meaning of "craftwork".) He suggests as a result that in any case never before had such a high degree of project-making and invention been achieved, "as it refers to Matters of Negoce, and Methods of Civil Polity" (Defoe 1697, 1–2).

At his time it teemed with such people "who besides the Innumerable Conceptions which dye in the bringing forth, and (like Abortions of the Brain) only come into the Air, and dissolve, do really every day produce new Contrivances, Engines, and Projects to get Money, never before thought of" (Defoe 1697, 4).

In one place in his work, Defoe makes the remark that the French "have not been so fruitful in Inventions and Practices" (Defoe 1697, 7) as the English. But in that he errs greatly. To the contrary, one is tempted to say that the classic land of the project maker is *France*, where at the same time as in England, say from the middle or end of the 17th century until deep into the 18th century, the same processes played out as on the other side of the Channel, and perhaps even, corresponding to the dispositions of the people, in somewhat more temperamental and dramatic form. Also and directly for France, good

570

experts of those periods of time establish even for the beginning of the 17th century "an urge to invent and enrich oneself quickly thereby"[625]. The projectors were called in France "donneurs d'avis" [advice givers] or "brasseurs d'affaires" [brewers of business].

The type of the projector had still not died out in France at the end of the 18th century, as the descriptions of Paris at the time make known to us[626].

The project-making also blossomed in other lands — thus in *Austria* at the time of Leopold I[627]; at the court of Maria Theresa a certain Caratto played a significant role, of whom Stupan remarked[628]: "The Caratto (who on 25th January 1765 had handed in a text over a few commercial suggestions) has already been practising the *handiwork of a projector* for more than forty years; his principles are good and irrefutable, but his conclusions exaggerated."

In *Saxony* (at the end of the 17th century), the "entrepreneur" Johann Daniel Krafft was a universally known personality[629]; from Saxony also came the manager of the Fayence factory at Mosbach in *Baden* — Tännich, who already formed the connecting link between the projector and the founder[630].

What position the projectors are entitled to in the genesis of the capitalist entrepreneur is quite clear — they are the progenitors of the Laws, the Pereire, the Lesseps, the Strousbergs, the Saccards, but also of the thousands of small "founder" souls with which our time is filled. What they still lacked, and what they in part already (as we can note at individual points) sought to create themselves was the sphere of activity itself — the enterprise. They still stood outside, they were themselves not yet businesspeople, were themselves not yet entrepreneurs. The ideas which should have been called on to produce the capitalist essence wavered about as it were still like lifeless shadows and awaited the hour of their birth. This could only come after the idea of the enterprise had connected itself with them. But this point in time now, so far as we can see, was reached towards the end of the 17th century. We learn that at the time already many of the projectors found a willing ear with the possessors of money, and that it consequently came to "foundings" of all sorts of enterprises which we have to describe as speculative enterprise. Defoe, whom we already more than once owe for valuable information, also informs us over this point.

But with it a new type of entrepreneur came into the world — precisely the "*founder*". He has as we see an entire illustrious series of spiritual forebears — socially he is completely rootless. He originates from any stratum of society you like, but what characterises him quite especially is that he does not receive a specific stamp from any social stratum from which he has arisen. He is as it were born free, fallen from heaven.

He is, however, completely different in his behaviour from all the previously considered types of entrepreneur. You can at most compare him to the bourgeois trader to the extent his talent lies in the same *direction*. But yet worlds separate him from his bourgeois brother.

Bourgeoisie and founders are like each other in that they both do without the external means of power which serve the state and estate owners in their entrepreneurial activity. With them the place of this external compulsion is taken by inner compulsion. But whereas the bourgeoisie sought to convince, the founders strove to persuade. The former calculated on success, the latter forced it. The founder dreamt gigantically. He lived as if in a constant fever. The exaggeration of his own ideas spurred him ever anew and kept him in permanent motion. The prevailing mood of his being was an enthusiastic lyricism. And out of this prevailing mood he completed his greatest work — he swept along other people with himself so that they helped him carry out his plans. When he was a great representative of his sort, a poetic ability possessed him, making pictures arise before the eyes of others of enticing charm and colourful splendour which gave an idea of the wonders he wanted to perform — what blessings the planned work meant for the world, what blessings for those who carried it out. He promised mountains of gold and knew how to make his promises believable. He stimulated the imagination, he awoke belief. And he awakened powerful instincts which he used to his advantage — he incited above all the addiction to gambling and placed it in his service. Opinion making is the key. And for that all means are proper which gain the attention, the curiosity, the desire to buy. Fuss becomes an end in itself.

And the work of the founder is completed, he has reached his goal, when wide circles get into a state of intoxication in which they are ready to grant all the means which he needs for the carrying out of his enterprise.

The less easy the plan of an enterprise is to be ignored, and the more the possible effects are of a general nature, the better suited it is for the founder, and the greater the wonders the spirit of speculation can perform. Hence great banking enterprises, great overseas enterprises, and great commercial enterprises were especially suited objects for the activity of the spirit of speculation from the beginning and have remained so up to today.

***

Chapter 60: The Heretics

Already with the listing of the last type of entrepreneur, I have abandoned the principle of classification which allowed me to distinguish the first three types. I will distance myself still further now from the pure social-genetic ordering of the individual types of entrepreneur when I now highlight a series of groups as places of origin of entrepreneurship, groups which are formed by the community of their faith as well as the external lot of their members. I repeat also once more what I have already said: that the circles from which I have the various types of capitalist entrepreneur emerge intersect each other in part, that thus the individual groups from which the entrepreneurs come do not generally stand in relation to each other in terms of the secondary order. That becomes apparent when we now attempt to evaluate the human domain of hereticism as one of the "birthplaces" of the entrepreneurial class. But the intelligent reader will not be led astray by this arrangement of the material, but rather, as I hope, directly receive strong stimulus from it.

The state has, as we have already established (see Chapter 28* of this volume), created — through the development of the state church especially — the concept and the appearance of the heretic or heterodoxies as a political or social category in Europe. With that it shall be said that in the modern states two categories of citizens were distinguished — full citizens and half citizens according to their confession of faith — of which those of one — the members of the church of the land — were thus in full possession of all rights of citizenship, whereas the members of other confessions were deemed "half citizens", to whom in particular the access to public offices

---

* [Tr.: corrected from the obviously erroneous reference to Chapter 25.]

and dignities was blocked or made difficult. The Jews were half citizens in this sense almost everywhere up until into the 18th century and mostly beyond; in the Catholic lands there were also the Protestants; in the Protestant lands conversely the Catholics and the factions not belonging to the state church; thus in Great Britain the Presbyterians, the Quakers, etc.; in the Presbyterian New England states of America, the adherents of the High Church, etc.

This *"hereticism" as such*, quite independently of the confession itself which was seen as heretic, was now obviously an important nursery of capitalist entrepreneurship because it massively strengthened the interest in acquisition and increased the business efficiency. And indeed for obvious reasons — excluded from participation in public life, the heretics had to expend their entire life power in business. This alone offered them the opportunity to obtain that respected position in the community which the state withheld from them. It was inevitable that in these circles of the "excluded" the significance of money possessions was valued more highly than under otherwise equal circumstances in the other strata of the population because for them money signified the *only* path to power.

On the other hand, it was inherent in their position as heterodoxies that they had to develop their economic capabilities more strongly because naturally for them the opportunities for acquisition proved more difficult. Only the most meticulous conscientiousness, only the most shifty accountability, only the most far-reaching adaptation to the needs of the clientele promised them business success. Persecuted and suspected, wrote Benoist of the Huguenots, how could they have otherwise survived than by "the wisdom of their behaviour and by their sense of honour" ("par la sagesse de leurs moeurs et par leur honnêteté")*.

It was obvious too that these heretics in the period of capitalism's beginnings dedicated themselves directly to *capitalist* enterprises with a particular zeal, since these indeed promised the most success, offered the safest handle for ob-

---

* [Tr.: perhaps from Benoist (1693; 1694), though I have been unable to trace this specific quote.]

taining wealth and through it status. Hence we find them in those critical times, thus particularly from the 16th to the 18th century, everywhere in prime position as bankers, as merchants, as industrialists. "Wheeling and dealing", "the trade" were directly dominated by them. The best judges recognised these connections correctly already during those centuries.

The Spaniards simply said heresy promotes the spirit of trade.

And a clear-sighted man like William Petty gave the following interesting judgement over the significance of "heresy" for the development of the capitalist spirit[631]: trade lies in all states and under any government in the hands of the heterodox party and such who represent a view different from the officially recognised one; thus in India, where the Muslim religion is recognised, the Hindus (the Banians) are the most significant merchants. In the Ottoman empire, the Jews and Christians. In Venice, Naples, Livorno, Genoa, and Lisbon, the Jews and non-Catholic. Even in France, the Huguenots are represented relatively more strongly in trade, whereas in Ireland, where the Catholic religion is not recognised by the state, the adherents of this religion have a large part of the trade in their hands. From which follows that *the spirit of trade is not connected with some religion as such*, but rather as was previously already stated *with heterodoxy* as a whole, as the example of all the great English trading cities also confirms ("Trade is not fixt to any Species of Religion as such; but rather [...] to the heterodox Part of the whole" (Petty 1755, 119)).

We frequently encounter similar verdicts, especially over the significance of the non-conformists for the development of trade and industry in Great Britain.

"They [the non-conformists] are not excluded from the nobility, among the gentry they are not a few; but none are of more importance than they in the trading part of the people and those that live by industry, upon whose hands the business of the nation lies much." (Corbet 1667, 23; cited in Hallam 1832, 3:152 n. 257)

That these observations, as these men shared them with us, were correct is taught by a look at the economic history of that time. We are especially well-informed over the relations in France by the reports of the intendants which were demanded by the king after the repeal of the Edict of Nantes and which Boulainvilliers collected and has shared in excerpts[632]. From that you see that in fact the perhaps greatest part of capitalist industry and overseas trade lay in the hands of the Reformed (or had lain up to that time which was so absolutely critical for France). The iron working in Sedan, the paper making in Auvergne, in Angoumois, in the Généralité of Bordeaux, the vegetable tanning in Touraine which competed with the English, were exclusively in their hands; in Normandy, Maine, and Brittany, "they had almost the majority share in the blossoming linen weaving"; in Tours and Lyon in the fabrication of silk, velvet, and taffeta; in Languedoc, Provence, Dauphinée, Champagne in the wool industry; in the Généralité of Paris in the making of lace, etc.

In Guyenne the wine trade lay in their hands; in two provinces (de Brouage and d'Oléron) a dozen families had the monopoly on the salt and wine trades; in Sancerre they were according to the statements of the intendant "superior in number, wealth, and significance to the Catholics". In the Généralité of Alençon 4,000 Protestants dominated almost the entire trade. The same picture in Rouen, Caen, Nimes, and Metz.

They most liked to run the external trade to Holland and Britain, and the Dutch and English liked to do business with them most of all, because they had more trust in them than with the Catholics — so suggests Benoist.

We also encounter numerous Reformed as bankers in the France of the time, and they also liked to undertake tax-farming, which they were permitted to do. It is known that Colbert bristled a lot against the edicts which forbade their use in the administration of taxes.

So that you may surely be permitted to endorse the verdict of Ranke over the Protestant heretics in France in the 17th century when he says in summing up[633]:

> Excluding the war and the essential offices of state, the Reformed took all the greater share in the administration of the finances, the farming of privileges, the issuing of bonds; it is remarkable with what zeal and success they devoted themselves to the rising manufacturing.

You will perhaps object that the Huguenots in France were the bearers of capitalist development not because they were heretics, but rather because they were *Protestants*, indeed in the way Max Weber has put forward the hypothesis quite generally that the membership of *specific* religious communities (the movements of "ascetic Protestantism") were the cause of the "capitalist spirit".

I deny now in no way the influence which the special structure of the religious confession has exercised on the economic disposition, as I of course also do not ignore the fact that the "heretics" in Europe were predominantly Protestants (and Jews). I do not doubt that specific dogmas have contributed to *stiffening* the capitalist spirit (although I also find many hindrances for its development directly in Puritanism and Quakerism).

With respect, however, to the unquestionable fact that "heretics" of another observance have also provided a large contingent for capitalist entrepreneurship, I am inclined to ascribe the main share in the influence to the heretics as such, and not to a specific system of religion or a specific sect. The following considerations strengthen me in this view. The entire formulation of the question of whether a specific religious confession has produced a specific economic disposition (and not rather, as others claim, vice versa) does not seem to me to be serendipitous. I think rather that *both* confessions (be it capitalism, be it Protestantism) are products of the same basic tendency so that only the "new" spirit, which we see at work everywhere it is about the development of modern Europe[634], finds its expression in both. Both — Protestantism and capitalism — are by their innermost nature "heretical spirit", spirit of rebellion against slackness, indolence, self-satisfaction, still life. Church reform and economic reform arise at base from the same spirit of "non-conformism"[635], which perhaps even (which we can only suspect) was connected to specific dispositions of blood. Obviously both these expressions of the same spirit then influenced each other mutually. And to that extent you can speak of an influence of specific systems of religion on capitalism (and vice versa).

In that I make heresy as such, not the membership of a specific religious community, responsible for the origin of capitalist entrepreneurship, I thus generalise the problem, on the other hand in accordance with the overall structure of this work, I do without exposing the origin of the new spirit and highlight only the social conditions under which we see this develop.

But now another social phenomenon stands in close relationship to the religious — and you can add: to the political — heresy, a social phenomenon which has had a much greater share in the construction of the capitalist economy than heresy itself — I mean the migrations from one land into another which we see those persecuted on religious or political grounds making in those centuries of early capitalism. The heretics became emigrants; the emigrant became a foreigner in the new homeland.

The problem of migrations, however, goes beyond the "emigrant" problem, to the extent such migrations were also pursued for other than religious or political grounds. Hence, I treat them separately and in context, and dedicate to them the entire following chapter.

***

Chapter 61: The Foreigners

Preliminary Remarks

It would be an appealing exercise to write all of human history from the point of view of "the foreigner" and his influence on the course of events. In fact we observe from the beginnings of history how in small and in large scale it is imputed to the impacts from outside that the national communities developed in a particular way. It may be a matter of systems of religion or technical inventions, of forms of everyday life or styles or garb, of state revolutions or stock exchange arrangements — always or at least very frequently we find that the stimulus emanates from "foreigners". Thus the foreigner also plays an outstandingly large role in the history of the capitalist entrepreneur. Constantly during the European Middle Ages and to a greater extent still in the later centuries, families left their hereditary residence in order to erect their hearth in another land. And they are precisely those economic subjects which we must identify in numerous cases as the founders and promoters of capitalist organisation. Hence it is surely rewarding to follow the connections which perhaps existed between the migrations and the history of the capitalist entrepreneur. At the same time you can differentiate between individual migrations and mass migrations.

Literature

We possess for *England* a systematic and comprehensive portrayal of the influence which the foreigners exercised on the culture of a land in Cunningham (1897). Further for Russia in several texts, amongst which Brüggen (1885) especially deserves to be named, as well as Jschchanian (1913), in which the other literature is also worked over. But then there is an abundance of writings over the history and the influence of individual migratory movements.

The *literature over the "emigrants"* is especially extensive and in part very good. It describes partly the fate of religiously persecuted *emigrants* from a land, partly that of *immigrants* into a land. Both types of depiction complement each other. From the almost incalculable abundance of writings I name the following as the most useful:

Weiss (1853) — fundamental and yet to be surpassed.

Berg (1845) — for our purposes only the *first* volume, which deals with the "handel en nijverheid" [trade and industry], essentially comes into consideration. A good, detailed portrayal.

Burn (1846). The great English literature over the emigrant problem has been worked over in essence by Cunningham in his comprehensive work mentioned above. Since 1887 a volume published by the Huguenot Society has appeared annually.

Erman and Reclam (1782) — a very in-depth portrayal of the fate of emigrants in German lands, particularly in Brandenburg-Prussia. Volumes V and VI contain the information which interests us here.

Baird (1885).

But then almost all writings of economic, and particularly industrial history come into consideration, since almost in every region, in every place, as we will see, the influence of foreigners made itself felt on the course of economic life and thus had to be noted by the literature. A list of individual works would be pointless. I will just name a few sources in the appropriate places.

I. The Suitability of Foreigners to be Capitalist Entrepreneurs

Whilst with the first three types of entrepreneurs which we distinguished according to their social origins we could only surmise *what* made them suited to be capitalist entrepreneurs, whilst with them we had to conclude their suitability from the fact that they had become capitalist entrepreneurs, we could already establish with the heretics *why* precisely they were called to become capitalist entrepreneurs, but we can establish that in a still more impressive way with foreigners. In other words, the grounds for selection to which we wanted to attribute all the development of entrepreneurship are perfectly clear with the last and still more with this type; just like the grounds which must have assisted the once selected type in the development of their entrepreneurial abilities.

Let us make clear that each change of place in the centuries which we are surveying here concerns a process of selection in which the capitalist variants start to move. The capitalist variants — that is the people who had either already developed into capitalist economic subjects or were best disposed (suited) for such. Those individuals who decided on emigration are — especially or perhaps *only* in the earlier times when each change of place and above all every move to a colonial land was still a bold undertaking — the most energetic, strongest willed, most daring, boldest, most calculating, least sentimental natures; no matter whether they decided on migration because of religious or political oppression or from occupational grounds. Precisely oppression in the homeland is, as we have already been able to establish, the best nursery for capitalist education. Through emigration, however, those from these oppressed who were fed up as it were with pre-serving their lives in their own land through accommodation and servility were selected. That it was also with these about a "selection" of the most able (in the sense understood here), we see already from the fact that a great part of those perse-cuted on religious or political grounds did *not* make the de-cision to emigrate, but rather preferred to seek to adapt at home — most Huguenots (four fifths) remained in France, just as many Jews remained for centuries in the East before they started to move.

Perhaps it can then also be established that, seen as a whole, those tribes in which the capitalist variants were fre-quently represented formed the actual migratory peoples — the Etruscans (Lombards!), the Jews, the Scots, other Ger-manic tribes (from which in France, for example, the Huguenots were formed), the Alemanni (Swiss), etc.

Furthermore we are placed before the question of whether and by what the abode in the new homeland — whether and by what thus "the foreign" as such — contributed to the devel-opment and intensification of capitalist abilities.

If you want to trace this indubitably present influence back to a single cause, then you can say the migration developed the capitalist spirit through the *severance of all old life habits and life relationships* which it led to. In fact it is not difficult to trace back all the psychological processes which we observe in the "foreigner" in the new homeland and which make him into a good capitalist entrepreneur to this one decisive fact; to the fact thus that for him the tribe, the land, the people, the state in which he had been embedded up to then with his en-tire being had stopped being a reality.

When we see the *interest in acquisition* achieve primacy with him, then we must immediately comprehend that this could not at all happen otherwise, since indeed an activity in other professions is not possible for the foreigner — in the old cultural state he is excluded from participation in public life, the colonial land has absolutely no other professions yet. Also all comfortable life was forbidden in the foreign land — the foreign land is wasteland. It has as it were no soul for the newcomer. The surroundings signified nothing to him. He can at most use it as a means to the goal — of acquisition. This fact seems to me to be of great importance for the development of a mind directed only at acquisition. That applies in particular for the settlement of colonial land. "Our streams and rivers turn mill wheels and carry rafts into the valley like the Scottish; but no ballads, not the simplest song reminds us that men and women also found themselves on their banks, loved, separated, that under every roof in their valleys lust and the sorrow of life was felt" — this lament of an American from the early times expresses clearly what I mean. This observation, that the only relationship of the Yankees to their surroundings was that of pure practical use-value (or at least was earlier), has often already been made, particularly by those who travelled around America at the beginning of the 19th century.

There was for the emigrant — it applies similarly for the emigrants as for the colonists — no past, there was for him no present. There was for him *only a future*. And if just once the focus of interest becomes money, then it appears almost to be obvious that for him the acquisition of money preserved the single sense as that means by help of which he wanted to build his future. He can only acquire money by the expansion of his entrepreneurial activity. And since he is a select able, daring person, his limitless urge for acquisition will soon convert him to a restless entrepreneurial activity. This also thus follows directly from the worthlessness of the present, the overvaluation of the future.

And the foreigner is *not hindered by any limitations* in the development of his entrepreneurial spirit, nor by any personal considerations — in the milieu in which he enters into relations, he only ever meets with foreigners. And it is amongst foreigners that profitable business is primarily to be made, whereas you help the comrades — you only give interest bearing loans to foreigners, Antonio says to Shylock, for only from foreigners can you demand back interest and principal irrespectively if they are not paid.

But some limitations of an objective nature also did not infect the entrepreneurial spirit in foreign lands. No tradition! No old business! Everything must be created anew, as it were from nothing — no ties to a place — in foreign lands every place is the same, or you exchanged what was once selected easily with something else if this offers more chances of profit.

From all that a pull must by necessity follow which on the other hand adheres to all the activities of the foreigner, be he a colonist, be he an emigrant — the resolve for a perfect *development of economic-technical rationalism*. He *must* carry this out because hardship impels him or because his hunger for the future impels him; he *can* apply it more easily because no tradition at all stands obstructing his path. Thus the fact, which we observe, that the emigrants in Europe were the promoters of commercial and industrial progress wherever they went is easily explained. Thus the well-known phenomenon that the new technical inventions were put into use nowhere as decisively as in America is explained no less effortlessly.

II. The Share of Foreigners in the Building of the Capitalist Economy

1. Individual Foreigners

Individual migrations, which are thus based on the fact that from individual causes a family (or even a few families) altered their place of residence, that is, settled in a different land or in a different landscape, have occurred of course in all ages. We are interested here in those to which some advancement of the capitalist spirit was tied, as we may especially then presume when we find the immigrants as bearers of a higher form of economic commerce or as founders of new industries ... I am thinking in the first case of the "Lombards" and other Italian money dealers who conducted their business during the High Middle Ages in France, England, and elsewhere; and I recall how, amongst other industries during the Middle Ages and later, the silk industry was advanced by foreign immigrants in particular. And indeed was advanced in the capitalist sense (for the transfer of craftsmen from one place to another does not concern us in this connection).

585

Thus we learn, for example, the following about the influence of the immigration of natives of Lucca on the development of the Venetian silk industry:

> A new phase of development occurred with the immigration of merchants and silk workers from Lucca, whereupon the industry first came to fruition; at the same time the mercantile element stepped more into the foreground — the merchants became managers of production; they consigned their own raw material to the masters for processing in the various stages of production. (Broglio d'Ajano 1893, 24)

And over the Genoese silk industry:

> Similar to in Venice with the immigration from Lucca, the silk industry in Genoa first made a great advance through the brothers Perolerii and other merchants who at the beginning of the 15th century brought into their service master drawers from Lucca. The introduction of the silk industry is even attributed to them in general. At the same time a social order in the Genoese silk industry was introduced — namely the capitalist cottage industry — which found its expression in 1432 in the founding of the silk guild. (Sieveking 1897, 102 f.)

In Bologna the perhaps first modern factory, a silk spinning mill, "in which a single machine performed the work of 4,000 spinners" was erected by a certain Bolognino di Barghesano from Lucca supposedly in the year 1341 (Alidosi Pasquali 1621, 27).

The silk industry of Lyon likewise traces its origin back to Italian immigrants who conducted it at first in a purely craftwork-like form. It is of interest to us that the crossing over into the capitalist organisation in the 16th century is again to be traced back to the initiative of two foreigners (E. Pariset 1901, 19–20).

The same applies to the Swiss silk industry — in 1575 the Pelegari opened a silk factory with 15, later 30 workers — "a firm of 15 or 30 journeymen was up to then unheard-of even with the paper and book printers" (Geering 1886, 471) — the same for the Austrian silk industry (Bujatti 1893, 16 ff.).

The silk industry is only the main example; alongside it, however, numerous industries were founded some here, some there, some by the French, some by the Germans, some by the Dutch, some by the Italians in foreign lands — and indeed most of those industries which were about to transform into the capitalist form.

2. The "Emigrants"

Even much more tangible, however, was the influence of "foreigners" on the course of economic life in the cases in

which it concerned *mass migration* from one land to another. We can distinguish from the 16th century in which they started the following three such mass migrations:
1. the migrations of the Jews;
2. the colonisation of overseas lands, particularly the United States of America; and
3. the migrations of religiously persecuted Christians, especially the Protestants — the "emigrants".

I will speak about the significance of the Jews in the context of the following chapter. To portray the share of "foreigners" in colonisation would be absurd, since *all* colonisers are "foreigners". The task remains to demonstrate the significance at least approximately which the "emigrants" had for the development of a capitalist entrepreneurship in Europe.

The migrations of the religiously persecuted Christians, especially the Protestants, assumed from the outbreak of the Reformation the character of mass migrations. Probably all lands gave and received, but it is known that the most losses were suffered by France, and that the other lands took in more French emigrants than they lost of their own citizens. An exact statistical working out of the extent of these migrations is not possible. But you can safely say that it concerned many hundreds of thousands who — only within the borders of Europe — changed their homeland because they did not want to change their faith. The number of those Protestants whom France alone lost *after* the repeal of the Edict of Nantes is estimated by Weiss[636] at 250–300,000 (of 1,000,000 Protestants all up who lived in France at the time). But the emigrations had already begun in the 16th century, and France was not the only land from which an emigration took place. But it was also not so much about knowing whether it was hundreds of thousands more or less who took part at the time in the migrations as about making clear the significance which these migrations had for the reorganisation of economic life (which is what concerns us here). And it is easy to measure when you take the trouble to follow the activity of emigrants in the lands of their destination. There the result is that they everywhere took the most active part in the construction of capitalism, and that in banking and especially in the industry of all lands an essential advancement was owed to the immigrants, as the following overview will show.

The *German* states received, as is known, refugees in great masses from Austria, Scotland, and France. The Scots and French come into consideration in particular as representatives of the capitalist spirit.

1. *Scots* came during the 16th and 17th centuries to East Prussia and Posen in great crowds. They were of Reformed and Catholic confession, but in both cases they left their homeland because they could not bear the oppression on account of their faith. The Scots in East Prussia were for the greater part "well off and intelligent" and were seen as dangerous competition (Sembrzjycki 1892). But they even advanced into the interior — at the close of the 16th century we find Scottish colonies resident in Cracow, Bromberg, Posen; everywhere the Scots were amongst the most respected merchants. At the beginning of the 17th century more than half the Posen merchants were Scots; in 1713 still amongst the 36 members of the merchants' guild 8 were Scots. In a petition of the Posen merchants to Count Hoym of 11th August 1795, it was stated:

> The city of Posen owes its former splendour and the extent of its trade to that part of its inhabitants who had emigrated from Scotland and had established themselves here as merchants under the preservation of many privileges. (G. St. A. Gen. Dir. Südpr. Ortsch. LXXII 98 cited in Jaffé 1909, 14)

Cf. Fischer (1902; 1903). Furthermore Rode (1905). A greater work over the Scots in Poland comes from the pen of Baskerville and Steuart (1915).

In the 16th century we encounter (resident?) Scots as lace and braid dealers in the Ore Mountains (E. Siegel 1892, 42).

They were just as at home in Silesia. In Breslau Scots were already being mentioned in 1596. The Brieger shopkeepers' law of 1629/1729 forbade *Scots*, Jews, Italians, etc. from hawking wares. In Hirschberg braids and veils were fetched from foreigners, "Jews, Scots, and Poles". They became settled by means of a "Scottish shopkeeper fairness" or "Scottish chamber fairness" (Anonymous 1796).

2. It was refugees from the Palatinate and Holland, Reformed and Mennonites, who laid the foundations for the (immediately established on a capitalist basis) Krefeld silk industry. Members of the immigrant family von der Leyen are looked on as founders of the silk industry in Krefeld. In the year 1768 the firm of Friedrich and Heinrich von der Leyen employed 2,800 people in the silk industry (Schulze 1904, 658; cf. Berg 1845, 1:285).

The Dutch were (next to Jews) the leading banking houses of the free imperial city of Frankfurt am Main.

The plush and fitted carpet industry in Gera was founded on a capitalist basis by Nicolas de Smit from Tournai (Doornik) in the year 1595 (Germann 1913, 19).

It was the Dutch (next to the Swedes and Huguenots) who in the 17th century brought about the steel and ironware industry in the Bergisches Land (Voye 1908, 4:276).

3. The role which the *French* emigrants played in the German economic life of the 17th and 18th centuries is well-known, that they mostly were the first everywhere here above all to found the capitalist industry and had individual large branches of trade (like, for example, those in the silk industry) almost entirely (together with the Jews) in their hands.

The most important colonies of French refugees were (Weiss 1853, 1:245 ff.) in the electorate of Saxony, in Frankfurt am Main, in Hamburg, in Brunswick, in the Landgraviate of Hessen (Kassel!), and — above all — in Brandenburg-Prussia. The number of French taken in under Frederick William I and Frederick III is estimated at 25,000, of which 10,000 were in Berlin alone. The refugees everywhere introduced the system of "Manufactures réunies" [united factories]; particularly in the production of woollen material, so in Magdeburg (in 1687 André Valentin from Nimes and Pierre Claparède from Montpellier employed 100 workers on weaving looms and 400 spinners), Halle an der Saale, Brandenburg, Westphalia, Berlin, just in the silk production. Other industries which owed their founding or further development in the capitalist sense on the French were the production of stockings, hats, (in 1782 the first hat factory with 37 workers was founded by a Frenchman in Berlin), leather, gloves, stationery, playing cards, linseed oil, luxury soap (in 1696 the first luxury soap factory was erected by a Frenchman in Berlin) (Wiedfeldt 1898, 386), candles, glass, mirrors, etc.

The industries founded by the French are enumerated in full in Erman and Reclam (1782, vols. 5 & 6).

The introduction of the making of fabric in Germany goes back to Dutch refugees in the 16th century; in the 17th century to Huguenot refugees — thus, for example, the factories in Göttingen, Kassel, Mühlhausen, Eisenach can be traced back in 1680–1720 to Huguenot residents. Journal für Fabriken und Manufakturen XXIII, 268, 277, 283[*].

Huguenots were the founders of industry in Baden and the Electoral Palatinate (Gothein 1892, 1:674 ff.), as well as in the French duchies (Schanz 1884).

Amongst the 386 members of the cloth and silk guild in Berlin, no less than 81 French names were still found at the beginning of the year 1808 (Arendt 1808).

4. We also find (Catholic) Italians among the founders of the capitalist economy in Germany. Like in Breisgau (Gothein 1892, 1:739 ff.).

Holland was from the separation of the seven provinces the place of refuge of all possible sorts of refugees. "La grande arche des fugitifs" [the great ark of the fugitives], Bayle called it. The religious interest was

---

[*]   [Tr.: I have been unable to precisely identify or locate this journal — it may be the Journal für Fabrik, Manufaktur, Handlung und Mode, see Anonymous (1802), but the contents do not line up.]

in no way always the decisive one; the Dutch states took in those who promised to bring them advantage for trade and industry — heathens, Jews, Christians, Catholics, and Protestants. "Eigenbelang [...] meer nog dan medelijden voor vervolgde geloofsgenooten [had] zijn deel in de edelmoedige en liefderijke ontvangst der vlugtelingen" [Self-interest [...] more than pity for persecuted fellow believers [had] its share in the generous and loving reception of the refugees] (Berg 1845, 1:167 ff.).

Thus under Mary Tudor 30,000 English Protestants came to Holland; during the Thirty Years War numerous Germans, during the Spanish despotism (thus already in the 16th century) Walloons, Flemings, and natives of Brabant came from the Spanish Netherlands; many Jews since their expulsion from Spain; from the 16th and 17th centuries great masses of French Protestants whose number was estimated towards the end of the 17th century at 55–75,000.

Interesting now is the statement that also in this land the foreigners took an especially strong part in the "upswing of economic life", thus in the founding and expansion of capitalism. How much in particular the stock market trade and the speculation had been advanced by the Jews, who almost completely dominated the Amsterdam stock exchange in the 17th and 18th centuries, is something I have explained in detail in my book on the Jews (Sombart 1911a; 1913d). But even the other immigrants soon took up a prominent place in trade and industry. Thus we find, for example, a Frenchman, the "genial and restless" Balthasar de Moucheron, as founder of trading companies alongside his brother Melchior who was likewise a famous merchant (Stoppelaar 1901; cited in Brakel 1908, 4).

But especially — as almost everywhere — the French emigrants proved to be skilled in the naturalisation of new capitalist industries. A contemporary writer of the 17th century established that more than twenty different manufacturers in Holland were led by refugees. "Hanno introdotto i Rifuggiati l'uso nel Paese [...] di più di venti specie differenti di Manifatture" [The refugees introduced to that country the use [...] of more than twenty different kinds of manufactures] (Leti 1690, 2:148; cited in Berg 1845, 1:212).

The flourishing of Amsterdam was traced by another writer of the time to the influence of foreigners. Scion wrote to the magistrate of Amsterdam:

> "toutes ces industries se sont établies en deux aus de temps et sans dépense [...] Cela remplit de plus en plus la ville d'habitants, accroît ses revenus publics, affermit ses murailles et ses boulevards, y multiple les arts et les fabriques, y établit les nouvelles modes, y fait rouler l'argent, y élève de nouveaux édifices, y fait fleurir de plus en plus le commerce, y fortifie la religion protestante, y porte encore plus l'abondance de toutes choses [...] Cela enfin contribue à rendre Amsterdam l'une des plus fameuses villes du monde"
> [all these industries were established in two years of time and without expense [...] This fills the city more and more with in-

habitants, increases its public revenues, strengthens its walls and its boulevards, multiplies the arts and factories there, establishes new fashions, makes money flow there, raises new buildings there, makes trade flourish there more and more, strengthens the Protestant religion there, brings there even more the abundance of all things [...] This finally contributes to make Amsterdam one of the most famous cities in the world]

(cited in Weiss 1853, 2:135-136).

Alongside Amsterdam, above all Leiden and Harlem drew advantage from them. The industries which were planted by the French refugees were, as usual, in the first line the textile (silk) industry, then hat making, paper manufacturing, and book printing. We can also distinctly perceive how the turn to the capitalist organisation is always traced back directly to the influence of immigrants: up until the 17th century craftwork was quite intact; then — particularly in the second half of the century — the contracts of the cities with foreign entrepreneurs started. In 1666 a contract of the magistrate of Harlem with an Englishman for the purpose of erecting a mirror factory, in 1678 with J. J. Becker for the purpose of founding a silk spinning factory, etc. An overview across the industry of emigrants in Holland is given by Berg (1845, 1:109 ff.). Cf. Pringsheim (1890, 32 f.).

That even in *England* the capitalist development was essentially advanced by foreign immigrants is less well-known and yet cannot be put in doubt. It remains to be seen what lasting traces the Italians who swamped England in the 14th century have left behind in the economic life of the English. As thorough an expert as Cunningham wants, for example, to see imitations of Italian models in the first English capitalist consortiums. But certainly the immigrants of the 16th and 17th centuries who came from Holland and France in particular drew deep furrows in the English economic life. Their number is considerable: in 1560 already 10,000 Flemish refugees shall have found residence in England, and in 1563 even 30,000 (according to the report of the Spanish envoy). Though these figures may also be exaggerated, we can yet assume that they are not far off from the reality, as credible statistics confirm: a census of the Lord Mayor of London from the year 1568 resulted in 6,704 foreigners in London, of which 5,225 were Dutch; in 1571 there were in Norwich 3,925 Dutch and Walloons, in 1587 the majority of the population (4,679) consisted of them. Sources in Campbell (1892, 1:269). There are good informants who claim that the history of English industry began with these Netherlanders. More considerable yet was the number of French refugees who came to England particularly in the 17th century. They are consistently estimated by Baird, Poole, and Cunningham at about 80,000, of whom half shall have migrated on to America. And indeed it was precisely the richer Huguenots who made their way to England (Jurieu 1686, 2:451; cited in Weiss 1853, 1:132).

The foreign immigrants now actuated their spirit of entrepreneurship in the most varied areas of trade and industry, for which they were frequently pioneering. Principally established by them were the silk industry, veil and cambric weaving, carpet weaving, hat making (earlier hats were obtained from Flanders, refugees founded a factory for felt and thrummed hats under 5 & 6 Edw. VI c. 24 (1551) "Making of hats, etc."), paper making (the production of luxury paper was introduced by a German, Spillmann, in 1598 — according to a poem by Thomas Churchyard he employed 600 people), the glass industry (privilege to Anthony Been and John Care (Netherlanders) for 21 years for the erection of glassworks "in order to make glass in the French, Burgundian, and Dutch manner"; in 1670 Venetians erected a large mirror factory), steel wire making (introduced in 1662 by Dutchmen), dyeing (in 1577 the Portuguese Pero Vaz Devora showed the English dyers indigo dyeing; in the 17th century the Fleming Kepler introduced the famous scarlet weaving; another Fleming, Bauer, brought wool dying to a great flowering in 1667), calico printing (introduced in 1690 by a Frenchman); cambric making (introduced in the 18th century by a Frenchmen of the Reformed Church to Edinburgh), the standard industry of England, the cotton industry was founded by foreigners in Manchester, the clockmaking industry (the Dutch made at first pendulum clocks which were called Dutch clocks), waterworks were planned for London by an Italian named Genelli, a company of German entrepreneurs conducted the copper mining and copper industry in the 16th century, the Sheffield knife industry was first made famous by Flemings, and so on ad infinitum. The cited facts according to Burn (1846, 254 ff.) and Cunningham (1897, 178 ff., 212 ff., 235, 263). Cf. also D. Campbell (1892, 1:489 f.) and Lecky (1879, 1:205 ff.; 1878, 1:191 ff.). I have only given a small sample from the abundance of material.

How great the influence of foreign immigrants was on the entire course of the *Swiss* economy has been shown in the beautiful book of Geering over the trade and industry of the city of Basel (Geering 1886), whose nineteenth chapter concerns the "Locarners and Huguenots". Cf. Wartmann (1870, 1:87 ff.). Peter Bion — the founder of the cotton industry of St Gallen — was a typical representative of the entrepreneurial and successful "foreigners".

That *Russia's* economic development was in essence the work of foreigners is well-known.

***

Chapter 62: The Jews

If I dedicate a special chapter to the Jews in this genetic portrayal of capitalist entrepreneurship, it happens thus because the role which they play in the history of modern capitalism is in fact a unique one — both their activity as capitalist entrepreneurs as well as the grounds for their prominent significance for the course of economic events exhibit a special case so much that no economic history which makes any claim to completeness can ignore them.

Now I believe I have given proof in my book on the Jews[637] that the particular significance of the Jews for modern history is to be sought in the advancement of those features of capitalist development which I have called the commercialisation of economic life. Their generalisation describes now, however, the transition to the age of high capitalism. The special and decisive significance of the Jews must thus be found in *that the accelerated transfer of early capitalist economic forms to high capitalist economic forms is to be attributed to their influence.*

This activity of the Jews will not yet be addressed here where we are only following the forming of the early capitalist economy.

The assumption now, however, that the Jews would have had no share at all in this first formation of capitalism would be erroneous. Rather we find them also in the early period of the modern economy very active as entrepreneurs, as I have likewise portrayed in detail in my above-mentioned book. And even in this period already specific forms of economic activity peculiar to the Jews are recorded in which as it were the germs of their later world historical mission are situated.

These are the following.

I. The Most Important Achievements of the Jews as Entrepreneurs in the Period of Early Capitalism

1. The Stimulation of the International Trade in Goods

The share which the Jews took in the reorganisation of trade as it took place after the alteration of the economic sphere was significant[638]. Significant firstly through the clearly purely *quantitatively prominent participation* in the effected sale of goods.

Thus the extent of the trade of the Jews, already before their acceptance, thus ran in the first half of the 17th century to a twelfth of the entire *English* trade[639]. Unfortunately we do not learn what source this figure is taken from. But that it is not all to far from the reality is proven by information which we find in a memorandum of the London merchants. It concerns whether the Jews should pay the foreign tolls on imported goods or not. The writer suggests that if it were rescinded the crown would suffer a loss annually of at least £10,000[640].

We are conspicuously well informed about the participation of Jews at the *Leipzig Messe* [market fair] which was indeed for a long time the centre of German trade and which forms a good gauge for its intensive and extensive development, but which also played an important role for a few of the bordering lands, particularly Poland and Bohemia. We find now here at the Leipzig Messe from the end of the 17th century Jews to a growing extent as market traders, and the processors of the statistical material agree completely that it was the Jews who established the splendour of the Leipzig Messe. When we survey the entire period of 1767–1839, it shows that the Messes were visited annually on average by 3,185 Jewish market traders, as opposed to 13,005 Christians — the number amounts accordingly to 24.49% or almost a quarter of the Christian merchants. In specific years, like e.g. between 1810 and 1820, the ratio of Jews to Christians climbed to 33⅓%: 4,896 Jews, 14,366 Christians[641].

During the 16th and 17th centuries and up well into the 18th century the *Levant trade* and the trade with and across *Spain-Portugal* still formed by far the most important branch of world trade. See Part 6 of the next volume. The Jews, however, played the leading role on these trade routes. Already

594

from Spain they had obtained control of the greatest part of the Levant trade; already at the time they had offices everywhere in the Levantine seaports. With the expulsion from the Iberian Peninsula a large part of the expelled Jews went themselves into the Orient; another part moved northwards and consequently the Orient trade slid quite imperceptibly over to the Northern peoples. They likewise led the newly developed colonial trade, to the extent it passed through Spain and Portugal, to the north and thereby made Antwerp at first into a site of world trade.

Later Holland became through the connecting of these relationships a power in world trade. The network of world trade became larger and more closely meshed precisely too the extent the Jews moved their offices to more distant and to closer to one another places[642]. Especially when the West of the earth was drawn into world trade.

We read an interesting report of the magistrate of *Antwerp* to the Bishop of Utrecht from 30 September 1546 in Uitterdijk (1904, LXIV f.). Within it is quite openly expressed that the Marranos* were the founders of the great overseas trade particularly in colonial goods, and that the commercial flourishing of the Netherlands was owing to them: "on veoit par expérience que la pluspairt des navires qu'arrivèrent en Zélande et la dicte ville d'Anvers du costel de Wetst, est de Portugal et des Isles d'Algarbe et le conduysent et le font venir ichy les dicts nouveaulx Chrestiens" [we see by experience that most of the ships that arrived in Zeeland and the said city of Antwerp from the west coast[?], are from Portugal and the islands of the Algarve and it is the said new Christians who conduct it and bring it here] (Uitterdijk 1904, LXV). What turnovers it concerned, we see from the following figures. Diego Mendes had in stock in pepper and other spices:

for his brother.............................for 60,000 ducats
for Georg Lopez...........................for 50,000 ducats
for Diego Rodriguez Pinto.........for 48,000 ducats

(Uitterdijk 1904, LXIII)

By the *nature of their trade* almost more than by its extent they obtained a large influence over the entire structure of economic life, and they had a partly revolutionary effect on the old forms of life.

Then we first encounter the significant fact that the Jews as good as monopolised the trade in important *luxury goods*

---

* [Tr.: Marranos were Jews who stayed in Spain during the Spanish Inquisition and practised Judaism in secret.]

for a long time. And during the aristocratic 17th and 18th centuries this trade meant the most. The luxury objects which the Jews above all had at their disposal were jewellery, precious stones, pearls, silk and silk goods — jewellery of gold and silver because they had dominated the precious metals market since time immemorial; precious stones and pearls because they had been the first to possess the source locations (particularly Brazil); silk and silk goods because of their ancient connections to the eastern trade regions.

Trade in jewels and pearls: in *Hamburg*: Griesheim (1759, 119). *Holland* (founders of diamond cutting!): Slijper (1906, 231); Denekamp (1895; cited in Goldstein 1907); in *Italy*: Kaufmann (1901).

Trade in silk and silk goods: The Jews fostered the silk trade (and the production of silk) for thousands of years. They brought the silk industry from Greece to Sicily and later to Spain and France. Some information in Graetz (1853, 5:244). In the 16th century we find them as masters of the silk trade in Italy: Kaufmann (1901); and in the 18th century in *France*, the centre of the silk industry as well as of the trade in silk and silk goods. In the year 1760 the board of the Lyon silk guild called the Jewish nation "Maitresse du commerce de toutes les provinces" [mistress of trade in all the provinces] (for silk and silk goods). See Godart (1899, 224). In 1755 there were 14 Jewish silk goods dealers in Paris, in 1759 22. See Kahn (1892, 63). In *Berlin* they dominated this branch of trade together with the French emigrants almost exclusively, as the following figures prove. In the half-year from 1st August 1753 to January 1754 in Berlin:

	in foreign silk goods brought in	taken from Berlin and Potsdam factories
Christian merchants	8,225 talers	2,522 talers
Jewish merchants	22,135 talers	22,473 talers

From the Report of the General Directorate in Berlin 11th March 1754 (Schmoller and Hintze 1892, 1:334 f. § 343; cf. 1:344 f. § 360).

On the other hand we find the Jews occupied everywhere with a predominant influence in trade where it concerns the distribution of *mass products*. A few of the large staples of the modern era, like grains, wool, flax, later spirits, tobacco, and particularly sugar were primarily brought to market by them.

The trade in new *articles revolutionising* old ways of behaviour then above all had a strongly provocative and overturning effect on the course of economic life, however, and was a trade in which again the Jews manifestly had an especially strong share. I am thinking of the trade in cotton[643], foreign cotton goods (calico)[644], indigo[645], etc. The preference for such articles, which was felt in the attitudes of the time to be a troublemaker for the domestic "nourishment", probably obtained for the trade of the Jews occasionally the reproach of "unpatriotic trade", of "commerce of Jews which employs few German hands usefully and for the most part rests on internal consumption"[646].

What otherwise characterised the "commerce of Jews" and made it exemplary for all trade which was directed thereby onto new paths was the *multifarious nature and extensiveness of the traded goods*. When the merchants of Montpellier complained about the competition which Jewish traders gave them, the intendant answer to them (1740) was: if they, the Christians, had just as well-stocked stores as the Jews, the customers would then like just as much to come to them as to the Jewish competition[647]. And Richard Markgraf draws up for us in his closing words the following description of the activity of the Jews at the Leipzig fair[648]: "Secondly, they [the Jewish traders] had an improving effect on the fair business through the multifarious nature of their purchases, to the extent they thereby shaped the fair trade in more and more varied ways and stimulated industry, especially the domestic industry, to ever greater variety in its production. At many fairs the Jews were even decisive on account of their various and comprehensive purchases."

Wherein I, however, above all see the significance which the "Jewish commerce" obtained during the early capitalist epoch for most economies in the circumstance that the Jews dominated almost exclusively precisely those areas of trade from which *large quantities of hard money* were to be obtained — thus the newly accessible silver and gold lands (Central and South America), be it in direct commerce, or be it indirectly through Spain and Portugal. Often enough we then hear it also reported that the Jews were bringing hard money into the land[649]. But founding of the modern economy meant in large part the drawing in of precious metals, and in that nobody was as highly involved as the Jewish merchants.

2. *The Share in the Colonisation of America*[650]

It is only natural that the Jews were deeply involved in all colonial foundings (since to them the New World, even if it also only refashioned the old, held the prospect of ever more personal fulfillment than the sullen old Europe, especially since here the last Dorado had also proven itself to be an inhospitable land). That applied just as much for the East as for the West and the South of the earth.

By far the most important area of colonisation of the Jews, however, was *Central and South America*, in particular the so-called "sugar colonies".

The first merchants in the newly discovered America were Jews. The first industrial establishments in the American colonies came from Jews. Already in 1492 Portuguese Jews settled in St Thomas and began there the plantation economy on a grand scale — they erected numerous sugar factories and soon employed 3,000 negro slaves. The influx of Jews to South America straight after the discovery was so large that in the year 1511 Queen Johanna considered it necessary to take action against it. But apparently this decree remained without effect, for the Jews over there increased more and more. By the law of 21st May 1577 then finally the ban on lawful emigration to the Spanish colonies was formally repealed.

In order to be able to evaluate entirely the lively effectiveness which the Jews displayed as founders of the colonial trade and colonial industry in the sphere of the South American region, you do well to follow the fate of a few colonies in detail.

The history of the Jews in the American colonies and with it the history of those colonies themselves splits into two large sections which were formed by the banishment of the Jews from Brazil (1654).

How the Jews founded the sugar industry in St Thomas straight after the discovery in the year 1492 has already been mentioned. Around 1550 we find this industry already in full flower on the island — 60 plantations, provided with sugar mills and boiling pans, produced, as the tenth paid to the king proves, annually 150,000 arrobas of sugar (each about 12 kg) (C. Ritter 1840, 94; cited in Lippmann 1890, 249). From here or from *Madeira* (according to Kohler (1894, 94)), where they had likewise carried on the sugar industry for a long time, the Jews transplanted this branch of industry into the largest of the American colonies — to *Brazil* which with it entered into its first period of its flourishing — which was defined by the dominance of the sugar industry.

The human material for the new colonies was provided in the first period almost exclusively by Jews and criminals, of whom annually two shiploads came across from Portugal (Brunner 1906; cf. Kohut 1895). The Jews very soon became the reigning caste — "no small part of the wealthiest Brazilian merchantry consisted of 'new Christians'" (Handelmann 1860, 412). It was also one of their tribe who as the first governor-general brought the administration of the colony into order — in fact the new possession only really began to flourish when in the year 1549 Thomé de Souza, a man of preeminent qualities, was sent over (Netscher 1853, 1). About the rich Jewish family of Souza, see Kayserling (1867, 307), and Grunwald (Grunwald 1902, 123). But the colony first began to develop its full brilliance when it passed into the hands of the Dutch (1624) and the rich Dutch Jews then began to stream across. In 1624 numerous American Jews united and founded in Brazil a colony in which 600 respected Jews from Holland settled (Kohler 1894, 94). Still in this first half of the 17th century all of the large sugar plantations were in the hands of Jews (Brunner 1906), of whose comprehensive efficiency and of whose wealth we are informed by travellers. Thus Nieuhoff, who travelled about Brazil from 1640 to 1649, commented as follows: "Among the Free-Inhabitants of *Brazil* that were not in the [Dutch West India] Companys Service, the Jews were the most considerable in number, who had transplanted themselves thither from Holland. They had a vast Traffick beyond all the rest, they purchased Sugar-Mills, and built stately houses in the Receif. They were all Traders, which would have been of great Consequence to the Dutch Brazil, had they kept themselves within the due Bounds of Traffick" (Nieuhoff et al. 1704, 2:146). And in Pyrard's travel report we read: "The profits they make after being nine or ten years in those lands are marvellous, for they all come back rich" (Kohler 1894, 95). Cf. also Netscher (1853, 103).

This domination of the Jewish element in the plantation business survived the episode of the Dutch reign over Brazil and extended up into the 18th century — despite the "expulsion" of the Jews in the year 1654. (An actual expulsion did not take place. The Jews were even granted amnesty in the peace treaty of 1654; but then the remark was added: "Jews and other non-Catholics shall be treated as in Portugal". That sufficed indeed! The peace treaty is printed verbatim in Aitzema*, cited in Netscher (1853, 163).) In any case, we learn even from the first half of the 18th century (Handelmann 1860, 412–13): at one time "when several of the most respected merchants of Rio de Janeiro fell into the hands of the Holy Office [the Inquisition!], the business on so many plantations faltered so that the production and trade of the province [i.e. Bahia] could not recover from this blow for a long period". By an edict of 2nd

---

*   [Tr.: I have been unable to expand on this reference. Presumably in one of the 14 volumes of Aitzema (1655).]

March 1768 then all registers over the new Christians were delivered for destruction; by the law of 25th March 1773 "the new Christians" were put entirely on the same level in civil affairs as the old Christians. Thus again apparently numerous crypto-Jews also preserved themselves in a preeminent position in Brazil after the seizure of the land *by the Portuguese* in the year 1654 and then gave the land in its sweet flourishing also the flourishing of gemstones since they submitted themselves very soon to the trade in gemstones as well.

But for that reason the year 1654 remained of epochal significance in Jewish-American history. For a very large part of the Brazilian Jews turned at the time to other regions of America and thereby transferred the economic focus there.

Above all now, however, it was a few important parts of the West Indies archipelago and the adjacent coast which first really came into bloom from the 17th century with the filling with the Jewish presence. Thus *Barbados* which was populated almost only by Jews. It had been taken possession of by the English in 1627; in 1641 sugar cane was introduced; in 1648 the export of sugar began. The sugar industry could not survive, however, since the sugar because of its bad quality did not cover the costs of transport to England. The "Dutch" driven out of Brazil were the first to introduce regular production and taught the inhabitants how to prepare dry and keepable sugar whose export soon increased in quick measure. In 1661 Charles II could already appoint as barons 13 owners who drew an income of £10,000 from Barbados, and around 1676 the island was already capable of annually loading 400 ships each with 180 tons of raw sugar (Hotten 1874, 449; Ligon 1673; cited in Lippmann 1890, 301 ff.; Reed 1866, 7; Moseley 1800; 1799; McCulloch 1880, 2:1087). For comparison there are also the general works of colonial history, above all Lucas (1905, 2:121 f., 2:274, 2:277).

In 1664 Thomas Modyford introduced sugar production from Barbados to *Jamaica*, which rapidly arrived at riches as a result. In 1656 the English had snatched it from the Spanish once and for all. Whilst there were at the time only three smaller boiling plants on Jamaica, in 1670 there were already 75 mills in operation which were producing some 100 tons of sugar and in the year 1700 sugar was the main article of Jamaica and the source of its wealth. How strongly the Jews participated in this development we can conclude from the fact that already in 1671 the proposal of exclusion was placed with the government by the Christian merchants, but it only had the effect that the settlement of Jews was promoted still more by the government. The governor reproached the petition with the words: "he was of opinion that His Majesty could not have more profitable subjects than the Jews and the Hollanders; they had great stocks and correspondance". From a letter of the governor on 17th December 1671 to the secretary of state Lord Arlington (Kayserling 1900, 710). Thus it happened that the Jews were not expelled from Jamaica, rather "they became the first traders and merchants of the English colony" (Lawrence-Archer 1875, 4; cited in Kohler 1894, 98). In the 18th century they bore all the taxes and had industry and trade for the most part in their hands (Kayserling 1900; Hyamson

1907, chap. XXVI). There is much evidence from contemporary sources in Kohler (1902, 59 ff.; 1894, 98).

Of the remaining English colonies, they especially favoured *Suriname*. Here Jews had sat since 1644 who were sometimes endowed with privileges, "whereas we have found that the Hebrew nation [...] have [...] proved themselves useful and beneficial to the colony". This favoured position of course persisted when Suriname passed over from England to Holland (1667). At the end of the 17th century the numerical ratio was like 1 to 3. In 1730 they possessed 115 of the 344 plantations in Suriname on which mostly sugar was farmed. The most important source for the history of the Jews in Suriname is De Leon et al. (1788). Koenen, who in his work on the Jews in the Netherlands (1843, 313 f.) shared a few things from it, called it "de hoofdbron [...] voor de geschiedenes der Joden in die gewesten" [the main source [...] for the history of the Jews in those regions]. Unfortunately I have not been able to see the original myself. The more recent literature has brought much new material to light: Gottheil (1901) contains excerpts from the cadastral maps; Roos (1905); Hilfman (1907). Over the relations between Suriname and Guiana, see S. Oppenheimer (1907). Cf. also Hyamson (1907, chap. XXVI) and Lucas (1905).

The same picture as the English and Dutch colonies is provided by the more important French ones — Martinique, Guadeloupe, and San Domingo. Here too the sugar industry was the source of "wealth" and here too the Jews were the rulers of this industry and the sugar traders.

In *Martinique* the first large plantation and boilers were instituted by Benjamin Dacosta in 1655, who had fled there from Brazil with 900 fellow believers and 1,100 slaves.

In *San Domingo* the sugar industry had already been begun in 1587, but the "Dutch" refugees from Brazil were first to bring it into full bloom.

Over Jews in *Martinique*, *Guadeloupe*, and *San Domingo*, see Lippmann (1890, 301 ff.), where sources and earlier literature is indicated; Cahen (1881; 1882); and Handelmann (1856).

You must now always keep in mind that in those critical centuries when the American colonial economy was founded, sugar production (apart from of course the silver production and the extraction of gold and precious stones in Brazil) formed the backbone of the entire colonial economy and with it indirectly that of the home economy, as I will attempt to show statistically in Part 6 of the following volume.

3. War Supplies

During the centuries in which the modern state arose, Jewish traders played a quite prominent role as suppliers of the army's demand so that you can almost say this branch of business was first properly developed by them, as it was on the other hand it which raised up very many Jews.

We encounter them at first in *England* during the 17th and 18th centuries in that capacity. During the Commonwealth the by far most significant supplier was Antonio Fernandez Carvajal, "the great Jew", who immigrated to London between 1630 and 1635 and soon rose up to be one of the leading merchants of the land. In the year 1649 he belonged to the five London merchants to whom the privy council conferred the supply of grain for the army[651]. He shall have brought £100,000 of silver to England annually. In the following period, namely in the wars of William III, Sir Solomon Medina, "the Jew Medina", appeared above all as "the great contractor" who was thereupon raised to the nobility — he was the first (unbaptised) noble Jew in England[652].

And likewise it was Jews who provided the armies with the necessities on the enemy side in the War of the Spanish Succession — "And *France* every time made use of their help to mount its cavalry in times of war"[653]. In 1716 the Jews of Strasbourg referred to the services which they had provided the army of Louis XIV through reports and provisions[654]. Jacob Worms was named the head war supplier of Louis XIV[655]. In the 18th century they then stood out in this capacity in France more and more. In the year 1727 the Jews of Metz had inside six weeks 2,000 horses brought into the city for consumption and more than 5,000 as remounts[656]. The marshal Moritz of Saxony, the victor at Fontenoy, stated that his armies had never been provisioned better than when he had turned to the Jews[657]. A prominent personality as supplier at the time of the last two Louis was Cerf Beer, of whom it was said in his patent of naturalisation: "que la dernière guerre ainsi que la disette, qui s'est fait sentir en Alsace pendant les années 1770 et 1771 lui ont donné l'occasion de donner des preuves de zèle dont il est animé pour notre service et celui de l'Etat" [that the last war, as well as the famine which made itself felt in Alsace during the years 1770 and 1771, gave him the opportunity to give proof of the zeal with which he is animated for our service and that of the State][658]. A global house of the first rank were the Gradis of Bordeaux — Abraham Gradis established large stores in Quebec in order to supply the French troops fighting in America[659]. The Jews in France played a prominent role as suppliers during the Revolution, during the

Directorate, and also in the Napoleonic Wars[660]. Nice evidence for their outstanding significance is the placard which was put up in 1795 in the streets of Paris when the latter was threatened by a famine, and in which the Jews were asked to show themselves grateful for the rights conferred on them by the Revolution by having grains brought into the city. "Eux seuls" [They alone], the author of the placard suggested, "peuvent mener cette entreprise à bonne fin, vu leurs nombreuses relations, dont ils doivent faire profiter leurs concitoyens" [can bring this enterprise to a successful conclusion, given their many connections which they must share with their fellow citizens][661].

A similar picture to how in the year 1720 the court Jew Jonas Meyer kept Dresden from starvation by the bringing in of large quantities of grain (the chronicler speaks of 40,000 bushels)[662].

Even in *Germany* we find the Jews early on and often exclusively in the positions of army suppliers. In the 16th century there was Isaak Meyer to whom Cardinal Albert of Brandenburg on his reception in Halberstadt in 1537 with respect to the threatening times placed the stipulation "of providing our foundation with good artillery and armour"; and Josel of Rosheim who in 1548 received an imperial letter of safe conduct because he had provided the king in France with money and provisions for the soldiers. In the 17th century (1633) the Bohemian Jew Lazarus testified that he "fetched or had fetched at his own cost news and advice on which the imperial armada placed much, and constantly endeavoured to supply all sorts of clothing and needed munitions to the imperial armada"[663]. In the year 1546 we encounter Bohemian Jews who delivered blankets and cloaks to the army[664]. The Great Elector made use of Leimann Gompertz and Salomon Elias "in his military operations with great effect, since they had to do with many supplies of artillery, arms, powder, mounting pieces, etc. for the needs of the armies"[665]. Samuel Julius, imperial supplier of horses (remounts) under the elector Frederick August of Saxony; the Model family, court and war suppliers in the Principality of Ansbach (17th and 18th centuries)[666]. "Hence all the Commissarii are Jews, and all the Jews are Commissarii", said Moscherosch apodictically in the visions of Philander von Sittenwald[667].

The first rich Jews who were permitted under Emperor Leopold to reside again in *Vienna* after the expulsion — the Oppenheimers, Wertheimers, Mayer Herschel, etc. — were also all army suppliers[668]. We possess for all the Austrian lands numerous sources for the activity of the army suppliers which was also continued into the 18th century[669].

Finally mention was yet made of Jewish suppliers who provisioned the *American* troops during the revolutionary war (just as likewise later in the Civil War)[670].

Now I have only listed here the achievements *peculiar to* the Jews as *entrepreneurs* of the epoch of early capitalism — hence I have *not* mentioned their prominence as *financiers*, because here no entrepreneurial activity was carried out, nor have I reported on their share in the erection of early capitalist *industry*, because nothing in that appears peculiar to the Jews. For rounding out the picture of the share of the Jews in the origin of capitalism this side of their activity may at any rate be taken into consideration.

II. The Aptitude of the Jews for Capitalism

The special status of the Jews in the history of European capitalism is founded both on the particular disposition of the Jewish people and on the particular situation in which the Jews found themselves during the centuries in which the capitalist economy was founded.

You might also frame the question, the discussion of which the greatest part of my book on the Jews is dedicated, as whether the spiritual structure in which we find the Jewish people at the end of the Middle Ages rests on an ancient disposition or was first formed by the more than thousand year old history of suffering in the exile — no doubt can reign amidst objective judges that *in the historical moment* in which capitalism began to unfold, the Jews were already equipped with an *abundance of characteristics* which made them suited to intervene decisively in the course of economic development. In particular it was trading and arithmetical abilities as well as the bourgeois virtues which distinguished their milieu from many others. They already thus possessed to a considerable extent in advance the characteristics which belong to the good capitalist entrepreneur and which in other peoples first had to be cultivated in the course of economic development.

To that was now added the circumstance that *the external life conditions* of the Jews were likewise of the sort which could not be thought more advantageous for the development of the capitalist entrepreneur. What we learn to recognise as such favourable conditions with heretics and foreigners recurs in the fate of the Jews which furthermore added still more beneficial moments to those.

What then distinguished the peculiar position in which the Jews of Western Europe and America found themselves from about the end of the 15th century?

The governor of Jamaica fittingly expressed it quite generally in a letter to the Secretary of State from 17th December 1671, when he wrote[671]: "he was of opinion that His Majesty could not have more profitable subjects than the Jews: *they had great stocks and correspondence*". In fact with both these special features a substantial part of the advantage is described which the Jews had over others. Only you must add for completeness their peculiar position within the national community in which they operated. It can be described as foreignness and as half-citizenship. I want thus to emphasise four circumstances which made (and make) the Jews especially suited to achieve such significance:

1. their spatial distribution;
2. their foreignness;
3. their half-citizenship;
4. their wealth; to which is added:
5. their money-lending.

1. Spatial Distribution

Of significance for the behaviour of the Jews was of course first and above all *their dispersion across all lands* of the inhabited earth, as indeed had been the case since the first exile, but as had now taken place again since their expulsion from Spain and Portugal and since their streaming back from Poland. We follow them in their wandering during the past centuries and find them settling afresh in Germany and in

France, in Italy and in England, in the Orient and in America, in Holland and in Austria, in South Africa and in East Asia.

The natural consequence of this repeated movement within culturally partly already highly developed lands was that parts of one and the same family settled in the most varied centres of economic life and formed great international houses with numerous affiliates. Just to name a few: the Lopez family had its seat in Bordeaux and branches in Spain, England, Antwerp, and Toulouse; the Mendès family, a banking house, likewise resided in Bordeaux and had branches in Portugal, France, and Flanders; the Gradis were a branch of the Mendès again with numerous branch businesses; we find the Carceres resident in Hamburg, in England, in Austria, the West Indies, Barbados, and Suriname; other well-known families with a world-spanning net of affiliates are the Costas (Acosta, D'Acosta), the Coneglianos, the Alhadibs, the Sassoons, the Pereires, and the Rothschilds. But there is no sense in lengthening the list — the Jewish business houses which were represented in at least two trading cities of the earth numbered in the hundreds and thousands. There was barely one of significance which had not had a foot in at least two different lands[672].

And what great significance this dispersal must have had for the advancement of the Jews need also hardly be established in detail — it is quite apparent. What Christian houses had to first obtain with effort, what they, however, only achieved in the rarest of cases in equally complete manner, that the Jews picked up along the way from the beginning of their activity — the fulcrum for all international trading and credit operations — the "great correspondence", this basic condition of successful international business activity, especially, as I will later demonstrate in detail, in the age of early capitalism.

I recall that which I have said about the participation of the Jews in the Spanish-Portuguese trade, in the Levant trade, and in the development of America: of quite special importance was the circumstance that a large part of them branched out directly from Spain — through that they directed the current of colonial trade and above all the current of silver into the beds of the newly rising powers: Holland, England, France, and Germany.

It was significant that they liked to turn directly to those lands which were on the point of experiencing a great economic boom, and with that directly bestowed on these lands the advantages of their international connections. It is well-known that the fugitive Jews diverted with forethought the current of trade from the lands which had expelled them, in order to supply those which had hospitably taken them in.

Thus they made Antwerp for a period the centre of world trade because they maintained the connections to Spain and Portugal especially briskly. A part of the trading significance of Antwerp was transferred then to London, to Amsterdam, to Hamburg, to Frankfurt — places to which they especially liked to move. But other cities also drew benefit from the extended trade connections of the immigrant Sephardic Jews. I am thinking of the especially instructive example of the Spanish Jew, Marco Perez, who, originally one of the first financiers of William of Orange, emigrated from Antwerp to Basel, where he set the entire merchant class in uproar by his new practices, whilst it must be acknowledged that he "traded to the benefit of the peoples with all lands and zones"[673].

This peculiar significance of Jewish internationalism for the development of modern capitalism is quite nicely illustrated by a picture which a spirited observer made use of in a study over the Jews two hundred years ago and which has fully preserved its freshness still today. In a correspondence of the Spectator of 27th September 1712 it states: "They are [...] so disseminated through all the trading Parts of the World, that they are become the Instruments by which the most distant Nations converse with one another and by which mankind are knit together in a general Correspondance: they are like the Pegs and Nails in a great Building, which, though they are but little valued in themselves, are absolutely necessary to keep the whole Frame together."

The "spatial distribution of the Jews" now is, however, not only significant in that it brings about the international dispersal of the Jews — it serves to explain many phenomena as well in so far as they apply to the *distribution across the interior of the lands*. If we, for example, have often encountered the Jews as suppliers of war material and provisions for the armies — they have also been thus since ancient times: with the siege of Naples by Belisarius, the Jews there declared they wanted to supply the city with provisions[674] — thus it has its basis certainly for the good part in the fact that they could gather together more easily than the Christians a large quantity of goods thanks to the connections which they maintained from city to city. "The Jewish entrepreneur must not shrink from all these difficulties. He may just electrify the Jews in the right place and right away he has as many helpers and helpers' helpers as he will ever need"[675]. For in fact the Jew of earlier times acted "never as an isolated individual, but rather as a member of the most spread out trading company in the world"[676]. "Ce sont des particules de vif argent qui courent, qui s'égarent et qui à la moindre pente se réunissent en un bloc principal" [They are particles of mercury which run, go astray, and at the slightest slope come together in a principal block], as it was said in a petition of the Parisian merchants from the second half of the 18th century[677].

2. Foreignness

The Jews were foreign during the last centuries in most lands firstly in the purely external sense of *the newly immigrated*. Right in the places where they displayed their most effective activity, they were not old-established, indeed there they had mostly not even arrived from the nearer surroundings, but rather from afar, from lands with different customs and habits, in part even different climates. They came to Holland, France, and England from Spain and Portugal, and then from Germany; to Hamburg and Frankfurt from the other German cities and then to all of Germany from the Russian-Polish east.

But Israel had been foreign amidst the peoples all through the centuries in yet another, you could say a psychological-social sense, in the sense of an *inward oppositionality* to the surrounding population, in the sense of an almost caste-like insularity towards the host peoples. They, the Jews, felt themselves to be something special and were felt by the host peoples to be such in turn. And as a result all the behaviours and attitudes were developed by the Jews to a state which by necessity had to arise in the commerce with "foreigners" especially in a time which still stood some distance from the concept of world citizenship.

The mere fact that you were involved with a "foreigner" has at all times which were not yet infiltrated by humanitarian valuations sufficed to relieve the conscience, and to loosen the bonds of moral duties. The commerce with foreigners has always been shaped in a "more ruthless" way. And the Jews were always involved, especially when they intervened in the great economic hustle and bustle, with "foreigners", with "non-comrades", because they were always to boot a small minority. When for a member of the host people every tenth or every hundredth act of commerce brought a connection to a "foreigner", then conversely with the Jews nine acts out of ten or ninety nine in a hundred resulted in commerce with foreigners — so that the "*morality of the foreign*", if I may use this expression without being misunderstood, was one that was practised again and again to which the entire business behaviour then had to adjust as it were. The commerce with foreigners was for Jews the "norm", whereas it remained the exception for the others.

Closely connected with their foreignness stood the peculiar and odd legal position in which they found themselves in all places. But that has as basis for its explanation its own significance and shall thus be treated in the following independent portrayal.

3. Half-Citizenship

It seems at first glance as if the bourgeois legal position of the Jews was especially of significance for their economic fate in that it imposed on them specific *limitations* in the choice of profession, particularly *in their gainful employment*. But I believe that the effect which the legal position exercised in this consideration has been overrated.

In *one* point only is the decisive effect of the old constitution of trade on the careers of the Jews proven — that is where economic life was influenced by the dominance of the corporate associations, or more correctly, where the economic processes played out in the framework of cooperative organisation. The Jews found no way into the guilds — the crucifix which was placed in every office of these associations, and about which all the members assembled, held them back. And therefore, *if* they wanted to practise a trade, they could only do so outside the circle which was kept occupied by the Christian cooperatives; regardless of whether an area of production or an area of trade was in question. And hence they were the born "interlopers", the moonlighters, the guild breakers, the "free traders", as we find them everywhere.

The fate of the Jews was apparently determined more decisively by those parts of the law which governed their relationship to the state, thus especially *their position in public life*. They demonstrate firstly in all states a conspicuous consensus, for they arrive in the final analysis all at excluding the Jews from participation in public life, thus barring them entry to the offices of state and local government, to the bar, to parliament, to the army, and to the universities. That applies also to the western states — France, Holland, England — and America up until the end of our epoch.

What effects this slight on the Jews must have had in public life can be seen from what I have said about the significance of hereticism for the development of the capitalist dispositions and abilities[678].

I will share here the fitting words of a contemporary of the 17th century, in which the prominent mercantile capabilities of the Jews were confirmed and described as the effect of that described under 2. and 3. He wrote[679]: "the Jews are held the most Mercuriall people in the World, by reason of their so often transmigrations, persecutions, and *Necessity*, which is the Mother of Wit".

4. Wealth

We can, without second thought for the conditions under which the Jews have fulfilled their economic mission during the last three or four centuries and whose peculiar form made their work itself into a peculiar one, work out the fact that, wherever and whenever they have played a role in economic life, they have had at their disposal a large monetary wealth.

A large number of the refugees who left the Pyrenean peninsula since the 16th century must have been immensely rich. We hear of an "exodo de capitaes", an emigration of capital which shall have been brought about by them. But we also know that on their expulsion they sold their numerous possessions and had themselves paid for them in bills of exchange for foreign places[680].

The richest of all probably turned to *Holland*. At least we learn here of the first settlers — Manuel Lopez Homen, Maria Nunez, Miguel Lopez, and others — that they possessed great wealth[681]. Whether then in the 17th century many rich Spanish Jews were still immigrating, or whether the old-established were arriving at ever greater wealth will be hard to establish as a whole. It also suffices to know that the Jews in Holland during the 17th and 18th century were famed for their wealth.

But even in other lands the Jews stood out for their wealth. The clever Savary confirms that for us with respect to the France of the 17th and the beginning of the 18th century in that he quite summarily shares a general judgement with the following content: "on dit qu'un marchand est *riche comme un Juif*, quand il a la réputation d'avoir amassé de grands biens" [a merchant is said to be as rich as a Jew, when he is reputed to have amassed great wealth][682].

And for *England* we even possess statistical data over the wealth of the rich Spanish Jews soon after their official approval. We learn that the half-year turnover of the rich Jewish business houses was already in the year 1663 swaying between £13,000 and £41,000[683].

In *Germany* the centres of Jewish life during the 17th and 18th centuries were Hamburg and Frankfurt am Main. For both cities we can precisely establish statistically the state of wealth of the Jews, and what we learn absolutely confirms our judgement[684].

When we ask now again what significance such prominent possession of money must have had for the economic fate of the Jews, this is obviously of a quite common sort as need not be explained in detail.

By comparison, a different circumstance which is likewise connected with the Jews' possession of money deserves to be illuminated somewhat more. I mean the extensive use which the Jews made of their money for *the purpose of lending*. This particular application namely (whose general diffusion cannot be doubted) obviously became one of the most important preparations for capitalism itself.

5. *Money-Lending*

If the Jews proved suited in every respect for advancing the development of capitalism, then they owe that quite certainly not in the least to their capacity as money-lenders (both large and small). *For the lending of money is one of the most important roots of capitalism.* Its basic idea is already contained in germ in money-lending; it received its most important features from money-lending.

In money-lending every quality is extinguished and the economic process appears to only be defined quantitatively.

In money-lending the contract-like nature of business became the substance — the negotiation over performance and consideration, the promising for the future, and the idea of delivery form its content.

In money-lending all that is sustenance-like vanishes.

In money-lending all corporeality (everything "technical") is eliminated — the economic action became of purely intellectual nature.

In money-lending the economic activity as such lost all sense — the occupation in money-lending stopped being a sensual activity of the body or the spirit. With that its value shifted from itself to its result. The result alone still has meaning.

In money-lending the possibility emerged for the first time quite distinctly of earning money by economic behaviour without your own sweat even; the possibility appears quite distinctly of having other people work for you without acts of violence even.

You see, in fact all these peculiar characteristics of money-lending are also peculiar characteristics of all capitalist economic organisation.

To that is now added that a quite considerable part of modern capitalism *historically* grew from money-lending (from the advance, from the loan). In fact everywhere we find putting-out as the archetype of the capitalist enterprise. But also where this grew from benefice relations. And finally also where they at first appeared in some form of shareholding.

For in its most fundamental construction the joint-stock company is nothing but a money-lending business with directly
productive content.

Thus to me once again a circumstance appears to lie in the
exercise of the money-lending business which enabled the
Jews objectively to create, to advance, and to spread the capitalist essence.

But all that will first come to life if we now follow in the
next volume how the edifices of the capitalist economy were
built on these foundations.

***

Bibliography

Adams, Brooks. 1895. *The Law of Civilisation and Decay: An Essay on History*. New York: The Macmillan Company.

———. 1907. *Die Gesetze der Zivilisation und des Verfalls*. Vienna & Leipzig: Akademischer Verlag.

Adler, Max. 1903. *Die Anfänge der merkantilistischen Gewerbepolitik in Österreich*. Wiener Staatswissenschaftliche Studien, 4.3. Vienna & Leipzig: Franz Deuticke.

Afanassiev, Georges. 1894. *Le Commerce des céréales en France au 18e siècle*. Translated by Paul Boyer. Paris: A. Picard et fils.

Agricola, Georgius. 1556. *De re metallica*. Basel: Hieronymus Froben & Nicolaus Episcopius.

———. 1912. *De Re Metallica*. Translated by Herbert Clark Hoover and Lou Henry Hoover. London: The Mining Magazine.

Ahrens, Felix Benjamin, C. Arndt, H. Brüggemann, H.W. Dahlen, G. Ebe, M. Gürtler, Hermann Hardicke, et al., eds. 1896. *Das Buch der Erfindungen, Gewerbe und Industrien; gesamtdarstellung aller gebiete der gewerblichen und industriellen Arbeit, sowie von Weltverkehr und Weltwirtschaft*. 9th ed. 10 vols. Leipzig: Otto Spamer.

Aitzema, Lieuwe van. 1655. *Saken van Staet en Oorlogh In, ende omtrent de Vereenigde Nederlanden: Verhael Vande Nederlandsche Vrede-Handeling*. Veely.

Alberi, Eugene, ed. 1839. *Relazioni degli ambasciatori veneti al Senato*. Società Editrice Fiorenta. 15 vols. Florence.

Albinus, Petrus. 1590. *Meißnische Land und Berg-Chronica, In welcher ein vollnstendige description des Landes, so zwischen der Elbe, Sala vnd Südödischen Behmischen gebirgen gelegen, So wol der dorinnen begriffenen auch anderer Bergwercken, sampt zugehörigen Metall un[d] Metallar beschreibungen*. Dresden: Gimelis Bergen.

Alexi, S. 1890. "Die Münzmeister der Calimala- und Wechslerzunft in Florenz." *Zeitschrift für Numismatik* 17: 258–69.

Alidosi Pasquali, Giovanni Nicolò. 1621. *Instruttione delle cose notabili della città di Bologna e altre particolari*. Bologna: Nicolo Tebaldini.

Alighieri, Dante. 1867. *The Divine Comedy*. Translated by Henry Wadsworth Longfellow. 3 vols. Boston: Ticknor & Fields.

———. 1876. *Göttliche Komödie*. Translated by Adolf Friedrich Karl Streckfuß. Leipzig: Philipp Reclam.

Altmann, Samuel Paul. 1909. "Quantitätstheorie." In *Handwörterbuch der Staatswissenschaften*, edited by Johann Conrad, Ludwig Elster, Wilhelm Lexis, and Edgar Loening, 3rd ed., 6:1257–65. Jena: G. Fischer.

Álvarez Osorio y Redín, Miguel. 1687. "Memoriales a Carlos II." Biblioteca Nacional de España.

Amiet, Jacob J. 1877. "Die französischen und lombardischen Geldwucherer des Mittelalters, namentlich in der Schweiz." *Jahrbuch für Schweizerische Geschichte* 2: 141–328.

Anderson, Adam. 1787. *An Historical and Chronological Deduction of the Origin of Commerce: From the Earliest Accounts*. Edited by William Combe. 2nd ed. 4 vols. London: J. Robson, T. Payne & Sons, et al.

Anderson, Christopher. 1845. *The Annals of the English Bible*. 2 vols. London: William Pickering.

Anderson, James S. M. 1856. *The History of the Church of England in the Colonies and Foreign Dependencies of the British Empire*. 2nd ed. 3 vols. London: F. & J. Rivington.

André, Jean-François. 1887. *Histoire de la papauté à Avignon*. 2nd ed. Avignon: Seguin.

Andree, Karl. 1867. *Geographie des Welthandels*. 3 vols. Stuttgart: J. Engelhorn.

Anonymous. 1675. *The Character of a Town-Gallant: Exposing the Extravagant Fopperies of Some Vain Self-Conceited Pretenders to Gentility and Good Breeding*. London: W.L.

———. 1716. *An Account of the Work-Houses in Great Britain, in the Year 1732*. 3rd ed. London.

———. 1786. "Kurze Bemerkungen über die polnischen und schlesischen Eisenhütten-Werke." *Schlesische Provinzialblätter* 3: 203–11.

———. 1787. "Es war sonst eben so." *Journal des Luxus und der Moden* 2 (5): 169–71.

———. 1788. "Noch einige ökonomische Bemerkungen über Oberschlesien." *Schlesische Provinzialblätter* 7: 228–39.

———. 1796. "Schotten. Schottenkram. Schottenkramgerechtigkeit." *Schlesische Provinzialblätter* 24: 459–62.

———. 1800. "Über die Betteley in Niederschlesien." *Schlesische Provinzialblätter* 31–32: 396-408;40-50.

———. 1802. "Thüringens Wollen-Manufakturen." *Journal für Fabrik, Manufaktur, Handlung und Mode* XXIII (4): 265–91.

———. 1803. "Briefe über einige wichtige Gegenstände." *Schlesische Provinzialblätter* 38: 197-221;389-396;485-525.

Archenholtz, Johann Wilhelm von. 1787. *England und Italien*. 3 vols. Leipzig: Dyk.

Archivio di Stato di Firenze. 1884. *Le carte strozziane del R. Archivio di stato in Firenze: inventario*. 2 vols. Firenze: Tipografia galileiana.

Arendt, Friedrich Wilhelm. 1808. *Verzeichniß der Vorsteher und sämmt-licher Mitglieder der teutsch und französisch vereinigten Kaufmannschaft der Tuch- und Seidenhandlung hiesiger Residenzien, von den Ältesten angefertigt.* Berlin: Wilhelm Dieterici.

Argelati, Filippo. 1750. *De monetis Italiae variorum illustrium virorum dissertationes.* 6 vols. Milan: Regia Curia in Aedibus Palatinis.

Arias, Gino. 1905. *Il sistema della costituzione economica e sociale italiana nell'età dei comuni.* Rome: Casa editrice nazionale.

Arnold, Carl Franklin. 1900. *Die Ausrottung des Protestantismus in Salzburg unter Erzbischof Firmian und seinen Nachfolgern: ein Beitrag zur Kirchengeschichte des achtzehnten Jahrhunderts.* 2 vols. Schriften zur Reformationsgeschichte 67 & 69. Halle: Verein für Reformationsgeschichte,.

Arnold, Samuel Greene. 1859. *History of the State of Rhode Island & Providence Plantations.* 2 vols. New York: D. Appleton & Co.

Arnold, Wilhelm. 1854. *Verfassungsgeschichte der deutschen Freistädte im Anschluss an die Verfassungsgeschichte der Stadt Worms.* 2 vols. Gotha: F. A. Perthes.

———. 1861. *Zur Geschichte des Eigentums in den deutschen Städten: mit Urkunden.* Basel: Georg.

Aronius, Julius, Albert Dresdner, and Ludwig Lewinski. 1902. *Regesten zur Geschichte der Juden im fränkischen und deutschen Reiche bis zum Jahre 1273.* Berlin: L. Simion.

Ashley, William James. 1887. *The Early History of the English Woollen Industry.* Baltimore: American Economic Association.

Aubert, L. M. B. 1893. "Beiträge zur Geschichte der deutschen Grundbücher." *Zeitschrift der Savigny-Stiftung für Rechtsgeschichte. Germanistische Abteilung* 14 (1): 1–74.

Audouin, Xavier. 1811. *Histoire de l'administration de la guerre.* 4 vols. Paris: Didot.

Aupetit, Albert. 1901. *Essai sur la théorie générale de la monnaie.* Paris: Guillaumin et Cie.

Baasch, Ernst. 1894. "Hamburgs Seeschiffahrt und Waarenhandel vom Ende des 16. bis zur Mitte des 17. Jahrhunderts." *Zeitschrift für Hamburgische Geschichte* 9: 295–420.

———. 1900. "Hamburgs Handel und Schifffahrt am Ende des 18. Jahrhunderts." In *Hamburg um die Jahrhundertwende 1800,* 156–73. Hamburg: Neue Börsen-Halle.

Baird, Charles Washington. 1885. *History of the Huguenot Emigration to America.* 2 vols. New York: Dodd, Mead & Co.

Ballagh, James Curtis. 1895. *White Servitude in the Colony of Virginia. A Study of the Systems of Indentured Labor in the American Colonies*. Baltimore: John Hopkins University Press.

Bandeau, Nicholas, ed. 1783. *Encyclopédie méthodique. Commerce*. 3 vols. Panckoucke.

Barre, Président la. 1622. *Formulaire des Elus, avec un Traité des Monnoyes & des Métaux*. Rouen: J. Osmont.

Baskerville, Beatrice C., and A. Francis Steuart, eds. 1915. *Papers Relating to the Scots in Poland, 1576-1793*. Publications of the Scottish History Society 59. Edinburgh: Scottish History Society.

Basnage, Jacques, ed. 1725. *Thesaurus monumentorum ecclesiasticorum et historicum, sive Henrici Canisii lectiones antique*. 4 vols. Antwerp: Apud Rudolphum & Gerhardum Wetstenios.

Bassermann-Jordan, Ernst von. 1905. *Die Geschichte der Räderuhr: unter besonderer Berücksichtigung der Uhren des Bayerischen Nationalmuseums*. Frankfurt am Main: H. Keller.

Bassett, John Spencer. 1896. *Slavery and Servitude in the Colony of North Carolina*. Baltimore: John Hopkins University Press.

Baudrillart, Henri. 1880. *Histoire du luxe privé et public depuis l'antiquité jusqu'à nos jours*. 2nd ed. 4 vols. Paris: Hachette et cie.

Baumstark, Eduard. 1853. *Zur Geschichte der arbeitenden Klasse: eine Rede zur Feier des Allerhöchsten Geburtsfestes Dr. Majestät des Königs von Preussen Friedrich Wilhelm IV am 15. October 1853 an der Universität zu Greifswald gehalten*. Greifswald: F. W. Kunike.

Beaupré, Jean Nicolas. 1846. *Les gentilshommes verriers, ou Recherches sur l'industrie et les priviléges des verriers dans l'ancienne Lorraine, aux XVe, XVIe et XVIIe siècles*. 2nd ed. Nancy: Hinzelin et cie.

Becher, Johann Joachim. 1682. *Närrische Weißheit Und Weise Narrheit*. Frankfurt: Johann Peter Zubrod.

Becher, Johann Philipp. 1789. *Mineralogische Beschreibung der Oranien-Nassauischen Lande nebst einer Geschichte des Siegischen Hütten- und Hammerwesens*. Marburg: Neue akademische Buchhandlung.

Beck, Ludwig. 1884. *Die Geschichte des Eisens in technischer und kulturgeschichtlicher Beziehung*. 5 vols. Brunswick: F. Vieweg.

Beck, Theodor. 1900. *Beiträge zur Geschichte des Maschinenbaues*. 2nd ed. Berlin: J. Springer.

Becker, George Ferdinand. 1888. *Geology of the Quicksilver Deposits of the Pacific Slope*. U. S. Geological Survey Monograph 13. Washington, D.C.: U.S. Government Printing Office.

Beckmann, Johann. 1777. *Beyträge zur Oekonomie, Technologie, Polizey- und Cameralwissenschaft.* 12 vols. Göttingen: Vandenhoeck & Ruprecht.

———. 1780. *Beyträge zur Geschichte der Erfindungen.* 5 vols. Leipzig: Kummer.

Beer, Adolf. 1894. *Die Staatsschulden und die Ordnung des Staatshaushaltes unter Maria Theresia.* Vienna: Tempsky.

———. 1895. "Studien zur Geschichte der österreichischen Volkswirtschaft unter Maria Theresia: I. Die Österreichische Industriepolitik." *Archiv für österreichische Geschichte* 81: 1–134.

———. 1899. "Die Österreichische Handelspolitik unter Maria Theresia und Joseph II." *Archiv für österreichische Geschichte* 86: 1–204.

Beer, George Louis. 1907. *British Colonial Policy 1754-1765.* New York: Macmillan Company.

———. 1912. *The Old Colonial System, 1660-1754.* 2 vols. New York: Macmillan.

Bein, Louis. 1884. *Die Industrie des sächsischen Voigtlandes, wirthschaftsgeschichtliche Studie.* 2 vols. Leipzig: Duncker & Humblot.

Beloch, Julius. 1895. "Die Entwicklung der Grossstädte in Europa." In *Huitième Congrès International D'hygiène Et de Démographie Tenu À Budapest Du 1 Au 9 Septembre 1894, Comptes-rendus Et Mémoires,* edited by Zsigmond Gerlóczy. Vol. 7. Budapest: Pesti könyvnyomda-részvénytársaság.

Below, Georg von. 1889. *Entstehung der deutschen Stadtgemeinde.* Düsseldorf: L. Voss.

———, ed. 1895. *Landtagsakten von Jülich-Berg. 1400-1610.* 2 vols. Publikationen der Gesellschaft für Rheinische Geschichtskunde 11. Düsseldorf: L. Voss & Cie.

———. 1900. "Der Untergang der mittelalterlichen Stadtwirtschaft: (über den Begriff der Territorialwirtschaft)." *Jahrbücher für Nationalökonomie und Statistik,* 3, 21: 449–73, 593–631.

———. 1903. "Die Entstehung des modernen Kapitalismus." *Historische Zeitschrift* 91: 432–85.

———. 1905a. *Das ältere deutsche Städtewesen und Bürgertum.* Edited by Wilhelm Heyd. Monographien zur Weltgeschichte, VI. Bielefeld & Leipzig: Velhagen & Klasing.

———. 1905b. *Die Ursachen der Rezeption des römischen Rechts in Deutschland.* Munich & Berlin: R. Oldenbourg.

Bender, Johann Heinrich. 1841. *Das Lotterierecht.* 2nd ed. Giessen: Georg Friedrich Heyer.

Benfey, Theodor. 1859. *Pantschatantra: fünf Bücher indischer Fabeln, Märchen und Erzählungen.* Leipzig: F. A. Brockhaus.

Benoist, Élie. 1693. *Histoire De L'Edit De Nantes*. 5 vols. Delft: Beman.

Benoist, Elie. 1694. *The History of the Famous Edict of Nantes*. Translated by Edward Cooke. 2 vols. London: J. Dunton.

Bensen, Heinrich Wilhelm. 1847. *Die Proletarier. Eine historische Denks- chrift*. Stuttgart: Franckh.

Berg, Willem Ernst Johan. 1845. *De réfugiés in de Nederlanden, na de her- roeping van het Edict van Nantes*. 2 vols. Amsterdam: Johannes Müller.

Berger, Louis Konstanz. 1895. *Der alte Harkort: ein westfälisches Lebens- und Zeitbild*. 3rd ed. Leipzig: J. Baedeker.

Bergius, Johann Heinrich Ludwig. 1775. *Neues Policey- und Cameral- Magazin nach alphabetischer Ordnung*. 6 vols. Leipzig: M. G. Weidmann.

Bernard, Lucie. 1802. *Neue Reise durch England und Portugal*. Hamburg: August Campe.

Bertheau, Franz R. 1912. *Chronologie zur Geschichte der geistigen Bildung und des Unterrichtswesens in Hamburg von 831 bis 1912*. Hamburg: Lucas Gräfe.

Bertin, Ernest. 1879. *Les mariages dans l'ancienne société française*. Paris: Hachette.

Besnard, François-Yves. 1880. *Mémoires de François-Yves Besnard: souvenirs d'un nonagénaire*. 2 vols. Paris: H. Champion.

Besoldus, Christopher. 1740. *Orbis Novus Literatorum, Praeprimis Jur- isconsultorum, Detectus, Sive Continuatio Thesauri Practici Be- soldiani*. Regensburg: Lentz.

Besson, Jacques. 1578. *Theatrum instrumentorum et machinarum*. Lyon: B. Vicentium.

Beugnot, Auguste-Arthur. 1854. *Mémoire sur le régime des terres dans les principautés fondées en Syrie par les Francs à la suite des Crois- ades*. Paris: J.-B. Dumoulin.

Beyer, Heinrich, ed. 1860. *Urkundenbuch zur Geschichte der, jetzt die preussischen Regierungsbezirke Coblenz und Trier bildenden mittelrheinischen Territorien*. 3 vols. Coblenz: J. Hölscher.

Beyerle, Konrad. 1900. *Grundeigentumsverhältnisse und Bürgerrecht im mittelalterlichen Konstanz*. 2 vols. Heidelberg: C. Winter.

Bezold, Friedrich von, Eberhard Gothein, and Reinhold Carl Bernhard Al- exander Koser. 1908. *Staat und Gesellschaft der neueren Zeit (bis zur französischen Revolution)*. Die Kultur der Gegenwart, Part II, Section V.1. Berlin & Leipzig: B.G. Teubner.

Bianchi, Tommasino de. 1862. *Cronaca modenese, di Jacopino de' Bianchi*. Monumenti di storia patria delle provincie modenesi: Serie delle cronache 1. Parma: Pietro Fiaccadori.

Bidermann, Hermann Ignaz. 1870. *Über den Merkantilismus*. Innsbruck: Wagner.

Bigot de Sainte-Croix, Claude. 1788. *Mémoire sur les corporations*. Paris: Broch.

Birch, Thomas, ed. 1754. *Memoirs of the Reign of Queen Elizabeth, from the Year 1581 Till Her Death*. 2 vols. London: A. Millar.

Biringuccio, Vannoccio. 1540. *De la pirotechnia*. Venice.

———. 1942. *The Pirotechnia of Vannoccio Biringuccio, Translated from the Italian with an Introduction and Notes by Cyril Stanley Smith & Martha Teach Gnudi*. Translated by Cyril Stanley Smith and Martha Teach Gnudi. New York: The American Institute of Mining and Metallurgical Engineers.

Bishop, John Leander. 1868. *A History of American Manufactures from 1608 to 1860*. 2nd ed. 3 vols. Philadelphia: Edward Young.

Bloch, Maurice. 1899. "Les juifs et la prosperètè publique à travers l'histoire." *Revue des études juives* 38: 14–51.

Böckler, Georg Andreas. 1673. *Theatrum machinarum novum, Das ist: Neu vermehrter Schauplatz der Mechanischen Künsten*. Nuremberg: Paulus Fürsten.

Bodin, Jean. 1586. *De Republica libri sex*. Paris: Jacob Du-Puys.

Böhmer, Johann Friedrich, ed. 1836. *Codex diplomaticus Moeno-Francofurtanus. Urkundenbuch der Reichsstadt Frankfurt*. 2 vols. Frankfurt am Main: Franz Varrentrap.

Boileau, Étienne. 1879. *Les métiers et corporations de la ville de Paris : XIIIe siècle. Le livre des métiers d'Étienne Boileau*. Edited by René de Lespinasse and François Bonnardot. Paris: Imprimerie Nationale.

Boislisle, Arthur-André-Gabriel Michel, ed. 1874. *Correspondance des contrôleurs généraux des finances avec les intendants des Provinces*. 3 vols. Paris: Imprimerie Nationale.

Boissonnade, Prosper. 1899. *L'Industrie du papier en Charente et son histoire*. Bibliothèque du Pays poitevin 9. Ligugé: Bureaux du "Pays Poitevin."

———. 1900. *Essai sur l'organisation du travail au Poitou: Depuis le XIe siècle jusqu'à la Révolution*. 2 vols. Paris: H. Champion.

———. 1902. "Colbert, son système et les entreprises industrielles en Languedoc (1661-1683)." *Annales du Midi* 14 (53): 5–49.

Boiteau, Paul. 1889. *État de la France en 1789*. 2nd ed. Paris: Librairie Guillaumin.

Bokemeyer, Heinrich. 1888. *Die Molukken. Geschichte und quellen-mässige Darstellung der Eroberung und Verwaltung der ostindischen Gewürzinseln durch die Niederländer.* Leipzig: F. A. Brockhaus.

Bond, Edward A. 1840. "XI. Extracts from the Liberate Rolls, Relative to Loans Supplied by Italian Merchants to the Kings of England, in the 13th and 14th Centuries; with an Introductory Memoir." *Archaeologia* 28 (2): 207–326.

Bondy, Gottlieb, and Franz Dworsky, eds. 1906. *Zur Geschichte der Juden in Böhmen, Mähren und Schlesien von 906 bis 1620.* 2 vols. Prague: G. Bondy.

Bonn, Moritz Julius. 1896. *Spaniens Niedergang während der Preisrevolution des 16. Jahrhunderts. Ein induktiver Versuch zur Geschichte der Quantitätstheorie.* Münchener volkswirtschaftliche Studien 12. Stuttgart: Cotta.

Bonnassieux, Louis Jean Pierre Marie. 1892. *Les grandes compagnies de commerce.* Paris: E. Plon Nourrit et cie.

Bonvallet-Desbrosses, Simon-Joseph-Louis. 1791. *Situation actuelle de la France.* Paris: L'Auteur & Denné.

Bonwick, James. 1887. *Romance of the Wool Trade.* London: Griffith, Farran, Okeden, and Welsh.

Bosio, Giacomo. 1621. *Historia della sacra religione et illustrissima militia di S. Giovanni Gierosolimitano.* 2 vols. Rome: Guglielo Facciotto.

Bothe, Friedrich. 1906. *Die Entwicklung der direkten Besteuerung in der Reichsstadt Frankfurt bis zur Revolution 1612-1614.* Staats- und socialwissenschaftliche Forschungen, 26.2. Leipzig: Duncker & Humblot.

Boulainvilliers, Henri de. 1737. *État de la France, dans lequel on voit tout ce qui regarde le gouvernement ecclésiastique, le militaire, la justice, les finances, le commerce, les manufactures, le nombre des habitans, & en général tout ce qui peut faire connoître à fond cette monarchie.* 6 vols. London: T. Wood & S. Palmer.

Bourdeille, Pierre de. 1864. *Oeuvres complètes de Pierre de Bourdeille seigneur de Brantôme.* Edited by Ludovic Lalanne. 11 vols. Paris.

Bourgoin, Jean. 1625. *La chasse aux larrons ou avant coureur de l'histoire de la chambre de justice.* Paris.

Boutaric, Edgard. 1861. *La France sous Philippe le Bel: étude sur les institutions politiques et administratives du Moyen âge.* Paris: H. Plon.

———. 1863. *Institutions militaires de la France avant les armées permanentes.* Paris: H. Plon.

Brakel, Simon van. 1908. *De Hollandsche handelscompagnieën der zeventiende eeuw: hun ontstaan - hunne inrichting*. Gravenhage: Martinus Nijhoff.

Branca, Giovanni. 1629. *Le Machine volume nuovo, et di molto artificio da fare effetti maravigliosi tanto Spiritali quanto di Animale Operatione, arichito di bellissime figure*. Rome: Giacomo Mascardi.

Brant, Sebastian. 1854. *Narrenschiff*. Edited by Friedrich Zarnke. Leipzig: Georg Wigand.

Bremner, David. 1869. *The Industries of Scotland: Their Rise, Progress, and Present Condition*. Edinburgh: Adam & Charles Black.

Brender à Brandis, Gerrit. 1786. *Vaderlandsch kabinet van koophandel, zeevaart, landbouw, fabrijken, enz.* 2 vols. Amsterdam: Arend Fokke.

Brentano, Lujo. 1872. *Die Arbeitergilden der Gegenwart*. Leipzig: Duncker & Humblot.

Brewer, John Sherren, ed. 1879. *Registrum Malmesburiense: The Register of Malmesbury Abbey: Preserved in the Public Record Office*. 2 vols. Rerum Britannicarum Medii Aevi Scriptores 72. London: Longman & Co.

Bridge, Cyprian, ed. 1889. *History of the Russian Fleet during the Reign of Peter The Great, by a Contemporary Englishman, 1724*. Publications of the Navy Records Society 15. Navy Records Society.

Broc, Hervé de. 1887. *La France sous l'ancien régime*. 2 vols. Paris: E. Plon, Nourrit et Cie.

Broglio d'Ajano, Romolo. 1893. *Die Venetianische Seidenindustrie und ihre Organisation bis zum Ausgang des Mittelalters*. Munchener Volkswirtschaftliche Studien 2. Stuttgart: Cotta.

Brougham, Henry. 1803. *An Inquiry into the Colonial Policy of the European Powers*. 2 vols. Edinburgh: E. Balfour, et al.

Brückner, Georg. 1856. "Die Bettler zu Effelder des Jahres 1667 und ihre Zeit: Ein Beitrag zur Geschichte des 30jährigen Krieges." *Zeitschrift für Kulturgeschichte* 1: 31–52.

Bruder, Adolf. 1886. *Studien über die Finanzpolitik Herzog Rudolf IV. von Oesterreich (1358–1365). Mit Benützung zweier ungedruckter Gutachten des XIV. Jahrhunderts*. Innsbruck: Wagner.

Brüggen, Ernst von der. 1885. *Wie Russland europäisch wurde. Studien zur Kulturgeschichte*. Leipzig: Veit.

Brünneck, Wilhelm von. 1880. "Zur Geschichte der Miete und Pacht in dem deutschen und germanischen Recht des Mittelalters." *Zeitschrift der Savigny-Stiftung für Rechtsgeschichte: Die Germanistische Abteilung* 1: 138–90.

Brunner, A. W. 1906. "America." In *The Jewish Encyclopedia: A Descriptive Record of the History, Religion, Literature, and Customs of the Jewish People from the Earliest Times to the Present Day*, edited by Cyrus Adler and Isidore Singer, 1:492–511. New York: Funk & Wagnalls.

Buchanan, Francis. 1807. *A Journey from Madras Through the Countries of Mysore, Canara, and Malabar*. 3 vols. London: T. Cadell and W. Davies, and Black, Parry, and Kingsbury.

Bücher, Karl. 1886. *Die Bevölkerung von Frankfurt am Main in 14. und 15. Jahrhundert*. Tübingen: Laupp.

Buchon, Jean Alexandre C. 1840. *Recherches et matériaux pour servir à une histoire de la domination française aux XIIIe, XIVe et XVe siècles dans les provinces démembrées de l'Empire grec à la suite de la quatrième croisade*. Paris: A. Desrez.

———. 1845. *Livre de la Conqueste*. Paris: De Plon frères.

Buckle, Henry Thomas. 1864. *History of Civilization in England*. 4th ed. 2 vols. London: Longman, Green, Longman, Roberts & Green.

Budel, Reinier. 1591. *De Monetis et re numaria*. 3 vols. Cologne: Coloniae Agrippinae, apud Joannem Gymnicum, sub Monocerote.

Bujatti, Franz. 1893. *Die Geschichte der Seidenindustrie Österreichs. Deren Ursprung und Entwicklung bis in die neueste Zeit*. Vienna: Hoelder.

Burckhardt, Jacob. 1860. *Die Kultur der Renaissance in Italien. Ein Versuch*. Basel: Schweighauser.

———. 1878. *The Civilisation of the Renaissance in Italy*. Translated by Samuel George Chetwynd Middlemore. 2 vols. London: C. Kegan Paul & Co.

Burn, John Southerden. 1846. *The History of the French, Walloon, Dutch, and Other Foreign Protestant Refugees Settled in England, From the Reign of Henry VIII. To the Revocation of the Edict of Nantes*. London: Longman, Brown, Green, and Longmans.

Burney, James. 1816. *History of the Buccaneers of America*. London: Payne & Foss.

Burnley, James. 1889. *The History of Wool and Woolcombing*. London: Low, Marston, Searle and Rivington.

Burrish, Onslow. 1728. *Batavia Illustrata: Or, A View of the Policy and Commerce of the United Provinces, Particularly of Holland : With an Enquiry into the Alliances of the States General with the Emperor, France, Spain, and Great Britain*. London: J. Osborn.

Bury Palliser, Fanny. 1865. *History of Lace*. London: Sampson Low, Son & Marston.

Busch, Gabriel Christoph Benjamin. 1797. *Almanach der Fortschritte in Wissenschaften, Künsten, Manufakturen und Handwerken.* 16 vols. Erfurt: Keyser.

———. 1802. *Handbuch der Erfindungen.* 12 vols. Eisenach: J.G.E. Wittekindt.

Büsch, Johann Georg. 1784. "Über die öffentlichen Handlungskompagnien." In *Handlungsbibliothek*, by Johann Georg Büsch and Christoph Daniel Ebeling, 1:9–240. Hamburg.

———. 1790. *Ueber die Hamburgischen Zukker-Fabriken und den vergeblichen Wetteifer der Nordischen Staaten mit denselben, auf Veranlassung der Fragmente des Herrn Ritters von Zimmermann über Friedrich den Grossen.* Hamburg: Carl Ernst Bohn.

Büttgenbach, Franz. 1898. *Der erste Steinkohlenbergbau in Europa. Geschichtliche Skizze.* Aachen: Ignaz Schweitzer.

Buxton, Thomas Fowell. 1840. *The African Slave Trade, and Its Remedy.* London: J. Murray.

Byington, Ezra Hoyt. 1896. *The Puritan in England and New England.* Boston: Roberts Brothers.

Cahen, Abraham. 1881. "Les Juifs de la Martinique au XVIIe siècle." *Revue des études juives* 2: 93–122.

———. 1882. "Les Juifs dans les Colonies françaises au XVIIIe siècle." *Revue des études juives* 4 & 5: 4:127-145, 236–48; 5:68-92, 258–72.

Cahn, Julius. 1895. *Münz- und Geldgeschichte der Stadt Straßburg im Mittelalter.* Strasbourg: Karl J. Trübner.

———, ed. 1911. *Münz- und Geldgeschichte von Konstanz und des Bodenseegebietes im Mittelalter bis zum Reichsmünzgesetz von 1559.* Münz- und Geldgeschichte der im Großherzogtum Baden vereinigten Gebiete 1. Heidelberg: Carl Winter.

Cairnes, John Elliott. 1863. *The Slave Power: Its Character, Career and Probable Designs: Being an Attempt to Explain the Real Issues Involved in the American Contest.* 2nd ed. London and Cambridge: Macmillan & Company.

Callery, Alphonse. 1882. "Les douanes avant Colbert et l'ordonnance de 1664." *Revue Historique* 18 (1): 49–91, 272.

Calonne, Albéric de. 1883. *La vie agricole sous l'ancien régime en Picardie et en Artois.* Paris: Guillaumin.

Calvin, Jean. 1554. *Defensio orthodoxae fidei de sacra Trinitate, contra prodigiosos errores Michaelis Serveti Hispani: ubi ostenditur haereticos jure gladii coercendos esse, & nominatim de homine hoc tam impio juste & merito sumptum Genevae fuisse supplicium.* Geneva: Oliva Roberti Stephani.

Camden, William. 1586. *Britannia siue Florentissimorum regnorum, Angliae, Scotiae, Hiberniae, et insularum adiacentium ex intima antiquitate chorographica descriptio*. London: George Bishop.

Campbell, Douglas. 1892. *The Puritan in Holland, England, and America: An Introduction to American History*. 2 vols. New York: Harper & Brothers.

Campbell, John. 1774. *A Political Survey of Britain: Being a Series of Reflections on the Situation, Lands, Inhabitants, Revenues, Colonies, and Commerce of This Island*. 2 vols. London: John Campbell.

Campomanes, Pedro Rodríguez. 1775. *Discurso sobre la educacion popular de los artesanos y su fomento*. Madrid: Antonio de Sancha.

Canot, Théodore. 1854. *Captain Canot or Twenty Years of an African Slaver*. Edited by Brantz Mayer. New York: D. Appleton and Co.

Capefigue, Jean Baptiste Honoré Raymond. 1855. *Banquiers, fournisseurs, acquéreurs des biens nationaux, emprunts, système financier de Pitt et Castelreagh*. Histoire des grandes opérations financières; banques, bourses, emprunts, compagnies industrielles, etc. 2. Paris: Amyot.

Cardonne, Denis-Dominique. 1765. *Histoire de l'Afrique et de l'Espagne sous la domination des Arabes*. 3 vols. Paris: Saillant.

———. 1770. *Geschichte von Afrika und Spanien unter der Herrschaft der Araber*. Translated by Johann Conrad Fäsi. Zurich: Orell, Geßner, Füeßlin.

Carey, B., ed. 1876. *La cour et la ville de Madrid vers la fin du XVIIe siècle. Relation du voyage d'Espagne par la comtesse d'Aulnoy*. Paris: E. Plon et cie.

Carli, Gian Rinaldo. 1804. *Delle monete e dell'instituzione delle zecche d'Italia*. Scrittori classici italiani anticlii e moderni di economia política: Parte Moderna 13. Milan: G.G. Destefanis.

Carlyle, Thomas, ed. 1902. *Oliver Cromwell's Letters and Speeches with Elucidations*. 4 vols. The Works of Thomas Carlyle in 30 Volumes 6–8. London: Chapman & Hall.

Caro, Georg. 1906. "Ländlicher Grundbesitz von Stadtbürgern im Mittelalter." *Jahrbücher für Nationalökonomie und Statistik*, III, 31: 721–43.

———. 1908. *Sozial- und Wirtschaftsgeschichte der Juden im Mittelalter und der Neuzeit*. 2 vols. Grundriss der Gesamtwissenschaft des Judentums. Leipzig: Gustav Fock.

Carqueja, Bento. 1908. *O Capitalismo Moderno e as suas origens em Portugal*. Porto: Chardron.

Casas, Bartolomé de las. 1552. *Brevisima relación de la destrucción de las Indias*. Seville: Sebastian Trugillo.

Cau, Cornelis, ed. 1658. *Groot Placcaetboek.* 9 vols. The Hague.

Caus, Salomon de. 1615. *Les Raisons des forces mouvantes, avec diverses machines tant utiles que plaisantes.* Frankfurt am Main: Jan Norton.

Cecchetti, Bartolomeo. 1870. *La vita dei Veneziani fino al 1200.* Venice: Naratovich.

Charnock, John. 1801. *An History of Marine Architecture: Including an Enlarged and Progressive View of the Nautical Regulations and Naval History, Both Civil and Military, of All Nations, Especially of Great Britain.* 3 vols. London: R. Faulder.

Chennevières, François de. 1750. *Détails militaires, dont la connoissance est nécessaire à tous les officiers, & principalement aux commissaires des guerres.* 4 vols. Paris: C.-A. Jombert.

Child, Josiah. 1698. *A New Discourse of Trade.* London: T. Sowle.

Chotard, H. 1898. "La mendicité en Auvergne au XVIII siècle." *Revue d'Auvergne* XV: 1–41.

Cibrario, Luigi. 1839. *Economia politica del medio evo.* Turin: Eredi Botta.

———. 1860. *Operette varie.* Turin: Botta.

———. 1868. *Della schiavitù e del servaggio e specialmente dei servi agricoltori.* 2 vols. Milan: Civelli.

Clamageran, Jean-Jules. 1867. *Histoire de l'impôt en France: depuis l'époque romaine jusqu'à 1774.* 3 vols. Paris: Guillaumin et Cie.

Clark, Henry William. 1911. *History of English Nonconformity from Wiclif to the Close of the Nineteenth Century.* 2 vols. London: Chapman and Hall.

Clarkson, Thomas. 1786. *An Essay on the Slavery and Commerce of the Human Species, Particularly the African, Translated from a Latin Dissertation, Which Was Honoured with the First Prize in the University of Cambridge, for the Year 1785, with Additions.* London: J. Phillips.

Clément, Pierre, ed. 1861. *Lettres, instructions, et Memoires de Colbert.* 7 vols. Paris: Imprimerie impériale.

———. 1892. *Histoire de Colbert et de son administration.* 3rd ed. 2 vols. Paris: Didier.

Clowes, W. Laird. 1897. *The Royal Navy, A History from the Earliest Times to 1900.* 7 vols. London: S. Low, Marston, Co.

Cobb, Sanford H. 1902. *The Rise of Religious Liberty in America: A History.* New York: Macmillan & Company.

Colmeiro, Manuel. 1863. *Historia de la economia politica en España.* 2 vols. Madrid: C. Lopez.

Conrad, Johann, Ludwig Elster, Wilhelm Lexis, and Edgar Loening, eds. 1898. *Handwörterbuch der Staatswissenschaften*. 2nd ed. 7 vols. Jena: G. Fischer.

Cooley, Henry Scofield. 1896. *A Study of Slavery in New Jersey*. Baltimore: John Hopkins University Press.

Corbet, John. 1667. *A Discourse of the Religion of England Asserting, That Reformed Christianity Setled in Its Due Latitude, Is the Stability and Advancement of This Kingdom*. London.

Corbier, Claude. 1870. "Notice Historique sur les forges de la Chaussade a Guérigny (Nièvre)." *Bulletin de la Société nivernaise*, 350–410.

Coronel, S. 1859. *Middelburg voorheen en thans*. Middelburg: Benthem en Jutting.

Cosack, Konrad. 1898. *Lehrbuch des Handelsrechts mit Einschluß des Seerechts*. 4th ed. Stuttgart: F. Enke.

Coulsom, Walter. 1818. "Mill's British India." *Edinburgh Review* 31 (December): 1–44.

Crome, August Friedrich Wilhelm. 1833. *Selbstbiographie: ein Beitrag zu den gelehrten und politischen Memoiren des vorigen und gegenwärtigen Jahrhunderts*. Stuttgart: Metzler.

Crousaz, Adolf Friedrich Johannes von. 1865. *Die Organisationen des Brandenburgischen und preussischen Heeres von 1640 bis 1863*. 2 vols. W. Dietze.

Cunningham, William. 1897. *Alien Immigrants to England*. Social England. London: S. Sonnenschein & Company.

———. 1907. *The Growth of English Industry and Commerce during the Early and Middle Ages*. 4th ed. 2 vols. Cambridge: Cambridge University Press.

D'Angerville, Mouffle. 1781a. *The Private Life of Lewis XV: In Which Are Contained the Principal Events, Remarkable Occurrences, and Anecdotes of His Reign*. 4 vols. London: Charles Dilly.

———. 1781b. *Vie privée de Louis xv, ou Principaux evéemens, particularités et anecdotes de son regne*. 4 vols. London: John Peter Lyton.

Dannenberg, Hermann. 1880. "Die Goldgulden vom Florentiner Gepräge." *Numismatische Zeitschrift* 12: 146–85.

Darigrand, Edme-François. 1763. *L'anti-financier ou Relevé de quelques-unes des malversations dont se rendent journellement coupables les fermiers-généraux, & des vexations qu'ils commettent dans les provinces: servant de réfutation à un écrit intitulé: Lettre servant de réponse aux remontrances du Parlement de Bordeaux, précédée d'une épitre au Parlement de France,accompagnée de notes historiques*. Amsterdam.

Darmstaedter, Ludwig, and René Du Bois-Reymond. 1904. *4000 Jahre Pionier-Arbeit in den exakten Wissenschaften*. Berlin: J.A. Stargardt.

Darmstaedter, Ludwig, René Du Bois-Reymond, and C. Schaefer. 1908. *Ludwig Darmstaedters Handbuch zur Geschichte der Naturwissenschaften und der Technik*. 2nd ed. Berlin: J. Springer.

D'Avenant, Charles. 1771. *The Political and Commercial Works of That Celebrated Writer Charles D'Avenant, LL. D., Relating to the Trade and Revenue of England, the Plantation Trade, the East-India Trade and African Trade*. Edited by Charles Whitworth. 5 vols. London: R. Horsfield.

D'Avenel, Georges. 1894. *Histoire économique de la propriété, des salaires, des denrées et de tous les prix en général, depuis l'an 1200 jusqu'en l'an 1800*. 7 vols. Paris: Imprimerie Nationale.

———. 1895. *La fortune privée à travers sept siècles*. Paris: Chamerot & Renouard.

Davidsohn, Robert. 1896a. *Forschungen zur alteren Geschichte von Florenz*. 4 vols. Berlin: Mittler & Sohn.

———. 1896b. *Geschichte von Florenz*. 4 vols. Berlin: Mittler & Sohn.

Davies, Charles Maurice. 1851. *The History of Holland and the Dutch Nation from the Beginning of the Tenth Century to the End of the Eighteenth*. 3 vols. London: G. Willis.

Dávila, Gil González. 1690. "Historia de la vida y hechos del Rey D. Felipe III." MSS/12177. Biblioteca Nacional de España, Madrid.

Day, Clive. 1904. *The Policy and Administration of the Dutch in Java*. London: Macmillan & Company.

De Jonge, Jan Karel Jacob, and Marinus Lodewijk van Deventer, eds. 1862. *De opkomst van het Nederlandsch gezag in Oost-Indië (1595-1610): verzameling van onuitgegeven stukken uit het Oud-koloniaal archief*. 13 vols. The Hague: Martinus Nijhoff.

De Jonge, Johannes Cornelis. 1858. *Geschiedenis van het Nederlandsche zeewezen*. 2nd ed. 10 vols. Haarlem: Kruseman.

De Leon, Moses Pereira, Samuele Henrico De la Parra, Ishak De la Parra, David de Isaac Cohen Nassy, and Samuel Wheler Brandon. 1788. *Essai historique sur la colonie de Surinam*. 2 vols. A Paramaribo.

Defoe, Daniel. 1697. *An Essay Upon Projects*. London: Thomas Cockerill.

———. 1704. *Giving Alms, No Charity And Employing the Poor A Grievance to the Nation Being an Essay Upon This Great Question*. London.

———. 1726. *The Complete English Tradesman*. 2 vols. London: Charles Rivington.

———. 1890. *The Compleat English Gentleman*. Edited by Karl Daniel Bül-bring. London: David Nutt.

Defoe, Daniel, and Samuel Richardson. 1778. *A Tour Through the Island of Great Britain Divided Into Circuits or Journies*. 8th ed. 4 vols. London: W. Strahan, J.F. and C. Rivington.

Del Campo Marin, Antonio. n.d. "Influxo del precio del azogue sobre su consumo."

Del Mar, Alexander. 1880. *A History of the Precious Metals: From Earliest Times to the Present*. London: George Bell and Sons.

———. 1886. *Money and Civilization: Or, A History of the Monetary Laws and Systems of Various States Since the Dark Ages, and Their Influence Upon Civilization*. London: George Bell and Sons.

Delbrück, Hans. 1876. "Ueber den politischen Charakter der englischen Kirchenspaltung im siebzehnten Jahrhundert." *Historische Zeitschrift* 36: 83–106.

———. 1886. *Historische und politische Aufsätze*. 3 vols. Berlin: Walther & Apolant.

———. 1907. *Geschichte der Kriegskunst im Rahmen der politischen Geschichte*. 4 vols. Berlin: G. Stilke.

———. 1990. *History of the Art of War within the Framework of Political History*. Translated by Walter J. Renfroe. 4 vols. Lincoln: University of Nebraska Press.

Demuth, Adolf. 1890. "Das Manufacturhaus in Weißwasser." *Mitteilungen des Vereins für Geschichte der Deutschen in Böhmen* 28: 293–333.

Denekamp, Emile Eduard. 1895. *Die Amsterdamer Diamantindustrie*. Heidelberg: J. Hörning.

Denton, William. 1888. *England in the Fifteenth Century*. London: George Bell and Sons.

Depping, Georg Bernhard, ed. 1850. *Correspondance administrative sous le règne de Louis XIV, entre le cabinet du roi, les secrétaires d'état, le chancelier de France*. 4 vols. Paris: Imprimerie Nationale.

Des Cilleuls, Alfred. 1898. *Histoire et régime de la grande industrie en France aux XVIIe et XVIIIe siècles*. Paris: V. Giard & E. Brière.

Des Marez, Guillaume. 1901. *La lettre de foire a Ypres au XIIIe siècle, contribution à l'étude des papiers de crédit.*. Brussels: H. Lamertin.

Detlefsen, Detlef. 1901. "Ein Beitrag zur Geschichte des Bettels." *Zeitschrift der Gesellschaft für Schleswig-Holsteinische Geschichte* 31: 116–35.

Deutsch, Helene. 1909. *Die Entwicklung der Seidenindustrie in Österreich 1660-1840*. Studien zur Sozial-, Wirtschafts- und Verwaltungsgeschichte 3. Vienna: C. Konegan.

Diderot, Denis, and Jean Le Rond D'Alembert, eds. 1751. "Mode (Arts)." In *L'Encyclopédie ou Dictionnaire raisonné des sciences, des arts et des métiers*, 10:598. Paris: Briasson, David, Le Breton, & Durand.

Dircks, Henry. 1865. *The Life, Times, and Scientific Labours of the Second Marquis of Worcester. To Which Is Added, a Reprint of His Century of Inventions, 1663, with a Commentary Thereon*. London: Bernard Quaritch.

Dixon, E. 1898. "The Florentine Wool Trade in the Middle Ages." *Transactions of the Royal Historical Society* 12 (December): 151–79.

Dobel, Friedrich. 1879. "Der Fugger Bergbau und Handel in Ungarn." *Zeitschrift des Historischen Vereins für Schwaben und Neuburg* 6: 33–50.

———. 1882. "Über den Bergbau und Handel des Jacob und Anton Fugger in Kärnten und Tirol." *Zeitschrift des Historischen Vereins für Schwaben und Neuburg* 9: 193–213.

Doenges, Willy. 1907. *Meißner Porzellan. Seine Geschichte und künstlerische Entwicklung*. Berlin: Marquardt & Co.

Dominik, Hans. 1915. "Die Anfänge der Berliner Maschinenindustrie." *Großberliner Kalender* 3: 303–11.

Dopsch, Alfons. 1912. *Die Wirtschaftsentwicklung der Karolingerzeit vornehmlich in Deutschland*. 2 vols. Weimar: Bohlau.

Doren, Alfred. 1901. *Studien aus der Florentiner Wirtschaftsgeschichte*. 2 vols. Stuttgart: Cotta.

Doüet d'Arcq, Louis. 1853. "Sur les comptes des ducs de Bourgogne, publiés par Mr de Laborde (deuxième article)." *Bibliothèque de l'École des chartes* 14 (1): 125–47.

Dreesbach, Emil. 1901. "Der Orient in der altfranzösischen Kreuzzugsliteratur." Breslau: University of Breslau.

Dressel, Hans. 1908. *Die Entwicklung von Handel und Industrie in Sonneberg*. Gotha: F. A. Perthes.

Droysen, Johann Gustav. 1875a. "Beiträge zur Geschichte des Militairwesens in Deutschland während der Epoche des dreißigjährigen Krieges." *Zeitschrift für deutsche Kulturgeschichte* 4: 375-420,449-470,570-645.

———. 1875b. *Beiträge zur Geschichte des Militärwesens in Deutschland während der Epoche des dreißigjährigen Krieges*. Hanover: Schlüter.

Du Bourg, Antoine. 1885. *Tableau de l'ancienne organisation du travail dans le midi de la France. Corporations ouvrieres de la ville de Toulouse de 1270 à 1791*. Toulouse: Imprimerie Catholique Saint-Cyprien.

Du Casse, Albert. 1862. *Histoire anecdotique de l'ancien théâtre en France*. 2 vols. Paris: E. Dentu.

Du Châtelet, Louis-Marie-Florent. 1798. *Voyage Du Ci-Devant Duc Du Chatelet, En Portugal*. Edited by Jean François de Bourgoing. 2 vols. Paris: Buisson.

Dubois, J. P. J. 1763. *Vies des gouverneurs généraux avec l'abrégé de l'histoire des établissemens Hollandois aux Indes orientales*. The Hague: Pierre de Hondt.

Duchesne, Henri Gabriel. 1776. *Dictionnaire de l'industrie, ou collection raisonnée des procédés utiles dans les sciences et dans les arts*. 3 vols. Paris: Lacombe.

Duchesne, Laurent. 1900. *L'evolution economique et sociale de l'industrie de la Laine en Angleterre*. Paris: Librairie de la Société du Recueil général des lois et des arrêts.

Dumas, François. 1894. *La généralité de Tours au XVIIIe siècle: administration de l'intendant Du Cluzel (1766-1783)*. Mémoires de la Société archéologique de Touraine 39. Touraine: L. Péricat.

Dunn, Matthias. 1844. *An Historical, Geological, and Descriptive View of the Coal Trade of the North of England; Comprehending Its Rise, Progress, Present State, and Future Prospects. To Which Are Appended a Concise Notice of the Peculiarities of Certain Coal Fields in Great Britain and Ireland; and Also a General Description of the Coal Mines of Belgium, Drawn up from Actual Inspection*. Newcastle upon Tyne: Pattison and Ross.

Dupré d'Aulnay, Louis. 1744. *Traité general des subsistances militaires, qui comprend la fourniture du pain de munition, des fourages & de la viande aux armées & aux troupes de garnisons; ensemble celle des hôpitaux & des équipages des vivres & de l'artillerie, par marché ou résultat du Conseil, à for-fait, ou par régie*. Paris: Prault pere.

Duro, Cesáreo Fernández. 1884. *La Armada Invencible*. 2 vols. Madrid: Sucesores de Rivadeneyra.

Dutil, Léon. 1911. *L'état économique du Languedoc à la fin de l'ancien régime (1750-1789)*. Paris: Hachette & cie.

Dutt, Romesh Chunder. 1908. *The Economic History of India Under Early British Rule: From the Rise of the British Power in 1757, to the Accession of Queen Victoria in 1837*. 3rd ed. London: Kegan Paul, Trench, Trübner & Company.

Eberstadt, Rudolph. 1899. *Das französische Gewerberecht und die Schaffung staatlicher Gesetzgebung und Verwaltung in Frankreich vom dreizehnten Jahrhundert bis 1581.* Staats- und socialwissenschaftliche Forschungen 17. Leipzig: Duncker & Humblot.

Eccardus. 1907. *Geschichte des niederen Volkes in Deutschland.* 2 vols. Berlin & Stuttgart: W. Spemann.

Eden, Frederick Morton. 1797. *The State of the Poor. Or, An History of the Labouring Classes in England, from the Conquest to the Present Period.* 3 vols. London: J. Davis.

Edwards, Thomas. 1646. *Gangraena, or, A Catalogue and Discovery of Many of the Errors, Heresies, Blasphemies and Pernicious Practices of the Sectaries of This Time, Vented and Acted in England in These Four Last Years: Also a Particular Narration of Divers Stories, Remarkable Passages, Letters; an Extract of Many Letters, All Concerning the Present Sects; Together with Some Observations upon, and Corollaries from All the Fore-Named Premises.* 3 vols. London: Ralph Smith.

Eheberg, Karl Theodor von. 1879. *Über das ältere deutsche Münzwesen und die Hausgenossenschaften besonders in volkswirthschaftlicher Beziehung. Mit einigen bisher ungedruckten Urkunden über die Strassburger Hausgenossen.* Staats- und socialwissenschaftliche Forschungen, 2.5. Leipzig: Duncker & Humblot.

Ehrenberg, Richard. 1899. "Die Banken von 11. bis zum 17. Jahrhundert." In *Handwörterbuch der Staatswissenschaften*, edited by Johann Conrad, Ludwig Elster, Wilhelm Lexis, and Edgar Loening, 2nd ed., 2:167–74. Jena: G. Fischer.

———. 1922. *Das Zeitalter der Fugger. Geldkapital und Kreditverkehr im 16. Jahrhundert.* 3rd ed. 2 vols. Jena: Gustav Fischer.

Ehrle, Franz. 1889. "Der Nachlaß Clemens' V. und der in Betreff desselben von Johann XXII. (1318-1321) geführte Process." *Archiv für Literatur- und Kirchengeschichte des Mittelalters* 4: 1–158.

Elgas, Barnett A. 1905. *The Jews of South Carolina.* Philadelphia: J. B. Lippincott.

Endemann, Wilhelm. 1862. "Beiträge zur Kenntnis des Handelsrechts im Mittelalter." *Zeitschrift für das gesamte Handelsrechts* 5: 333–414.

Engel, Arthur, and Raymond Serrure. 1891. *Traité de numismatique du Moyen Âge.* 3 vols. Paris: E. Leroux.

———. 1897. *Traité de numismatique moderne et contemporaine.* 2 vols.

Ennen, Leonard. 1863. *Geschichte Der Stadt Köln, Meist Aus Den Quellen Des Kölner Stadt-Archivs.* Vol. 1. Cologne & Neuß: L. Schwann.

Erman, Jean Pierre, and Pierre Christian Frédéric Reclam. 1782. *Mémoires pour servir à l'histoire des réfugiés François dans les états du roi.* 9 vols. Berlin: J. Jasperd.

Ermisch, Hubert. 1883. *Urkundenbuch der Stadt Freiberg in Sachsen.* 3 vols. Codex diplomaticus Saxoniae regiae 2. Hauptteil 12–14. Leipzig: Giesecke & Devrient.

———. 1887. *Das sächsische Bergrecht des Mittelalters.* Leipzig: Giesecke & Devrient.

Ernst, Carl von. 1880. "Die Kunst des Münzens von der ältesten Zeiten bis zur Gegenwart." *Numismatische Zeitschrift* 12: 22–67.

Eschwege, Wilhelm Ludwig von. 1833. *Pluto brasiliensis: eine Reihe von Abhandlungen über Brasiliens Gold-, Diamanten- und anderen mineralischen Reichthum, über die Geschichte seiner Entdeckung, über das Vorkommen seiner Lagerstätten, des Betriebs, der Ausbeute und die daraufbezügliche Gesetzgebung u.s.w.* Berlin: G. Reimer.

Eulenburg, Franz. 1893. "Das Wiener Zunftwesen. I." *Zeitschrift für Social- und Wirtschaftsgeschichte* 1 (2/3): 264–317.

———. 1906. Review of *Review of Die überseeischen Unternehmungen der Welser und ihrer Gesellschafter,* by Konrad Häbler. *Historische Zeitschrift* 96 (1): 104–6.

Euler, Leonhard. 1776. *Théorie complète de la construction et de la manoeuvre des vaisseaux , mise à la portée de ceux qui s'appliquent à la navigation.* Paris: C.-A. Jombert.

Eversmann, Friedrich August Alexander. 1804. *Uebersicht der Eisen- und Stahl-Erzeugung auf Wasserwerken in den Ländern zwischen Lahn und Lippe.* Dortmund: Mallinckrodt.

Exner, Wilhelm Franz. 1869. *Die Tapeten- und Buntpapier-Industrie für Fabrikanten und Gewerbtreibende, sowie für technische Institute.* Weimar: Voigt.

Exquemelin, Alexandre Olivier. 1744. *Histoire des aventuriers flibustiers qui se sont signalés dans les Indes.* 4 vols. A. Trevoux.

Faber, Richard. 1888. *Die Entstehung des Agrarschutzes in England: Ein Versuch.* Abhandlungen aus dem Staatswissenschaftlichen Seminar zu Strassburg i.E. 5. Strasbourg: Karl J. Trübner.

Fagniez, Gustave. 1897. *L'économie sociale de la France sous Henri IV, 1589-1610.* Paris: Hachette et Cie.

Falconbridge, Alexander. 1788. *An Account of the Slave Trade on the Coast of Africa.* London: J. Phillips.

Faulhaber, Carl. 1896. *Die ehemalige schlesische Goldproduktion mit besonderer Berücksichtigung des Reichensteiner Bergreviers.* Breslau: W. Korbner.

Fechner, Hermann. 1907. *Wirtschaftsgeschichte der preussischen Provinz Schlesien in der Zeit ihrer provinziellen Selbstandigkeit, 1741-1806. Nach den Akten des Geheimen Staatsarchivs und des Handeslministeriums in Berlin, des Staatsarchivs und des Oberbergamtsarchivs in Breslau.* Breslau: S. Schottlaender.

Feilchenfeld, A. 1899. "Anfang und Blütezeit der Portugiesengemeinde in Hamburg." *Zeitschrift für Hamburgische Geschichte* 10: 199–240.

Feillet, Alphonse. 1865. *La misère au temps de la Fronde et Saint Vincent de Paul.* Paris: Didier.

Feldhaus, Franz Maria. 1904. *Lexikon der Erfindungen und Entdeckungen auf den Gebieten der Naturwissenschaften und Technik in chronologischer Übersicht mit Personen- und Sachregister.* Heidelberg: C. Winter.

———. 1910. *Ruhmesblätter der Technik von den Urerfindungen bis zur Gegenwart.* Leipzig: Friedrich Brandstetter.

———. 1914. *Die Technik der Vorzeit, der geschichtlichen Zeit und der Naturvölker.* Leipzig & Berlin: W. Engelmann.

Fenaille, Maurice. 1903. *État général des tapisseries de la manufacture des Gobelins depuis son origine jusqu'à nos jours, 1600-1900.* 6 vols. Paris: Imprimerie Nationale.

Ferrara, F. 1871. "Documenti per servire alla Storia de' Banchi veneziani." *Archivio Veneto* 1: 107–55, 332–63.

Ferrari, J. 1860. *Histoire de la Raison d'Etat.* Paris: Michel Lévy.

Fichard, Johann Karl von. 1819. *Die Entstehung der Reichsstadt Frankfurt am Main und die Verhältnisse ihrer Bewohner.* Frankfurt am Main: Andreä.

Fink, Erich. 1894. "Die Bergwerksunternehmungen der Fugger in Schlesien." *Zeitschrift des Vereins für Geschichte (und Alterthum) Schlesiens* 28: 294–340.

Fischer, Thomas Alfred. 1902. *The Scots in Germany: Being a Contribution Towards the History of the Scots Abroad.* Edinburgh: O. Schulze & Company.

———. 1903. *The Scots in Eastern and Western Prussia: A Sequel to "The Scots in Germany, a Contribution Towards the History of the Scot Abroad."* Edinburgh: O. Schulze & Company.

Fisher, Irving. 1911. *The Purchasing Power of Money: Its Determination and Relation to Credit, Interest, and Crises.* New York: The Macmillan Company.

Flach, Jacques. 1893. *Les Origines de l'ancienne France.* 2 vols. Paris: L. Larose et Forcel.

Flamm, Hermann. 1905. *Der wirtschaftliche Niedergang Freiburg im Br. und die Lage des städtischen Grundeigentums im 14. und 15. Jahrhundert. Ein Beitrag zur Geschichte der geschlossenen Stadtwirtschaft.* Volkswirtschaftliche Abhandlungen der Badischen Hochschulen, 8.3. Karlsruhe: Braun.

Fleetwood, William. 1745. *Chronicon Preciosum: Or, an Account of English Gold and Silver Money; The Price of Corn and Other Commodities; and of Stipends, Salaries, Wages, Jointures, Portions, Day-Labour, &c. in England for Six Hundred Years Last Past.* London: T. Osbourne.

Fletcher, Andrew. 1698. *Two Discourses Concerning the Affairs of Scotland.* Edinburgh.

Flörke, Heinrich Gustav. 1803. "Mode." In *Oekonomisch-Technologische Encyklopädie, Oder Allgemeines System Der Staats- Stadt- Haus- Und Landwirthschaft Und Der Kunstgeschichte,* 92:367–517. Berlin: Joachim Pauli.

Forbes, Urquhart Atwell, and W. H. R. Ashford. 1906. *Our Waterways: A History of Inland Navigation Considered as a Branch of Water Conservancy.* London: J. Murray.

Forbonnais, François Véron Duverger de. 1758. *Recherches et considérations sur les finances de France depuis l'année 1595 jusqu'à l'année 1721.* 2 vols. Basel: Cramer.

Forestié, Édouard, ed. 1890. *Les livres de comptes des Frères Bonis, marchands montalbanais du XIVe siècle.* 2 vols. Archives historiques de la Gascogne 20, 23. Paris: H. Champion.

Förster, Friedrich Christoph. 1834. *Wallenstein, Herzog zu Mecklenburg, Friedland und Sagan, als Feldherr und Landesfürst in seinem öffentlichen und Privat-Leben: Eine Biographie.* Potsdam: Riegel.

Forster, George. 1794. *Ansichten vom Niederrhein, von Brabant, Flandern, Holland, England und Frankreich, im April, Mai und Junius 1790.* 3 vols. Berlin: Voss.

Fortescue, John William. 1899. *A History of the British Army.* 13 vols. London: Macmillan & Company.

Fournier, August. 1887. "Handel und Verkehr in Ungarn und Polen um die Mitte des 18. Jahrhunderts. Ein Beitrag zur Geschichte der österreichischen Commerzialpolitik." *Archiv für österreichische Geschichte* 69: 317–481.

Fournier, Édouard, ed. 1855. *Les Caquets de l'Accouchée.* Paris: P. Jannet.

Fournier, Edouard. 1877. *Le Vieux-Neuf. Histoire ancienne des inventions et découvertes modernes.* 2nd ed. 3 vols. Paris: Librairie de la Société des Gens de Lettres.

Fox Bourne, Henry Richard. 1886. *English Merchants: Memoirs in Illustration of the Progress of British Commerce*. 2nd ed. 2 vols. London: Chatto & Windus.

Fraas, Carl. 1865. *Geschichte der Landbau- und Forstwissenschaft. Seit dem sechzehnten Jahrhundert bis zur Gegenwart*. Geschichte der Wissenschaften in Deutschland 3. Munich: Cotta.

France. 1578. *Ordonnance du Roy, sur le faict de la police generale de son Royaume*. Lyon: Michel Jove & Jean Pillehotte.

———. 1730. *Recueil des règlemens généraux et particuliers concernant les manufactures et fabriques du royaume*. 6 vols. Paris: L'Imprimerie Royale.

———. 1788. *Code du fabricant, ou résumé sommaire des principaux règlemens concernant les arts et métiers*. 2 vols. Paris: Prévôt.

Frauenstädt, Paul. 1897a. "Bettel- und Vagabundenwesen in Schlesien vom 16. bis 18. Jahrhundert." *Zeitschrift für die gesamte Strafrechtswissenschaft* 17: 712–35.

———. 1897b. "Bettel- und Vagabundenwesen in Schlesien vom 16. bis 18. Jahrhundert." *Preussische Jahrbücher* 89.

Frégier, Honoré Antoine. 1850. *Histoire de l'administration de la police de Paris*. 2 vols. Paris: Guillaumin et Cie.

Frensdorff, Ferdinand, Matthias von Lexer, and Friedrich Roth, eds. 1865. *Die Chroniken der schwäbischen Städte: Augsburg*. 9 vols. Die Chroniken der deutschen Städte vom 14. ins 16. Jahrhundert. Leipzig: S. Hirzel.

Freudenthal, Max. 1901. "Leipziger Messgäste." *Monatsschrift für Geschichte und Wissenschaft des Judenthums* 45 (10/12): 460–509.

Freymark, Hermann. 1897. "Zur preussischen Handels- und Zollpolitik von 1648-1818." Halle: Vereinigte Friedrichs-Universität Halle-Wittenberg.

Freytag, Gustav. 1859. *Bilder aus der deutschen Vergangenheit*. 5 vols. Leipzig: S. Hirzel.

Friedenwald, Herbert. 1893. "Jews Mentioned in the Journal of the Continental Congress." *American Jewish Historical Society* 1: 65–89.

Friedländer, Ludwig Heinrich. 1881. *Darstellungen aus der Sittengeschichte Roms in der Zeit von August bis zum Ausgang der Antonine*. 5th ed. 3 vols. Leipzig: S. Hirzel.

Friedmann, S. 1860. *Niederländisch- Ost- und Westindien: Ihre Neueste Gestaltung in Geographischer, Statistischer, und Culturhistorischer Hinsicht, Mit Besonderer Darstellung Der Klimatischen und Sanitätischen Verhältnisse*. Munich: G. Franz.

Friedrichs II. von Preußen. 1846. *Œuvres de Frédéric le Grand*. 30 vols. Berlin: Decker.

Froude, James Anthony. 1858. *History of England from the Fall of Wolsey to the Death of Elizabeth*. 12 vols. London: J.W. Parker & Son.

Froumenteau, Nicholás. 1581. *Le Thrésor des thresors de France ou Preparatif propre et nécessaire*.

Fugger, Markus. 1578. *Von der Gestüterey: Das ist Ein gründtliche beschreibung wie vnnd wa man ein Gestüt von guten edlen Kriegsrossen auffrichten, vnderhalten, vnd wie man die jungen von einem Jar zu dem andern erziehen soll, biß sie einem Bereitter zum abrichten zuvndergeben, vnnd so sie abgericht in langwiriger Gesundhait zuerhalten*. Frankfurt am Main: Feyerabend.

Funck-Brentano, Frantz. 1897. *Les origines de la guerre de Cent ans: Philippe le Bel en Flandre*. Paris: H. Champion.

Gallo, Emanuele. 1914. *Il valore sociale dell'abbigliamento*. Turin: Fratelli Bocca.

Gardiner, Ralph. 1796. *England's Grievance Discovered: In Relation to the Coal-Trade; the Tyrannical Oppression of the Magistrates of Newcastle; Their Charters and Grants; the Several Tryals, Depositions, and Judgements Obtained Against Them; with a Breviate of Several Statutes Proving Repugnant to Their Actings; with Proposals for Reducing the Excessive Rates of Coals for the Future; and the Rise of Their Grants Appearing in This Book*. D. Akenhead & Sons.

Gardiner, Samuel Rawson. 1897. *History of the Commonwealth and Protectorate, 1649–1660*. 4 vols. London: Longman, Green and Co.

Garnier, Russell Montague. 1892. *History of the English Landed Interest, Its Customs, Laws and Agriculture*. 2 vols. London: Swan Sonnenschein & Co.

Garsault, François A. de. 1771. *L'art de la lingere*. Paris: L. F. Delatour.

Garve, Christian. 1792. *Versuche über verschiedene Gegenstände aus der Moral, der Litteratur und dem gesellschaftlichen Leben*. 5 vols. Breslau: Korn.

Gasquet, Francis Aidan. 1889. *Henry VIII and the English Monasteries: An Attempt to Illustrate the History of Their Suppression*. 2 vols. London: John Hodges.

Geering, Traugott. 1886. *Handel und Industrie der Stadt Basel. Zunftwesen und Wirtschaftsgeschichte bis zum Ende des XVII. Jahrhunderts*. Basel: Felix Schneider.

———. 1903. "Die Entwicklung des Zeugdrucks im Abendland seit dem XVII. Jahrhundert." *Vierteljahrsschrift für Social- und Wirtschaftsgeschichte* 1: 397–433.

Geijerstam, Gustaf af. 1897. *Anteckningar rörande arbetarnes ställning vid fyra svenska grufvor.* Stockholm.

Gelcich, Eugen. 1882. *Studien über die Entwicklungsgeschichte der Schifffahrt mit besonderer Berücksichtigung der nautischen Wissenschaften, nebst einem Anhang über die nautische Literatur des 16. und 17. Jahrhunderts und über die Entwicklungsgeschichte der Formeln zur Reduction der Monddistanzen.* Laibach: Kleinmayr & Bamberg.

———. 1892. "Die Instrumente und die wissenschaftlichen Hülfsmittel der Nautik zur Zeit der grossen Länder-Entdeckung." In *Hamburgische Festschrift zur Erinnerung an die Entdeckung Amerikas*, edited by Wissenschaftliche Ausschuss des Komités für die Amerika-Feier. Vol. 1.2. Hamburg: L. Friederichsen.

Gérando, Joseph-Marie de. 1839. *De la bienfaisance publique.* 4 vols. Paris: Jules Renouard et Cie.

Germann, Karl. 1913. *Die deutsche Möbelplüsch- und Moquette-Industrie. Geschichtliche Entwicklung und gegenwärtige Lage.* Leipzig: Veit.

Gerson, Johannes. 1483. *Opera.* 4 vols. Cologne: Johann Koelhoff.

Gersprach, E. 1892. *La manufacture nationale des Gobelins.* Paris: Delagrave.

Gerstmann, Bruno E. H., ed. 1909. *Beiträge zur Kulturgeschichte Schlesiens, 14. bis 20. Jahrhundert: aus den Familiengeschichten der Mentzel- und der Gerstmann'schen Nachkommenschaft, aus Staats-, Stadt-, Handels-, Gewerbe-, Vereins- und anderen Archiven, sowie vielen privaten, zeitgenössischen Aufzeichnungen, mit 17 Tafeln, Abbildungen von Personen, Liegenschaften, Plänen, Wappen, Siegeln, Münzen und mit Stammtafeln und Ahnentafeln.* Leipzig: B. E. H. Gerstmann.

Gibbins, H. de B. 1897. *Industry In England: Historical Outlines.* London: Methuen And Company Limited.

Glanvill, Joseph. 1681. *The Zealous and Impartial Protestant.* London: H. Brome.

Gleichen-Russwurm, Alexander von. 1911. *Das galante Europa: Geselligkeit der grossen Welt, 1600-1789.* Stuttgart: J. Hoffmann.

Gmelin, Johann Friedrich. 1783. *Beyträge zur Geschichte des teutschen Bergbaus, vornehmlich aus den mittlern und spätern Jahrhunderten unserer Zeitrechnung.* Halle: Johann Jacob Gebauer.

Gobbers, Joseph. 1883. "Die Erbleihe und ihr Verhältnis zum Rentenkauf im mittelalterlichen Köln des 12.-14. Jahrhunderts." *Zeitschrift der Savigny-Stiftung für Rechtsgeschichte: Die Germanistische Abteilung* 4: 130–214.

Godart, Justin. 1899. *L'Ouvrier en soie. Monographie du tisseur lyonnais. Étude historique, économique et sociale.* 3 vols. Lyon: Bernoux & Cumin.

Goethe, Johann Wolfgang von. 1808. *Faust. Eine Tragödie.* Tübingen: Cotta.

———. 1832. *Faust - Der Tragödie zweiter Teil.* Goethe's Werke. Vollständige Ausgabe aus letzter Hand 41. Stuttgart & Tübingen: Cotta.

———. 1890. *Faust: A Tragedy.* Translated by Bayard Taylor. 3rd ed. London: Ward, Lock & Co.

Goetze, Walter. 1912. "Das Wiederaufleben des römischen Rechts im 12. Jahrhundert." *Archiv für Kulturgeschichte* 10: 25 ff.

Goldast, Melchior. 1620. *Catholicon rei monetariae, sive Leges monarchicae generales de rebus nummariis et pecuniariis.* Frankfurt am Main: impensis Rulandiorum.

Goldstein, N. W. 1907. "Die Juden in der Amsterdamer Diamantindustrie." *Zeitschrift für Demographie und Statistik der Juden* 3 (12): 178–84.

Goncourt, Edmond de, and Jules de Goncourt. 1878. *La Du Barry.* Paris: G. Charpentier.

Gonner, Edward Carter Kersey. 1912. *Common Land and Inclosure.* London: Macmillan.

Gothein, Eberhard. 1892. *Wirtschaftsgeschichte des Schwarzwaldes und der angrenzenden Landschaften.* Strasbourg: Karl J. Trübner.

Gottheil, Richard James Horatio. 1901. "Contributions to the History of the Jews in Surinam." *American Jewish Historical Society* 9: 129–42.

Gottlob, Adolf. 1889. *Aus der Camera Apostolica des 15. Jahrhunderts: ein Beitrag zur Geschichte des päpstlichen Finanzwesens und des endenden Mittelalters.* Innsbruck: Wagner.

———. 1892. *Die päpstlichen Kreuzzugs-Steuern des 13. Jahrhunderts, ihre rechtliche Grundlage, politische Geschichte und technische Verwaltung.* Heiligenstadt: F.H. Cordier.

———. 1899. "Päpstliche Darlehensschulden des 13. Jahrhunderts." *Historisches Jahrbuch* 20: 665–717.

Götz, Wilhelm. 1888. *Die Verkehrswege im Dienste des Welthandels: Eine historisch-geographische Untersuchung.* Stuttgart: F. Enke.

Gouraud, Charles. 1854. *Histoire de la politique commerciale de la France et de son influence sur le progrès de la richesse publique.* 2 vols. Paris: A. Durand.

Gourville, J. Hérault de. 1838. *Mémoires concernant les affaires auxquelles il à été employé par la cour depuis jusqu'à 1698.* Mémoires pour servir à l'histoire de France 5. Paris.

Graetz, Heinrich. 1853. *Geschichte der Juden von den Anfängen bis auf die Gegenwart.* 11 vols. Berlin: Veit & Comp.

———. 1875. "Die Familie Gradis." *Monatsschrift für die Geschichte und Wissenschaft des Judenthums* 24 & 25: 24:447-459, 25:78-85.

Great Britain House of Commons. 1773. *Further [i.e. the Fourth] Report from the Committee of Secrecy Appointed by the House of Commons, Assembled at Westminster in the Sixth Session of the Thirteenth Parliament of Great Britain, to Enquire into the State of the East India Company.* London: T. Evans.

———. 1785. *Ninth Report from the Select Committee, Appointed to Take Into Consideration the State of the Administration of Justice in the Provinces of Bengal, Bahar and Orissa.* London: J. Debrett.

———. 1791. *An Abstract of the Evidence Delivered Before a Select Committee of the House of Commons in the Years 1790, and 1791, on the Part of the Petitioners for the Abolition of the Slave Trade.* London: James Phillips.

Great Britain Royal Commission on Historical Manuscripts. 1876. *Historical Manuscripts Commission Fifth Report.* London: H.M.S.O.

———, ed. 1888. *The Manuscripts of the Earl Cowper, K.G.: Preserved at Melbourne Hall, Derbyshire.* 3 vols. Historical Manuscripts Commission, 12th Report, Appendix. London: Royal Commission on Historical Manuscripts.

Green, Alice Stopford. 1894. *Town Life in the Fifteenth Century.* London: Macmillan & Company.

Gregorovius, Ferdinand. 1859. *Geschichte der Stadt Rom im Mittelalter: Vom fünften Jahrhundert bis zum sechzehnten Jahrhundert.* 8 vols. Stuttgart: Cotta.

Greppi, Emanuele. 1883. "Il Banco di S. Ambrogio." *Archivio storico lombardo* 10: 514–48.

Griesheim, Christian Ludwig von. 1759. *Die Stadt Hamburg in ihrem politischen, öconomischen und sittlichen Zustande; nebst Nachträgen zu diesem Tractate; und Beyträgen zu der Abhandlung: Anmerk. u. Zugaben über den Tractat die Stadt Hamburg, welche selbigen ebenfalls verbessern und gewisser machen.* Hamburg: Drese.

Griffen, Appleton P.C. 1900. *List of Books (with References to Periodicals) Relating to the Theory of Colonization, Government of Dependencies, Protectorates, and Related Topics.* Washington, D.C.: U.S. Government Printing Office.

Griselle, Eugène, ed. 1913. "[unknown]." *Documents d'histoire: XVIIe, XVIIIe, XIXe siècles* 4.

Grose, Francis. 1786. *Military Antiquities Respecting a History of the English Army, from the Conquest to the Present Time*. 2 vols. London: S. Hooper.

Grote, Hermann. 1857. *Münzstudien*. 9 vols. Leipzig: Hahn.

Grothe, Hermann. 1874. *Leonardo da Vinci als Ingenieur und Philosoph. Ein Beitrag zur Geschichte der Technik und der induktiven Wissenschaften*. Berlin: Nicolaische Verlag.

Grünberg, Carl. 1893. *Die Bauernbefreiung und die Auflösung des gutsherrlichbäuerlichen Verhältnisses in Böhmen, Mähren und Schlesien*. 2 vols. Leipzig: Duncker & Humblot.

———. 1901. "Unfreiheit." In *Handwörterbuch der Staatswissenschaften*, edited by Johann Conrad, Ludwig Elster, Wilhelm Lexis, and Edgar Loening, 2nd ed., 7:317–37. Jena: G. Fischer.

Grünhagen, Colmar. 1894. "Ueber den grundherrlichen Charakter des hausindustriellen Leinengewerbes in Schlesien und die Webernöte." *Zeitschrift für Social- und Wirtschaftsgeschichte* 2 (2): 241–61.

Grunwald, Max. 1902. *Portugiesengräber auf deutscher Erde: Beiträge zur Kultur-und Kunstgeschichte*. Hamburg: Alfred Janssen.

Guiffrey, Jules. 1881. *Comptes des bâtiments du roi sous le règne de Louis XIV*. 5 vols. Paris: Imprimerie Nationale.

———. 1885. *Inventaire général du mobilier de la couronne sous Louis XIV (1663-1715)*. 2 vols. Paris: La Société d'encouragement pour la propagation des livres d'art.

———. 1886. *Histoire de la tapisserie depuis le moyen âge jusqu'à nos jours*. Tours: Alfred Mame et fils.

Guillaume, Henri Louis Gustave. 1848. *Histoire de l'organisation militaire sous les ducs de Bourgogne*. Brussels: Académie Royale de Belgique.

Guizot, François, ed. 1825. *Vie de Philippe Auguste / Rigord. Vie de Philippe Auguste / Guillaume le Breton. Vie de Louis VIII*. Collection des mémoires relatifs à l'histoire de France, XI. Paris: J.-L.-J. Brière.

Häbler, Konrad. 1888. *Die wirtschaftliche Blüte Spaniens im 16. Jahrhundert*. Historische Untersuchungen, IX. Berlin: R. Gaertner.

———. 1894. "Welser und Ehinger in Venezuela." *Zeitschrift des historischen Vereins für Schwaben und Neuburg* 21: 66–86.

———. 1896. "Die Anfänge Der Sklaverei in Amerika." *Zeitschrift Für Social- Und Wirtschaftsgeschichte* 4: 176–223.

———. 1897. *Die Geschichte der Fugger'schen Handlung in Spanien*. Weimar: Emil Felber.

———. 1899. "Amerika." In *Weltgeschichte*, edited by Hans Ferdinand Helmolt, 1:181–574. Leipzig & Vienna: Bibliographisches Institut.

———. 1900. "Zur Geschichte des spanischen Kolonialhandels im 16. und 17. Jahrhundert." *Zeitschrift für Social- und Wirthschaftsgeschichte* 7: 373–437.

———. 1903. *Die überseeischen Unternehmungen der Welser und ihrer Gesellschafter.* Leipzig: C.L. Hirschfield.

———. 1907. *Geschichte Spaniens unter den Habsburgern.* Vol. 1. Allgemeine Staatengeschichte. 1. Abteilung: Geschichte der europäischen Staaten 36. Gotha: F. A. Perthes.

Haenle, Siegfried. 1867. *Geschichte der Juden im ehemaligen Fürstenthum Ansbach. Mit Urkunden und Regesten.* Ansbach: C. Junge.

Hahl, Albert. 1893. *Zur Geschichte der volkswirtschaftlichen Ideen in England gegen Ausgang des Mittelalters.* Jena: Gustav Fischer.

Hakluyt, Richard. 1598. *The Principall Navigations, Voyages, Traffiques, and Discoveries of the English Nation.* 3 vols. London: G. Bishop, R. Newberie & R. Barker.

Hale, Matthew. 1683. *A Discourse Touching Provision for the Poor.* London: W. Shrowsbery.

Hale, Thomas. 1758. *A Compleat Body of Husbandry.* 2nd ed. 4 vols. London: Thomas Osborne.

Hale, Thomas, and William Petty. 1691. *An Account of Several New Inventions and Improvements Now Necessary for England, in a Discourse by Way of Letter to the Earl of Marlbourgh, Relating to Building of Our English Shipping, Planting of Oaken Timber in the Forrests, Apportioning of Publick Taxes, the Conservacy of All Our Royal Rivers, in Particular That of the Thames, the Surveys of the Thames, &c. Herewith Is Also Published at Large The Proceedings Relating to the Mill'd-Lead-Sheathing, and the Excellency and Cheapness of Mill'd-Lead in Preference to Cast Sheet-Lead for All Other Purposes Whatsoever. Also A Treatise of Naval Philosophy.* London: James Astwood.

Hall, Hubert. 1901. *Society in the Elizabethan Age.* 4th ed. London: S. Sonnenschein, Lowrey & Company.

Hallam, Henry. 1818. *View of the State of Europe during the Middle Ages.* 3 vols. London: John Murray.

———. 1832. *Constitutional History of England from Henry VII to George II.* 3rd ed. 3 vols. London: J.M. Dent & Co.

Halle, Ernst von. 1891. *Die Hamburger Giro-Bank: und ihr Ausgang.* Studien zur Hamburgischen Handelsgeschichte 1. Berlin: Puttkammer & Mühlbrecht.

Halliwell-Phillipps, James Orchard. 1852. *Some Account of a Collection of Several Thousand Bills, Accounts, and Inventories, Illustrating the History of Prices between the Years 1650 and 1750*. Brixton Hill: C. & J. Adlard.

Hallwich, Hermann, ed. 1879. *Wallenstein's Ende: ungedruckte Briefe und Acten*. 2 vols. Leipzig: Duncker & Humblot.

Hamilton, Alexander. 1727. *A New Account of the East Indies. Being the Observations and Remarks of Capt. Alexander Hamilton, Who Spent His Time There from the Year 1688. to 1723. Trading and Travelling, by Sea and Land, to Most of the Countries and Islands of Commerce and Navigation, between the Cape of Goodhope, and the Island of Japon*. 2 vols. Edinburgh: J. Mosman.

Hanauer, Auguste. 1876. *Études économiques sur l'Alsace ancienne et moderne*. 2 vols. Strasbourg: Simon.

Handelmann, Heinrich. 1856. *Geschichte der Insel Hayti*. Kiel: Verlag der Schwersschen Buchhandlung.

———. 1860. *Geschichte von Brasilien*. Berlin: Springer.

Hantzsch, Viktor. 1895. *Deutsche Reisende des sechzehnten Jahrhunderts*. Leipziger Studien aus dem Gebiet der Geschichte, 1.4. Leipzig: Duncker & Humblot.

Häpke, Rudolf. 1905. "Die Entstehung der grossen bürgerlichen Vermögen im Mittelalter." *Jahrbuch für Gesetzgebung, Verwaltung und Volkswirtschaft im Deutschen Reiche* 29: 1052–87.

Harms, Bernhard. 1907. *Das Münz- und Geldpolitik der Stadt Basel im Mittelalter*. Zeitschrift für die gesamte Staatswissenschaft. Ergänzungsheft 23. Tübingen: H. Laupp.

Hartlib, Samuel. 1655. *Samuel Hartlib His Legacy of Husbandry*. London: Richard Wodnothe.

Hartmann, Ludo Moritz. 1900. *Geschichte Italiens im Mittelalter*. 2 vols. 32. Gotha: F. A. Perthes.

———. 1904. *Zur Wirtschaftsgeschichte Italiens im frühen Mittelalter: Analekten*. Gotha: F. A. Perthes.

Hartung, Johannes. 1898. "Aus dem Geheimbuche eines deutschen Handelshauses im 16. Jahrhundert." *Zeitschrift für Social- und Wirthschaftsgeschichte* 6: 36–87.

Hatschek, Hans J. 1887. *Das Manufakturhaus auf dem Tabor in Wien: Ein Beitrag zur österreichischen Wirthschaftsgeschichte des 17. Jahrhunderts*. Leipzig: Duncker & Humblot.

Haudecoeur, A. 1896. *Vie populaire de Saint Remi, évêque de Reims et apôtre des Francs*. Abbeville.

Hauser, Henri. 1903. "Les questions industrielles et commerciales dans les cahiers de la Ville et des communautés de Paris aux Etats généraux de 1614." *Vierteljahrsschrift für Social- und Wirtschaftsgeschichte* 1 (3/4): 372–96.

Haynes, Hopton. 1700. "Briefe Memoirs Relating to the Silver and Gold Coins of England; with an Account of the Corruption of the Hammered Moneys and of the Reform by the Late Grand Coynage at the Tower and the Five County Mints in the Years 1696, 1697, 1698 and 1699." Lansdowne MSS DCCCI. British Museum, London.

Hegel, Karl, Hermann Cardauns, and Karl Gustav Theodor Schröder, eds. 1875. *Die Chroniken der niederrheinischen Städte. Cöln.* 3 vols. Die Chroniken der deutschen Städte vom 14. ins 16. Jahrhundert 12–14. Leipzig: Hirzel.

Hegel, Karl, and Matthias von Lexer, eds. 1862. *Die Chroniken der fränkischen Städte: Nürnberg.* 5 vols. Die Chroniken der deutschen Städte vom 14. ins 16. Jahrhundert. Leipzig: S. Hirzel.

Hegel, Karl von. 1847. *Geschichte der Städteverfassung von Italien: seit der Zeit der römischen Herrschaft bis zum Ausgang des zwölften Jahrhunderts.* 2 vols. Leipzig: Weidmannsche Buchhandlung.

Heilmann, Johann. 1850. *Das Kriegswesen der Kaiserlichen und Schweden zur Zeit des dreißigjährigen Krieges.* Leipzig & Meissen: Goedsche.

Heineken, Hermann. 1908. *Der Salzhandel Lüneburgs mit Lübeck bis zum Anfang des 15. Jahrhunderts.* Historische Studien 63. Berlin: E. Ebering.

Heiss, Alois. 1865. *Descripcion general de las monedas Hispano-cristianas desde la invasion de los Arabes.* 3 vols. Madrid: R. N. Milagro.

Held, Adolf. 1871. "Noch einmal über den Preis des Geldes. Ein Beitrag zur Münzfrage." *Jahrbücher für Nationalökonomie und Statistik* 16: 315–40.

———. 1881. *Zwei Bücher zur Sozialen Geschichte Englands.* Leipzig: Duncker & Humblot.

Helferich, J. 1843. *Von den periodischen Schwankungen im Werth der edeln Metalle von der Entdeckung Amerikas bis 1830.* Nuremberg: J. L. Schrag.

Helps, Arthur. 1855. *The Spanish Conquest in America, and Its Relation to the History of Slavery and the Government of Colonies.* 4 vols. London: John W. Parker.

Hennert, Karl Wilhelm. 1790. *Beitrage zur brandenburgischen Kriegsgeschichte unter Kurfürst Friedrich dem Dritten nachherigem erstem Könige von Preussen.* Berlin & Stettin: Friedrich Nicolai.

Hentzner, Paul. 1757. *A Journey into England by Paul Hentzner In the Year MDXCVIII*. Edited by Horace Walpole. Translated by Richard Bentley. Strawberry-Hill.

Herbert, Edward, John Hayward, Francis Godwin, William Camden, and Arthur Wilson. 1706. *A Complete History Of England: With The Lives Of All The Kings and Queens Thereof; From the Earliest Account of Time, to the Death of His Late Majesty King William III. Containing a Faithful Relation of All Affairs of State, Ecclesiastical and Civil. The Whole Illustrated with Large and Useful Notes, Taken from Divers Manuscripts, and Other Good Authors: And Effigies of the Kings and Queens, from the Originals, Engraven by the Best Masters*. Vol. 2. 3 vols. London: Brab. Aylmer.

Herrera y Tordesillas, Antonio de. 1601. *Historia general de los hechos de los castellanos en las Islas y Tierra Firme del mar Océano que llaman Indias Occidentales*. 4 vols. Madrid: Juan Flamenco.

Herrmann, Ferdinand. 1900. *Schilderung und Beurteilung der gesellschaftlichen Verhältnisse Frankreichs in der Fabliauxdichtung des 12. und 13. Jahrhunderts*. Coburg: Rossteutscher.

Hertzberg, Gustav Friedrich. 1889. *Geschichte der Stadt Halle an der Saale von den Anfängen bis zur Neuzeit*. 3 vols. Halle: Buchhandlung des Waisenhauses.

Herzfeld, Marie. 1906. *Leonardo da Vinci. Der Denker, Forscher und Poet*. 2nd ed. Jena: E. Diederichs.

Herzog, Johann Jakob, ed. 1854. *Real-Encyklopädie für protestantische Theologie und Kirche*. 22 vols.

Herzog, Johann Jakob, Gustav Leopold Plitt, and Albert Hauck, eds. 1877. *Real-Encyklopädie für protestantische Theologie und Kirche*. 2nd ed. 18 vols. Leipzig: J.C.Hinrichs.

Hessus, Helius Eobanus. 1532. *Urbs Noriberga illustrata carmine heroico*. Joannes Petreius.

Heusler, Andreas, trans. 1900. *Die Geschichte vom Hühnerthorir: eine altisländische Saga*. Berlin: Wiegandt & Grieben.

Hewins, William Albert Samuel. 1892. *English Trade and Finance Chiefly in the Seventeenth Century*. University Extension Series. London: Methuen.

Heyck, Eduard. 1886. *Genua und seine Marine im Zeitalter der Kreuzzüge*. Innsbruck: Wagner.

Heyd, Wilhelm. 1879. *Geschichte des Levantehandels im Mittelalter*. 2 vols. Stuttgart: J.G. Cotta.

Heyking, Edmund Freiherr von. 1880. *Zur Geschichte Der Handelsbilanztheorie*. Berlin: Puttkammer & Mühlbrecht.

Heynen, Reinhard. 1905. *Zur Entstehung des Kapitalismus in Venedig.* Stuttgart & Berlin: Cotta.

Hilfman, P. A. 1907. "Some Further Notes on the History of the Jews in Surinam." *American Jewish Historical Society* 16: 7–22.

Hilliger, Benno. 1900. "Studien zu mittelalterlichen Massen und Gewichten." *Historische Vierteljahrsschrift* 3: 161–215.

Himly, Auguste. 1876. *Histoire de la Formation Territoriale des États de l'Europe Centrale.* 2 vols. Paris: Hachette et cie.

Hintze, Otto. 1906. "Die Epochen des evangelischen Kirchenregiments in Preußen." *Historische Zeitschrift* 97: 67–119.

———. 1910. "Der Commissarius und seine Bedeutung in der allgemeinen Verwaltungsgeschichte." In *Historische Aufsätze: Karl Zeumer zum sechzigsten Geburtstag als Festgabe dargebracht von Freunden und Schülern*, edited by Mario Krammer. Weimar: Böhlau.

Hippeau, Célestin. 1870. *L'industrie: le commerce et les travaux publics en Normandie au XVIIe et au XVIIIe siècles. Documents inédits.* Paris: A. Aubry.

Hirsch, Johann Christoph. 1756. *Des Teutschen Reichs Münz-Archiv.* 9 vols. Nuremberg: Adam Jonathon Felßeckers.

Histoire de l'hôpital général de Paris. 1676. Paris: F. Muguet.

Hitzinger, Peter. 1860. *Das Quecksilber-Bergwerk Idria, von seinem Beginne bis zur Gegenwart.* Laibach: Kleinmayr.

Hoffmann, Friedrich. 1907. *Kritische Dogmengeschichte der Geldwerttheorien.* Leipzig: C.L. Hirschfield.

Hopf, Carl. 1859. "Giustiniani (Familie aus Genua)." In *Allgemeine Encyclopädie der Wissenschaften und Künste, in alphabetischer Folge von genannten Schriftstellern*, edited by J. S. Ersch, J. G. Gruber, G. Hassel, and A. G. Hoffmann, 1.68 Giro – Glarus:308–41. Leipzig: F. A. Brockhaus.

Hoppensack, Johann Martin. 1796. *Ueber den Bergbau in Spanien überhaupt und den Quecksilber-Bergbau zu Almaden insbesondere.* Weimar: Industrie-Comptoir.

Hörnigk, Philipp Wilhelm von. 1750. *Oesterreich über alles, wann es nur will.* Frankfurt & Leipzig.

Hoste, Paul. 1697. *Théorie de la construction des vaisseaux, qui contient plusieurs traitez de mathématique sur des matières nouvelles et curieuses.* Lyon: Anisson & Posuel.

Hotten, John Camden, ed. 1874. *The Original Lists of Persons of Quality, Emigrants, Religious Exiles, Political Rebels, Serving Men Sold for a Term of Years, Apprentices, Children Stolen, Maidens Pressed, and Others Who Went from Great Britain to the American Plantations, 1600-1700. With Their Ages, the Localities Where They Formerly Lived in the Mother Country, the Names of the Ships in Which They Embarked, and Other Interesting Particulars, from Mss. Preserved in the State Paper Department of Her Majesty's Public Record Office, England.* London: John Camden Hotten.

Houtte, Hubert van. 1902. *Documents pour servir à l'histoire des prix de 1381 à 1794.* Brussels: Académie Royale des Sciences, des Lettres et des Beaux-Arts de Belgique, Commission Royale d'Histoire.

Houzé de l'Aulnoit, Aimé. 1889. *La finance d'un bourgeois de Lille au XVIIme siècle: livre de raison de François-Daniel Le Comte (1664-1717).* Lille: L. Danel.

Howard, John. 1777. *State of the Prisons in England and Wales, with Preliminary Observations, and an Account of Some Foreign Prisons.* London: W. Eyres.

Howell, James. 1869. *Instructions and Directions for Forreine Travell 1642. Collated with the Second Edition of 1650.* Edited by Edward Arber. English Reprints. London.

Hubert Hall. 1885. *A History of the Custom-Revenue in England: From the Earliest Times to the Year 1827.* 2 vols. London: Elliot Stock.

Hübner, Otto. 1853. *Die Banken.* Leipzig: Heinrich Hübner.

Hue, Otto. 1910. *Die Bergarbeiter: historische Darstellung der Bergarbeiter-Verhältnisse von der ältesten bis in die neueste Zeit.* 2 vols. Stuttgart: Dietz.

Hughson, Shirley Carter. 1894. *The Carolina Pirates and Colonial Commerce, 1670-1740.* Baltimore: The Johns Hopkins Press.

Hulme, Edward Wyndham. 1896. "The History of the Patent System under the Prerogative and at Common Law. Part I." *Law Quarterly Review* 12: 141–54.

———. 1900. "The History of the Patent System under the Prerogative and at Common Law. Part II." *Law Quarterly Review* 16: 44–56.

Humboldt, Alexander von. 1811. *Essai politique sur le royaume de la Nouvelle-Espagne.* 5 vols. Paris: F. Schoell.

———. 1814. *Political Essay on the Kingdom of New Spain.* Translated by John Black. 2nd ed. 4 vols. London: Longman, Hurst, Rees, Orme, & Brown.

———. 1838. "Ueber die Schwankungen der Goldproduktion mit Rücksicht auf staatswirthschaftliche Probleme." *Deutsche Vierteljahrs Schrift* 4: 1–40.

———. 1845. *Kosmos: Entwurf einer physischen Weltbeschreibung.* 5 vols. Stuttgart & Tübingen: Cotta.

Hume Brown, Peter. 1904. *Scotland in the Time of Queen Mary.* London: Methuen & Co.

Hume, David. 1754. *History of England.* 6 vols. London: A. Millar.

Hundeshagen, C. B. 1861. "Ueber einige Hauptmomente in der geschichtlichen Entwicklung des Verhältnisses zwischen Staat und Kirche, in Doves Zeitschrift für Kirche." Edited by Richard Dove. *Zeitschrift für Kirchenrecht* 1: 232–66; 444–90.

Hüne, Albert. 1820. *Vollständige historisch-philosophische Darstellung aller Veränderungen des Negersclavenhandels.* 2 vols. Göttingen: Johann Friedrich Röwer.

Hyamson, Albert Montefiore. 1907. *A History of the Jews in England.* London: Macmillan & Company.

Hyndman, Henry Mayers. 1883. *The Historical Basis of Socialism in England.* London: K. Paul, Trench & Co.

Inama-Sternegg, Karl Theodor. 1879. *Deutsche Wirtschaftsgeschichte.* 3 vols. Leipzig: Duncker & Humblot.

———. 1899. "Bevölkerung des Mittelalters und der neueren Zeit bis Ende des 18. Jahrhunderts in Europa." In *Handwörterbuch der Staatswissenschaften*, edited by Johann Conrad, Wilhelm Lexis, Ludwig Elster, and Edgar Loening, 2nd ed., 2:660–74. Jena: G. Fischer.

Inama-Sternegg, Karl Theodor von. 1895. "Die Goldwährung im deutschen Reiche während des Mittelalters." *Zeitschrift für Social- und Wirtschaftsgeschichte* 3: 1–60.

Ingram, John Kells. 1895. *A History of Slavery and Serfdom.* London: A. and C. Black.

Innocent VIII, Pope. 1538. *Liber aureus Practicis ipsis utilissimus: Regulas Cancellariae Apostolicae Innocentii VIII. nuperrime castigatas: ac earundem subtiles glorias: cum marginalibus Adnotametis, nec non Indice Alphabetico articulatim complectens: quibus ordinatim subjecte sunt Regulae Cacellariae Iuly II. cum uberrimis glossematibus. Ite Regulae apostolicae Clementis VIII.*

Jacob, William. 1831. *Historical Inquiry into the Production and Consumption of Precious Metals.* 2 vols. London: John Murray.

———. 1838. *Ueber Production und Consumtion der edlen Metalle: eine geschichtliche Untersuchung.* Translated by Carl Theodor von Kleinschrod. 2 vols. Rein'sche Buchhandlung.

Jacobs, Joseph. 1906a. "Banking." In *The Jewish Encyclopedia: A Descriptive Record of the History, Religion, Literature, and Customs of the Jewish People from the Earliest Times to the Present Day*, edited by Cyrus Adler and Isidore Singer, 2:491–93. New York: Funk & Wagnalls.

———. 1906b. "South Carolina." In *The Jewish Encyclopedia: A Descriptive Record of the History, Religion, Literature, and Customs of the Jewish People from the Earliest Times to the Present Day*, edited by Cyrus Adler and Isidore Singer, 11:480–81. New York: Funk & Wagnalls.

Jaffé, Moritz. 1909. *Die Stadt Posen unter preussischer Herrschaft: ein Beitrag zur Geschichte des deutschen Ostens.* Schriften des Vereins für Sozialpolitik, 119.2. Leipzig: Duncker & Humblot.

Jäger, Carl. 1831. *Ulms Verfassung, bürgerliches und commercielles Leben im Mittelalter.* Stuttgart & Heilbronn: F.C. Löflund & J.D. Claß.

Jäger, Eugen. 1890. *Die französische Revolution und die sociale Bewegung.* 2 vols. Berlin: Puttkammer und Mühlbrecht.

Jähns, Max. 1889. *Geschichte der Kriegswissenschaften: Vornehmlich in Deutschland.* 3 vols. Geschichte der Wissenschaften in Deutschland 21. Munich & Leipzig: R. Oldenbourg.

James, John. 1857. *History of the Worsted Manufacture in England, from the Earliest Times.* London: Longman, Brown, et al.

Janssen, Johannes. 1874. *Geschichte des deutschen Volkes seit dem Ausgang des Mittelalters.* 8 vols. Freiburg im Breisgau: Herder.

Jany, Curt. 1901. *Die Anfänge der alten Armee.* Urkundliche Beiträge und Forschungen zur Geschichte des Preußischen Heeres 1. Berlin: E.S. Mittler & Sohn.

Jars, Gabriel. 1774. *Voyages metallurgiques, ou Recherches et Observations.* 2 vols. Lyon: Gabriel Regnault.

Jastrow, J. 1914. "Kopernikus Münz- und Geldtheorie." *Archiv für Sozialwissenschaft und Sozialpolitik* 38: 734–51.

Jeffery, Reginald Welbury. 1908. *The History of the Thirteen Colonies of North America 1497-1763.* London: Methuen & Company.

Jellinek, Georg. 1895. *Die Erklärung der Menschen- und Bürgerrechte: Ein Beitrag zur modernen Verfassungsgeschichte.* Leipzig: Duncker & Humblot.

———. 1914. *Allgemeine Staatslehre.* 3rd ed. Berlin: O. Häring.

Joinville, Jean. 1906. *The Memoirs of the Lord of Joinville: A New English Version*. Translated by Ethel Kate Bowen-Wedgwood. London: J. Murray.

Joinville, Jean de. 1858. *Mémoires de Jean, sire de Joinville, ou Histoire et chronique du très-chrétien roi saint Louis*. Edited by Francisque Michel. Paris: Firmin Didot Freres, Fils et Cie.

Joneli, Hans. 1907. "Arbeitslosenfürsorge im alten Basel." *Basler Zeitschrift für Geschichte und Altertumskunde* 6: 180–283.

Jourdan, Athanase-Jean-Léger, Decrusy, François-André Isambert, Armet, and Alphonse-Honoré Taillandier, eds. 1822. *Recueil général des anciennes lois françaises, depuis l'an 420 jusqu'à la révolution de 1789*. 29 vols. Paris: Belin-Le-Prieur & Verdiere.

Jschchanian, B. 1913. *Die ausländischen Elemente in der russischen Volkswirtschaft*. Berlin: Franz Siemenroth.

Jurieu, Pierre. 1686. *Lettres pastorales addressées aux fideles de France, qui gemissent sous la captivité de Babylon*. 3 vols. Rotterdam: Acher.

Justi, Johann Heinrich Gottlobs von. 1758. *Staatswirtschaft oder systematische Abhandlung aller Oekonomischen un Cameralwissenschaften, die zur Regierung eines Landes erfordert werden*. 2nd ed. 2 vols. Leipzig: Bernhard Christoph Breitkopf.

———. 1760. *Gesammelte chymische Schriften worinnen das Wesen der Metalle und die wichtigsten chymischen Arbeiten vor dem Nahrungstand und das Bergwesen ausführlich abgehandelt werden*. 2 vols. Berlin & Leipzig: Buchladen der Real-Schule.

———. 1761. *Gesammlete politische und Finanzschriften über wichtige Gegenstände der Staatskunst, der Kriegswissenschaften und des Cameral- und Finanzwesens*. 3 vols. Copenhagen & Leipzig: Rothe.

Kaeppelin, Paul. 1908. *La Compagnie des Indes orientales et François Martin*. Paris: A. Challamel.

Kahn, Léon. 1892. *Les Juifs de Paris sous Louis XV (1721-1760)*. Paris: A. Durlacher.

Karajan, Theodor Georg von. 1838. "Beyträge zur Geschichte der landesfürstlichen Münze Wiens im Mittelalter." In *Der österreichische Geschichtsforscher*, edited by Joseph Chmel, 1:274–330, 401–500. Vienna: Carl Gerold.

Kaufmann, David. 1901. "Die Vertreibung der Marranen aus Venedig im Jahre 1550." *The Jewish Quarterly Review* 13 (3): 520–32.

Kautsky, Karl, and Eduard Bernstein. 1895. *Die Vorläufer des neueren Sozialismus: Von Thomas More bis zum Vorabend der französischen Revolution*. 2 vols. Stuttgart: J.H.W. Dietz.

Kayserling, Meyer. 1867. *Geschichte der Juden in Portugal*. Leipzig: Oskar Leiner.

———. 1900. "The Jews in Jamaica and Daniel Lopez Laguna." *Jewish Quarterly Review* 9: 708–17.

Keller, Ludwig. 1900. "Der Grosse Kurfürst und die Begründung des modernen Toleranzstaates." In *Der Protestantismus am Ende des XIX. Jahrhunderts in Wort und Bild*, edited by C. Werckshagen, 1:229–52. Berlin: Wartburg.

King, Gregory. 1804. *Natural and Political Observations and Conclusions upon the State and Condition of England 1696, by Gregory King, Esq., Lancaster Herald, to Which Is Prefixed a Life of the Author*. Edited by George Chalmers. London: J. Stockdale.

Kirchhoff, Alfred. 1870. *Die ältesten Weistümer der Stadt Erfurt über ihre Stellung zum Erzstift Mainz aus den Handschriften hg., erklärt und mit ausführlichen Abhandlungen versehen. Ein Beitrag zur Verfassungs- und Kulturgeschichte der deutschen Städte*. Halle: Buchhandlung des Waisenhauses.

Kirsch, Johann Peter. 1894. *Die päpstlichen Kollektorien in Deutschland während des 14. Jahrhunderts*. Quellen und Forschungen aus dem Gebiet der Geschichte 3. Paderborn: Ferdinand Schöningh.

Klein, Johann Wilhelm. 1792. *Ueber Armuth, Abstellung des Bettelns und Versorgung der Armen*. Nördlingen: Beck.

Klerk de Reus, Gerardus Cornelius. 1894. *Geschichtlicher Ueberblick der administrativen: rechtlichen und finanziellen Entwicklung der Niederländisch-Ostindischen Compagnie*. Batavia-Solo: Albrecht & Rusche.

Kling, Constantin. 1906. *Geschichte der Bekleidung, Bewaffnung und Ausrüstung des Königlich preussischen Heeres*. 3 vols. Weimar: Putze & Hölzer.

Klose, Samuel Benjamin. 1781. *Von Breslau: Dokumentirte Geschichte und Beschreibung. In Briefen*. 3 vols. Breslau: Korn.

Knapp, Georg Friedrich. 1891. "Ursprung der Sklaverei in den Kolonien." *Archiv für soziale Gesetzgebung und Statistik* 2: 129–45.

———. 1905. *Staatliche Theorie des Geldes*. Leipzig: Duncker & Humblot.

———. 1924. *The State Theory of Money*. Translated by H.M. Lucas and James Bonar. London: Macmillan & Company.

Koch, Anton. 1914. *Wesen und Wertung des Luxus*. Tübingen: J. C. B. Mohr.

Koch-Sternfels, Joseph Ernst von. 1820. *Die Tauern, insbesondere das Gasteiner Thal und seine Heilquellen*. Munich: Lindauer.

Koegel, Rudolf. 1897. *Geschichte der deutschen Literatur bis zum Ausgang des Mittelalters*. Vol. 1.2. Strasbourg: Karl J. Trübner.

Koehne, Carl. 1905. "[Review of Strieder's Zur Genesis des modernen Kapitalismus (1905)]." *Mitteilungen aus der historischen Literatur* 33: 178 ff.

Koenen, Hendrik Jakob. 1843. *Geschiedenis der Joden in Nederland.* Utrecht: C. van der Post.

Kohl, Dieter. 1910. "Überseeische Handelsunternehmungen oldenburgischer Grafen im 16. Jahrhundert." *Hansische Geschichtsblätter* 16: 417–39.

Kohler, Max James. 1894. "Phases of Jewish Life in New York Before 1800." *American Jewish Historical Society* 2: 77–100.

———. 1902. "Jewish Activity in American Colonial Commerce." *American Jewish Historical Quarterly* 10: 47–64.

Kohut, George A. 1895. "Les Juifs dans les colonies Hollandaises." *Révue des Études Juives* 31: 293–97.

König, Albin. 1899. *Die sächsische Baumwollindustrie am Ende des vorigen Jahrhunderts und während der Kontinentalsperre.* Leipzig: Teubner.

König, Anton Balthasar. 1787. *Alte und neue Denkwürdigkeiten der königlich preussischen Armee.* Berlin: Siegismund Friedrich Hesse.

———. 1790. *Annalen der Juden in den preußischen Staaten besonders in der Mark Brandenburg.* Berlin: Unger.

Kortum, Ernst Traugott von. 1795. *Über Judenthum und Juden: hauptsächlich in Rüksicht ihres Einflusses auf bürgerlichen Wohlstand.* Nuremberg: Raspe.

Kostanecki, Anton von. 1889. *Der öffentliche Kredit im Mittelalter. Nach Urkunden der Herzogtümer Braunschweig und Lüneburg.* Staats- und socialwissenschaftliche Forschungen 9. Leipzig: Duncker & Humblot.

———. 1909. *Arbeit und Armut. Ein Beitrag zur Entwicklungsgeschichte sozialer Ideen.* Freiburg im Breisgau: Herder.

———. 1912. *Dantes Philosophie des Eigentums.* Berlin & Leipzig: Rothschild.

Kowalewsky, Maxime. 1909. *La France économique à la veille de la Révolution.* 2 vols. Paris: V. Giard & E. Brière.

Krafft, Hans Ulrich. 1862. *Ein deutscher Kaufmann des sechzehnten Jahrhunderts: Hans Ulrich Krafft's Denkwürdigkeiten.* Edited and translated by Adolf Cohn. Göttingen: Vandenhoeck & Ruprecht.

Krause, Johann Heinrich. 1869. *Die Byzantiner des Mittelalters in ihrem Staats-, Hof- und Privatleben: insbesondere vom Ende des zehnten bis gegen Ende des vierzehnten Jahrhunderts nach den byzantinischen Quellen.* Halle: Schwetschke.

Kremer, Alfred von. 1875. *Culturgeschichte des Orients unter des Chalifen.* 2 vols. Vienna: Braumüller.

———. 1888. "Ueber das Budget der Einnahmen unter der Regierung des Hârûn alraśîd nach einer neu aufgefundenen Urkunde." In *Verhandlungen des VII Internationalen Orientalisten-Congresses gehalten in Wien, 1886. Semitische Sektion*, 1–18. Vienna: Alfred Hölder.

Kropatschek, Joseph, ed. 1804. *Oesterreichs Gesetze, welche den Commerzialgewerben und den Gewerbsleuten insbesondere vorgeschrieben worden sind, nebst Beifügung der Artikel und Ordnungen für jede Zunft und Innung.* 2 vols. Vienna.

Krügern, Johann Friedrich, ed. 1763. "Rede von den Ursachen und Würkungen des Mangels an Menschen, nebst den Hülfsmittel dawieder, gehalten den 10. May 1758." *Daniel Gottfried Schrebers Sammlung verschiedener Schriften, welche in die öconomischen, Policey- und Cameral-, auch andere verwandte Wissenschaften einschlagen* 10: 361–92.

Krünitz, Johann Georg, Friedrich Jakob Floerken, Heinrich Gustav Flörke, Johann Wilhelm David Korth, Ludwig Koßarski, and Carl Otto Hoffmann, eds. 1773. *Oeconomische Encyclopädie.* 242 vols. Berlin: Joachim Pauli.

Kulischer, Josef. 1908. "Warenhändler und Geldausleiher im Mittelalter." *Zeitschrift für Volkswirtschaft, Socialpolitik und Verwaltung* 17: 29–71, 201–54.

Kunckel von Löwenstern, Johann. 1767. *Vollständiges Laboratorium chymicum worinnen von den wahren Principiis in der Natur, der Erzeugung, den Eigenschaften und der Scheidung der Vegetabilien, Mineralien und Metalle wie auch von Verbesserung der Metalle gehandelt wird.* 4th ed. Berlin: Rüdiger.

Kunstmann, Friedrich. 1850. *Die Handelsverbindungen der Portugiesen mit Timbuktu im XV. Jahrhunderte.* Abhandlungen der III. Klasse der Königlichen bayrischen Akademie der Wissenheit, VI.1. Munich: Königliche bayrische Akademie der Wissenheit.

Kuske, Bruno. 1914. *Die städtischen Handels- und Verkehrsarbeiter und die Anfänge städtischer Sozialpolitik in Köln bis zum Ende des 18. Jahrhunderts.* Kölner Studien zum Staats-und Wirtschaftsleben. Bonn: A. Marcus & E. Webers.

Kuss, Henri. 1878. *Mémoire sur les mines et usines d'Almaden.* Paris: Dunod.

La Bruyère, Jean de. 1880. *Les caractères de La Bruyère.* Paris: Ernest Flammarion.

La Treille, François de. 1563. *Discours des villes, châteaux, et forteresses battues, assaillies et prises par la force de l'artillerie, durant les règnes des très-chrétiens rois Henri second et Charles IX, étant grand-maître et capitaine général d'icelle le seigneur Destrées, chevalier de l'ordre de leur Majesté.* Paris: G. Buon.

Labat, Jean-Baptiste. 1728. *Nouvelle relation de l'Afrique occidentale.* 5 vols. Paris: Guillaume Cavelier.

———. 1742. *Nouveau voyage aux isles de l'Amérique.* 8 vols. Paris: C.J.B. Delespine.

Laiglesia y Auset, Francisco de. 1904. *Los caudales de Indias en la primera mitad del siglo XVI.* Madrid: L. Aguado.

Lallemand, Léon. 1902. *Histoire de la charité.* 5 vols. Paris: Alphonse Picard et Fils.

Lamond, Elizabeth. 1893. *A Discourse of the Common Weal of This Realm of England.* Cambridge: Cambridge University Press.

Lamprecht, Karl. 1885. *Deutsches Wirtschaftsleben im Mittelalter. Untersuchungen über die Entwicklung der materiellen Kultur des Platten Landes auf Grund der Quellen zunächst des Mosellandes.* 4 vols. Leipzig: Alphons Dürr.

———. 1893. "Zum Verständniss der wirthschaftlichen und socialen Wandlungen in Deutschland vom 14. zum 16. Jahrhundert." *Zeitschrift für Social- und Wirtschaftsgeschichte* 1: 191–263.

Landau, Helene. 1906. "Die Entwicklung des Warenhandels in Österreich." *Zeitschrift für Volkswirtschaft, Socialpolitik und Verwaltung* 15: 1–29.

Landwehr, Hugo. 1894. *Die Kirchenpolitik Friedrich Wilhelms: des Großen Kurfüsten: Auf Grund archivalischer Quellen.* Berlin: E. Hofmann.

Lange, Friedrich Albert. 1910. *Die Arbeiterfrage.* Sozialistische Neudrucke, IV. Berlin: Vorwärts.

Langegg, Ferdinand Adalbert von. 1888. *El Dorado: Geschichte der Entdeckungsreisen nach dem Goldlande El Dorado im XVI. und XVII.* Leipzig: W. Friedrich.

Langer, Otto. 1891. *Sklaverei in Europa während der letzten Jahrhunderte des Mittelalters.* Bautzen: E.M.M. Monse.

Langlade, Émile. 1911. *La marchande de modes de Marie-Antoinette: Rose Bertin.* Paris: A. Michel.

———. 1913. *Rose Bertin: The Creator of Fashion at the Court of Marie-Antoinette.* London: J. Long.

Lappenberg, Johann Martin. 1842. *Hamburgisches Urkundenbuch.* 4 vols. Hamburg: Leopold Voss.

Lapsley, G. T. 1889. "The Account Roll of a Fifteenth Century Iron Master." *English Historical Review* 14: 509–29.

Laspeyres, Étienne. 1863. *Geschichte der volkswirthschaftlichen Anschauungen der Niederländer und ihrer Litteratur zur Zeit der Republik.* Leipzig: Hirzel.

Lastig, Gustav. 1879. "Beiträge zur Geschichte des Handelsrechts." *Zeitschrift für das gesamte Handelsrecht* 24: 387–449.

Lattes, Alessandro. 1882. *Il diritto commerciale nella legislazione statutaria delle città italiane.* Milan: Hoepli.

Lau, Theodor Ludwig. 1719. *Aufrichtiger Vorschlag von glücklicher, vorteilhafter und beständiger Einrichtung der Intraden und Einkünfte der Souveräne und ihrer Untertanen.* Frankfurt am Main.

Law, Alice. 1895. "The English Nouveaux-Riches in the Fourteenth Century." *Transactions of the Royal Historical Society* New Series, Vol. 9: 49–73.

Lawrence-Archer, James Henry. 1875. *Monumental Inscriptions of the British West Indies from the Earliest Date, with Genealogical and Historical Annotations, from Original, Local, and Other Sources, Illustrative of the Histories and Genealogies of the Seventeenth Century, the Calendars of State Papers, Peerages and Baronetages; with Engravings of the Arms of the Principal Families.* London: Chatto & Windus.

Lazari, Vincenzo. 1862. "Del traffico e delle condizioni degli schiavi in Venezia nei tempi di mezzo." *Miscellanea di storia italiana* 1: 463–501.

Le Blanc, François. 1690. *Traité historique des monnoyes de France , avec leurs figures, depuis le commencement de la monarchie jusqu'à présent.* Paris: Charles Robustel.

Leadam, Isaac Saunders, ed. 1897. *The Domesday of Inclosures, 1517-1518: Being the Extant Returns to Chancery for Berks, Bucks, Cheshire, Essex, Leicestershire, Lincolnshire, Northants, Oxon, and Warwickshire by the Commissioners of Inclosures in 1517 and for Bedfordshire in 1518; Together with Dugdale's Ms. Notes of the Warwickshire Inquisitions in 1517, 1518, and 1549.* 2 vols. London: Longmans, Green, and Co.

Leber, Constant. 1847. *Essai sur l'appréciation de la fortune privée au moyen âge.* 2nd ed. Paris: Guillaumin et cie.

Lecky, William Edward Hartpole. 1865. *History of the Rise and Influence of the Spirit of Rationalism in Europe.* 2nd ed. 2 vols. London: Longmans, Green and Co.

———. 1878. *A History of England in the Eighteenth Century*. 8 vols. London: Longman, Green and Co.

———. 1879. *Geschichte Englands im 18. Jahrhundert*. Translated by Ferdinand Löwe. 4 vols. Leipzig & Heidelberg: Winter.

Lecornu, Léon François Alfred. 1884a. *Sur la métallurgie du fer en basse-Normandie*. Caen: F. Le Blanc-Hardel.

———. 1884b. "Sur la métallurgie du fer en basse-Normandie." *Mémoires de l'Académie nationale des Sciences, Arts et Belles-Lettres de Caen*, 88–108.

Lenel, Walter. 1897. *Die Entstehung der Vorherrschaft Venedigs an der Adria mit Beiträgen zur Verfassungsgeschichte*. Strasbourg: Trübner.

Lenz, Friedrich, and Otto Unholtz. 1912. *Die Geschichte des Bankhauses Gebrüder Schickler. Festschrift zum 200 jährigen Bestehen*. Berlin: Gebrüder Schickler.

Leonard, E. M. 1900. *The Early History of English Poor Relief*. Cambridge: University Press.

Leonhard, Rudolf, Theodor Vogelstein, Moritz Julius Bonn, and Edgar Jaffé. 1913. *Grundfragen der englischen Volkswirtschaft*. Veröffentlichungen der Handelhochschule München 1. Munich & Leipzig: Duncker & Humblot.

Léris, Antoine de. 1754. *Dictionnaire portatif des théâtres, contenant l'origine des différens théâtres de Paris*. Paris: C.A. Jombert.

Leroy-Beaulieu, Paul. 1886. *De la colonisation chez les peuples modernes*. 3rd ed. Économistes et publicistes contemporains. Paris: Guillaumin et Cie.

L'Espine, Jacques Le Moine de. 1710. *Le negoce d'Amsterdam, ou, traité de sa banque: de ses changes, des compagnies orientales & occidentales, des marchandises qu'on tire de cette ville, & qu'on y porte de toutes les parties du monde, des poids, des mesures des aunages & du tarif*. Amsterdam: Chez Pierre Brunel.

L'Estoile, Pierre de. 1741. *Journal du regne de Henry IV. roi de France et de Navarre*. 4 vols. Paris: Vaillant.

Letaconnoux, J. 1906. "La question des subsistances et le commerce des grains en France au XVIIIe siècle." *Revue d'histoire moderne et contemporaine* VIII.

Leti, Gregorio. 1690. *Teatro Belgico, o vero ritratti historici, chronologici, politici, e geografici, delle sette Provincie Unite*. 2 vols. Amsterdam: Guglielmo de Jonge.

Levasseur, Emile. 1900. *Histoire des classes ouvrières et de l'industrie en France avant 1789*. 2 vols. Paris: Arthur Rousseau.

Levy, Alphonse. 1900. *Geschichte der Juden in Sachsen*. Berlin: S. Calvary & Co.

Levy, Hermann. 1909. *Monopole, Kartelle und Trusts in ihren Beziehungen zur Organisation der kapitalistischen Industrie, dargestellt an der Entwicklung in Grossbritannien*. Jena: G. Fischer.

———. 1912. *Die Grundlagen des ökonomischen Liberalismus in der Geschichte der englischen Volkswirtschaft*. Jena: Gustav Fischer.

Lewis, George Randall. 1908. *The Stannaries. A Study of the English Tin Miner*. Boston & New York: Houghton, Mifflin and Company.

Lexis, Wilhelm. 1879. "Beiträge zur Statistik der Edelmetalle nebst einigen Bemerkungen über die Werthrelationen." *Jahrbücher für Nationalökonomie und Statistik* 34 (5): 361–417.

———. 1900a. "Doppelwährung." In *Handwörterbuch der Staatswissenschaften*, edited by Johann Conrad, Ludwig Elster, Wilhelm Lexis, and Edgar Loening, 2nd ed., 3:237–52. Jena: G. Fischer.

———. 1900b. "Edelmetalle." In *Handwörterbuch der Staatswissenschaften*, edited by Johann Conrad, Ludwig Elster, Wilhelm Lexis, and Edgar Loening, 2nd ed., 3:260–65. Jena: G. Fischer.

———. 1900c. "Gold und Goldwährung." In *Handwörterbuch der Staatswissenschaften*, edited by Johann Conrad, Ludwig Elster, Wilhelm Lexis, and Edgar Loening, 2nd ed., 4:748–64. Jena: G. Fischer.

———. 1901a. "Schifffahrt." In *Handwörterbuch der Staatswissenschaften*, edited by Johann Conrad, Ludwig Elster, Wilhelm Lexis, and Edgar Loening, 2nd ed., 6:539–76. Jena: G. Fischer.

———. 1901b. "Silber und Silberwährung." In *Handwörterbuch der Staatswissenschaften*, edited by Johann Conrad, Ludwig Elster, Wilhelm Lexis, and Edgar Loening, 2nd ed., 6:725–46. Jena: G. Fischer.

Lexis, Wilhelm, Eduard Meyer, B. Pick, and Theo Sommerlad. 1900. "Münzwesen." In *Handwörterbuch der Staatswissenschaften*, edited by Johann Conrad, Ludwig Elster, Wilhelm Lexis, and Edgar Loening, 2nd ed., 5:898–933. Jena: G. Fischer.

Lexis, Wilhelm, and Theo Sommerlad. 1901. "Zur Geschichte der Preise." In *Handwörterbuch der Staatswissenschaften*, edited by Johann Conrad, Ludwig Elster, Wilhelm Lexis, and Edgar Loening, 2nd ed., 6:205–24. Jena: G. Fischer.

Libočan, Václav Hájek z. 1596. *Böhmische Chronica: Von Ursprung der Böhmen von irer Hertzogen und Konige Graffen Adels und Geschlechter Ankunfft, von jhren löblichen Ritterlichen Thaten, Item von der Städte und Schlösser Fundation und Anfang*. Translated by Johannes Sandel. 2 vols. Prague: Weidlich.

Liebe, Georg. 1899. *Der Soldat in der deutschen Vergangenheit*. Monographien zur deutschen Kulturgeschichte 1. Leipzig: E. Diederichs.
———. 1903. *Das Judentum in der deutschen Vergangenheit: aus dem fun-
fzehnten bis achtzehnten Jahrhundert*. Monographien zur
deutschen Kulturgeschichte 11. Leipzig: E. Diderichs.
Liebig, Justus von. 1878. *Chemische Briefe*. 6th ed. Leipzig: C. F. Winter.
Ligon, Richard. 1673. *A True And Exact History Of the Island of Bar-
badoes. Illustrated with a Map of the Island, as Also the Principal
Trees and Plants There, Set Forth in Their Due Proportions and
Shapes, Drawn out by Their Several and Respective Scales. To-
gether with the Ingenio That Makes the Sugar, with the Plots of
the Several Houses, Rooms, and Other Places, That Are Used in
the Whole Process of Sugar-Making; Viz. the Grinding-Room, the
Boyling-Room, the Filling-Room, the Curing-House, Still-House,
and Furnaces; All Cut in Copper*. London: Parker.
Lindner, Theodor. 1901. *Weltgeschichte seit der Völkerwanderung*. 9 vols.
Stuttgart & Berlin: Cotta.
Lingard, John. 1820. *A History of England from the First Invasion by the
Romans to the Accession of Henry 8*. 8 vols. London: J. Mawman.
Lipold, Marko Vincenc, ed. 1881. *Das K. K. Quecksilberbergwerk zu Idria
zur Feier des 300 jährigen staatlichen Besitzes*. Vienna: K. K. Ber-
gdirection zu Idria.
Lippert, Julius. 1896. *Social-Geschichte Böhmens in vorhussitischer zeit:
Ausschliesslich aus quellen*. 2 vols. Vienna: F. Tempsky.
Lippmann, Edmund Oskar. 1890. *Geschichte des Zuckers: seiner Darstel-
lung und Verwendung, seit den ältesten Zeiten bis zum Beginne
der Rübenzuckerfabrikation. Ein Beitrag zur Kulturgeschichte*.
Leipzig: Max Hesse.
Livi, Ridolfo. 1907. "La schiavitù medioevale: e la sua influenza sui caratteri
antropologici degli italiani." *Rivista italiana di sociologia* IX (IV–
V): 557–81.
Llorente, Juan Antonio. 1817. *Histoire critique de l'Inquisition espagnole*. 4
vols. Paris: Treuttel & Wurtz.
———. 1826. *The History of the Inquisition of Spain, from the Time of Its
Establishment to the Reign of Ferdinand VII*. London: G. B. Whit-
taker.
Lochner, Georg Wolfgang Karl. 1845. *Lochner, Nürnbergs Vorzeit und Gegenwart*. Nürnberg: Campe.
Loewe, Victor. 1895. *Die Organisation und Verwaltung der Wallen-
steinschen Heere*. Freiburg im Breisgau: Mohr.

Lohmann, Friedrich. 1900. *Die staatliche Regelung der englischen Wollindustrie vom XV. bis zum XVIII. Jahrhundert*. Staats- und socialwissenschaftliche Forschungen, 18.1. Leipzig: Duncker & Humblot.

Löhneisen, Georg Engelhard von. 1609. *Della cavalleria: gründtlicher Bericht von allem was zu der Reutterei gehörig und einem Cavallier davon zu wissen geburt*. Remlingen.

Loria, Achille. 1896. "Die Sklavenwirtschaft im modernen Amerika und im europaischen Altertume." *Zeitschrift für Social- und Wirthschaftsgeschichte* 4: 67–118.

———. 1901. *Il capitalismo e la scienza: studj e polemiche*. Turin: Fratelli Bocca.

Lorini, Buonaiuto. 1609. *Le fortificationi di Buonaiuto Lorini nobile fiorentino*. Venice: Francesco Rampazetto.

Louis XIV. 1860. *Mémoires de Louis XIV pour l'instruction du Dauphin: D'après les textes originaux avec une étude sur leur composition, des notes et des éclaircissements*. Edited by Charles Dreyss. 2 vols. Paris: Didier.

Loyseau, Charles. 1610. *Le traité des ordres et simples dignités*. Paris: Abel L'Angelier.

Luard, Henry Richards, ed. 1872. *Matthaei Parisiensis, Monachi Sancti Albani, Chronica Majora*. 7 vols. Rerum brittanicarum medii Aevi Scriptores. London: Longman & Co, et al.

Luard, John Dalbiac. 1852. *A History of the Dress of the British Soldier from the Earliest Period to the Present Time*. London: William Clowes & Sons.

Lübke, Wilhelm. 1868. *Geschichte der Renaissance Frankreichs*. Geschichte der neueren Baukunst, 4.2. Stuttgart: Ebner & Seubert.

Lucas, Charles Prestwood. 1905. *A Historical Geography of the British Colonies*. 2nd ed. 6 vols. Oxford: Clarendon Press.

Ludovici, Carl Günther. 1741. *Allgemeine Schatzkammer der Kaufmannschaft oder Vollständiges Lexikon aller Handlungen und Gewerbe so wohl in Deutschland als auswärtigen Königreichen und Ländern*. 4 vols. Leipzig: Heinsius.

———. 1768. *Grundriss eines vollständigen Kaufmanns-Systems, nebst den Anfangsgründen der Handlungswissenschaft, und angehängter kurzen Geschichte der Handlung zu Wasser und zu Lande woraus man zugleich den gegenwärtigen Zustand der Handlung von Europa, auch bis in die andern Welttheile, erkennen kann, zum Dienste der Handlungsbeflissene entworfen*. 2nd ed. Leipzig: Bernhard Christoph Breitkopf.

Lueder, August Ferdinand. 1808. *Ueber die Industrie und Kultur der Portugiesen*. Berlin: Duncker & Humblot.

Luschin von Ebengreuth, Arnold. 1904. *Allgemeine Münzkunde und Geldgeschichte des Mittelalters und der neuren Zeit*. Handbuch der mittelalterlichen und neueren Geschichte 5. Munich & Berlin: R. Oldenbourg.

Luther, Martin. 1909. *D. Martin Luthers Werke. Kritische Gesamtausgabe*. Vol. 30.2. Weimar: Hermann Böhlaus Nachfolger.

Macaulay, Thomas Babington. 1855. *The History of England from the Accession of James II*. 5 vols. London: Longman, Brown, et al.

Mackintosh, John. 1892. *The History of Civilisation in Scotland*. 2nd ed. 4 vols. London: Alexander Gardner.

Macpherson, David, and Adam Anderson. 1805. *Annals of Commerce, Manufactures, Fisheries, and Navigation, with Brief Notices of the Arts and Sciences Connected with Them. Containing the Commercial Transactions of the British Empire and Other Countries, from the Earliest Accounts to the Meeting of the Union Parliament in January, 1801; and Comprehending the Most Valuable Part of the Late Mr. Anderson's History of Commerce with a Large Appendix*. 4 vols. London: Nichols.

Macquer, Philippe. 1766. *Dictionnaire Portatif Des Arts Et Métiers: Contenant en abrégé L'Histoire, La Description & La Police Des Arts Et Métiers, Des Fabriques Et Manufactures de France & des Pays Etrangers*. 3 vols. Paris: Lacombe.

Madox, Thomas. 1769. *The History and Antiquities of the Exchequer of the Kings of England*. 2 vols. London: William Owen & Benjamin White.

Main, A. 1893. *I Pisani alle prime Crociate*. Livorno: Meucci.

Maitland, Frederic William. 1907. *Domesday Book and Beyond: Three Essays in the Early History of England*. Cambridge: Cambridge University Press.

Maliniak, Julian. 1913. *Die Entstehung der Exportindustrie und des Unternehmerstandes in Zürich im XVI. und XVII. Jahrhundert*. Zurich & Leipzig: Rascher.

Malvezin, Théophile. 1875. *Histoire des Juifs à Bordeaux*. Bordeaux: C. Lefebvre.

Malynes, Gerard. 1623. *The Center of the Circle of Commerce*. London: W. Jones.

Mandeville, Bernard. 1723. *The Fable of the Bees: Or, Private Vices, Publick Benefits*. 2nd ed. London: E. Parker.

Marbault, Pierre. 1837. *Remarques sur les mémoires des sages et royales oeconomies d'estat, domestiques, politiques et militaires de Henry le Grand, etc., de Maximilian de Béthune, duc de Sully*. Paris: Didot.

Marin, Carlo Antonio. 1798. *Storia Civile E Politica Del Commercio de' Veneziani*. 8 vols. Venice: Coleti.

Markgraf, Richard. 1894. *Zur Geschichte der Juden auf den Messen in Leipzig von 1664-1839. Ein Beitrag zur Geschichte Leipzigs*. Bischofswerda: Friedrich Wey.

Marmont Du Hautchamp, Barthélemy. 1739. *Histoire du système des finances, sous la minorité de Louis XV. Pendant les années 1719 & 1720*. 6 vols. La Haye: Pierre de Hondt.

Marperger, Paul Jacob. 1704. *Der Geöffnete Ritter-Platz*. Hamburg: Benjamin Schiller.

———. 1717. *Beschreibung Der Banquen Und deroselben Wie auch Der Banquiers Ihrem Recht*. Leipzig: Johann Christian Martini.

———. 1721. *Das neu-eröffnete Manufacturen-Haus*. Hamburg: Johann Christoph Kisner.

Marquart, Johann. 1662. *Tractatus politico-juridicus de jure mercatorum et commerciorum singulari*. Frankfurt am Main: Thomae Matthiae Gotzii.

Martin, Germain. 1899. *La grande industrie sous le regne de Louis XIV*. Paris: Rousseau.

———. 1900. *La grande industrie en France sous le règne de Louis XV*. Paris: A. Fontemoing.

———. 1913. *L'histoire du crédit en France sous le règne de Louis XIV*. Paris: J.-B. Sirey.

Martin, Robert Montgomery. 1838. *The History, Antiquities, Topography, and Statistics of Eastern India*. 3 vols. London: W. H. Allen and Company.

Marx, Karl. 1859. *Zur Kritik der politischen Ökonomie*. Berlin: F. Duncker.

———. 1903. *Das Kapital: Kritik Der Politischen Ökonomie*. 5th ed. 4 vols. Hamburg: Otto Meissner.

———. 1904. *A Contribution to the Critique of Political Economy*. Translated by N.I. Stone. Chicago: Charles H. Kerr.

———. 1906. *Capital. A Critique of Political Economy*. Edited by Frederick Engels. Translated by Samuel Moore and Edward Aveling. New York: The Modern Library.

März, Johannes. 1906. *Die Fayencefabrik zu Mosbach in Baden*. Jena: G. Fischer.

Mas Latrie, Jaques Marie Joseph Louis. 1852. *Histoire de l'île de Chypre sous le règne des princes de la maison de Lusignan*. 3 vols. Paris: L'Imprimerie Impériale.

Masetti Bencini, Ida. 1897. "Firenze e le isole della Capraia e della Pianosa." In *Archivio Storico Italiano*, 5/19:110–12. Florence: G.P. Vieusseux.

Masson, Paul. 1908. *Les compagnies du corail: étude historique sur le commerce de Marseille au XVIe siècle et les origines de la colonisation française en Algérie-Tunisie*. Paris & Marseille: Fontemoing & Barlatier.

Matagrin, Amédée. 1905. *Histoire de la tolérance religieuse: évolution d'un principe social*. Paris: Librairie Fischbacher.

Mathesius, Johann. 1587. *Bergpostilla, Oder SAREPTA*. Nuremberg: Gerlachin.

Matschoss, Conrad. 1912. *Friedrich der Große als Beförderer des Gewerbefleißes. Zur 200. Wiederkehr des Geburtstages Friedrichs des Großen im Auftrage des Vereins zur Beförderung des Gewerbfleißes verfasst*. Berlin: Leonhard Simon.

Maurer, Georg Ludwig von. 1870. *Geschichte der Städteverfassung in Deutschland*. 4 vols. Erlangen: Ferdinand Enke.

Mavor, James. 1914. *An Economic History of Russia*. 2 vols. London and Toronto: J.M. Dent & Sons.

Mayet, Etienne. 1786. *Mémoire sur les manufactures de Lyon*. London: Moutard.

McCormac, Eugene Irving. 1904. *White Servitude in Maryland, 1634-1820*. Baltimore: Johns Hopkins Press.

McCulloch, John Ramsay. 1880. *A Dictionary, Practical, Theoretical and Historical of Commerce and Commercial Navigation*. Edited by Hugh G. Reid. New. London: Longman, Green and Co.

Meinardus, Otto. 1891. "Beiträge Zur Geschichte Der Handelspolitik Des Grossen Kurfürsten." *Historische Zeitschrift* 66 (3): 444–95.

Meitzen, August. 1895. *Siedelung Und Agrarwesen Der Westgermanen Und Ostgermanen, Der Kelten, Römer, Finnen Und Slawen*. 3 vols. Wanderungen, Anbau Und Agrarrecht Der Völker Europas Nördlich Der Alpen 1. Berlin: Wilhelm Hertz.

Mélamed, Sam Max. 1910. *Der Staat im Wandel der Jahrtausende*. Studien zur Geschichte des Staatsgedankens. Stuttgart: Enke.

Meltzing, Otto. 1906. *Das Bankhaus der Medici und seine Vorläufer*. Volkswirtschaftliche und wirtschaftsgeschichtliche Abhandlungen: Neue Folge 6. Jena: Gustav Fischer.

Mensi, Franz von. 1890. *Die Finanzen Oesterreichs von 1701 bis 1740*. Vienna: Manz'sche K.u.K. Hof-Verlags- und Universitäts-Buchhandlung.

Mention, Léon. 1900. *L'Armée de l'ancien régime: de Louis XIV à la Révolution*. Paris: L.H. May.

Mercado, Tomás de. 1569. *Tratos y contratos de mercaderes y tratantes decididos y determinados*. Salamanca: Mathias Gast.

Mercier, Louis-Sébastien. 1782. *Tableau de Paris*. 12 vols. Amsterdam.

Merivale, Herman. 1861. *Lectures on Colonization and Colonies: Delivered Before the University of Oxford in 1839, 1840, & 1841*. London: Longman, Green, Longman and Roberts.

Meyer, Martin. 1668. "24 October 1666." *Philemeri Irenici Elisii Diarium Europaeum* 16 (1).

Michel, Francisque. 1852. *Recherches sur le commerce, la fabrication et l'usage des étoffes de soie, d'or et d'argent et autres tissus précieux en Occident, principalement en France, pendant le Moyen Age*. Vol. 1. Paris: Crapelet.

Michelet, Jules. 1893. *Histoire de France*. 16 vols. Paris: E. Flammarion.

Mirabeau, Honoré Gabriel Riquetti, Comte de. 1788. *De la monarchie prussienne sous Frédéric le Grand*. Vol. 1. London.

Mises, Ludwig von. 1905. "Zur Geschichte der österriechischen Fabrikgesetzgebung." *Zeitschrift für Volkswirtschaft, Sozialpolitik und Verwaltung* 14: 209–71.

Möllenberg, Walter. 1911. *Die Eroberung des Weltmarkts durch das mansfeldische Kupfer*. Gotha: F. A. Perthes.

Mollwo, Carl, ed. 1901. *Das Handlungsbuch von Hermann und Johann Wittenborg*. Leipzig: Dyk.

Monin, Hippolyte. 1891. "Les Juifs de Paris à la fin d l'Ancien Régime." *Revue des études juives* 23: 85–98.

Monson, William. 1902. *The Naval Tracts of Sir William Monson in Six Books*. Edited by Michael Oppenheim. 5 vols. London: Navy Records Society.

Montaigne, Michel de. 1820. *Essais*. Edited by Amaury Duval. 6 vols. Paris: Chassérian.

———. 1842. *The Essays of Montaigne*. Edited by William Hazlitt. Translated by Charles Cotton. London: John Templeman.

Montesquieu, Charles Louis. 1721. *Lettres persanes*. Cologne: Pierre Marteau.

Montvéran, Tournachon de. 1833. *Essai de statistique raisonnée sur les colonies européennes des tropiques et sur les questions coloniales*. Paris: Delaunay.

Moranvillé, Henri. 1887. "Rapports à Philippe VI sur l'état de ses finances." *Bibliothèque de l'École des chartes* 48: 380–95.

Moreau, C. 1853. *Choix de mazarinades*. 2 vols. Paris: Jules Renouard et Cie.

Moreau de Jonnès, Alexandre. 1837. *Statistique de la Grande-Bretagne et de l'Irlande*. 2 vols. Paris: Bourgogne et Martinet.

———. 1842. *Recherches statistiques sur l'esclavage colonial et sur les moyens de le supprimer*. Paris: Bourgogne et Martinet.

———. 1867. *État économique et social de la France depuis Henri IV jusqu'à Louis XIV, 1589 à 1715*. Paris: C. Reinwald.

Morris, Henry C. 1900. *The History of Colonization, from the Earliest Times to the Present Day*. 2 vols. New York and London: Macmillan & Company.

Moscherosch, Hans Michel. 1900. *Gesichte Philanders von Sittenwald*. Edited by Felix Bobertag. Deutsche National-Literatur 32. Berlin & Stuttgart: W. Spemann.

Moseley, Benjamin. 1799. *A Treatise on Sugar*. London: G.G. & J. Robinson.

———. 1800. *Abhandlung über den Zucker*. Translated by Karl August Nöldechen. Berlin & Stettin: Friedrich Nicolai.

Mosnier, L. 1898. *Origines et développement de la grande industrie en France du xv siècle à la Révolution*. Paris: A. Fontemoing.

Mothe-Fénelon, François de Pons de Salignac de La. 1825. *Lettre de Fénelon à Louis XIV*. Paris: Antoine-Augustin Renouard.

Motley, John Lothrop. 1860. *History of the United Netherlands*. 4 vols. London: John Murray.

Muffat, Karl August. 1868. "Beiträge zur Geschichte des bayerischen Münzwesens unter dem Hause Wittelsbach vom Ende des zwölften bis in das sechzehnte Jahrhundert." *Abhandlungen der Königlichen bayrischen Akademie der Wissenschaft, III Klasse* IX (I): 204–69.

Müllner, Alfons. 1909. *Geschichte Des Eisens in Inner-Österreich von Der Urzeit Bis Zum Anfange Des XIX. Jahrhunderts*. Vol. 1. Vienna and Leipzig: Helm und Goldmann.

Mun, Thomas. 1895. *England's Treasure by Forraign Trade*. New York: Macmillan & Company.

Müntz, Eugène. 1899. "L'argent et le luxe a la cour pontificale d'Avignon." *Revue des questions historiques* 66: 5–44, 378–406.

Muratori, Lodovico Antonio. 1738. *Antiquitates italicæ medii ævi, sive Dissertationes*. 6 vols. Rome: Mediolani.

Mylius, Christian Otto, ed. 1737. *Corpus Constitutionum Marchicarum, Oder Königl. Preußis. und Churfürstl. Brandenburgische in der Chur- und Marck Brandenburg, auch incorporirten Landen publicirte und ergangene Ordnungen, Edicta, Mandata, Rescripta etc. Von Zeiten Friedrichs I. Churfürstens zu Brandenburg, etc. biß ietzo unter der Regierung Friderich Wilhelms, Königs in Preußen etc. ad annum 1736 inclusivè.* 6 vols. Berlin & Halle: Buchladen des Waisenhauses.

Naudé, Wilhelm. 1896. *Die Getreidehandelspolitik der Europäischen Staaten vom 13. bis zum 18. Jahrhundert, als Einleitung in die Preußische Getreidehandelspolitik.* Acta Borussica, Getreidehandelspolitik 1. Berlin: Paul Parey.

———. 1901. *Die Getreidehandelspolitik und Kriegsmagazinverwaltung Brandenburg-Preussens bis 1740.* Edited by Gustav von Schmoller. Acta Borussica, Getreidehandelspolitik 2. Berlin: Paul Parey.

Naville, François Marc Louis. 1836. *De la charité légale, de ses effets, de ses causes.* 2 vols. Paris: Dufart.

Neal, Daniel. 1822. *The History of the Puritans; or, Protestant Nonconformists; from the Reformation in 1517, to the Revolution in 1688.* Edited by Joshua Toulmin. 5 vols. London: W. Baynes and Son.

Nebenius, Carl Friedrich. 1829. *Ueber die Natur und die Ursachen des öffentlichen Credits, Staatsanlehen, die Tilgung der öffentlichen Schulden, den Handel mit Staatspapieren und die Wechselwirkung zwischen den Creditoperationen der Staaten und dem ökonomischen und politischen Zustande der Länder.* Karlsruhe: Marx.

Necker, Jacques. 1781. *Compte rendu au roi.* Paris: Imprimerie Royale.

———. 1784. *De l'administration des finances de la France.* 3 vols. Paris: Panckouke.

———. 1788. *Sur le compte rendu au Roi en 1781. Nouveaux éclaircissemens.* Paris: Hotel de Thou.

Nemnich, Philipp Andreas. 1800. *Beschreibung einer im Sommer 1799 von Hamburg nach und durch England geschehenen Reise.* Tübingen: Cotta.

Netscher, Pieter Marinus. 1853. *Les Hollandais au Brésil: notice historique sur les Pays-Bas et le Brésil au XVIIe siècle.* La Haye: Belinfante.

Neubauer, Theodor Thilo. 1916. "Wirtschaftsleben im mittelalterlichen Erfurt." *Vierteljahrsschrift für Sozial- und Wirtschaftsgeschichte* 13: 132–52.

Neuburg, Clamor. 1892. *Goslars Bergbau Bis 1552.Ein Beitrag Zur Wirthschafts- Und Verfassungsgeschichte Des Mittelalters.* Hanover.

Neuburger, Otto. 1913. *Die Mode. Wesen, Entstehen und Wirken*. Berlin: Franz Siemenroth.

Neudörffer, Johann. 1875. *Des Johann Neudörfer Schreib- und Rechenmeisters zu Nürnberg Nachrichten von Künstlern und Werkleuten daselbst aus dem Jahre 1547*. Edited by G.W. Lochner. Quellenschriften für Kunstgeschichte und Kunsttechnik des Mittelalters und der Renaissance 10. Vienna: W. Braumüller.

Neumann, Bernhard. 1904. *Die Metalle: Geschichte, Vorkommen und Gewinnung, nebst ausführlicher Produktions- und Preis-Statistik*. Halle: W. Knapp.

Neumann, Max. 1865. *Geschichte des Wuchers in Deutschland bis zur Begründung der heutigen Zinsengesetze (1654)*. Halle: Buchhandlung des Waisenhauses.

Nicolai, Friedrich. 1783. *Beschreibung einer Reise durch Deutschland und die Schweiz im Jahre 1781*. 12 vols. Berlin & Stettin: Friedrich Nicolai.

Nieuhoff, John, John Smith, La Peyrere, Thomas James, Feodor Iskowitz Backhoff, Zachary Wagener, Ferdinand Colombus, and John Greaves. 1704. *A Collection of Voyages and Travels, Some Now First Printed from Original Manuscripts. Others Translated out of Foreign Languages, and Now First Publish'd in English. To Which Are Added Some Few That Have Formerly Appear'd in English, but Do Now for Their Excellency and Scarceness Deserve to Be Re-Printed*. Vol. 2. 4 vols. London: Awnsham & John Churchill.

Nirrnheim, Hans, ed. 1895. *Das Handlungsbuch Vickos von Geldersen*. Hamburg & Leipzig: L. Voss.

Nöggerath, Adalbert. 1862. "Mittheilungen über die Quecksilberbergwerke zu Almadén und Almadenejos in Spanien nebst einen Ueberblick der Vorkommnisse von Quecksilber im Allgemeinen." *Zeitschrift für das Berg-, Hütten- und Salinenwesen im preussischen Staate* 10: 361–92.

Noiret, Hippolyte, ed. 1892. *Documents inédits pour servir à l'histoire de la domination vénitienne en Crète de 1380 à 1485: tirés des archives de Venise*. Bibliothèque des Écoles Françaises d'Athènes et de Rome 61. Paris: Thorin & Fils.

Nopp, Johann. 1632. *Aacher Chronick, das ist eine kurtze, historische Beschreibung aller gedenckwürdiger Antiquitäten und Geschichten, sampt zugefügten Privilegien und Statuten*. 3 vols. Cologne: Hartger Woringen.

Normand, Charles. 1908. *La Bourgeoisie française au XVII siècle*. Paris: Félix Alcan.

Normand, Jacques, and Gaston Raynaud, eds. 1877. *Aiol: chanson de geste.* Société des Anciens Textes Français. Paris: Firmin Didot.

North, Roger. 1742. *The Life of the Right Honourable Francis North, Baron of Guilford, Lord Keeper of the Great Seal, under King Charles II. and King James II. Wherein Are Inserted the Characters of Sir Matthew Hale, Sir George Jeffries, Sir Leoline Jenkins, Sidney Godolphin, and Others, the Most Eminent Lawyers and Statesmen of That Time.* London: J. Whiston.

Nübling, Eugen. 1903. *Zur Währungsgeschichte des Merkantilzeitalters: Ein Beitrag zur Deutschen Wirtschaftsgeschichte.* Ulm: Gebrüder Nübling.

Nuglisch, Adolf. 1904. "Zur Frage nach der Entstehung des modernen Kapitalismus." *Jahrbücher für Nationalökonomie und Statistik,* 3, 28 (2): 238–50.

O'Callaghan, Edmund Bailey, and Berthold Fernow, eds. 1853. *Documents Relative to the Colonial History of the State of New York; Procured in Holland, England, and France.* 15 vols. Albany: Weed, Parsons & Co.

Ochenkowski, Władyslaw von. 1879. *Englands wirtschaftliche Entwickelung im Ausgange des Mittelalters.* Making of the Modern World 2. Jena: G. Fischer.

Oppenheim, Michael. 1896. *A History of the Administration of the Royal Navy and of Merchant Shipping in Relation to the Navy.* Vol. 1. London and New York: John Lane.

Oppenheimer, Franz. 1907. *Der Staat.* Frankfurt am Main: Rütten & Loening.

———. 1926. *The State: Its History and Development Viewed Sociologically.* Translated by John M. Gitterman. New York: Vanguard Press.

Oppenheimer, Samuel. 1907. "An Early Jewish Colony in Western Guiana, 1658-1666; And Its Relation to the Jewsin Surinam, Cayenne and Tobago." *American Jewish Historical Society* 16: 95–186.

Ouvrard, Gabriel Julien. 1827. *Mémoires de G. J. Ouvrard sur sa vie et ses diverses opérations financières.* 4th ed. 3 vols. Brussels: Galand et Lejeune.

Owen, Robert. 1813. *A New View of Society: Or, Essays on the Principle of the Formation of the Human Character, and the Application of the Principle to Practice.* London: Cadell & Davies.

Pacheco, Joaquín F., Francisco de Cárdenas, and Luis Torres de Mendoza, eds. 1864. *Colección de documentos inéditos relativos al descubrimiento, conquista y colonización de las posesiones españolas en América y Oceanía.* 42 vols. Madrid: Bernaldo de Quirós.

Pagnini, Giovanni Francesco. 1765. *Della Decima e di varie altre Gravezze Imposte dal Comune di Firenze.* 4 vols. Lisbon & Lucca: G. Bouchard.

Palissy, Bernard. 1580. *Discours admirables de la nature des eaux et fontaines tant naturelles qu'artificielles, des metaux, des sels & salines, des pierres, des terres, du feu & des emaux.* Paris: Martin le Jeune.

Palmieri, Arturo. 1909. *I lavoratori del contado bolognese durante la signorie.* 2 vols. Atti e memorie della R. Deputazione di storia patria per le provincie di Romagna 3. Bologna: Zanichelli.

Pariset, Ernest. 1901. *Histoire de la fabrique lyonnaise. Étude sur le Régime social et économique de l'Industrie de la Soie à Lyon, depuis le XVIe siècle.* Lyon: A. Rey.

Pariset, Georges Auguste. 1897. *L'État et les Églises en Prusse sous Frédéric-Guillaume Ier (1713-1740).* Paris: Armand Colin et Cie.

Pascal, Blaise. 1670. *Pensées de M. Pascal sur la religion et sur quelques autres sujets, qui ont esté trouvées après sa mort parmy ses papiers.* 2nd ed. Paris: Guillaume Desprez.

———. 1688. *Monsieur Pascall's Thoughts, Meditations, and Prayers, Touching Matters Moral and Divine as They Were Found in His Papers after His Death: Together with a Discourse upon Monsieur Pascall's, Thoughts ... as Also Another Discourse on the Proofs of the Truth of the Books of Moses: And a Treatise, Wherein Is Made Appear That There Are Demonstrations of a Different Nature but as Certain as Those of Geometry, and That Such May Be given of the Christian Religion.* Translated by Jacob Tonson. London: J. Tonson.

Pashley, Robert. 1852. *Pauperism and Poor Laws.* London: Longman, Brown, Green, and Longmans.

Patent Office. 1868. *Patents for Inventions: Abridgments of Specifications Relating to Roads and Ways. A.D. 1619-1866.* London: Office of the Commissioners of Patents for Inventions.

———. 1871. *Patents for Inventions: Abridgments of Specifications Relating to Weaving. Part II - A.D. 1860-1866.* London: Office of the Commissioners of Patents for Inventions.

———. 1876. *Patents for Inventions: Abridgments of Specifications Relating to Harbours, Docks, Canals, Etc. A.D. 1617-1866.* London: Office of the Commissioners of Patents for Inventions.

Pauli, Carl Wilhelm. 1847. *Lübeckische Zustände Zu Anfang Des Vierzehnten Jahrhunderts.* Lübeck: F. Aschenfelde.

Paultre, Christian. 1906. *De la répression de la mendicité et du vagabondage en France sous l'Ancien régime.* Paris: L. Larose & L. Tenin.

Peetz, Hartwig. 1883. *Volkswissenschaftliche Studien*. Augsburg: Lampart & Co.

Pegolotti, Francesco Balducci. 1766. "Pratica della Mercatura." In *Della Decima e di varie altre Gravezze Imposte dal Comune di Firenze*, by Giovanni Francesco Pagnini. Vol. 3. Lisbon & Lucca: G. Bouchard.

Peltzer, Rudolph Arthur. 1908. "Die Geschichte der Messingindustrie und der künstlerischen Arbeiten in Messing (Dinanderies) in Aachen und den Ländern zwischen Maas und Rhein von der Römerzeit bis zur Gegenwart." *Zeitschrift des Aacheners Geschichtsvereins* 30: 235–463.

Perthes, Clemens Theodor. 1862. *Politische Zustände und Personen in Deutschland zur Zeit der französischen Herrschaft*. 2 vols. Gotha: F.A. Perthes.

Peruzzi, Simone Luigi. 1868. *Storia del commercio e dei banchieri di Firenze in tutto il mondo conosciuto (1200–1345)*. Florence: Cellini.

Peschel, Oscar. 1853. "Über die Schwankungen der Werthrelationen zwischen den edlen Metallen und den übrigen Handelsgütern." *Deutsche Vierteljahrs Schrift* 4: 1 ff.

———. 1858. *Geschichte des Zeitalters der Entdeckungen*. Stuttgart & Augsburg: Cotta.

Petitot, Claude Bernard, ed. 1819. *Collection des mémoires relatifs à l'histoire de France*. 52 vols. Paris: Foucault.

Petty, Sir William. 1755. *Several Essays in Political Arithmetick*. 4th ed. London: D. Browne.

Petyt, William, Thomas Dring, and Samuel Crouch. 1680. *Britannia Languens, or, A Discourse of Trade: Shewing the Grounds and Reasons of the Increase and Decay of Land-Rents, National Wealth and Strength: With Application to the Late and Present State and Condition of England, France, and the United Provinces*. London: Printed for Tho. Dring, at the Harrow at Chancery-Lane end in Fleetstreet and Sam. Crouch in Popes-Head-Alley near the Royal Exchange in Corn-hill.

Peytraud, Lucien Pierre. 1897. *L'esclavage aux Antilles françaises avant 1789: d'après des documents inédits des archives coloniales*. Paris: Hachette et Cie.

Pfaff, Karl. 1857. "Die Landstreicher und Bettler in Schwaben vom sechszehnten bis in das achtzehnte Jahrhundert." *Zeitschrift für Kulturgeschichte* 2: 431–66.

Philippovich, Eugen von. 1893. *Grundriß der politischen Oekonomie*. 2 vols. Tübingen: Mohr.

Picciotto, James. 1875. *Sketches of Anglo-Jewish History*. London: Trübner & Company.

Pigeonneau, Henri. 1887. *Histoire du commerce de la France*. 2 vols. Paris: Leopold Cerf.

Pimentel, M. Henriquez. 1876. *Geschiedkundige aanteekeningen, betreffende de Portugesche Israelieten in den Haag en hunne synagogen aldaar*. Gravenhage: Gebroeders Belinfante.

Pirenne, Henri. 1899. *Geschichte Belgiens*. 4 vols. Geschichte der europäischen Staaten 30. Gotha: F. A. Perthes.

Piton, Camille. 1892. *Les Lombards à Paris et en France*. 2 vols. Paris: H. Champion.

Platière, Jean-Marie Roland de La, ed. 1785. *Encyclopédie méthodique. Manufactures, arts et métiers*. 7 vols. Panckoucke.

Polenz, Gottlieb von. 1857. *Geschichte des französischen Calvinismus bis zur Nationalversammlung im Jahre 1789. Zum Theil aus handschriftlichen Quellen*. 5 vols. Gotha: F. A. Perthes.

Polifilo. 1903. *La guardaroba di Lucrezia Borgia: Dell'Archivisto di Stato di Modena*. Milan: Umberto Allegretti.

Pontano, Giovanni. 1520. *Opere*. 6 vols. Florence: Filippo Giunta.

Poppe, Johann Heinrich Moritz von. 1807. *Geschichte der Technologie seit der Wiederherstellung der Wissenschaften bis an das Ende des achtzehnten Jahrhunderts*. 3 vols. Göttingen: Johann Friedrich Röwer.

———. 1837. *Geschichte aller Erfindungen und Entdeckungen im Bereiche der Gewerbe, Künste und Wissenschaften: von der frühesten Zeit bis auf unsere Tage*. Stuttgart: Hoffmann.

Postlethwayt, Malachy. 1774. *The Universal Dictionary of Trade and Commerce: With Large Additions and Improvements, Adapting the Same to the Present State of British Affairs in America, since the Last Treaty of Peace Made in the Year 1763*. 4th ed. 2 vols. London: W. Strahan, et al.

Prato, Giuseppe. 1907. *Costo della guerra di Successione Spagnuola e le spese pubbliche in Piemonte dal 1700 al 1713*. Turin: Fratelli Bocca.

———. 1908. *La vita economica in Piemonte a mezzo il secolo XVIII*. Turin: Societa Tipografico-Editrice Nazionale.

Prescott, William Hickling. 1843. *History of the Conquest of Mexico, with a Preliminary View of the Ancient Mexican Civilization, and the Life of the Conqueror, Hernando Cortés*. 3 vols. New York: Harper & Brothers.

———. 1847. *History of the Conquest of Peru, with a Preliminary View of the Civilization of the Incas*. 2 vols. New York: Harper & Brothers.

Preußischen Akademie der Wissenschaften. 1892. *Acta Borussica. Denk-mäler der Preußischen Staatsverwaltung im 18. Jahrhundert.* 42 vols. Berlin.

Přibram, Karl. 1907. *Geschichte der österreichischen Gewerbepolitik von 1740 bis 1860.* 2 vols. Duncker & Humblot.

Price, William Hyde. 1906. *The English Patents of Monopoly.* Harvard Economic Studies 1. Boston & New York: Houghton, Mifflin and Company.

Pringsheim, Otto. 1890. *Beiträge zur wirtschaftlichen Entwicklungs-geschichte der Vereinigten Niederlande im 17. und 18. Jahrhundert.* Leipzig: Duncker & Humblot.

Prutz, Hans. 1877. *Die Besitzungen des Deutschen Ordens im Heiligen Lande: ein Beitrag zur Culturgeschichte der Franken in Syrien.* Leipzig: Brockhaus.

———. 1881. "Die Besitzungen des Johanniterordens in Palästina und Syrien." *Zeitschrift des Deutschen Palästina-Vereins* 4: 157–93.

———. 1883. *Kulturgeschichte der Kreuzzüge.* Berlin: E.S. Mittler & Sohn.

———. 1906. "Die finanziellen Operationen der Hospitaliter." *Sitzungs-berichte der Bayerischen Akademie der Wissenschaften, phil.-hist. Klasse,* 9–47.

Public Record Office of Great Britain. 1856. *Calendar of State Papers. Domestic Series.* Edited by Mary Anne Everett Green and Robert Lemon. 12 vols. London: Longman, Green, Longman, Roberts & Green.

———. 1860. *Calendar of State Papers. Colonial Series.* 46 vols. London: Her Majesty's Stationery Office.

Pyle, Howard, ed. 1891. *The Buccaneers and Marooners of America: Being an Account of the Famous Adventures and Daring Deeds of Certain Notorious Freebooters of the Spanish Main.* London: T. Fisher Unwin.

Quarient und Raal, Franz Anton von, ed. 1704. *Codex Austriacus.* 6 vols. Vienna: Leopold Voigt.

Quintana, José Manuel. 1830. *Vidas de los españoles célebres.* 3 vols. Madrid: Imprenta Central.

Rabbeno, Ugo. 1895. *The American Commercial Policy: Three Historical Essays.* 2nd ed. Cleveland: Arthur H. Clark Company.

Raffles, Thomas Stamford. 1817. *The History of Java.* 2 vols. London: Black, Parbury, and Allen.

Ramelli, Agostino. 1588. *Le Diverse Et Artificiose Machine Del Capitano Agostino Ramelli Dal Ponte Della Tresia, Ingegniero del Christianissimo Re di Francia et di pollonia.* Paris: A. Ramelli.

———. 1994. *The Various and Ingenious Machines of Agostino Ramelli: A Classic Sixteenth-Century Illustrated Treatise on Technology.* Translated by Martha Teach Gnudi. New York: Dover.

Ramusio, Giovanni Battista. 1550. *Delle navigationi et viaggi.* 3 vols. Venice: Lucantonio de Giunti.

Ranke, Leopold von. 1856. *Französische Geschichte vornehmlich im sechzehnten und siebzehnten Jahrhundert.* 2nd ed. 5 vols. Stuttgart: Cotta.

———. 1857. *Fürsten und Völker von Süd-Europa im sechszehnten und siebzehnten Jahrhundert: vornehmlich aus ungedruckten Gesandtschafts-Berichten.* 3rd ed. 4 vols. Berlin: Duncker & Humblot.

Raumer, Freidrich von. 1857. *Geschichte der Hohenstaufen und ihre Zeit.* 3rd ed. 6 vols. Leipzig: Brockhaus.

Raynal, Guillaume Thomas. 1775. *Histoire philosophique et politique des établissemens & du commerce des européens dans les deux Indes.* 3 vols. Geneva: Libraires associés.

Real Academia de la Historia (Spain). 1842. *Colección de documentos inéditos para la historia de España.* 113 vols. Madrid: Academia de la Historia.

Reed, William Reed. 1866. *The History of Sugar and Sugar Yielding Plants, Together with an Epitome of Every Notable Process of Sugar Extraction, and Manufacture, from the Earliest Times to the Present.* London: Longman, Green and Co.

Rehme, Paul. 1895. *Das Lübecker Ober-Stadtbuch: ein Beitrag zur Geschichte der Rechtsquellen und des Liegenschaftsrechtes, mit einem Urkundenbuche.* Hanover: Helwing.

Reinaud, Joseph. 1829. "Traités de commerce entre la république de Venise et les derniers sultans mameloucs d'Égypte, traduits de l'italien et accompagnés d'éclaircissements." *Journal asiatique* Série 2 Tome 4: 22–50.

Rey, Emmanuel Guillaume. 1883. *Les colonies franques de Syrie aux XIIme et XIIIme siècles.* Paris: Picard.

Ribbe, Charles de. 1874. *Les Familles et la société en France avant la révolution.* 3rd ed. 2 vols. Paris: J. Albanel.

———. 1889. *Une grande dame dans son ménage au temps de Louis XIV: d'après le journal de la Comtesse de Rochefort (1689).* Paris: Victor Palmé.

Ricard, Jean-Pierre. 1722. *Le négoce d'Amsterdam: contenant tout ce que doivent savoir le marchands & banquiers, tant ceux qui sont établis à Amsterdam que ceux des pays étrangers.* Amsterdam: N.Etienne Lucas.

Richter, Ämilius Ludwig. 1846. *Die evangelischen Kirchenordnungen des sechszehnten Jahrhunderts.* 2 vols. Weimar: Verlag des Landes-Industriecomptoirs.

Richthofen, Emil Carl Heinrich Freiherr von. 1839. *Der Haushalt der Kriegsheere, in seinen militärischen, politischen und staatswirtschaftlichen Beziehungen.* Handbibliothek für Offiziere, oder populaire Kriegslehre für Eingeweihte und Laien 5. Berlin: Herbig.

Riedel, Adolph Friedrich Johann, ed. 1838. *Codex diplomaticus Brandenburgensis.* 41 vols. Berlin: F. H. Morin.

Rietschel, Siegfried. 1905. "Strieder, Jacob, Zur Genesis des modernen Kapitalismus." *Zeitschrift der Savigny-Stiftung für Rechtsgeschichte. Germanistische Abteilung* 26 (1): 298–300.

Risbeck, Johann Kaspar. 1783. *Briefe eines reisenden Franzosen über Deutschland an seinen Bruder in Paris.* 2 vols. Zurich: Geßner.

Ritter, Carl. 1822. *Die Erdkunde im Verhältniß zur Natur und zur Geschichte des Menschen: oder allgemeine, vergleichende Geographie, als sichere Grundlage des Studiums und Unterrichts in physikalischen und historischen Wissenschaften.* 2nd ed. 21 vols. Berlin: Reimer.

———. 1840. *Über die geographische Verbreitung des Zuckerrohrs.* Berlin: Königliche Akademie der Wissenschaften.

Ritter, Moritz. 1903. "Das Kontributionssystem Wallensteins." *Historische Zeitschrift* 90: 193–249.

Rizzi, Hans. 1903. "Das österreichische Gewerbe im Zeitalter des Merkantilismus." *Zeitschrift für Volkswirtschaft, Socialpolitik und Verwaltung* 12: 71–101.

Robiquet, Paul. 1880. *Histoire municipale de Paris depuis les origines jusqu'à l'avènement de Henri III.* Paris: C. Reinwald.

Rochow, Friedrich Eberhard von. 1789. *Versuch über Armen-Anstalten und Abschaffung aller Betteley.* Berlin: Friedrich Nicolai.

Rode, Albert. 1905. *Robert Bargrave: Ein englischer Reisender des XVII. Jahrhunderts. Mit Bisher nicht veröffentlichten Auszügen aus seiner Reisebeschreibung.* Hamburg: Lütcke & Wulff.

Rodolico, Niccolò. 1904. "Il sistema monetario e le classi sociali nel medioevo." *Rivista Italiana di Sociologia* VIII: 462–69.

Roger-Miles, Leon. 1910. *Les createurs de la mode dessins et documents de Jungbluth.* Paris: C. Eggimann.

Rogers, James Edwin Thorold. 1866. *A History of Agriculture and Prices in England: From the Year after the Oxford Parliament (1259) to the Commencement of the Continental War (1793).* 7 vols. Oxford: Clarendon Press.

————. 1884. *Six Centuries of Work and Wages; the History of English Labour*. London: Putnam.

————. 1898. *The Industrial and Commercial History of England (Lectures Delivered to the University of Oxford)*. Edited by Arthur George Liddon Rogers. London: T. Fisher Unwin.

Rohrscheidt, Kurt von. 1898. *Vom Zunftzwang zur Gewerbefreiheit. Eine Studie nach der Quellen*. Berlin: Carl Heymann.

Roller, Otto Konrad. 1907. *Die Einwohnerschaft der Stadt Durlach im 18. Jahrhundert in ihren wirtschaftlichen und kulturgeschichtlichen Verhältnissen dargestellt aus ihren Stammtafeln*. Karlsruhe: Braun.

Roncière, Charles de la. 1899. *Histoire de la marine française*. 6 vols. Paris: Plon-Nourrit et Cie.

Roos, J. S. 1905. "Additional Notes on the History of the Jews in Surinam." *American Jewish Historical Society* 13: 127–36.

Roscher, Wilhelm Georg Friedrich. 1854. *System der Volkswirthschaft*. 5 vols. Stuttgart: Cotta.

————. 1856. *Kolonien, Kolonialpolitik und Auswanderung*. Leipzig & Heidelberg: Winter.

————. 1874. *Geschichte der National-Oekonomik in Deutschland*. Geschichte der Wissenschaften in Deutschland 14. Munich: Oldenbourg.

Roscoe, William I. 1805. *The Life and Pontificate of Leo X*. 4 vols. Liverpool: Creery.

Rosenthal, Eduard. 1879. *Zur Geschichte des Eigentums in der Stadt Würzburg*. Würzburg: Thein.

Roth, Johann Ferdinand. 1800. *Geschichte des Nürnbergischen Handels - Ein Versuch*. 4 vols. Leipzig: Böhme.

Round, John Horace. 1888. "Danegeld and the Finance of Domesday." In *Domesday Commemoration, 1085-1886: Domesday Studies*, edited by P. E. Dove, 1:98–104. London and New York: Longman, Green and Co.

Ruding, Rogers. 1840. *The Annals of the Coinage of Britain and Its Dependencies*. 3rd ed. 3 vols. London: John Hearne.

Ruffini, Francesco. 1901. *La libertà religiosa*. Vol. 1. Turin: Fratelli Bocca Editori.

————. 1912. *Religious Liberty*. Translated by J. Parker Heyes. New York: G.P. Putnam's Sons.

Ruge, Sophus. 1881. *Geschichte des Zeitalters der Entdeckungen*. Allgemeine Geschichte in Einzeldarstellungen 9. Berlin: G. Grote.

Rymer, Thomas. 1727. *Foedera, conventiones, literæ, et cujuscumque generis acta publica, inter reges Angliæ, et alios quosvis imperatores, reges, pontifices, principes, vel communitates, ab Ineunte sæculo duodecimo, viz. ab Anno 1101. Ad nostra usque tempora, habita aut tractata: Ex Autographis, infra Secretiores archivorum regiorum thesaurarius per multa Sæcula reconditis, fidelitur exscripta, in lucem missa de mandato nuperæ reginæ.* 2nd ed. 20 vols. London: J. Tonson.

Saalfeld, Friedrich. 1810. *Geschichte des portugiesischen Kolonialwesens in Ostindien.* Göttingen: J.F. Röwer.

———. 1812. *Geschichte des holländischen Kolonialwesens in Ostindien.* 2 vols. Göttingen: Heinrich Dieterich.

Sackur, Ernst. 1893. "Beiträge zur Wirtschaftsgeschichte französischer und lothringischer Klöster im 10. und 11. Jahrhundert." *Zeitschrift für Social- und Wirtschaftsgeschichte* 1: 154–90.

Sägmüller, Johann Baptist. 1897. "Der Schatz Johanns XXII." *Historisches Jahrbuch* 18: 37–57.

Saint-Gelais, Octovien de. 1525. *Le Vergier d'honneur de l'entreprise de Charles VIII à Naples, en prose et en vers par Octavien de S. Gelais, évêque d'Angoulême, et André Lavigne.* Paris: Philippe Le Noir.

Saint-Maur, Nicolas-François Dupré de. 1746. *Essai sur les monnoies ou réflexions sur le rapport entre l'argent et les denrées.* Paris: Jean-Baptiste Coignard & De Bure.

Saint-Simon, Louis de Rouvroy, duc de. 1857. *Mémoires complets et authentiques du Duc de Saint-Simon sur le siècle de Louis XIV at la Régence.* Edited by Adolphe Chéruel. 20 vols. Paris: Hachette et Cie.

———. 1889. *The Memoirs of the Duke of Saint-Simon on the Reign of Louis XIV and the Regency.* Translated by Bayle St John. 5th ed. 3 vols. London: Swan Sonnenschein.

Salvioni, Giovanni Battista. 1899. "Sul valore della Lira Bolognese." In *Atti e memorie della R. Deputazione di Storia Patria per le Provincie di Romagna*, 253–340. Series III, XVII. Bologna: R. Deputazione di Storia Patria per le Provincie di Romagna.

Salz, Arthur. 1913. *Geschichte der böhmischen Industrie in der Neuzeit.* Munich & Leipzig: Duncker & Humblot.

Saunier, Claudius. 1903. *Die Geschichte der Zeitmeßkunst von den ältesten Zeiten bis zur Gegenwart.* Translated by Gustav Speckhart. 3 vols. Bautzen: Emil Hübner.

Savary des Brûlons, Jacques, and Philémon Louis Savary. 1723. *Diction-naire universel de commerce: d'histoire naturelle, & des arts & métiers*. 3 vols. Paris: Jacques Estienne.

Savary, Jacques. 1675. *Le parfait négociant ou Instruction générale pour ce qui regarde le commerce des marchandises de France et des pays étrangers*. Paris: Jean Guignard.

Savine, Albert. 1908. *La Cour Galante de Charles II: D'après les Documents d'Archives et les Mémoires*. Paris: Louis-Michaud.

Savine, Alexander. 1909. *English Monasteries on the Eve of the Dissolution*. Oxford Studies in Social and Legal History 1. Oxford: Clarendon Press.

Scelle, Georges. 1906. "Histoire politique de la traite négrière aux Indes de Castille: Contrats et Traités d'Assiento." Paris: University of Paris.

Schäfer, Ernst. 1902. *Beiträge zur Geschichte des spanischen Protestantismus und der Inquisition im sechzehnten Jahrhundert*. 3 vols. Gütersloh: C. Bertelsmann.

Schalk, Carl. 1880. "Der Münzfuss der Wiener Pfennige in den Jahren 1424 bis 1480." *Numismatische Zeitschrift* 12: 186–282, 324–78.

Schanz, Georg. 1884. *Zur Geschichte der Colonisation und Industrie in Franken*. Bayerische Wirthschafts- und Verwaltungsstudien 1. Erlangen: A. Deichert.

Schanz, Georg von. 1881. *Englische Handelspolitik gegen Ende des Mittelalters, mit besonderer Berücksichtigung des Zeitalters der beiden ersten Tudors Heinrich VII. und Heinrich VIII.* 2 vols. Leipzig: Duncker & Humblot.

Schaube, Adolf. 1897. "Ein Italienischer Coursbericht von Der Messe von Troyes Aus Dem 13. Jahrhundert." *Zeitschrift Für Social- Und Wirtschaftsgeschichte* 5 (2): 248–308.

———. 1898. "Die Wechselbriefe König Ludwigs Des Heiligen Von Seinem Ersten Kreuzzuge Und Ihre Rolle Auf Dem Geldmarkte Von Genua." *Jahrbücher für Nationalökonomie und Statistik* 15: 603–21, 730–48.

Scherer, Hermann. 1852. *Allgemeine Geschichte des Welthandels: Von den frühen Zeiten bis zur Entdeckung Amerikas*. Leipzig: Schultze.

Scheube, H. 1873. *Aus den Tagen unserer Grossväter. Culturgeschichtliche Zeit- und Lebensbilder*. Berlin: F. Berggold.

Scheurl, Albrecht von. 1884. "Christoph Scheurl, Dr. Christoph Scheurls Vater." *Mitteilungen des Vereins für Geschichte der Stadt Nürnberg* 5: 13–46.

Schipper, Ignacy. 1907. *Anfänge Des Kapitalismus Bei Den Abendländischen Juden Im Früheren Mittelalter (Bis Zum Ausgang Des XII. Jahrhunderts)*. Vienna & Leipzig: Wilhelm Branmüller.

Schlesinger, Ludwig. 1865. "Zur Geschichte der Industrie in Oberleutensdorf." *Mitteilungen des Vereins für Geschichte der Deutschen in Böhmen* 3: 87-96;133-148.

Schlözer, August Ludwig. 1777. *August Ludwig Schlözer's Briefwechsel meist historischen und politischen Inhalts.* 10 vols. Göttingen: Vandenhoekschen Buchhandlung.

———. 1782. "Nachricht von der Hamburger Bank. Hamburg, 3. April 1782." *Stats-Anzeigen* 1: 73–84.

———. 1787. "Ueber Papirgeld." *Stats-Anzeigen* 11: 369–84.

Schmidt, Alfred. 1914. *Geschichte des englischen Geldwesens im 17. und 18. Jahrhundert.* Abhandlungen: Staatswissenschaftliches Seminar, Universität Straßburg 32. Strasbourg: Karl J. Trübner.

Schmoller, Gustav. 1884a. "Studien über die wirtschaftliche Politik Friedrichs des Großen und Preußens überhaupt von 1680-1786. Teil I." *Jahrbuch für Gesetzgebung, Verwaltung und Volkswirtschaft im Deutschen Reiche* 8: 1–62, 345–421, 999–1091.

———. 1886. "Studien über die wirtschaftliche Politik Friedrichs des Großen und Preußens überhaupt von 1680-1786. Teil II." *Jahrbuch für Gesetzgebung, Verwaltung und Volkswirtschaft im Deutschen Reiche* 10: 1–46, 327–73, 675–727.

———. 1887a. "Studien über die wirtschaftliche Politik Friedrichs des Großen und Preußens überhaupt von 1680-1786. Teil III." *Jahrbuch für Gesetzgebung, Verwaltung und Volkswirtschaft im Deutschen Reiche* 11: 1–58, 789–883.

———. 1891. "Die geschichtliche Entwickelung der Unternehmung." *Jahrbuch für Gesetzgebung, Verwaltung und Volkswirtschaft im Deutschen Reiche* 15: 1-48,635-710,1001-1030.

———. 1898a. "Das brandenburg-preussische Innungswesen von 1640-1800." In *Umrisse und Untersuchungen zur Verfassungs-, Verwaltungs- und Wirtschaftsgeschichte besonders des Preußischen Staates im 17. und 18. Jahrhundert,* by Gustav Schmoller, 314–456. Leipzig: Duncker & Humblot.

———. 1898b. *Umrisse und Untersuchungen zur Verfassungs-, Verwaltungs- und Wirtschaftsgeschichte besonders des Preußischen Staates im 17. und 18. Jahrhundert.* Leipzig: Duncker & Humblot.

Schmoller, Gustav, and Otto Hintze. 1892. *Die preußische Seidenindustrie im 18. Jahrhundert und ihre Begründung durch Friedrich den Großen.* 3 vols. Acta Borussica, Seidenindustrie 1–3. Berlin: Paul Parey.

Schmoller, Gustav von. 1877. "Die Entstehung des preußischen Heeres von 1640 bis 1740." Edited by Julius Rodenberg. *Deutscher Rundschau* XII: 248–73.

———. 1884b. "Das Merkantilsystem in seiner historischen Bedeutung: städtische, territoriale und staatliche Wirtschaftspolitik." *Jahrbuch für Gesetzgebung, Verwaltung und Volkswirtschaft im Deutschen Reiche* 8 (1): 15–61.

———. 1887b. "Die Hausindustrie und ihre älteren Ordnungen und Reglements." *Jahrbuch für Gesetzgebung, Verwaltung und Volkswirtschaft im Deutschen Reiche* 11 (1): 369–75.

———. 1897. *Die Strassburger Tucher und Weberzunft. Urkunden und Darstellung nebst Regesten und Glossar. Ein Beitrag zur Geschichte der deutschen Weberei und des deutschen Gewerberechts, vom XIII-XVII Jahrhundert.* Strasbourg: Karl J. Trübner.

———. 1900. *Grundriß der allgemeinen Volkswirtschaftslehre. Erster größerer Teil. Begriff. Psychologische und sittliche Grundlage. Litteratur und Methode. Land, Leute und Technik. Die gesellschaftliche Verfassung der Volkswirtschaft.* Vol. 1. 2 vols. Leipzig: Duncker & Humblot.

———. 1902. *The Mercantile System and Its Historical Significance, Illustrated Chiefly from Prussian History.* Translated by William James Ashley. New York: Macmillan & Company.

Schneider, Philipp. 1885. *Die bischöflichen Domkapitel, ihre Entwicklung und rechtliche Stellung im Organismus der Kirche.* Mainz: Kirchheim.

Schoelcher, Victor. 1842. *Des colonies françaises: abolition immédiate de l'esclavage.* Paris: Pagnerre.

Schönlank, Bruno. 1894. *Sociale Kämpfe vor dreihundert Jahren.* Leipzig: Duncker & Humblot.

Schorer, Hans. 1904. "Das Bettlertum in Kurbayern in der zweiten Halfte des 18. Jahrhundert." *Forschungen zur geschichte Bayerns* 12: 176–207.

Schott, Theodor. 1885. *Die Aufhebung des Edikts von Nantes im Jahre 1685.* Halle: Verein für Reformationsgeschichte.

Schrötter, Friedrich Freiherr von. 1904. *Das Preußische Münzwesen im 18. Jahrhundert. Münzgeschichtlicher Teil.* Edited by Gustav Schmoller. 4 vols. Acta Borussica. Münzwesen 2. Berlin: Paul Parey.

Schudt, Johann Jakob. 1714. *Jüdische Merkwürdigkeiten: vorstellend, was sich Denkwürdiges in den neuen Zeiten bey einigen Jahrhunderten mit den in alle 4 Theile der Welt, sonderlich durch Teutschland zerstreuten Juden zugetragen. Sammt einer vollständigen Franckfurter Juden-Chronik.* 4 vols. Frankfurt & Leipzig: Wolfgang Christoph Multzen.

Schuhmacher, Hermann Albert. 1892. "Die amerikanischen Unternehmungen der Augsburger Welser in Venezuela." In *Hamburgische Festschrift zur Erinnerung an die Entdeckung Amerikas*, edited by Wissenschaftliche Ausschuss des Komités für die Amerika-Feier. Vol. 2.1. Hamburg: L. Friederichsen.

Schulte, Aloys. 1900. *Geschichte des mittelalterlichen Handels und Verkehrs zwischen Westdeutschland und Italien mit Ausschluss von Venedig.* 2 vols. Leipzig: Duncker & Humblot.

Schulze, Paul. 1904. "32. Die Seidenindustrie." In *Handbuch der Wirtschaftskunde Deutschlands*, 3:652–70. Leipzig: B.G. Teubner.

Schulze-Gävernitz, Gerhart von. 1892. *Der Grossbetrieb: ein wirtschaftlicher und socialer Fortschritt. Eine Studie auf dem gebiete der Baumwollindustrie.* Leipzig: Duncker & Humblot.

Schwartzen, Heinrich Engelbert, ed. 1744. *Historische Nachlese zu denen Geschichten der Stadt Leipzig.* Leipzig: August Stopffeln.

Schweizer, Franz August. 1903. *Merkantilismus von Colbert.* Geschichte der Nationalökonomik in vier Monographien über Colbert, Turgot, Smith, Marx, nebst einer philosoph. Systematik der Nationalökonomie 1. Ravensburg: Dorn.

Sée, Henri. 1906. *Les classes rurales en Bretagne du XVIe siècle a La Révolution.* Paris: V. Giard & E. Brière.

Sélincourt, Hugh De. 1908. *Great Raleigh.* London: Methuen & Co.

Sella, Quintino. 1887. *Codex Astensis qui de Malabayla Communiter Nuncupatur. Vol. I: Del Codice D'Asti Detto de Malabayla.* Atti della Reale Accademia dei Lincei, Ser. 2a, Vol. 4. Rome: Accademia nazionale dei Lincei.

Sembrzjycki, Johannes. 1892. "Die Schotten und Engländer in Ostpreußen und die 'Brüderschaft Gross-Brittanischer Nation' zu Königsberg." *Altpreussische Monatsschrift* 29: 228–47.

Semino, Prospero. 1798. "Memorie sopra il commercio de' Genovesi negli scali marittimi e terre del Levante, dal secolo X fino al secolo XV." Genoa. Manoscritti, Ricci, 146. Archivio Storico del Comune di Genova.

Senckenberg, Heinrich Christian von, and Johann Jacob Schmauß, eds. 1747. *Neue und vollständigere Sammlung der Reichs-Abschiede, Welche von den Zeiten Kayser Conrads des II. bis jetzo, auf den Teutschen Reichs-Tägen abgefasset worden, sammt den wichtigsten Reichs-Schlüssen, so auf dem noch fürwährenden Reichs-Tage zur Richtigkeit gekommen sind, in vier Teilen.* 4 vols. Frankfurt am Main: Koch.

Sérionne, Jacques Accarias de. 1768. *Le commerce de la Hollande, ou tableau du commerce des Hollandois dans les quatre parties du monde.* 3 vols. Amsterdam: Changuion.

———. 1778. *La richesse de la Hollande.* 2 vols. London: Aux dépens de la Compagnie.

Serres, Olivier de. 1600. *Le Théâtre d'agriculture et mesnage des champs.* Paris.

Shaw, William Arthur. 1895. *The History of Currency, 1252 to 1894: Being an Account of the Gold and Silver Monies and Monetary Standards of Europe and America, Together with an Examination of the Effects of Currency and Exchange Phenomena on Commercial and National Progress and Well-Being.* London: Wilsons & Milne.

———, ed. 1896. *Select Tracts and Documents Illustrative of English Monetary History 1626-1730.* London: Clement Wilson.

Siegel, Eduin. 1892. *Zur Geschichte des Posamentiergewerbes mit besonderen Rücksichtnahme auf die erzgebirgische Posamentenindustrie.* Annaberg: Graser.

Siegel, Johann Gottlieb. 1742. *Corpus iuris cambialis.* 2 vols. Leipzig: Heinsius.

———. 1751. *Einleitung zum Wechselrecht überhaupt, darinnen aus den neuesten in Europa üblichen Wechselordnungen gezogene Sätze nach ihrer natürlichen Ordnung sowohl unterschiedener Wechselgesetze dunkler Stellen deutliche Erklärung, und in Ermangelung der Vorschrift in den Wechselordnungen, aus denen allgemeinen Rechten entlehnte Principia, nebst vielen den usum fori erläuternden Principiis, zu befinden.* Leipzig: Heinsius.

Sieveking, Heinrich. 1897. "Die Genueser Seidenindustrie im 15. und 16. Jahrhundert." *Jahrbuch für Gesetzgebung, Verwaltung und Volkswirtschaft im Deutschen Reiche* 21: 101–34.

———. 1898. *Genueser Finanzwesen.* 2 vols. Volkswirtschaftliche Abhandlungen der Badischen Hochschulen. Freiburg im Breisgau: J. C. B. Mohr.

———. 1904. "Die mittelalterliche Stadt. Ein Beitrag zur Theorie der Wirtschaftsgeschichte." *Vierteljahrsschrift für Sozial- und Wirtschaftsgeschichte* 2: 177–218.

———. 1907. *Grundzüge der neueren Wirtschaftsgeschichte vom 17. Jahrhundert bis zur Gegenwart.* Grundrisse der Geschichte der Wissenschaft, II.2. Leipzig: B.G. Teubner.

———. 1909. "Die kapitalistische Entwicklung in den italienischen Städten des Mittelalters." *Vierteljahrsschrift für Sozial- und Wirtschaftsgeschichte* 7: 64–93.

Simmel, Georg. 1905. *Philosophie der Mode*. Berlin: Pan.

Simon, Jules. 1859. *La Liberté*. 2nd ed. 2 vols. Paris: Hachette et Cie.

Simonsfeld, Henry. 1878. *Venetianische Studien I: Das Chronicon Altinate*. Munich: Theodor Ackermann.

Sinclair, John. 1803. *The History of the Public Revenue of the British Empire*. 3rd ed. 2 vols. London: Cadell & Davies.

Slijper, E. 1906. "Netherlands." In *The Jewish Encyclopedia: A Descriptive Record of the History, Religion, Literature, and Customs of the Jewish People from the Earliest Times to the Present Day*, edited by Cyrus Adler and Isidore Singer, 9:231–33. New York: Funk & Wagnalls.

Slokar, Johann. 1914. *Geschichte der österreichischen Industrie und ihrer Förderung unter Kaiser Franz I. Mit besonderer Berücksichtigung der Grossindustrie und unter Benützung archivalischer Quellen verfasst*. Vienna: F. Tempsky.

Smith, Adam. 1776. *An Inquiry Into the Nature and Causes of the Wealth of Nations*. 3 vols. London: A. Strahan and T. Cadell.

Soetbeer, Adolf. 1862. "Beiträge zur Geschichte des Geld- und Munzwesens in Deutchland." *Forschungen zur deutschen Geschichte* 1, 2, 4, 6.

———. 1879. *Edelmetall-Produktion und Werthverhältniss zwischen Gold and Silber seit der Entdeckung Amerika's bis zur Gegenwart*. Ergänzungsheft zu "Petermann's Mitteilungen" 57. Gotha: Justus Perthes.

———. 1880. "Dr A. Petermann's Mitteilungen aus Justus Perthes' geographischer Anstalt. Ergänzungsband XIII, 1879-1880." In *Edelmetall-Produktion und Wertverhältnis zwischen Gold und Silber seit der Entdeckung Amerika's bis zur Gegenwart*, edited by E. Behm, 1–156. Gotha: Justus Perthes.

Solórzano Pereira, Juan de. 1736. *Politica indiana*. 2 vols. Madrid: Matheo Sacristan.

Sombart, Werner. 1893. "Studien zur Entwicklungsgeschichte des italienischen Proletariats." *Archiv für Soziale Gesetzgebung und Statistik* 6: 177–258.

———. 1902a. *Der moderne Kapitalismus*. 1st ed. 2 vols. Leipzig: Duncker & Humblot.

———. 1902b. *Wirtschaft und Mode. Ein Beitrag zur Theorie der modernen Bedarfsgestaltung*. Grenzfragen des Nerven- und Seelenlebens 12. Wiesbaden: J. F. Bergmann.

———. 1903. *Die deutsche Volkswirtschaft im neunzehnten Jahrhundert*. Berlin: Bondi.

———. 1911a. *Die Juden und das Wirtschaftsleben*. Leipzig: Leipzig Duncker & Humblot.

———. 1911b. "Technik und Kultur." *Archiv für Sozialwissenschaft und Sozialpolitik* 33: 305–47.

———. 1913a. *Der Bourgeois: Zur Geistesgeschichte Des Modernen Wirtschaftsmenschen.* Munich & Leipzig: Duncker & Humblot.

———. 1913b. *Krieg und Kapitalismus.* Studien zur Entwicklungsgeschichte des modernen Kapitalismus 2. Munich & Leipzig: Duncker & Humblot.

———. 1913c. *Luxus und Kapitalismus.* Translated by W.R. Dittmar. Studien zur Entwicklungsgeschichte des modernen Kapitalismus 1. Munich & Leipzig: Duncker & Humblot.

———. 1913d. *The Jews and Modern Capitalism.* Translated by Mortimer Epstein. London: T. Fisher Unwin.

———. 1915. *The Quintessence of Capitalism: A Study of the History and Psychology of the Modern Business Man.* Translated by Mortimer Epstein. London: T. Fisher Unwin.

———. 1925. "Prinzipielle Eigenart des modernen Kapitalismus." In *Spezifische Elemente der modernen kapitalistischen Wirtschaft. 1. Teil,* 2–26. Grundriss der Sozialökonomik, IV. Tübingen: J. C. B. Mohr.

———. 1967. *Luxury and Capitalism.* Translated by W.R. Dittmar. Ann Arbor: University of Michigan Press.

Somerset, Edward. 1663. *A Century of the Names and Scantlings of Such Inventions as at Present I Can Call to Mind to Have Tried and Perfected Which (My Former Notes Being Lost) I Have, at the Instance of a Powerful Friend, Endeavored Now, in the Year 1655, to Set These down in Such a Way, as May Sufficiently Instruct Me to Put Any of Them to Practice.* London: J. Grismond.

Sommerhausen, Hirsch. 1853. "Die Geschichte der Niederlassung der Juden in Holland und den niederländischen Colonien. Nach der öffentlich gekrönten Preisschrift des Herrn J. Koenen." *Monatsschrift für Geschichte und Wissenschaft des Judenthums* 2 (4): 121–45.

Sommerlad, Theo. 1900. "Münzwesen. IV. Mittelälterliches Münzwesen." In *Handwörterbuch der Staatswissenschaften,* edited by Johann Conrad, Ludwig Elster, Wilhelm Lexis, and Edgar Loening, 2nd ed., 5:921–28. Jena: G. Fischer.

Sorel, Charles. 1644. *Les Loix de la Galanterie.* Paris: Auguste Aubry.

Spain. 1640. *Recopilacion de Las Leyes Destos Reynos Hecha Por Mandado de La Magestad Catolica Del Rey Don Felipe Segundo Nuestro Señor, Que Se Ha Mandado Imprimir, Con Las Leyes Que Despues de La Vltima Impression Se Han Publicado, Por La Magestad Catolica Del Rey Don Felipe Quarto El Grandenuestroseñor.* 3 vols. Madrid: Catalina de Barrio Angulo & Diego Diaz de la Carrera.

Sparke, Michael. 1903. "Leather: A Discourse Tendered to the High Court of Parliament." In *Social England Illustrated: A Collection of XVIIth Century Tracts*, edited by Edward Arber, Thomas Seccombe, and Andrew Lang, 317–36. An English Garner 9. Westminster: A. Constable.

Spears, John Randolph. 1900. *The American Slave-Trade: An Account of Its Origin, Growth and Suppression.* New York: C. Scribner's Sons.

Spengler, Oswald. 1920. *Der Untergang des Abendlandes: Umrisse einer Morphologie der Weltgeschichte.* 2 vols. Munich: C. H. Beck.

———. 1922. *The Decline of the West.* Translated by Charles Francis Atkinson. 2 vols. London: G. Allen & Unwin.

Sperges, Joseph von. 1765. *Tyrolische Bergwerksgeschichte, mit alten Urkunden, und einem Anhange, worinn das Bergwerk zu Schwaz beschrieben wird.* Vienna: Johann Thomas Edlen von Trattnern.

Spix, Johann Baptist von, and Karl Friedrich Philipp von Martius. 1823. *Reise in Brasilien auf befehl Sr. Majestät Maximilian Joseph I.* 3 vols. München: M. Lindauer.

Sprengel, Matthias Christian. 1779. *Vom Ursprung des Negerhandels: ein Antrittsprogramm.* Halle: J.C. Hendel.

Sprengel, Peter Nathanael, and D.L. Hartwig. 1773. *Handwerke und Künste in Tabellen.* 2nd ed. 17 vols. Berlin: Buchhandlung der Realschule.

Srbik, Heinrich von. 1907. *Der staatliche Exporthandel Österreichs von Leopold I bis Maria Theresia.* Vienna & Leipzig: W. Braumüller.

———. 1910. "Abenteurer am Hofe Kaiser Leopold I. Alchemie, Technik und Merkantilismus." *Archiv für Kulturgeschichte* 8: 52–71.

Stafford, William. 1876. *William Stafford's Compendious or Briefe Examination of Certayne Ordinary Complaints of Diuers of Our Countrymen in These Our Dayes, A.D. 1581, (Otherwise Calld "A Briefe Conceipt of English Pollicy").* Edited by Frederick James Furnivall. London: N. Trübner.

———. 1895. *William Stafford's drei Gespräche über die in der Bevölkerung verbreiteten Klagen 1581.* Edited by Emanuel Leser. Translated by Johann Hoops. Leipzig: Duncker & Humblot.

Steffen, Gustaf Fredrik. 1901. *Studien zur Geschichte der englischen Lohnarbeiter mit besonderer Berücksichtigung der Veränderungen ihrer Lebenshaltungen.* Translated by Margarete Langfeldt. 3 vols. Stuttgart: Hobbing & Büchle.

Steinbeck, Aemil. 1857. *Geschichte des schlesischen Bergbaues, seiner Verfassung, seines Betriebes.* 2 vols. Breslau: J.U. Kern.

Steiner, Bernard Christian. 1893. *History of Slavery in Connecticut.* Baltimore: John Hopkins University Press.

Sternberg, Kaspar Maria Graf von. 1836. *Umrisse einer Geschichte der böhmischen Bergwerke.* 2 vols. Prague: G. Haase.

Stetten, Paul von. 1779. *Kunst-, Gewerb- und Handwerks-Geschichte der Reichs-Stadt Augsburg.* 2 vols. Augsburg: Stage.

Stieda, Wilhelm. 1887. *Revaler Zollbücher und -Quittungen des 14. Jahrhunderts.* Hansische Geschichtsquellen, V. Halle: Buchhandlung des Waisenhauses.

———. 1889. *Litteratur, heutige Zustände und Entstehung der deutschen Hausindustrie. Nach den vorliegenden gedruckten Quellen.* Leipzig: Duncker & Humblot.

———. 1894. *Hansisch-Venetianische Handelsbeziehungen im 15. Jahrhundert. Festschrift der Landes-Universität Rostock zur zweiten Säcularfeier der Universität Halle a. S.* Leipzig: Jäh & Schunke.

———. 1899. "Städtische Finanzen im Mittelalter." *Jahrbücher für Nationalökonomie und Statistik* 17: 1–54.

———. 1901. "Zunftwesen." In *Handwörterbuch der Staatswissenschaften,* edited by Johann Conrad, Ludwig Elster, Wilhelm Lexis, and Edgar Loening, 2nd ed., 7:1022–33. Jena: G. Fischer.

———. 1902. *Die Anfänge der Porzellanfabrikation auf dem Thüringerwalde.* Jena: G. Fischer.

Stobbe, Otto. 1866. *Die Juden in Deutschland während des Mittelalters in politischer, socialer und rechtlicher Beziehung.* Brunswick: Schwetschke.

Stoppelaar, Johannes Hermanus de. 1901. *Balthasar de Moucheron: een bladzijde uit de Nederlandsche handelsgeschiedenis tijdens den tachtigjarigen oorlog.* Gravenhage: Martinus Nijhoff.

Storch, Heinrich Friedrich von. 1797. *Historisch-statistisches Gemälde des Russischen Reichs am Ende des 18. Jahrhunderts.* 8 vols. Riga: Hartknoch.

Strada, Jacobus. 1618. *Kunstliche Abriß allerhand Wasser Wind Roß und Handt Mühlen: beneben schönen und nützlichen Pompen, auch andern Machinen, damit das Wasser in Höhe zuerheben, auch lustige Brunnen und Wasserwerck, dergleichen vor diesem nie gesehen worden. Nicht allein den Liebhabern zur Ubung und Nachrichtung, sondern auch dem gantzen gemeinen Vatterland, zu Dienst und Wolgefallen, so wol in Kriegs- als Friedenszeiten zugebrauchen.* Frankfurt am Main: Strada.

Strieder, Jacob. 1904. *Zur Genesis des modernen Kapitalismus: Forschungen zur Entstehung der grossen burgerlichen Kapitalvermogen am Ausgang des Mittelalters und zu Beginn der Neuzeit, zunachst in Augsburg.* Leipzig: Duncker & Humblot.

———. 1914. *Studien zur Geschichte kapitalistischer Organisationsformen: Monopole, Kartelle, und Aktiengesellschaften im Mittelalter und zu Beginn der Neuzeit.* Munich & Leipzig: Duncker & Humblot.

Strype, John. 1725. *Annals of the Reformation and Establishment of Religion, And Other Various Occurrences in the Church of England; During the First Twelve Years Queen Elizabeth's Happy Reign.* 2nd ed. 4 vols. London: Thomas Edlin.

Stubbs, William. 1874. *The Constitutional History of England in Its Origin and Development.* 5th ed. 3 vols. Oxford: Clarendon Press.

Sturz, Helfrich Peter. 1786. *Schriften von Helfrich Peter Sturz.* New improved edition. 2 vols. Leipzig: Weidmann Erben und Reich.

Stüwe, Friedrich. 1836. *Die Handelszüge der Araber unter den Abbassiden durch Afrika, Asien und Osteuropa.* Berlin: Dunker und Humblot.

Sue, Eugène. 1835. *Histoire de la marine française.* 4 vols. Paris: Béthune et Plon.

Suess, Eduard. 1877. *Die Zukunft des Goldes.* Vienna: W. Braumüller.

Sully, Maximilien de Béthune duc de. 1747. *Memoires de Maximilien de Bethune: Duc de Sully, principal ministre de Henry le Grand.* 5 vols. Geneva: Barrilot.

———. 1837. *Memoires ou œconomies royales destat domestiques, politiques et militaires de Henry le grand.* Edited by Joseph François Michaud and Jean Joseph François Poujoulat. 2 vols. Nouvelle collection des mémoires pour servir a l'histoire de France depuis le XIIIe siècle jusqu'a la fin du XVIIIe, Ser. 2, vols. 2–3. Paris: Didot.

Supan, Alexander. 1906. *Die territoriale Entwicklung der europäischen Kolonien.* Gotha: Justus Perthes.

Süßmann, Arthur. 1907. *Die Judenschuldentilgungen unter König Wenzel.* Schriften der Gesellschaft zur Förderung der Wissenschaft des Judentums 2. Berlin: L. Lamm.

Tafel, Gottlieb Lukas Friedrich, and Georg Martin Thomas, eds. 1856. *Urkunden zur älteren Handels- und Staatsgeschichte der Republik Venedig, mit besonderer Beziehung auf Byzanz und die Levante. Vom neunten bis zum Ausgang des fünfzehnten Jahrhunderts.* 3 vols. Fontes Rerum Austriacarum 12–14. Vienna: Hof- und Staatsdruckerei.

Taine, Hippolyte. 1875. *Les origines de la France contemporaine.* 14th ed. 12 vols. Paris: Hachette.

———. 1876. *The Origins of Contemporary France.* 6 vols. New York: Henry Holt & Co.

Tallemant des Réaux, Gédéon. 1910. *Les Historiettes de Tallemant des Réaux.* Edited by Louis Jean Nicholas Monmerqué. Paris: Garnier.

Talon, Omer. 1821. *Oeuvres d'Omer et de Denis Talon.* 6 vols. Paris: A. Egron.

Tamassia, Nino. 1910. *La famiglia Italiana nei secoli decimoquinto e decimosesto.* Milano: Sandron.

Tarello, Camillo. 1567. *Ricordo d'agricoltura di M. Camillo Tarello da Lonato.* Venice: Francesco Rampazetto.

Taussig, Frank William. 1888. *The Tariff History of the United States: A Series of Essays.* New York & London: G. P. Putnam's Sons.

Tawney, Richard Henry. 1912. *The Agrarian Problem in the Sixteenth Century.* London: Longmans, Green and Company.

———. 1913. "The Assessment of Wages in England by the Justices of the Peace." *Vierteljahrsschrift Für Social- Und Wirtschaftsgeschichte* 11: 307–37, 533–64.

Temple, Sir William. 1685. *Remarques sur l'estat des Provinces unies des Païs-Bas.* The Hague: Chez Jean & Daniel Steucker.

———. 1754. *The Works of Sir William Temple, Bart.* 4 vols. Edinburgh: G. Hamilton & J. Balfour, A. Kincaid & A. Donaldson et al.

Terry, Schuyler Baldwin. 1914. *The Financing of the Hundred Years' War: 1337-1360.* London: London School of Economics.

Thierbach, Moritz. 1886. *Die geschichtliche Entwicklung der Handfeuerwaffen.* Dresden: C. Höckner.

Thirion, Henri. 1895. *La vie privée des financiers au XVIIIe siècle.* Paris: E. Plon, Nourrit et Cie.

Thomson, Thomas, and Cosmo Innes, eds. 1814. *The Acts of the Parliament of Scotland, 1424–1707.* 11 vols. London: Record Commission.

Thun, Alphons. 1879. *Die Industrie am Niederrhein und ihre Arbeiter.* 2 vols. Staats- und socialwissenschaftliche Forschungen 2. Leipzig: Duncker & Humblot.

Tölner, Johann. 1885. *Johann Tölners Handlungsbuch von 1345-1350*. Edited by Karl Koppmann. Geschichtsquellen der Stadt Rostock 1. Rostock: Werther.

Toniolo, Guiseppe. 1895. "L'economia di credito e le origini del capitalismo nella Repubblica Fiorentina." *Rivista internazionale di science sociali e discipline ausiliarie* 8: 560–76.

Tönnies, Ferdinand. 1905. "Die Entwicklung der Technik." In *Festgabe für Adolph Wagner zur 70. Wiederkehr seines Geburtstages*, edited by G. Adler, 127–48. Leipzig: Winter.

———. 1915. "Die historisch-geographischen Richtungen der Neuzeit." *Weltwirtschaftliches Archiv* 6: 307–19.

Tooke, Thomas, and William Newmarch. 1838. *A History of Prices and of the State of the Circulation during the Years 1793–1856*. 6 vols. London: Longman, Orme, Brown, Green, and Longmans.

———. 1862. *Die Geschichte und Bestimmung der Preise während der Jahre 1793-1857*. Translated by Carl Wilhelm Asher. 2 vols. Dresden: R. Kuntze.

Tovey, D'Blossiers. 1738. *Anglia Judaica: Or the History and Antiquities of the Jews in England, Collected from All Our Historians, Both Printed and Manuscript, as Also from the Records in the Tower, and Other Publick Repositories*. Oxford: James Fletcher.

Troeltsch, Ernst. 1919. *Die Soziallehren der christlichen Kirchen und Gruppen*. Gesammelte Schriften of Ernst Troeltsch 1. Tübingen: J.C.B. Mohr (Paul Siebeck).

———. 1931. *The Social Teaching Of The Christian Churches*. Translated by Olive Wyon. 2 vols. Halley Stewart Publications 1. London: George Allen & Unwin Ltd.

Troeltsch, Walter. 1897. *Die Calwer Zeughandlungskompagnie und ihre Arbeiter: Studien zur Gewerbe- und Sozialgeschichte Altwürttembergs*. Jena: G. Fischer.

Tugan-Baranowski, Michael von. 1900. *Geschichte der russischen Fabrik*. Berlin: Emil Felber.

Turner, G. J. 1898. "The Sheriff's Farm." *Transactions of the Royal Historical Society* 12: 117–49.

Tzschoppe, Gustav Adolf, and Gustav Adolf Harald Stenzel, eds. 1832. *Urkundensammlung zur Geschichte des Ursprungs der Städte und der Einführung und Verbreitung deutscher Kolonisten und Rechte in Schlesien und der Oberlausitz*. Hamburg: F. A. Perthes.

Uhl, Johann Ludwig. 1758. *Erste Fortsetzung des Corpus Juris Cambialis*. Leipzig: Heinsius.

———. 1764. *Zweite Fortsetzung des Siegelschen Corpus Juris Cambialis*. Leipzig: Heinsius.

Uhlhorn, Gerhard. 1890. "Armenwesen (Geschichte der öffentlichen Armenpflege)." In *Handwörterbuch der Staatswissenschaften*, edited by Johann Conrad, Ludwig Elster, Wilhelm Lexis, and Edgar Loening, 2nd ed., 1:1056–76. Jena: G. Fischer.

Uitterdijk, J. Nanninga. 1904. *Een Kamper handelshuis te Lissabon 1572-1594. Handelscorrespondentie, rekeningen en bescheiden.* Zwolle: J. J. Tijl.

Ulbach, Louis, Louis Fortoul, Alphonse Pagès, and Armand Parrot-Larivière. 1884. *La Hollande et la liberté de penser au XVIIe et au XVIIIe siècle.* Paris: Calmann Lévy.

Ullmann, Salomon. 1909. *Studien zur Geschichte der Juden in Belgien bis zum XVIII Jahrundert.* Antwerp: S. Kahan.

Ulloa, Bernardo de. 1753. *Rétablissement des manufactures et du commerce d'Espagne.* Amsterdam: Chez les Freres Estienne.

Unger, Franz, and Theodor Kotschy. 1865. *Die Insel Cypern, ihrer Physischen und Organischen Natur nach mit Rücksicht auf ihre frühere Geschichte.* Vienna: W. Braumüller.

Ungern-Sternberg, Wilhelm von. 1835. *Geschichte des Goldes.* Dresden: E. Blochmann.

Unwin, George. 1904. *Industrial Organisation in the Sixteenth and Seventeenth Centuries.* Oxford: Clarendon Press.

Ure, Andrew. 1839. *Dictionary of Arts, Manufactures and Mines.* 3rd ed. 3 vols. London: D. Appleton & Co.

Usselincx, William. 1608. *Naerder bedenckingen, over de zee-vaerdt, coophandel ende neeringhe, als mede de versekeringhe vanden staet deser vereenichde landen, inde teghenwoordighe vrede-handelinghe met den coninck van Spangnien ende de aerts-hertoghen.*

Uzielli, Gustavo. 1901. *Cenni storici sulle imprese scientifiche, marittime e coloniali di Ferdinando I Granduca di Toscana: (1587 - 1609).* Tipografia Spinelli.

Uztáriz, Gerónimo de. 1753. *Théorie et pratique du commerce et de la marine . Traduction libre sur l'espagnol de don Geronymo de Ustariz, sur la seconde édition de ce livre à Madrid en 1742.* Translated by François Véron Forbonnais. Paris: Veuve Estienne & Fils.

Uzzano, Giovanni di Bernardo da. 1440. *Pratica della mercatura.*

Valran, Gaston. 1899. *Misère et charité en Provence au XVIII. siècle.* Paris: Arthur Rousseau.

Vanderkindere, Léon. 1879. *Le siècle des Artevelde: etudes sur la civilisation morale et politique de la Flandre et du Brabant.* Brussels: A-N. Lebègue.

Var, Robert du. 1845. *Histoire de la classe ouvrière: depuis l'esclave jusqu'au prolétaire de nos jours*. 4 vols. Paris: Michel.

Varenbergh, Émile. 1874. *Histoire des relations diplomatiques entre le compté de Flandre et l'Angleterre au moyen âge*. Brussels: C. Muquardt.

Vauban, Sébastien Le Prestre de. 1851. *La Dîme royale*. Edited by Eugène Daire. Paris: Alcan.

Veer, Gustav de. 1864. *Prinz Heinrich der Seefahrer und seine Zeit*. Danzig: Kafemann.

Velho, Álvaro. 1838. *Roteiro da viagem que em descobrimento da India pelo Cabo da Boa Esperança fez dom Vasco da Gama em 1497*. Porto: Typographia commercial portuense.

Veranzio, Fausto. 1616. *Machinae Novae*. Venice.

Verein für Hamburgische Geschichte. 1890. "Baggermaschinenbetrieb in Hamburg im Jahre 1634." *Mitteilungen des Vereins für Hamburgische Geschichte* 13: 101–3.

Vetter, Arno. 1910. *Bevölkerungsverhältnisse der ehemals Freien Reichsstadt Mühlhausen in Thüringen im 15. und 16. Jahrhundert*. Leipziger historische Abhandlungen 17. Leipzig: Quelle & Meyer.

Vigne, Marcel. 1903. *La banque à Lyon du XVe au XVIIIe siècle*. Lyon: A. Rey.

Vignon, E. J. M. 1862. *Études historiques sur l'administration des voies publiques en France aux dix-septième et dix-huitième siècles*. 4 vols. Dunod.

Villani, Giovanni. 1728. "Istorie Fiorentine." In *Rerum Italicarum scriptores*. Vol. XIII. Milan: Societatis Palatinae in Regia Curia.

Villard, Amédée. 1882. *Histoire du prolétariat ancien et moderne*. Paris: Guillaumin.

Virgil, Polydore. 1576. *Polydori Virgilii Urbinatis de rerum inventoribus libri octo*. Rome: Antonij Bladij.

Vischer, Friedrich Theodor. 1888. *Mode und Cynismus. Beiträge zur Kenntniss unserer Culturformen und Sittenbegriffe*. 3rd ed. Stuttgart: K. Wittwer.

Volger, Wilhelm Friedrich, ed. 1872. *Urkundenbuch der Stadt Lüneburg*. 3 vols. Hanover: Hahn.

Volkelt, Johann Gottlieb. 1775. *Gesammlete Nachrichten von Schlesischen Bergwerken*. Breslau & Leipzig: C.F. Gutsch.

Voltaire. 1877. *Oeuvres completes de Voltaire, avec des notes et une notice historique sur la vie de Voltaire*. 50 vols. Paris: Garnier.

Voltelini, Hans von. 1913. *Die Anfänge der Stadt Wien*. Vienna: C. Fromme.

Voye, Ernst. 1908. *Geschichte der Industrie im märkischen Sauerland.* 4 vols. Hagen: Otto Hammerschmidt.

Vuitry, Adolphe. 1883. *Etudes sur le régime financier de la France, avant la Révolution de 1789. Nouvelle Série.* 3 vols. Paris: Guillaumin et Cie.

Waentig, Heinrich. 1898. *Gewerbliche Mittelstandspolitik. Eine rechtshistorisch-wirtschaftspolitische Studie auf Grund österreichischer Quellen.* Leipzig: Duncker & Humblot.

Wagemann, Ludwig Gerhard. 1789a. "Über die erste Arbeitsschule in Hessen." *Göttingisches Magazin für Indüstrie und Armenpflege* 1: 35–44.

———. 1789b. "Über einige vorzügliche Ursachen des Verarmens und Bettelns, nebst Angabe theils erprobter, theils brauchbarer Mittel dagegen, besonders in Beziehung auf Göttingen." *Göttingisches Magazin für Indüstrie und Armenpflege* 1: 63–89.

———. 1789c. "Über Industrieschulen im allgemeinen und über die Göttingische insbesondere." *Göttingisches Magazin für Indüstrie und Armenpflege* 1: 1–34.

Wagenaar, Jan. 1762. *Amsterdam, in zyne opkomst, aanwas, geschiedenissen, voorregten, koophandel, gebouwen, kerkenstaat, schoolen, schutterye, gilden en regeeringe, beschreeven.* 13 vols. Amsterdam: Isaak Tirion.

Wagner, Adolph. 1892. *Grundlegung der politischen Oekonomie.* 2 vols. Leipzig: C. F. Winter.

———. 1907. *Theoretische Sozialökonomik oder allgemeine und theoretische Volkswirtschaftslehre.* 2 vols. Leipzig: C. F. Winter.

Wagner, Thomas. 1791. *Corpus Juris Metallici recentissimi et antiquioris.* Leipzig.

Wailly, Natalis de. 1855. "Dissertation sur les dépenses et les recettes ordinaires de Saint Louis." *Recuiel des Histoires des Gaules et de la France* XXI: LIII–LXXVII.

Waltershausen, August Sartorius von. 1894. *Die Arbeits-Verfassung der englischen kolonien in Nordamerika.* Strasbourg: K. J. Trübner.

Walther, Andreas. 1912. "Geldwert in der Geschichte. Ein methodologischer Versuch." *Vierteljahrsschrift für Sozial- und Wirtschaftsgeschichte* 10 (1/2): 1–52.

Wartmann, Hermann. 1870. *Industrie und Handel des Kantons St. Gallen auf Ende 1866: ein Beitrag zur Kenntnis der schweizerischen Volkswirtschaft und zur schweizerischen Handelsgeschichte.* 2 vols. St Gallen: Huber & Company.

Wätjen, Hermann. 1913. "Das Judentum und die Anfänge der modernen Kolonisation." *Vierteljahrsschrift für Sozial- und Wirtschaftsgeschichte* 11: 338–68.

Wattenbach, Wilhelm. 1874. "Sklavenhandel im Mittelalter." *Journal Anzeiger für Kunde der deutschen Vorzeit* N.F. 21: 37–40.

Webb, Sidney, and Beatrice Potter Webb. 1894. *The History of Trade Unionism.* London and New York: Longmans, Green and Co.

Weeden, William Babcock. 1890. *Economic and Social History of New England 1620-1789.* 2 vols. Boston & New York: Houghton, Mifflin and Company.

Weigel, Christoff. 1698. *Abbildung Der Gemein-Nützlichen Haupt-Stände Von denen Regenten Und ihren So in Friedens- als Kriegs-Zeiten zugeordneten Bedienten an, bis auf alle Künstler Und Handwerker.* Regensburg: Christoff Weigel.

Weiss, Charles. 1853. *Histoire des réfugiés protestants de France depuis la révolution de l'Edit de Nantes jusqu'à nos jours.* 2 vols. Paris: Charpentier.

Weisse, Karl Georg. 1794. *Über das Field-Kommissariat der königlichen preußisch Armee.*

Wekebrod, Franz Xavier, ed. 1799. *Sammlung der Verordnungen und Generalien für sämmtliche Zünfte und Innungen.* Gastl: Brünn.

Wetzer, Heinrich Joseph, and Benedict Welte, eds. 1847. *Kirchenlexikon: oder Encyklopädie der katholischen Theologie und ihrer Hilfswissenschaften.* 13 vols. Herder.

Wheeler, John. 1601. *A Treatise of Commerce, Wherin Are Shewed the Commodies Arising by a Wel Ordered, and Ruled Trade.* Middelburch: R. Schilders.

White, John. 1773. *Art's Treasury of Rarities: And Curious Inventions.* 6th ed. Glasgow: John Tait.

Whitworth, Charles. 1764. *A Collection of the Supplies, and Ways and Means; from the Revolution to the Present Time.* London: R. Davis.

Wichmann, Max. 1885. *Über die Metalle bei den altamexikanischen Kulturvölkern.* Halle: C. Colbatzky.

Wiebe, Georg. 1895. *Zur Geschichte der Preisrevolution des XVI. und XVII. Jahrhunderts.* Staats- und socialwissenschaftliche Beiträge, 2.2. Leipzig: Duncker & Humblot.

Wiedfeldt, Otto. 1898. *Statistische Studien zur Entwickelungsgeschichte der Berliner Industrie von 1720 bis 1890.* Staats- und socialwissenschaftliche Forschungen 69. Leipzig: Duncker & Humblot.

Wiegand, Wilhelm, Aloys Schulte, Georg Wolfram, Hans Witte, and Johann Fritz, eds. 1879. *Urkundenbuch der Stadt Strassburg*. 7 vols. Strasbourg: J. H. Ed. Heitz.

Wilcke, Ferdinand. 1860. *Geschichte des Ordens der Tempelherren: nebst Bericht über seine Beziehungen zu den Freimaurern und den neuern pariser Templern*. 2nd ed. 2 vols. Halle: Schwetschke.

Wilcke, Friedrich Wilhelm. 1792. *Über Entstehung, Behandlung und Erwehrung der Armuth: Eine Preisschrift*. Halle: Johann Jacob Gebauer.

Wilczek, E. 1907. *Beiträge zur Geschichte des Berg- und Hüttenbetriebes im Unterharz unter spezieller Berücksichtigung des "Rammelsberger Bergbaues" und der "Frau Marien-Saigerhütte" zu Oker im Harz*. Sammlung berg- und hüttenmännischer Abhandlungen 10. Kattowitz O.-S.: Gebrüder Böhm.

Wild, Albert. 1862. *Die öffentlichen Glücksspiele mit EInschluss der Lotterie-Anlehen oder Anleitung zur Berechnung der Vortheile, Nachtheile etc. bei den Spielen*. Munich: E. A. Fleischmann.

Wilda, Hans. 1889. "Zur sizilischen Gesetzgebung, Steuer- und Finanzverwaltung unter Kaiser Friedrich II. und seinen normannischen Vorfahren." Halle: Vereinigte Friedrichs-Universität Halle-Wittenberg.

Wilkins, John. 1691. *Mathematical Magick, or, The Wonders That May by Performed by Mechanical Geometry*. London: Richard Baldwin.

William Edward Hartpole Lecky. 1873. *Geschichte des Ursprungs und Einflusses der Auflärung in Europa*. Translated by H. Jolowicz. 2 vols. Leipzig & Heidelberg: C.F. Winter.

Williams, Gomer. 1897. *History of the Liverpool Privateers and Letters of Marque: With an Account of the Liverpool Slave Trade, 1744–1812*. London: Heinemann.

Wilson, Henry. 1872. *History of the Rise and Fall of the Slave Power in America*. 2 vols. Boston & New York: Houghton, Mifflin and Company.

Winckler, Paul. 1697. *Der Edelmann*. 2nd ed. Nuremberg: Christoph Riegel.

Winthrop, John. 1825. *The History of New England from 1630 to 1649. With Notes by J. Savage*. 2 vols. Boston: Phelps & Farnham.

Wobly, Karl. 1909. "Beitrag zur Wirtschaftsgeschichte Polens." *Zeitschrift für Volkswirtschaft, Socialpolitik und Verwaltung* 18: 355–89.

Woker, Philipp. 1878. *Das kirchliche Finanzwesen der Päpste: ein Beitrag zur Geschichte des Papstthums*. Nördlingen: C. H. Beck.

Wolf, Gerson. 1876. *Geschichte der Juden in Wien (1156-1876)*. Vienna: Alfred Hölder.

Wolf, Lucien. 1894. "The First English Jew: Notes on Antonio Fernandes Carvajal with Some Biographical Documents." *Transactions of the Jewish Historical Society of England* 2: 15–28.

———. 1902. *The Jewry of the Restoration, 1660-1664*. London: Jewish Chronicle Office.

Wolfstrigl-Wolfskron, Max von. 1903. *Die Tiroler Bergbau 1301-1665*. Innsbruck: Wagner.

Worms, Stephen. 1904. *Schwazer Bergbau in fünfzehnten Jahrhundert*. Vienna: Manz.

Young, Arthur. 1770. *A Six Months Tour Through the North of England*. 4 vols. London: W. Strahan.

Zamboni, Filippo. 1897. *Gli Ezzelini, Dante e gli Schiavi*. Nuova. Florence: Landi.

Zeising, Heinrich. 1607. *Theatrum Machinarum*. 6 vols. Leipzig: Henning Grosse.

Zenker, Luise. 1906. *Zur volkswirtschaftlichen Bedeutung der Lüneburger Saline für die Zeit von 950-1370*. Forschungen zur Geschichte Niedersachsens, 1.2. Hanover: Hahn.

Zetzner, Johann Eberhard. 1913. *Reiss-Journal und Glücks- und Unglücks-fälle von Johann Eberhard Zetzner: Aus dem Leben eines Strass-burger Kaufmanns des 17. und 18. Jahrhunderts (1677-1735)*. Edited by Rudolf Reuss. Beiträge zur Landes- und Volkskunde von Elsaß-Lothringen und der angrenzenden Gebieten, XLIII. Leipzig: Heitz.

Zillner, Franz Valentin. 1890. *Geschichte der Stadt Salzburg*. 2 vols. Salzburg: Gesellschaft für Salzburger Landeskunde.

Zimmermann, Alfred. 1885. *Blüthe und Verfall des Leinengewerbes in Schlesien: Gewerbe- und Handelspolitik dreier Jahrhunderte*. Breslau: W.G. Korn.

———. 1896. *Die Europäischen Kolonien*. 5 vols. Berlin: Ernst Siegfried Mittler und Sohn.

———. 1905. *Kolonialpolitik*. Hand- und Lehrbuch der Staatswis-senschaften in selbständigen Bänden. Abteilung 1, Volk-swirtschaftslehre 18. Leipzig: C.L. Hirschfield.

Zimmermann, Paul. 1905. "Herzog Julius in Volkswirtschaftlicher Bez-iehung." *Hansische Geschichtsblätter* 32: 33–62.

Zincke, Georg Heinrich, ed. 1742. *Leipziger Sammlungen von Wirth-schafftlichen- Policey- Cammer- und Finantz-Sachen*. Leipzig: Jacobi.

———, ed. 1744. "Sendschreiben, die Nutzbarkeit des Cameral-Studii und die Art und Weise betreffende, wie der Leute auf dem Lande zum Anbau wüster Gegenden zu vermehren." *Leipziger Sammlungen von Wirthschafftlichen- Policey- Cammer- und Finantz-Sachen* 2: 613–20.

———, ed. 1745. "Ein Beyspiel zwar wohlgemeynter aber leerer Projecte, um fleißige Arbeiter zu Manufacturen zu bekommen, und denen fleißigen Armen zu helffen." *Leipziger Sammlungen von Wirthschafftlichen- Policey- Cammer- und Finantz-Sachen* 2: 365–78.

———, ed. 1746a. "Gedancken von der Einrichtungen eines Arbeits- Werck- oder sogenannten Zucht-Hauses." *Leipziger Sammlungen von Wirthschafftlichen- Policey- Cammer- und Finantz-Sachen* 3: 803–76.

———, ed. 1746b. "Vorstellungen an einen Regenten, wegen des Zustandes einer an einem um An. 1676 herum versuchten und nun wieder längst verschwunden Seyden-Manufactur." *Leipziger Sammlungen von Wirthschafftlichen- Policey- Cammer- und Finantz-Sachen* 3: 157–87.

———, ed. 1757. "Nachricht von der zu Wittenberg neu angelegten und ferner zu entrichtenden Anstalt der Armenschulen, eines Waisenhauses, und einer abermaligen Realschule." *Leipziger Sammlungen von Wirthschafftlichen- Policey- Cammer- und Finantz-Sachen* 12: 713–28.

Zirkel. 1887. "Zur Geschichte des sachsischen Bergbaus." *Zeitschrift für Bergrecht* 28: 344–65.

Zonca, Vittorio. 1607. *Novo Teatro di Machine et Edificii*. Padua: Pietro Bertelli.

Zwiedineck-Südenhorst, Otto von. 1900. *Lohnpolitik und Lohntheorie, mit besonderer Berücksichtigung des Minimallohnes*. Leipzig: Duncker & Humblot.

End Notes

1   See chapter 3 of the first volume.
2   Supplemental information for this chapter can be provided by my de-piction in the fourth volume of the *Grundriss der Sozialökonomik* (Sombart 1925), where I have developed in fuller detail all the ideas whch are here described only in their essential features.
3   I have made clear these complicated connections, which are not visible to common reason, in the place named in the previous note. There the reader will also find the only elaboration, necessary for the understand-ing of the economy of High Capitalism, of the forms of development of the economic orientation implicit in in the idea of acquisition.
4   In detail in the 1st edition (Sombart 1902a, 199 ff.) and in *Grundriss der Sozialökonomik* (Sombart 1925) [Tr.: the physical volume being trans-lated from claims to be the third 'unaltered' edition and has a copyright date of 1916, and the date 1919 on its title page, so how a work from 1925 came to be referenced in it is a mystery]. Cf. also the chapter "The Origin of the Capitalist Enterprise" in the next volume of this work (chapter 10 of the second volume of the original work).
5   In more detail in the 1st edition (Sombart 1902a, 204 ff.).
6   In more detail in the 1st edition (Sombart 1902a, 204 ff.).
7   Wilda (1889).
8   [Tr.: not referenced by Sombart. See Luther (1909, 30.2:508).]
9   [Tr.: not referenced by Sombart. See Burckhardt (1860, 7–8; 1878, 12–13).]
10 [Tr.: not referenced by Sombart. See Bezold et al (1908, 38).]
11 [Tr.: not referenced by Sombart. See Bezold et al (1908, 224).]
12 These connections are demonstrated with much spirit by C. B. Hun-deshagen (1861, 232 ff., 444 ff.).
13 E. Laspeyres (1863, 124 ff., 134ff.).
14 Ranke demonstrates this in the clearest and shortest manner (1856, 1:55 ff.). Cf. Sombart (1913b, 5 f.).
15 Fortescue (1899, 1:204).
16 Jany (1901, 118 f.).
17 Turned to account for the first time by M. Jähns (1889, 2:1554). Cf. G. Schmoller (1877, 267).
18 Sombart (1913b, 35).
19 Sombart (1913b, 35).
20 Thus in England, see Laird Clowes (1897), and for France, Sombart (1913b, 36 f.).
21 Delbrück (1907, Vol. 3; 1990, Vol. 3).
22 For these and the earlier numbers, see Delbrück (1907, 3:153, 3:229, 3:344, 3:363 ,3:404).
23 Delbrück (1907, 3:476). Cf. also Sombart (1913b, 37 ff.).
24 Heyck (1886). A first-rate work.
25 Duro (1884, 2:85 ff., Doc. 110), cited by Clowes (1897, 1:560).
26 According to the official lists (Sue 1835, 4:170).
27 De Jonge (1858, 1:Bijlage XII).
28 Appendix A in Bridge (ed.) (1889, 133 ff.).
29 Portrayed in detail in Sombart (1913b, 46 ff.).

30 See the detailed portrayal in Sombart (1913b, 66 ff.).

31 Boutaric (1863, 360 ff.).

32 Guillaume (1848, 78, 102–3).

33 Forming a part of Marberger (1704).

34 Thierbach (1886, 20 f.).

35 Example in Droysen (1875b, 20 ff.; 1875a, 404 ff.).

36 Example in Jany (1901, 45).

37 Example in Kling (1906, 2:277).

38 Jany (1901, 55) and Kling (1906, 2:203).

39 Franç. 16691, Fol. 102vo cited in (1899, 2:493; 1563).

40 Liebe (1899, 21).

41 Jähns (1889, 1:662).

42 Sombart (1913b, 84 f.).

43 We are informed over the upkeep of the armies of Wallenstein by (both not very precisely) Heilmann (1850), and Loewe (1895). Cf. Förster (1834) (with important material), and Ritter (1903).

44 For the development of the organs of state authority entrusted with the care of the work of provision (war commissioners!), see Sombart (1913b, 118 ff.). Cf., in addition to the literature named there, Hintze (1910, 493 ff.), and also Below (1895, 2:ix f.).

45 Delbrück (1907, 3:608 f.).

46 Boutaric (1863, 277–80).

47 Droysen (1875b, 112 ff.; 1875a, 623 ff.).

48 Boutaric (1863, 277).

49 Boutaric (1863, 311), citing the MS in the British Museum, No. 11542.

50 Boutaric (1863, 384).

51 Naudé (1901, 272).

52 Naudé (1901, 87 ff.).

53 For example, in Genoa in the 13th century (Heyck 1886, 158, 160, 169).

54 For *France*, see "Principes de Mr Colbert sur la marine", printed in Sue (1835, 1:317). For *England*, see Close Rolls 48, 71 and 15 John 158, cited in Clowes (1897, 1:119).

55 Guillaume (1848, 140).

56 Oppenheim (1896, 1:138–39).

57 Clowes (1897, 2:20). St. P. D. 11 December 1655; St. P. D. CXXXIV, 64; St. P. D. September 1656, in Oppenheim (1896, 1:329).

58 For *England*, see handwritten sources in Grose (1786, 1:310 f.); and Fortescue (1899, 1:283 f.). For *France*, see Mention (1900, 255). For *Brandenburg-Prussia*, see Kling (1906, 2:3-4).

59 Jany (1901, 33). Richthofen (1839, 628 ff.).

60 See, for example, the contract over the clothing of the Anhalt Foot Regiment from 23 January 1681 (1906, 2:212).

61 Examples for *England*, see Grose (1786, 1:310 ff.), and Hall (1901, 127). For *France*, see Mention (1900, 255 f.).

62 Richthofen (1839, 628 ff.).

63 The multifarious nature of clothing extends still into the 17th century. Over the motley look of Swedish troops in the Thirty Years War, see for example Heilmann (1850, 18); and for the army of the Great Elector,

see Kling (1906, 2:213). For why the army still bore in the 17ᵗʰ century distinctive marks of any type, see Kling (1906, 2:4), cf. appendices 41-43.

64 Over its origins, see Sombart (1913b, 156 ff.).

65 "Memoires pour servir a l'histoire de la maison de Brandebourg 1767 par Frédéric II", printed in Kling (1906, 2:201).

66 The gradual victory of uniforms in the various armies is described by the following: Audouin (1811, 1:52 f.), de Chennevières (1750, 2:116 ff.), Boutaric (1863, 359, 425), Fortescue (1899, 3:213), Clowes (1897, 3:20), A. B. König (1787, 24) cited in Kling (1906, 2:211), Jany (1901, 45 f.), Kling (1906, 2:3), and Crousaz (1865, 1:11 ff.). Cf. Sombart (1913b, 161 ff.).

67 These ideas, which were most highly developed in France, have been portrayed masterfully by Ranke in his history of France [Tr.: Sombart is probably referring here to Ranke (1856)].

68 Jähns (1889, 1:686).

69 Clément (1861, 2:ccvii).

70 The mercantilist theories formed earliest of all probably in *England* where, for example, the poem "Libelle of Englyshe Polycye" appearing in 1436 already equated money and welfare (Hahl 1893, 45 f.; Petyt, Dring, and Crouch 1680).

71 Evidence in Schmoller (1891, 1001 ff.).

72 Hörnigk (1750, 30, 173). Other occurrences in Roscher (1854, 3:179 n.6).

73 Hofkammer-Referat 16/III 1700 (2/VI 1710), Hoff. 13917, cited in Sbrik (1907, 290 n.2).

74 Manuscript cited in Levasseur (1900, 2:37). [Tr.: Henry II of France died in 1559, so Levasseur is mistaken in attributing the letter of 1568 to him — Charles IX is more likely.]

75 The granting of privileges during the mercantilist period in the form of monopolisation differentiates itself from the granting of privileges of our own time in the form of the granting of patents in that the former took place under the authority of the government with the expressed intention of promoting by each individual act of granting privileges the public (or princely) interests, whereas the granting of patents for an invention rest on an individual (private) right whose granting cannot be refused. This is dealt with in Hulme (1896; 1900).

76 That *various* legal sources have fed regalism (in addition to feudalism, imperialism) is very probable.

77 Burckhardt (1860, 1:35 ff.).

78 Eberstadt (1899, 325 ff.).

79 Unwin (1904, 164 ff.) and passim H. Levy (1909, 38).

80 Savary des Brûlons and Savary (1723, s.h.v.).

81 R. Gardiner (1796, 55–56).

82 Cf. the depiction of the economic forms in the next volume. In the argument over monopolies this question — whether monopolies were with or without numerus clausus — played a leading role of course. Thus, for example, Child (1698, Ch. 3, 102 ff.) defends the trade mono-

poly, but without numerus clausus.

83 A list of patents is in Hulme (1896; 1900). Cf. Cunningham (1907, 2:58 ff., 2:76 ff.), and the new, thorough work of Price (1906).

84 Levasseur (1900, 2:37).

85 Thun (1879, 2:27).

86 Pigeonneau (1887, 1:435).

87 Rymer (1727, 19:583). Cf. James (1857, 148).

88 Cf. the depiction of economic forms in the next volume.

89 Cited in Přibram (1907, 273).

90 See, for *France*, Callery (1882); for *England*, Hall (1885).

91 Savary des Brûlons and Savary (1723, 2:632).

92 They advanced (1667) 400,000 livre to make up 200 serge chairs; in the following years they continued with the subventions (Levasseur 1900, 2:241).

93 Cunningham (1907, 2:516).

94 Lewis (1908).

95 Přibram (1907, 71 ff., 132).

96 The text of the orders is from Rymer (1727, 19:187-235).

97 See the list of new statutes in Levasseur (1900, 2:461 f.).

98 Unwin (1904, 103 ff.).

99 See, for example, Stieda (1901).

100 Savary des Brûlons and Savary (1723).

101 Boissonade (1900, 2:6, 15).

102 Depping (1850, 3:iv-vi).

103 Depping (1850, 3:iv-vi).

104 "C'est l'époque d'un délire dont on n'aurait jamais cru l'esprit humain susceptible." (Platière 1785, 1:4). There you will also find under the keyword *Réglement* the very detailed regulations of the 1770s and 1780s verbatim.

105 Přibram (1907, 76 ff.).

106 Srbik (1907, 304; cf. 286 ff.).

107 See, for example, the Saxon electorate's regulations of 1660 and 1666 (Ludovici 1741, 1:585-586).

108 See, for example, the regulations of 1671, 1730, 1739, and 1741 which regulate the paper industry of Angoumois in the most exact detail (Boissonnade 1899, 13 ff.).

109 A. Anderson (1787, 2:318).

110 Cunningham (1907, 2:483 ff.).

111 See the precise figures of expenditure for improvement of roads and waterways in the years 1600–1661 in Vignon (1862, 4:2).

112 Vignon (1862, 1:61).

113 Vignon (1862, 1:133).

114 Cunningham (1907, 2:532 ff.).

115 Forbes and Ashford (1906, 61 f., 64 f.).

116 It is impossible instead, as Knapp does, to use the word money only for the concept of state money or in his terminology "cash means of payment", so as to then certainly need to expect without contradiction to be able to show that "the money" is a state institution. That means do-

ing violence though to common usage, perhaps even to logic.

117 Knapp (1905, 30–31; 1924).

118 Ernst (1880, 55 ff. esp.).

119 The regulated class of workers amounted in 1497 in the mint of Seville to 170, in that of Granada 100, of Burgos 98, in addition to which there were 62 minters. [Tr.: no source given by Sombart.]

120 Schmoller (1900, 1:532). In Basel during the 14th and 15th centuries 5.72–11.83% of the coin's value (Harms 1907, 178).

121 Haynes (1700, 63) shared by Cunningham (1907, 2:434).

122 Over the comparatively high grade of the insights into monetary theory of Copernicus see the informative essay by Jastrow (1914). By contrast Oresimus [Nicole Oresme] is quite the swallow who does not make a summer. (Counterpart to the position of Leonardo in the history of technology! See Chapter 29.)

123 In the year 1606 the Dutch placards contained images and rates for almost 1,000 foreign coins! It is one the merits of Shaw's book to have made clear these connections. In particular he has described with diligence the role which Antwerp played as a central "pieces market". A corresponding work for Florence has yet to be done. Some material is now being brought out by Arias (1905, 159).

124 "havendo in Firenze grande difetto, e nulla moneta d'argento [...] che tutte le monete d'argento si fondieno, e portavansi oltre mare." [having a great defect in Florence, and no silver coins [...] in that all the silver coins were melted down and carried overseas] (Villani 1728, 914 Bk. XII, Ch. LII) (A very instructive chapter.)

125 Hilliger (1900, 202 ff.). See the article on Finance (Middle Ages) [*Münzwesen (Mittelalter)*] by Sommerlad (1900).

126 See, for example, the reasons which Henry V gave in the year 1411 for his worsening of the money: "because of the great scarcity of money at the time" he wanted to now have 50 nobles minted from the pound of gold and 30 shillings from the pound of silver (whereby the weight of the silver penny sank from 18 to 15 grains, that of the gold nobles from 120 to 108 grains) (Shaw 1895, 55). Cf. Chapter 31.

127 Madox (1769, 1:274 f.).

128 Inama-Sternegg (1879, 3.2:390 ff.).

129 Inama-Sternegg (1879, 3.2:391). Ban on bar money: "in civitatibus et aliis locis, ubi propria et iusta moneta esse consuevit, nemo mercatum aliquod facere debeat cum argento, sed cum denariis proprie sue monete" [in the cities and other places where their own good money is customary, no market works with silver, but with the denares in their own money] in "Sententia de cambio et imaginibus denariorum" (MGH Const., Vol. 2, 416, §302) from the year 1231.

130 Carli expresses it thus in his treatise over money (1804, 323).

131 The best specialist study known to me about the medieval gold (guilder) exchange is the work of Schalk (1880).

132 See in this regard Section Four, in particular Chapter 31.

133 The coin law of 1551 limited the acceptance obligation with pfennigs to 10 fl., the coin edict of 1559 determined even that: "nobody in an

agreed large payment is obliged to accept few or many pfennigs against his will" (Goldast 1620, 184).

134 Over this see Vigne (1903, 84).

135 Sieveking (1898, 2:202, 2:205 ff.).

136 Greppi (1883).

137 See Ludovici (1741, 4:540 ff.).

138 Cf. also Schlözer (1787; 1782, 76).

139 Article XIII of the Navigation Act 1660 (12 Cha. 2 c.18), confirmed by 25 Cha. II c.7 (Navigation Act 1673).

140 Rey (1883).

141 Prutz (1883, 377 ff.).

142 Prutz (1883, 390) and Heyd (1879, 1:170 f.).

143 "Vint à la part de Venise la quarte part et la moitié de la quarte part de tout l'empire de Romanie" [To Venice came the fourth part and half of the fourth part of the whole Roman Empire] (Buchon 1845, 21). The references named in that are in Buchon (1840, 13 ff.). The documents are published in Thomas and Tafel (1856, 1:452 ff.).

144 Here the Sanudos reigned, who called themselves "ducs des douze îles" [dukes of the twelve islands] until Crispo removed them in 1372 (Buchon 1840, 352 ff., 357 f.). This is called the "conquête de familles" [conquest of families].

145 We are informed in passing about the Genoese colonial possessions by Heyck (1886, 154); Sieveking (1898, 1:178 f., 2:102); Cibrario (1839, 280) who cites Semino (1798)), and of course also Heyd (1879).

146 Over the possessions of the Genoese family the Centarioni in Greece, cf. Buchon (1840, 304 ff.).

147 Main (1893, 37 f.) cited in Toniolo (1895).

148 Toniolo (1895), Davidsohn (1896b, 1:282), Masetti Bencini (1897).

149 In the 14th century the Acciaiuoli family obtained the Duchy of Athens (Buchon 1840, 346 ff.).

150 You will find the facts of the newer colonial history put together most lucidly in the above-mentioned work of Supan (1906, 14 ff.).

151 Heyd (1879, 2:376).

152 Postlethwayt (1774, 1:241).

153 Burrish (1728, 327). Cf., in the next volume of this work, chapter 22 on maritime shipping in the epoch of early capitalism.

154 Great Britain House of Commons (1773, 535), cited in Dutt (1908, 46).

155 A "report of the lords commissioners of trade and plantations", cited in MacPherson & Anderson (1805, 3:200-201). An exact overview of the state of the forts, equipment, munitions, garrison, etc. on the African coast is found in Postlethwayt (1774, 1:728).

156 "Los Indias desta isla española eran y son la riqueza della" [The Indians of this Spanish island are the riches of it], a memorial from the year 1505.

157 That was derived again from the nature of the teachings of Luther not long ago and with fine intellect by Troeltsch (1919, 516 f. and elsewhere; 1931, 2:518 f. and elsewhere).

158 See the subtle remarks of Hundeshagen (1861).

159 Troeltsch (1919, 472; 1931, 2:494).
160 From the well-known polemic of Edwards (1646, 1:121), cited in J. Anderson (1856, 2:233).
161 Delbrück (1876; 1886, 2:1-24).
162 "C'est moins peut-être par le fanatisme de la cour de Louis XIV que par les scrupules du roi, luttant alors contre la papauté pour l'Eglise gallicane, qui'il faut expliquer le paroxisme de persécutions qui précéda la révocation de l'édit de Nantes" [It is less perhaps by the fanaticism of the court of Louis XIV than by the scruples of the king, then fighting against the papacy for the French national church, which must explain the paroxism of persecutions which preceded the revocation of the edict of Nantes] (Michelet 1893, 12:245). [Tr.: this text does not appear at the reference given or anywhere else in Michelet's history of France (or anywhere else), as far as I can tell.]
163 Hallam (1832, 1:173).
164 Hallam (1832, 1:129 ff.).
165 J. Anderson (1856, 1:425-428).
166 Cf. H. Levy (1912, 8 ff.).
167 J. Anderson (1856, 2:211 ff.). Cf. J. Anderson (1856, 2:157 ff., 2:175 ff., 2:210 ff.).
168 J. Anderson (1856, 1:462).
169 J. Anderson (1856, 2:7 ff.).
170 Neal (1822, 3:124).
171 Přibram (1907, 1:146).
172 As is well-known, a fierce argument has existed for as long as anyone can remember over the motive which shall have caused Frederick William I to that step — whether calculated policy or religious sympathy. Even now Arnold polemicises against Pariset. To me Pariset seems to hit on the correct view for this case when he writes that with the Prussian Kings there existed "une intime union des sentiments réligieux et des intérêts materiels" [an intimate union of religious feelings and material interests] (G. A. Pariset 1897, 797).
173 Cited in Koenen (1843, 156–57).
174 Motley (1860, 4:109).
175 In J. Anderson (1856, 1:488). In a single state (Providence), Roger Williams, an Independent driven out of Massachusetts, preached shortly beforehand (1636), in the foundational treaty of the secessionists, that unlimited freedom of religious conviction would only be established by the founders of this state promising this state obedience to the law "only in civil things". Arnold (1859, 1:103) cited in Jellinek (1895, 35).
176 J. Anderson (1856, 2:29).
177 J. Anderson (1856, 2:317 ff.).
178 J. Anderson (1856, 2:324).
179 J. Anderson (1856, 2:423 ff.).
180 That is demonstrated with good reasons by Keller (1900).
181 More about this in my book on the Jews (Sombart 1911a; 1913d).
182 Keller (1900, 251).

183 See the survey of Cosack (1898, 12 §4 II 2a). The edicts of the French kings in the 16ᵗʰ century (e.g. the edict of Charles IX from 1563 by which the Parisian commercial court was regulated) had an administrative law bent, whereas the regulation of private commercial law only took place through the named codification.

184 They are collected in J. G. Siegel (1742), alongside Uhl's two continuations (Uhl 1758; 1764). Cf. Ludovici (1768, 193 f. §389), and J. G. Siegel (1751).

185 See, for example, Endemann (1862, 333 ff., 393 ff.). Cf. Marquart (1662, 421 ff. Lib. III Cap. VII ff.).

186 See the overview of the current literature by Below (1905b). Below himself rejects decisively the view according to which Roman Law was introduced to Germany to satisfy the "demands of commerce" which supposedly the German law was not capable of satisfying.

187 Goetze (1912).

188 An article titled "Projector" is included in Postlethwayt (1774, 2552 ff.; Defoe 1697), and in which he expresses the same ideas as Defoe. The article is, however, only a literal printing of the introduction and first chapter of Defoe's essay.

189 The scientific and technological works of Leonardo have for the most part been printed. An overview of the various editions as well as a selection of important places is given by Herzfeld (1906), to which she has written a quite sensible introduction. Cf. Grothe (1874), and the three treatises over Leonardo now united in T. Beck (1900).

190 New knowledge has been spread about him, see Feldhaus (1910, 106 ff.). [Tr.: also see note on page 161.]

191 Becher (1682, 87).

192 Becher (1682, 247–48).

193 Becher (1682, 232).

194 Fraas (1865, 134).

195 Beck (1900) in his "contributions" gives with each of the works commented on by him a short biography of the author.

196 Over Fausto Veranzio, see Beck (1900, 513 ff.).

197 Register of the Privy Council; Acts of Parliament of Scotland, Vol. IX, pp. 419-420; cited in Mackintosh (1892, 3:333). [Tr.: Mackintosh's references given here could not be found in the named places of the Register of the Privy Council of Scotland nor in the Acts of Parliament of Scotland.]

198 Becher (1682, 213 f.).

199 Cf. Tönnies (1905, 130 f.).

200 The "machinery books" cited on page 163 can be considered as sources here. Beck reports critically over their content in Beck (1900).

201 Fraas (1865, 134).

202 The main work of Olivier de Serres was *Théatre d'agriculture* (1600) which underwent 19 editions up to 1675. Over Olivier de Serres see Fagniez (1897, 36 ff.), Fournier (1877, 2:179 ff.); over the introduction of artificial meadows, see Fraas (1865, 206 ff.).

203 D'Avenel (1894, 1:293 ff.).

204 Their invention is set at the year 1560. The attempts by comparison are of older date. Interesting details in Wolfstrigl-Wolfskron (1903, 39 ff., 50). Over the state of "waterworks" about 1680, Becher (1682, 181 ff.).

205 Ahrens et. al. (1896, 5:). Also cf. Zirkel (1887, 367). Zirkel concurs with that information on the dating of the — finished — invention "around 1690". The reasons which Neuburg (1892, 212) cites for powder already having been used for explosions in Rammelsberg towards the end of the 15th century appear much less conclusive to me.

206 North (1742, 137), cited in Fournier (1877, 1:60).

207 The year of 1519 is given by Albinus (1590, 75) for the installation of a stamping mill by Paul Grommesdetter in Joachimsthal. Agricola reports that Sigmund Malthiz, to whom in 1512 the right to all earth extracted from the pits was conferred, invented the wet stamping "in thanks" — the invention falls thus between 1512 and 1519. For the history of the stamping mill, cf. also Beckmann (1780, 5:101 ff.).

208 Cf. below on page 193.

209 Beckmann (1780, 1:319 ff.).

210 Beck (1884, 2:12 f.). This significant work covers the history of iron (its preparation and its use) exhaustively. The transition to blast furnaces and to iron casting is depicted at the conclusion of the first volume; the second volume covers the 16th and 17th centuries. With the third volume the depiction already begins to go over the ground-breaking innovations which the epoch of high capitalism introduced and do not yet come into consideration here.

211 Neumann (1904, 169). Ahrens et. al. (1896, 5:532). A very in-depth description of the patio process is found in Humboldt (1811, 4:106 ff.; 1814, 3:250 ff.). Cf. also Beckmann (1780, 1:44 ff.).

212 See the illustrations in the first volume of Platière (1785) under the keyword "ancre".

213 I found the best descriptions of these pre-steam machine hammers in Volkelt (1775, 265); Becher (1789, 560 f.); and Lecornu (1884a, 9; 1884b, 94).

214 Fournier (1877, 2:377). Cf. Beckmann (1780, 1:55 ff.).

215 According to Beckmann (1780, 2:527), with it the art of rolling came into use for the first time.

216 The index volume of the English patent collection relating to spinning contains eight inventions for mechanical spinning in the 17th century, among them (in the year 1678), "a new spinning engine never used in England" by means of which you could spin in one day the same quantity as previously in two or three days.

217 Becher (1682, 19).

218 Bergius (1775, 1:191 ff.), where a detailed description of the state of "ribbon manufacturing" at the time and its history is to be found. Cf. Beckmann (1780, 1:122 ff.).

219 Patent Office (1871, ix).

220 Geering (1903, 400).

221 Savary des Brûlons and Savary (1723, 1:274). According to them a Frenchman was supposed to have been the inventor of the knitwear

machine — a view which may have its basis in that the English inventor, who found little sympathy in his fatherland, soon made his way
to France to exploit his invention. Cf. also Fournier (1877, 2:240 ff.).

222 In 1616 woad was still produced in 300 Thuringian villages, in 1629
only still in 30 (Poppe 1837, 191).

223 Over the history of clocks there is much material in Beckmann (1780,
1:149 ff., 1:301 ff., 2:465 ff.). From the more recent literature Saunier
(1903) and Bassermann-Jordan (1905) are suitable for an introduction.
The latter indeed written predominantly from an art history perspect-
ive, though also valuable for the history of technology.

224 According to the newer research, spring-driven clocks already existed
as table clocks in the 15th century — the hall clock of Philip the Good,
Duke of Burgundy was probably a spring-driven clock (Bassermann-
Jordan 1905, 26 f.).

225 See Sombart (1913a, 421; 1915, 326). Cf. also in the next volume of this
work the chapter on the origin of the capitalist enterprise (chapter 10 of
the second volume of the original work). There I also give an overview
of the history of the origin of clocks and their spread.

226 The metric measurement developing from the 17th century belongs in
the following period (Ahrens et al. 1896, 2:195 ff.).

227 Feldhaus (1910, 431 ff.).

228 Several Jews participated in these important inventions, as has already
emerged from the portrayal. Jewish historians keep watch jealously in
consequence for the share of their compatriots in this work of invention being belittled — see Graetz (1853, 8:361), who gathers together
the sources and polemicises against Alexander von Humboldt, who
ascribed the compiling of astronomical tables and the improvement of
the astrolabe to Martin von Beheim alone (Humboldt 1845, 2:296).

229 Ahrens et al. (1896, 2:384).

230 Gelcich (1882; 1892) has the best information over these things.

231 Ungern-Sternberg (1835, 23).

232 See the few sources referenced in Soetbeer (1862, Vol. 6 esp.), and cf.
Hanauer (1876, 1:177) and Inama-Sternegg (1879, 1:465).

233 Ten years after the conquest the Caliph was presented with a map of
Spain on which the production of minerals was recorded — Cardonne
(1765, 1:116; 1770, 53–54) cited in Del Mar (1886, 80).

234 Del Mar (1886, 81).

235 Document of Henry IV (Holy Roman Emperor) from 1189 (Goldast
1620, 98–99).

236 Steinbeck (1857, 2:125 ff.).

237 Davidsohn (1896b; 1896a, 3:3).

238 Pigeonneau (1887, 1:264).

239 Also occasional figures confirm that assumption — thus the Kuttenberg
yield amounted to 20–40,000 marks of fine silver in the first period.

240 Peschel (1853, 35). A dissenting view was strangely held by Alexander
von Humboldt (1838). He has, however, already been conclusively re-
futed by Helferich (1843, 49 ff.).

241 See Chapter 27 above.

242 I refer for Byzantium to Krause (1869, 49, 51 ff., 55 f., 280); for the caliphate to the portrayals of Kremer (1875, 2:194 f., 2:300 f.); cf. Kremer (1888, 12).

243 Heyd (1879, 1:224, 1:252, 1:260, 1:265) gives information on the honour gifts and the role they played in the Levant colonies.

244 The spoils which were taken with the conquest of Antioch in the year 1098 are reported in Luard (1872, 2:78-79).

245 The documentary evidence for the decline of Goslar from the beginning of the 14th century (from which the causes identified in the text mainly took effect) is provided by Neuburg (1892, 49 ff.).

246 In Sternberg (1836, 1:52).

247 Jacob (1831); for *Italy* Salvioni (1899, 334 f.), cited in Arias (1905, 158); for *England* Shaw (1895, 54 ff.). For other references see Chapter 42.

248 Ruding (1840, 1:135); cf. Jacob (1838, 1:244 ff.). How the entire English mint and currency policies of the 14th and 15th centuries were defined by this fact of increasing scarcity of precious metals is described by Shaw (1895, 54 ff.). In the year 1453 the Commons petitioned that the operation of the silver mines in Devon and Cornwall, after having been suspended for a long time, might be taken up again so as to influence the lack of silver.

249 "Germania [...] yields [...] in wealth of all metals to no other soil; for all foreign, Gallic, Hispanic, and other nations have almost all their silver from the German merchants." (Janssen 1874, 1:419).

250 The coinage export of precious metals from Venice to Alexandria amounted in the 15th century to 300,000 ducats annually in the expert opinion of the Venetian ambassador Trevisan, according to Reinaud (1829, 29) cited in Peschel (1858, 28).

251 That applies, for example, to Goslar, where from the 1450s they succeeded in controlling the water flooding in so as to thereby increase the yield considerably compared to previously (Neuburg 1892, 105 ff., 149). Cf. Chapter 30 above.

252 Koch-Sternfels (1820), cited in Soetbeer (1879, 30).

253 According to more recent research 1446 (Worms 1904, 11).

254 See Worms (1904, 86), with which you can compare Wolfstrigl-Wolfskron (1903, 35) (where the supply of Schwaz smelted silver within the years 1470–1623 is described exactly according to the files of the Imperial State Archive Innsbruck-Pest (Arch. Suppl. 897)). The information of Soetbeer and Schmoller [Tr.: specific works not referenced by Sombart] which relies on Sperges (1765) are to be corrected according to this new research.

255 Neither in Soetbeer (1880), nor in Suess (1877) does Asia come into consideration as a land of gold. But even Del Mar (1880) knows only Japan as a source of gold. The same applies to Lexis (1900c).

256 I have compiled the sources in Sombart (1902a, 1:373 ff.), where those who are especially interested may check them.

257 See the previous note.

258 These figures, in my opinion, depict only a minimum, which results from the above considerations. Certainly Soetbeer would have assumed a higher amount if the information of Lopez over the yields of the Sofala mines had been known to him. These were, when the Portuguese themselves arrived, already estimated at 2 million mitkal (at 1⅓ ducats, so about 24 million marks) per year. But the Europeans then certainly obtained greater yields than the Arabs (Ramusio 1550, 1:134C). That agrees with the information which Saalfeld (1810, 174) gives us on the basis of other sources, according to which the yield shall have amounted to £1½ million.

259 See the descriptions of the wealth in gold and silver treasure of *Peru* in Prescott (1847, Vol. 1); likewise for *Mexico* in Prescott (1843, Vol. 1); likewise for the *land of the Chibcha*, in particular in the empire of the Zippa of Bogotà and the Zaque in Tunja, in Häbler (1899, 300). A good survey is in Wichmann (1885, 27 ff.).

260 Humboldt calculates the total amount of yield which fell into the hands of the conquerors up to the opening of the Potosi mines at 106,000 gold marks, that is around 25 million piasters or 130 million francs in the currency of the time (Humboldt 1811, 4:253 ff.; 1814, 3:428). Lexis (1900c), on the other hand, calculates only 20 million marks for it.

261 Del Mar (1886, 166 ff.).

262 In France at the time of Henry IV more Spanish gold doubloons, ducats, and pistoles were in circulation than small silver coins in the time of Charles IX — one exaggerated (Bourdeille 1864, 3:197 ff.).

263 See over this the sixth part of the next volume which deals with international economic relations.

264 Dávila (1690, 35). Ranke, who imparts this information, suggests it sounds unbelievable, but "a credible man" confirms it (Ranke 1857, 1:428).

265 Exact information over this is also contained in the aforementioned sixth part of the next volume.

266 Handelmann (1860, 579–80); Eschwege (1833, 145).

267 Suess (1877, 172).

268 See the depiction in the next volume.

269 See chapter 25 of Sombart (1913a; 1915).

270 Roscher (1874, 1:§122).

271 The proof has already been produced ofttimes. Good explanations over it, to which I refer, are found in Philippovich (1893, Vol. 1). My argument deviates in essential points from the usual ones, but borrows from them on other important points.

272 See the compilation of the estimates in Wiebe (1895, 180): "It is notable that in general every new investigation comes up with ever smaller numbers for the size of the [money] devaluation."

273 Aupetit (1901, 245), cited in Fisher (1911, 234 f.).

274 Sternberg (1836, 2:92 note).

275 Published in Worms (1904, Doc. 1).

276 In T. Wagner (1791, 133 ff.).

277 Inama-Sternegg (1879, 3.2:195).

278 Over the forms of mint administration in general, see Luschin von Ebengreuth (1904, 85 f.); over the mint cooperative members in particular, see Karajan (1838). There also see the main source: *Das Wiener Münzbuch* [Viennese Mint Book] from the 15th century. Cf. Eheberg (1879). The content of Eheberg's book is, however, — so far as it does not use Karajan — essentially consitutional history.

279 In Breslau a ducal smelting house [*Brenngaden*] in which gold and silver was smelted, redeemed, tested, and weighed, is already demonstrable in 1203 — it has the preemptive purchase right for all precious metals (Tzschoppe and Stenzel 1832, 278).

280 When with the flourishing of Schneeberg (thus towards the end of the 15th century), which had its ore smelted at first in Zwickau, the mint erected there could not mint all the silver, they had to allow the miners for a time to freely sell and export silver (Schmoller 1891, 978).

281 Mint law of King George of Poděbrady in 1469 (Sternberg 1836, 2:175). Directive of King Vladislaus II of Bohemia (1492), Kuttenberg Copiar. No. 205 in Sternberg (1836, 1:86). Repeated in 1494 (Sternberg 1836, 2:135).

282 Compare with that of Count Schlick (Sternberg 1836, 1:322 ff.). The state edict of Ferdinand I (1534) determines that only when the royal mints cannot accept the offered silver, "estate owners and mining co-operatives" shall have the right to sell their silver elsewhere. But even in this case they must supply the amount which they receive over 7 guilders, 14 white groschen, and 6 white pfennigs for the mark to the royal treasury (Goldast 1620, 103 f.).

283 See Worms (1904, 87).

284 Metal ingots were not permitted to be exported. Hence a large part of the silver coins of Europe and Asia came through the form of piasters.

285 That of course happened to a broad extent. In order to properly draw many foreign coins to themselves, the coin *exchange* was declared a monopoly of the minters or the minting cooperatives in many places. That is proven with much source material for the German cities in the Middle Ages by Eheberg (1879, 59 ff., 142 ff.).

286 "Sententia de argento vendendo" (MGH Const., Vol. 2, 397-398, §283) from 1224.

287 See the long list of such determinations in Eheberg (1879, 59 ff., 142 ff.).

288 Karajan (1838, 316). From the highest chambers complaints were made that the Viennese mint cooperative members traded gold and silver on their own account, for years their silver was used not in support of the mint, but in their own interests (Karajan 1838, 325 and doc. XLVI).

289 "Ordenunge der münsser" [Laws of the mint] from the year 1470 (Eheberg 1879, 200 No. 5).

290 Worms (1904, 87).

291 Sternberg (1836, 1:223, 1:225).

292 Ehrenberg (1922, freq.).

293 Steinbeck (1857, 2:233-234).

294 An astounding fact: in the 419 large octave pages of Wiebe's thick book, which took on as its special task the investigation of the connection between money value and price, the word "Produktionskosten" [production costs] (if I have read correctly) does not occur at all! Just as little in the book of Bonn which bears the subtitle of "an inductive attempt at the history of the quantity theory"; just as little in the latest monograph comprising 515 pages over the quantity theory, the work of Irving Fisher mentioned above on page 231 (at least not with reference to the production of coinage!).

295 Humboldt (1811, 3:413; 1814, 3:112).

296 One livre tourn. at the time was perhaps 0.95 francs in present-day [1916] currency.

297 Nöggerath (1862). Kuss (1878).

298 Lipold (1881).

299 Neumann (1904, 267 f.).

300 According to the information of Becker (1888) and completed by Neumann (1904, 281).

301 Humboldt (1811, 4:89; 1814, 3:283).

302 Del Campo Marin (n.d.).

303 Srbik (1907, 230 ff.).

304 Basnage (1725, vol. 3), cited in Sperges (1765, 87).

305 Eschwege (1833, 15, 59, 88, 90).

306 About 10 marks in present-day [1916] currency.

307 Lamprecht (1885, 1:602 ff.).

308 D'Avenel (1894, 1:237 ff.).

309 See, for example, Meitzen (1895, 2:341, 2:639).

310 Over their well-known wealth, information is given by Hegel (1847, 2:80 f.).

311 Given, for example, in Stubbs (1874, 3:557).

312 In Denton (1888, 266).

313 King (1804); see on the same the critical remarks of Rogers (1866, 5:90 f.).

314 Carte Strozziane Ms., cited in Gregorovius (1859, 7:342–343).

315 See Davidsohn (1896b, 1:762).

316 According to a "Relatione di tutti li stati signori e principi d'Italia" and Leoni cited by Ranke (1857, 1:469).

317 Ranke (1857, 1:266).

318 Taine (1875, 1:18; 1876, 1:13). For the period of Louis XIV, the incomes of the French nobility was estimated at 520 million livres — 100 million from feudal rights, 420 million from the use of landed property (Moreau de Jonnès 1867, 402).

319 Pirenne (1899, 1:148 ff.). Cf. Sackur (1893, 167 f.).

320 See, for example, the document of donation in Marin (1798, 1:273 f.).

321 Doüet d'Arcq (1853).

322 The income of the Church amounted to 224,800,000 livres according to Bonvallet-Desbrosses (1791, 147) referred to in Boiteau (1889, 41).

323 Note to Regula 66 in Innocent VIII (1538, fol. lviii), cited in Woker (1878, 2). Woker's book is still today the most comprehensive work on

papal finance. It is in the individual parts exceeded by the works of Kirsch, Gottlob, Müntz, among others, but as a whole not yet replaced. Regrettable is the frequent deterioration which the judgement of the author experiences through his (Protestant) party fanaticism, a reproach which is not at all to be made for the more recent scholarly portrayals stemming from Catholic pens. Among these towers up Gottlob (1889; 1899), Kirsch (1894), and Müntz (1899, 5 ff.).

324 Gottlob (1892, 236).

325 Gottlob (1892, 236).

326 Gottlob (1892, 237).

327 Gottlob (1892, 135).

328 Gottlob (1889, 257; 1899, 669). Gottlob relies on Ehrle (1889, 147).

329 According to Sägmüller (1897).

330 We are informed about *the finances of the religious orders of knights* in large strokes by Prutz (1883, 244 ff.). Elsewhere the same author treats in detail the possessions of the Knights Hospitaller (Prutz 1881); and the financial operations of that order (Prutz 1906). An overview of the estate possessions of the Templars at the beginning of the 14th century is given by Wilcke (1860, 2:7 ff.).

331 Leber (1847, 28).

332 Wailly (1855, LXXVI).

333 See the "Ordonnance fixant le budget des recettes et des dépenses de l'État" (1311), printed in Boutaric (1861, 342 f.). Cf. also Vuitry (1883, 1:311 ff.).

334 Clamageran (1867, 1:xxiv, 1:407 n.1). Vuitry (1883, 2:652 ff.).

335 Forbonnais (1758).

336 According to the precise investigations of Sinclair (1803).

337 See Archivio di Stato di Firenze (1884, 2:833); cited in Gregorovius (1859, 7:342-343).

338 According to [Tr.: Bernardino?] Corio, cited in Cibrario (1839, 3:200). Cibrario converts the florin with 14.51 L.; in my opinion too high.

339 Alidosi Pasquali (1621, 35–36).

340 [Tr.: Villani (1728, 12:§92).]

341 Hegel and Lexer (1862, vol. I). Cf. Lochner (1845, 84).

342 According to Stieda (1899, 11–12).

343 Rogers (1866, 4:502 ff.).

344 See the previous volume, Chapter 18, p. 295 f.

345 Translated by Heusler (1900).

346 Great Britain Royal Commission on Historical Manuscripts (1876, 523–31), cited in Green (1894, 2:60).

347 See the source material in Maliniak (1913, 43 ff.).

348 Flach (1893, 2:369).

349 "When the Cologne craftsmen in the Middle Ages were affluent or even rich, it did not rest on their activity in the workshop, but rather on them growing into the general goods and money trade with the turnover of their little commercial surplus on the out-of-town markets, bringing the principal force of their labours to this, and only incidentally retaining their commercial operation." (Kuske 1914, 82)

350 Hartmann (1900, 2.2:102). Inama-Sternegg (1879, 2:341 ff., 2:361 f.) gives general information over the revenue of the salt works; Schmoller (1891, 654 ff.) the same; over the particular development in *Salzburg*, see: Zillner (1890, 139, 157); in *Halle*: Hertzberg (1889, 1:55); in *Lüneburg*: Zenker (1906) (good); Heineken (1908).

351 "Incipit leges quas Ahistulf Rex adiuncxit" (MGH LL, Vol. 4, 196, §3).

352 Hartmann (1904, 75).

353 In the business reports of the commercial traveller Gherardi of the Florentine firm Spigliati-Spini from the year 1284, 24 monasteries in England were mentioned which had sold for 4–11 years their wool to the named house (Pagnini 1765, 2:324 f.). In a little notebook of [Francesco] Balducci Pegolotti from the 14th century are listed some 200 names of English abbeys and monasteries which delivered wool to the Florentine traders. The list (Ms. 2441 of the Biblioteca Riccardiana) is shared by Peruzzi (1868, 71 ff.). The list by Peruzzi is more extensive than than in Varenbergh (1874, 214–17) which is taken from the Archives de Douai, cartulaire L, fol. 44; but is considered incorrect according to the investigations of Dixon (1898, 151).

354 See, for example, Prutz (1883, 45).

355 Lippert (1896, 2:361).

356 Strieder (1914, 182 ff.).

357 Prutz (1883, 100 ff.).

358 A rich source material is to be found in Dopsch (1912, 2:234 ff.).

359 According to Villani (1728) who is certainly to be relied on for these figures. In 1320 the Knights of St John of Jerusalem owed both the named banking houses 575,000 gold guilders (Bosio 1621, 2:28).

360 Calculated according to the taxation amounts beyond doubt. See, for example, Clamageran (1867, 1:300); Moranvillé (1887, 387).

361 Piton (1892, 21).

362 Schaube (1898, 608).

363 Stobbe (1866, 137).

364 See the testament of Christian Mentzel (d. 1748) in Gerstmann (1909, 26 ff.).

365 See, for example, the interest table in Davidsohn (1896a, 1:158 f.): min. 10, max. 50, median 20.26%.

366 Heynen (1905, 99).

367 Law (1895, 66).

368 Schneider (1885, 37); Gottlob (1892, 249); Davidsohn (1896a, vol. 3 No. 771, 787).

369 Evidence in Bender, *Die öffentlichen Glückspiele*, 1862 [Tr.: Sombart may have mixed up here the reference of Bender (1841) with Wild (1862)]. Cf. Meitzen (1895, 2:637).

370 Joinville (1858, 235; 1906, 380).

371 Clamageran (1867, 1:264).

372 Froumenteau (1581, 2:45) in Levasseur (1900, 2:127).

373 Law (1895, 63 f.).

374 According to the pamphlet "Catéchsime des partisans" (Moreau 1853, 1:227-289; Ranke 1856, 3:50–51).

375 Darigrand (1763, 59 f.).

376 Forbonnais (1758, 1:475, 1:476, 2:122, 2:123).

377 Compiled from Häbler (1897, 72 ff., 82 ff., 145, 169, 176, 193).

378 Examples in Sombart (1902a, 1:224).

379 The information is taken entirely from Aronius et al. (1902).

380 From the "Chronik des Burkard Zink", in Frensdorff et al. (1865, 2:13, 2:27, 2:30). For further evidence for the "appraisals" of Jews in Germany see Neumann (1865, 328 ff.). Cf. also Süßmann (1907).

381 Hegel & Lexer (1862, 1:121 ff.). Stobbe (1866, 37).

382 It is always about the weight mark here (so far as nothing else is noted), which in silver is the same as 42.8 marks in present-day [1916] currency. The amounts are taken from the seventh chapter of the first volume of Madox (1769), where an enormous mass of source materials lie stacked up awaiting use.

383 Guizot (1825, 22).

384 Boutaric (1861, 303).

385 Boutaric (1861, 304).

386 Vuitry (1883, 1:96).

387 Petitot (1819, 13:352).

388 See under Chapter 62: The Jews (in Section 8).

389 Strieder (1904). This text is one of the most valuable of the works which my Modern Capitalism has to thank for its development.

390 To a very considerable extent certainly, the means of these people, to the extent they were *officials* without recourse to money-lending, was produced directly by fraudulent administration — they then belong in Chapter 43. Mazarin!

391 Shared by Thirion (1895, 19–20).

392 Normand (1908).

393 Fournier (1855, 54).

394 It is printed in full in D'Angerville (1781b, 1:171-196; not included in 1781a). Cf. also the information in Sombart (1913c, 9 f.; 1967, 7 f.).

395 In the first edition (Sombart 1902a, 1:271 ff.) I provided a series of datapoints over the productivity of personal lending in the Middle Ages, to which I refer the reader.

396 Hall (1901, 48 ff.).

397 Below (1889, 50).

398 Maurer (1870, 2:235 f.). Arnold (1854, 2:192 ff.). More recent investigations have established these facts in their significance for the foundation of the entire civic development. See, for example, for *Cologne* the introduction to Hegel (1875, vol. 3); and for *Constance*, the especially informative studies of Beyerle (1900, 1:66 ff.).

399 For information, see Aubert (1893).

400 See, for example, for *Hamburg*: Lib. act. a. a. o. XVIII, 13 f. LXXII, 12. CXLVII, 9, 26 [Tr.: I have been unable to source a full reference for this – Sombart cites it as "Liber actorum (Hamburgensis)" on p.1184 of the Anonymenregister concluding his second volume – possible candidate is *Liber actorum coram consulibus in resignatione haereditatum* (1248-1273)]; for *Frankfurt*: Fichard (1819, 150–51), and Böhmer

(1836, 2:217, 247, 288, 350, 352, 384); for *Augsburg*: Stetten (1779, 1:4); for *Würzburg*, Rosenthal (1879, 44); for *Breslau*: Klose (1781, 1:501, 516, 632), Tzschoppe and Stenzel (1832, 259).

401 Maurer (1870, 2:179).

402 For *Cologne*: Hegel et al. (1875, 3:XXIII).

403 We are best informed over this point thanks to the wealth of literature on legal history.

404 For example, Wiegand et al. (1879, 3:71 §225, 3:98 f. §313). Also see the excellent introduction by Schulte to Wiegand et al. (1879, vol. 3).

405 Wiegand et al. (1879, 3:2 §3, 3:26 §75, 3:41 f. §120, 3:56 §173). Cf. Gobbers (1883).

406 Many examples of it are contained in Rehme (1895).

407 See, for example, for *Würzburg*: Rosenthal (1879, 49).

408 The objection of Strieder — that the first owners of the land would *not* have drawn advantage from the rise in value, because they would have given away *everything* as hereditary leases at an earlier period — is not to be held in so far as that even the remission, which certainly happened in numerous cases, took place *gradually* and only really with the blossoming of the cities. That is also emphasised by Häpke (1905, 1059).

409 For *Basel*: Arnold (1861, 64). For *Lübeck*: Pauli (1847, 1:46).

410 Bücher (1886, 340).

411 With amounts twenty times, in some cases even twenty five times as large (Pauli 1847, 48).

412 With amounts 12½ times as large (Eulenburg 1893, 287).

413 Bruder (1886, 99); cf. Inama-Sternegg (1879, 3.2:469).

414 The most distinguished have made my thesis their own at least in part; an especially valuable testimony is that of Below who wrote in summary:

> The residents of the old cities who had large property ownership at their disposal could arrive at wealth effortlessly with the rapid growth of the communities, as we observe in the 12th and 13th centuries — in the numerous arrivals they found willing buyers for housing sites. At the time a significant commerce in land was already developing. (Below 1905a, 116)

415 Libočan (1596, 1:95).

416 Mathesius (1587, 16r).

417 Mathesius (1587, 16v).

418 Humboldt (1811, 3:404, 4:20; 1814, 3:195, 3:224-225).

419 The share of the mine lords were measured in the various mining areas quite differently. In general they had a tendency to diminish.

420 Del Mar (1886, 149).

421 In the year 1447 the miners in the *Freiberg* district complained that the wealthy citizens of the city did not participate in mining. "Thus poor me must just work my dear mine alone with a few poor handworkers." (Ermisch 1883, 2:102)

422 In *Silesia* the alternative was frequently given to field owners (not just to the estate owners) of demanding instead of land compensation acceptance into the cooperative at ⅛ of their mine possession (thus with 12½ shares). It thereby happened that estate owners and farmers (only with exclusion of the mere farmers of inheritable leases) became collaborators (Steinbeck 1857, 2:186). A similar right occurred in *Saxony*. Here the heir (i.e. the free farmer) could claim his "field share", that is, he was free to "participate in the mine" with 1/32 (Ermisch 1887, XXXV). Analogous in *Bohemia*.

423 The gold panning in the *Black Forest* was practised by all members of the mark the land belonged to (Gothein 1892, 609–12).

424 Gothein (1892, 603, 637).

425 See the compilation of places in the chronicles by Sternberg (1836, 1.2:32 ff.).

426 Mathesius (1587, 17v).

427 Sperges (1765, 120).

428 Peetz (1883, 68).

429 Sperges (1765, 97–98).

430 Sperges (1765, 105 ff.).

431 Cf. now also Strieder (1914, 3 ff., 13 ff.).

432 Fink (1894) and Faulhaber (1896).

433 Ehrenberg (1922, 1:187 ff.).

434 Scheurl (1884, 30).

435 "Augsburg bankers had their hand in play everywhere; even in the mining of the Münster valley the Fuggers took over from the Freiburg patricians." (Gothein 1892, 599)

436 After Soriano (Ranke 1857, 1:407).

437 Humboldt (1811, 2:25 ff.; 1814, 1:224 ff.).

438 In Suess (1877, 173).

439 Schmoller (1891, 692).

440 Tzschoppe and Stenzel (1832, Doc. 108).

441 Over the lucrative "coin debasements" for *Germany*: Eheberg (1879, 50 ff., 55 ff.); for *England*: Cunningham (1907, 1:301 ff.); for *France*: Vuitry (1883, 2:261); for *Bohemia*: Sternberg (1836, 2:57 ff.); for the *Crusader States*: Prutz (1906, 21 ff.). Cf. in addition Chapter 26.

442 Ermisch (1883, 2:106-109 § 1003).

443 Stafford (1895, 119 f.). [Tr.: the German translation was from an original manuscript, and the section quoted is excluded from the English edition (Stafford 1876) and thus translated back from the German here.]

444 At base the entire content of, for example, Ehrenberg's investigations amounts to proving that the enormous commerce in credit of that time developed hand in hand with the import of silver into Spain (Ehrenberg 1922, 2:222 ff.). (Ehrenberg himself says nothing of these connections.)

445 Colmeiro (1863, 2:403 f.).

446 Colmeiro (1863, 2:402).

447 Häbler (1888, 69). Cf. also Häbler (1900, 413 ff.).

448 Handelmann (1860, 581).

449 Eschwege (1833, 15, 59, 88).

450 For *England*: Jacob (1838, 2:69; 1831, 2:90 ff.). That is strangely the only reference which Marx knew or at least expressly raised between the increase in precious metals and the "original accumulation" (Marx 1903, 1:709; 1906, 1:815 f.).

451 Goldast (1620, 228).

452 Cunningham (1907, 2:141).

453 Shaw (1895, 73). The book by Shaw made it its particular task to show how the "bullionist, financiers and arbitragist", and "the merchant exchangers" took advantage of the chaos in the currencies and obtained wealth.

454 For *Flanders*: Vanderkindere (1879, 140). For *Cologne*: Hegel (1875, vol. 3 Intro.). For the *French* cities in the 16ᵗʰ and 17ᵗʰ centuries: Normand (1908, 149).

455 D'Avenel (1894, 1:149, 1:154).

456 Shared without source by Salz (1913, 405).

457 Cited in Gmelin (1783, 69).

458 "E cosa grande il considerare le smisurate richezze che molti di essi sono stati soliti di accumulare in brevissimo tempo." [It is extraordinary to consider the enormous wealth that many of them have been accustomed to accumulate in a very short time.] Letter to Cardinal Borgia in Ranke (1857, 1:477).

459 Cunningham (1907, 2:181 ff.).

460 Hall (1901, 128 ff.). There the swindling of the military suppliers is also treated in detail (Hall 1901, 124 ff.).

461 Great Britain Royal Commission on Historical Manuscripts (1888, 1:45), cited in Oppenheim (1896, 1:192–93).

462 Over the corruption in the New England states during the colonial period, see O'Callaghan & Fernow (1853, 4:317 f. & passim).

463 Hamilton (1727).

464 Cited in Leroy-Beaulieu (1886, 4:73). More recent figures in Bokemeyer (1888, 279 f.).

465 Bokemeyer (1888, 279). Cf. Saalfeld (1812, 254).

466 Weisse (1794, 35 f.). The author is indeed a wrinkled, state's haemorrhage who went on a lot about the hordes above him, but who yet gives the impression of a well-informed and honest judge.

467 "When such a judge as Sir John Fortescue could exult that more Englishmen were hanged for robbery in one year than French in seven, and that, 'if an Englishman be poor and see another having riches which may be taken away from him by might, he will not spare to do so', it may be perceived how thoroughly these sentiments had pervaded the public mind." (Hallam 1818, 3:163)

468 "Should townsmen, merchants, and shopkeepers prescribe us laws and become our lords?", the robber barons speak when in 1254 the Rhenish city federation formed to protect the land against their violent acts. Staindel's Albert. Stadensis., cited in Raumer (1857, 4:414).

469 See the sources in Fagniez (1897, 15, 164 ff.); and Pigeonneau (1887, 2:34).

470 For the 12th and 13th centuries, a rich source of material is provided by Heyck (1886, 182 ff.).

471 Heyd (1879, 1:255 ff., 1:258, 1:263, 1:487 f., 1:489, 2:16) has in the main digested what we possess in source material for the history of robbery and plunder in the Italian cities during the Middle Ages.
Probably the best source is formed by the records of a commission of investigation which the Doge Jacopo Contarini sat down in the year 1278 — for investigating all the robbery and mistreatment which the Venetians had tolerated in the previous ten years from the side of the Greeks and their allies. We learn there alone of the stories of about 90 freebooters. Published in Tafel & Thomas (1856, 3:159-281).

472 See page 216 f.

473 See the descriptions of Herrera, Xerez, and Gomara, excerpts of which are provided to us by Prescott (1843; 1847), and Helps (1855), among others.

474 Peschel (1858, 605), source? Odoardo Barbosa speaks only of a "Sacco d'incredibili ricchezze in oro e mercanzie" [Lots of incredible riches in gold and merchandise], cited in Ramusio (1550, 1:318D).

475 Schuhmacher (1892, 72, 124) and Langegg (1888, 13–14).

476 Prescott (1843, 1:541).

477 Herrera y Tordesillas (1601, 4:3, 4:8).

478 Shared by Soetbeer (1880).

479 Häbler (1900, 392 f.).

480 Prescott (1847, 1:356-357). It agrees quite exactly with the table of "Acta de reparticion del rescate de Atuahalpa" [record of the distribution of the ransom of Atuahalpa] which is printed in Quintana (1830, 2:407 f.).

481 "Testimonio de la Acta de reparticion del rescate de Atuahalpa, otorgado por el escribano Pedro Sancho" in Quintana (1830, 2:407 ff.).

482 Printed in Pacheco et al. (1864); excerpted in Soetbeer (1880, 65–66).

483 Roscher (1854, 1:§122) (citation is not right). According to Herrera y Tordesillas (1601, 4:108-109), the estates of Gonzalo Pizarro were more profitable than the bishopric of Toledo.

484 Humboldt (1811, 2:324-325; 1814, 2:194).

485 Saalfeld (1810, 174).

486 According to Herrera y Tordesillas — see A. Anderson (1787, 2:73 anno 1454). [Tr.: Sombart miscited as anno 1554, hence the incorrect reference to the 16th century.]

487 Published in Sue (1835, 4:Lib. VII, Ch. 1 & 2).

488 According to the documents of Sue (1835, 4:1 ff.).

489 Sinclair (1803, 2:42).

490 Principal works are Exquemelin (1744), originally written in Dutch in 1678, then translated into French and Spanish; Pyle (1891) [Tr.: a translation of Exquemelin (1744) with additional materials.]; Burney (1816); and Handelmann (1856, 22 ff.).

491 Burrish (1728, 333).

492 Uzielli (1901, 35).

493 Froude (1858, 8:451).

494 Register Privy Council 1, 471; 2, 500, and elsewhere, cited in Hume Brown (1904, 69 ff.). Yet more sources are also provided there.

495 D. Campbell (1892, 1:389 f.).

496 Hentzner (1757, 46).

497 Froude (1858, 11:177).

498 Hume Brown (1904, 72).

499 S. R. Gardiner (1897, 1:330), cited in Cunningham (1907, 2:188).

500 Strypes (1725, 4:129), cited in D. Campbell (1892, 1:374).

501 According to Hakluyt (1598): see Froude (1858, 9:360).

502 State Papers Domestic (1650, 9:34), cited in Cunningham (1907, 2:189). [Tr.: these references appear to be incorrect.]

503 Captain Francis Allen to Anthony Bacon, August the 17th 1589, in Birch (1754, 1:57), cited in D. Campbell (1892, 2:120).

504 The most important documents, namely the reports of the Earl of Bellomont, are published in O'Callaghan & Fernow (1853, 4:306 ff., 4:323, 4:447, 4:480, 4:512 ff.). Cf. also Macaulay (1855, 5:259 ff.), where the pretty story of Captain Kidd is told, who as 'privateer' was sent by the government to battle the sea piracy, and came back with a rich booty as 'pirate', since he had thought to himself along the way that it would be much more profitable to capture peaceful merchants than to battle belligerent sea pirates.

505 Hughson (1894, 59). The study treats the object with great love and thoroughness. In the view of Hughson, the preferential treatment of sea piracy by the American colonies was a consequence of the English maritime policy which sacrificed the colonies to the motherland — sea piracy offered the best means of buying cheap wares (Hughson 1894, 17).

506 Hughson (1894, 39).

507 J. Campbell (1774, 2:599).

508 See above page 294 f. To the confiscated land were also added still other items of means so that the amount of ecclesiastical income which Henry VIII confiscated rose to £160,000.

509 Cf. in addition to the literature cited on page 294 f.: Rogers (1866, 4:113), Garnier (1892, 1:286 ff.), and Gasquet (1889, 2:387 ff.).

510 How much a large part of the *Arab* wealth rested on the commercial exploitation of African and especially Asian peoples is taught by any depiction of history. Cf. especially Stüwe (1836), and in particular Kremer (1875, 2:274 ff., 2:189) (wealth of the businesspeople; means of 20 to 30 million francs).

511 We are well-informed about the whole variety of graded conditions of servitude in the later Eastern Roman Empire. That even slavery persisted in the Byzantine Empire during the entire Middle Ages, we now assume to be verified. See Langer (1891, 8–10).

512 Noiret (1892), and also Haudecoeur [Tr.: exact reference by Sombart is unclear, but may be Haudecouer (1896, Intro.)].

513 Hopf (1859, 338 ff.).

514 Kremer (1875, 2:152 f.).

515 Kremer (1875, 2:152).

516 There had been Negro slavery right through the Middle Ages; the trade in Negroes was driven for the longest time over land by the Moors (M. C. Sprengel 1779, 14 ff.); from 1445 the Portuguese stepped into their place (Peschel 1858, 68 ff.). Cf. also the texts named under Literature on page 379 f.

517 Solórzano Pereira (1736, 1:60), cited in Helps (1855, 4:381).

518 In the instructions of Ovandos from September 1500 it states, "que los Indios pagasen tributos y derechos como los demas vasallas à sus altezas y que serviesen en coger el oro pagandoles su trabajo" [that the Indians pay tribute and give rights like the other vassals to their masters and that they serve in catching the gold as payment by work] (Schuhmacher 1892, 300).

519 Peschel (1858, 303).

520 "Navigatione da Lisbona all' isola di san Thome", in Ramusio (1550, 117A).

521 See the excerpts in Dutt (1908, 264 f.). Cf. J. Campbell (1774, 2:613 and elsewhere).

522 Dutt (1908, 267).

523 Cf. the descriptions in Heyd (1879, 1:195 ff.); Prutz (1883, 315 ff.); Rey (1883, 235 ff.); Beugnot (1854, 258 ff.); and Kremer (1875, 2:320 ff.). A survey of the judgements of contemporary writers is found in Dreesbach (1901, 24 ff., 49 ff.).

524 Heyd (1879, 1:197). Cf. Rey (1883, 211 ff.).

525 Michel (1852, 1:306 ff.).

526 A. Beer (1899, 188–89).

527 Heyd (1879, 1:197).

528 Hopf (1859, 310).

529 [Tr.: Sombart gives a reference of "Pegolotti, loc. cit. 370", but no previous reference to Pegolotti exists — it is assumed that this may refer to Pegolotti (1766), but the page number does not match up.]

530 Only you must never look for it in the works which ex professo portray the history of the colonies. But perhaps consult from the older writings Barläus [Tr.: Sombart does not give a more precise reference here], D'Avenant (1771), A. Anderson (1787), Postlethwayt (1774), J. Campbell (1774), Buchanan (1807), Humboldt (1811; 1814), Usselincx (1608), and Saalfeld (1810; 1812); and from the newer Handelmann (1856; 1860), Lippmann (1890), Bokemeyer (1888), and Peytraud (1897), to just mention a few of the more important.

531 See the precise statistics in Sombart (1913c, 172; 1967, 144–45).

532 Buxton (1840).

533 Schipper (1907, 19 ff.); and Caro (1908, 1:137 ff.). Cf. Heyd (1879, 2:542 ff.).

534 References in Heyden (1905, 32 ff.).

535 A. Anderson (1787, 4:130) (according to a "French author").

536 Recently again by Loria (1896), where the views of the author are presented in detail. Cf. with it Loria (1901, 218 ff.). The two best theor-

etical discussions of the economic problem of slave labour are found in Cairnes (1863), and in A. Wagner (1892, 2:43 ff., esp. 2:60 ff.).

537 Grünberg (1901, 334).

538 The best portrayal of the slave trade is now Spears (1900). The main source for the end of the 18th century, which unfortunately contains almost no statistical information, is the survey organised by the English House of Commons in the years 1790 and 1791. The conclusions are summarised in Great Britain House of Commons (1791).

539 According to the report of Valentin Ferdinaud over Arguim (Kunstmann 1850, 179).

540 Merivale (1861, 1:297-298), where the theory later posited so often of the influence of stopping the terra libera on the formation of wages was also developed.

541 Cited in Handelmann (1860, 344).

542 Defoe (1726, 1:316). Cf. also G. L. Beer (1912), where much new and interesting material has been worked up. Over the rapid increase in the wealth of the planters in Barbados see, for example, G. L. Beer (1912, 2:9).

543 That occurs most of the time. See now again the lecture of Koch (1914).

544 For further information, see Sombart (1913c, 177 ff.; 1967, 148 ff.).

545 We are informed about the luxury which was pursued at these courts at the time by the diary which André de la Vigne, the secretary of Anne of Brittany, recorded on the journey with Charles VIII through Italy (Saint-Gelais 1525; excerpts in Roscoe 1805, 1:160 f. and App. XXIX).

546 See the figures on page 298 f. above.

547 Forbonnais (1758, 2:101).

548 Guiffrey (1881). Cf. Guiffrey (1885).

549 Meyer (1668), cited in Ranke (1856, 3:241).

550 Archives Nationales O¹, 3792−94, shared in the very informative book by Langlade (1911, 29, 122; 1913, 26 ff., 112).

551 Thirion (1895, 156−57).

552 "État des dépenses de Mme la Marquise de Pompadour du 9 sept. 1745 au 15 avr. 1769 jour de sa mort", by Leroy, cited in Baudrillat (1880, 4:327).

553 Real Academia de la Historia (Spain) (1842, 3:545-561) [Tr.: Sombart cited volume 4, Carey volume 3, but neither seem to relate], cited in Carey (1876, 408 ff.). Cf. Ranke (1857, 1:131 ff.).

554 Nice description of the luxurious court-life of William of Orange, when he was not yet King of England, in Berg (1845, 269 f.).

555 See the figures above on page 299 f.

556 This charming expression is found in Camden (1586, 106).

557 From the "Livre de raison de Pierre-César de Cadenet de Charleval, commencé en 1728 et continué en 1763 par son fils" in Ribbe (1874, 2:144). The Smithsonian in Washington possesses an absolutely valuable collection of English household budgets from the period 1650−1750. A few excerpts from it have been shared by the owner of this collection, who gathered them together and gifted them to the Smithsonian, Halliwell-Phillipps (1852).

558 See the surveys in Chapter 40.

559 Defoe (1726, 55 f.). Cf. Defoe (1890, 257).

560 See further information in Sombart (1913c, 100 ff.; 1967, 84 ff.).

561 See the evidence in Sombart (1913c, 75 ff.; 1967, 62 ff.).

562 The latest book over the history of luxury clothing — Gallo (1914) — is light literature. Its value lies in a chronology of consumption laws in the appendix and a good bibliography.

563 See, for example, "Inventaire des merveilles du monde rencontrées dans le palais du Cardinal Mazarin" [Inventory of the wonders of the world encountered in the palace of Cardinal Mazarin] in Moreau (1853, 1:143 ff.).

564 I have dedicated an especially detailed portrayal to the origin and inner organisation of the big cities in Sombart (1913c; 1967), to which I refer the reader. Cf. also Chapters 9, 10, and 15 of that volume.

565 See in Defoe (1726) the chapter "Of fine shops and shows".

566 For further information, see Sombart (1913c; 1967).

567 Orderici Vitalis in 1092: "Militares viri mores paternos in vestitu et capillorum tonsura dereliquerunt, quos paulo post burgenses et rustici et paene totum vulgus imitati sunt" [The military men discarded their fathers' customs in clothing and haircuts, and shortly afterwards the townspeople, and the peasants, and almost the whole population imitated them]. Cited in Raumer (1857, 6:520).

568 La Bruyère (1880, 291–307).

569 In Diderot and D'Alembert (1751), fashion is defined as: "tout ce qui sert à la parure et au luxe" [everything used for adornment and luxury]. The "bourgeoisie" (let alone the underclasses) had not yet been drawn into the whirlpool in which "society" lived, and was hence also even less affected by the rapid changes in fashion. I do not doubt that the memory of a ninety year old man in the first half of the 19th century – in his time fashion changed at most every 4, 5, or 6 years — was representative for *his* circle: "Les modes changeaient bien quelquefois, mais ce n'était guère qu'au bout de 4, 5, 6 ans et même après un plus long intervalle de temps" [Fashions changed sometimes, but only after 4, 5, or 6 years, and sometimes after an even longer period of time] (Besnard 1880, 1:137; cited in Levasseur 1900, 2:780). "Usually the well-to-do citizens got to know etiquette and the luxury of the noble world only by and by [...] As soon as a bourgeois family made a claim to be quite fashionable, just as soon did the greater difficulty which they had in achieving it, and the more frequent failures of the efforts they put into it become for them just as much a source of worry and displeasure as a cause for missteps" (Krünitz et al. 1773, 92:465).

570 See, for example, Mercier (1782, chaps. 173, 176, 177). I will give my view over the quite different role which fashion plays in the period of high capitalism in a later volume of this work.

571 Another explanation of the preference for foreign goods which is not to be rejected out of hand either is given by the author of the article on fashion in Krünitz (1773, 92:435) — the recognising of foreign fashion the earliest was a sign of noble position: first the court, then the nobil-

ity, etc. Apart from that, no attempt at interpreting this important phenomenon has become known to me.

572 "Quodque tolerari vix potest, nullum fere vestimenti genus probatur,
quod e Gallis non fuerit adductum, in quibus levia pleraque in pretio
sunt tametsi nostri persaepe homines modum illis et quasi formulam
quandam praescribant" [And what can barely be tolerated is that there
is proven to be almost no kind of garment which was not brought from
the French, which are most trifling in price, although our men very often prescribe to them a fashion, and as it were a certain formula.] (Pontano 1520, 1:71r; cited in Burckhardt 1860, 366; 1878, 2:175).

573 For *Portugal*, it is confirmed, for example, by Du Châtelet (1798, 1:75);
while another travel writer of the time believes in being able to establish the influence of London fashion on the taste of the Portuguese
(Bernard 1802, 277; cf. Lueder 1808, 50).

574 Heyck (1886, 177).

575 Duro (1884, Doc. 109).

576 Public Record Office of Great Britain (1856, 30:10), cited in Oppenheim (1896, 1:325). Cf. also the complete "inventaire d'armament" [in-
ventory of armament] in the supplement to Savary des Brûlons and
Savary (1723).

577 De Jonge (1858).

578 Heyck (1886, 65 ff.).

579 Ann. Jan. [Tr.: a Genuese yearbook?] 183, 35; 112, 3; 124, 30. Cited in
Heyck (1886, 129).

580 Public Record Office of Great Britain (1856, 62:19) cited in Oppenheim
(1896, 1:134).

581 See the sources in Sombart (1913b). For England, I add the following
nice compilation: Whitworth (1764).

582 The depiction of this object which I gave in Sombart (1913b) serves as a
base for the above, but has been augmented at various points by better
and more substantial material.

583 Dutt (1908, 47).

584 Great Britain House of Commons (1773), cited in Dutt (1908, 46).

585 "Abounding in herself with all the Necessaries and Conveniencies of
Life, she [the country of Bengal] scarce took any thing in exchange but
Gold and Silver, if we except sometimes for the Supply of Manufactures
to be again exported, Cotton from Surat." (J. Campbell 1774, 2:611)

586 Spain (1640, 4 tit. XXVI lib. IV), cited in Colmeiro (1863, 2:395 ff.).

587 See page 140 above.

588 Campomanes (1775, 406), cited in Bonn (1896, 109–10).

589 Mercado (1569).

590 90% of the rich French plantation owners resided in the colonies,
whereas the English admittedly followed a different practice — the entrepreneurs who became rich moved away from their colonies in order
to have their plantations managed from London via agents (Raynal
1775, 3:85, 3:82).

591 See, for example, the information in Raynal (1775, 3:316-317, 3:347,
3:366), and compare with what Vogelstein (see note on page 471) fur-

nishes in the way of material from other sources.

592 A. Anderson (1787, 4:178).

593 J. Campbell (1774, 2:639 ff.) and Raynal (1775, vol. 2 passim).

594 More recent researchers come to much lower figures. Thus Savine (1909) assumes that at most 35,000 poor (namely five times the 7,000 monks) were maintained by the monasteries, whose charity consisted for the most part in extraordinary material performances (festive feasts and the like).

595 "The expropriation of the agricultural producer, of the peasant, from the soil, is the basis of the whole process. The history of this expropriation, in different countries, assumes different aspects, and runs through its various phases in different orders of succession [?], and at different periods. In England alone, which we take as our example [!], has it the classic form." (Marx 1903, 1:682; 1906, 787)

596 Detlefsen (1901, 117 ff.).

597 They have been made the object of special investigations by amongst others Schulze-Gävernitz (1892), and recently in the interesting book by Kostanecki (1909).

598 Sombart (1893).

599 4 Hen. 7 c.19 (1488); 6 Hen. 8 c.5 (1514); 7 Hen. 8 c.1 (1515). See the depiction and evaluation of this legislation in Leadam (1897, 6 ff.).

600 Justi (1758, § 310). Cf. also the excerpts from Rumpfort essays in Gérando (1839, 3:522).

601 G. Martin (1900, 300).

602 See page 22 ff. Cf. Sombart (1913a, 256 ff.; 1915, 202 ff.).

603 Bezold (1908, 64).

604 Sélincourt (1908, 259).

605 Unwin (1904, 168 f.).

606 Strieder (1914).

607 Fournier (1887, 344).

608 Schweizer (1903, 10 n.1).

609 Zincke (1742, 9:973). Cited by Schmoller (1891, 8); the citation could not be found in the edition used by me [Tr.: Schmoller appears to have miscited here].

610 Zincke (1744, 616). As for the previous note [Tr.: page number of citation has been corrected].

611 The interesting report is printed in Fournier (1887, 373 ff.). Over the events of this sort, see Fournier (1887, 317 ff.). Cf. also the information in Beer (1895, 107 f.).

612 Over measures of a similar sort in *Russia* under Peter the Great, see Tugan-Baranowski (1900, 13 f.).

613 See Chapter 24 in this volume.

614 Hatschek (1887, 35 ff.).

615 Büttgenbach (1898, 167).

616 See such cases in Savary des Brûlons and Savary (1723, art. Société), and in Depping (1850, 3:LIV). Further in G. Martin (1900, 109 and elsewhere), Des Cilleuls (1898, 64 and elsewhere), Postlethwayt (1774, 2:778), A. Anderson (1787, 2:594), and Unwin (1904, 145 f., 165 f.).

617 See the detailed depiction in Sombart (1913a, 135 ff.; 1915, 103 ff.).
618 The next volume instructs about the various forms of capital formation.
619 Vividly described by Büsch (1790, 9 f.).
620 Wiedfeldt (1898, 79).
621 J. Savary (1675, 1:17).
622 The topic is covered in more detail by me in Sombart (1913a, 53 ff.; 1915, 40 ff.). The reader is referred to that depiction of which I only give an extract here.
623 Ranke (1857, 1:410). That Benevento about whom Ranke tells us also appeared by Pius V who, however, did not trust his arts.
624 That it was already rife at the start of the century is supported by Ben Jonson's comedy "The Devil is an Ass" in which the projector Meercraft plays the main role.
625 "Fièvre d'invention et d'enrichessement rapide" [Fever of invention and of rapid enrichment] according to Fagniez (1897, 333). [Tr.: Sombart erroneously cites Marbault (1837, 35; included at the end of Sully 1837; cited in Fagniez 1897, 333).] Cf. Normand (1908, 185 ff., 13). This good book contains much which makes the donneurs d'avis [advice givers] familiar to us.
626 Mercier (1782, 1:222).
627 Srbik (1910).
628 Cited in Beer (1894, 37 f.). Cf. also Justi (1761, 1:256 ff.).
629 Zincke (1745, 366 ff.).
630 See his characterisation in März (1906, 8 f.).
631 Petty (1755, 118 f.).
632 Boulainvilliers (1737).
633 Ranke (1856, 3:456).
634 See Chapter 20 of this volume.
635 The good book of Clark (1911) is supported by the construction of such a general spirit of "non-conformism".
636 Weiss (1853, 1:104).
637 Sombart (1911a; 1913d).
638 For all the details, I refer to Sombart (1911a, 25 ff.; 1913d, 22 ff.).
639 Hyamson (1907, 178).
640 Tovey (1738, 292).
641 Markgraf (1894). Freudenthal (1901).
642 Koenen (1843, 176 ff.) discusses in detail these connections. For comparison see perhaps Sommerhausen (1853).
643 Brunner (1906, 495 ff.).
644 Demonstrable, for example, for Hamburg: Feilchenfeld (1899, 211).
645 Moses Lindo, main promoter of indigo extraction, came in 1756 to South Carolina and invested £120,000 in indigo. From 1756 to 1776 indigo production increased fivefold. Lindo became general inspector of indigo (Elgas 1905; cited in Jacobs 1906b, 480).
646 Risbeck (1783). Extracts in Scheube (1873, 382 ff.).
647 The text is in Bloch (1899, 47).
648 Markgraf (1894, 93).

649 See, for example, Hyamson (1907, 174 f., 178), or the report of the magistrates of Antwerp to the Bishop of Arras in Ullmann (1909, 35) ("they brought great riches from their native land, especially silver, jewels, and many ducats"). Cf. Part 6 of the next volume.

650 The related study by Wätjen (1913) now serves to supplement my depiction in Sombart (1911a; 1913d).

651 L. Wolf (1894). Cf. Hyamson (1907, 171–73).

652 Hyamson (1907, 269). Picciotto (1875, 58 ff.).

653 Lau (1719, 258).

654 Cited in Liebe (1903, 75).

655 Jacobs (1906a).

656 Mémoire of the Jews of Metz from 24th March 1733, printed in excerpt in Bloch (1899, 35).

657 Cited in Bloch (1899, 23).

658 Excerpts from the Lettres patentes in Bloch (1899, 24).

659 Over the Gradis, see Malvezin (1875, 241 ff.), and Graetz (1875). Both depictions, based on good sources, are independent of one another.

660 Capefigue (1855, 68, 214, and elsewhere).

661 From the *Revue de la Révolution française* of 16th January 1892, cited in Bloch (1899, 34–35).

662 Schwartzen (1744, 122–23), cited in A. Levy (1900, 58).

663 I have extracted all three cases from Liebe (1903, 43 f., 70), who shares them without giving sources.

664 Bondy & Dworsky (1906, 1:388).

665 A. B. König (1790, 93–94).

666 Rescript of 28th June 1777; printed in Levy (1900, 74); and Haenle (1867, 70).

667 Moscherosch (1900, 372).

668 Mensi (1890, 132 ff.). Samuel Oppenheimer, "Imperial Army Chief Supervisor and Jew", as he was officially described and also tended to sign himself, concluded namely "almost all significant provisions and munitions supply contracts" in the campaigns of Prince Eugen (Mensi 1890, 133).

669 See, for example, the petition to the Viennese central government of 12th May 1762 in G. Wolf (1876, 70); Komitatsarchiv Neutra Iratok XII/3336 (for Moravia), according to information from Joseph Reizmann; for the supplying with provisions the fortresses of Raab, Ofen, and Komorn by Breslau Jews (in 1716), see G. Wolf (1876, 61).

670 Friedenwald (1893).

671 Kayserling (1900).

672 An overview of the Jewish international houses of his time and their branchings is given by Manasseh ben Israel in his memorandum to Cromwell. The history of the individual families is found portrayed in detail in the Jewish Encyclopedia, which is naturally especially valuable precisely in its biographical parts. In addition the general and specialist works of Jewish studies are to be referred to.

673 The effectiveness of Marco Perez is graphically described in Geering (1886, 454 ff.).

674 According to Procopius B. G. I. 8 and 16 in Friedländer (1881, 3:577).

675 Kortum (1795, 165).

676 Kortum (1795, 90).

677 Monin (1891, 90).

678 See above on page 575 ff.

679 Howell (1869, 41).

680 See, for example, Carqueja (1908, 73 ff., 82 ff., 91 ff.).

681 Wagenaar (1762, 8:127 f.), cited in Koenen (1843, 142). Aside from the sources mentioned by Koenen, we are instructed over the wealth of the Dutch Jews (naturally with greatly exaggerated nonsense — see, for example, the figures from the testament of De Pintos on page 292) by Schudt (1714, 1:277 ff., 4:208 f.). From the more recent literature, also to be named is Pimentel (1876, 34 ff.).

682 Savary des Brûlons and Savary (1723, 2:448).

683 L. Wolf (1902, 11).

684 See the data in Sombart (1911a, 214 ff.; 1913d, 185 ff.).

Milton Keynes UK
Ingram Content Group UK Ltd.
UKHW040706171024
2227UKWH00022B/112